MW01251289

Web Publishing with Microsoft FrontPage 97,
Second Edition

About the Author:

Martin S. Matthews is the author of *The Microsoft Outlook Handbook*, *The Official Guide to CorelDRAW!6 for Windows 95*, *Windows 95 Answers: Certified Tech Support*, *Excel for Windows Made Easy*, and numerous other titles. Martin, who has over 25 years of computer experience, also does consulting and training on a wide variety of computer topics with a number of firms nationwide.

Web Publishing with Microsoft FrontPage 97,
Second Edition

Martin S. Matthews

Osborne **McGraw-Hill**

Berkeley   New York   St. Louis   San Francisco
Auckland   Bogotá   Hamburg   London   Madrid
Mexico City   Milan   Montreal   New Delhi   Panama City
Paris   São Paulo   Singapore   Sydney
Tokyo   Toronto

Osborne **McGraw-Hill**
2600 Tenth Street
Berkeley, California 94710
U.S.A.

For information on translations or book distributors outside the U.S.A., or to arrange bulk purchase discounts for sales promotions, premiums, or fund-raisers, please contact Osborne/**McGraw-Hill** at the above address.

Web Publishing with Microsoft FrontPage 97, Second Edition

Copyright © 1997 by Martin S. Matthews and Carole Boggs Matthews. All rights reserved. Printed in the United States of America. Except as permitted under the Copyright Act of 1976, no part of this publication may be reproduced or distributed in any form or by any means, or stored in a database or retrieval system, without the prior written permission of the publisher, with the exception that the program listings may be entered, stored, and executed in a computer system, but they may not be reproduced for publication.

1234567890 DOC 9987

ISBN 0-07-882312-9

Publisher	**Copy Editor**
Brandon A. Nordin	Jan Jue
Editor in Chief	**Proofreader**
Scott Rogers	Karen Mead
Acquisitions Editor	**Indexer**
Wendy Rinaldi	David Heiret
Project Editors	**Computer Designer**
Janet Walden	Jani Beckwith
Heidi Poulin	
Judith Brown	**Illustrator**
	Lance Ravella
Editorial Assistant	
Ann Sellers	**Quality Control Specialist**
	Joe Scuderi
Technical Editor	
John Cronan	**Cover Designer**
	Hae Youn Kim, Tobi Design

Information has been obtained by Osborne/**McGraw-Hill** from sources believed to be reliable. However, because of the possibility of human or mechanical error by our sources, Osborne/**McGraw-Hill**, or others, Osborne/**McGraw-Hill** does not guarantee the accuracy, adequacy, or completeness of any information and is not responsible for any errors or omissions or the results obtained from use of such information.

Dedication:

Daniel G. Gestaut

Of all my friends, only a very few have been such for the better part of my life. Dan Gestaut is one. Quite simply, he is always there.

1 Designing and Creating Quality Web Pages 1

2 Exploring FrontPage 27

3 Using Wizards 71

4 Using Templates 103

5 Creating and Formatting a Web Page from Scratch 153

6 Using Microsoft Image Composer 197

7 Adding and Managing Hyperlinks and Hotspots 237

8 Using Tables and Frames 263

9 Working with Forms 299

10 Using WebBots 329

11 Importing and Integrating Office and Other Files 349

12 Working with HTML 389

13 Working with Databases 441

14 Security on the Web 499

15 Activating Your Webs 533

16 Setting Up an Intranet Web Site 595

17 Publishing and Promoting Webs on the Internet 617

A Installing FrontPage 97 with Bonus Pack 641

B FrontPage 97 Software Developer's Kit 669

Index 683

CONTENTS AT A GLANCE

Acknowledgments xvii

Introduction xix

1 Designing and Creating Quality Web Pages 1

The Internet and the World Wide Web 2

LANs and an Intranet 3

What Is a Web Page? 4

The Birth of the Internet 8

The World Wide Web 9

Designing for the Web 13

Monitor Resolution 14

Data Throughput 17

Web Browsers 18

Content 22

Working with Graphics 23

GIF 23

JPEG 24

GIF or JPEG? 24

Multimedia Files 25

2 Exploring FrontPage 27

Creating a Web 30

FrontPage Components 32

FrontPage Explorer 33

FrontPage Editor 38

To Do List 64

Personal Web Server 65

FrontPage Server Extensions 66

FrontPage on the Web: Surfrider Foundation Australia 67

Web Site 67

Webmaster Q & A 69

3 Using Wizards 71

Web Wizards 72

Using the Corporate Presence Wizard 74

Working with the Discussion Web Wizard 94

Using the Import Web Wizard 98

CONTENTS

Page Wizards.. 99
    Personal Home Page Wizard 99

4 Using Templates 103
Web Templates 104
    Applying the Normal Web Template 104
    Creating a Personal Web 107
    Using the Project Web Template 111
    Applying the Customer Support Web
        Template 116
Page Templates 118
    Confirmation Form Template 119
    Feedback Form Template 120
    Glossary of Terms Template 121
    Search Page Template 122
    Table of Contents Template 123
Creating Your Own FrontPage Templates 125
    Types of Templates 126
    FrontPage Directory Structure.. 126
    The .INF Information File 127
Building Templates 133
    Creating Single-Page Templates.. 134
    Constructing Web Templates 138

5 Creating and Formatting a Web Page from Scratch 153
Planning a Web 154
    What Are Your Goals?... 154
    What Is the Content? 155
    How Is It Organized?.. 155
    What Will It Look Like? 155
Starting a Web.. 157
Adding and Formatting Text.. 160
    Entering the Footer 161
    Creating the Home Page Title 163
    Listing the Current Specials 163
    Adding the Travel Options 165
    Building the Title for Pages 2 and 3... 167
    Entering the Offerings for a Travel Option 170

Importing the Details of a Travel Offering 172
Obtaining and Working with Graphics 177
   Creating and Inserting Graphics 177
   Adding Horizontal Lines 180
   Placing Clip Art 181
   Adding a Background 182
   Using Scanned Images 188

FrontPage on the Web: Jay's Seafood Restaurant **191**
   Web Site 191
   Webmaster Q & A 194

6 Using Microsoft Image Composer **197**
   The Image Composer Window 198
     Image Composer Toolbar and Menus 199
     Image Composer Toolbox and Palettes 200
   Working with Image Objects or Sprites 207
     Setting Up the Image Composer 207
     Inserting Sprites 209
     Selecting Sprites 211
     Moving, Sizing, Duplicating, and
       Rotating Sprites 215
     Adding Text Sprites 219
     Adding Geometric Shapes 225
     Working with Other Tools 230

7 Adding and Managing Hyperlinks and Hotspots **237**
   Adding Hyperlinks to Text and Graphics 239
     Assigning Hyperlinks to Text 239
     Assigning Hyperlinks to a Graphic 251
   Managing Hyperlinks 258

8 Using Tables and Frames **263**
   Designing with Tables 264
     Displaying Tabular Data in a Table 265
     Using a Table to Enhance a Layout 281
   Laying Out with Frames 286

FrontPage on the Web: Winnov, Ltd 294

Web Site 294

Webmaster Q & A 298

9 Working with Forms 299

Using Forms 300

Creating Forms with the Form Page Wizard 301

Building Forms from Scratch 316

Handling Form Input 324

10 Using WebBots 329

Incorporating WebBots in Your Webs 331

Comment Bot 331

Confirmation Field Bot 332

Include and Scheduled Include Bots 336

Scheduled Image Bot 337

Search Bot 339

Substitution Bot 341

Table of Contents Bot 344

Timestamp Bot 346

11 Importing and Integrating Office and Other Files 349

Importing Microsoft Office and
Other Productivity Files 350

Using Text from Microsoft Word and
Other Word Processors 351

Drag and Drop 368

Bringing Files from Other Productivity
Applications 370

Using Legacy Files on an Intranet 377

Looking at Imported Files in a Browser 378

Importing Multimedia Files 381

FrontPage on the Web: The BookBay 384

Web Site 384

Webmaster Q & A 386

12 Working with HTML 389

Introducing HTML 390

Using Basic Tags 391

Setting Paragraph Styles... 392

Applying Character Styles... 395

Displaying Characters 398

Style Sheets.. 401

Working with Images and Image Maps................................ 402

Adding Hyperlinks and Bookmarks.................................... 404

Defining Forms 407

Creating Tables 409

Incorporating Frames... 410

Using Multimedia 418

Understanding FrontPage-Generated HTML 418

How to Look at FrontPage HTML 421

Looking at a Simple HTML Example 425

Looking at Fantasy Travel HTML..................................... 426

Looking at the Corporate Presence HTML 428

Adding Capability to a FrontPage
Web with HTML... 433

How to Add HTML to FrontPage 433

Adding HTML to Display a Floating Frame 434

Inserting HTML to Modify a Table 435

HTML Authoring Resources 437

13 Working with Databases 441

Understanding Databases on the Web 442

Microsoft Access 445

Microsoft SQL Server.. 445

Internet Database Connector Files 446

Hypertext Extension Files 447

Structured Query Language Statements 448

Open Database Connectivity (ODBC) 451

How the Web Server Handles a Request 451

Building the Access Database.. 452

Creating Database Relationships....................................... 462

Adding Records to the Database 465

Defining a System Data Source Name 469

Creating Database Webs with FrontPage............................. 472

Creating an .IDC File.. 475

Creating a Hypertext Extension File 482

Finding Specific Products 485

Adding a Product to the Database 490

Deleting a Record 495

14 Security on the Web **499**

Areas Where Security Is Needed 500

Controlling Access 503

Securing Transmission 519

Authenticating People, Servers, and Data 523

Bibliography 524

FrontPage on the Web: NeedhamOnline 526

Web Site 526

Webmaster Q & A 530

15 Activating Your Webs **533**

Active Browser Features 534

Adding a Scrolling Marquee 535

Java 537

Object-Oriented Programming 537

Finding Java Applets 540

Installing the Java Software
         Development Kit 542

Working with Java 547

Compiling Java Applets 553

ActiveX 558

ActiveX and FrontPage 561

ActiveX and Netscape Navigator 566

Web Scripting Languages 575

JavaScript 576

VBScript 588

The FrontPage Script Wizard 591

The Microsoft Script Debugger 592

16 Setting Up an Intranet Web Site **595**

What Is an Intranet Site? 596

Why Have an Intranet? 598

What to Put on an Intranet 600

Building a FrontPage Intranet 602

    Installing TCP/IP on Your Network 602

    Configuring TCP/IP 605

    Using Your FrontPage Intranet 608

    Putting Information on Your Intranet 612

Web Page Version Control with SourceSafe 613

Security and Firewalls 615

17   Publishing and Promoting Webs on the Internet 617

Publishing Your Web Pages 618

    FrontPage Server Extensions 619

    Posting to a Host with FrontPage Server
    Extensions 623

    Posting to a Host Without
    FrontPage Server Extensions 626

Promoting Your Web Site 632

FrontPage on the Web: Bar Net 635

    Web Site 635

    Webmaster Q & A 639

A   Installing FrontPage 97 with Bonus Pack 641

What You Need to Install FrontPage 97
with Bonus Pack 643

What Components You'll Find in FrontPage 644

Installing Internet Explorer 3.0 645

Choosing and Installing a Server 647

Installing FrontPage 97 651

    Performing a Typical Installation 652

    Performing a Custom Installation 659

Checking Your Network Setup 662

Installing the Microsoft Image Composer 664

Installing the Web Publishing Wizard 666

B   FrontPage 97 Software Developer's Kit 669

Installing the FrontPage SDK 670

    Using the Common Gateway Interface (CGI) 673

Working with Designer HTML 674

Building your Own Templates 675

Applying the SDK Utilities 675

Creating Your Own WebBots 680

Using the SDK's Wizards 681

Index 683

Erik Poulsen, who is webmaster of Moms Online, (http://www.momsonline.com) in Port Townsend, Washington, not only excellently did much of the revision for this edition of the book, but also superbly wrote Chapters 13 and 15—two very significant additions to this edition. Erik not only knows the Web and the Internet, he knows what it takes to get a book out and he makes it happen. There is a lot of Erik in this book. Thanks, Erik!

John Cronan, who did the technical review of this book, did so with much expertise. He corrected many errors, added many tips and notes, and otherwise significantly improved the book. Thanks, John!

Janet Walden, Osborne's senior project editor, is among those people who are just fun to work with, who always have a smile in their voice, who are so competent at what they do that it always seems easy no matter how hard it is, and who have a caring respect for others that tells them they are valued. In the first edition, Janet had the job of turning a very rough manuscript into a great book in an unbelievably short time—and throughout it all, it was fun to work with her. In the second edition, she was capably assisted by **Judith Brown**. Thanks, Janet and Judith!

Jan Jue, the book's copy editor, is one of the best of her profession at finding those little inconsistencies that are so easy for the author to let slip by and yet can drive a reader crazy. In addition, Jan did a yeomen's job of removing all the grammatical, spelling, and stylistic errors that the author in his ignorance left in. Jan made a very major contribution to this book. Thanks, Jan!

Ann Sellers and **Heidi Poulin**, editorial assistant and associate project editor respectively, both put substantial effort into moving this book through the editorial process and handling all the little things that often get overlooked. And as important, they both did this with a friendly and gracious nature that made working with them a joy. Thanks Ann and Heidi!

George Henny, **Jeff Wallace**, and **Julie O'Brien** of WhidbeyNet, my Internet service provider, have been helpful in trying to set up the FrontPage server extensions and in answering my questions. Thanks, George, Jeff, and Julie!

Carole Boggs Matthews, life partner and sharer of our parenting thrills and spills, and an author in her own right, provided the all necessary support without which no project like this could ever get done. Thanks, my love!

As the interest in the Internet and its World Wide Web has skyrocketed, so has the desire of both organizations and individuals to have a presence there, to put up their own web sites and be a part of the Internet phenomenon. At the same time, organizations are using the same technology to install intranets at a geometric rate, and therefore they have the need to create their own web sites to use internally. The problem has been that the tools to create both Internet and intranet web sites have been very crude and anything but easy to use. FrontPage has changed all of that. FrontPage provides a very easy-to-use, full-featured set of tools for the expert creation, delivery, and maintenance of web sites. And FrontPage does this in a WYSIWYG environment where you can see what you are doing as you are doing it.

Unfortunately, FrontPage comes with a slim manual that gives only the briefest of instructions. *Web Publishing with Microsoft FrontPage 97, Second Edition* fills this void by giving you a clear, concise, hands-on guide to this extremely powerful product.

About This Book

Web Publishing with Microsoft FrontPage 97, Second Edition leads you through the planning, creation, testing, deployment, and maintenance of both intranet and Internet web sites with FrontPage. It does this using substantial real-world examples and clear, step-by-step instructions. All of the major features of FrontPage are explained and demonstrated in such a way that you can follow along and see for yourself how each is used, including the new database connectivity and the incorporation of Java, ActiveX, JavaScript, and Visual Basic Script. In addition, this book takes you beyond basic FrontPage web site creation and introduces you to HTML and how to use it with FrontPage, as well as how to set up an intranet site, how to manage Internet and intranet security, and how to publish and promote your web site. *Web Publishing with Microsoft FrontPage 97, Second Edition* provides the one complete reference on how to make the most of FrontPage. If you are going to purchase FrontPage, or if you already use it, you need this book!

How This Book Is Organized

Web Publishing with Microsoft FrontPage 97, Second Edition is written the way most people learn. It starts by reviewing the basic concepts and then uses a learn-by-doing method to demonstrate the major features of the product.

Throughout, the book uses detailed examples and clear explanations to give you the insight needed to make the fullest use of FrontPage.

The book begins by introducing you to web sites and FrontPage:

■ Chapter 1, "Designing and Creating Quality Web Pages," explores the world of the Internet and intranets and looks at what makes good web pages.

■ Chapter 2, "Exploring FrontPage," takes you on a tour of the major FrontPage features, giving you a taste of the power inherent in this product.

The next nine chapters demonstrate each of the major features of FrontPage by leading you through examples of their implementation:

■ Chapter 3, "Using Wizards," shows you how to create webs and web pages with these powerful tools.

■ Chapter 4, "Using Templates," not only demonstrates the use of templates in creating both webs and web pages, but also how to create templates themselves.

■ Chapter 5, "Creating and Formatting a Web Page from Scratch," sets aside the wizards and templates and looks at the steps necessary to create a full-featured web on your own.

■ Chapter 6, "Using Microsoft Image Composer," shows you how to create and edit graphics that can be used in webs.

■ Chapter 7, "Adding and Managing Hyperlinks and Hotspots," explores how to add interactivity and interconnectedness to your web.

■ Chapter 8, "Using Tables and Frames," describes two completely different methods of segmenting a page and shows how you can make the best use of these tools.

■ Chapter 9, "Working with Forms," explains ways to let the web user communicate back to you, the web creator.

■ Chapter 10, "Using WebBots," describes how to both automate some of the web creation process, as well as extend a web's interactive features.

■ Chapter 11, "Importing and Integrating Office and Other Files," shows you how to use existing or legacy files in your intranet and Internet webs.

The final six chapters cover ways of extending and enhancing what you can do with FrontPage.

- Chapter 12, "Working with HTML," provides an extensive introduction to the HTML language and how to use it with FrontPage.

- Chapter 13, "Working with Databases," introduces you to databases and shows you how to incorporate them in your own FrontPage webs.

- Chapter 14, "Security on the Web," looks at what the Internet and intranet security issues are and explains what you can do to minimize the risks.

- Chapter 15, "Activating Your Webs," describes the Java, ActiveX, JavaScript, and Visual Basic Script technologies that are being used to activate web sites and then shows you how to incorporate them in your own webs.

- Chapter 16, "Setting Up an Intranet Web Site," leads you through the steps to create an intranet in your organization.

- Chapter 17, "Publishing and Promoting Webs on the Internet," looks at how to locate an Internet service provider, how to transfer your completed webs to their servers, and then how to promote your webs once they're online.

Web Publishing with Microsoft FrontPage 97, Second Edition concludes with two appendixes:

- Appendix A provides a detailed set of instructions on how to install all the components on the Microsoft FrontPage 97 with Bonus Pack CD under different circumstances.

- Appendix B describes how to obtain, install, and use the FrontPage 97 Software Developer's kit that Microsoft makes available for advanced users.

See for Yourself: FrontPage on the Web

Scattered throughout the book are six "FrontPage on the Web" sections that showcase actual commercial web sites that have been created with FrontPage. In addition to discussing the sites, each section also includes a question and answer session with the webmaster(s), all of whom have been using FrontPage since early

1996. The webmasters share what their experiences with FrontPage have been and offer helpful tips on, as well as their likes and dislikes of, the program. These people have all done what you are setting out to do.

Internet Site Provides Files and Links

The Osborne/McGraw-Hill Internet site (http://www.osborne.com) and, in particular, the web page for this book (http://www.osborne.com/int/frontpa.htm) provide access to many of the files that were used or created in this book. You can find all of the resulting web files that were created by the exercises here, as well as many of the starting files used to produce the web pages (some of the photos, logos, and text from the cruise lines used in several chapters is proprietary material and cannot be placed on the Internet). Also, the web page for the book has many of the Internet links mentioned, allowing you to simply click an get to the reference. Make **http://www.osborne.com/int/frontpa.htm** a bookmark or favorite, and quickly get to the resources you need.

Conventions Used in This Book

Web Publishing with Microsoft FrontPage 97, Second Edition uses several conventions designed to make the book easier for you to follow. Among these are

- **Bold type** is used for text that you are to type from the keyboard.

- *Italic type* is used for a word or phrase that is being defined or otherwise deserves special emphasis.

- The Courier typeface is used for the HTML code that is either produced by FrontPage or entered by the user.

- SMALL CAPITAL LETTERS are used for keys on the keyboard such as ENTER and SHIFT.

- When you are expected to enter a command, you are told to press the key(s). If you are to enter text or numbers, you are told to type them.

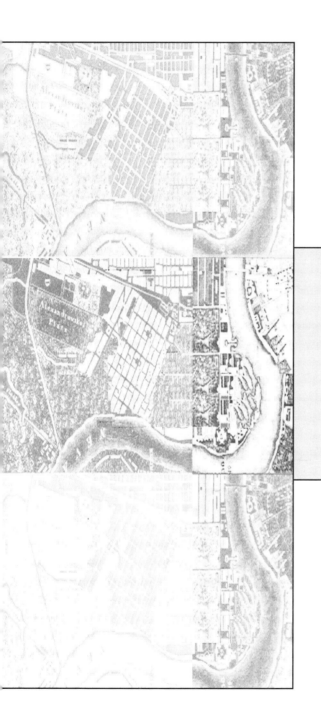

Designing and Creating Quality Web Pages

Communication, whether it be within a small group, throughout a large organization, or among many organizations, can almost always be improved—made faster, easier to receive, and easier to respond to. One recent improvement is the *web page,* a text and graphics form of communication transmitted by computers. While computers sit on the sending and receiving ends of web page communication, it is what *links* the computers that gives web pages one of their most important features. The link means that senders and receivers can operate independently—senders can put the web page up according to their schedule, and receivers can get it anytime thereafter. The link used for the transmission of web pages is one of two forms of networking, either the public *Internet,* which uses phone lines, or a private *intranet,* which uses a *local area network (LAN),* generally within an organization.

The Internet and the World Wide Web

Not long ago, using "Information Superhighway," "the Internet," or "the Web" in everyday conversation might have produced blank looks. Now the Internet and the *World Wide Web* (also known as "WWW" or simply, "the Web") are talked about daily in the news, in schools, and in conversations among friends and coworkers. Many people still don't really understand what the Internet and the Web are, but they know they're out there and will affect how people live, work, and communicate.

Being able to access the resources of the Internet and having a presence on the World Wide Web are becoming as necessary as having a telephone. You could certainly get by without a telephone, but by doing so you would cut yourself off from communicating with the millions of people who do have telephones. As this is written (at the end of 1996) there are over 30 million sites on the World Wide Web, hosted on 275,600 servers. These range from personal pages, where individuals can share their opinions or interests with the world, to educational and corporate sites getting hundreds of thousands of *hits* (connections made to a web site) a day.

The Internet and the World Wide Web form the foundation of a global communications revolution that will change the way people communicate, work, and conduct business. They will make it easier and cheaper to exchange information, ideas, and products around the globe. Accessing a web site in Australia is as easy as accessing a web site across the street.

In this book you will learn how you can be part of this revolution. You will learn how to use FrontPage to create and maintain a presence on the Web for your business, your organization, or for yourself. This book will take you through all the steps necessary to create your own web page—from initial design to placing your page on a web server where it can be accessed by anyone on the Web.

LANs and an Intranet

As important as the Internet has become to society, local area networks (LANs) have become even more important to the exchange of information and communication within organizations. LANs started out as a means to share programs and data files among several people in an organization. This was then augmented by electronic mail (e-mail) for sending and receiving messages over the LAN. Recently, *intranets* have been added to LANs to provide a miniature version of the World Wide Web within an organization—a place for people to post and read text and graphics documents if and when they choose.

A good example of an intranet web page is a project report. Instead of e-mailing a weekly report to a long list of potentially interested people (and filling up everybody's in-basket in the process), you could create a web page that would not only give the current status, but also other, more static information, such as the people working on the project, its goals, and its funding. In this way, those people who are truly interested can get the information.

With the Internet Database Connector (IDC) included with Microsoft's Internet Information Server (IIS) even more intranet interactivity is possible. Any Microsoft Office document can be included in a web page. Access databases can be queried, and custom web pages can automatically be generated to display the results of the query. Integrating Office and other files with your FrontPage web sites is covered in Chapter 11, and databases are covered in Chapter 13.

NOTE: *Internet Information Server (IIS) is included with Microsoft's Windows NT 4.0 Server. IIS and FrontPage provide all the software tools you need to set up an intranet or World Wide Web site.*

Except for possibly the content, there is no difference between a web page on the World Wide Web and a web page on an intranet. They are created the same way and can have the same features and components. The discussion and instructions throughout this book are aimed equally at the Web and an intranet, and there are examples of each. So in learning to create a web page, you can apply that knowledge to either form of dissemination.

TIP: *Think of the Internet and a LAN as equivalent means of information transmission, one public and the other private. And think of the Web and an intranet as equivalent means of posting and reading information being transmitted over the Internet or a LAN, respectively. The Web and an intranet are just advanced electronic bulletin boards, and a web page is an electronic document posted on that bulletin board.*

What Is a Web Page?

Since the focus of this book is how to create web pages, here's a more detailed definition of what a web page is. A good starting place is that a *web page* is a text file containing HyperText Markup Language (HTML) formatting tags, and links to graphics files and other web pages. The text file is stored on a *web server* and can be accessed by other computers connected to the server, via the Internet or a LAN. The file can also be accessed by use of *web browsers*—programs that download the file to your computer, interpret the HTML tags and links, and display the results on your monitor. Another definition is that a web page is an interactive form of communication that uses a computer network.

There are two properties of web pages that make them unique: they are interactive and they can use multimedia. The term *multimedia* is used to describe text, audio, animation, and video files that are combined to present information—for example, in an interactive encyclopedia or a game. When those same types of files are distributed over the Internet or a LAN, you can use the term *hypermedia* to describe them. With the World Wide Web it is now possible to have true multimedia over the Internet. However, unless your clients have a high-speed service, such as the Integrated Services Digital Network's (ISDN) 128-Kbps service, downloading the large hypermedia files takes too long to routinely use them. On most LANs, which are considerably faster, this is much more doable, but there are still limitations and a potential need to keep the LAN open for high-volume data traffic.

Web pages are interactive because the reader or user can send information or commands to a web site that will control an application running on the web server.

For example, Figure 1-1 shows the home page of Digital's AltaVista web index. The AltaVista home page gives you access to an application that searches the AltaVista index of web sites. You can use this and other search engines to locate sites on the Web. From this web page you can select which part of the Internet to search, how the results of the search will be displayed, and the keywords that the search will be based on. When you click on the Submit button, the information you've entered is sent to the AltaVista web server. The database is then searched, and the results are used to create a new web page, which is displayed by your web browser. Figure 1-2 shows the results of a search using the keyword "origami."

Each web page has an address called the *Uniform Resource Locator (URL)*. The URL for the AltaVista home page is *http://www.altavista.digital.com.* The URL is displayed in the Address *combo* box (a combination of a text box and a drop-down menu) at the top of the screen (below the toolbar). A URL is the path on the Internet to a specific web page. It is used in the same way you use a path name to locate files on your computer. In this case, the URL tells you that the web page is located on a web server named *altavista.digital.com* connected to the World Wide Web (WWW).

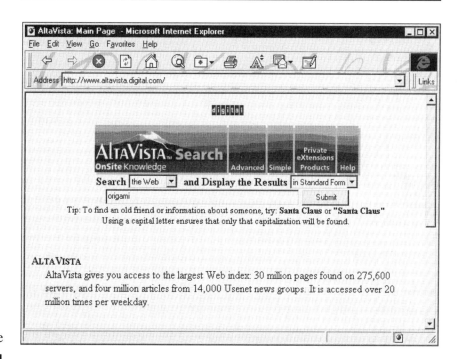

AltaVista
home page

FIGURE 1-1

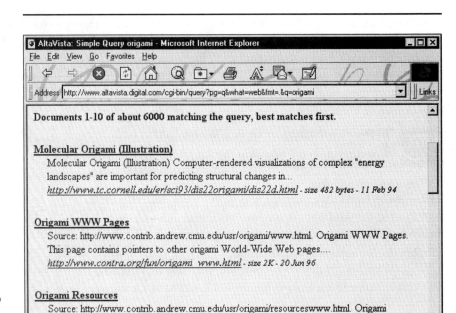

AltaVista web page created to display results of search

FIGURE 1-2

The actual filename of the home page is usually either *default.htm* or *index.htm;* it is implied by being unstated. On a LAN the URL is similar; it uses the server name in a format like *http://servername/directory/homepage filename.* The home page file can also be left off if it is *index.htm* or *default.htm.*

 NOTE: *Web pages located on web servers using the UNIX operating system generally have an .HTML extension, while web pages located on Windows NT web servers generally have an .HTM extension.*

AltaVista found about 6,000 web pages containing the keyword "origami." The web page created by the AltaVista server displays the title of each web page, an excerpt from the text on the page, and the URL for the page. Both the title of the page and the URL are displayed in a different color than the other text and are underlined. This indicates they are *hyperlinks.* Clicking on a hyperlink will cause your browser to load the location (web page) specified in the hyperlink. The hyperlink may take you to an actual location, or *bookmark,* within the same document, the way a bookmark works in a word processor file, or it may link you to a web site anywhere in the world. In fact, if a web page doesn't have an obvious identifier to its location, you may not even be aware of what country the web server you are connected to is in. You may start "surfing" the Web by clicking on hyperlinks on various pages to follow a train of thought and end up "traveling" around the world.

TIP: *With the latest Microsoft (3.0) and Netscape (3.0) browsers it is not necessary to enter* http:// *in the Address text box. With Microsoft's Internet Explorer 3.0 you can also search the Yahoo! search engine by typing* **go** *followed by the keywords in the Address text box. For example,* **go origami***.*

NOTE: *Hyperlinks do not have to be underlined, although they will be displayed in a different color than the body text. With most web browsers you can use the Preferences option to control whether hyperlinks will be underlined, and you can also set the color they will be displayed in.*

When you submit keywords or other information to a web site, such as AltaVista, you are actually running an application on the web server. Web servers can also download applications, for example, a Java applet, to your computer. *Java* is programming language that extends the flexibility and functions of the Web. *Applets* are small programs that are downloaded to your computer and then executed. An example of a Java applet is a currency-conversion program. When you click on the hyperlink to the applet, it is downloaded to your computer. You then enter the amount and type of currency you want to convert and the type of currency you want to convert it to, and the applet performs the conversion. You do not have to know how to program in Java in order to use a Java applet—a growing library of applets is already available on the Web. A good place to start is the Java home page (http://www.javasoft.com) or the Gamelan home page (http://www.gamelan.com). Java, JavaScript, ActiveX, and Visual BasicScript are all described in Chapter 15.

TIP: *You can turn support for Java applets on or off in Internet Explorer 3.0 by opening the Options dialog box from the View menu, selecting the Advanced tab, and clicking on the Enable Java JIT Compiler check box. In Netscape Navigator 3.0 you can turn support for Java applets and JavaScript on or off by opening the Network Preferences dialog box from the Options menu, selecting the Languages tab, and then clicking on the Enable Java and Enable JavaScript check boxes.*

As you can see, the World Wide Web is a flexible and powerful means of communication. How did this new medium come about?

The Birth of the Internet

The Internet is simply a set of computer hardware and software standards, or *protocols,* that allow computers to exchange data with other computers. The computers can be in the same room, or they can be located around the world from each other. They can use the same operating system software, such as Windows 95, or each can use a different computer operating system, such as Macintosh System 7.5 or UNIX. The standards that make up the Internet have become a modern *lingua franca*—a language enabling any computer connected to the Internet to exchange information with any other computer also connected to the Internet, regardless of the operating systems the computers use.

The birth of the Internet can be traced back to the launch of the first Sputnik by the Soviet Union in 1957. Concerned about losing the space race, the U.S. government created the Advanced Research Projects Agency (ARPA). By the late 1960s the use of computers by ARPA and other government agencies had expanded so much that a way for the computer systems to share data was needed. ARPANET, the predecessor to what we now know as the Internet, was created to meet this need.

The early growth of the Internet was funded by the government, but just as important as the money provided for research was the ability to impose standards on the computer industry. In the 1960s computers made by different manufacturers were, for the most part, unable to exchange data because of differences in their software. As ARPA defined the standards that have become the foundation of the Internet, it required manufacturers to support those standards if they wanted to do business with the government. This ensured that all computers would be able to exchange data with each other.

Another milestone in the history of the Internet came in the mid-1980s, when the National Science Foundation (NSF) added its five supercomputing centers (NSFNET) to the Internet. This gave educational centers, the military, and other NSF grantees access to the power of these supercomputers and, more importantly, created the *backbone* of today's Information Superhighway. This backbone is made up of all the high-capacity (or *wide-bandwidth)* phone lines and data links needed to effectively transfer all the information now on the Internet. Until this wide-bandwidth infrastructure existed, the potential of ARPANET, NSFNET, and now the Internet couldn't be realized. By the end of the 1980s almost all the pieces were in place for a global telecommunications revolution.

The World Wide Web

Before 1990 the Internet had grown to be a highway linking computers across the United States and around the world, but it was still a character-based system. That is, what appeared on computer screens connected to the Internet was simply text. There were no graphics or hyperlinks. A graphical user interface (GUI) to the Internet needed to be developed. Tim Berners-Lee, a scientist working at the European Laboratory for Particle Physics (CERN) in Geneva, Switzerland, proposed a set of protocols for the transfer of graphical information over the Internet in 1989. Berners-Lee's proposals were adopted by other groups, and the World Wide Web was born.

The Internet is a wide area network (WAN), as compared with a local area network (LAN) among computers in proximity. For computers to share information over a WAN, there must be a physical connection (the communications infrastructure created by ARPA and the NSF and now maintained by private industry) and a common software standard that the computers use to transfer data. The physical connection depends on whether you use a modem to dial up to the Internet, or whether your computer is part of a LAN with an Internet connection. The physical layer includes the modem or network interface card in your computer. You also need a phone or dedicated network line that connects you to the Internet backbone. In either case, your computer, connected to the Internet either with a dialup or network connection, has the potential to share information with any other computer connected to the Internet anywhere in the world.

The Internet and the Web are built upon several protocols:

- **Transmission Control Protocol/Internet Protocol (TCP/IP)** controls how information is packaged to be transferred between computers connected through the Internet.

- **HyperText Transfer Protocol (HTTP)** is the language the computers use to exchange information on the Web.

- **HyperText Markup Language (HTML)** is the programming language used to create the documents that are distributed on the Web and displayed on your monitor.

TCP/IP

To transfer information over the Internet or within a LAN, several requirements must be met. These include a way to assign each computer or site on the network a unique address (just like having a unique postal address) and "packaging" the information for transmission. These functions are handled by the Transmission Control Protocol and the Internet Protocol.

INTERNET PROTOCOL   The foundation of the system is the Internet Protocol (IP). The IP converts data into *packets* and provides an address for each site on the Internet. Packets are like the pages of a book. An entire book contains too much information to be printed on one page, so it is divided into multiple pages. This makes the information in the book much more manageable. The Internet Protocol does the same thing with the information in a file that is to be transmitted over the Internet or a LAN. It divides the information into packets that can be handled more easily by the network.

The other primary function of the IP is to provide addresses for the computers connected to the Internet. Each computer needs its own *IP address,* a group of four decimal numbers that provides a unique address for the computer. Examples of IP addresses are 198.68.191.10 and 204.250.144.70. These IP addresses are actually decimal representations of single 32-bit binary numbers. While a computer may be comfortable with 11000110 01000100 10111111 00001010 or 11001100 11111010 10010000 01000110 as an address, most people find decimal numbers easier to work with. This system of numbering allows for about 4.3 billion (2^{32}) possible combinations. If you are setting up a web server, you will need to get an IP address. These are assigned by the Internet Network Information Center (InterNIC, http://www.internic.net). Your Internet service provider (ISP) can help you get an IP address. If you will be using an existing web server, the network administrator or *webmaster* will be able to tell you what the IP addresses are.

TRANSMISSION CONTROL PROTOCOL   While the Internet Protocol provides the basics for sharing information over the Internet, it leaves some things to be desired. The two most important are ensuring that all the packets reach their destination and that they arrive in the proper order. This is where the Transmission Control Protocol (TCP) steps in. To understand how it works, assume you want to send a book to someone and you have to mail it one page (or packet) at a time. Also assume that there are no page numbers in the book.

How will recipients know that they received all the pages, and how will they know the proper order of the pages? TCP solves these problems by creating an "envelope" for each packet generated by the IP. Each envelope has a serialized number that identifies the packet inside it. As each packet is sent, the TCP assigns it a number that increases by 1 for each packet sent. When the packets are received, the numbers are checked for continuity and sequence. If any numbers are missing,

the receiving computer requests that the missing packet be ré-sent. If the packets are out of sequence, the receiving computer puts them back in order. TCP also makes sure the information arrives in the same condition it was sent (that the data was not corrupted in transit).

TCP/IP provides the basic tools for transferring information over the Internet. The next layer up the ladder is the HyperText Transfer Protocol, the traffic director for the Web.

NOTE: *To set up an intranet on a LAN, you must add the TCP/IP protocols to the existing networking protocols (probably either IPX/SPX or NetBEUI) on both the server and all clients. Chapter 17 tells you how to do this.*

HyperText Transfer Protocol

The HyperText Transfer Protocol (HTTP) is the heart of the World Wide Web and is also used with an intranet. HTTP composes the messages and handles the information that is sent between computers on the Internet using TCP/IP. To understand how HTTP works, you first need to understand the nature of client/server relationships.

CLIENT/SERVER RELATIONSHIPS   The basic function of the Internet or a LAN is to provide a means for transferring information between computers. To do this, one computer (the *server*) will contain information and another (the *client*) will request it. The server will process a client's request and transfer the information. The server may be required to process the request before it can be filled. For example, if the request is for information contained in a database, such as a request submitted to the AltaVista web index, the server would first have to extract the information from the database before it could be sent to the client.

The passing of information between a client and a server has four basic steps:

1. A connection is made between the client and the server. This is handled by TCP/IP.

2. The client sends a request to the server. The request is in the form of an HTTP message.

3. The server processes the request and responds to the client. Again, this is in the form of an HTTP message.

4. The connection between the client and the server is terminated.

To access information on the Web or an intranet, you need an application that can send requests to a server and that can process and display the server's response. This is the function of *web browsers*. The two most common web browsers are Microsoft's Internet Explorer and Netscape's Navigator.

HyperText Markup Language

The parts of the Web or an intranet covered so far, TCP/IP and HTTP, control how information is transferred over the network. HyperText Markup Language (HTML) is the component that controls how the information is displayed. The information sent from a web server is an HTML document. Here's what a simple HTML document looks like:

```
<HTML>
<HEAD>
<TITLE>A Simple HTML Document</TITLE>
</HEAD>
<BODY>
<H1>A Simple HTML Document</H1>
<B>This text is bold</B> and <I>this text is italic.</I>
</BODY>
</HTML>
```

Figure 1-3 shows how this HTML document is displayed by a web browser. Web browsers interpret the HTML document and display the results on your monitor. HTML files are simple ASCII text files that contain formatting tags which control how information (text and graphics) is displayed and how other file types are executed (audio and video files, for example).

HTML tags are usually used in pairs. An HTML document must begin with the <HTML> opening tag and end with the </HTML> closing tag. The <HEAD> </HEAD> tags enclose information about the web page, such as the title, which is defined by the <TITLE> </TITLE> tags and displayed in the title bar of the web browser. The body of the web page is enclosed by the <BODY> </BODY> tags. The <H1> </H1> tags define the enclosed text as a level-1 heading. The <B> </B> and <I> </I> tags respectively define text as bold or italic, as you can see in Figure 1-3.

 NOTE: *HTML tags are not case sensitive. They can be upper- or lowercase, or mixed case, such as <Body>.*

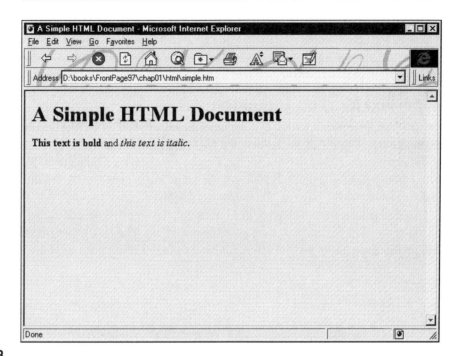

A simple
HTML
document
FIGURE 1-3

In the early days of the Web, these tags were typed in by use of a simple text editor to create web pages. This was time-consuming and not much fun. Today you can use FrontPage, a true WYSIWYG (what you see is what you get) HTML editor, to create your web pages. Gone are the days when you had to learn all the HTML tags and proper syntax. With FrontPage you design a page, and the proper HTML is created automatically. It's never been easier to create your own web site.

In the next section you will learn what makes a good web site.

Designing for the Web

Like any other medium, the Web has idiosyncrasies that the good designer has to be aware of and compensate for. Because the Web is strictly a computer-based medium, the hardware your work will be displayed on (the video card, monitor, and settings) and the particular web browser used will have a tremendous impact on how your work appears.

Monitor Resolution

If you've designed works for paper, you are used to having a fixed-size "canvas" to work with. As you lay out the elements of the design, you know exactly how the design will appear when finished and viewed by the audience. This is not the case when you design for the Web. Your work may be displayed on a Macintosh with a 512x342 pixel monochrome display, or a PC with a 1024x768 pixel SVGA display. On the Web, graphics are displayed at a resolution chosen when they are added to a page. A graphic that fills the screen at a 640x480 resolution will only use a quarter of the screen at a 1024x768 resolution. Figure 1-4 shows a web page displayed at a 640x480 resolution. Figure 1-5 shows the same page at 800x600 resolution, and Figure 1-6 shows the page at 1024x768 resolution.

As you can see, the web page in Figures 1-4 through 1-6 was designed so that it would be a cohesive design at each possible resolution. The best way to tell how your design will appear is to view it on monitors at different resolutions as you work on it.

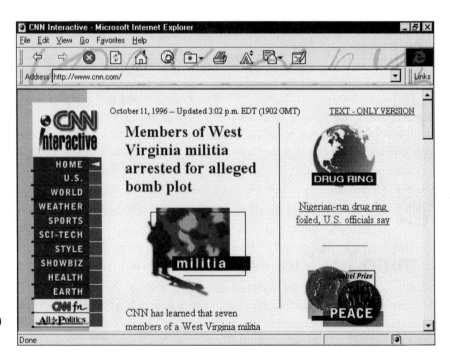

Web page at 640x480 resolution

FIGURE 1-4

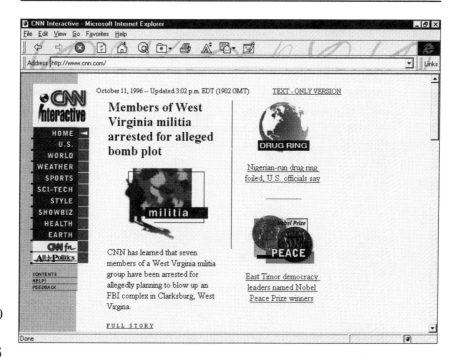

Web page
at 800x600
resolution

FIGURE 1-5

Since this isn't always easy to do (your computer may need to be rebooted each time you change your video resolution), the next best thing is to work at 640x480 resolution and check your work at the different resolutions when you're done. In all probability, your work will be viewed at 640x480 resolution most of the time.

TIP: *If you are using Windows 95, you can often change your resolution without rebooting by right-clicking on the desktop, choosing Properties, selecting Settings, and changing the Desktop Area. Also, there is a free utility available from Microsoft's Power Toys web page (http://www.microsoft .com/windows/software/powertoy.htm) called QuickRes. This utility allows you to change your video resolution more often without rebooting your system.*

Monitor Color Settings

On a PC, the number of colors a monitor can display can be 16 or 256 or 64,000 (16-bit High Color) or 16 million (24-bit True Color). Again, you have no control

Web page
at 1024
x768
resolution

FIGURE 1-6

over how many colors your work will be displayed with, and it is inevitable that
your work will be displayed on some monitors with only 16 colors.

The decision you have as a web page designer is whether to limit yourself to the
lowest common denominator (16-color, 640x480 resolution) or to work at a higher
standard. If you are designing a simple page with limited graphics, limiting your
design to 16 colors may make sense. It ensures compatibility with virtually all the
systems your work will be displayed on. (If someone is using a monochrome monitor
to view your work, the point is moot, of course.)

However, if you limit yourself to 16 colors, you will not be able to effectively
use scanned photographs or graphics with subtle shadings. In that case it would be
better to use at least 256 colors. You cannot limit yourself to the lowest common
denominator in every case. You simply have to accept that your work will not look
its best on lower-end systems. The people with these systems hopefully will upgrade
them as they discover that other people's systems look a lot better!

Another point to remember about color is that every monitor will display colors
a little differently. There are many factors that affect how colors are displayed on a

monitor, ranging from the age of the monitor to the light in the room. If you've worked with programs like Photoshop and have output to color printers, you know how difficult it can be to get the printed output to exactly match the colors you see on the monitor. If it's important that a particular color appear exactly the correct shade on a web page—when it's part of a logo, for example—you're simply out of luck. You can calibrate your own monitor and ensure the color is correct on a calibrated system, but once you turn it loose on the Web, you have no control over how it will appear.

If you design your web pages to be displayed on a 256-color, 640x480 resolution monitor and remember it will look different at other video resolutions, you can count on most people seeing your work the way you intended.

Data Throughput

Another factor that must be considered in the design of a web page is *data throughput*—how long it will take the page to be downloaded and displayed. People tend to have short attention spans. If your page is taking too long to download, the user is likely to go on to another page without waiting for your page to finish loading. The two primary factors in the time it takes for a web page to be transferred are the size of the page, including graphics and other files, and the speed of the user's modem or network. You should remember that there are still quite a few 14,400 baud (14.4 Kbps) modems in use. (Anything slower, such as 2,400 or 9,600 baud modems, is almost useless for accessing the Web.) If everyone had ISDN (128 Kbps) lines, this would be less of a problem, but it will be a while before that happens.

The text portion of a web page (the HTML) is rarely large enough to cause long downloads; the usual culprits are graphic and multimedia files. There are several things you can do to minimize the problem. The first is to keep your graphic and multimedia files as small as possible. Some of the ways you can do that are discussed later in this chapter in the section "Working with Graphics." You can also create several smaller pages, rather than one large page. You then use hyperlinks to connect the pages. This breaks up the loading time (the theory being that the user will tolerate several short delays better than one long delay).

TIP: *FrontPage has a way of including the contents of one page on another (as you'll see in Chapter 2) that both makes repeated elements like headings easy to do and speeds loading.*

Another factor is the bandwidth of the web server where the page is located. If the server has a narrow bandwidth connection to the Internet (such as a 56-Kbps analog line), it can be easily overloaded when it's accessed by several users at the same time. If the server has a wide-bandwidth connection—a full T1 (1.544 Mbps), for example—it is much less likely to be overloaded. However, the Internet has grown to the point where popular web servers are noticeably slower at peak times of the day and on weekends, even with wide-bandwidth connections.

Web Browsers

All web browsers interpret and display HTML-encoded files. Currently, HTML 2.0 is the last accepted standard, and HTML 3.2 is being developed (HTML 3.0 was never finalized). The manufacturers of web browsers, principally Microsoft and Netscape, chose not to wait for HTML 3.0 to be defined and implemented their own versions of HTML 3.0. This has been good for the Web to the extent that advances in browser capabilities have been made faster, but the compatibility of browsers has suffered. Some of the extensions offered by Microsoft and Netscape are compatible with each other, while others will only work with their own browser. Figure 1-7 shows a web page that uses some of the HTML tags introduced by Microsoft and Netscape displayed by use of Microsoft's Internet Explorer 3.0. Figure 1-8 shows the same page displayed with Netscape Navigator 3.0, Figure 1-9 shows the page displayed with NCSA Mosaic 2.1.1, and Figure 1-10 shows the page in the FrontPage 97 Editor. As you can see, each browser, using its default settings, displays the HTML file slightly differently. Today, visible differences between the major browsers are minor. The largest differences are for support of technologies such as Java and ActiveX, and scripting languages such as JavaScript and VBScript (see Chapter 15).

At the top of the page are a level-1 heading followed by a level-2 heading. Below the heads are two tables separated by a horizontal rule. Tables were introduced in the draft specification of HTML 3.0. All three browsers support tables (with some differences). The first table has one row and one column. The first table illustrates two important differences between the three browsers. Internet Explorer and Navigator allow you to change the background color of a cell in a table and the typeface (font) of text, while NCSA Mosaic does not. Internet Explorer and Navigator also allow you to change the width of borders in tables; NCSA Mosaic doesn't. Another difference is the amount of space inserted by the browser after a table or other element. Internet Explorer and Mosaic add space between elements; Navigator does not.

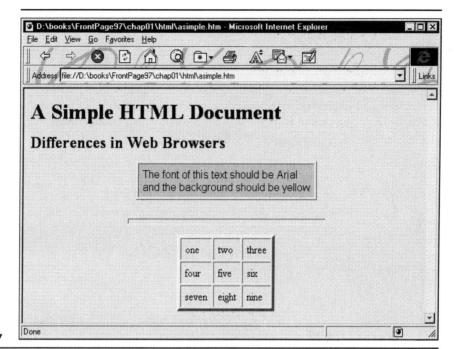

A simple web page displayed with Internet Explorer (v 3.0)

FIGURE 1-7

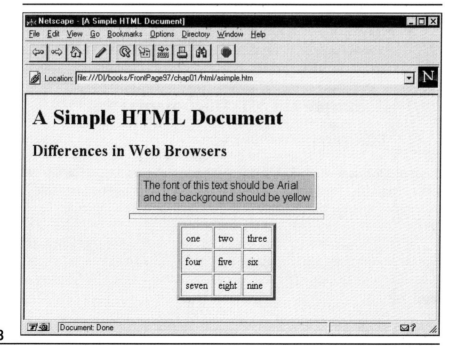

A simple web page displayed with Netscape Navigator (v 3.0)

FIGURE 1-8

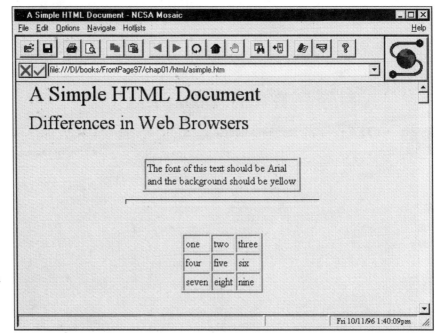

A simple
web page
displayed
with NCSA
Mosaic (v
2.1.1)

FIGURE 1-9

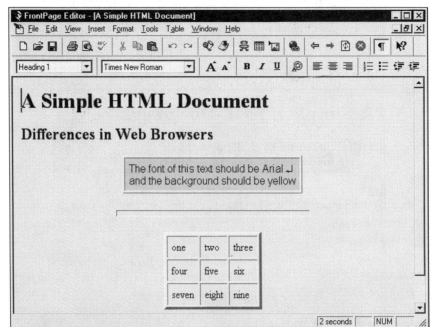

A simple
web page
displayed
with the
FrontPage
97 Editor

FIGURE 1-10

All three browsers interpret horizontal rules the same. In this example, the width of the rule is 50 percent of the window and the size (height) is 8 pixels. The final element of the page is a table with three rows and three columns. Internet Explorer and Navigator display the table in the same way, with a wider border than the first table, while NCSA Mosaic displays the same border for both tables. The Frame feature also reveals differences in browsers (see Chapter 8).

 NOTE: *This example web page was written to illustrate the differences between web browsers. By being careful, you can minimize many, but not all, of the differences between web browsers.*

Since you will have no control over which web browser your work will be displayed with, what HTML features should you use? Should you never use some features like fonts and cell background colors because some browsers don't support them? The short answer is no. HTML is actually a very limited language for page layout and design, and limiting yourself to the lowest common denominator will produce some very boring pages. Both Internet Explorer and Netscape Navigator have features not supported by any other browser. If you decide that you want to use one of the unsupported features, you have to encourage the user to use the browser you tailored your design to. This is not as difficult as it may sound. Microsoft and Netscape together dominate the web browser market, and both offer free versions of their browsers on the Web for downloading. At the top of your web page you can simply create a hyperlink to either the Internet Explorer or Navigator download sites, and tell users they need one or the other. In fact, both companies provide graphics (shown here) that you can insert in your page to link to the downloadable files.

As a web designer, you need to use all the tools at your disposal. By checking how your work will appear with different web browsers, you can minimize many design problems. When you need to use an unsupported HTML element, you can make it easy for users to download the web browser they need. What you cannot do, if you really want to create good work, is limit yourself to the lowest common denominator.

Content

Good graphic design for your web pages is only half the battle. Your web pages also need to be interesting—there has to be a reason for people to visit your web site. The content of your web site is just as important, if not more important, than the design.

First and foremost, your web site has to be rich in content, not hype. For example, if your site was created for marketing your line of kayaks, include the history of the sport, stories (with photos) of trips your users have taken, information for people new to the sport, hyperlinks to related sites (not necessarily your competitors), and anything else you can think of that might be interesting to kayakers. Don't just put up an online catalog and expect people to come back.

Next, be organized. Give people the tools they need to navigate your site. Before you start the graphic design for your site, plan the information flow. How will content areas be linked? How will users get around the site? Will they be able to get to any area in one hop, or will they have to traverse a convoluted series of links? Make it easy for your users. If they get frustrated trying to navigate your site, they won't be back. If people can download audio files from your site, make sure they can also download whatever player they need for the file. Don't make them search the Web, or even your site, for it.

Keep your site fresh. Update as often as you can. People are not going to come back to see the same old stuff. In the kayaking example, consider updating the trips featured every month. In winter (in the Northern Hemisphere) feature trips in New Zealand. Compare your web site to a magazine—no one would subscribe to a magazine that was exactly the same every month; it would be boring. Your web site is no different.

Make sure your visitors know who you are. Identify every page in your site—don't rely on just the page title displayed in the web browser title bar. You don't have to have your name in a level-1 heading on each page, but make sure that if someone is following a link from another site, they know where they are.

Do it today. If you don't, someone else will. The Web is a fast moving, extremely competitive environment. You don't have time to rest on your laurels. With over 30 million web sites already in existence, you have plenty of competition for people's attention. You can create a world-class web site, but it will take effort, planning, and creativity. Give people content and make it as easy as possible for them to get it.

Working with Graphics

Graphic images are an important element of your web site. On the Web, graphics come in two basic flavors: GIF and JPEG. Each format has its advantages and disadvantages.

TIP: *FrontPage allows you to bring in graphics in several standard formats such as PCX, TIF, and EPS, and FrontPage will convert them to GIF and JPEG formats.*

GIF

The Graphic Interchange Format (GIF) was originally developed by CompuServe to minimize the size of graphics files. The smaller the file size, the less time needed to transfer the file. GIF was the first file type widely supported by web browsers. That is, GIF files could be displayed by the browser without using an accessory, or *helper,* application.

GIFs are indexed color bitmap files containing up to 256 colors (8-bit color). *Indexed color* simply means the graphic file uses a palette of up to 256 colors. The colors in the palette can be defined by the user, and the palette can contain fewer than the full 256 colors. When fewer colors are used, the file size is reduced. GIF files are compressed by use of a *lossless* compression algorithm. This means that no image data is removed by the compression process.

There are two versions of the GIF format currently in use: 87 and 89a. The 89a format has three features not found in the older 87 GIF or JPEG format—transparent backgrounds, interlaced images, and animations. Transparent backgrounds are created when one color in the GIF is replaced by the color of the background it is displayed on. This is a very useful feature for creating irregular-shaped images, such as text that you want to have floating over the background, rather than being in a rectangular box. You could create a similar look by using the same background color in the GIF as you use on your web page, but not all web browsers will display the colors exactly the same, and you may end up with an undesirable effect. You would also have to change the background color in the GIF if you changed the web page background. FrontPage has a graphics tool that allows you to make one color transparent (see Chapter 5).

When an image is *interlaced,* it is loaded and displayed at full size, but not all the information is used. The image appears "out of focus" and gets sharper in a series of passes. It takes four passes to display an interlaced GIF in its final form. Noninterlaced GIFs are displayed one stripe at a time, and each stripe is displayed at the final resolution. FrontPage has an option that allows you to make a GIF file interlaced (see Chapter 5).

Animated GIFs are a combination of GIF images that are displayed in sequence. An example of an animated GIF is the Microsoft Internet Explorer logo button. Animated GIFs are supported by Netscape Navigator 2.0 and later, and Internet Explorer 3.0. To create animated GIFs, you need a program such as the GIF Construction Set for Windows (available at http://www.mindworkshop.com/alchemy/alchemy.html). Also, Microsoft has a program called GIF animator that can be downloaded for free from http://www.microsoft.com/msdownload/giffanimator.htm.

JPEG

The Joint Photographic Experts Group (JPEG) graphic format is a bitmap that can display up to 16.7 million colors (24-bit color). JPEG images are compressed by use of a *lossy* compression scheme. This makes the file smaller at the cost of some of the data in the image. Originally, web browsers used a helper application to display JPEG images, which meant that a separate window would be opened to display the image. Most current web browsers now display JPEG images without using a helper application.

GIF or JPEG?

Each format has its advantages and disadvantages. Which format you should use will depend on the specific use of the image.

GIF images are preferable when the image will contain fewer than 256 colors. For example, a graphic with only a few colors, like the "at work" graphic shown here that contains only three colors, works best by use of GIF. This example also benefits from having a transparent background. This image is often used to indicate that a web page is "under construction." With a transparent background, it can be used without modification on any web page, regardless of background color. On the other hand, if your image is a scanned color photograph, you would probably use JPEG, so it could have more than 256 colors.

GIFs are also the preferred choice for simple animations. Animations can be created with ActiveX, Java, and other technologies (see Chapter 15), but animated GIFs do not require any applets or scripting other than browser support.

NOTE: *At one time it was common to find web pages that were "under construction." This is not recommended practice. Your web pages should be finished when they are put online.*

Whichever graphic format you use, you will need a good graphics program to work with and convert graphic images. Microsoft Image Composer (see Chapter 6), included with the FrontPage 97 Bonus Pack, can create and edit both GIF and JPEG images. Adobe Photoshop and Fractal Design Painter are also good choices.

Multimedia Files

The Web is a rapidly evolving medium, and support for audio and video files is a major factor in that growth. This is another area where the real world has left the Internet Engineering Task Force behind. Just a few months ago it was necessary to add helper applications to your web browser in order to play and view most audio and video files. Today, both Microsoft's Internet Explorer 3.0 and Netscape's Navigator 3.0 include built-in, or *native,* support for AIFF, AU, MIDI, and WAV sound files, and AVI video files.

The Motion Picture Experts Group (MPEG) has also developed standards for audio and video files that are used on the Internet. Internet Explorer provides native support for MPEG files, while Navigator requires a plug-in. Netscape plug-ins are readily available on Netscape's web site (http://home.netscape.com) and are easy to install, but it is an extra step required of the user. When designing your web pages, using file types that have native support from both Netscape and Microsoft will ensure greater compatibility.

A number of other companies and organizations are developing products for utilizing the Internet for full multimedia broadcasting. Cornell University has

developed CU-SeeMe (for information see http://www.wpine.com), a video conferencing application for the Internet. CU-SeeMe is capable of transmitting both audio and video. Video requires a 28.8-Kbps or faster modem, while audio can function well at 14.4 Kbps.

Progressive Networks' RealAudio (http://www.realaudio.com) provides higher-quality audio by use of the RealAudio player. NPR, ESPN, CNN, and ABC all provide RealAudio files of their news broadcasts on their web sites. You can even hear a "live" simulcast of a Seattle classical music radio station on RealAudio's web site. A growing number of record companies are also using RealAudio on their web sites. Internet Explorer provides support for RealAudio with an ActiveX control, while Netscape uses a plug-in. Xing Technology's StreamWorks (http://www.xingtech.com) is another program that provides audio and video feeds over the Internet.

The potential of the World Wide Web and an intranet seems almost limitless. It will affect society as fundamentally as the printing press, radio, and television. Your ability to use these facilities to create and maintain a presence for your organization, business, or just for yourself, will become an essential skill for the next millennium.

In the next chapter you will see the tools FrontPage provides to help you master the Web and an intranet.

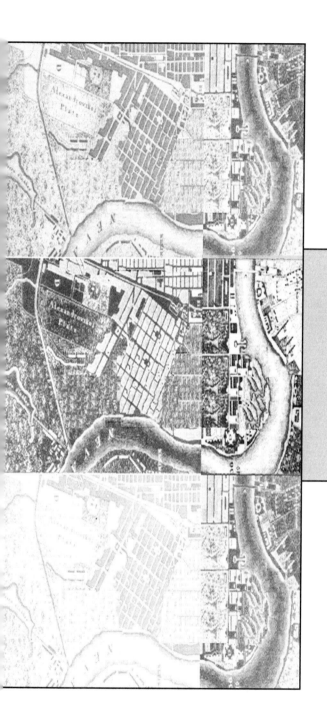

Exploring
FrontPage

Microsoft FrontPage is an authoring and publishing system for creating and delivering formatted content over the Internet or over a local area network (LAN). FrontPage provides the means to design, organize, and deliver an online publication, called a *web,* which may be one or more pages on the Internet's World Wide Web (the *Web*) or on an intranet. FrontPage uses six major components to organize, create, manage, and deliver webs.

- The **FrontPage Explorer** allows you to organize your webs and their links by using several views of the pages in a web in a drag-and-drop environment. It is normally the place where you start a new web; use wizards and templates to create a structure; set permissions for end users, authors, and administrators; and copy a web from one server to another.

- The **FrontPage Editor** allows you to create, format, and lay out text; add graphics created outside of FrontPage; and establish hyperlinks with other areas of the same web or with other webs. It provides a WYSIWYG (what you see is what you get) editing environment where you can edit existing webs, including those created elsewhere on the Web, as well as new webs. In the FrontPage Editor you can use page wizards and page templates, apply *WebBots* for interactive functions, create forms and tables, add image maps with clickable hotspots, and convert popular image formats into GIF and JPEG formats used on the Web.

- The **To Do List** provides a means to manage the tasks required to create a web, who those tasks are assigned to, the task's priority, and the page in a web to which the task is assigned.

- The **FrontPage Personal Web Server (FPPWS)** allows you to directly deliver your webs to someone seeking them, as well as to provide file-management support for your webs.

- The **Microsoft Personal Web Server (MSPWS)** also allows you to directly deliver your webs to someone seeking them, as well as to provide file-management support for your webs. It offers more functionality than the FrontPage Personal Web Server.

■ **FrontPage Server Extensions**, which are available for most popular Internet servers, add the functionality needed to implement the interactive parts of a FrontPage web.

There are significant differences between the Microsoft Personal Web Server and the FrontPage Personal Web Server. The FPPWS is designed to function only with FrontPage, while the MSPWS is based on Microsoft's Internet Information Server (IIS) and is more tightly integrated with Windows 95. IIS is included with Windows NT 4.0 Server and is all the web server you need to run a full World Wide Web site. Consequently, the MSPWS offers a broader range of features. For example, it allows you to also have an FTP (File Transfer Protocol) server available on your computer for the transfer of files between computers on your network in addition to a web server.

There is no default server for FrontPage, so you may use either one for your web development. If you are upgrading from FrontPage 1.1 or if you're not connected to a network, you may want to use the FPPWS. If you are connected to a network and you want to make your webs available to others on the network, the MSPWS should be your choice. Appendix A details the installation and setup of both servers but recommends that you use MSPWS, and this book will assume that MSPWS is running.

While either the Microsoft Personal Web Server or the FrontPage Personal Web Server and the Server Extensions allow you to use all of FrontPage's interactive features in your webs, you can also create *disk-based webs* that do not require either a personal web server or the server extensions. There are two primary reasons for using disk-based webs: if the web server your pages will be published on does not use the server extensions, and if you are using an older computer (386 or a slower 486, such as a 33 MHz or slower), editing your webs will be faster without a personal web server. The trade-off in features between using either personal web server and using disk-based webs is significant. Working on a slow computer is always frustrating; if you plan on doing any amount of web creation, you need the tools to do the job right. Fast 486s, Pentiums, and Pentium Pros will not have any problems running either personal web server. If your web presence provider is not using the FrontPage Server Extensions, you should suggest that they do so (see Chapter 17 for information on using the server extensions on a web server). The server extensions are available from Microsoft (http://www.microsoft.com/frontpage/softlib/fs_fp_extensions.htm) for virtually every popular Windows NT- and UNIX-based server. If your presence provider doesn't want to run the server extensions, then you might consider changing providers.

Microsoft maintains a rapidly growing list of web presence providers that do have the FrontPage Server Extensions installed (http://www.microsoft.com/frontpage/wpp/list/), and from this list you should be able to locate a suitable provider. Also remember that, with the Web, it is not necessary to be physically close to your provider in order to have a successful working relationship. Quality of service and features are more important.

The focus of this book is on creating webs that use the Microsoft Personal Web Server on your local machine and the FrontPage Server Extensions on the web server your webs will be hosted on.

Creating a Web

The FrontPage process of creating a web is unique and uses the following steps:

1. Plan the web. What are the goals; what text, graphics, forms, and hyperlinks will it contain; how will it flow; how will the user get around; and roughly what will the pages look like.

2. If you followed the instructions on installing FrontPage in Appendix A, the Microsoft Personal Web Server should automatically start when you start your computer. If not, start your personal web server, and then start the FrontPage Explorer.

3. In the Explorer create the structure of the new web by using a wizard and/or template, or simply by creating a blank page.

4. Also in the Explorer set the permissions—who can administer, author, and use the web you are about to create.

5. From the Explorer open the To Do List, and create the items you want to include on the list. If you used a wizard to create your structure, you will automatically have items in the To Do List that you can edit.

6. Back in the Explorer select the first page you want to work on, and open the FrontPage Editor with that page.

7. In the FrontPage Editor enter, format, and position the text you want to use. Insert the graphics, sound, video, hyperlinks, frames, tables, and forms. If desired, import existing webs into yours.

2

8. As each page is completed, save it, mark the To Do task as complete, and from the FrontPage Explorer, select the next page you want to work on, and reopen the FrontPage Editor.

9. Periodically open a web browser such as the Microsoft Internet Explorer or the Netscape Navigator from the FrontPage Editor with the Preview In Browser feature, and look at the web you are creating (better yet, use both browsers to see what your web will look like). This allows you to test the full functionality of your web with the personal web server you are using. You will be able to see and interact with the web as the user will. You can then revise the web by changing or updating the content, adjusting the page layouts, and reordering the pages and sections.

10. Verify the hyperlinks that you have placed in your web by using the Verify Hyperlinks command in the FrontPage Explorer Tools menu.

11. When you are satisfied with your web, release it for use by publishing it on the server from which you want to make it available. (That server must have the FrontPage Server Extensions installed on it to use many of the interactive features available in FrontPage, such as forms.)

12. Using your browsers, download, view, and manipulate the web as the user would. Note the load times and the impression you are getting of the web. Ask others to view and use the web and give you their impressions and suggestions.

13. Revise and maintain the web as necessary, either by directly editing the copy on the server, or by editing your local copy and then replacing the server copy.

TIP: *If someone other than you has permission to edit a web you are about to work on, you should copy the current version from the server and then edit it, rather than trusting the copy on your local machine. This avoids the "Twilight Zone Effect," where a web is edited by more than one person at one time. Also see Chapter 16 for information on SourceSafe, which prevents this effect on intranets.*

Creating a web with FrontPage gives you important advantages over other authoring systems. You can

- Graphically visualize and organize a complex web with a number of pages, images, and other elements by using the FrontPage Explorer.

- Create and edit a complex web page in a WYSIWYG environment by using the FrontPage Editor without having to use or know HTML, the language of the Web.

- Easily manage the tasks that are required to build a web, who has responsibility for them, and their completion by using the To Do List.

- Quickly create an entire web, page, or element on a page by using wizards or templates.

- Easily add interactive functions such as forms, text searches, and discussion forums without the use of programming, by using WebBots.

- Directly view and use a web on your hard disk by using your personal web server.

FrontPage Components

FrontPage is a true client/server application that provides all of the pieces necessary to create and deliver formatted text and graphical information over both a LAN and the Internet. From the client side, FrontPage provides

- The **FrontPage Explorer** to create, visualize, and manage an entire web with its many elements.

- The **FrontPage Editor** to create and edit a web page by adding formatted text, graphics, sounds, video, frames, tables, forms, hyperlinks to other pages and webs, and other interactive elements.

- The **To Do List** to track the tasks required to produce a web, identifying who is responsible for them, their priority, and status.

If you have the FrontPage Bonus Pack, you also have the Microsoft Image Composer to allow you to create and modify graphics for your webs (see Chapter 6). From the server side, FrontPage provides

- The **FrontPage Personal Web Server (FPPWS)** to allow you and others on a LAN connected to you to use your webs from your hard disk.

- The **Microsoft Personal Web Server (MSPWS)** to allow you and others on a LAN to use your webs and to transfer files between computers.

- The **FrontPage Server Extensions** to allow the implementation of the FrontPage interactive features on a commercial server.

In the next several sections of this chapter you will further explore the FrontPage components. While it is not mandatory, it will be beneficial if you are looking at these components on your own computer. To do that, start the FrontPage Explorer with these instructions:

NOTE: *The Microsoft Personal Web Server starts automatically upon startup of Windows 95. You can tell it's running by the icon that appears in the notification area on the right end of the taskbar. If yours is not running, see Appendix A for more information on how the MSPWS is started and controlled.*

1. Open the Start and then Programs menus, and select Microsoft FrontPage.

2. The Getting Started With Microsoft FrontPage dialog box is displayed. Click on the Cancel button, and the FrontPage Explorer window will appear, as you'll see in a moment.

FrontPage Explorer

The FrontPage Explorer is the normal starting place for creating a new web or editing an existing one. When you open an existing web in the FrontPage Explorer, you get a graphical view of the web, as you can see in Figure 2-1. The FrontPage Explorer is similar in a number of ways to the Windows 95 Explorer. In Hyperlink view, shown in Figure 2-1, a list of the files supporting the web is displayed in the left pane, and a graphical representation of the hyperlinks is shown in the right pane. In

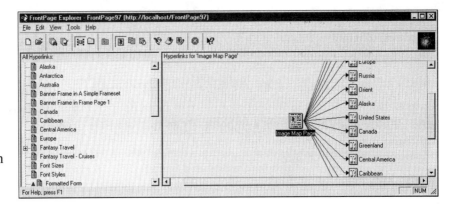

FrontPage
Explorer in
Hyperlink
view

FIGURE 2-1

Folder view, the left pane displays a hierarchical structure of folders, while the right pane displays a list of the files supporting the web as shown here:

Name	Title	Size	Type	Modified Date
africa.htm	Africa	278	htm	10/14/96 3:58:09 PM
alaska.htm	Alaska	278	htm	10/14/96 3:53:06 PM
antartica.htm	Antartica	281	htm	10/14/96 3:46:07 PM

Contents of 'chap2'

By clicking on the plus and minus icons in the left pane, you can expand or collapse the view of the hierarchy. If you right-click on an object in either pane, its context menu will open, which, among other options, allows you to open the object's Properties dialog box. A final way that the FrontPage Explorer is like the Windows 95 Explorer is that in Folder view you can sort the list of files by clicking on the field name immediately above the list, although you can only sort in ascending order.

A web contains one or more web pages with links among them. Web pages and their links create a hierarchical structure that is shown in the left pane of the FrontPage Explorer. You create this structure either by adding pages one at a time and then linking them, or by using one of the web wizards or templates to automatically create the desired pages and their links. You begin web wizards and templates, as well as custom webs with your own pages, by clicking on the New FrontPage Web button in the toolbar, or by choosing New FrontPage Web in the File menu. This opens the New FrontPage Web dialog box that contains a list of web wizards and templates, as shown in the following illustration:

```
┌─────────────────────────────────────────────────┐
│ New FrontPage Web                            [X] │
│                                                   │
│  Template or Wizard:                              │
│  ┌──────────────────────────┐   ┌─────────────┐ │
│  │ Normal Web               │   │     OK      │ │
│  │ Corporate Presence Wizard│   └─────────────┘ │
│  │ Customer Support Web     │                    │
│  │ Discussion Web Wizard    │   ┌─────────────┐ │
│  │ Empty Web                │   │   Cancel    │ │
│  │ Import Web Wizard        │   └─────────────┘ │
│  │ Learning FrontPage       │                    │
│  │ Personal Web             │   ┌─────────────┐ │
│  │ Project Web              │   │    Help     │ │
│  └──────────────────────────┘   └─────────────┘ │
│                                                   │
│   ☐ Add to the current web                       │
│                                                   │
│  ┌ Description ─────────────────────────────────┐│
│  │ Create a new web with a single blank page.   ││
│  │                                              ││
│  └──────────────────────────────────────────────┘│
└─────────────────────────────────────────────────┘
```

Web wizards and templates, both of which automatically create entire webs including a full set of pages, links, and other elements, differ only in the amount of interaction between you and the computer during the creation process. *Templates* create a ready-made web without interactin with you. *Wizards* use one or more dialog boxes, such as the one shown in Figure 2-2, to ask you a series of questions during creation. Based on your answers to these questions, a customized web is created. In both cases, you can customize the resultant web pages and elements.

The web templates and wizards that are currently available in FrontPage are shown in Table 2-1.

Wizards and templates can create either new webs or additions to existing webs. Also, wizards and templates automatically create the tasks in the To Do List that

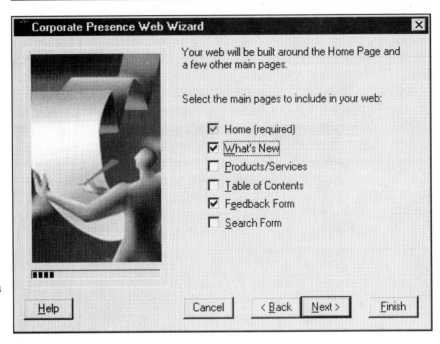

Wizards
use your
choices to
customize a
web they
build

FIGURE 2-2

support the pages that are created. As you'll see in a later chapter, you can build your own wizards and templates to, for example, create a standard look across all departments in a corporation.

As you are working on your web, you can open the FrontPage Editor or the To Do List by using either the Show FrontPage Editor or Show To Do List option in the Tools menu (or the related buttons on the toolbar). You can also open the FrontPage Editor by double-clicking on the page you want to edit in the right-hand pane of the FrontPage Explorer. When you are done creating a web, you can test all of the hyperlinks to external webs by selecting the Verify Hyperlinks option in the Tools menu. Also, if you have edited a web and removed or changed some of the pages, use the Recalculate Hyperlinks option in the Tools menu to update all of the internal links so there is no reference to a nonexistent page. Finally, when everything is the way you want it, you can copy your web to the server, provided you weren't already working on the server, by using the Publish FrontPage Web command in the File menu.

Template or Wizard	What Is Created
Templates	
Normal Web	Single blank page, used in starting or adding to a custom web.
Customer Support Web	Web that tells customers how to contact you and provides a form where they can leave information so you can contact them. Includes an FTP download area, a frequently asked questions (FAQ) area, and a form for leaving suggestions and contact information.
Empty Web	Web without pages, so you can import pages from another web.
Personal Web	Single page with personal and professional information and ways to be contacted.
Project Web	Web that provides a way to communicate the status of a project including its schedule, who is working on it, and its accomplishments.
Wizards	
Corporate Presence Wizard	Web that provides information about a company, including what it does, what its products and services are, how to contact it, and a means to leave feedback for it.
Discussion Web Wizard	Page that is an electronic bulletin board where users can leave messages and others can reply to those messages.
Import Web Wizard	Imports and converts existing webs into FrontPage 97 webs.

Web Templates and Wizards Available in FrontPage Explorer

TABLE 2-1

FrontPage Editor

The normal way to get to the FrontPage Editor is to select a page in the FrontPage Explorer, use one of the techniques discussed earlier to open the FrontPage Editor, and then use the File menu to open a particular page that is an HTML (.HTM) file. In any case, when you open the FrontPage Editor, you'll see a window that looks very much like most word processors, in particular, Microsoft Word for Windows, as you can see in Figure 2-3. This is where you can enter and edit text. It is also where you can add graphics; frames; tables; forms; sound; video; hyperlinks, including hotspots on graphics; and WebBots to your page, as you'll read about in a moment.

As you saw in Chapter 1, a web page is a lot of HTML (HyperText Markup Language) and a little bit of text. If you use a normal word processor or text editor (without any optional HTML features added) to create a web page, you must learn and use HTML. With the FrontPage Editor, you don't need to know HTML. You simply enter the text you want, format it the way you want using normal word processing formatting tools, and add graphics, forms, and other elements. When you are done, FrontPage will generate the HTML for you. It is no harder than creating

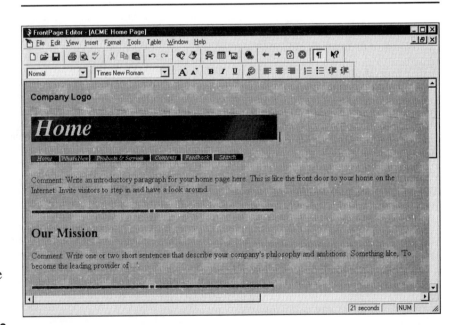

FrontPage
Editor
window

FIGURE 2-3

and formatting any other document, and what you see on the screen is very close to what you would see in a web browser. Not only does the FrontPage Editor convert the text and formatting that you enter to HTML, but you can also import RFT, ASCII, and Microsoft Office files into the FrontPage Editor, and they will have the HTML added to them.

TIP: *If you want to see the HTML behind a web page, choose HTML from the View menu. If you are comfortable with directly editing HTML, you can do so in the HTML Editor displayed by choosing HTML from the View menu. If you're not familiar with editing HTML, this could get you into trouble.*

Formatting Text

The formatting that is available from the FrontPage Editor is quite extensive, but it is limited to the type of formatting that is available with HTML. For example, HTML predefines a number of formatting styles whose name and definition are unique to the Web. Some formatting tags are dependent on the web browser being used to display your web page. For example, both Internet Explorer and Netscape Navigator accept a FONT tag that allows you to change the font (for example, <FONT FACE="Arial"></FONT>), but other browsers may not. (In Figure 1-9 in Chapter 1 you can see that NCSA Mosaic 2.1.1 does not support the FONT tag.) The paragraph styles supported in FrontPage are described in Table 2-2 and shown in Figure 2-4. They are applied either from the toolbar or the Format menu.

Paragraph Style	How It Looks
Normal	Displayed with the proportional font, normally Times Roman.
Formatted	Displayed with the fixed-width font, normally Courier.
Address	Displayed with the proportional font in an italic style. Named because it is often used to display information on how to contact the owner of the web.
Heading 1-6	Displayed with the proportional font in a bold style in six sizes.

Paragraph Styles

TABLE 2-2

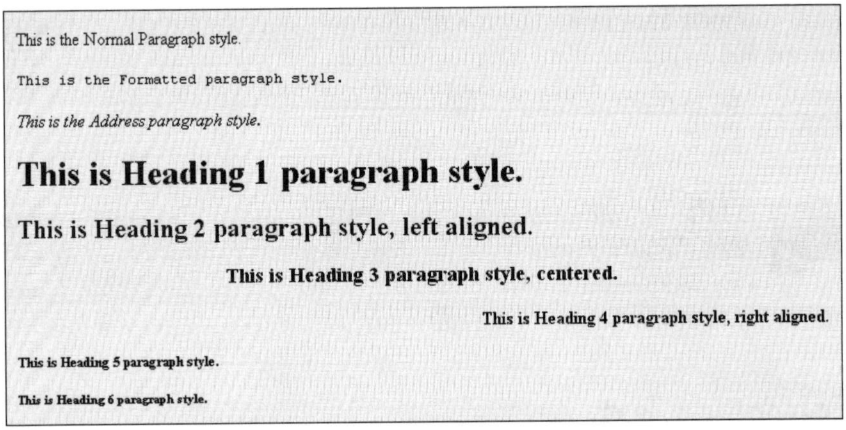

This is the Normal Paragraph style.

This is the Formatted paragraph style.

This is the Address paragraph style.

This is Heading 1 paragraph style.

This is Heading 2 paragraph style, left aligned.

This is Heading 3 paragraph style, centered.

This is Heading 4 paragraph style, right aligned.

This is Heading 5 paragraph style.

This is Heading 6 paragraph style.

Examples
of
paragraph
styles

FIGURE 2-4

TIP: *To have text displayed in a specified font, the browser must support the FONT tag, and the specified font must be installed on the user's computer. More information about using fonts on the Web, as well as a selection of fonts that can be downloaded, can be found on Microsoft's web site (http://www.microsoft.com/truetype/).*

NOTE: *The Formatted paragraph style is the only tag that allows you to use multiple spaces in text. HTML throws out all but one space when it encounters multiple spaces, except when the Formatted style is used. This can be used for forms to get the labels to right align and the text boxes to left align. You can also use tables to align labels and form fields (see Chapter 8).*

   Any of the paragraph styles can use left, center, or right paragraph alignment applied either from the Format menu Paragraph Properties dialog box or with the alignment buttons in the toolbar.

Font (or character) styles, which are described in Table 2-3 and some samples of which are shown in Figure 2-5, are applied through either the Change Style drop-down list on the left of the Formatting toolbar, the appropriate buttons on the toolbar, or the Format menu, which opens the Font dialog box.

Strong, Emphasis, Citation, Sample, Definition, Code, Variable, and Keyboard are logical styles. The appearance of the text with these tags is determined by the browser. Strong, for example, could be defined as italic if the user wanted to. Older browsers

Font Style	How It Looks
Bold (Strong)	Makes text bold
Italic (Emphasis)	Makes text italic
Underlined	Makes text underlined
Strikethrough	Puts a line through text
Typewriter	Puts text in the fixed-width font
Citation	Formats text in the Citation style, normally italic
Sample	Formats text in the Sample style, normally in a fixed-width font
Definition	Formats text in the Definition style, normally italic
Blink	Makes text blink (defined only in Netscape Navigator)
Code	Formats text in the Code style, normally the fixed-width font
Variable	Formats text in the Variable style, which is either italic (Netscape) or the fixed-width font (Microsoft)
Bold	Formats text in a bold style
Italic	Formats text in italic
Keyboard	Formats text in the Keyboard style, normally the fixed-width font with a bold style

Font Styles

TABLE 2-3

allowed you to change the defaults for these tags, but this seems to be a feature that has disappeared. Bold, Italic, Underlined, Blink, Typewriter, Strikethrough, and the font size are physical styles that are not changeable by the browser.

TIP: *FrontPage allows you to use either the logical or physical styles for the Bold and Italic font styles. If you select Bold from the toolbar or from the Font tab of the Font dialog box, the <STRONG> tag is used. If you select Bold from the Special Styles tab of the Font dialog box, the <B> (bold) tag is used instead. With the Italic style, the <EM> (emphasis) tag is used when selected from the toolbar or Font tab, and the <I> (italic) tag is used when selected from the Special Styles tab.*

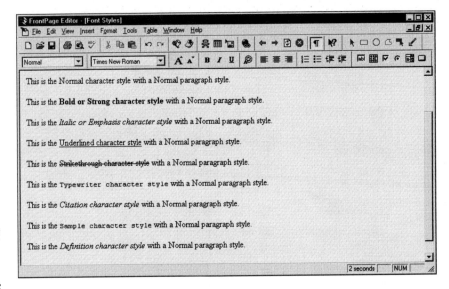

Examples
of some of
the font
styles

FIGURE 2-5

Characters in any style can be one of seven preset sizes from 8 points to 36 points, as shown in Figure 2-6; one of 48 preselected colors or a custom color; and either

  superscript or subscript position. Character size and color can be changed with the respective toolbar buttons, shown here, or though the Character Style dialog box.

In addition to the paragraph style that you have already seen, HTML and FrontPage allow you to define several types of lists. Table 2-4 describes the available list styles, which are shown in Figure 2-7. Note that at this time there is no difference between bulleted, directory, and menu lists. It is possible that this will change in the future.

 TIP: *You can end any list by pressing CTRL-ENTER.*

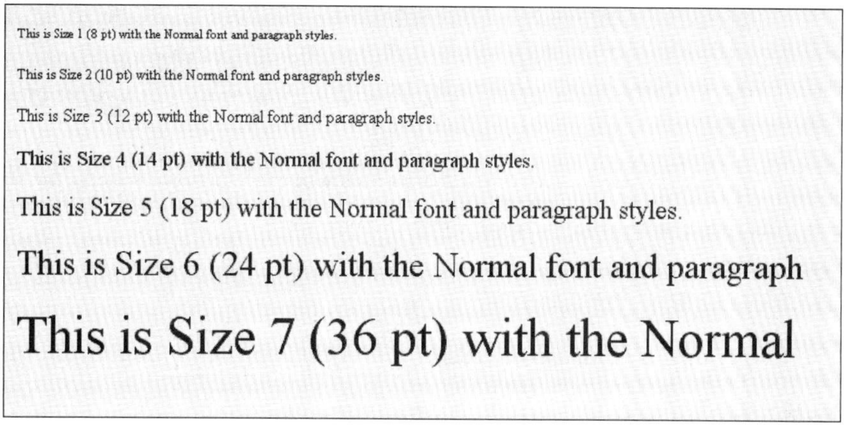

This is Size 1 (8 pt) with the Normal font and paragraph styles.

This is Size 2 (10 pt) with the Normal font and paragraph styles.

This is Size 3 (12 pt) with the Normal font and paragraph styles.

This is Size 4 (14 pt) with the Normal font and paragraph styles.

This is Size 5 (18 pt) with the Normal font and paragraph styles.

This is Size 6 (24 pt) with the Normal font and paragraph

This is Size 7 (36 pt) with the Normal

Examples
of font sizes

FIGURE 2-6

Not all web browsers treat the formatting in a web the same; they may even ignore some formatting. Blink, in particular, is a style that is ignored by all but the

List Style	How It Looks
Bulleted List	Series of paragraphs with a hanging indent and a bullet on the left
Numbered List	Series of paragraphs with a hanging indent and a number on the left
Directory List	Series of short (normally less than 20 characters) paragraphs
Menu List	Series of paragraphs, one line or less in length, in a vertically compact format
Definition	Pairs of paragraphs as terms, which are left aligned, and definitions, which are indented similarly to dictionary definitions

List Styles

TABLE 2-4

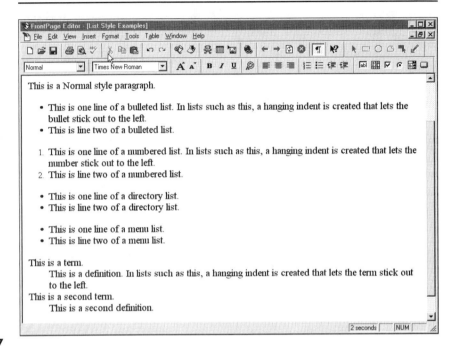

List style
examples

FIGURE 2-7

Netscape Navigator. Also, several styles may produce exactly the same effect in many browsers. For example, in most instances, the Emphasis, Citation, Definition, and Italic styles often produce the same effect. If you are creating a web for a broad public audience, it is worthwhile to test it in recent versions of the two primary web browsers: Netscape Navigator and Microsoft Internet Explorer.

 TIP: *Use only the physical styles excluding Blink to be assured of the widest usability.*

The Font dialog box or the Text Color button on the toolbar allows you to set the color of selected text. You can also set the color of text for an entire page through the Background tab on the Page Properties dialog box, which is opened from the File menu and shown in Figure 2-8. Colored text is useful on colored backgrounds, as you can see in Figure 2-9, and to create an unusual look on a page.

2

Page
Properties
dialog box

FIGURE 2-8

Colored
text on
graphic
background

FIGURE 2-9

TIP: *You can open the Page Properties dialog box by right-clicking on the page and selecting Page Properties from the context menu.*

Inserting Graphics

FrontPage allows you to add graphics to a web page in two ways:

■ You can add a background image that fills a page, which you can identify in the Page Properties dialog box you saw earlier. By placing a graphic in the background, you can enter text on top of it.

NOTE: *A background graphic will be tiled if it doesn't fill the screen. Even if it fills the screen at 640x480, it may be tiled at higher resolutions.*

■ You can add a stand-alone graphic image that you can identify in the Image dialog box opened from the Insert menu or the Insert Image button on the toolbar. You can either size the graphic before you insert it (using a graphics program) or after using FrontPage. Once it is inserted, you can right-click on the graphic and select Image Properties to open the Image Properties dialog box shown in Figure 2-10. Here you can enter the alignment, the amount of space to place on the top and to the left of a graphic, the thickness of a border, if any, and, on the General tab, the alternative text to display if the graphic is not displayed. You can also identify a hyperlink to follow if the user clicks on the graphic. Figure 2-11 shows the results of the settings in the dialog box shown in Figure 2-10.

TIP: *You can left or right align a graphic by selecting it and clicking on the Left Align or Right Align button in the toolbar.*

Graphics that are included in web pages must be either GIF or JPEG format. This has presented a problem in the past, because most clip-art and graphics programs use other formats. FrontPage has solved this problem by allowing you to import other file formats that FrontPage will convert to GIF or JPEG. The file formats that FrontPage can accept are

GIF (.GIF)
JPEG (.JPG or .JFF)
PCX (.PCX)
Encapsulated PostScript (.EPS)
SUN Raster (.RAS)
Targa (.TGA)
TIFF (.TIF)
Windows Metafile (.WMF)
Windows or OS/2 BMP (.BMP)

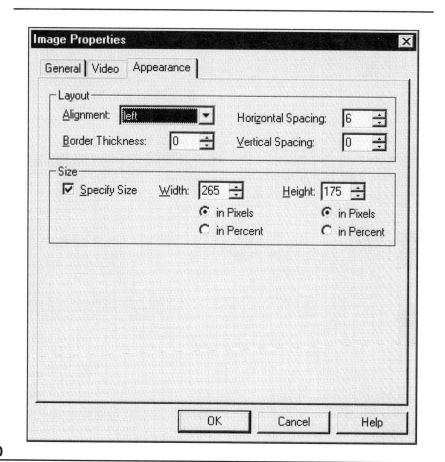

Image
Properties
dialog box

FIGURE 2-10

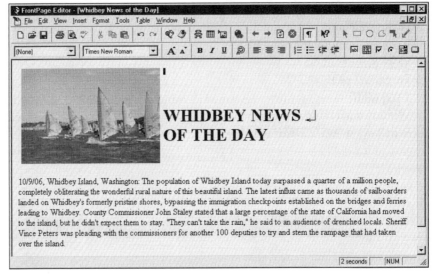

A graphic
aligned
with the
settings
shown in
Figure 2-10

FIGURE 2-11

It's important to remember that graphics take a long time to download and therefore become frustrating for the user who has to wait for them. Even though a graphic may look really neat, if users have to wait several minutes for it to download, they probably are not going to appreciate it or stick around to look at it.

 NOTE: *FrontPage converts graphics with fewer than 256 colors to GIF files and graphics with more than 256 colors to JPEG files. Also, WMF files can be imported only when they are part of an RTF file.*

 TIP: *You can tell how long a page will take to download by the number of seconds on the right of the status bar.*

Adding Forms

So far you have seen how to display text and graphics on a web page—how to deliver information to the user. In the FrontPage Editor you can also add a form in which the user of your web can send you information. You can create a form either field-by-field or all at once by using the Form Page Wizard. You'll see how the Form Page Wizard works in a later section. Here, look at the field-by-field approach. You can use either the Form Field option on the Insert menu, or more easily, the buttons in the Forms toolbar. The Forms toolbar is displayed by selecting Forms Toolbar from the View menu.

To use the Forms toolbar, described in Table 2-5, simply place the insertion point where you want the field, and then click on the button for the field you want. A dialog box will open and ask you to name the field and specify other aspects of it, such as the width of the box on the form and the number of characters that can be entered. Figure 2-12 shows one way a form can be built. In Chapter 9 you'll go through the detailed steps of designing and building a form.

Button	Description	Example in Figure 2-12
`abl`	One-line text box	Address
	Scrolling text box	Comments
	Check box	Using our products?
	Radio button	Age
	Drop-down menu	Which products?
	Push button	Submit and Reset

Form Field
Creation
Buttons

TABLE 2-5

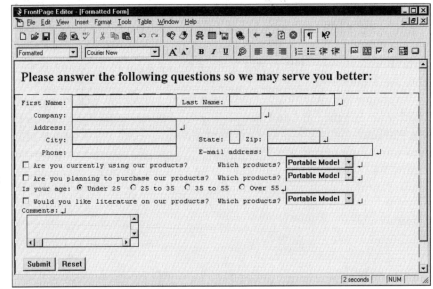

All form
fields are in
the same
block and
use the
Formatted
paragraph
style

FIGURE 2-12

TIP: *If you put form fields in the same form block (area enclosed by a dashed line) and use SHIFT-ENTER to create a new line, you can stack the fields closer together, and they will all have the same form properties.*

TIP: *If you format form fields with the Formatted paragraph style, you can align the labels and text boxes using multiple spaces as shown in Figure 2-12.*

When you create a form field-by-field, you need to provide a means of gathering the data that is entered on it. With FrontPage the best way to do this is with the Save Results WebBot. This is a piece of code that is in the FrontPage Server Extensions residing on your web server. When the user fills out and submits your form, the Save Results WebBot (or just "bot") accepts the information and stores it in a file that you can read. To activate the Save Results bot, right-click on the form, and then choose Form Properties. This opens the Form Properties dialog box, where you can open the Form Handler drop-down menu, and choose the WebBot Save Results Component. Then click on Settings to open the Settings For Saving Results Of Form dialog box shown in Figure 2-13. Here you need to enter the filename and file format that you want to use to contain the information that is returned. You may or may not want to include the field names in the output or in the additional information. You must do this for each field that is in a separate form block (the area enclosed with a dashed line).

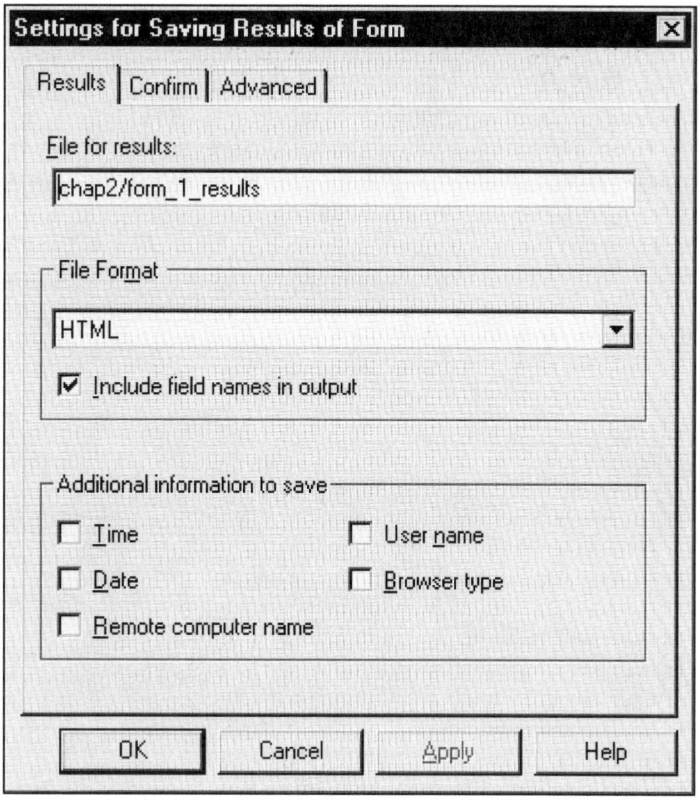

Settings for Saving Results of Form

Results | Confirm | Advanced

File for results:

chap2/form_1_results

File Format

HTML

☑ Include field names in output

Additional information to save

☐ Time   ☐ User name
☐ Date   ☐ Browser type
☐ Remote computer name

OK   Cancel   Apply   Help

Settings
For Saving
Results Of
Form
dialog box

FIGURE 2-13

When you create a form, you may have certain fields that must be filled in (such as first and last name) or fields that have to contain a certain type of information (such as numeric for a phone number). To force the user to enter the proper type of information where required, you can create validation rules for each form field. You do this by right-clicking on the form field you want validated, then selecting Form Field Validation from the context menu to open the Validation dialog box. The Text Box Validation dialog box is shown in Figure 2-14. (Different types of form fields will display different Validation dialog boxes.)

Using Tables

In webs, tables provide a means of dividing some or all of a page into rows and columns. Tables can be used to display tabular data as well as to simply position information on a page, perhaps with a border around it. In Chapter 1, you saw two

Text Box Validation   ✕

Display Name: [   ]

Data Type: [Text   ▼]

┌─ Text Format ──┐
│ ☑ Letters   ☐ Whitespace   │
│ ☐ Digits   ☐ Other: [   ] │
└──┘

┌─ Numeric Format ───┐
│ Grouping: ◉ Comma   ○ Period   ○ None   │
│ Decimal: ○ Comma   ◉ Period   │
└──┘

┌─ Data Length ──┐
│ ☑ Required   Min Length: [   ]   Max Length: [   ] │
└──┘

┌─ Data Value ───┐
│ ☑ Field Must Be: [Greater than or equal to ▼] Value: [   ] │
│ ☐ And Must Be: [Less than or equal to   ▼] Value: [   ] │
└──┘

[OK   ]   [Cancel   ]   [Help   ]

Text Box
Validation
dialog box

■ FIGURE 2-14

| Table | Window | Help |

Insert Table...
Insert Rows or Columns...
Insert Cell
Insert Caption
Merge Cells
Split Cells...

Select Cell
Select Row
Select Column
Select Table

Caption Properties...
Cell Properties...
Table Properties...

examples of tables, and how three different web browsers displayed them (in Figures 1-7 through 1-9). FrontPage has an extensive capability for creating and working with tables such as the one shown in Figure 2-15.

Tables are created by use of either the Insert Table button in the toolbar (which allows you to set the number of rows and columns in the table) or the Insert Table option on the Table menu, which opens the Insert Table dialog box. This allows you to specify the size, layout, and width of the table you are creating. Once a table is created, you can modify it through the Table menu, you can right-click on the table and choose Table Properties to change the

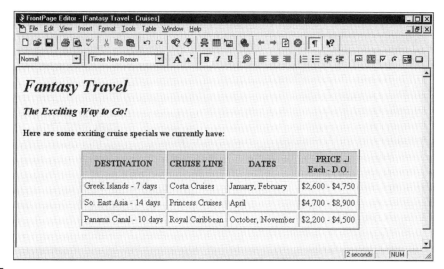

Table
created in
FrontPage

FIGURE 2-15

overall properties of the table, or you can choose Cell Properties from the context menu to change the properties of a single cell. Chapter 8 will go in-depth into tables.

Working with Wizards and Templates

In the New Page dialog box, the FrontPage Editor provides a number of *page* wizards

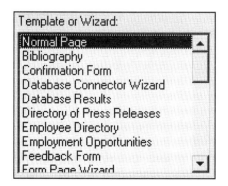

and templates (as distinct from the *web* wizards and templates available in the FrontPage Explorer) to help you create many specialized pages.

For example, to use a wizard to create a custom form similar to the one created earlier, you would select the Form Page Wizard from the New Page dialog box that is opened only from the File menu. This opens a series of dialog boxes that ask you questions about what you want on the form

you want to build, an example of which is shown in Figure 2-16. When you are done, a form is automatically created such as that in Figure 2-17.

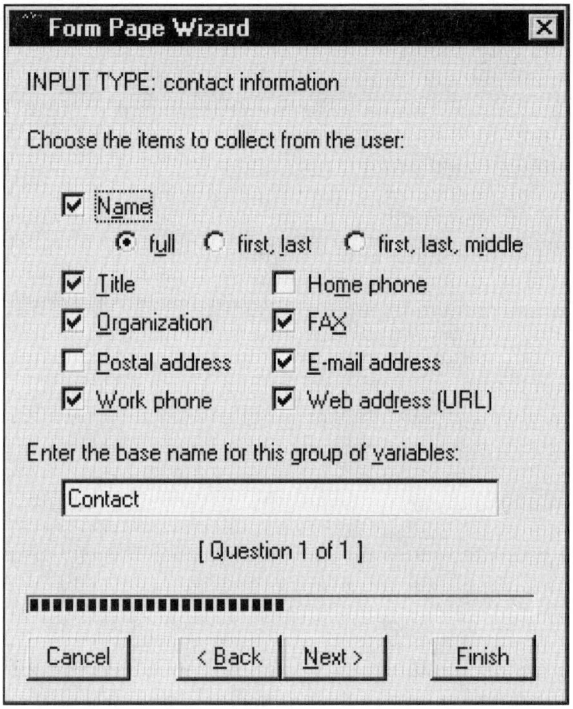

Form Page Wizard

INPUT TYPE: contact information

Choose the items to collect from the user:

☑ Name
    ◉ full   ○ first, last   ○ first, last, middle
☑ Title   ☐ Home phone
☑ Organization   ☑ FAX
☐ Postal address   ☑ E-mail address
☑ Work phone   ☑ Web address (URL)

Enter the base name for this group of variables:

Contact

[Question 1 of 1]

Cancel   < Back   Next >   Finish

One of a
series of
questions
leading to
the creation
of a form

FIGURE 2-16

NOTE: *The form in Figure 2-17 was created by use of Formatted text. The Form Wizard can also generate a table for aligning the labels and form fields.*

NOTE: *The New Page button on the toolbar directly gives you a new page using the Normal Page template and does not open the New Page dialog box.*

The page templates, like their counterparts in the FrontPage Explorer, simply create a new formatted page for you without any input from you. With both wizards and templates, though, you can customize the resulting web page as you see fit. The wizards and templates provide an excellent way to get a quick start on a large variety of web pages, as shown in Table 2-6.

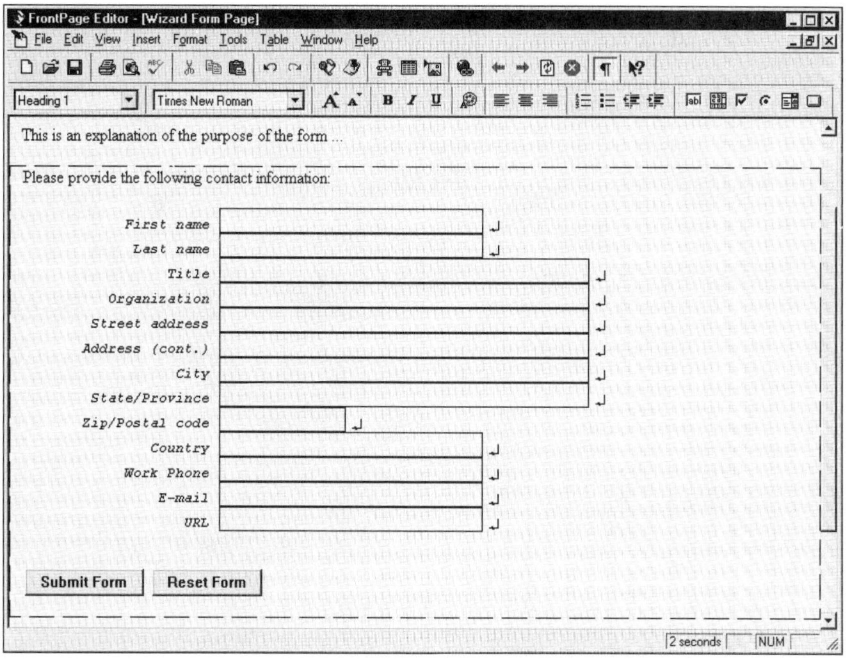

A form
created by
the Form
Page
Wizard

FIGURE 2-17

TIP: *Wizards and templates quickly get you over the "where do I start" hurdle and give you a "first cut" that you can customize.*

Frames are a powerful way to organize a web page by combining several pages on one page, each in a tile or *frame,* as you can see in Figure 2-18. FrontPage uses the Frames Wizard to create the several pages necessary for a given layout. With the Frames Wizard you can choose one of several canned layouts, as shown in Figure 2-19, or you can create a custom layout with the rows, columns, and dimensions that you want. When you use frames, you cannot see the finished product in FrontPage, you will only see and edit the individual pages (the example in Figure 2-18 uses three pages). You must open a browser, such as Netscape Navigator 3.0 or Internet Explorer 3.0, to see the finished product. Frames will be discussed in-depth in Chapter 8.

Wizard or Template	What Is Created on a New Page
Normal Page	Blank page
Bibliography	List of references to other pages or works
Confirmation Form	Acknowledgment of the receipt of input from the user
Database Connector Wizard	Creates an Internet Database Connector (.IDC) file for querying a database
Database Results	Creates a HyperText Extension file (.HTX) for displaying the results from an IDC file
Directory of Press Releases	Date-ordered list of hyperlinks to press releases
Employee Directory	Alphabetical list of employees with a table of contents containing hyperlinks to each employee
Employment Opportunities	Alphabetical list of job openings with a form for the user to ask for further information
Feedback Form	Form for a user to give you comments
Form Page Wizard	Custom form you have designed using this wizard
Frames Wizard	Page made up of other pages that are arranged in tiles or frames
Frequently Asked Questions	List of questions and their answers
Glossary of Terms	Alphabetical list of terms and their definitions
Guest Book	Form for users of your web to leave their identification and comments
Hot List	Categorized list of hyperlinks to other web sites

Wizards
and
Templates
Available
in the
FrontPage
Editor

TABLE 2-6

2

Wizard or Template	What Is Created on a New Page
HyperDocument Page	List of document subsections meant to be hyperlink destinations
Lecture Abstract	Announcement of an upcoming seminar, lecture, or workshop
Meeting Agenda	Announcement of a meeting with a list of topics for discussion
Office Directory	Geographical list of company offices with hyperlinks to countries and regions
Personal Home Page Wizard	Custom home page you have designed using this wizard
Press Release	Normal press release format that can be linked to the Directory of Press Releases
Product Description	Description of a product including its features, benefits, and specifications
Product or Event Registration	Registration form for an event or for product support
Search Page	Search engine for finding keywords within the pages of a web
Seminar Schedule	Description of a seminar that is meant to be linked to a Lecture Abstract page
Software Data Sheet	Software product description including the features and benefits of the product
Survey Form	Form to collect information from users of your web
Table of Contents	List, in outline format, of hyperlinks to the other pages in your web
User Registration	Form for registering to use a secure web
What's New	List, in date order, of recent changes and announcements

Wizards and Templates Available in the FrontPage Editor (*continued*)

TABLE 2-6

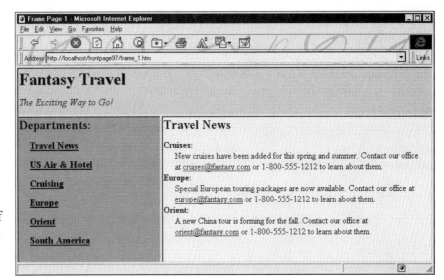

Example of
a web page
using
frames

FIGURE 2-18

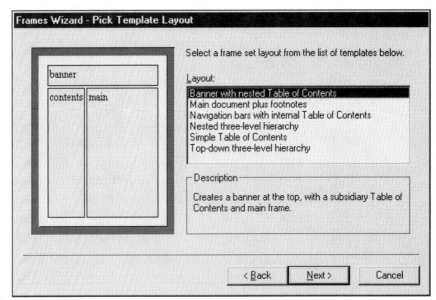

Canned
layouts
available in
the Frames
Wizard

FIGURE 2-19

NOTE: *Frames are another area of HTML programming that is not supported by all browsers. Both Navigator 3.0 and Internet Explorer 3.0 support frames. As you will learn in Chapter 8, you can create alternate pages that will be loaded by browsers that do not support frames when a frameset page is encountered. (A* frameset *defines a frame page and identifies the set of pages, each containing the contents of one frame, that go together to create the single frame page in a browser.)*

Using WebBots

WebBots provide automation in a web—the ability to do more than just provide text and graphics on a page. For example, WebBots let the users search a web, return information to you that has been entered on a form, and participate in a discussion group. Most of FrontPage's bots, though, just make creating and maintaining a web easier. In other web-authoring packages, this same capability requires various levels of programming. In FrontPage you simply have to set up and enable a WebBot.

The Discussion WebBot is automatically enabled when you create a new web from the FrontPage Explorer by using the Discussion Web Wizard. The Save Results WebBot is automatically enabled when you use the Form Page Wizard in the FrontPage Editor or, as you saw earlier, you can enable it manually in the Forms Properties dialog box. All other bots are enabled through the Insert WebBot Component dialog box (shown next) opened by choosing WebBot Component from the Insert menu. The bots that you can place on a page are described in Table 2-7.

Insert WebBot Component	
Select a component:	
Confirmation Field	OK
Include	
Scheduled Image	Cancel
Scheduled Include	
Search	Help
Substitution	
Table of Contents	
Timestamp	

WebBot	Capability Added to a Web Page
Confirmation Field	Echoes the information entered on a form by users, so you can show users what they entered.
Include	Allows you to include one web page on another. If you want to have a constant header on every page, you can put the header on a web page and then include that page on all others in the web.
Scheduled Image	Allows you to display an image in a web page for a given period. When the time expires, the image is not displayed.
Scheduled Include	Allows you to include one page on another for a given period. When the time expires, the included page is not displayed.
Search	Creates a form in which the user can enter a word or words to search for in the current web, carries out the search, and returns the elements matching the criteria.
Substitution	Substitutes a value on a web page with a configuration variable when the page is viewed by the user.
Table of Contents	Creates and maintains a Table of Contents page with links to all the other pages in the web.
Timestamp	Places on a page the date and time the page was last edited or updated.

WebBots that Can Be Inserted on a Page from FrontPage Editor

TABLE 2-7

Adding Hyperlinks and Mapping Hotspots

In the FrontPage Editor you can add hyperlinks (or "links"), which allow the user of a web to quickly jump from one page to another, or to a particular element on the same or another page (called a "bookmark"), or to a different web or web site. You can make either text or a graphic be the element the user clicks on to make the link, and you can map certain areas of a graphic to be different links (called "hotspots"). You create a link by first selecting the object that you want the user to click on and then clicking on the Create Or Edit Hyperlink button, or by choosing Hyperlink from the Edit menu. In either case, the Create Hyperlink dialog box will open as shown in Figure 2-20.

Within the Create Hyperlink dialog box, you can select a bookmark on any open page or just an open page without a bookmark, any page in the current web with or without a bookmark, any URL or address on the World Wide Web, or a new page yet to be defined in the current web. The address on the Web can be another web or HTTP site, or an FTP, Gopher, Mail, News, Telnet, or Wais site. When you have created a hyperlink, the object on which the user is to click changes to a different color and may become underlined as you can see in the words "Africa," "Caribbean," and "Europe" in Figure 2-21.

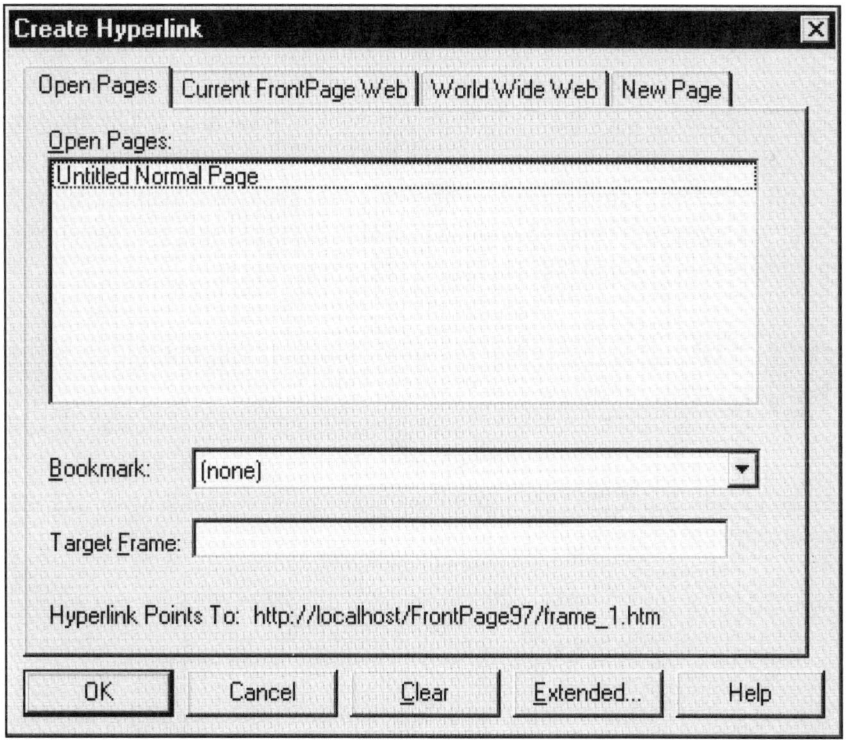

Create
Hyperlink
dialog box

FIGURE 2-20

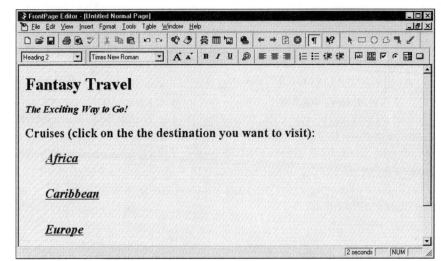

Hyperlinks
are
underlined
and a
different
color

FIGURE 2-21

A graphic can have its entire area defined as a link, or you can identify specific areas in a graphic as separate links, while any unidentified areas are assigned a default link. For example, a travel agency could provide a map that allows the user to quickly get to information about a particular area of the world by simply clicking on that area, as you can see in Figure 2-22.

TIP: *The left end of the status bar tells you the link under the mouse pointer (Hawaii.htm in Figure 2-22).*

You identify hotspots on a graphic by using the drawing tools (shown here) in the upper right of the toolbar.

First select the graphic, then select the rectangle, circle, or polygon tool. Use it to draw a border around the area of the graphic you want to be the hotspot. When you

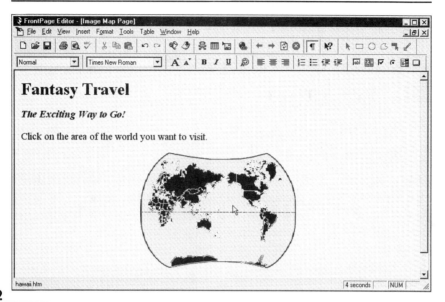

Selecting a
hyperlink
within a
graphic

FIGURE 2-22

are done identifying all the hotspots, your graphic will look something like this
(although users won't see the lines in a browser):

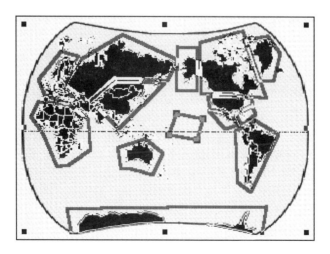

The rightmost pair of drawing tools provides two unique functions. The second
tool from the right turns off the graphic and shows you just the hotspots, and the

rightmost tool allows you to click on any color in the graphic and make it transparent, allowing the page background to show through.

 NOTE: *Transparent backgrounds only work with GIF 89a files. If you try using a transparent background with a JPEG, you get a dialog box that says the JPEG will be converted to a GIF.*

To Do List

 To open the To Do List, you must have a web open. Then from either the FrontPage Explorer or the FrontPage Editor you can click on the Show To Do List button in the toolbar, or select Show To Do List from the Tools menu. In either case the To Do List window opens, as you can see in the following illustration:

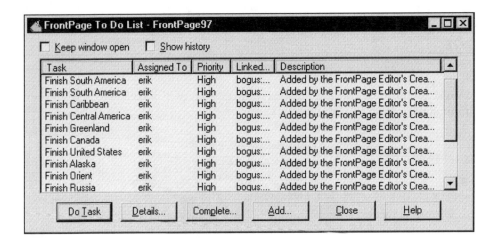

The items on the To Do List are placed there either by a web wizard or by you, which you can do with either the Add button in the To Do List window or by choosing Add To Do Task from the Edit menu in either the FrontPage Explorer or the FrontPage Editor. When you add a new task, you give it a name, assign it to an individual, give it a priority, and type in a description in the Add To Do Task dialog box shown in Figure 2-23.

Once you have a complete To Do List, you can use it to go to the various sections of a web that still require work by selecting a task and clicking on the Do Task button. This will open the FrontPage Editor and display the page that needs work. When you have completed the task, you can return to the To Do List window and select

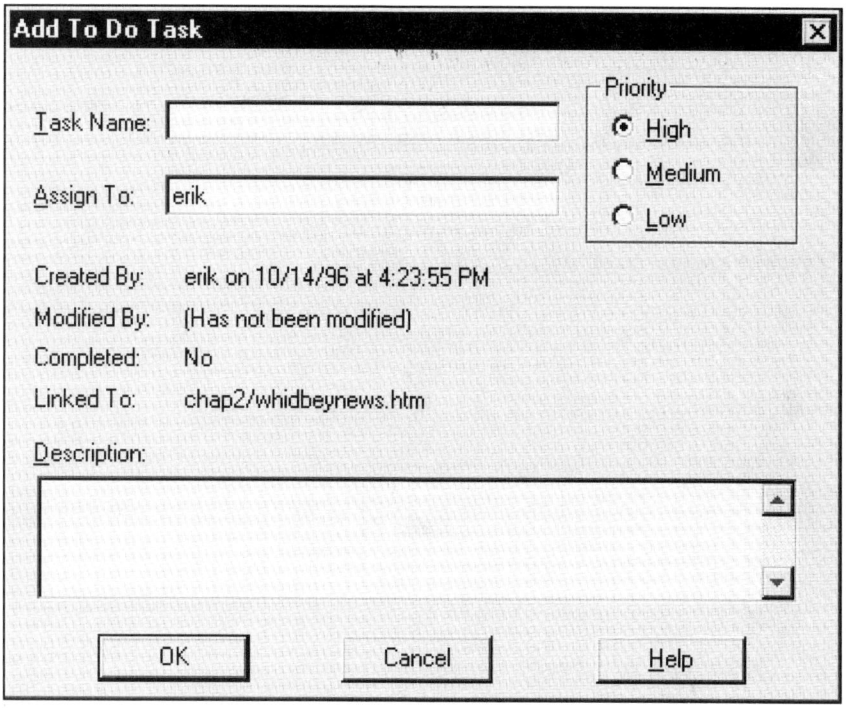

Add To Do
Task dialog
box

FIGURE 2-23

Complete, where you can either mark the task as completed and leave it in the list, or delete the task from the list. By clicking on Details in the To Do List window, you can modify who the task is assigned to, its priority, and its description, but not the task name.

TIP: *You can sort the tasks in the To Do List on any field by clicking on the field name at the top of the list.*

Personal Web Server

The personal web server, either the Microsoft Personal Web Server or the FrontPage Personal Web Server, provides the file management for a web (as distinct from an individual page) in FrontPage. You need to have it running if you want to create or edit a web on your computer, unless you have some other Internet server software

running along with the FrontPage Server Extensions for that server, or you are using a disk-based web. The personal web server simply sits in the background as a task.

TIP: *The personal web server can be all the server you need for a small intranet linking six to ten workstations.*

FrontPage Server Extensions

The FrontPage Server Extensions must be installed on the server that is distributing a web that contains many of the advance features in FrontPage. Among these are

- Forms
- Hotspot image maps
- WebBots that are active while a web is being used is a browser, such as:
  - Confirmation Field bot
  - Discussion bot
  - Registration bot
  - Save Results bot
  - Search bot

FrontPage Server Extensions are available from Microsoft for most of the popular Internet servers, both UNIX- and Windows NT-based systems, at *http://www.microsoft.com/frontpage/softlib/fs_fp_extensions.htm.*

In the following chapters you will use all of the components of FrontPage and many of their features to build your own webs.

FrontPage on the Web

Surfrider Foundation Australia

URL: *http://www.midcoast.com.au/users/surfrider*
Webmasters: Wayne F. Ryan and Dane B. Clarke
E-mail: *surfrider@midcoast.com.au,*
            wryan10@scu.edu.au, dane@yacc.dialix.oz.au

P.O. Box 6348
Coffs Harbour, NSW Australia 2450
or
P.O. Box 417
Nambucca Heads, NSW Australia 2448
B/H 066 513 078
A/H 066 516 206
B/H 065 686 467
065 686 556 (Fax)

Web Site

The Surfrider Foundation Australia web site is a winner of the Microsoft Great Web Sites Contest. The Home page, shown in Figure 1, has a number of neat features, including unique background music (added with <bgsound src="zep.mid" loop="infinite">); a "News Flash" marquee (between the pair of *NEW!*s), shown in Listing 1; automated GIF marbles for bullets in the table; and automated GIF stars. Also, the counter in the lower right is really an automated GIF that spins the numbers.

Listing 1
uee HTML

```
<marquee bgcolor="#00FFFF" height="19" width="50%">NEWS FLASH -----
THIS SITE WAS A WINNER IN THE MICROSOFT FRONTPAGE GREAT WEB SITES
CONTEST ----- NEWS FLASH ----- CHECK OUT THE S.O.S. REPORT ON THE
RESEARCH PAGE ----- NEWS FLASH ----- NEW LINK TO THE A.S.P. ON
THE EDUCATION PAGE ----- NEWS FLASH ----- REMEMBER IF YOU ARE NOT
PART OF THE SOLUTION, YOU ARE PART OF THE PROBLEM! ----- SUPPORT
THE SURFRIDER FOUNDATION * JOIN TODAY * -----</marquee>
```

Figure 2 shows the Surfrider Foundation web site's second page. At the bottom of that page, which (like all the pages) has its own music, includes a form

FrontPage on the Web (cont.)

Surfrider
Foundation
Home page

FIGURE 1

Why not become a member? *At least find out more!*

To join the Surfrider Foundation, send $25 to:
Surfrider Foundation
Visa: give Surfrider a call 02 9972 3533 and do it on the phone

If you would like more information about how you can help please fill in this form and submit.

Name

Address

Town   State   Postcode

Please send me more information!   No, please clear the form so I can start again

RESPECT THE BEACH

Page 2:
form for
joining the
organization

FIGURE 2

FrontPage on the Web (cont.)

for joining the organization. This form was created with the HTML in Listing 2. All of the pages have a simple beauty with subtle colors and exquisite graphics like those shown in Figure 3.

Listing 2
Form HTML

```
<form action= http://www.midcoast.com.au/htbin/formmail method="POST">
    <input type="hidden" name="mailto"
    value="surfrider@midcoast.com.au"><input type="hidden"
    name="message1" value="Thankyou for your interest."><input
    type="hidden" name="message2" value="We'll be in contact shortly.">
    <input type="hidden" name="returnpage"
    value="Surfrider Foundation (Mid North Coast branch).">
    <input type="hidden" name="returnpath"
    value="http://www.midcoast.com.au/user/surfrider/index.html">
    <p align="left"><font color="#0000FF"><strong>Name</strong></font>
    <font color="#FFFFFF">. </font>
    <input type="text" size="41" maxlength="256" name="address"></p>
    <p align="left"><font color="#0000FF"><strong>Address</strong></font>
    <input type="text" size="40" maxlength="256" name="street"></p>
    <p align="left"><font color="#0000FF"><strong>Town</strong></font>
    <font color="#FFFFFF">. </font><input type="text" size="20"
    maxlength="256" name="town">
    <font color="#0000FF"><strong>State</strong></font>
    <input type="text" size="10" maxlength="256" name="state">
    <font color="#0000FF"><strong>Postcode</strong></font>
    <input type="text" size="12" maxlength="256" name="postcode"></p>
    <p align="center"><input type="submit" name="Submit"
    value="Please send me more information!"> <input type="reset"
    value="No, please clear the form so I can start again"> </p></form>
```

Webmaster Q & A

WHY FRONTPAGE?   We decided to use FrontPage originally to speed up some of the design work, then we found it to be very clever and useful. I thought it was like desktop publishing for the Web, and I suppose that's what it is.

FrontPage on the Web (cont.)

S.O.S. Report

Human Impact on Australian Beaches

Results from the SOS95 Beach Survey
Michael Leggi-Wilkinson, Surfrider Foundation Australia

During the last 20 years population growth in the non metropolitan coastal zone of Australia has exceeded that of the capital cities. Consequently, there is a ribbon pattern of urban development emerging in blocks and hugging the coast between Cairns and Adelaide. Similar blocks of development are emerging north and south of Perth Western Australia and along parts of Tasmania. Urbanisation of the coastal fringe impacts heavily on the coastal environment.

The results indicate that approximately eight per cent of Australia's 7529 mainland beaches are in urban areas. 24 per cent of the beach areas surveyed have stormwater pipes to the beach and/or its lagoon. Three thousand million litres of sewage a day are being discharged into the ocean environment.

This extensive report covers aspects such as

- Property and infrastructure development along the Australian coastline.
- How many beaches are affected by new development proposals?
- How many beaches have lost their dunal system to urban or infrastructure development?
- How many sewage outfalls are discharging effluent into estuarine or marine environments?
- Where are the sewage outfalls and what quality effluent do they discharge?
- How many beaches are affected by stormwater discharge pipes?
- Which rivers, creeks, lakes, lagoons and harbours are sources of beach pollution via their catchments?

Simple beauty of page 3

FIGURE 3

LIKES AND DISLIKES   We like almost everything most about FrontPage except that using the FrontPage Web Server Extensions is a little more complicated than it could be, especially compared with the ease of the editor.

NEATEST FEATURES OF THIS SITE   Background music, animated GIFs, and tables

TIPS

- Pay attention to your code.
- Watch for case-sensitive web servers (UNIX).
- Remember that not all viewers will have Microsoft Internet Explorer and your same screen resolution.
- Test a lot before you post your pages.

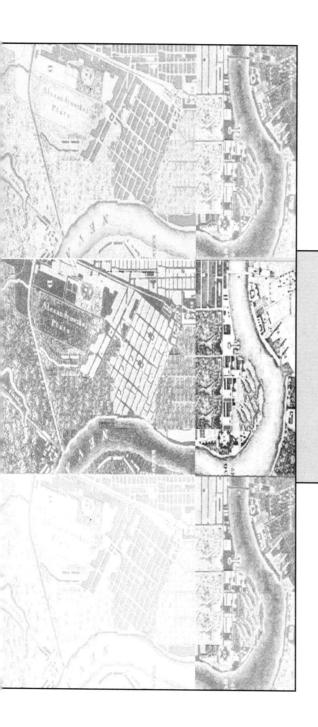

Using Wizards

As you saw in Chapter 2, the easiest way to create a web with FrontPage is by using a wizard or a template. You'll remember that *wizards* ask you questions about the web you want to create and then build a web based on your answers, whereas *templates* create a particular kind of web without input from you. In this chapter you'll see how to use wizards in both webs and pages, and the results that they produce. (Templates are covered in Chapter 4.) The purpose of this is twofold: it gets you acquainted with the wizards, and it demonstrates many of FrontPage's features, which have been included in the webs produced by the wizards.

Web Wizards

FrontPage provides wizards at both the web level and the page level. Begin looking at the web level by loading the FrontPage Explorer as you did in Chapter 2. (It is assumed that you are using the Microsoft Personal Web Server and have it set to start up automatically when you turn on your computer, as explained in Appendix A. If you are using the FrontPage Personal Web Server, it should load automatically when you load the FrontPage Explorer. In the remainder of this book it will be assumed that you have one of the personal web servers running and that you have handled its loading.)

When the program loading is complete, the Getting Started With Microsoft FrontPage dialog box will be displayed as shown in Figure 3-1. This dialog box is displayed when you load the FrontPage Explorer, unless you clear the Show Getting Started Dialog check box. Click on Cancel, then click on the New FrontPage Web button in the toolbar; or open the File menu and choose New FrontPage Web. The New FrontPage Web dialog box, shown here, will open and display a list of templates and wizards.

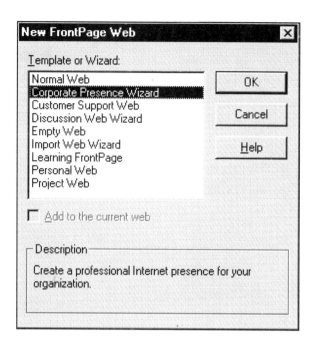

The New FrontPage Web dialog box contains three web wizards: the Corporate Presence Wizard, the Discussion Web Wizard, and the Import Web Wizard. The Corporate Presence Wizard allows you to create a complete web site to promote your company or business. With it you can create web pages that tell customers what's new with your company (such as press releases), inform customers about your products and services, create a table of contents to help visitors navigate your web site, provide a feedback form so your customers can give you their opinions, and provide a search form that visitors to your web site can use to quickly find specific information on your site.

The Discussion Web Wizard creates web pages for the user to submit comments to a discussion, a table of contents, a search form, a page to follow *threaded replies*, and a confirmation page so users know their comments have been received. Threaded replies link multiple comments on the same subject. This allows the reader to go directly from one comment to the next on a given subject.

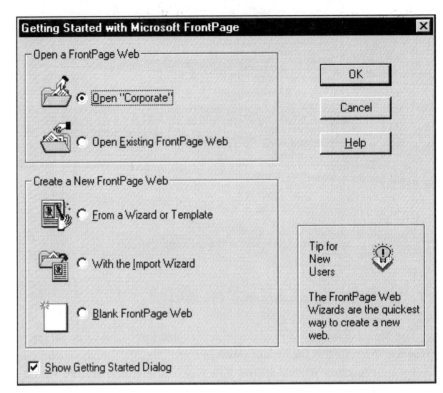

Getting
Started
With
Microsoft
FrontPage
dialog box

FIGURE 3-1

With the Import Web Wizard you can quickly convert existing non-FrontPage web pages and content into a FrontPage web. This is an important feature if you need to convert into FrontPage a number of existing webs, to update them, or to incorporate any of FrontPage's WebBots in them.

Using the Corporate Presence Wizard

The Corporate Presence web is one of the more sophisticated webs that FrontPage creates. By using a wizard, you get to do a lot of customizing as you build. In this section you will create a Corporate Presence web ("Corporate web," for short). Do that now with these instructions (the New FrontPage Web dialog box should still be open on your screen):

1. Choose Corporate Presence Wizard in the New FrontPage Web dialog box and click on OK. The Corporate Presence Wizard dialog box shown here will be displayed. The Corporate Presence Wizard dialog box has two functions: to set the server on which the web will reside and to name the web.

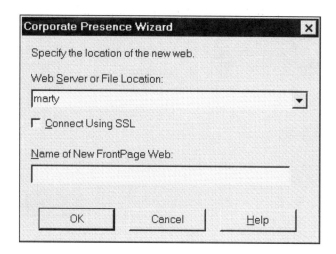

2. Select the web server you want to use. If you will be normally working directly on your web server, this should be its domain name. If you are working on your local computer and intend to publish your web on your web server later, this would be the name of your computer, as shown in the preceding illustration. (You may also use "localhost" for your web server. Localhost is a default network name for your computer—see the discussion of installing a personal web server in Appendix A.) If you were creating a disk-based web, you would enter the path of the web on your hard drive. (Since disk-based webs do not support many FrontPage features, they are not covered in this book.) If you do not have a server name entered, select or enter the domain name of the server or computer where your web will reside. The Connect Using SSL (Secure Sockets Layer) check box should be unchecked. See Chapter 14 for an explanation of using SSL.

3. Name the new web **Corporate** and click on OK. The first Corporate Web Presence Wizard dialog box will be displayed, like this.

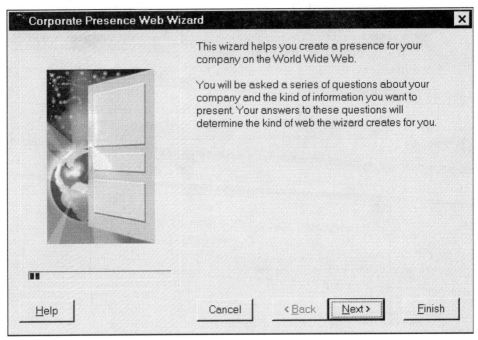

4. Click on Next in the first wizard dialog box, opening the list of pages that can be included in the web as shown in Figure 3-2.

5. Select all of the options to include all the possible pages, and click on Next. This brings up a list of topics that can be included on the Home page. Accept the defaults for this and the next seven dialog boxes, which ask you what you want on each type of page, until you reach the dialog box (shown in Figure 3-3) that asks for the presentation style you want to use in your web. As you go through each of the dialog boxes, note the options; you have significant flexibility.

6. Look at each of the options—Plain, Conservative, Flashy, and Cool—that you have for the presentation style, and choose the one you want (Flashy is used in the illustrations later in this chapter).

7. Click on Next. You'll be asked for the background and text colors you want to use. This will create a web style sheet that will be applied to all the pages you create in this web. You can easily change it later, and thereby change all the pages in the web, by changing the Web Colors page in the FrontPage Editor.

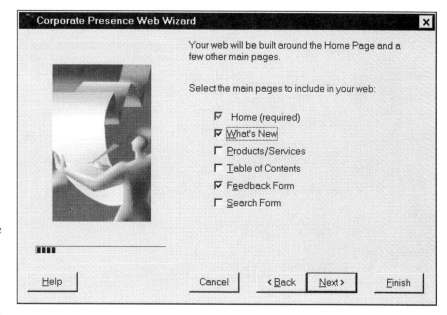

Choosing
the web
pages to be
included
in the
Corporate
web

FIGURE 3-2

8. Make the selections you want and click on Next. When you are asked if you want to initially mark your pages with the Under Construction icon, make your choice and click on Next.

TIP: *Using the Under Construction icon is generally not a good idea. If at all possible, finish the web before putting it on the server for public consumption. (It is shown on the screen shots later in this chapter so you can see what it looks like.)*

9. Enter the company name and address (any name and address is fine for this exercise) or accept the defaults, click on Next, enter the phone numbers and e-mail addresses to use, and again click on Next.

10. Make sure the Show To Do List is checked and then click on Finish. The web will be created and displayed in both the FrontPage Explorer and the FrontPage To Do List. If necessary, open the To Do List by clicking on its button in the FrontPage Explorer's toolbar, so both the Explorer and the To Do List are visible, as you can see in Figure 3-4.

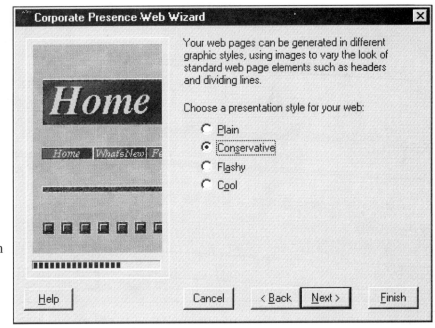

Your web pages can be generated in different graphic styles, using images to vary the look of standard web page elements such as headers and dividing lines.

Choose a presentation style for your web:

- ○ Plain
- ◉ Conservative
- ○ Flashy
- ○ Cool

Choosing the desired presentation style for a Corporate Presence web

FIGURE 3-3

11. Close the To Do List window and click on the FrontPage Folder View toolbar button to show the Corporate web in Folder view, as you can see in Figure 3-5. This shows all of the folders and files, one for each web page, that have been created by the Corporate Presence Wizard.

12. Return to Hyperlink view by clicking on the Hyperlink View button on the toolbar. As you can see in Figure 3-4 the Corporate Presence Wizard has not only created all the pages you selected in the wizard, it has also created the basic hyperlinks between the pages, represented by the arrows in the right pane of the FrontPage Explorer.

13. Right-click on the Home Page icon in either pane of the Explorer, and choose Properties from the context menu that opens as a result of right-clicking. The Properties dialog box for the home page, similar to the one shown in Figure 3-6, will open. Here you can see the filename and URL that have been generated for the home page. In the Summary tab you can see when and by whom the page was created and modified. You can also add comments.

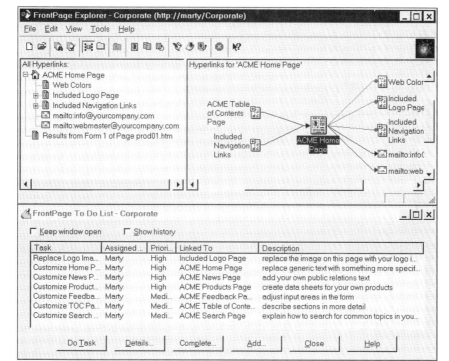

Corporate
web in
both the
FrontPage
Explorer
and
FrontPage
To Do List

FIGURE 3-4

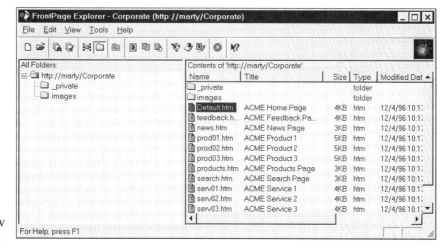

Corporate
web in the
FrontPage
Explorer
Folder view

FIGURE 3-5

Default.htm Properties   ☒

General │ Summary │

File
Name: Default.htm

Title: │ACME Home Page│

Type: Internet Document (HTML)

Size: 4.30KB (4406 bytes)

Location:
http://marty/Corporate/Default.htm

│   OK   │ │   Cancel   │ │   Apply   │ │   Help   │

The
Properties
dialog box
for the
Corporate
web

▮ FIGURE 3-6

NOTE: *By default FrontPage names the home page for a web*
Default.htm. The name of the home page for a web is important since this
will determine whether your web server will display the home page when
accessed without the home page filename (http://webname/) or whether the full URL
will be required (http://webname/pagename.htm). Different web servers have
different default settings for the home page name. Check with your web server
administrator for the default home page name on your web server.

14. Close the Properties dialog box, and then double-click on the home page
in the right pane to open the page in the FrontPage Editor. The FrontPage
Editor will open with the home page displayed, as shown in Figure 3-7.

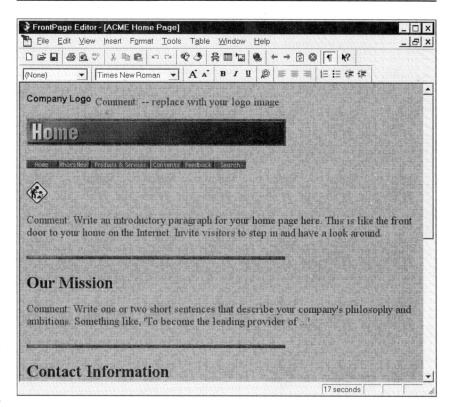

Corporate
web home
page in the
FrontPage
Editor

FIGURE 3-7

On the home page you can see some of the features incorporated in this web (scroll through the page to make sure you see everything). Here are some of the features to note (see Figure 3-7 for the first four features):

■ The "Company Logo" is an included page where you would put your company logo and name so they will appear on every page.

■ The page title "Home" and its background are a graphic, hhome.gif. It is one of a series of graphics on each page. You can create such graphics in Microsoft Image Composer, CorelDraw, Adobe Photoshop, Fractal Design Painter, or other graphics packages and then place them in FrontPage. Chapter 5 will further discuss placing graphics, and Chapter 6 will demonstrate how to use the Microsoft Image Composer.

- The *navigation bar* (also called a *navbar*) is a series of graphics, one for each of the hyperlinks, and is an included page that is used at the top of each regular web page.

- The line above "Our Mission" is a graphic.

- The phone numbers, postal address, e-mail addresses, and company name are entered and maintained through the Substitution bot. WebBots are discussed in depth in Chapter 10.

 15. Select Open from the File menu or click on the Open button on the toolbar to display the Open File dialog box shown next.

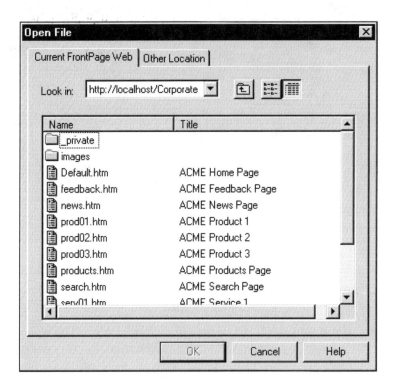

16. Select news.htm and click on OK. When the news.htm file is loaded in the FrontPage Editor, you can see the common elements that are included on each page created with the Corporate Presence Wizard. Notice that the Home banner below the company logo on the home page has been replaced by one that says, "What's New?" Each page in the Corporate web will have its own banner graphic to identify it.

3

On any of the pages you can enter and format any text you want, insert graphics, and add forms, tables, and other elements as you saw in Chapter 2. In later chapters you will do all of these tasks. The purpose here is simply to see that the Corporate Presence Web Wizard does in fact create a complete web. It also creates all of the structure (shown in Figure 3-4) that is behind a web in FrontPage. (If you used the default directories when you installed FrontPage, your Corporate web is stored under C:\Webshare\Wwwroot\Corporate with the MSPWS, and C:\FrontPage Webs\Content\Corporate with the FPPWS.)

Products & Services

The Products & Services page of your Corporate web serves as a central location to list your products and services, include a brief description, and to provide hyperlinks to the individual pages describing them in more detail. Open the Products & Services page now (products.htm in the Open File dialog box), and look at it in the FrontPage Editor.

Each element on the page has its own properties you can view and change by right-clicking on the object and selecting Properties from the context menu. In the following steps you will look at the Properties dialog boxes for the different types of objects on the Products & Services page.

1. Right-click on the words "Company Logo" at the top of the page to open the context menu shown here.

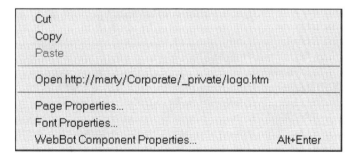

From this menu you can open in the FrontPage Editor the logo.htm page that you would modify to place your own logo at the top of each page. The logo.htm page can contain text, graphics, or any other type of FrontPage object.

 NOTE: *When you point at the Company Logo text, the mouse pointer turns into a robot to indicate the object is a WebBot.*

2. Click outside the context menu to close it, and then right-click on the Products & Services banner. In the context menu select Image Properties to open the Image Properties dialog box you see in Figure 3-8.

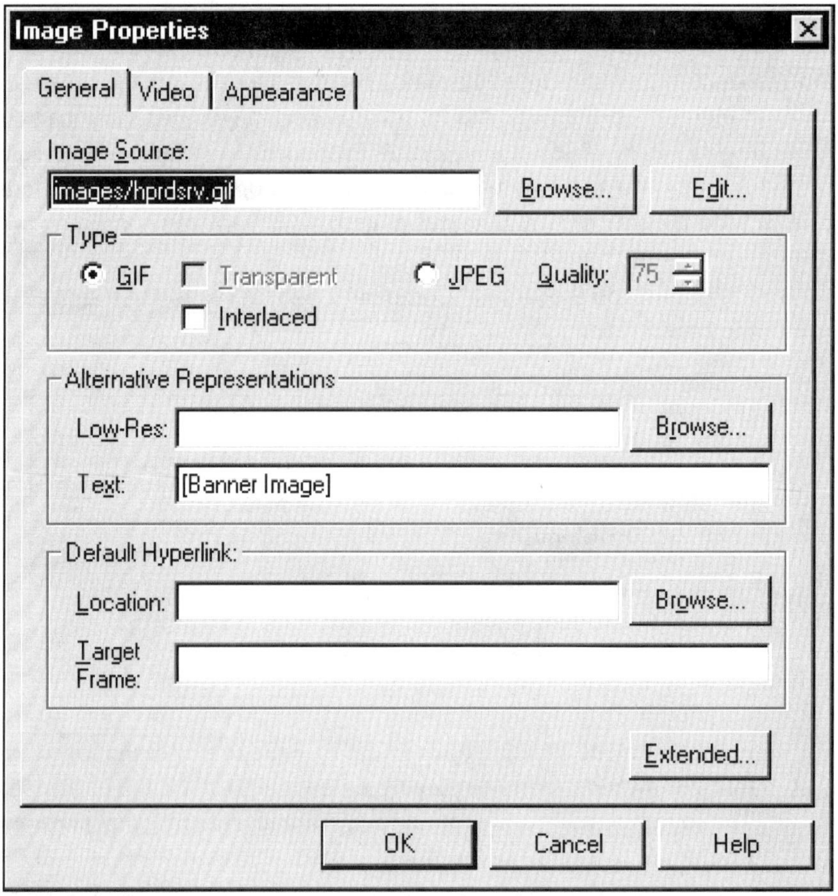

Image Properties   ☒

General | Video | Appearance

Image Source:

`images/hprdsrv.gif`   Browse...   Edit...

┌ Type ──┐
│ ⦿ GIF   ☐ Transparent   ○ JPEG   Quality: 75 ⬍ │
│   ☐ Interlaced   │
└──┘

┌ Alternative Representations ───────────────────┐
│ Low-Res: [   ]   Browse... │
│ Text: [Banner Image]   │
└───┘

┌ Default Hyperlink: ─────────────────────────────┐
│ Location: [   ]   Browse... │
│ Target   │
│ Frame: [   ]   │
└───┘

                              Extended...

        OK   Cancel   Help

Image
Properties
dialog box

FIGURE 3-8

3. In the Image Properties dialog box General tab you select the image to be displayed, provide text to be displayed in browsers that do not display graphics (this text will also be displayed for a few seconds if you point on the graphic in a browser), and create a hyperlink for the graphic. In the Appearance tab you can set the alignment of the graphic on the page, horizontal and vertical spacing around the graphic, and create a border for it.

4. Close the Image Properties dialog box, and right-click on the navbar below the Products & Services banner. The context menu displayed is similar to the one you saw by right-clicking on the company logo. The navbar is also a web page that is included on each page of the Corporate web. To change the navbar, you edit the navbar.htm page, opened from the context menu.

5. Right-click on the first hyperlink, Name Of Product 1. Select Hyperlink Properties to display the Edit Hyperlink dialog box shown here. You use this dialog box to set hyperlinks between text and graphics on your web pages and other web pages (both in your web and in other webs on the Web). You can also set hyperlinks to bookmarks on the same page.

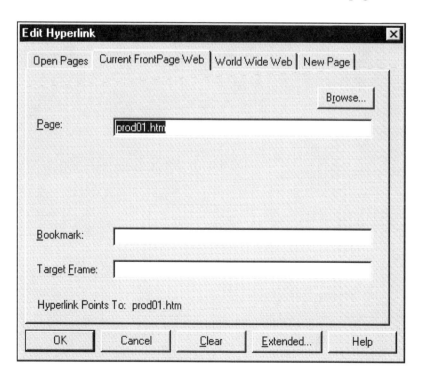

6. Click on Cancel to close the Edit Hyperlinks dialog box. Right-click on the first hyperlink again, and select Follow Hyperlink in the context menu to open the first product page (prod01.htm) in the FrontPage Editor, as shown in Figure 3-9. The Product 1 page includes a definition list to itemize the key benefits of the product and a table with columns for the product description, SKU number, and price. Each item in the definition list also has a graphic bullet. You can see the properties for the bullet by opening the Image Properties dialog box from its context menu.

 TIP: *In the FrontPage Editor you have to open the context menu and select Follow Hyperlink to open the target of a link. In a Web browser you simply click on the hyperlink itself.*

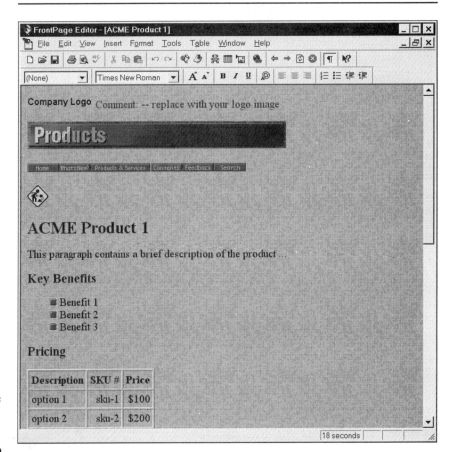

Product 1 page in the FrontPage Editor

FIGURE 3-9

7. Close the Product 1 page by selecting Close from the File menu.

The Table of Contents Page

The Table of Contents page provides the user with a single location to open any page in a web.

1. Open the Table of Contents page in the FrontPage Editor by selecting toc.htm in the Open File dialog box, which is opened by use of either the Open toolbar button or by selecting Open in the File menu. Figure 3-10 shows the page in the FrontPage Editor.

The listings on the Table of Contents page are created by the Table of Contents WebBot. In the FrontPage Editor this does not look like much, but in a browser this is automatically expanded to include references to each page and each bookmark on each page.

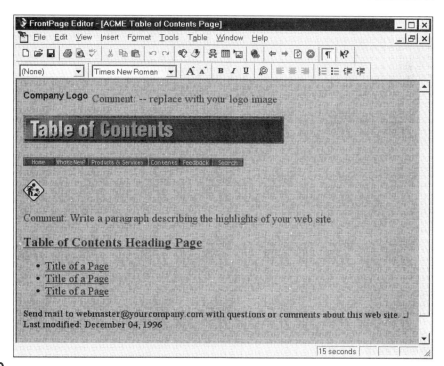

Table of Contents page in FrontPage Editor

FIGURE 3-10

2. Open the File menu and select Preview In Browser. In the Preview In Browser dialog box that is displayed, shown next, you can select a web browser to view your page, add a browser you have installed on your computer, and select the size at which the browser will be opened.

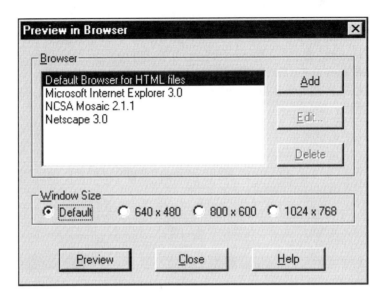

3. Click on Preview to open the Table of Contents page in your selected browser. Figure 3-11 shows the Table of Contents page after the WebBot has created the hyperlinks.

4. Close your browser, return to the FrontPage Editor, and close the Table of Contents page.

The Feedback Page

There are many reasons to get feedback from the people who visit your web site. If your site is designed to promote a product or service, you will want to know what they think of your products, and to give users a simple method to contact you with questions. The Feedback page in the Corporate web does exactly that, as you will see by following these instructions:

1. Open the Feedback page in the FrontPage Editor by selecting feedback.htm in the Open File dialog box and clicking on OK.

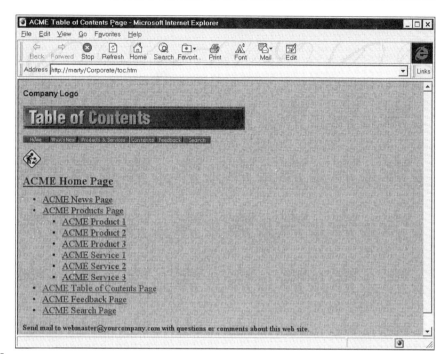

Table of
Contents
page in
web
browser

FIGURE 3-11

2. When the Feedback page is opened, scroll through it to see all the
elements. The lower part of the page should look like Figure 3-12.

The body of the Feedback page is a form. As you saw in Chapter 2, a
form is used to gather information on a web page and then transfer the
information to a WebBot or another application. The feedback form
includes a scrolling text box to enter the users' comments, a drop-down
menu for users to select the subject of their comments, five one-line text
boxes for users to enter information about themselves, and buttons to
submit or clear the form.

IP: *To see the contents of a drop-down menu on a form in the FrontPage
Editor, right-click on the drop-down menu and select Form Field Properties
from the context menu.*

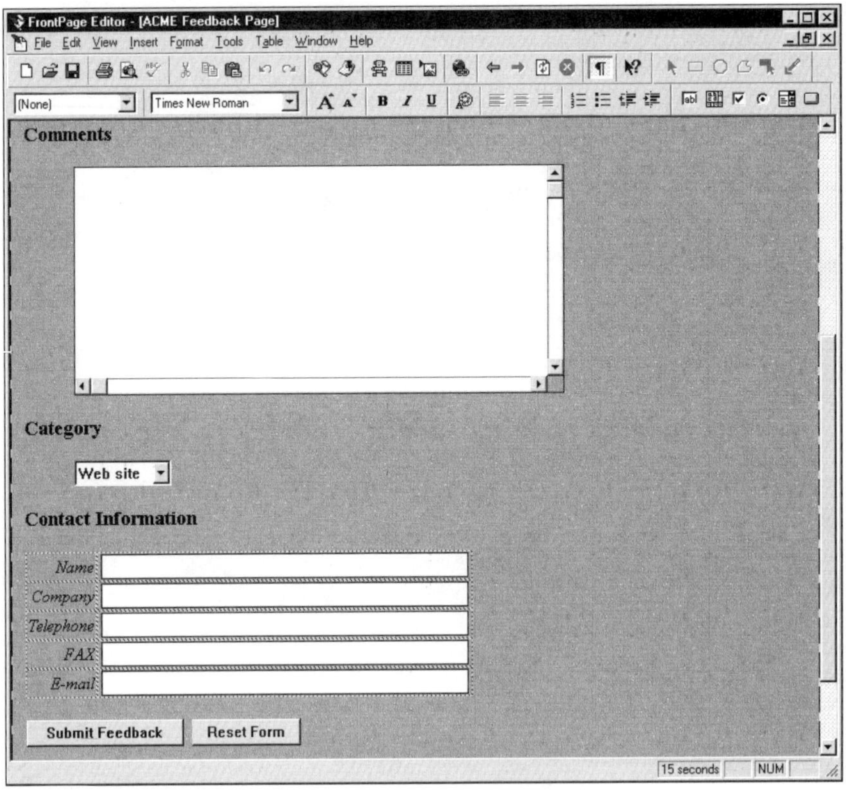

Feedback
page
form in
FrontPage
Editor

FIGURE 3-12

3. Right-click anywhere on the form except one of the form fields, and
select Form Properties from the context menu. The Form Handler
drop-down list box on the Form Properties dialog box contains a list
of the WebBot components that can be used to process the results
of the form.

4. Click on the Settings button to open the Settings For Saving Results Of
Form dialog box shown next. Here you can set the location of the file
created by the WebBot, the format of the file, and additional information
(for example, date, time, user name) to be included in the file.

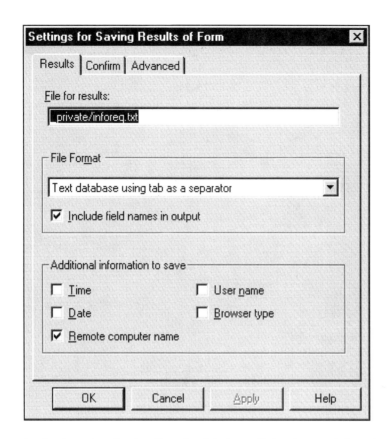

3

5. Close the Settings For Saving Results Of Form dialog box and then the Form Properties dialog box. Then close the Feedback page in the FrontPage Editor.

The Search Page

In a large web site a table of contents does not always provide the quickest method for a user to find specific information. The Search page allows users to search your web using any of the keywords that describe the information they are looking for. The Search page uses the WebBot Search component to search the web and generate a results page. The search results page will contain hyperlinks to the web pages that match the search criterion. Figure 3-13 shows the results of a search of the Corporate web for the word "products."

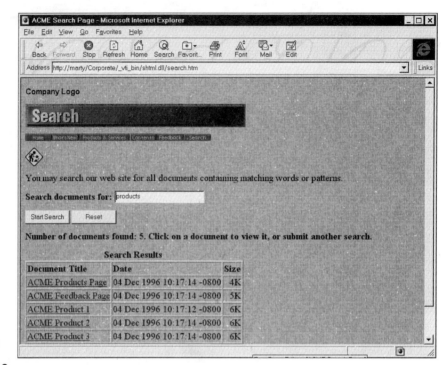

Search results for the word "products"

FIGURE 3-13

TIP: *You can hide pages, such as style pages or pages that you are only using to include in other pages, from the Search WebBot by placing the pages in the special web folder webname_private. The Search WebBot does not search this folder.*

1. Open the Corporate web Search page in the FrontPage Editor (search.htm in the Open File dialog box) as shown in Figure 3-14.

   The body of the Search page is a simple form with a single text box and two buttons. The user enters the words to search on in the text box and then clicks on the Start Search button.

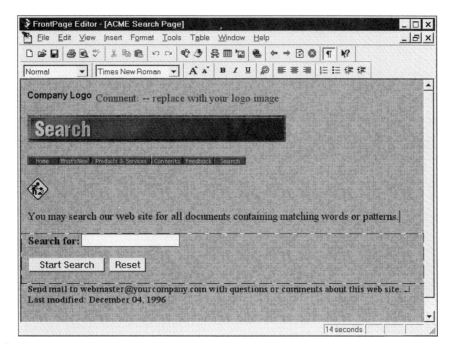

Search
page in
FrontPage
Editor

FIGURE 3-14

2. Right-click on the form (the Search for text box), and select WebBot
Component Properties from the context menu. In the WebBot Search
Component Properties dialog box, shown next, you can set the labels for
the text box and the buttons, set the width of the text box, and set the
options for the search results.

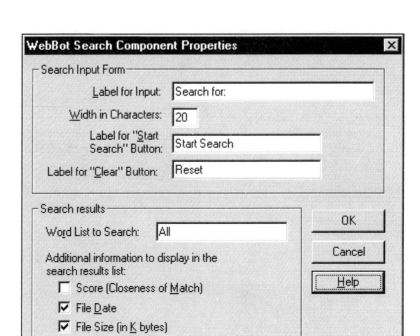

3. Click on Cancel to close the WebBot Search Component Properties dialog box.

Open your browser and try the features of the Corporate Presence web. In particular, try those noted earlier, especially the Table of Contents and Search pages. When you are finished viewing the Corporate web in your browser, close your browser, close the FrontPage Editor, and then delete the Corporate web by selecting Delete FrontPage Web in the FrontPage Explorer File menu and clicking on Yes in the Confirm Delete dialog box that will appear.

The Corporate Presence web shows how easy it is to create a complete web site with the FrontPage wizards. To actually put the web on the World Wide Web, you would only need to change the logo.htm file to insert your logo on each page and to add your content to the pages. In Chapter 11 you learn how to import word processor and other documents into a FrontPage web.

Working with the Discussion Web Wizard

Discussion groups are used to provide a place for people to carry on online conversations. They provide a simple method for you to link comments about a single subject, or to find comments about a specific subject in the discussion group. You can create a separate discussion web or incorporate a discussion group in another web by using the Discussion Web Wizard:

1. From the FrontPage Explorer, open the New FrontPage Web dialog box, choose Discussion Web Wizard, and click on OK. Type the filename for the web, **DiscussionGroup,** and click on OK. The first Discussion Web Wizard dialog box will explain how the wizard works.

2. Click on Next. The second dialog box will ask you the features of a discussion group that you want to include, as you can see in Figure 3-15. Your choices include the following:

- **Submission Form** is the form used to submit comments to the discussion and is required to have a discussion group.

- **Table of Contents** provides a means of organizing and finding previously submitted comments by subject. If you want readers to read and comment on what previous contributors have submitted, then you need to include a table of contents.

- **Search Form** is an alternative way for readers to find previously contributed information. It allows a reader to find a contribution containing words other than those in the subject.

- **Threaded Replies** links multiple comments on the same subject. This allows the reader to go directly from one comment to the next on a given subject.

- **Confirmation Page** shows the person making a submission what the system has received.

3. Keep all of the options checked, so you can look at them, and click on Next. The third dialog box will open and ask for the title you want to use and the folder name for the discussion group messages. Type **Discussion Group** for the title, and accept the default folder name (note that discussion folder names must begin with an underscore).

4. Again click on Next. The fourth Discussion Web Wizard dialog box will ask for the fields you want to start with on the submission form. You will be able to add more later with the FrontPage Editor.

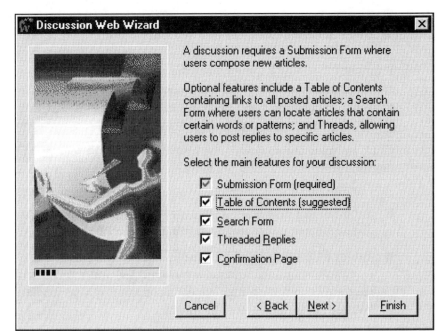

Second
Discussion
Web
Wizard
dialog box

FIGURE 3-15

5. Keep the default Subject and Comments and click on Next. The fifth
   dialog box will ask if you want to restrict the contributors to the
   discussion group.

6. Accept the default, No, Anyone Can Post Articles, and click on Next.
   Also accept the defaults in the next five dialog boxes by clicking on Next
   in each of them, and then click on Finish in the final dialog box. The web
   will then be displayed in the FrontPage Explorer.

7. You can, of course, open the pages of the web in the FrontPage Editor and
   make any changes you desire. To really look at the Discussion web and
   try it, you need to look at it in a browser. Since one of the defaults chosen
   was to use frames, you need to use Netscape Navigator 2.0 or later, or
   Internet Explorer 3.0 or later to see the frames.

8. Open Netscape Navigator or Internet Explorer and load DiscussionGroup
   (type **http://*your server name*/DiscussionGroup**), and your Discussion
   Group web will appear as shown in Figure 3-16.

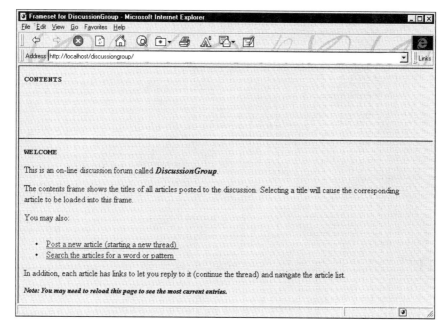

The
Discussion
Group
frameset
viewed in
a web
browser

FIGURE 3-16

9. Click on Post A New Article (you should see a form similar to that shown in Figure 3-17), enter a subject, your name, and some comments, and click on Post Article. (If you get a message saying you are about to send information over the Internet and it is insecure, click on Yes.) The confirmation should appear showing the subject you entered.

10. Click on the Refresh The Main Page hyperlink. Back at the Contents page you should again see the subject you entered under Contents. Click on your subject and you will see your name, the date and time you made the submission, and the comments you entered.

11. The navbar now has several new entries: Post (to start a new thread), Reply (to add a comment to an existing thread), Next and Previous (to go forward and backward, respectively, in the current thread), and Up (to go to the next thread).

12. Try these new navbar entries by making several submissions, both independent and in reply to another submission, so you can see how the navigation works. When you are done, close the browser and delete the web.

DiscussionGroup

[Contents | Search | Post]

POST ARTICLE

Subject:

From:

Comments:

Post Article   Reset Form

Form for
posting
an article
on the
Discussion
Group web

FIGURE 3-17

A discussion group can be a powerful means to communicate among a group, and FrontPage offers an easy way to create one.

Using the Import Web Wizard

If FrontPage 97 is the first version of FrontPage that you've used, you may have a number of existing webs that you will want to convert to FrontPage webs. The process is extremely simple when you use the Import Web Wizard.

1. From the FrontPage Explorer, open the New FrontPage Web dialog box and choose Import Web Wizard, and click on OK.

2. In the Import Web Wizard dialog box select your server and type the name of the new web. Click on OK and the first wizard dialog box will be displayed.

3. Enter the complete path name of the folder where the web is located, or click on the Browse button to locate the folder. The Include Subdirectories check box should be selected. Then click on Next.

4. The next dialog box will display a list of the files located in the selected folder. Select the files you want to import into the new web. Click on Next and then click on Finish.

That's all there is to it. Your imported web will be displayed in the FrontPage Explorer ready for you to work on.

Page Wizards

The web wizards are grand in their scope, with many different page types and features on each page. Sometimes, though, what you want is a single page or a single feature. For that purpose, FrontPage provides the page wizards. Table 3-1 lists the four types of pages or features you can create with them.

The Database Connector Wizard requires some knowledge of databases and is covered in Chapter 13. You used both the Frames Wizard and Form Page Wizard in Chapter 2 and will work with them again in Chapters 8 and 9, respectively. In the remainder of this chapter you will see how to use the Personal Home Page Wizard.

Personal Home Page Wizard

The Personal Home Page Wizard leads you through the creation of a single personal home page, giving you many options on what to include on the page as it is built,

Page Wizard	Function
Database Connector Wizard	Creates an Internet Database Connector (.IDC) file
Form Page Wizard	Creates a form
Frames Wizard	Creates a frameset and the required web pages
Personal Home Page Wizard	Creates a home page for yourself

Page Wizards

TABLE 3-1

saving you time in customizing. A personal home page can be used to promote you, a small organization, a product or service, or a concept. See the many options you have with the Personal Home Page Wizard:

1. First close any web you may have open in the FrontPage Explorer. If the FrontPage Editor isn't already open, click on the Show FrontPage Editor button in the Explorer's toolbar.

2. In the FrontPage Editor select New from the File menu, select Personal Home Page Wizard from the New Page dialog box, and then click on OK. In the first Personal Home Page Wizard dialog box, shown here, you are asked to select the major sections that you want on this page. Select all of the suggested sections so you can see what they offer, and then click on Next.

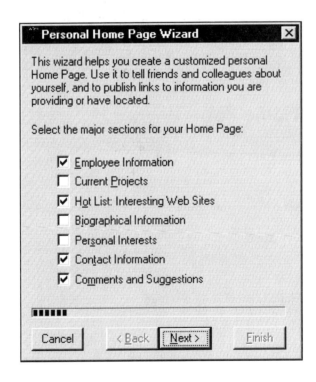

3. In the second dialog box you are asked for the page URL (the page's filename) and the page title that will appear in the title bar of a browser. For this example, accept the defaults and click on Next.

4. The third dialog box asks you the information to include in the Employee Information section. Select all of the topics, and click on Next.

5. You are then asked to enter the name of the projects (could be anything) that you want to include on your page. Enter these, decide if you want them in a bulleted, numbered, or definition list, and then click on Next.

6. In the next several dialog boxes choose how you want a "Hot List" presented, the format of a biography section, a list of items for the Personal Interests section and how it is to be presented, your various addresses and phone numbers, and how you want to get the comments and suggestions that are submitted. In each case click on Next after making the necessary entries.

7. In the next to the last dialog box, you are asked the order of the sections on your page and are given a list of the sections. To change the order, click on a section you want to move, and then click on Up or Down the number of times it takes to move the section to where you want it.

8. When you have the sections in the order you want, click on Next, and then click on Finish to create your home page. One possible result is shown in Figure 3-18.

There are many things that you can do to customize this page. One of the more likely changes is to add additional pages to this home page and refer to them from the home page. If you are going to do that, you'll need to first create a web in the FrontPage Explorer, then create your home page, and finally create the additions, all from within the web. As you are looking at this page, keep in mind that it has many uses other than just for an individual.

The wizards available in FrontPage for both webs and pages are an exceptionally valuable resource for creating the webs you want. If you use your imagination as you build a web, you will find that the wizards will save you considerable work.

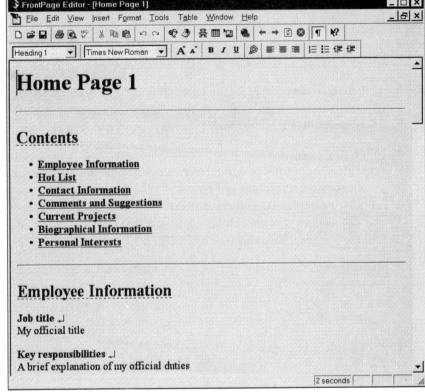

A personal home page created with the Personal Home Page Wizard

FIGURE 3-18

They also will give you a number of ideas on how to utilize the features of FrontPage in your webs. Look through the wizards before and as you are working on your web to get all you can out of them.

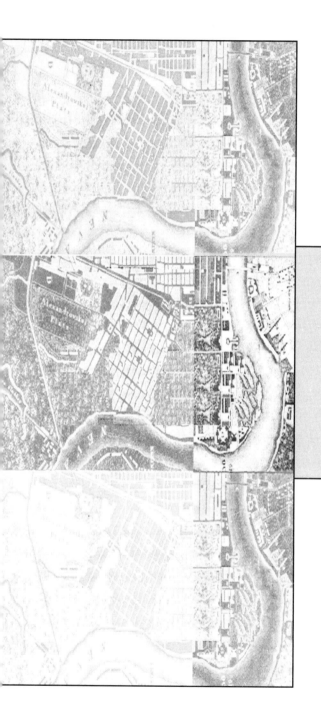

Using Templates

As you saw in Chapter 2, the easiest way to create a web with FrontPage is by using a wizard or a template. You'll remember that *wizards* ask you questions about the web you want to create and then build a web based on your answers. *Templates* create a particular kind of web without input from you. In Chapter 3 you used wizards to create complete webs and pages. In the first half of this chapter you'll see how to use templates in both webs and pages, and the results that they produce. In the second half you will learn how to create your own templates for webs and pages. By creating your own templates you can easily create new webs or add pages to existing webs without having to re-create a design or layout each time.

Web Templates

FrontPage provides templates at both the web level and the page level. Begin looking at the web level by loading the FrontPage Explorer. When the program loading is complete, click on the From A Wizard Or Template option, and click on OK in the Getting Started With Microsoft FrontPage dialog box, or open the File menu and choose New FrontPage Web. The New FrontPage Web dialog box will open and display a list of templates and wizards.

Applying the Normal Web Template

The starting place for creating a general-purpose web is with the Normal Web template. This template creates a single web page on which you can place anything. Do that now with these instructions (the New FrontPage Web dialog box should be open on your screen):

1. Double-click on Normal Web in the New FrontPage Web dialog box or, assuming that Normal Web is already selected, just click on OK. The Normal Web Template dialog box will open.

2. Select the web server that you want to use; then enter the name you want to give this web. This name cannot use spaces, but can be longer than

eight characters. For this example, the web will be referred to as
"Normal1," so if you do not have another name you want to use, enter
Normal1 for the Name of New FrontPage Web and then click on OK.

3. Right-click on the Home Page representation in either Folder or
   Hyperlink view, and choose Properties from the context menu that opens
   as a result of right-clicking. The Properties dialog box for the Home Page,
   similar to the one shown in Figure 4-1, will open. Here you can see the
   filename and URL that have been generated for the new web. In the
   Summary tab you can see when and by whom the web was created and
   modified. You can also add comments.

4. Close the Properties dialog box, and then double-click on the page in the
   right pane to open the page in the FrontPage Editor. The FrontPage Editor
   will open with a blank page.

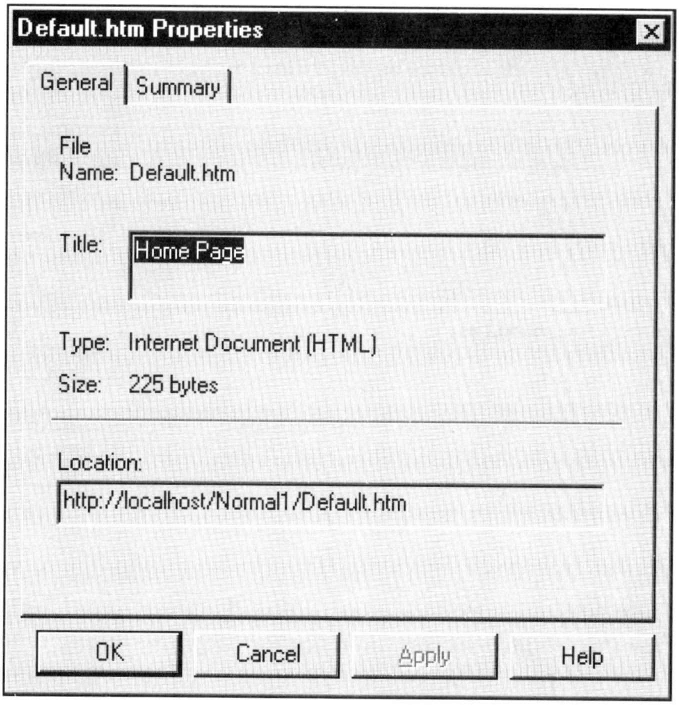

4

Home Page
Properties
dialog box

FIGURE 4-1

Default.htm Properties   ✕

General | Summary |

File
Name: Default.htm

Title: | Home Page

Type: Internet Document (HTML)
Size: 225 bytes

Location:
http://localhost/Normal1/Default.htm

| OK | Cancel | Apply | Help |

On the blank page you can enter and format any text you want, insert graphics, and add forms, tables, and other elements as you saw in Chapter 2. In later chapters you will do all of these tasks. The purpose here is simply to see that the Normal Web template does in fact create a single blank web page. It also creates all of the structure that is behind a web in FrontPage.

Why go to all this trouble for a single web page? FrontPage needs the structure to perform its functions. Since most webs have a number of pages and other functions such as forms, the structure is needed for organizing the web and making it easy to use and maintain.

You can easily add pages to a web created with the Normal Web template by using the FrontPage Editor. Try the following instructions, go back to the FrontPage Explorer, and see how the new page is automatically integrated into the web that was created.

1. Open the FrontPage Editor's File menu, and choose New to open the New Page dialog box. Normal Page should be selected as the template. Click on OK to create a new page in your Normal1 web.

2. Again open the File menu, and choose Save to open the Save As dialog box. Type **Second Page** as the Page Title. The page URL should automatically change to "second.htm," as you can see:

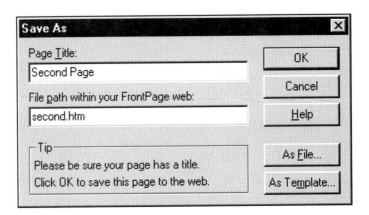

3. Click on OK to save the page, and then click on the FrontPage Editor's Close button, or open the File menu and choose Exit to leave the FrontPage Editor and return to the FrontPage Explorer. When the FrontPage Explorer opens, you'll see a new page, "Second Page" (shown in Figure 4-2), has been added to the web you created earlier.

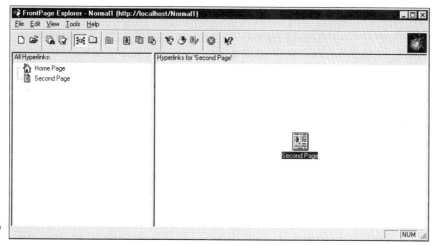

A second
page
integrated
into the
original web

4

FIGURE 4-2

4. Open the FrontPage Explorer's File menu and choose Delete FrontPage Web. You'll be informed that deleting a web is a permanent action, and there is no undo for it. Click on Yes to delete the Normal1 web.

As you create your own webs, you'll probably use the Normal Web template often to create the small or custom webs that you'll need.

Creating a Personal Web

The Personal Web template available in FrontPage creates a basic single-page web to publicize a person or small organization. Build that next as your second project, with the following steps:

1. From the FrontPage Explorer, open the File menu, choose New FrontPage Web, select Personal Web, and click on OK. Make sure the Web Server is correct, enter a name such as MyWeb, and click on OK. The new web appears with a number of hyperlinks that you can customize, as you can see in Figure 4-3.

2. Double-click on My Home Page in the right pane to open it in the FrontPage Editor.

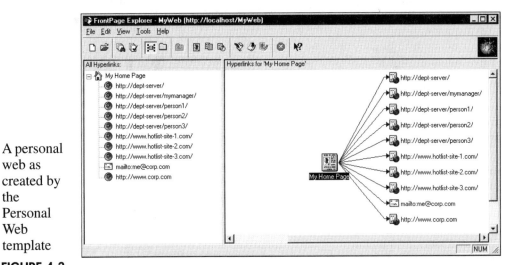

A personal web as created by the Personal Web template

FIGURE 4-3

The page that opens has a lot of features incorporated in it, some of which are shown in Figure 4-4. These features are only suggestions and can be customized. They provide a starting place that you can use or delete depending on your needs, and you can add any other features that you want. Use the scroll bar to review the following features:

NOTE: *The page created with the Personal Web template is very similar to the personal web page you created in Chapter 3 with the Personal Web wizard. Unlike the Personal Web template, the Personal Web wizard lets you choose what features to include.*

■ **Plain text** is text that you can replace with your own words. For example, Michael Smith might replace "My Home Page" with "Michael Smith's Page."

■ **Bookmarks**, text with a dashed underline, are references to which you can jump using a hyperlink. You can see the name of the bookmark by right-clicking on text that has a dashed underline and selecting Bookmark Properties. For example, right-clicking on Contents and selecting

Bookmark Properties opens the Bookmark dialog box shown next, which tells you the bookmark attached to Contents is "top."

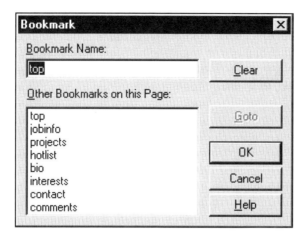

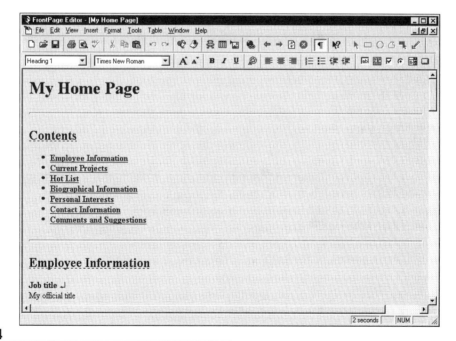

Page created with the Personal Web template

FIGURE 4-4

■ **Hyperlinks,** text of a different color with a solid underline, are links to bookmarks or other pages in the current web, or to other webs. Again, you can open the Hyperlinks Properties dialog box and see where the link is pointing. The "Employee Information" in the Contents list, for example, is pointing to a bookmark named "jobinfo" in the open page, as you can see in the dialog box in Figure 4-5, which was opened by right-clicking on "Employee Information" in the Contents list and then selecting Hyperlinks Properties.

 NOTE: *Bookmarks and hyperlinks can be graphics as well as text.*

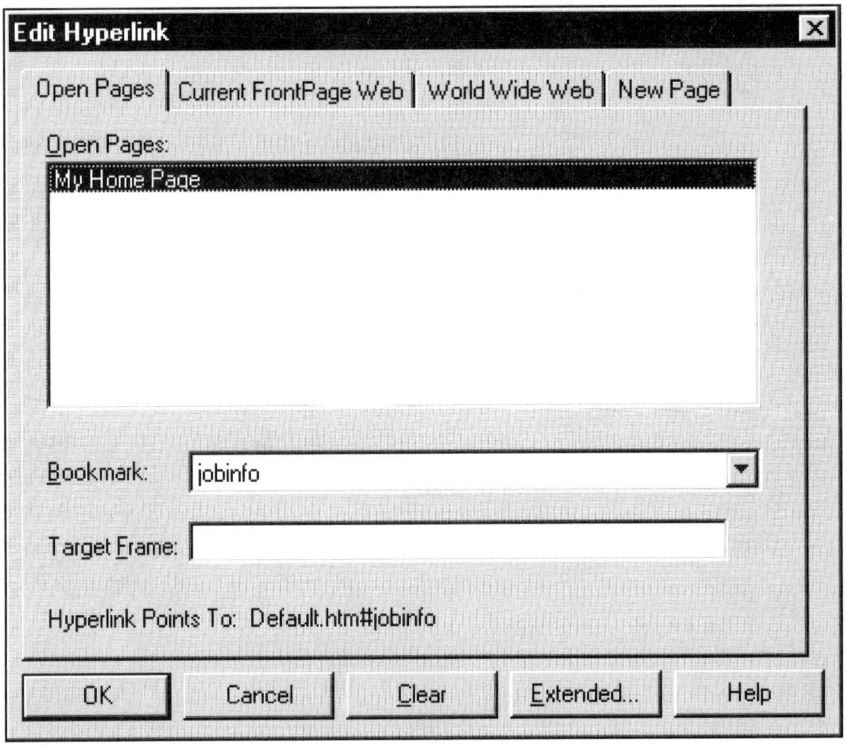

Edit Hyperlink ☒

Open Pages | Current FrontPage Web | World Wide Web | New Page

Open Pages:

My Home Page

Bookmark: jobinfo ▼

Target Frame:

Hyperlink Points To: Default.htm#jobinfo

| OK | Cancel | Clear | Extended... | Help |

Edit
Hyperlink
dialog box

FIGURE 4-5

- **Annotation text**, which is in a third color and causes the mouse pointer to turn into a little robot, like the one shown here, does not appear when the web is viewed with a browser. This text is created with the Annotation WebBot. It is meant for notes to the web authors and editors.

> **Department or workgroup** ↵
> My department's name Comment: ... with a link to its home page
>
> **Manager** ↵
> My manager's name Comment: ... with a link to his or her home page

- **URLs** or Internet addresses are just hyperlinks to that address but with a specific protocol such as mailto for e-mail or FTP for file transfer. The Hyperlink Properties dialog box for the link will show you the full address and protocol and let you change them.

- **Forms** for entering comments and the reader's name, or preferably, e-mail address, allow your reader to communicate with you. Note that responses from the form are stored in the file homeresp.txt. You can change this and other aspects of the form by opening the Form Properties dialog box and clicking on Settings.

- **Timestamp**, at the bottom of the page, is created with the Timestamp WebBot. You can change its format and the way it is set through its WebBot Component Properties dialog box.

When you are done looking at the personal web page, close the FrontPage Editor and then delete MyWeb in the FrontPage Explorer. The "simple" personal web you can create with the Personal Web template is a good starting point for many webs and offers a number of useful features. Consider it as you create your own webs.

Using the Project Web Template

The Project Web template creates a multipage web, shown in Figure 4-6, that is used to keep people up to date on a project. It lists a project's staff members, schedule, and status, and provides independent page headers and footers, an archive, a search

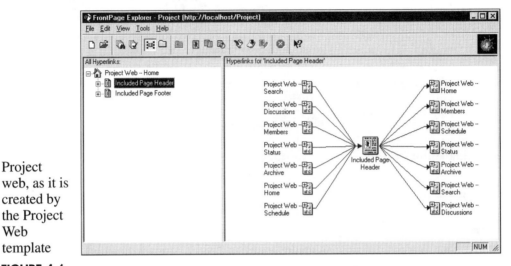

Project web, as it is created by the Project Web template

FIGURE 4-6

engine, and a discussion bulletin board. (You've seen how some of these features were used in the webs you created with wizards in Chapter 3.) Follow these steps to look at some of the features that are unique to this template:

1. From the FrontPage Explorer open the New FrontPage Web dialog box, select Project Web, and then click on OK. Select a server and name for the web, such as "Project." A new web will be created and will appear in the FrontPage Explorer. Click on the plus sign on the left of the Included Page Header page to expand the directory tree so it looks like Figure 4-6.

2. Click on Project Web—Home in the left pane, and then double-click the same page in the right pane to open the FrontPage Editor with that page. The page shown in Figure 4-7 will be displayed.

Included Pages

FrontPage has a WebBot that allows you to include one page on another. Thus, if you want the same information or objects to be on several pages, you can put that information on one page and then include that page on all the others where you want

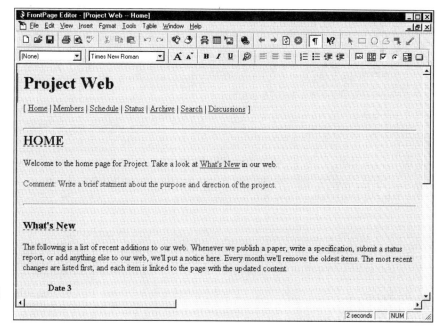

Project
Web home
page with
an included
header

FIGURE 4-7

it. This is done with the Include WebBot (WebBots will be discussed in Chapter 10). This is how the included pages work:

1. Move the mouse pointer to the top of the page; the WebBot icon appears. That is because the top of the page is a separate header page (named header.htm in this case) applied to all pages in the web.

NOTE: *You cannot edit the contents of a header page on a regular page. You must open the header page itself.*

2. Right-click on the top of the page and select Open header.htm. (The context menu will show the complete path, http://localhost/Project/ header.htm, in this example.) The header page will open as you can see next. Here you can edit the title and navigation bar (or "navbar") that will appear on every page of the web.

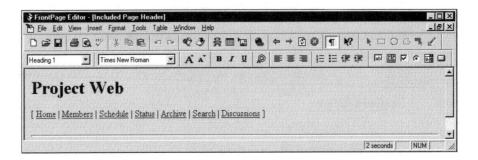

3. Move the mouse pointer through the navbar, and in the lower-left corner of the window you'll see the pages to which the links will jump when they are clicked. In this case the navbar is just a series of words, each a hyperlink to a different page. You can also make a navbar out of a graphic or a series of graphics and use hotspots for the hyperlinks. You can edit both the words and the links—the words directly, and the links through the Edit Hyperlink dialog box.

4. In the Included Page Header you just opened, right-click on Members in the navbar and choose Hyperlink Properties. The Edit Hyperlink dialog box will open and show you the link to the Members.htm page. This is the link you would change if you wanted a different link. Click on Cancel to close the Edit Hyperlink dialog box.

5. Close the Included Page Header. Go to the bottom of the home page, and you'll see a footer page that is also included on every web page. You can edit it as you can the header page.

6. Close the FrontPage Editor with the home page, and return to the FrontPage Explorer.

7. Open and review the Members, Schedule, Status, and Archive pages. On each you'll see the header and footer placed there by the Include WebBot, as well as many features you saw on the Personal Web page.

Searches and Discussion Groups

The Project web that you created incorporates two other WebBot-created features—text searches and discussion groups—which add interactivity to the web. You saw how these features worked in the Corporate Presence web you created in Chapter 3. You can review how these work in the Project web next:

1. Open the Project Web—Search page in the FrontPage Editor. Your screen should look like Figure 4-8. In the second section of this page is a one-field form that allows you to search the documents in the current web for a particular text string that you have entered in the form. This search form has been created by the Search bot. You can edit its characteristics by right-clicking in the search area and choosing WebBot Component Properties. The bottom part of the Search page contains instructions on how to structure a search query.

2. Close the Search page and open the Project Web—Discussions page, which contains links to two discussion groups. The discussion groups are separate webs and are created with the Discussion bot. These allow people to enter comments, and others to comment on their comments, thereby creating threads on a given subject. Most online forums follow this format.

3. Close the FrontPage Editor. To get a better perspective of the Project web, open it in a browser. And then when you are done, delete the Project web in the FrontPage Explorer.

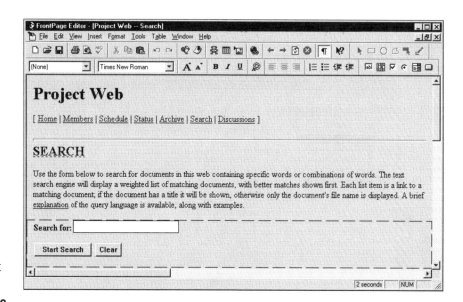

Search page for doing text searches

FIGURE 4-8

A web that has been created with the Project Web template provides an excellent communications tool, not only for projects, but also for any team, operation, or department.

Applying the Customer Support Web Template

The Customer Support Web template, shown in Figure 4-9, makes a lot of information available to the user in several ways and allows the user to provide information to you in two ways. In doing this, the web uses FrontPage features you have already seen, but with different twists. Look at those differences now:

1. In the FrontPage Explorer create a Customer Support web from the New FrontPage Web dialog box. Your result should look like Figure 4-9.

2. Open the Customer Support—Welcome page, the home page for this web. As you have seen before, this page has an included header and footer, with a navbar in the header.

3. Close the Welcome page and then open, look at, and close the What's New and FAQ (frequently asked questions) pages. These pages, well-designed for their purposes, are simply combinations of text and hyperlinks with the included header and footer.

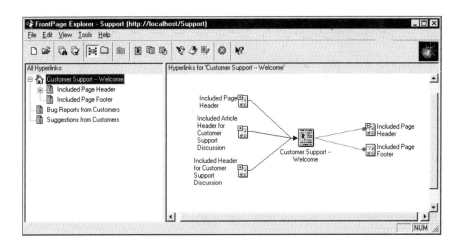

Customer
Support
Web
template

FIGURE 4-9

4. Open the Customer Support—Bugs page. If you scroll down the page, you'll see a special form for collecting errors in computer software ("bugs"). As with all other features in a wizard- or template-created web, you can customize this, changing the text, size, and content of the fields. In the last case, right-click on the field and choose Form Field Properties. The field's Properties dialog box will open, as shown in Figure 4-10 for the second field. Here you can change the name of the field in the top text box and change the choices the field presents to the user by using the Add, Modify, and Remove buttons.

5. Close the Bugs page; open, look at, and close the Suggestions page, which contains another form; and then open the Download page. The purpose of the Download page is to allow users to transfer software or documents to their computers from your server. This is done with the FTP (file transfer protocol) Internet protocol.

6. If you scroll down the page and then move the mouse pointer over the links for these transfers, you'll see in the status bar the URL to effect the FTP transfer, like that shown in the lower-left corner of Figure 4-11.

Drop-Down Menu Properties dialog box

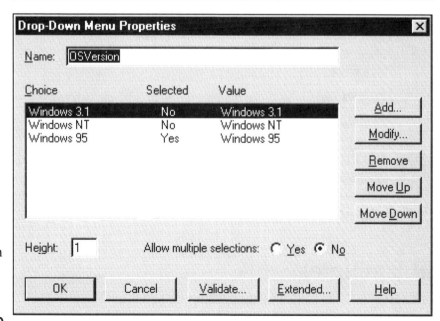

FIGURE 4-10

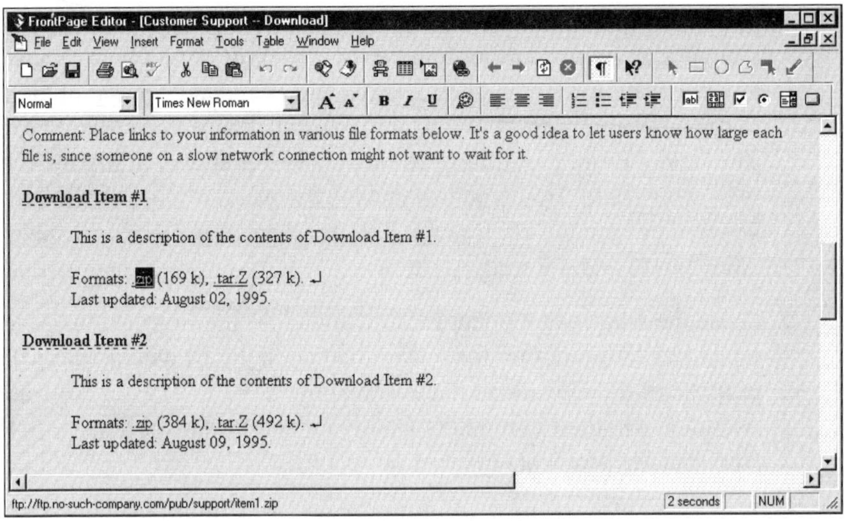

URL for an
FTP
transfer of
software or
a document

FIGURE 4-11

7. Close the Download page and then open, look at, and close the Discussion and Search pages. These contain a discussion group and a search form similar to those you saw in the Project web.

8. Open your Customer Support web in a browser and try its features, submitting a bug report and a suggestion. This will show you how these work.

9. When you are done, close the FrontPage Editor, and delete the Customer Support web.

> **NOTE:** *The reason each of these webs is being deleted after you are done looking at them is that they take a fair amount of disk space. The Customer Support web, as it is created by the template, takes 369K, and the Project web takes 417K.*

Page Templates

The web templates create webs with many different page types and many different features on each page. Sometimes, though, what you want is a single page. For that purpose, FrontPage provides the page templates. In the next section you'll see some of the more useful page templates. Begin with these steps:

1. In the FrontPage Explorer create a new web using the Normal Web template; name it **TestPages**.

2. Double-click on the Home Page in the right-hand pane of the Explorer to open the FrontPage Editor.

3. Open the File menu and choose New. The New Page dialog box appears.

The 30 wizards and templates listed in the New Page dialog box represent a tremendous resource that you can use to build your own webs. Chapter 2 provided a brief description of all the page wizards and templates. Many are differentiated only by their layout and content. Let's look at five of the more general-purpose ones. As each template is discussed, use the template to create a page and look at the results, at least in the FrontPage Editor, and possibly in your browser.

Confirmation Form Template

A confirmation page is used to show someone submitting information to you that their submission was received. When you create a submission form—for example, a feedback form or a registration form—a default confirmation page is automatically generated by FrontPage. You can create a custom confirmation page by using the Confirmation Form template, but you must specify that you want to use your confirmation page in the Form Properties dialog box of the submission form (from a form field's context menu, click on Form Properties, click again on Settings, select the Confirm tab, and fill in the URL of the confirmation page). In the FrontPage Explorer you can see the link between the submission form and the confirmation page it uses.

The Confirmation Form template creates a confirmation page using Confirmation Field bots as shown in Figure 4-12. These are used to place fields from the submission anywhere on the confirmation page. You can add additional fields to a confirmation page by using the WebBot Component option on the Insert menu, as well as change the text and move the existing confirmation fields. Several submission forms can share the same confirmation page if the forms use the same field names.

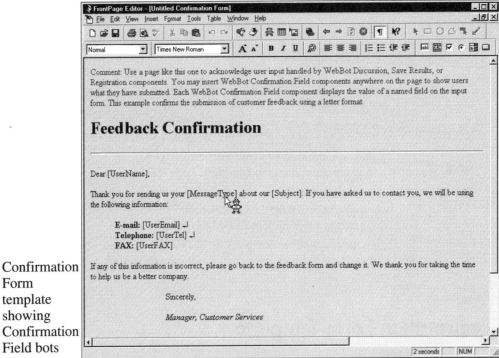

Confirmation Form template showing Confirmation Field bots

FIGURE 4-12

NOTE: *You must know the field names from the submission form when you are building the confirmation page, because the Confirmation Field bot, which requires the field name, does not allow you to browse for them.*

Feedback Form Template

The Feedback Form template creates a general-purpose form page that allows a user to send you comments, as you can see in Figure 4-13. The template creates several types of fields, gives them names that are also used in the Confirmation Form template, and activates the Save Results bot to capture the information submitted and to save it in the Feedback.txt file in the _Private subdirectory under the web's directory. (If you use the default directory scheme and your web is named TestPages, then the full path for Feedback.txt is C:\WebShare\Wwwroot\TestPages_private\Feedback.txt

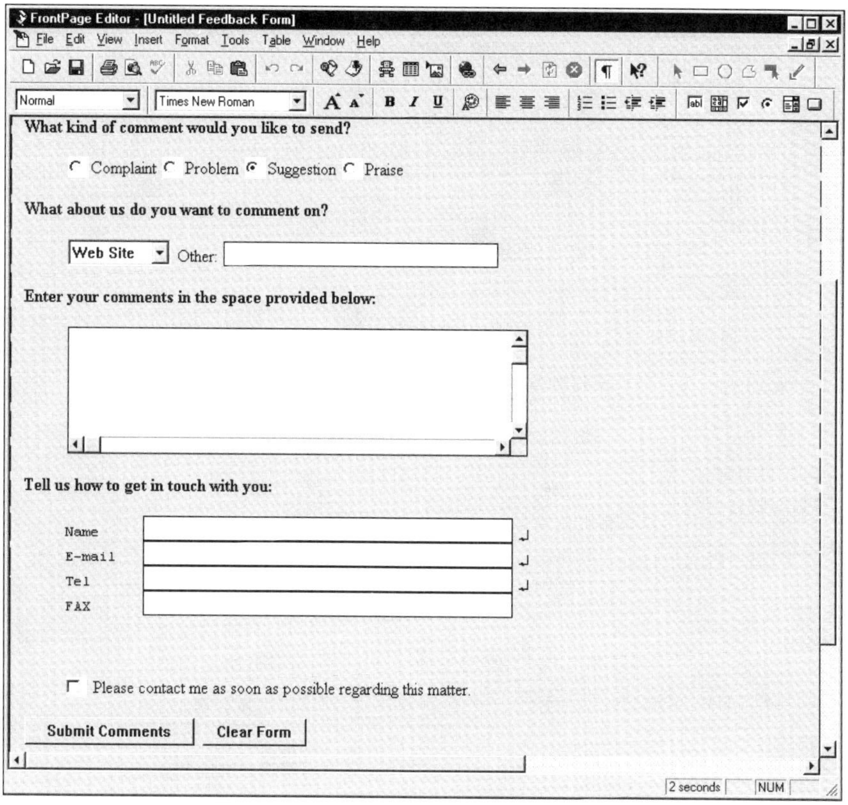

Form page created with Feedback Form template

FIGURE 4-13

with the MSPWS or C:\FrontPage Webs\Content\TestPages_Private\ Feedback.txt with the FPPWS.)

NOTE: *FrontPage is not consistent in its use of "folder" vs. "directory." To put some order to this I'll use directory when talking about the file structure and folder when referring to the Explorer in Folder view.*

Glossary of Terms Template

The page that you see in Figure 4-14, created by the Glossary of Terms template, has an indexing scheme that is useful in many situations other than a glossary. This is particularly true for longer lists, such as lists of parts, employees, and publications.

Comment: Create new entries in alphabetical order inside the appropriate section according to the first letter of the word or phrase. First insert a Definition Term and type the new entry. Then insert a Definition immediately after it, but press Shift+Enter to leave a blank line between the term and definition. Make the term bold, and create a bookmark for it.

Glossary of Terms

A B C D E F G H I J K L M N O P Q R S T U V W X Y Z #

Select the first letter of the word from the list above to jump to appropriate section of the glossary. If the term you are looking for starts with a digit or symbol, choose the '#' link.

- A -

aardvark

    Animal commonly referred to as an "ant-eater."

apple

    A popular fruit.

Alphabetized reference created by Glossary of Terms template

FIGURE 4-14

While it is very simple to create from scratch, the template still saves you from creating 27 bookmarks and 27 links.

Search Page Template

The Search Page template provides all the text search features that you saw in the webs earlier in this chapter. It is completely self-contained, including the query language instructions, as you can see in Figure 4-15. When you include this page in a web, it will search all of the text in the web without any further effort on your part. (As you saw when looking at the Normal Web template at the beginning of this chapter, you can add a page like the Search Page to a web by opening the web in the FrontPage Explorer, double-clicking on an existing page to open the FrontPage Editor or by clicking on the toolbar button, choosing New from the File menu, and then selecting the template or wizard you want to use to create the page.)

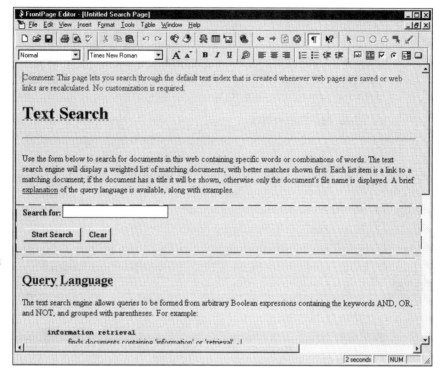

Text Search page created with the Search Page template

FIGURE 4-15

Table of Contents Template

The page, or more likely a portion thereof, created by the Table of Contents template is probably one of the more useful page templates. When you have finished adding all of the pages to a web, giving them each names, and creating links from a home page, add a table of contents page, or incorporate its contents on another page. This will not look like much in the FrontPage Editor (see Figure 4-16), but when you open the page in a browser, you'll have a complete table of contents of all the pages in the web. If there are links to the pages, they are shown in the hierarchical structure of their links. If the pages are not linked, they are listed after the linked pages, as you can see in Figure 4-17. The Table of Contents, then, creates a link to all the unlinked pages.

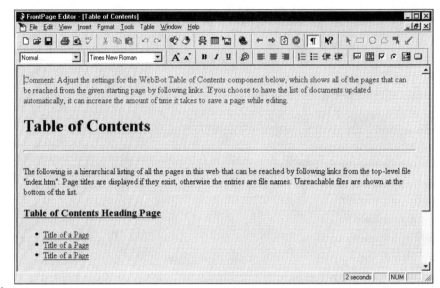

Table of
Contents
page in the
FrontPage
Editor

FIGURE 4-16

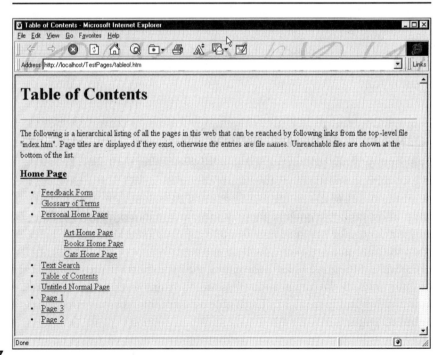

Table of
Contents
page in a
browser

FIGURE 4-17

NOTE: *Unlinked pages are listed in alphabetical order by their URL or filename, not their title.*

Figure 4-17 was created from a web that contained the six pages created from templates and discussed here, plus a normal page used as the home page of the web and containing the links in a custom navbar shown in Figure 4-18. Additionally, three pages were created and linked to the projects area of the personal home page, as well as three more pages that were unlinked. The creation, use, and management of hyperlinks, including navbars, will be fully discussed in Chapter 5.

Before going on to create your own templates, close and delete your TestPages web you have been using.

Creating Your Own FrontPage Templates

As you have been working with templates, you have probably had some ideas for FrontPage templates that you wished were available. If you are setting up an intranet, this is especially true, because it makes excellent sense to have a template for each part of the organization to use to get a consistent web across the company. In any situation where several similar webs are needed, it makes sense to use a template to create them. If you are creating a large web with a number of pages that look alike, it makes sense to create a page template that will speed up the process.

In the next couple of sections you'll look at the types of templates you can create and their common characteristics, and then see how to build the different types. Building templates does not require programming, as does creating your own wizards, but templates do require considerable file manipulation—making sure the right files are in the right place. We'll spend some time making the file management clear and leading you through complete examples so you can see how templates are built.

A navigation bar (or navbar) used to link the five pages created here

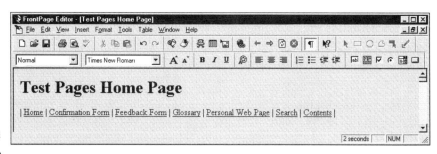

FIGURE 4-18

Types of Templates

Templates are model or prototype webs or web pages, identical in every detail to an actual web or web page. The only thing that distinguishes them is that they are in a special directory or folder. You can view a template in a browser and use it like any other web or web page. In fact, a template is just a web or web page that has been set aside to serve as a model for other webs or web pages.

Because they are stored in different directories, think of web templates and page templates as two distinct types of templates, although there are many similarities. *Page* templates create a single page that becomes part of a separately created web. A page template is a single .HTM file. A *web* template creates one or more interconnected pages within a full FrontPage web, which means that it includes all of the directory structure that is a part of FrontPage. In both cases, though, you create the web or the page in the same way that you would create any other web or page. When the web or page is the way you want it, you then place it in a special directory set up for templates with the extension .TEM. For example, Test.tem is a directory or folder containing the files for a template named "Test." The files within the template folder are just the normal .HTM HTML web files plus an .INF template information file.

FrontPage Directory Structure

The .TEM template folders are stored in different directories depending on whether they are pages or webs. Where these directories are depends on how you installed FrontPage and requires an understanding of the FrontPage directory structure.

FrontPage has two primary directories. One is called the FrontPage *root* directory and has the name "Microsoft FrontPage." The other directory is called the FrontPage *server* directory. If you are using the Microsoft Personal Web Server, this has the name "WebShare." If you are using the FrontPage Personal Web Server, the directory has the name "FrontPage Webs." During installation you are asked where you want to place these directories. The default is to place the FrontPage root directory under the Program Files directory so it has the path:

C:\Program Files\Microsoft FrontPage

Also, by default, the server directory is placed directly under your drive's root directory and so has the path:

C:\WebShare

or

C:\FrontPage Webs

The FrontPage server directory contains a subdirectory for your content ("Wwwroot" with MSPWS and "Content" with FPPWS), which stores all of the FrontPage webs that you create. It is *not* used to store templates, but comes into play when you create them, as you'll see later in this chapter. The FrontPage root directory is used to store templates and is central to the current discussion.

If you don't remember where you or someone else placed the FrontPage root directory during installation, you can find that information in the Frontpg.ini file, which is in your Windows directory. You can use Notepad to open this file. When you do that, look for the [FrontPage 2.0] section. In the line immediately under that heading you should see something like

FrontPageRoot=C:\Program Files\Microsoft FrontPage

as shown in Figure 4-19. Of course, your path may be different.

Within the FrontPage root directory are two subdirectories named "Pages" and "Webs." The Pages subdirectory is used to contain all of the page templates and wizards, as you can see in Figure 4-20, and the Webs subdirectory contains all of the web templates and wizards.

Open your Pages subdirectory now, and then open one of the .TEM template folders. Within the template folder you should see two files. One of these files is an .HTM web file that, if you double-click on it, will open your default browser and display a normal web page. In any other directory, this file would be considered just another web page; there is nothing to distinguish it except the directory it is in. The other file within the template folder is an .INF template information file. Look at it next.

The .INF Information File

The .INF template information file is used to hold descriptive information about the template. It is similar to a Windows .INI file and is read by the FrontPage Editor and FrontPage Explorer when they are working with templates. The .INF file must have

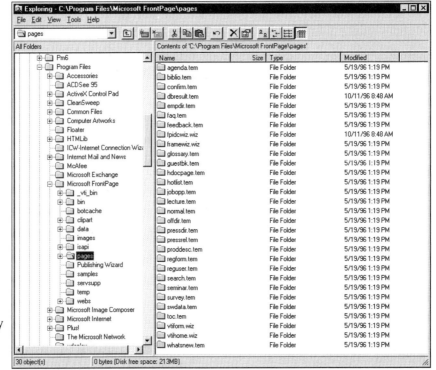

Frontpg.ini
file
showing
the location
of the
FrontPage
root
directory

FIGURE 4-19

the same name as the .TEM folder it is in, so the Test.tem folder will contain the
Test.inf file.

Microsoft
FrontPage
directory
and its
Pages
subdirectory
containing
templates

FIGURE 4-20

In the Pages directory, open the Agenda.tem folder, and then double-click on the Agenda.inf file. If the .INF file type is not associated with an application that can read it on your computer, select the Windows Notepad as that application. Notepad will open and display the file's short contents, like this:

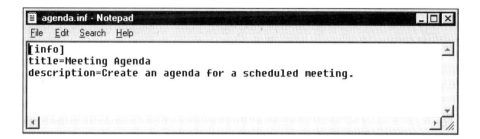

The Information File [info] Section

The .INF information file will always have an [info] section with at least two items in it—the title of the template and its description—as you just saw. These items are used in the New FrontPage Web or New Page dialog boxes to provide the name of the template and its description (as you can see next).

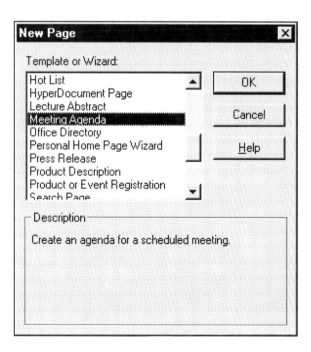

If the .INF file is not included, FrontPage uses the base name of the template folder ("Test" if the template folder is Test.tem) as the title and leaves the description blank.

The format of the .INF file is important and must match what you saw earlier. There must be a section named [info], and it must contain the title and description lines spelled correctly and with the equal signs. Whatever is on the right of the equal sign is data and will appear in the New Page Or Web dialog box. Each of the fields in the [info] section can be up to 255 characters long, including the attribute name ("title" and "description") and equal sign. As a practical matter, though, to be completely visible within the New Page or New FrontPage Web dialog box, the title should be fewer than 30 characters, and the description should be fewer than 100 characters. Under most circumstances, this file will automatically be created for you, as you will see in later sections of this chapter.

 TIP: *If you do have to create an .INF file, the easiest way is to copy an existing file and change the name, title, and description.*

For page templates, which are displayed in the FrontPage Editor, only the [info] section of the .INF file is used. For web templates, which are displayed in the FrontPage Explorer, the .INF file can have three additional sections that are used when the template is loaded into a server. These sections are a [FileList] section, a [MetaInfo] section, and a [TaskList] section.

The Information File [FileList] Section

The [FileList] section, which is shown in Figure 4-21, allows you to tell the FrontPage Explorer how you want the files in the template stored in a web. If you do not include a [FileList], the FrontPage Explorer loads all of the files in the .TEM directory, but does nothing with any subdirectories. The filenames in the .TEM directory are converted to all lowercase and become URLs in the web. Also, any .JPG, .JPEG, or .GIF files in the .TEM directory are placed in the Images subdirectory of the web. You need to include the [FileList] section if you have any of the following situations:

- You have subdirectories to the .TEM directory containing files you want in the web.

- You want to specify the URL and/or the case it uses.

- You want to specify the specific files in the .TEM directory to be placed in the web (files in the .TEM directory and not in [FileList] are ignored).

- You want the files to go to directories in the web other than the root directory for the .HTM files and the images subdirectory for the .JPG and .GIF files. The other available subdirectories are _private and cgi-bin.

When you use the [FileList], you must list all of the files you want transferred. If you do not want to change the filename or the path, list just the filename with an equal sign after it, as you see in Figure 4-21. If you want to specify the path, you need to switch from the MS-DOS/Windows use of the backslash between subdirectories on the left of the file list to the URL use of a slash between subdirectories on the right side, as shown in the entries from the Images directory in Figure 4-21.

NOTE: *While all of the examples of page templates that have images with them in FrontPage have an Images subdirectory, the subdirectory is not required. It is nevertheless recommended that web templates use the Images subdirectory for any image files.*

An .INF information file with a [FileList] section

```
custsupp.inf - Notepad
File  Edit  Search  Help
[info]
title=Customer Support Web
description=Create a web to improve your customer support services, particularly for
software companies.
[FileList]
buglist.htm=
bugrep.htm=
cusuaftr.htm=
cusuahdr.htm=
cusucfrm.htm=
cusufoot.htm=
cusuhead.htm=
cusupost.htm=
cususrch.htm=
cusutoc.htm=
discuss.htm=
download.htm=
faq.htm=
feedback.htm=
footer.htm=
header.htm=
images\scrnshot.gif=images/scrnshot.gif
images\undercon.gif=images/undercon.gif
index.htm=
search.htm=
suggest.htm=
tn-001.htm=
whatsnew.htm=
```

FIGURE 4-21

The Information File [MetaInfo] Section

The [MetaInfo] section can be used to store configuration variables used in the Substitution bot (see the discussion of the Substitution bot in Chapter 10). In this way the [MetaInfo] section supplies the custom configuration variables that would otherwise have to be manually loaded into the Parameters tab of the FrontPage Web Settings dialog box for each web (opened by selecting Web Settings from the FrontPage Explorer Tools menu). For example, you might provide the following company information for all users of a template:

```
[MetaInfo]
CompanyName=Fantasy Travel
CompanyAddress=1234 West Bayside Drive, Seattle, WA 98123
CompanyPhone=(206) 555-1234 or (800) 555-1234
```

The Information File [TaskList] Section

The [TaskList] section is used to provide a list of tasks to be placed in the FrontPage To Do List for a web template. The tasks in the list have the following format:

```
TaskNumber=TaskName|Priority|CreatedBy|URL|Cookie|Comment
```

The elements in the task list are separated by a vertical bar and are described in Table 4-1. Figure 4-22 shows a To Do List Task Details dialog box in which you can see how the elements are used.

TIP: *Adding the To Do tasks to a web template adds significantly to its value and can reduce the amount of support that is needed to help organizations use your template.*

Home Page Renaming

As a default, FrontPage names the home page in its webs Default.htm if you are using MSPWS or Index.htm FPPWS. On an NCSA server, the name "Index.htm" is implied and can be left off the URL for a web. For example, the URL http:www.fairmountain.com/wine opens the Index.htm page in the Wine web on the Fairmountain server. Depending on the server to which the web is eventually uploaded, the implied name for a home page can differ. On a CERN server it normally is Welcome.htm, and on an Internet Information Server it is Default.htm.

Element	Description	Comments
TaskNumber	A unique number or a key	For example, "t01," "t02," "t03," and so on
TaskName	A short task description	A 3- or 4-word phrase used as the task name
Priority	An integer describing relative importance	1 = High, 2 = Medium, 3 = Low
CreatedBy	Name of template	Used in the Created By field
URL	The URL for the task	The page or image that the task refers to
Cookie	The location on the page where work is required	Only bookmarks are supported, in the form *#bookmark*
Comment	Description of task	A longer description of what needs to be done (*cannot contain new-line characters*)

Description of [TaskList] Elements

TABLE 4-1

When the FrontPage Explorer creates a web from a web template, it will automatically rename any file named "Index.htm" to the name appropriate for the current server. The FrontPage Explorer, though, *does not change any links to the home page*. To use the automatic renaming feature, you can make all links to the home page be a special ./ (period-slash) link that will force the server to locate the correct home page. If you do not want to use the automatic renaming feature, put the following line in the [info] section of the .INF information file:

NoIndexRenaming=1

Building Templates

Depending on whether you are building a single-page template or a web template, the procedures vary. Therefore, to get a feeling for both of these, build one of each in the following sections.

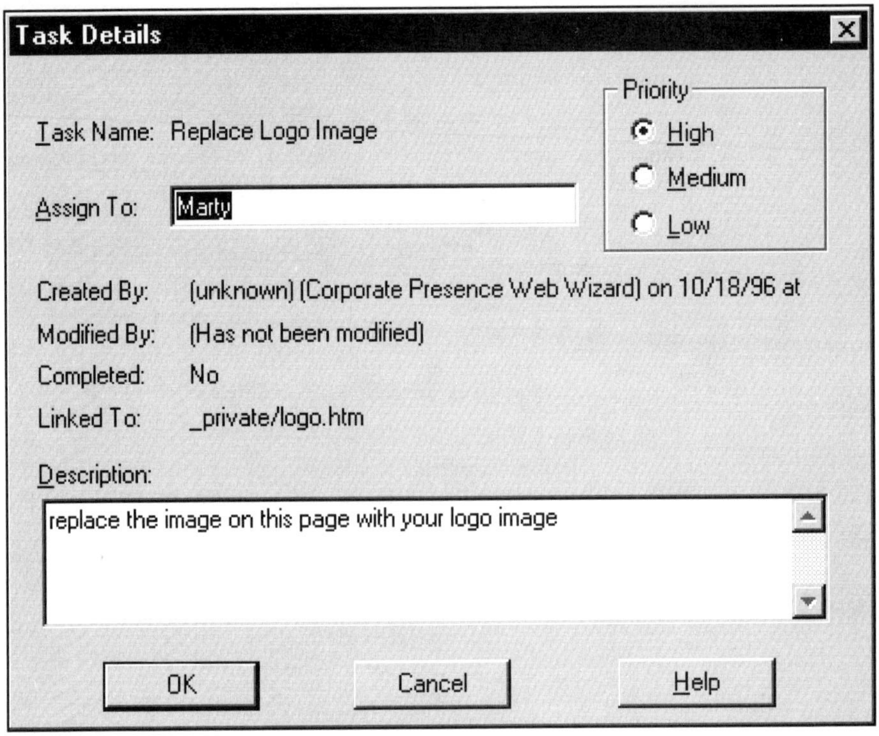

Task Details ✕

Task Name: Replace Logo Image

┌─ Priority ─┐
◉ High
○ Medium
○ Low

Assign To: [Marty]

Created By: (unknown) (Corporate Presence Web Wizard) on 10/18/96 at

Modified By: (Has not been modified)

Completed: No

Linked To: _private/logo.htm

Description:

replace the image on this page with your logo image

[OK]   [Cancel]   [Help]

To Do List
Task
Details
dialog box

FIGURE 4-22

Creating Single-Page Templates

Building a single-page template is simplicity itself. Just create a normal web page with the material you want on it, and then save it as a template. That's all there is to it! Before you go on to the next section, though, try it for yourself:

1. If it isn't already, load the FrontPage Explorer.

2. In the FrontPage Explorer, create a new Normal web named **Templates**.

3. Double-click on the Home Page in the right pane of the FrontPage Explorer to open the page in the FrontPage Editor.

4. At the top of the page in the FrontPage Editor type **PAGE TITLE**. With the cursor still on the same line as the text, select Heading 1 from the Change Style drop-down menu, as shown next. Your page should look similar to Figure 4-23.

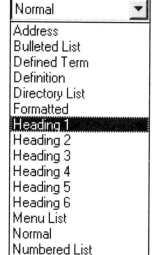

5. Press ENTER and type **| Option 1 | Option 2 | Option 3 |** (the vertical bar character is entered by pressing SHIFT-\). Press ENTER and type **Subject 1**. Select Heading 2 from the Change Style drop-down menu, and then press ENTER.

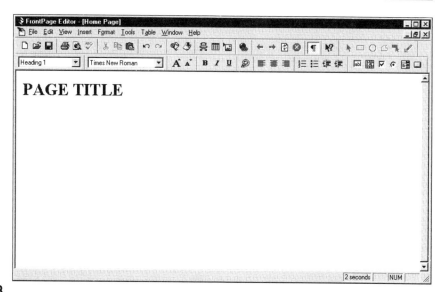

Home Page
template
with
Heading 1
title

FIGURE 4-23

6. Type **Option 1** and press SHIFT-ENTER. Type **Option 2**, press SHIFT-ENTER again, type **Option 3**, and press ENTER.

7. Type **Subject 2** and select Heading 2 from the Change Style drop-down menu. Create another list of options using the instructions in step 6. Your page should look similar to Figure 4-24.

8. From the File menu, click on Save As, type **Home Page Template** for the Page Title, type **hometem.htm** for the File path within your FrontPage web, and click on As Template. The Save As Template dialog box will open as shown here:

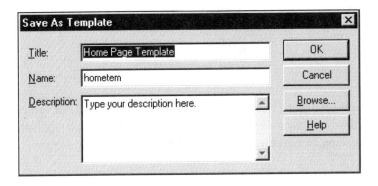

9. Copy the title to the Name box, type **Create a custom home page** in the Description box, and click on OK.

10. Close the template file in the FrontPage Editor, open the Windows Explorer, and locate the new template. If you used the default directory structure, it will be in C:\Program Files\Microsoft FrontPage\pages, like this:

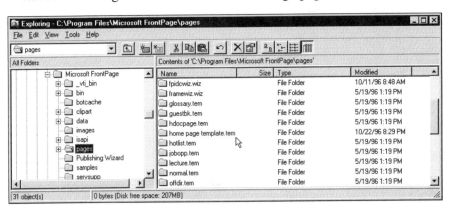

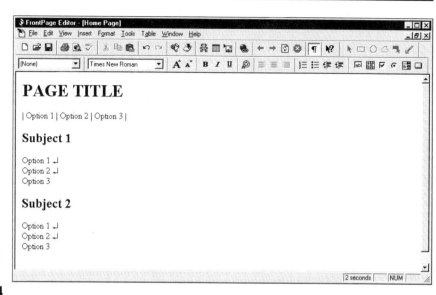

Home Page template

FIGURE 4-24

TIP: *If you do not see the template name appear in the \pages subdirectory, press F5 to refresh the Windows Explorer.*

11. Open the Home Page Template.tem. You should see two files: the .HTM web file and the .INF information file. Double-click on the .INF file. It should open as you see here:

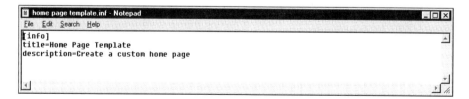

12. Close Notepad and return to the FrontPage Editor. Open the File menu, choose New, and scroll the Template Or Wizard list box until you can see the Home Page Template, as shown next:

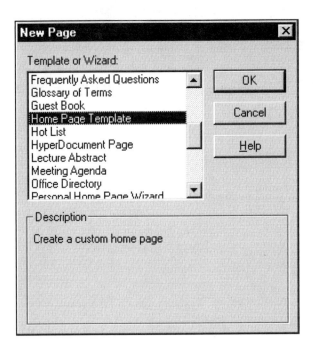

13. Double-click on Home Page Template, and a new page based on your template will open ready for you to customize. When you are ready, save the page with a unique name and by clicking on OK to save it as a part of your web.

14. Close the FrontPage Editor, and then delete the Templates web.

Although this example was very simple, you can see that with your template you should be able to substantially reduce the time it will take to create additional pages, and that all of the pages created that way will be very consistent. In Chapter 5 you will learn about the various elements you can use to customize your web pages and templates.

Constructing Web Templates

Constructing a web template, while inherently more complex than a single page template, is not much more difficult to create. Basically you create and save a web as you normally would. You can then either use a special program to copy the new web to a web template, or you can manually copy the files. The next exercise will show you how to use both the manual steps and the special program to build a web template based on a table for displaying budgeting information.

1. From the FrontPage Explorer create a new web based on the Normal Web template. Name it **BudgetTemplate**. When it opens, double-click on the home page to open the FrontPage Editor.

2. In the FrontPage Editor, select Image from the Insert menu. Click on the Clip Art tab, and select Icons from the drop-down menu. Select one of the icons and click on OK. Sales.gif is selected here. Type **BUDGETING HOME PAGE**, format it as a Heading 1, and then use Save As to save the page. For the Page Title, type **Budget Home Page**, leave the File path within your FrontPage web as Default.htm, and then click on OK. Answer Yes to save the image in the web. Your page should look like Figure 4-25.

4

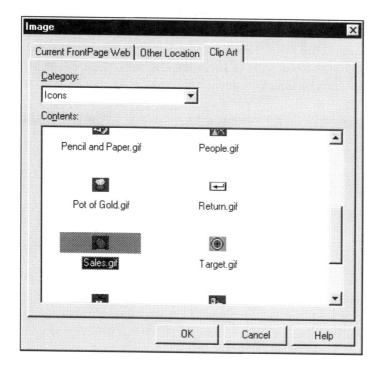

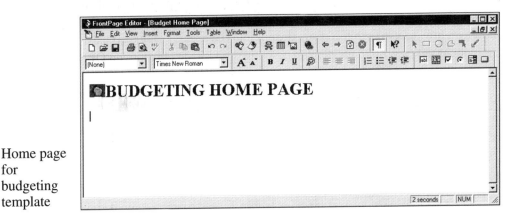

Home page
for
budgeting
template

FIGURE 4-25

3. Click on the New button in the Standard toolbar, type **DEPARTMENTAL BUDGET**, format it as a Heading 2, press DOWN ARROW to go to the next line, type | **Home** | **Department 1** | **Department 2** |, format it as Heading 4, select the word "Home," and link it to the Budget Home page. Save the page with a page title of **Included Header** and a URL of **Inclhead.htm** and click on OK. Your Included Header page should look like this:

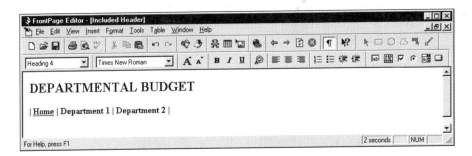

4. Open a new page, open the Insert menu, choose WebBot Component, and double-click on Include. In the WebBot Include Properties dialog box, browse to find and double-click on the Included Header, and then click on OK. The Included Header should appear on your new page.

5. On the line immediately following the header, type **DEPARTMENT 1**, format it as Heading 1, and center it.

6. Move down to the next line and select Insert Table from the Table menu. In the Insert Table dialog box make the Rows **8**, the Columns **6**, the Alignment **Center**, the Border Size **3**, the Cell Padding **3**, and leave the Cell Spacing **2**. Turn off (uncheck) Specify Width and click on OK.

Insert Table	✕
Size	
Rows: 8	OK
Columns: 6	Cancel
Layout	Extended...
Alignment: Center ▼	Help
Border Size: 3	
Cell Padding: 3	
Cell Spacing: 2	
Width	
☐ Specify Width 100	
○ in Pixels ● in Percent	

7. Type in the top row and left column as shown in Figure 4-26, and then save the page with a Page Title of **Department 1** and a page URL of **Depart1.htm**.

8. From the Edit menu choose Select All, click on Copy, open a new page, click on Paste, change the title to **Department 2**, and then save the page with the title of **Department 2** and URL of **Depart2.htm**.

9. Open the Included Header page, and set the links to both the Department 1 and Department 2 references in the navbar. Resave this page.

10. Open the Budget Home page, and insert the Table of Contents bot under the title. If the Page URL For Starting Point Of Table is not set to

Default.htm, click on the Browse button and select it in the Current Web dialog box. Click on OK. Save the Budget Home page and close the FrontPage Editor.

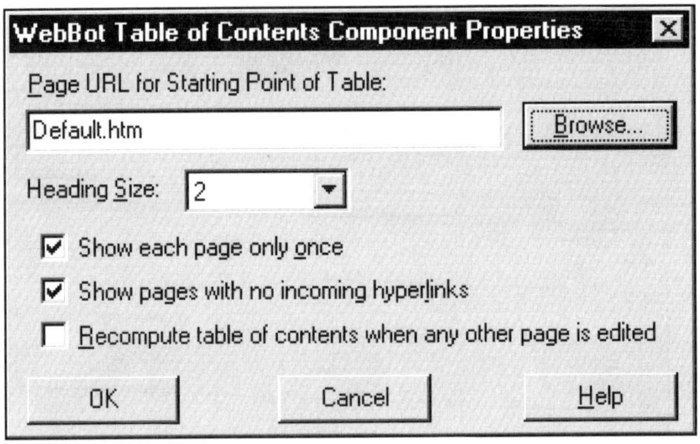

WebBot Table of Contents Component Properties

_P_age URL for Starting Point of Table:

Default.htm   [Browse...]

Heading _S_ize: [2   ▼]

☑ Show each page only _o_nce

☑ Show pages with no incoming hyper_l_inks

☐ _R_ecompute table of contents when any other page is edited

[OK]   [Cancel]   [_H_elp]

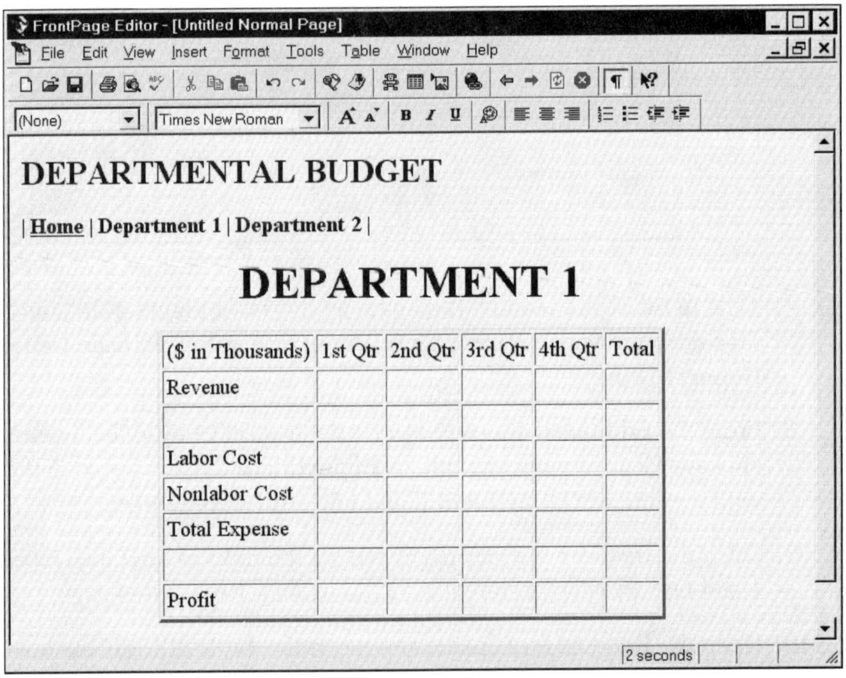

FrontPage Editor - [Untitled Normal Page]

File Edit View Insert Format Tools Table Window Help

(None) ▼   Times New Roman ▼

DEPARTMENTAL BUDGET

| **Home** | Department 1 | Department 2 |

DEPARTMENT 1

($ in Thousands)	1st Qtr	2nd Qtr	3rd Qtr	4th Qtr	Total
Revenue					
Labor Cost					
Nonlabor Cost					
Total Expense					
Profit					

2 seconds

Departmental
budget page

FIGURE 4-26

11. Try the web in a browser to make sure all is well. When you are done, close the browser.

At this point, you have completed a fairly complex web, as shown in Figure 4-27. It is important to have several pages, two bots, and an image in this example to see how all of these elements are handled. (If the hyperlink to the graphic is not shown, click on the Hyperlinks To Images button on the toolbar.) In two later sections you'll turn this web into a web template, using manual procedures in one section, and using a program in the FrontPage Software Developer's Kit (FDK) in the other section. First, look at the file structure and see what files are in which directory.

A Web's Directory and File Structure

Figure 4-28 shows the directories created for a web by FrontPage and the files in the "root" directory. All four page (.HTM) files and the graphic file are there in the right-hand pane. Also, in the left pane there are six to eight directories for the web. The use of each directory is shown in Table 4-2. Open each directory as you read through the table.

Since you need to make copies of some of these files when you are creating a template, you need to have an understanding of this directory structure. Fortunately, you only need to worry about what is in _private, _vti_shm, cgi-bin, images, and the web's root directory (but that's still five of the nine possibilities).

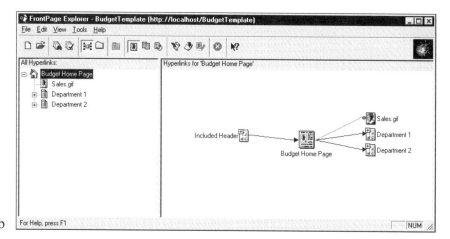

Completed
Budget web

FIGURE 4-27

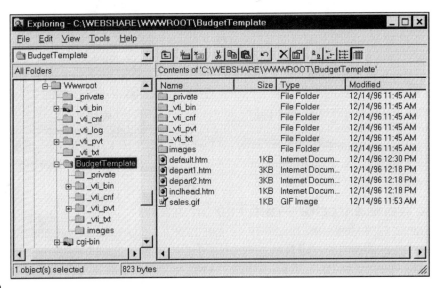

Web
directory
structure

FIGURE 4-28

Manually Creating a Web Template

Manually creating a web template means creating the necessary directories, copying the correct files to them, and then manually creating the .INF file. Do that as explained in the following steps.

NOTE: *The instructions given here for manually creating a web template, while referencing the specific files in the current example, are all the steps needed in the general case to create a web template. Some of the steps are not needed in this example, but are included for reference.*

1. Using the Windows Explorer, locate the Webs subdirectory within the FrontPage root directory. By default this is C:\Program Files\Microsoft FrontPage\Webs. Open the Webs directory so its contents are displayed in the right pane of the Windows Explorer.

2. Right-click in the right pane, choose New, and then select Folder. Type **Budget.tem** as the name of the new folder and press ENTER.

Directory	Contents
_private	Pages that you don't want available to a browser or to searches; for example, included pages
_vti_bin	FrontPage-created Common Gateway Interface (CGI) programs for controlling browse-time behavior, administrator, and author operations on the server
_vti_cnf	A configuration page for every page in the web, containing the name of the page, the created-by and modified-by names, and the creation and modification dates, among other variables
_vti_pvt	Several subdirectories with both the current and historical To Do List files, meta-information for the web, and the dependency database
_vti_shm	The source page for every page in the web that contains bots; the source is the page without the bots (only used with the FrontPage Personal Web Server)
_vti_txt	Text indexes for use by the Search bot
images	All images associated with a web (only used with the FrontPage Personal Web Server)
cgi-bin	Custom CGI scripts and other executable pages

FrontPage
Web
Directory
Structure

TABLE 4-2

3. Still in the Windows Explorer, locate the new BudgetTemplate subdirectory (by default this is C:\WebShare\Wwwroot\BudgetTemplate with the MSPWS and C:\FrontPage Webs\Content\BudgetTemplate with the FPPWS), and open it in the right pane.

4. Select the .GIF file and all the .HTM files. (If you are using the FrontPage Personal Web Server, you'll also have to copy the Images subdirectory, but do not copy the #haccess.ctl file.) While holding down CTRL, drag the files and directory to the new Budget.tem directory. Holding down CTRL is important, because otherwise you will move the files and not copy them.

5. If you are using the FrontPage Personal Web Server (FPPWS), locate and open the _vti_shm subdirectory within the original BudgetTemplate directory (by default C:\FrontPage Webs\ Content\BudgetTemplate_vti_shm). Select all the .HTM files, and while holding down CTRL, drag the files to the new Budget.tem directory. When asked if you would like to replace an existing file, click on Yes in response to all such queries in this step.

NOTE: *With the FPPWS, the web's root directory holds the expanded version of all page files (the version used in a browser), while the _vti_shm subdirectory holds the source version of all pages that have bots. For templates, you want only the source version. So the pages on which you use bots will have their source version copied over the expanded version.*

6. Open the Custsupp.tem subdirectory within the Webs directory (C:\Program Files\Microsoft FrontPage\Webs\Custsupp.tem). Select the Custsupp.inf file, and while holding down CTRL, drag it to the Budget.tem directory to copy the file there.

7. In the Budget.tem directory, select the Custsupp.inf file and rename it **Budget.inf**.

8. Double-click on Budget.inf to open it in Windows Notepad. Change the title to **Budgeting Web**. Change the description to **Create a quarterly departmental budget**. Replace all of the .HTM files in the FileList with the depart1.htm, depart2.htm, inclhead.htm, and default.htm files that are in the budgeting web. Finally, on *both* sides of the equal sign, replace the image file named "scrnshot.gif" with the name of the image file that you used. When you are done, your Budget.inf file should look like Figure 4-29. Save and close your .INF file.

NOTE: *You only need a [FileList] section in the .INF file if you have files in one or more of the images, cgi-bin, or _private subdirectory.*

9. Although it isn't necessary in this example, if you use either the _private or cgi-bin subdirectory, you will need to copy it to the template directory. It is possible to have bots on the pages in the _private subdirectory, in which case, if you are using FPPWS, there will be a _vti_shm

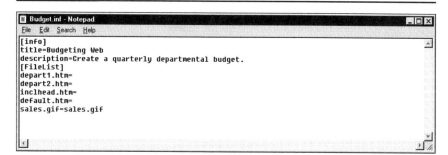

Budget.inf
file in
Notepad

FIGURE 4-29

subdirectory under it with the source files that you want to place in the
_private subdirectory (*not* _vti_shm) of your template. The easiest way to
do this, if it is necessary, is to copy the _private and cgi-bin subdirectories
to your template directory. If there is a _vti_shm subdirectory under
_private, copy its contents to _private, accept any replacement, and delete
_vti_shm.

10. Open the FrontPage Explorer, select New FrontPage Web from the File
menu, and you should see your Budgeting Web displayed in the New
FrontPage Web dialog box, like this:

11. Select the Budgeting Web, and then click on OK to create a new web based on the template. Give the new web some name like "Budget97," and it will open in the Explorer as shown in Figure 4-30. Open the home page in the FrontPage Editor. Everything should be there, just as you originally created it.

12. Close the FrontPage Editor, open the new web in a browser, and click on one of the department links in the table of contents to see if it works. It should appear as shown in Figure 4-31.

13. Close the browser and delete the new web you just created.

If your new web does not work as you would expect, look at the files in the template. Make sure that all your files are placed where they should be and that the .INF file is as shown earlier. Those are about the only things that can go wrong.

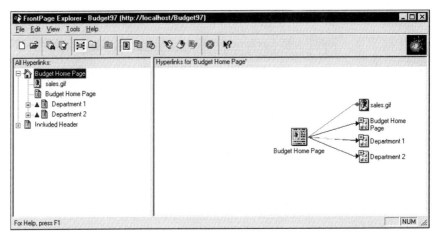

Budget
web
created
from the
template

FIGURE 4-30

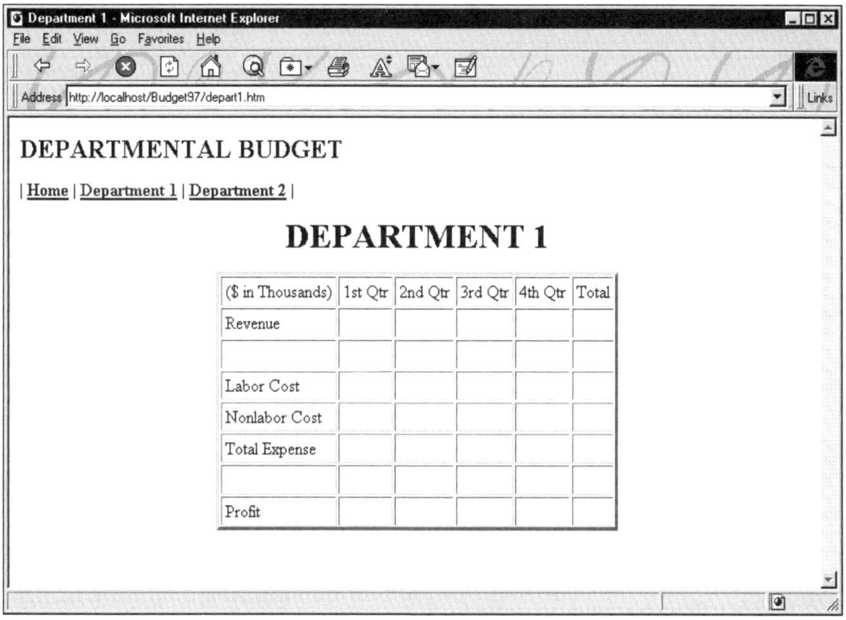

New
budget web
in a browser

FIGURE 4-31

Automatically Creating a Web Template

The FrontPage Developer's Kit includes a program, Webtmpl.exe, that automatically does most of the work you just did in the last section. Before you burn this book, there are at least three good reasons for doing the manual approach first:

- It familiarizes you with the web structure of FrontPage and how webs and web templates are stored, so that you are in a position to check what the program does.

- Webtmpl.exe only works with the FrontPage Personal Web Server.

- Webtmpl.exe requires that you have Microsoft Visual Basic installed.

The Webtmpl.exe program lets you select an existing web on your computer from which a web will be made. It then creates the template web in the correct directory; copies all the .HTM files in the original web's root directory plus the images, cgi-bin, and _private subdirectories; properly handles bots; and creates the .INF file including any configuration variables and active To Do List tasks. So while you do need to check it, the program does a lot for you.

This program is in the FrontPage Software Developer's Kit, which is available on the FrontPage 97 with Bonus Pack CD and as a free download from http://microsoft.com/frontpage/sdk/fs_fp_sdkdwnld.htm. So it will be available, download it now with the following steps (see Appendix B for a more detailed description of the Sdk):

1. After downloading Fp97sdk.exe, create a new directory such as **FpSdk** and move Fp97sdk.exe to the new directory. Then use a program such as PKUnzip or WinZip to unpack it. Since there are subdirectories that must be created, be sure to use whatever your archive program requires to have it create the directories that are included in the file (-d for PKUnzip).

2. When the file has been unpacked, open the directories so you can see the Utility and Webtmpl directories and the Webtmpl.exe program, like this:

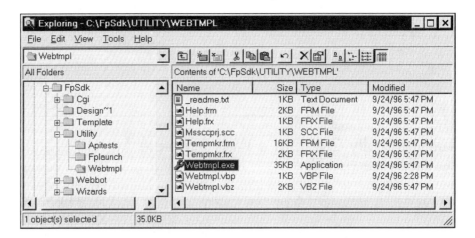

3. Double-click on Webtmpl.exe to start the program. The FrontPage Web Template Maker will open, as you can see in Figure 4-32.

4. Click on BudgetTemplate, change the title to **Budgeting Web**, the name to **Budgeting**, and the description to **Create a departmental budgeting web**.

5. Click on Make Web Template. In about the time it takes you to remove your hand from the mouse, the program will be done. Click on the Close button to get rid of it.

6. Open the Windows Explorer and under Webs, you should see the Budgeting.tem directory immediately below the Budget.tem directory you

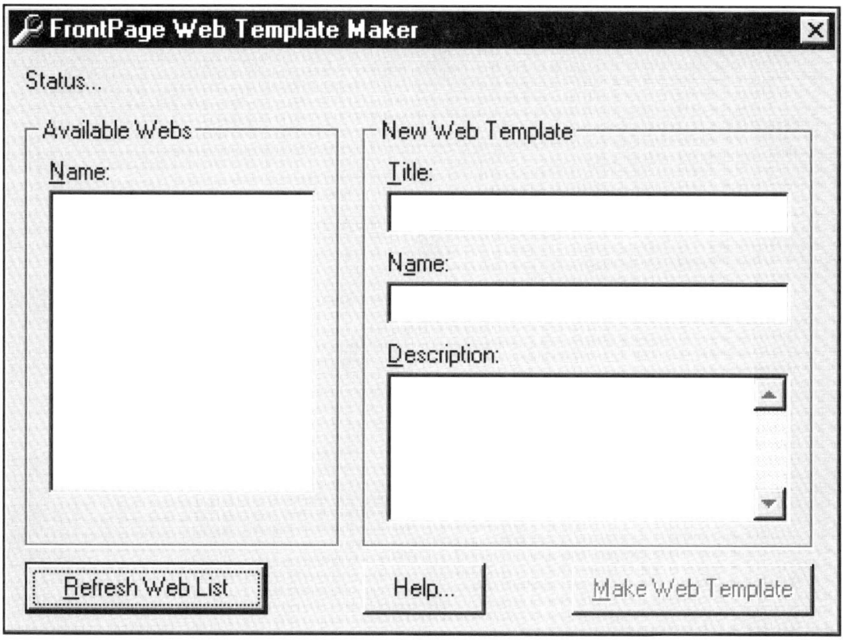

FrontPage
Web
Template
Maker

FIGURE 4-32

created earlier. Notice how the _private and cgi-bin directories were copied in this case, although there is nothing in them.

7. Double-click on Budgeting.inf to open it in Notepad. Except for the different wording for the title and description and the fact that the filenames are repeated (which is not necessary), it is the same as the .INF file that you created.

8. Open the FrontPage Explorer and click on New FrontPage Web. The New FrontPage Web dialog box will now show two Budgeting Web templates. If you wish, create a new web based on this template, and then open it in a browser. You should see that the results are the same as you saw earlier.

Creating your own templates is another very significant bit of leverage that FrontPage gives you to quickly and effectively create webs. As you work through the remainder of this book, you will have your own ideas for templates you can create.

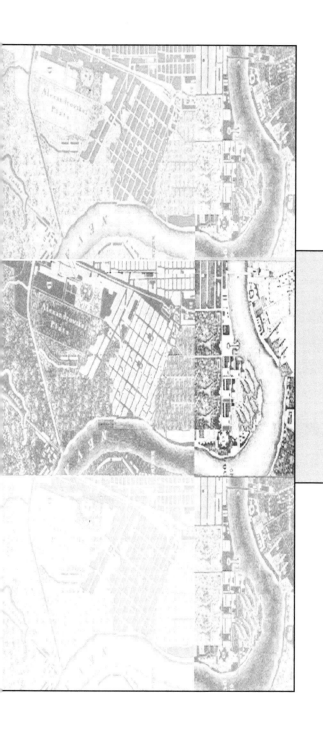

Creating and Formatting a Web Page from Scratch

In Chapters 3 and 4 you saw how to build a web and its pages by using a wizard or a template. You learned that using a wizard or template is the easiest way to create a web that uses many FrontPage features. Occasionally, you may want to build a web from scratch (and consequently increase your knowledge of the parts of a web). Create a web now from scratch, beginning with the planning.

Planning a Web

In Chapter 2 you were given a list of steps to build a web. You may remember that planning was the first and probably most important step in making a good web—and the one most often shortchanged. Planning seeks to answer four questions:

- What are the goals of the web?

- What will its content be?

- How will it be organized?

- What do you want it to look like?

Suppose you work for a large travel agency named Fantasy Travel[1] and have been given the task of creating an intranet web to communicate with the company's agents. Go through each of the four questions with that in mind. (With only small changes you could alternatively look at this as an Internet web to communicate with your potential clients.)

What Are Your Goals?

Setting the goals of a web is very important—if the goals are well thought out, you will probably end up with an effective web. Keep it simple. Having one or two obtainable goals for your web is better than having a number of goals that cannot all be met. Too many goals will scatter the focus of the web, making it much more difficult to accomplish any one of them.

For Fantasy Travel, there is one primary goal for their intranet web: to give their agents a competitive advantage by providing access to a consolidated list of the latest travel offerings. (An Internet web goal might be to get the user to call Fantasy and

---

While the Fantasy Travel used here is fictitious, there is an actual travel agency named Fantasy Travel located in Los Angeles, CA, and they do have a web site at http://www.fantasytravel.com.

inquire about a possible trip.) There is a secondary and supporting goal: to keep the web frequently updated so the agents will look at it often.

What Is the Content?

To accomplish Fantasy Travel's goals, you'll need to include information about current travel specials over a broad range of travel options. The information needs to be complete enough to capture the agents' interest but concise enough for them to read quickly. Therefore, the content needs to include not only a brief description of current packages, but also general information the agents might need, such as the current exchange rates, climates, and current travel conditions.

How Is It Organized?

How well a web is organized determines how easily users can get the information they seek. This means that the desired information should be within one or two clicks of your home page, and the path should be clear—users won't have to guess how to get what they want. The home page mainly provides links to other pages. The pages behind the home page contain the desired information and are a single link away from the home page. The home page's links to detailed information give relatively quick answers to those agents who are willing to take a couple of minutes, but following the links may not appeal to those who are in a hurry. For quick answers, you need to have some low-priced specials briefly but prominently listed on the home page.

The structure of your web needs to be a simple and obvious tree structure, so that users always know where they are and how they got there. While a cross-link between two third-level branches may seem like a quick way to get users from one place to another, it is also a quick way to confuse users about where they are. It is better to force users back up the tree and down another branch. If you never have more than two levels from your home page, it is not a big chore to backtrack. Besides, the previously visited pages are already on the user's disk in their browser's cache, so they can quickly backtrack.

What Will It Look Like?

With all the concepts just discussed, what will this web look like? The best approach is to sketch the primary types of pages that you will be using. Figure 5-1 shows one way that the information in this web could be laid out to satisfy

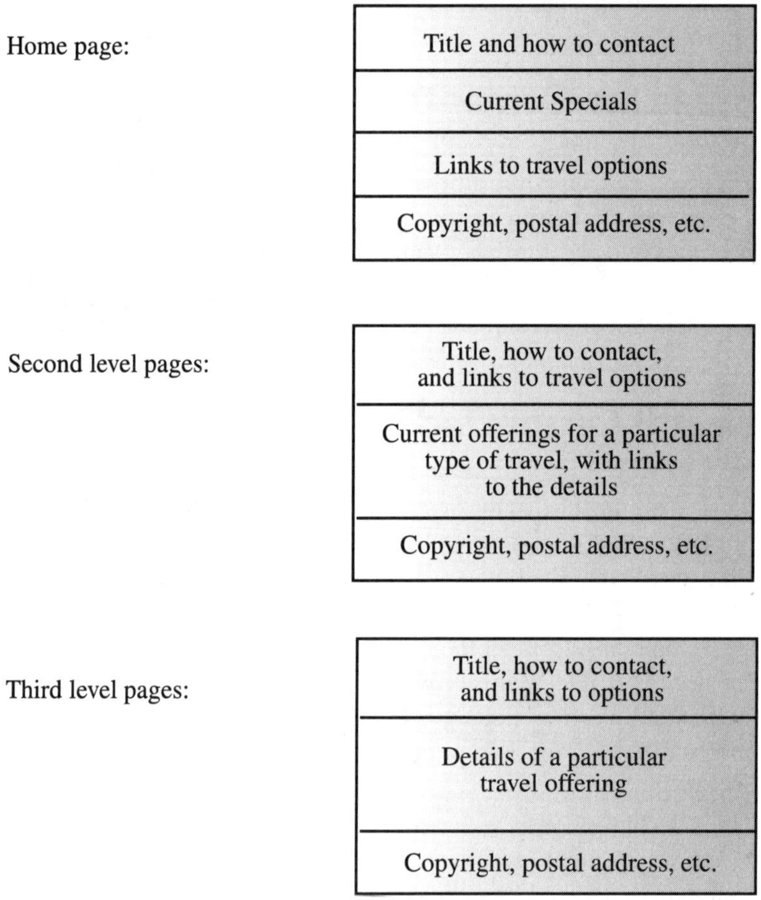

Home page:

| Title and how to contact |
| Current Specials |
| Links to travel options |
| Copyright, postal address, etc. |

Second level pages:

| Title, how to contact, and links to travel options |
| Current offerings for a particular type of travel, with links to the details |
| Copyright, postal address, etc. |

Third level pages:

| Title, how to contact, and links to options |
| Details of a particular travel offering |
| Copyright, postal address, etc. |

One way to
lay out the
Fantasy
Travel web

◼ FIGURE 5-1

the desired points brought out in the plan. To keep to the desired three levels, there will be three types of pages:

◼ A home page with a list of interesting specials and links to all the different types of travel

- A second-level page for a type of travel with links to the details for a particular offering

- A third-level page for the details of a travel offering

All three pages will have the same footer, which will have a copyright notice, the date last updated, a postal address, and information on how to contact the webmaster (the person responsible for maintaining the web). The second- and third-level pages, of which there will be many, will share the same heading, which will have company and contact information as well as links to other pages. The home page will have a unique header and larger, separate sections with a number of links in each.

The web will begin with major travel options such as Alaskan cruises, China tours, and African safaris, which will be located on the home page. The web will flow to a list of specific offerings for a travel option, such as a list of Alaskan cruises, on the second-level pages. These will lead to the details of a specific offering, such as the specifics of a particular cruise, on the third-level pages. The "Current Specials" on the home page will link directly to the third-level details of those offerings.

This gives you a general view of what your web will look like, which is enough for the planning process. As you actually create the pages, you will fine-tune that look with the placing of graphics and the positioning of text.

Starting a Web

The Fantasy Travel web will be created over this and the following five chapters. This chapter will look at working with text and graphics. Chapter 6 will demonstrate how to create and modify graphics using the Microsoft Image Composer. Chapter 7 will deal with hyperlinks and hotspots, Chapter 8 will add tables and frames, Chapter 9 will work with forms, and Chapter 10 will address WebBots. The reason for this approach is to focus on one topic at a time. As a result, you'll see areas, especially in this chapter, that may be better handled with, for example, a table or a WebBot. That discussion will be put off until the appropriate chapter, so each topic can be fully developed without interfering with others.

Developing all but the simplest webs is a long and tedious chore. Look at this proposed travel web—there will be a second-level page for each type of travel, of which there are probably six to ten types. There are then probably six to ten offerings

for each type. That means at a minimum that there will be 36 third-level pages (not counting those that may be referred to directly from the home page), six second-level pages, and a home page—a total of at least 43 pages! You can let out your breath; in this chapter you'll only do one of each type of page. It is important to consider, though, how the page count explodes as you develop a web and how adding levels makes the web grow geometrically.

TIP: *Leave enough time to complete the development of a web. One way to speed the process is to scan literature that you want incorporated (like travel brochures for the details of a travel offering) and then use optical character recognition (OCR) to convert them to text. Be sure to carefully edit any OCR-generated text (the process is less than perfect), and make sure you have written permission to reproduce other people's copyrighted material.*

To start the Fantasy Travel web:

1. Start the FrontPage Explorer.

2. In the Getting Started With Microsoft FrontPage dialog box, select Blank FrontPage Web and click on OK. Alternatively, open the File menu and choose New FrontPage Web, select Normal Web from the New FrontPage Web dialog box, and click on OK.

3. In the Normal Web Template dialog box, select the web server you want to use, type **FantasyTravel** for the name of the web, and click on OK.

4. In the right pane of the FrontPage Explorer, double-click on the Home Page icon to open the FrontPage Editor.

5. Open the File menu and choose Page Properties. Observe that the URL for this page includes the page's filename of Default.htm, as shown next. The home page of a web will normally have the filename Default.htm or Index.htm. The filename of the home page should match the default for the server your web will be hosted on (check with the webmaster of your server if you're not sure). Default.htm is the default filename for the MSPWS.

 NOTE: *It is recommended that you build this web site from scratch, but if you wish, you can download it from http://www.osborne.com/int/frontpa.htm.*

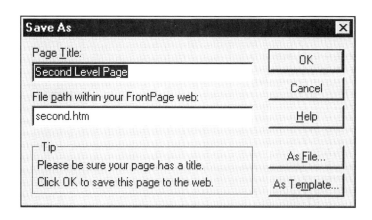

6. Click on OK to close the Page Properties dialog box. Open the File menu, choose New, select Normal Page from the New Page dialog box, and click on OK.

7. Open the Page Properties dialog box, change the Title to **Second Level Page** (ignore the fact that the Location text box is not filled in), and click on OK to close the Page Properties dialog box.

8. Open the File menu and choose Save. You'll see that the Page Title has been picked up and the page URL has been automatically filled in, like this:

9. Click on OK to close the Save As dialog box. Open the File menu, choose New, select Normal Page from the New Page dialog box, and click on OK.

10. Open the Save As dialog box, change the Page Title to **Third Level Page** (note that the URL automatically changes as you type), and click on OK.

11. If you open the Window menu, you'll see three open pages appropriately named. If you open the FrontPage Explorer, you'll see that your web now incorporates three pages, as shown in Figure 5-2.

12. Back in the FrontPage Editor, open the Window menu, and choose Home Page to prepare for the addition of text.

Adding and Formatting Text

The text will be entered in sections corresponding to the Home page sections shown in Figure 5-1—for example, the title, the footer (copyright, postal address, etc.), and the current specials. Where applicable, this information will be entered and formatted on the home page and then copied to other pages. Begin by entering the footer.

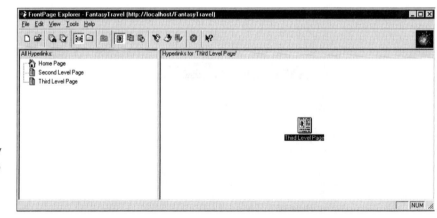

FrontPage Explorer showing the Fantasy Travel web with three pages

FIGURE 5-2

Entering the Footer

The footer goes at the bottom of all the pages and contains the copyright notice, the postal address, phone numbers, information on how to contact the webmaster, and the date last revised. To create the footer:

1. On the Home Page in the FrontPage Editor, press ENTER several times to leave some room at the top of the page for the other information to be entered. (The other information will take more than several lines, but this will get you started.)

2. Type the following information, just as it is shown here. Press SHIFT-ENTER (new line) at the ends of each of the first two lines.

   Copyright 1996, Fantasy Travel, Inc. All rights reserved.
   1234 West Bayside Drive, Seattle, WA 98123, (206) 555-1234
   **   or (800) 555-1234**
   Send comments on this web site to webmaster@fantasytravel.com.
   Last revised 11/1/96.

NOTE: *Using SHIFT-ENTER instead of ENTER reduces the amount of space between lines and helps group related material.*

3. If you look at the paragraph style in the Format toolbar, it should be Normal. This is a little large for the footer, so click on the down arrow in the Change Style drop-down menu, and select Heading 5. This reduces the size, but it is still easy to read, as you can see in Figure 5-3.

 4. Click on the Save button in the toolbar, or press CTRL-S to save your home page with its new footer.

NOTE: *The e-mail address will be in blue and underlined. The FrontPage Editor recognizes that these are e-mail addresses and automatically creates mailto hyperlinks. A mailto hyperlink will open the user's default e-mail program when the hyperlink is selected in a browser.*

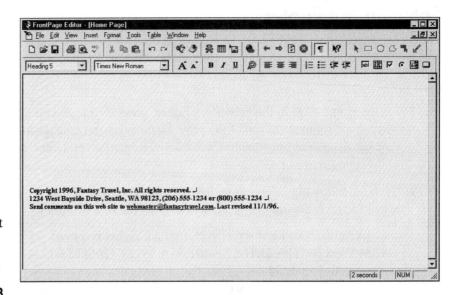

Footer text
formatted
as
Heading 5

FIGURE 5-3

 5. Drag across the text you just entered so all of it is highlighted. Click on the Copy button in the toolbar, or press CTRL-C to copy the footer to the Clipboard.

6. Open the Window menu and choose Second Level Page.

 7. Click on the page, press ENTER several times, and then click on the Paste button in the toolbar, or press CTRL-V to paste the footer onto the second page.

8. You can see that the paragraph style has reverted to Normal, so open the drop-down menu and choose Heading 5, and then click on the Save button in the toolbar or press CTRL-S to save the second page.

9. Open the Window menu, choose Third Level Page, click on the page, press ENTER several times, click on Paste in the toolbar or press CTRL-V, select the Heading 5 style, and click on Save in the toolbar or press CTRL-S.

You now have the footer entered and correctly formatted on each page. Next work on the home page title.

Creating the Home Page Title

The home page title is the introduction to this web. It needs to be inviting and to reflect the company. It also needs to communicate how certain people can be reached. That is a big order and one that you'll revisit again in this chapter and in later chapters. To use text only:

1. Open the Window menu, choose Home Page, and press CTRL-HOME to return to the top of the home page in preparation for creating the title.

2. Type the following text, pressing SHIFT-ENTER at the end of the first and third lines, and pressing ENTER at the end of the second and fourth lines:

   FANTASY TRAVEL
   "The Exciting Way To Go!"
   For the latest fares, contact Julie Bergan at 555-1234
      or John Donald at 555-1235
      or through e-mail at julieb@fantasytravel.com or
      jmd@fantasytravel.com

3. Drag across all the text to select it, and then click on the Center Align button. If the paragraph style isn't Normal, open the Style drop-down menu and select Normal.

4. Drag across the first two lines to select them, open the Change Style drop-down menu, select Heading 1, and then click on the Italic button in the Format toolbar.

5. Drag across just the first line, and click on the Increase Text Size button in the Format toolbar to increase the size of the first line to the 36-point maximum.

6. Click on the Save toolbar button to protect your work. Your final product should look like Figure 5-4. (The figures and illustrations in this book were taken at a resolution of 1024×768. If you are running at a different resolution, your screen will look different.)

Listing the Current Specials

The current specials are promotional fares for a particular week. Listing them gives agents immediate access to the latest and lowest fares.

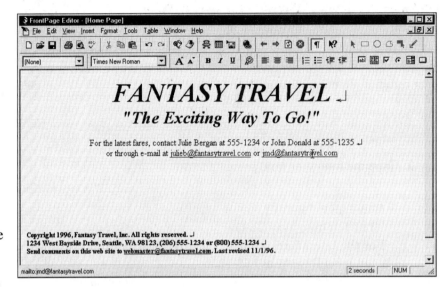

The
completed
Home page
in its text
form

FIGURE 5-4

TIP: *It is very important to keep the list of specials updated. First, it provides a reason for people to come back and look at the page. Second, it prevents information in the list from getting out of date.*

To create the list of current specials:

1. With the blinking insertion point on the line immediately following the fourth line of the title text, press ENTER once to leave a blank line, and make sure that the paragraph style is Normal and the text is left aligned.

2. Type the following text as it is shown. Press ENTER at the end of each line.

> **CURRENT SPECIALS**
> **Super airfares to San Francisco: $75,**
>   **LA: $175, New York: $275, & Miami: $375**
> **Hawaii, on the Kona beach, 1-bedroom deluxe condo,**
>   **all amenities, $100 / night**
> **Fiji, air plus 6 nights in beautiful beach front bungalow**
>   **with breakfast, $850**
> **Disneyland, air, 1 day Disneyland pass, 2 nights hotel, rental car,**

> and more, $285
> London, air, 5 nights first-class hotel, breakfast, 2 city tours,
> and more, $750
> (Some restrictions may apply to the above fares.)

NOTE: *A single paragraph cannot have more than one paragraph style, nor can a single paragraph contain more than one bulleted or numbered line. For that reason, all of the lines in both the Current Specials and Travel Options sections have* ENTER *placed at the end of each line, even though it takes more space.*

3. Click on line 1, and from the Paragraph Style drop-down menu box, choose Heading 2.

4. Drag across lines 2 through 6, and click on the Bulleted List button in the Format toolbar.

5. Drag over the last line, click on the Decrease Text Size button, and then click on the Increase Indent button twice (both buttons are in the Format toolbar).

6. Click on the Save button in the toolbar. Your Current Specials section should look like Figure 5-5.

Adding the Travel Options

The Travel Options section provides a list, really an index, of the travel options that are available from this travel agency. In Chapter 7, you'll come back and make these links to the second-level pages.

To create the Travel Options section:

1. With the blinking insertion point on the line immediately below the last line typed, type the following text. Press ENTER at the end of each line. You can copy the list of options on line 2 and use it on lines 4 through 7.

TIP: *If you press* ENTER *at the end of the last line typed, the next line will also be indented twice; if you press the* DOWN ARROW *key, the line will be left aligned without the indents.*

AVAILABLE TRAVEL OPTIONS
AIR TRAVEL:
  Domestic, Canada, Europe, So. America, Africa, Asia, So. Pacific
CRUISES: Alaska, Panama Canal, Caribbean,
  Europe, So. America, Asia, So. Pacific
TOURS: Domestic, Canada, Europe, So. America,
  Africa, Asia, So. Pacific
HOTELS: Domestic, Canada, Europe, So. America,
  Africa, Asia, So. Pacific
AUTO: Domestic, Canada, Europe, So. America, Africa,
  Asia, So. Pacific
RAIL: Domestic, Canada, Europe, So. America, Africa,
  Asia, So. Pacific

2. Click on line 1 and choose the Heading 2 style.

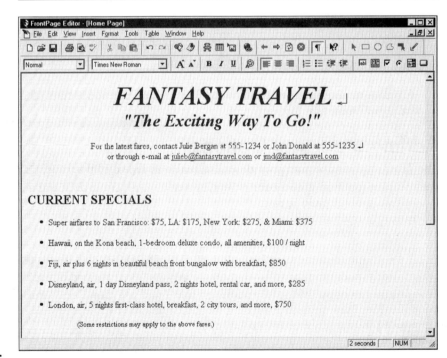

The
completed
Current
Specials
section

FIGURE 5-5

3. Select lines 2 through 7, and click on the Numbered List button in the Format toolbar.

4. Delete all but one blank line between the last line of the travel options and the beginning of the footer.

5. Save the Home page. The bottom of your Home page should look like Figure 5-6.

This completes the text that you will need on the Home page.

Building the Title for Pages 2 and 3

On all but the Home page, you want to have a brief title or heading with the ways to contact the specialists and the links to other pages. This keeps the contacts in front of the agents and gives them the primary way to navigate or get around the web. Use the next set of instructions to enter the text related to these items on page 2 and copy them to page 3. Later in this chapter you'll do some graphics work on this, and in Chapter 7 you'll establish the actual links to implement the navigation.

1. On the Home page, drag over the first four lines of text that represent the title of the web, and click on the Copy button in the toolbar.

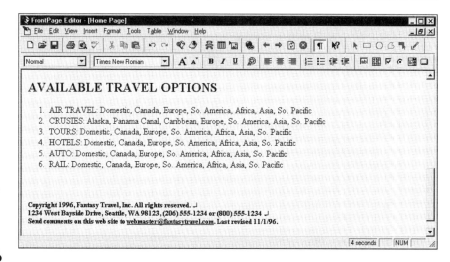

The completed Travel Options section

FIGURE 5-6

2. Open the Window menu and choose Second Level Page. After the page opens, click in the top left corner to place the insertion point there, and click on the Paste button in the toolbar. The title appears on page 2.

3. If you have an extra blank line above the just-pasted title, press CTRL-HOME to move the insertion point to the very top of the page, and then press DEL to delete the leading paragraph mark.

4. Select the words "Fantasy Travel," and choose Heading 2 as the paragraph style. The size doesn't change, because you applied the special character size to these words. The size of the second line ("The Exciting Way To Go") changes because it is part of the same paragraph, and you did not apply a special character size to it.

5. Open the Format menu, choose Font, select Normal for the Font Size (as shown in the following illustration) to change the first line to the actual Heading 2 size.

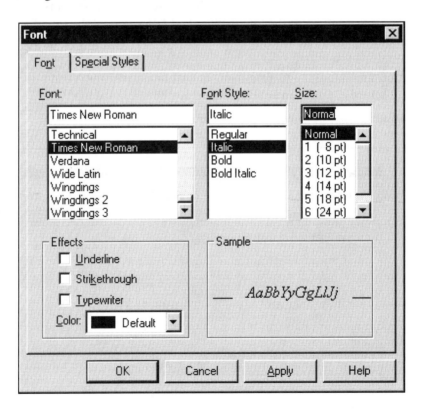

This changes the first line to the actual Heading 2 size, as you can see next. Click on OK to close the Font dialog box.

FANTASY TRAVEL ↵
"The Exciting Way To Go!"

NOTE: *"Normal" font size is not a particular size, but rather allows the default size of a given paragraph style to take precedence.*

6. Select the second line and press DEL twice to delete the line as well as the paragraph mark. This also changes the phone numbers and e-mail addresses to Heading 2.

7. Select the words "For the latest fares, c" (include the comma, the space following it, and the letter "c" from the word "contact") and type an uppercase **C**.

8. After the first phone number, type a space and **(julieb)**. After the second phone number, add another space and type **(jmd)** to add the e-mail addresses.

9. Delete the new-line symbol and the remainder of the contact information.

10. Select all of the words in the title *except* "Fantasy Travel," and click on the Decrease Text Size button once so all of the contact information fits on one line like this (it may wrap to two lines with a different resolution):

FANTASY TRAVEL ↵
Contact Julie Bergan at 555-1234 (julieb) or John Donald at 555-1235 (jmd)

---

11. Click on the Align Left button to left align the title, and then move the insertion point to the first line after the title.

12. Type the following text, which in Chapter 7 will become a navbar with links to the rest of the web. (Note that there is a space, a vertical bar, and a space between each option.)

5

| **Home** | **Air Travel** | **Cruises** | **Tours** | **Hotels** | **Auto** | **Rail** |

13. With the insertion point still in the future navbar, choose Heading 3 for the paragraph style. Your second page heading should now look like Figure 5-7. Click on the Save button to save the changes to page 2.

14. Select all three lines of the heading, and click on the Copy button in the toolbar.

15. Open the Window menu, choose Third Level Page, click in the top left corner of the page to place the insertion point there, and click on the Paste button in the toolbar. The heading appears on page 3.

16. If you have an extra blank line above the just-pasted title, press CTRL-HOME to move the insertion point to the top of the page. Then press DEL to delete the leading invisible paragraph mark.

17. Click on the Save button to save page 3.

Entering the Offerings for a Travel Option

The body of information on the second-level pages is a listing of specific offerings for a particular type of travel—for example, a geographically ordered listing of the

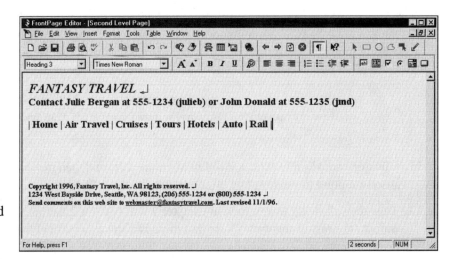

The completed second and third page headings

FIGURE 5-7

cruises. That is, of course, a long list. For this example, to keep the typing to a minimum, you'll work on the page for cruises, with only a couple of geographic areas and a couple of cruises in each.

1. Open the Window menu and choose Second Level Page. When the page opens, place the insertion point at the end of the navbar, and press ENTER twice to leave a blank line.

2. Type **CRUISES**, choose Heading 1, click on Center, and press ENTER.

3. Type **ALASKA**, choose Heading 3, click on Align Left, and press ENTER.

4. Choose Heading 5 and click on the Increase Indent button in the Format toolbar to format and indent the list of cruises.

5. Type the following cruise list, pressing SHIFT-ENTER after each of the first two lines and ENTER after the third line:

   > **Royal Caribbean, Legend of the Seas, 7 nights,**
   >   **Vancouver to Skagway & rtn, May-Sept**
   > **Princess Cruises, Sun Princess, 7 nights,**
   >   **Vancouver to Skagway & rtn, May-Sept**
   > **Holland American, Nieuw Amsterdam, 7 nights,**
   >   **Vancouver to Sitka & rtn, May-Sept**

6. Click on the Decrease Indent button, choose Heading 3, type **SOUTH PACIFIC**, and press ENTER.

7. Choose Heading 5, click on the Increase Indent button, and type the following cruise list, pressing SHIFT-ENTER after the first line and ENTER after the last line:

   > **Princess Cruises, Pacific Princess, 16 days,**
   >   **Los Angeles-Hawaii-Papeete, Jan. 7 only**
   >   **Royal Caribbean, Legend of the Seas, 10 nights,**
   >   **Vancouver to Honolulu, Sept 15 only**

8. Choose Heading 4, and type the following notice:

   > **Note: Excellent prices are available on these cruises, call for the latest ones.**

When you are done, your second-level page should look like Figure 5-8.

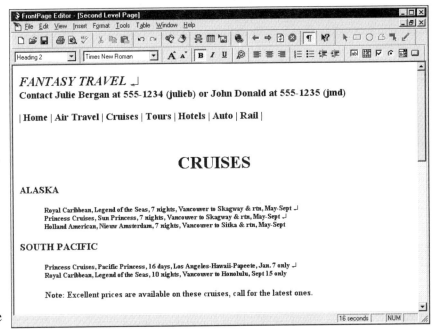

Completed second page

FIGURE 5-8

9. Delete all but one blank line between the last line entered and the beginning of the footer, and then save the page.

Importing the Details of a Travel Offering

The Third-Level page contains the detailed description of one particular travel option. Since this is often better described by the travel provider, it may be helpful to use their material if you have permission to do so (check with your legal department or advisor on the need for this). You can do this by typing in the material, or in some cases it might be faster to scan it in.

> **NOTE:** *Scanning text from brochures and other promotional pieces and then using optical character recognition (OCR) has a much lower success rate than if the text were on plain white paper. For small amounts of text, it is often easier to type it.*

In the following exercise you will use a combination of scanned and typed text to enter the information for the third page. If you have a scanner with OCR capability, you are encouraged to use it with something like a brochure or catalog—anything that is on slick paper with a mixture of text and pictures, and possibly with the text printed on a background image (the material can be about anything; it does not have to be related to travel). You'll then get an understanding of how that works. Of course, if you do not have access to a scanner, then you can import any text in place of that used here. That will at least give you experience importing.

The trip used for this detailed description is a cruise from Los Angeles to Papeete, Tahiti, offered by Princess Cruises in their Fall '95–Spring '96 catalog (and is used by permission of Princess Cruises, a P&O Company). Several segments of text from this catalog will be scanned into Microsoft Word for Windows 97 and then inserted into the Fantasy Travel web.

REMEMBER: *You may use any text to replace that used here. If possible, use a scanner as directed, but if that is unavailable, import any text you have. You can also download it from http://www.osborne.com/int/frontpa.htm.*

NOTE: *FrontPage can import files from almost any word processor. Chapter 11 will cover in detail how to import word processor and other files into FrontPage.*

To build the body of the third page by use of scanned and typed text:

1. Using your scanner and its software in the normal manner, scan an article of approximately 100 words. Use your OCR program (most scanners come with an OCR program) to convert the text so that it can be read by Microsoft Word 97 for Windows or your word processing program.

2. Similarly scan and convert to text a table of approximately four columns and ten rows, and then scan and convert to text two articles of 20 to 30 words each.

3. In Microsoft Word 97 for Windows or your word processing program, edit the articles and table for scanning errors and any changes that you want to make. Then save the articles.

4. From the second page of the Fantasy Travel web in the FrontPage Editor, open the Window menu and choose Third Level Page.

5. On the second line below the navbar (leaving a blank line below the navbar), type the following text. Use SHIFT-ENTER at the end of the first line and ENTER on the second. Format these lines with Heading 2.

> **Princess Cruises' Pacific Princess**
> **16 Days, Los Angeles to Papeete via Hawaii, 1/7/96 Departure**

6. Move the insertion point below the heading you just typed, and then from the Insert menu, choose File. In the Select A File dialog box, shown in the following illustration, open the Files Of Type drop-down menu, and choose the type of word processor file you used.

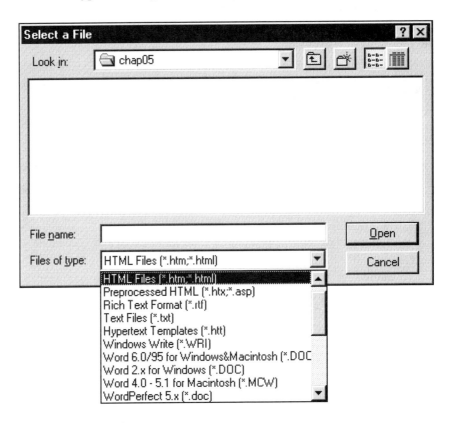

7. Locate the folder and select the name of your 100-word article and click on Open. The article will appear on your page, as you can see in Figure 5-9.

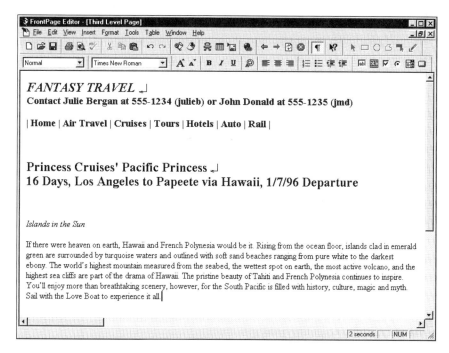

Imported article

FIGURE 5-9

8. In a similar way, import your table and then the two short articles.

9. If necessary, add or remove lines so that there is a single blank line before and after your two short articles.

10. On the second line after your short articles, type the following text:

Material on this page originated from and is used with the permission of Princess Cruises.

TIP: *Getting permission to use other people's work generally depends on whether it is to the advantage of the originator. For example, permission for the material used here from Princess Cruises was easy to get because it publicizes them and one of their cruises.*

11. Select the line you just typed, and click on the Italic button on the Format toolbar.

12. Eliminate all but one line between the line you just typed and the page footer, and then save the page. The bottom of the page should look like Figure 5-10.

The table in this example was created in Word for Windows 97. When it was imported, the FrontPage Editor automatically generated an HTML table with the same rows and columns, as shown in Figure 5-10. In Chapter 8 you'll see how to create FrontPage tables.

This completes the entry of all the text you need in this web. Now look at sprucing up the text with graphics.

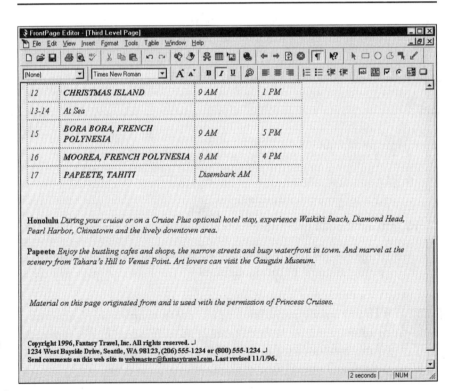

Text at the bottom of page 3

FIGURE 5-10

Obtaining and Working with Graphics

There are three sources of graphics for a web: you can create graphics with programs like Microsoft Image Composer, CorelDraw, Windows Paint, or Adobe Photoshop; you can import clip art included with FrontPage (clip art is also available in most places software is sold and with many packages, especially CorelDraw); and you can use a scanner to scan existing printed art. All of these have advantages and disadvantages. Using clip art is fast and easy, but it is often difficult to find exactly what you want. Scanned art gives you a lot of versatility, but you must have access to a scanner, and you must get permission from the art's creator to copy it. Creating your own art has the ultimate versatility, but it takes time and skill. This section will look at all three types of graphics.

Graphics can communicate a lot very quickly, and to some people graphics are far better at communicating than text. Therefore, make graphics an important part of your web, whether it is on the Internet or on an intranet. Adding graphics to an intranet page is slightly different from adding them to an Internet page. Intranet pages, for internal consumption, usually emphasize information. Internet pages, for external consumption, usually emphasize selling. Also, local area network (LAN) connections used by most intranets are much faster at downloading graphics than the modem connections generally used on the Internet. Just keep in mind the objectives of your web and the time graphics take to load.

Creating and Inserting Graphics

In creating graphics for your web pages, you are limited only by your skill, imagination, and time. One type of graphic that is fairly easy to do with a number of programs is *word art*—a graphic created out of one or more words. To use word art for the web's title (Microsoft Image Composer is described here, but you can use any program you wish):

 NOTE: *The following Microsoft Image Composer instructions are very cursory. The Microsoft Image Composer will be covered in depth in Chapter 6.*

1. Open Microsoft Image Composer. Select Properties from the Edit menu, and set the size of your composition to 404 pixels wide and 62 pixels high.

2. Select the Text tool and click on the Select Font button in the Text tool palette.

3. Set the defaults for the text to be Garamond, 48-point, and bold. Click on OK. Type **Fantasy Travel**, as shown here:

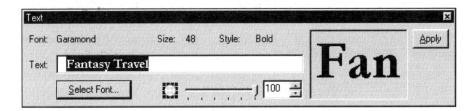

4. Click on Apply, and then select the Warps And Filters tool.

5. In the Warps And Filters tool palette select Outlines from the drop-down menu, and then select Relief, as shown here:

6. Click on Apply and a relief effect will be applied to your text, as you can see next:

7. Save your image in its native file format with the name **Title**, and then select Send To FrontPage from the File menu. Your graphic will be converted to a GIF file and added to your web.

NOTE: *The Send To FrontPage menu option only works when the FrontPage Explorer is running.*

TIP: *Before exporting a graphic from a graphics program to a web, it's best to size the graphic as desired. Even though you can resize the graphic in FrontPage, you cannot add more pixels. Enlarging a graphic will make it appear jagged. Also, choose a moderate number of colors or even grayscale to reduce the file size and therefore the download time.*

8. In the FrontPage Editor with the Fantasy Travel web, choose Home Page from the Window menu, select the two words in the first line of the title (leaving the new-line symbol), and press DEL.

9. From the Insert menu, choose Image, select your file (Title.gif, if you followed the preceding instructions), and click on OK. The new title will appear, as you can see in Figure 5-11.

 10. One problem with the graphic as imported is that it has a colored background. Suppose you wanted it to be the same as the rest of the background. FrontPage has a Make Transparent tool at the far right of the toolbar that will remove any one color in a graphic. Click on the graphic to select it, click on the Make Transparent tool, and then click on the colored background. The result looks like this:

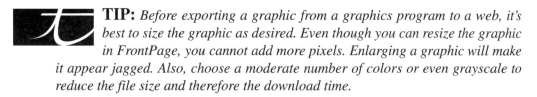

11. Save the changes to the Home page. You'll be asked if you want to save the images you are using in this web (the title, in this case) with the web files; click on Replace. Even though the image is already in your web, this will update the links to it. Close Microsoft Image Composer.

The word-art title as originally imported

FIGURE 5-11

 CAUTION: *Always save your images with your web files, so that when you copy the web to a server, they will all be together and the FrontPage Explorer can do the copying for you.*

Adding Horizontal Lines

Horizontal lines help separate sections of a web page. FrontPage provides an easy way to add such lines through the Insert menu, and you can add your own lines by placing them as graphics. Try both techniques now with these steps:

1. With the Fantasy Travel home page displayed in the FrontPage Editor, place the insertion point on the blank line just above "CURRENT SPECIALS."

2. Open the Insert menu and choose Horizontal Line. A horizontal line will appear on your page.

3. Delete the original blank line (the horizontal line creates its own line ending). You now have a line separating the top two sections on your Home page, like this:

For the latest fares, contact Julie Bergan at 555-1234 or John Donald at 555-1235 ↵
or through e-mail at julieb@fantasytravel.com or jmd@fantasytravel.com

---

CURRENT SPECIALS

- Super airfares to San Francisco: $75, LA: $175, New York: $275, & Miami: $375

---

4. Move the insertion point down to the left end of the line that reads "AVAILABLE TRAVEL OPTIONS." Press ENTER to create a blank line just above it. Here you'll add a horizontal line graphic that comes with FrontPage.

5. Open the Insert menu, choose Image, click on the Clip Art tab, and select Lines from the Category drop-down menu.

6. In the Contents display box, select Elegant Double.gif and click on OK.

7. Click on Center, to center the rule, so that it looks like this:

(Some restrictions may apply to the above fares.)

═══

AVAILABLE TRAVEL OPTIONS

1. AIR TRAVEL: Domestic, Canada, Europe, So. America, Africa, Asia, So. Pacific

---

8. Save your Home page.

Placing Clip Art

Clip art gives you that quick little something to jazz up a page. There are many sources of clip art, and some are bundled with FrontPage and Microsoft Office, Corel WordPerfect, and CorelDraw. To add a firecracker next to the CURRENT SPECIALS heading by using art from the CorelDraw clip-art collection or any other piece of clip art you have available:

1. Open your graphics package such as CorelDraw, and import a firecracker-like piece of clip art (the \Clipart\Celebrat\Crack032.cmx file on the fourth CorelDraw 6 CD was used here).

2. While still in your graphics package, export your firecracker as a .TIF file, sizing it quite small (I used 59×53 pixels) and with 256 colors.

3. In the FrontPage Editor with the Fantasy Travel home page, move the insertion point to the left edge of the CURRENT SPECIALS heading.

4. From the Insert menu, choose Image, click on the Other Location tab, select From File, and then click on the Browse button to locate the file. Click on OK when the file is selected.

5. Remove the background by using the Make Transparent tool as you did earlier. It should appear as you see it here:

6. Save the home page. A Save Image To FrontPage Web dialog box appears, asking if you want to save the graphic to the current FrontPage web. Click on Yes to do so.

It's easy to get carried away with adding small clip-art images. They are neat and don't use much memory (the firecracker image you see here is only 2K compared with the title, which is over 5K), so people think that they add little to the load time. But if you put a bunch of them on a page, such as one for every paragraph, all of a sudden you have a problem.

Adding a Background

The default background used by FrontPage is white, which you have seen in all the figures and illustrations so far in this chapter. You can change this to any color you wish or to a background image by using the Page Properties dialog box. Again, you have to be aware of the load-time impact as your background gets more sophisticated. Next, several possibilities for a background will be discussed.

Creating a Solid Color Background

Begin by looking at solid color backgrounds:

TIP: *If you keep to black for your text—and there is no reason you must—then your backgrounds should be very light colors. In any case you should maintain a very high contrast between the background and text colors so they are easy to read.*

1. With the Fantasy Travel home page in the FrontPage Editor, open the File menu, choose Page Properties, and then the Background tab. The Page Properties dialog box Background tab will appear as shown in Figure 5-12.

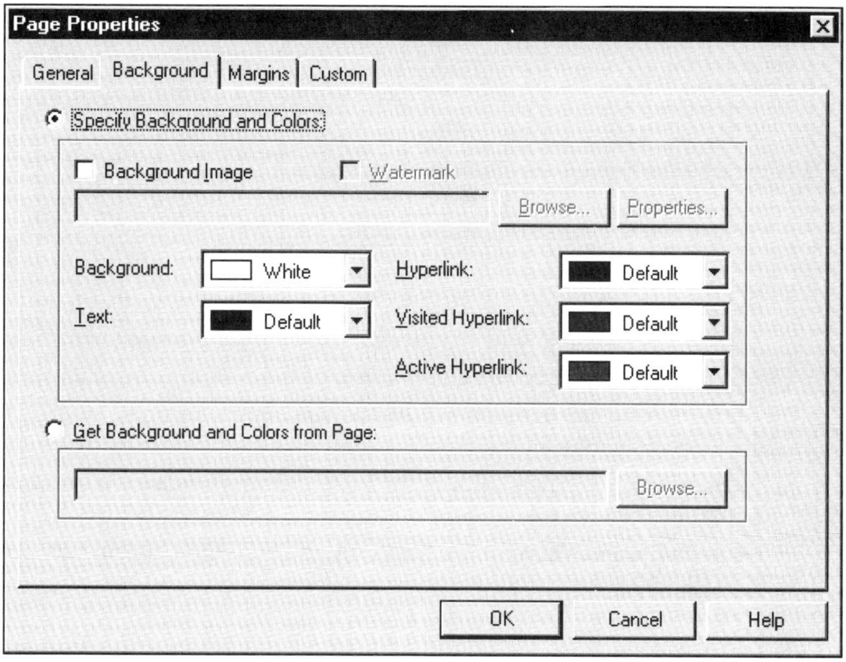

5

The Page Properties dialog box Background tab

FIGURE 5-12

2. Click on the down arrow for the Background drop-down menu. A menu of 16 colors, the default color, and a Custom option is displayed, as you see here:

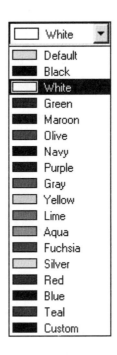

3. By selecting Custom you display the Color dialog box, shown in Figure 5-13. You can use any of the predefined 48 colors, or you can define up to 16 additional colors and use one of them. You can create your own colors by using either of two numerical schemes, or more simply by clicking on a color in the color selector and then adjusting the brightness on the right. One such color is the light yellow you can see being created in Figure 5-13. Create a color of your own, and then click on Add To Custom Colors. You will see the color added to the Custom colors below the Basic colors.

4. Click on your new color in the Custom Colors on the left and then click on OK. The color appears in the Page Properties dialog box; click on OK. The color appears on the web page.

 TIP: *Be sure to check how both the Netscape Navigator and Microsoft Internet Explorer display any custom color you create. Some colors may end up being dithered and won't look right.*

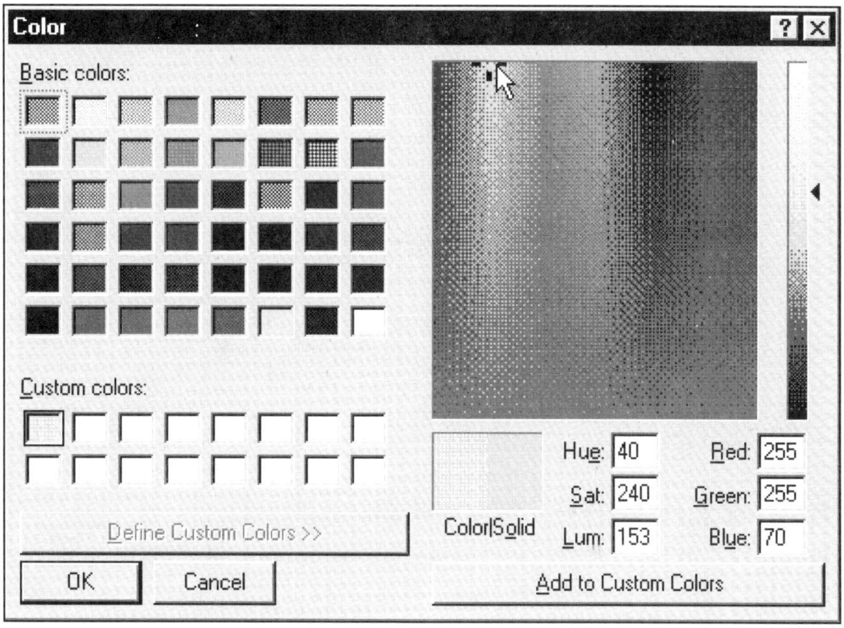

5

Defining a
custom
color in the
Color
dialog box

FIGURE 5-13

5. Save your home page.

> **TIP:** *If you want to make the background the same on several pages in a web, then, after getting the first page the way you want it, open the second page, open its Page Properties dialog box Background tab, click on Get Background And Colors From Page, and select the first page.*

Using a Textured Background

Another choice for a background is one of the many textured backgrounds available on the Internet and from other sources. Within FrontPage there are 19 choices for a textured background. These textured backgrounds are used in some of the web wizards.

> **NOTE:** *Most textured backgrounds are made by tiling a small graphic. You can make your own with any small image, optimally 96×96 pixels. If the image has a repeatable pattern, it is possible to get it to be reasonably seamless, as FrontPage has done in its samples.*

To add a textured background:

1. Select the Second Level Page from the Window menu of the FrontPage Editor.

2. Open the File menu, choose Page Properties, then the Background tab, and click on Background Image.

3. Click on Browse, select Clip Art, select Backgrounds from the Category drop-down menu, and then double-click on Pink and White.gif.

4. Click on OK in the Page Properties dialog box, and the background appears as shown in Figure 5-14.

5. Save page 2 and answer Yes that you want the background image saved with your web.

Using a Single Background Image

You can also use a single background image to cover a page. In most circumstances this is not advised, because the image is quite large (the image used in this example is over 130K) and therefore will take a long time to download. Also, it is hard to get

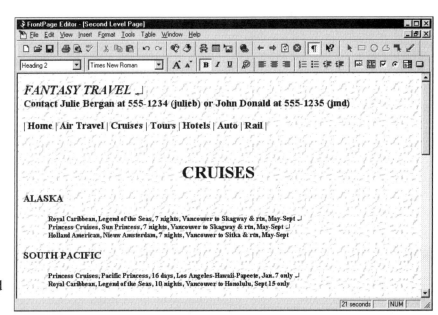

A textured background on page 2

FIGURE 5-14

a single text color that shows up well against a multicolored image. Nevertheless, if you know that all your readers have high-speed connections, as they might in an intranet, a single background image can be quite striking. Try it:

1. Select Third Level Page from the Window menu of the FrontPage Editor.

2. Open the Page Properties dialog box, click on Background Image in the Background, and browse to locate a large photographic image. (The image I've used was scanned out of the Princess Cruises catalog.) Click on OK to close the dialog box and import the image.

3. After you have imported an image, reopen the Page Properties dialog box, and click on the Properties button to open the Image Properties dialog box. Under Type, click on Interlaced, as shown here, which allows the image to be progressively downloaded. People seem better able to wait for an image downloaded this way.

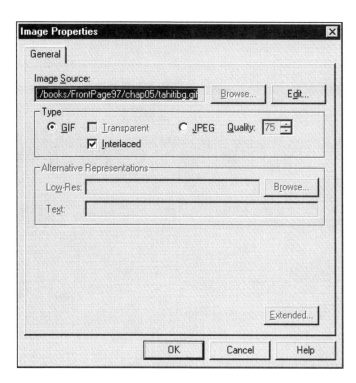

4. Click on OK to close the Image Properties dialog box, open the Text drop-down menu, and then select white.

5. Click on OK to close the Page Properties dialog box. Your background image with white text over it will appear as shown in Figure 5-15.

6. Save your page 3, answering Yes to saving the image with the web.

Using Scanned Images

Using scanned images on web pages is very similar to using other graphics, except for what you can do to the image before bringing it into FrontPage. For example, you can scan an image into Adobe Photoshop, where you can crop it or otherwise edit it. To try that:

1. Using your scanner and its software in the normal manner, scan a picture that you want to bring into your web (I used an image of the Pacific Princess from the Princess Cruises catalog). This will create a .TIF or other bitmap file.

A single image used as a background image

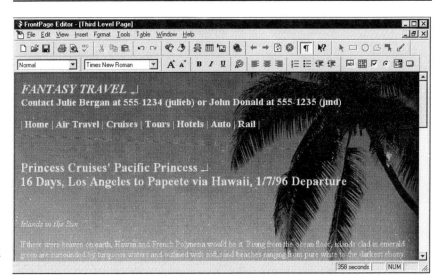

■ FIGURE 5-15

Scanned image used by permission of Princess Cruises.

2. Open Adobe Photoshop or another program that can edit bitmap files, and crop the image to the size you want. Do any other editing and then resave the file.

3. In the FrontPage Editor, use the Windows menu to choose the Second Level Page.

4. Place the insertion point to the left of the word "CRUISES." Open the Insert menu, choose Image, select From File, click on Browse, choose the type of file you are bringing in, and then double-click on the file you want to import. Your result will look something like Figure 5-16.

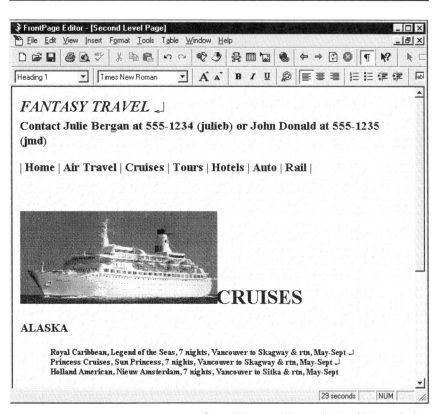

Page 2 with a scanned image placed on it

FIGURE 5-16

Scanned image used by permission of Princess Cruises.

5. Save page 2, answering Yes that you do want to save the new image with the current web. Also, close the FrontPage Editor and the FrontPage Explorer.

Text and graphics are the foundation of any web, whether you create the web or it is created with a template or wizard. In Chapter 6 you will see how to use Microsoft's Image Composer to create and modify graphics for your webs.

FrontPage on the Web

Jay's Seafood Restaurant

URL: *http://www.jays.com*
Webmaster: Bruce Lindsey
E-mail: *jays@erinet.com*

225 E Sixth Street
Dayton, OH 45402
(937) 222-2892
(937) 222-7547 (Fax)

5

Web Site

The Jay's Seafood Restaurant web site is a winner of the Microsoft Great Web Sites Contest. The Home page, shown in Figure 1, has an attractive background created from the logo. Following the logo, a borderless table, shown in Listing 1, provides an attractive way to separate the two elements.

Jay's Home
page

FIGURE 1

FrontPage on the Web (cont.)

Listing 1
Short table
HTML

```
<<table border="0" width="100%">
    <tr><td valign="top" width="33%"><p align="center"><img
        src="images/homepage.gif" alt="Home Page" width="118"
        height="65"> </p></td>
    <td valign="top" width="33%"><p align="center">
    <a href="Contents.htm"><img src="images/contentpage.gif"
    alt="Contents Page" border="0" width="128" height="65"></a>
    <br><a href="Contents.htm"><em><strong>Enter Jay's
        Restaurant</strong></em></a></p>
    </td></tr>
</table>
```

The second page provides a table of contents, as you can see in Figure 2. This was created using an image map with the HTML in Listing 2. The wine list, shown

Table of
contents
using an
image map

FIGURE 2

FrontPage on the Web (cont.)

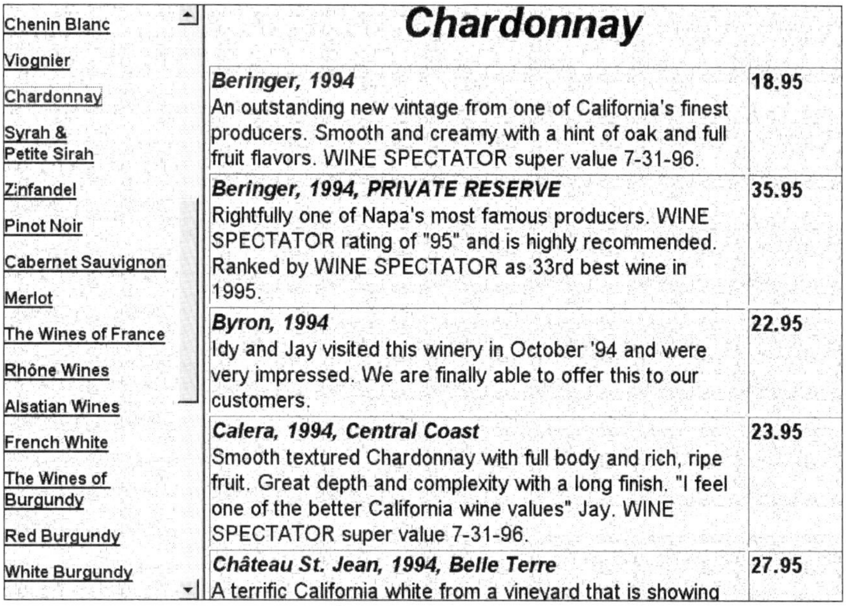

Chenin Blanc	**Chardonnay**	
Viognier		
Chardonnay	**Beringer, 1994**	**18.95**
Syrah & Petite Sirah	An outstanding new vintage from one of California's finest producers. Smooth and creamy with a hint of oak and full fruit flavors. WINE SPECTATOR super value 7-31-96.	
Zinfandel	**Beringer, 1994, PRIVATE RESERVE**	**35.95**
Pinot Noir	Rightfully one of Napa's most famous producers. WINE SPECTATOR rating of "95" and is highly recommended. Ranked by WINE SPECTATOR as 33rd best wine in 1995.	
Cabernet Sauvignon		
Merlot		
The Wines of France	**Byron, 1994**	**22.95**
Rhône Wines	Idy and Jay visited this winery in October '94 and were very impressed. We are finally able to offer this to our customers.	
Alsatian Wines		
French White	**Calera, 1994, Central Coast**	**23.95**
The Wines of Burgundy	Smooth textured Chardonnay with full body and rich, ripe fruit. Great depth and complexity with a long finish. "I feel one of the better California wine values" Jay. WINE SPECTATOR super value 7-31-96.	
Red Burgundy		
White Burgundy	**Château St. Jean, 1994, Belle Terre**	**27.95**
	A terrific California white from a vineyard that is showing	

Wine list built using frames

FIGURE 3

in Figure 3, was built using frames. You select a type of wine in the left frame, which is independently scrollable, and see a list of that type of wine in the right frame.

Listing 2
rm HTML

```
<table border="0" cellpadding="0" cellspacing="0" width="100%">
    <tr><td align="center" colspan="4"><font face="Arial"> 
        <!--webbot bot="ImageMap"
        rectangle=" (152,176) (394, 214)  upcoming.htm"
        rectangle=" (317,124) (473, 159)  links.htm"
        rectangle=" (54,125) (270, 161)  WineFeatures.htm"
        rectangle=" (363,77) (537, 111)  JaysHistory.htm"
        rectangle=" (192,77) (356, 113)  receptions.htm"
        rectangle=" (5,75) (176, 111)  JaysUpdate.htm"
        rectangle=" (353,25) (533, 61)  KitchenDoor.htm"
        rectangle=" (187,25) (326, 63)  wineframe.htm"
        rectangle=" (409,182) (531, 257)  JaysHome.htm"
        rectangle=" (43,23) (143, 62)  JaysMenu.htm"
        src="images/menumap1.jpg" alt="Menu Map" border="0"
        width="549" height="285" startspan --><MAP NAME="FrontPageMap">
```

FrontPage on the Web (cont.)

```
        <AREA SHAPE="RECT" COORDS="152, 176, 394, 214" HREF="upcoming.htm">
      <AREA SHAPE="RECT" COORDS="317, 124, 473, 159" HREF="links.htm">
       <AREA SHAPE="RECT" COORDS="54, 125, 270, 161" HREF="WineFeatures.htm">
       <AREA SHAPE="RECT" COORDS="363, 77, 537, 111" HREF="JaysHistory.htm">
       <AREA SHAPE="RECT" COORDS="192, 77, 356, 113" HREF="receptions.htm">
       <AREA SHAPE="RECT" COORDS="5, 75, 176, 111" HREF="JaysUpdate.htm">
       <AREA SHAPE="RECT" COORDS="353, 25, 533, 61" HREF="KitchenDoor.htm">
       <AREA SHAPE="RECT" COORDS="187, 25, 326, 63" HREF="wineframe.htm">
       <AREA SHAPE="RECT" COORDS="409, 182, 531, 257" HREF="JaysHome.htm">
       <AREA SHAPE="RECT" COORDS="43, 23, 143, 62" HREF="JaysMenu.htm"></MAP>
       <a href="_vti_bin/shtml.exe/Contents.htm/map">
       <img src="images/menumap1.jpg" width="549" alt="Menu Map"
       ismap usemap="#FrontPageMap" height="285" border="0"></a>
       <!--webbot bot="ImageMap" endspan i-checksum="41427" -->
</font></td></tr>
</table>
```

Webmaster Q & A

WHY FRONTPAGE? I received an announcement that FrontPage v1.1 beta was available to download for free about the time Jay's decided to investigate getting on the Web. The software had the familiar feel of Microsoft Word. Many of the documents that ended up on our web site were already in Word format, so it was simple to import them into FrontPage without having to learn HTML. I found FrontPage easy to learn and use. In many ways it is as simple to lay out a page in FrontPage as in Word. FrontPage 97 has added many new features, streamlined many of the old ones, and promises to streamline integration with the entire Office 97 suite.

LIKES AND DISLIKES I'm not a trained web author. In fact, Jay's web site is my first attempt at it. The beta version I used to do the site originally didn't even have complete help files available, so, as you can see from the outcome, using the software is pretty intuitive.

FrontPage on the Web (cont.)

NEATEST FEATURES OF THIS SITE   The wine list in frames with the index on the left and the associated page on the right. It also features a musical accompaniment written by a friend of mine. Some sections of the web site are from publications originally done in Microsoft Publisher. Since I began using Publisher 97 and FrontPage 97 together, I can copy from Publisher 97 into FrontPage 97, and the text is automatically converted into HTML.

TIPS   Take some time and play around with the software. Make a few sample web sites and see what you can do with the software before doing some serious work. If you see web pages you find particularly interesting and wonder how they were put together, simply save them as files and import them into FrontPage so you can see how they are done. Learn not only from other successful web sites, but take note of sites you didn't like and avoid their mistakes. One mistake I made that I am still gradually correcting is using caps in filenames. Try to always use lowercase and never use spaces.

5

Using Microsoft
Image Composer

In Chapter 5, if you followed the instructions, you quickly and without much explanation used the Microsoft Image Composer to create a new title for your Fantasy Travel web site. In this chapter you'll look at the Image Composer in some depth with an eye to creating and editing graphics that you can use in the webs you create.

The Image Composer is a full-featured application for creating and manipulating bitmapped images. As the name implies, a bitmapped image is one that is composed of numerous bits—*pixels*—that are of various colors and transparencies. Bitmapped images can be created by use of many different "paint" programs, by scanning a photograph into your computer, or by taking a photograph with a digital camera. There are also many libraries of bitmapped images, including one that comes with FrontPage 97 (you'll explore it later in this chapter), that you can use and modify. The Image Composer has its own file format with the extension of .MIC, but it can open and save images in a number of different bitmapped formats including

- Adobe Photoshop 3.0 (*.PSD)
- Altamira Composer (*.ACC)—open only
- CompuServe GIF (*.GIF)
- JPEG (*.JPG)
- Targa (*.TGA)
- TIFF (*.TIF, *.TIFF)
- Windows bitmap (*.BMP, *.DIB)—.DIB open only

The Image Composer Window

The Image Composer window, which is shown in Figure 6-1, contains a number of unique features. In addition to the normal toolbar below the menus at the top, there is a *toolbox* running down the left edge. At the bottom of the toolbox is the *Color Swatch,* which shows the current color you are working with. Within the working area of the window there is a white area called the *composition guide,* which shows the desired area of the image you're working on (the default is 640×480 pixels). At the bottom of the window is the status bar, which shows the X and Y coordinates of the current mouse position on the right, the position and size of the currently selected object, and other information.

NOTE: *The area of the composition guide is the* only *area that is saved when you save to a GIF, JPEG, Targa, TIFF, or Windows BMP format. Only the Image Composer's MIC or Adobe Photoshop PSD formats save the entire composition you are working on.*

As a default, the Image Composer window contains a dialog box with the palette for the currently selected tool (the Arrange tool palette is shown in Figure 6-1). This dialog box cannot be covered by the Image Composer's window, but it can be dragged outside of the Image Composer and can be closed.

Image Composer Toolbar and Menus

The Image Composer toolbar contains standard Windows 95 buttons from the leftmost button through the Undo arrow. To the right of the Undo arrow are eight buttons or drop-down menus unique to Image Composer. They are described in Table 6-1.

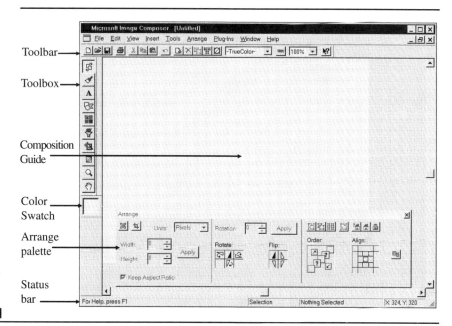

FIGURE 6-1

Icon	Name	Description
	Insert Image File	Opens the Insert From File dialog box, allowing you to select an image that you want to add to the current composition
	Delete	Deletes the current selection
	Duplicate	Duplicates the current selection
	Select All	Selects all of the objects currently displayed in the Image Composer
	Clear Selection	Removes the focus from the currently selected object
-TrueColor-	Color Format	Allows the selection of the color palette that you want to use
100%	Actual Size	Returns the display to actual size
100%	Zoom Percent	Zooms the display to a selected percentage of actual size

Image Composer's Unique Toolbar Buttons

TABLE 6-1

The Image Composer's menus include a number of standard Windows 95 options, plus options that duplicate the toolbar and toolbox buttons and tools, and a few unique options not available elsewhere. The latter are described as they are used later in this chapter.

Image Composer Toolbox and Palettes

The tools in the toolbox allow you to manipulate the objects you are working on in many ways, including arranging, painting, warping, and coloring existing objects, plus adding shapes and text as additional objects.

Arrange Tool and Palette

The Arrange tool and palette allows you to size, crop, rotate, flip, order, align, group/ungroup, flatten, and position the selected object(s).

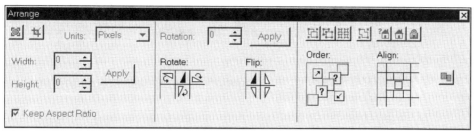

Paint Tool and Palette

The Paint tool and palette allows you to apply the current color to the currently selected objects using a variety of tools, point sizes, and opacity.

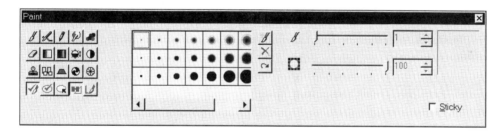

6

Text Tool and Palette

The Text tool and palette allows you to create a line of text up to 80 characters long; to select the font, font size, and font style from those available on your computer; and to set the opacity.

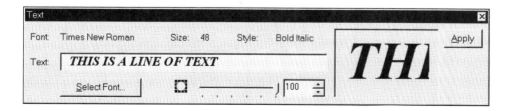

Shapes Tool and Palette

The Shapes tool and palette allows you to create rectangles, ovals, splines, and polygons; to set the opacity of a shape; and to edit the points or nodes in a spline or polygon. You can also copy a specific color within a composition using the Colorlift option.

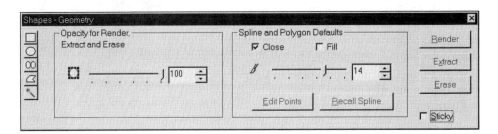

Patterns And Fills Tool and Palette

The Patterns And Fills tool and palette allows you to apply a different color, color gradient, or pattern to an existing object or its complement. You can also set the opacity of all the options and the characteristics of some of them.

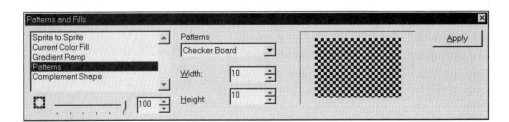

Warps And Filters Tool and Palette

The Warps And Filters tool and palette allows you to apply specific transformations to the selected object. The transformations include bending an object, adding outlines around it, changing the sharpness of the image, and changing the properties of the object's color.

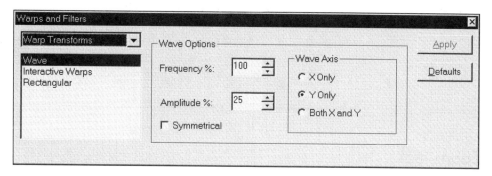

Art Effects Tool and Palette

The Art Effects tool and palette allows you to apply a number of special effects to the selected object. For example, you can make it look like a watercolor piece, a spatter painting, a charcoal or smudge stick drawing, or like it was made with stained glass. You can also give the selected object the appearance of torn or glowing edges, bas relief, or a neon glow.

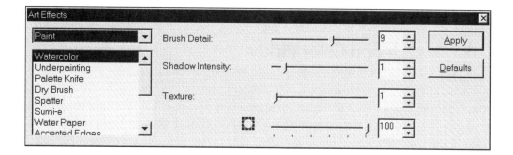

Color Tuning Tool and Palette

The Color Tuning tool and palette allows you to change the color of an object by shifting a color through changes to its brightness, contrast, hue, and saturation; by changing the highlights and shadows on the object; or by changing the dynamic range of a color.

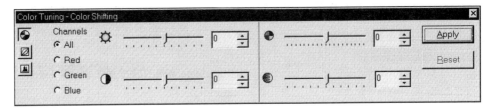

Zoom Tool

Clicking on the Zoom tool in the toolbox changes the mouse pointer to a magnifying glass, which, when clicked anywhere in the workspace, increases the magnification of the objects by 100 percent. (Return to actual size by clicking on the Actual Size button in the toolbar.)

Pan Tool

Clicking on the Pan tool in the toolbox changes the mouse pointer to a grabber hand with which you can move or *pan* the contents of the window's workspace. (The Pan tool moves the entire workspace, not individual objects—do that with the Arrange tool.)

Color Swatch and Color Picker

Clicking on the Color Swatch beneath the toolbox opens the Color Picker dialog box (commonly referred to as the *Color Picker*), shown in Figure 6-2, which allows you to choose a color for the objects you create or whose color you want to change, or to create a custom palette from which you can choose colors. You can choose a color in the Color Picker in three ways:

- By dragging on the small circle in the square (called the *Hue Ramp*) on the left of the dialog box if the *Whiteness Ramp* (the vertical rectangle next to the Hue Ramp) is high enough to produce a color. (The Hue Ramp and Whiteness Ramp together are called the *Color Ramp*.)

- By clicking in the Hue Ramp and/or Whiteness Ramp, or by dragging the handles on the edges.

- By dragging any combination of the Red, Green, or Blue sliders, or by clicking on the corresponding spinners.

Blackness handle · Hue handle · Whiteness Ramp · Current color · New color

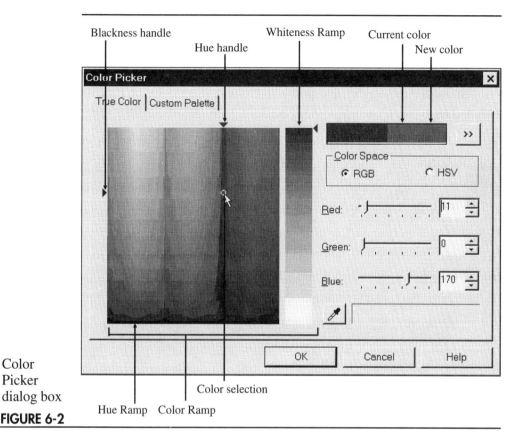

Color
Picker
dialog box

FIGURE 6-2

Color selection · Hue Ramp · Color Ramp

The Red, Green, Blue (RGB) color model is the most common and is the default when you first start Image Composer. You can alternatively pick the Hue, Saturation, Value (HSV) model, which better corresponds with the edge markers in the Color Ramps on the left of the dialog box.

In the lower right of the True Color tab of the Color Picker dialog box is a button with an eye dropper icon. If you click on this button, the mouse pointer changes into an eye dropper that you can move to any color on your desktop (not just within the Image Composer window) and click on a color to capture that color for application in the Image Composer.

NOTE: *Color Picker only provides the current color. It does not apply it to an object. To do that, you must either create an object while the color you want is selected, or paint an existing object.*

The Custom Palette tab allows you to create your own pallets, as shown in Figure 6-3. If you click on New and name a palette, a set of empty color positions is created. You can then automatically generate the number of colors to fill those positions, or you can double-click on a color position and open another dialog box from which you can choose a color for that position. If you close the Color Picker with the Custom Palette tab open, the Color Picker will reopen displaying the Custom Palette tab, so it is easy to use it if you choose.

 TIP: *Experiment by using the tools and their palettes. If something undesirable occurs, simply press CTRL-Z to undo the last command. Be sure to save your work before starting to experiment, so you can return to a beginning state.*

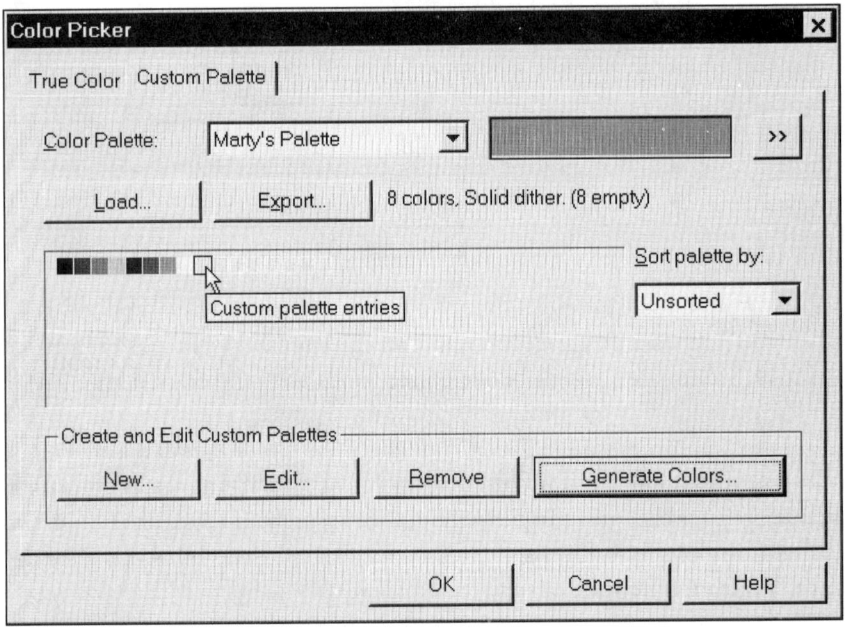

Custom Palette tab of the Color Picker

FIGURE 6-3

Working with Image Objects or Sprites

In the Image Composer there are only three ways to produce an initial image:

- By inserting an image from a file on your disk or from an image on a PhotoCD.

- By creating text with the Text tool.

- By creating shapes with the Shapes tool.

Each image that you insert or create by one of these methods becomes a separate object that contributes to the final *composition* that you are creating. These image objects are called *sprites* in Image Composer, and are the building blocks that you can manipulate with the various tools and features that you have been reading about. Although you can group sprites and manipulate them together, until you do the grouping, each sprite is independent and can be selected, moved, and otherwise manipulated separately.

When you add a second sprite to a composition, it may or may not overlap the first sprite, but in either case the two sprites are on separate *layers* in a *stack* of sprites. For this reason, the opacity of a sprite becomes an important property. When you move a sprite, you can do so in three dimensions, as you will read about later in this chapter.

6

Setting Up the Image Composer

Before you insert or create sprites in the Image Composer, you need to set the defaults to reflect the way you want your final composition to look. There are two aspects to this—the image size and the default color. Begin the creation of a new Fantasy Travel web page title by setting the image size and the default color with the following instructions:

1. Start the Microsoft Image Composer if it is not already running.

2. Open the File menu and choose the Composition Properties option to open the Composition Properties dialog box shown in Figure 6-4.

3. Drag across the number in the Width numeric box and type **508**.

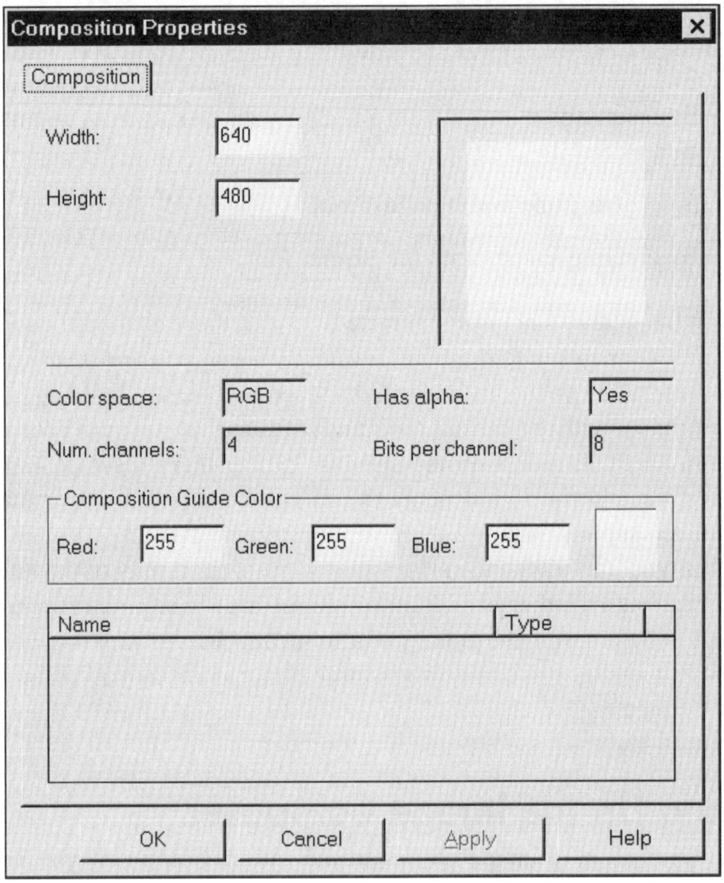

Composition Properties ☒

Composition

Width: 640

Height: 480

Color space: RGB   Has alpha: Yes

Num. channels: 4   Bits per channel: 8

┌─ Composition Guide Color ──────────────────────

Red: 255   Green: 255   Blue: 255

Name   Type

| OK | Cancel | Apply | Help |

Setting the initial image size

FIGURE 6-4

4. Drag across the number in the Height numeric box and type **78**.

5. Click on OK to close the dialog box and return to the Image Composer.

6. Click on the Color Swatch under the toolbox to open the Color Picker.

7. Click on the True Color tab, and select a pure blue by using either the sliders or the spinners to set Red to **0**, Green to **0**, and Blue to **255**.

8. Click on OK to close the dialog box and return to the Image Composer. Your composition guide should be a wide, short band across the top of the workspace, and your Color Swatch should show the pure blue, as you can see (except for the color) in Figure 6-5.

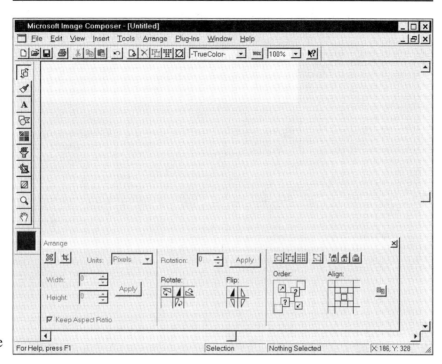

Image
Composer
set up to
create a title

FIGURE 6-5

Inserting Sprites

The easiest way to begin to work with the Image Composer is by bringing in an
existing image. Since the Image Composer comes with a number of images you can
use, this is also very convenient. Bring in several existing images by using the
following instructions. You will then manipulate the resulting sprites in later sections
of this chapter.

1. Place your FrontPage 97 CD in its drive or connect to the server site
   containing the FrontPage 97 files, so you can retrieve some of the Image
   Composer clip art that it contains.

2. Open the Insert menu and choose From File to open the Insert From
   File dialog box. Select your CD-ROM drive, and then choose the
   \ImgComp\Mmfiles\Photos\Metaphor\PhotoDsc folder and the
   Champagn.mic file as you can see next. Click on OK, and a large
   champagne bottle in an ice bucket appears on your screen, similar
   to Figure 6-6.

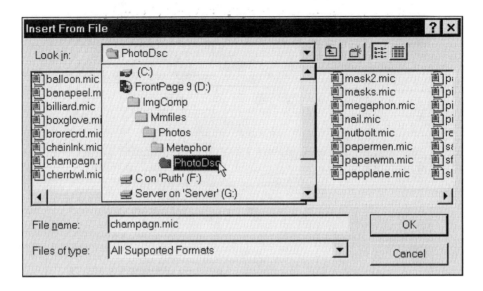

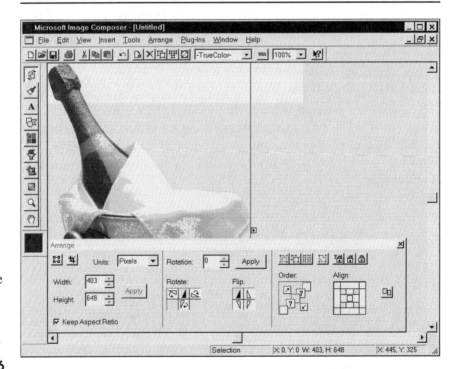

First sprite
brought
into the
Image
Composer

FIGURE 6-6

3. Open the Insert menu, choose From File, and select your CD-ROM drive and the \ImgComp\Mmfiles\Photos\Flags\PhotoDsc folder. Then press and hold CTRL while clicking on France.mic, Gbritain.mic, Germany.mic, and Italy.mic. When all four flags are selected, click on OK. The four flags will come into your Image Composer, one on top of the other.

You now have five objects or sprites in your workspace: the champagne bottle and four flags, all on top of one another. It doesn't look like much at the present, but in the next several sections, you'll manipulate the sprites so that they become a border for your title.

Selecting Sprites

To do anything with sprites, you must select them. When you bring a sprite into the Image Composer, it is automatically selected, but when you bring in a second sprite, you can select the first, if it is not covered by another sprite, by clicking on it. When a sprite is selected, it has a box drawn around it called a *selection box,* with eight small boxes called *sizing handles* (one on each side and one more in each corner), like this:

When a sprite is selected, you can move it by placing the mouse pointer inside the selection box until it becomes a four-headed arrow, and then dragging the sprite where you want it. You can also size a sprite by moving the mouse pointer to any of the seven sizing handles with a straight arrow until the mouse pointer becomes a two-headed arrow, and then dragging the side or corner in the direction in which you want to change the side. By pointing on the eighth sizing handle (the one in the

upper-right corner with the circular arrow) and dragging, you can rotate the sprite either clockwise or counterclockwise.

Currently the French flag (if you followed the suggested order) is selected. It was the last sprite brought in and is therefore on the top layer. All the other sprites are on different layers in the stack. To select a sprite hidden by one or more layers above it, you can use one of the following methods:

- Click on any part of the sprite that is exposed.

- Press TAB to select the next layer down. When the bottom sprite is selected, pressing TAB again will select the top layer.

- The Arrange menu and Arrange palette contain commands and tools, such as Bring To Front and Send Backward, to change the position of a selected sprite in the stack.

Although a layer may be selected, you cannot see it unless it is either the top layer or is not covered by a higher layer.

 TIP: *Although you cannot see a layer, if you can select it (and you always can with TAB), you can move it by pointing inside the selection box and dragging.*

Use the following steps to practice selecting the sprites you have in your workspace:

1. Click on the Pan tool in the toolbox to select it, and then use it to move the workspace so the sprites are away from the top and left edges, as shown in Figure 6-7.

2. Click on the Arrange toolbox tool, and then drag the Arrange palette as far out of the Image Composer window as possible. When you are done, click on the French flag to reselect it.

3. Press TAB slowly five times to move down through the stack and then back to the top.

4. Click on the part of the ice bucket sticking beneath the current flag selection box, then click on a flag outside of the champagne and ice bucket selection. Click on the French flag to select it again.

5. Click on the orange bit of the German flag sticking out from beneath the French flag. You should be able to select it even though it is within the selection box of the French flag. Try clicking on other bits of sprites that you can see. Only some of the time can you select a different sprite.

6. Select the French flag again and drag the Arrange dialog box so you can see all of it. In the right-hand third of the dialog box there is a section titled "Order," like this:

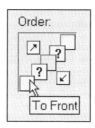

6

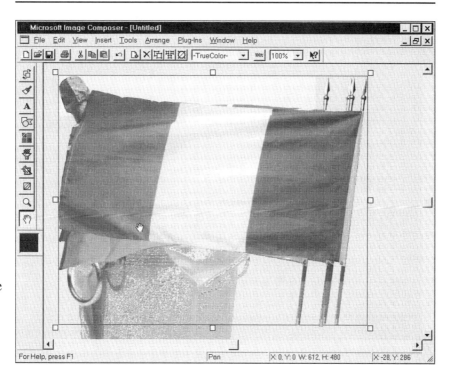

Moving the sprites away from the top and left edges

FIGURE 6-7

7. Click on the arrow in the upper-left labeled "Send Backward." The French flag will go behind the German flag, but still be selected. It has gone from the top of the stack to the second from the top position. Click on Send Backward again, and the French flag will move to the third position behind the British flag.

8. Click on the white box in the upper-right of the Arrange Order tool labeled "To Back." The French flag will move to the very back of the stack behind the champagne and ice bucket.

9. Select the champagne and ice bucket, and click on the lower-left question mark in the Arrange Order tool labeled "Before." A Hint message will open as shown next. You need to select the sprite that you want the selected sprite to be in front of. Click on OK and then click on the British flag to place the champagne and ice bucket between the German and British flags, as shown in Figure 6-8.

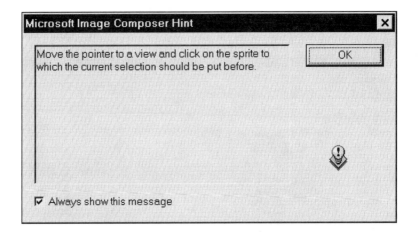

10. With the champagne and ice bucket still selected, open the Arrange menu, and click on Send To Back to return this sprite to the bottom of the stack.

11. Select the French flag, open the Arrange menu, and click on Bring To Front to restore the original order of the stack.

Although the concept of a stack of sprites with the upper ones hiding the lower ones seems like it might be difficult to work with, Image Composer has a powerful set of tools that makes it easy.

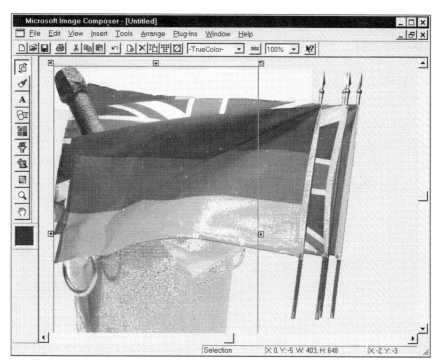

Placing the champagne and ice bucket between the German and British flags

FIGURE 6-8

Moving, Sizing, Duplicating, and Rotating Sprites

The objective is to place the flags and champagne on either end of the composition guide that will become the title block for the web title that you will create. To do that, you must reduce the size of all the objects, move and rotate the flags, and duplicate, flip, and move the champagne to get this final image:

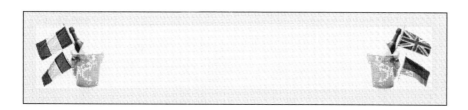

Sizing the Flags

The Image Composer also has a powerful set of tools for manipulating sprites. Begin using them by sizing and moving the flags:

1. With the French flag selected, click on the Units drop-down list on the left of the Arrange palette, and select Percent.

2. Drag over the "100" in the Width spinner and type **8**. Make sure that Keep Aspect Ratio is checked, as shown next, and click on Apply. The French flag will become comparatively small.

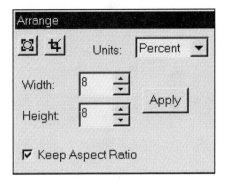

3. Drag the French flag so it is out of the way, say, in the upper-right of the workspace.

4. Repeat Steps 1 and 2 to size each of the other three flags to 8 percent of their original size, and then drag them out of the way to the upper right.

Sizing, Duplicating, and Flipping the Champagne

Next, reduce the size of the champagne and ice bucket, duplicate it so there is a copy at either end of the title, and then flip the right-hand copy, so the two are pointing in opposite directions:

1. Select the champagne and ice bucket, choose Percent as the units in the Arrange sizing tools, enter **12** as the percent, and with Keep Aspect Ratio checked, click on Apply.

2. Drag the champagne and ice bucket up to the left side of the composition guide, about a quarter of an inch in, like this:

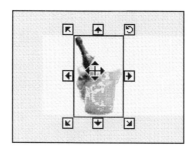

3. With the champagne and ice bucket still selected, click on the Duplicate toolbar button. A second champagne and ice bucket appears, slightly offset from the original.

4. Drag the second champagne and ice bucket to the right side of the composition guide, about a quarter of an inch from the end.

5. With the right-hand champagne and ice bucket selected, click on the Flip Horizontally tool in the Arrange palette, as you can see next. The Champagne flips so that it is pointing to the right.

6

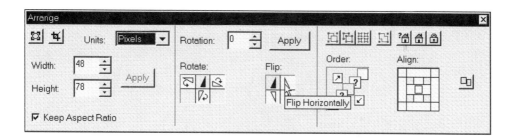

6. Open the File menu and save your work as **title2.mic**.

Moving and Rotating the Flags on the Left

Now move the French and Italian flags to the left end, and rotate them to fit the space.

1. Drag the French flag to the upper-left of the composition guide.

2. With the French flag still selected, click on the down arrow in the Rotation spinner in the Arrange palette until you get –25, and then click on Apply. The French flag will rotate to the left.

3. Click on To Back in the Arrange palette, causing the French flag to go behind the champagne and ice bucket, like this:

4. Drag the Italian flag to the lower-left corner of the composition guide.

5. With the Italian flag still selected, set the Rotation spinner to -27 and click on Apply.

6. Click on To Back in the Arrange palette so that the Italian flag goes behind the French flag and the champagne and ice bucket. Adjust the positioning of the French flag, Italian flag, and champagne until you are happy with them, similar to what you can see here:

7. Click on the Save toolbar button to again save your work.

Flipping and Positioning the Flags on the Right

The final task with the flags is to flip and position the final two on the right.

1. Select the British flag and click on Flip Horizontally in the Arrange palette.

2. With the British flag still selected, set the Rotation spinner to 25 and click on Apply.

3. Drag the British flag to the upper-right corner of the composition guide, and click on To Back in the Arrange palette to place it behind the champagne and ice bucket.

4. Select the German flag, flip it horizontally, rotate it 25 degrees, position it in the lower right of the composition guide, and send it to the back.

5. Adjust the positioning of the flags and champagne and ice bucket on the right until you are satisfied with them. It should resemble this:

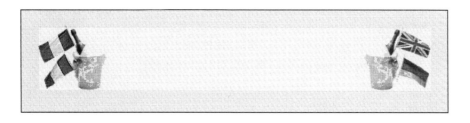

6. When you are happy with the flags and champagne, click on the Select All toolbar button, open the Arrange menu, and choose Flatten Selection. This creates one sprite on one level out of the six sprites and six levels that previously existed. It is easier to work with a single sprite as you build the remainder of the title block.

7. Open the Arrange menu, and choose Lock Position to keep the flags and champagne in their current position. Save your work once more.

Adding Text Sprites

Text sprites are simply any text that you create with the Text tool and place in the workspace. One aspect of creating text sprites is selecting the font that you will use. You can, of course, use any font, but FrontPage also includes some on its CD.

Fonts on FrontPage CD-ROM

The fonts available on the FrontPage CD include several that are unique and possibly interesting for a web page. See what is available and copy one to your hard disk for use in the title block you are building.

1. With the FrontPage 97 CD in its drive, open the Windows Explorer, select your CD-ROM drive, and then select the \ImgComp\Mmfiles\Fonts folder. Within that folder you'll see a number of folders, each with a different font, as you can see in Figure 6-9.

2. Open several of these folders and double-click on one or more fonts to see what they look like. For example, Calisto MT Bold is shown in Figure 6-10.

3. When you have gotten an idea of the fonts available, open the Start menu, choose Settings Control Panel, and then double-click on Fonts. Your Fonts folder will open, showing you the fonts that you have available on your hard disk.

4. Open the File menu and choose Install New Font. Specify your CD-ROM drive, and then select the \ImgComp\Mmfiles\Fonts\Eras folder. Five fonts will appear as you can see in Figure 6-11.

Fonts available on the FrontPage CD

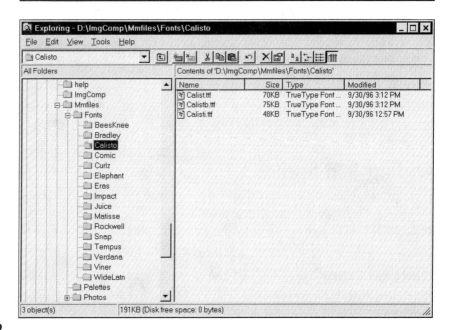

FIGURE 6-9

Looking at one of the available fonts

FIGURE 6-10

---

5. Select Eras Demi for use in the title block you are creating, and select any of the other fonts that you want (used CTRL to select more than one font). Click on OK to copy the fonts.

6. Close the Fonts folder window, the Control Panel, and the Windows Explorer to get back to the Image Composer.

Creating Text Sprites

Creating text sprites is fairly easy, as you saw in Chapter 5. Use your new font to create the Fantasy Travel name:

1. Click on the Text toolbox tool to open the Text palette.

Fonts to be
copied
from the
CD-ROM

Add Fonts

List of fonts:

Eras Bold ITC (TrueType)
Eras Demi ITC (TrueType)
Eras Light ITC (TrueType)
Eras Medium ITC (TrueType)
Eras Ultra ITC (TrueType)

OK

Cancel

Select All

Help

Network...

Folders:
D:\ImgComp\Mmfiles\...\Eras

Drives:

d:\
ImgComp
Mmfiles
Fonts
Eras

d:

☑ Copy fonts to Fonts folder

FIGURE 6-11

2. Click on Select Font in the Text palette to open the Font dialog box.

3. Select Eras Demi and accept the default Regular style and 48 points, as shown in Figure 6-12, and then click on OK.

4. Type **Fantasy Travel** and make sure 100 percent opacity is set, so your Text palette looks like this:

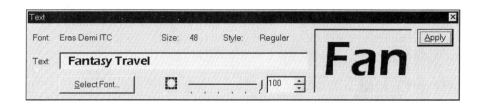

5. Click on Apply. The words "Fantasy Travel" appear in the upper corner of your workspace.

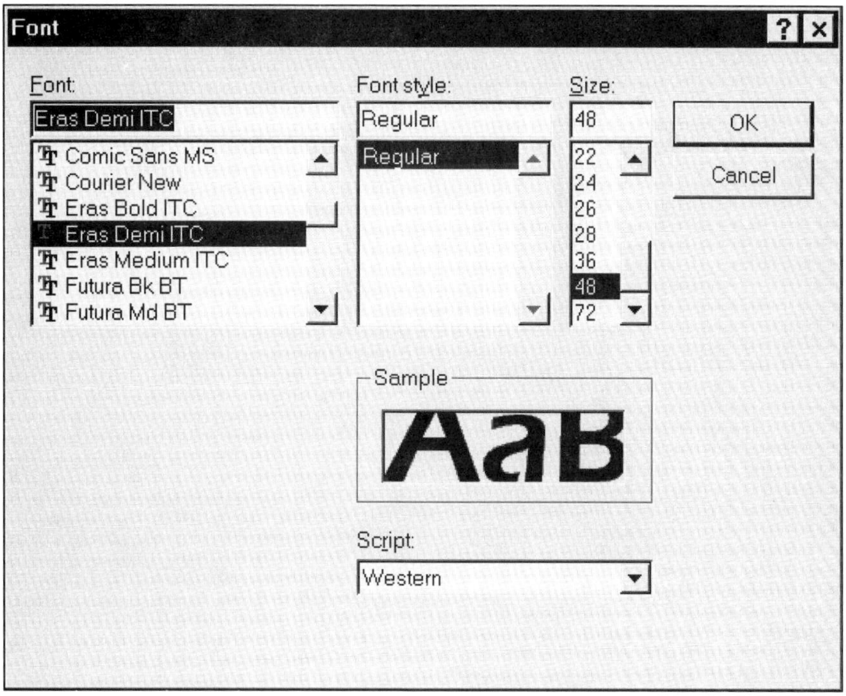

Selecting
the font for
the title
block

FIGURE 6-12

6. Drag the text so that it is approximately centered in the composition guide. It will overlap the two champagne bottles, as you can see here:

7. To reduce the width of the text, drag its left-center sizing handle to the right until it is just to the right of the right edge of the left ice bucket. Then drag its right-center sizing handle to the left until it is just to the left of the left edge of the right ice bucket. The final results should look like Figure 6-13.

8. Save your work.

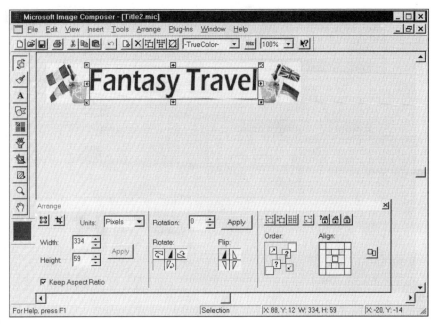

Text in its correct position

FIGURE 6-13

Enhancing Text Sprites

There are, of course, many things that you can do to "enhance" text from its original two-dimensional appearance. Two of the things that you can do are to add an outline and to add a drop shadow:

1. With the title text still selected, click on the Warps And Filters toolbox tool to open that palette.

2. In the Warps And Filters palette, open the drop-down list box in the upper-left corner and choose Outlines.

3. Choose Edge from the list, make sure the Thickness is 1 and the opacity is 100, and click on the Color Swatch in the palette. The Color Picker dialog box will open.

4. Move the Red slider all the way to the right, making Red **255**. Move Green and Blue all the way to the left, so they are **0**, as you can see in Figure 6-14. Click on OK.

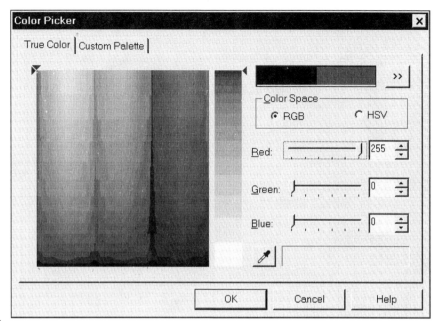

Color
Picker
dialog box
selecting
red

FIGURE 6-14

5. Click on Apply. A thin red border appears around the blue letters.

6. Keeping the text selected, go back to the Warp And Filters palette, and choose Shadows from the list.

7. Set the X and Y offsets to **2**, leave the opacity at 100, and click on the Color Swatch in the palette to open the Color Picker.

8. Set Red at **60**, Green at **0**, and Blue at **100** to create a purple, and click on OK.

9. Click on Apply to give a small drop shadow to the characters, as shown in Figure 6-15.

10. Save your title block by clicking on Save in the toolbar.

Adding Geometric Shapes

The final element you need to add to the title block you are building is some confetti around the title and champagne bottles. Do that by creating several geometric shapes, reducing their size, coloring them, and flipping and rotating them.

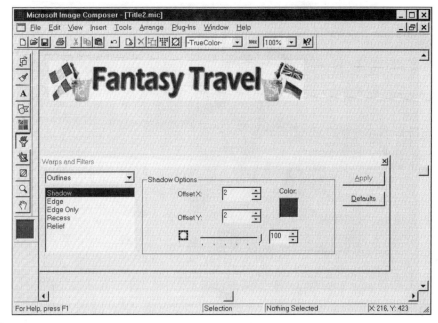

Finished
text with a
border and
drop
shadow

FIGURE 6-15

Creating Geometric Shapes

Use the Shapes tool to create several geometric shapes in different colors. You will
then use the shapes to make confetti.

 1. Click on the Shapes toolbox tool to open the Shapes palette shown next.
This palette allows you to create four types of shapes: rectangles and
squares, ovals and circles, splines or curved shapes, and polygons or
multi-straight-sided shapes.

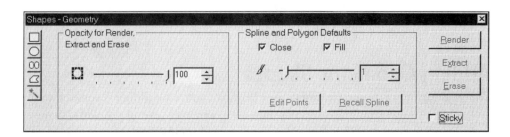

2. Click on the Color Swatch below the toolbox to open the Color Picker. Create yellow, which is Red **255**, Green **255**, and Blue **0**. Click on OK.

3. Click on the Rectangle tool, and draw a small square in the workspace below the composition guide by pressing and holding SHIFT while drawing the shape (holding down **SHIFT** keeps the sides equal). When the square is complete, click on Render to finish it.

 TIP: *If you don't like your first square, simply delete it and try again.*

4. Open the Color Picker and change the current color to pure red (Red **255**, Green and Blue **0**).

5. Click on the Oval tool, and draw a circle the same size as and next to the square by again holding down SHIFT. (While you are drawing it, it looks like a square.) When you are done, click on Render and you'll see the circle.

6. Change the current color to pure green (Red and Blue **0**, and Green **255**).

7. Click on the Polygon tool and draw a small triangle next to and the same size as the square. Do this by clicking on an initial point, moving the mouse a very short distance, clicking a second point, moving a short distance perpendicular to your first move, and clicking a third point. A triangle will be formed by drawing three lines between the points. Click on Render when you are ready.

8. Change the current color to pure blue (Red and Green **0**, and Blue **255**).

9. Click on the Spline tool, click on Close to uncheck it, and set the Spline line width (the slider on the right) to **1**.

10. Draw a double curlicue going from bottom right to upper left as follows: click an initial point; move a short distance to the upper left and then click the top of the first curlicue; move slightly to the right and back down, and click at the bottom of the first curlicue; move to the left and click at the outside of the first curlicue; move to the upper left and click at the top of the second curlicue; move slightly to the right and back down, and click at the bottom of the second curlicue; move to the left and click at the outside of the second curlicue; move up to the upper left and click a final point. Your result should look like this:

11. When your double curlicue is ready, click on Render.

12. Click on the Arrange tool, and use the Arrange palette to reduce the size of the curlicue to about 50 percent and the square, circle, and triangle to about 60 percent so that on a relative-size basis they should compare to the flags and champagne, as shown here:

NOTE: *Use trial and error in sizing your shapes. Try a percentage reduction and if it isn't correct, immediately press CTRL-Z to undo it and try another percentage.*

Manipulating Geometric Shapes

The objective is to use the four shapes you have created and create the random look of confetti around the name. Do that by duplicating, flipping, rotating, and placing these objects:

1. Select the four shape sprites by "rubber banding" them. Point the mouse in the upper left of the shapes and drag to the lower right of them, as you can see here. When you release the mouse button, you'll see that all of the shapes are selected. (If for some reason one or more of the sprites did not get selected, you can press and hold SHIFT while clicking on the unselected sprites.)

2. Click on the Duplicate toolbar button, and then drag the copy off to the right. Do that seven more times to create a total of nine sets of four shapes.

3. Click on the curlicue in the second set, and use the Arrange palette to flip it horizontally. Flip the third curlicue vertically, and flip the fourth both vertically and horizontally.

4. Rotate the fifth, sixth, seventh, and eighth curlicues by 45, 135, 225, and 315 degrees, respectively.

5. Flip and then rotate the triangle as you did the curlicue.

6. Individually select the second, fourth, sixth, and eighth squares (you can't do it all at once) and rotate them 45 degrees. When you are done, your shape sprites should look like this:

7. Tightly group each of the eight sets of shapes. The two sets with horizontal curlicues should be duplicated, since these fit best on the top and bottom of the name, giving you a total of ten sets.

8. Position the sets of shapes on the composition guide around the names, as you can see here:

9. When you are done positioning, save your work under the original name, Title2.mic, and then save it again under **Webtitle.mic**.

10. Click on the Select All toolbar button to select all of the pieces of the title block, open the Arrange menu, and choose Flatten Selection. Save your work a third time under the name Webtitle.mic.

11. Open the Windows Explorer, and locate the two files Title2.mic and Webtitle.mic. You'll notice a very significant difference in their size. In my case (yours could be a little different), Title2.mic was 774K and Webtitle.mic was 127K.

12. In the Image Composer, open the File menu and choose Save As. In the Save As dialog box, open the Save As Type drop-down list box, choose TIFF, and click on Save. A message box will open telling you that the file format you are using will flatten the sprites and crop the result to the

composition guide. Since you want to do that in this case, click on OK. Repeat this Save As process, and choose JPEG as the type.

13. Look in the Explorer, and you'll see the file sizes reduced once more. In my case, the JPEG file was 21K and the TIFF file was 62K, as you can see next:

Title2.mic	774KB	Image Compos...
Webtitle.jpg	21KB	JPEG Image
Webtitle.mic	127KB	Image Compos...
Webtitle.tif	62KB	TIF File

NOTE: *The flattening process is important for saving file space on your disk, but once you flatten, you cannot reverse the process—and it is very difficult to do much editing of a flattened file. You can create the same size TIFF and JPEG files from an unflattened .MIC file as you can from a flattened one.*

Working with Other Tools

While the Fantasy Travel title block is complete, there are several of the tools that you haven't yet used. Try several of these in the remaining sections of this chapter.

Applying Patterns and Fills

The Patterns And Fills toolbox tool and palette allows you to apply solid colors and patterns to a sprite in your workspace. It is one of two ways of changing a sprite's color after you have created it (the other is with the Paint tool).

1. In the Image Composer, open the File menu and choose New. The title block will be removed from your screen, and a new, blank 640×480 composition guide will open in the Image Composer. Since you are not working on an end product, but just want to try out some of the tools, you don't care about the size of the composition guide.

2. Click on the Shapes tool, draw a rectangle about 2 by 4 inches (it is not important where it is, so long as you can see it—and the size can really be anything that you want it to be). Click on Render. A rectangle will appear filled with the last color you used (pure blue in this book).

3. Click on the Patterns And Fills toolbox tool to open the Patterns And Fills palette.

4. If it is not already selected, click on the rectangle you just drew, and then select the Gradient Ramp from the list on the left of the Patterns And Fills palette.

NOTE: *You can only apply a pattern or a fill to an existing sprite. You must create the sprite first, and then add the pattern or fill.*

5. Open the Ramp Name drop-down list box, choose Gold, and then click on Apply. Your Image Composer window should look like Figure 6-16.

6. Open the Ramp Name list again, choose Sunrise, and click on Apply. Your rectangle will now look like a sunrise.

6

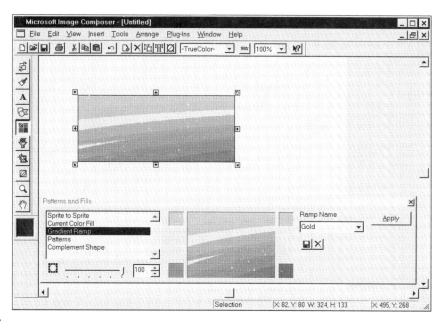

Rectangle filled with a gold gradient ramp

FIGURE 6-16

7. In the Patterns And Fills palette, click on Current Color Fill in the list box, and then click on Apply. Your rectangle will fill with pure blue again.

8. Click on Patterns in the list box, open the Patterns drop-down list, choose Hue/Blackness, and click on Apply. A rainbow of colors going to black at the bottom will fill your rectangle.

9. Click on the Text toolbox tool, accept the current font (it should be the last one you used), type **This is text!**, and click on Apply. Move the text below the rectangle you created earlier and leave it selected.

10. Open the Patterns And Fills palette again, choose Sprite To Sprite in the list on the left, select Transfer Full in the drop-down list, and click on Apply. A Hint message box will appear asking you to click on the source sprite.

11. Click on OK and then click on the rectangle you created earlier. Another Hint message box will appear telling you that the two sprites need to overlap. Click on OK.

12. Move the text so that it is on top of the rectangle, and click on Apply again in the Patterns And Fills palette. Acknowledge the first hint and click on the rectangle. The part of the text within the rectangle will disappear.

13. Drag the text off the rectangle, and you'll see that the part of the text that was inside the rectangle has exactly the same coloration as the part of the rectangle it covered, which you can get some idea of (it's in shades of gray!) in Figure 6-17.

14. With the text still selected, choose Complement Shape in the Patterns And Fills list box, and click on Apply. The area around the text will change to the current color. If the text is white, for example, and the current color is blue, you'll get this image:

15. Select the rectangle, change the current color to white (click on the Color Swatch to open the Color Picker, move all three color sliders to **255**, and click on OK), choose Current Color Fill in the Patterns And Fills list box, and click on Apply. (This sets up the rectangle to use in the next section.)

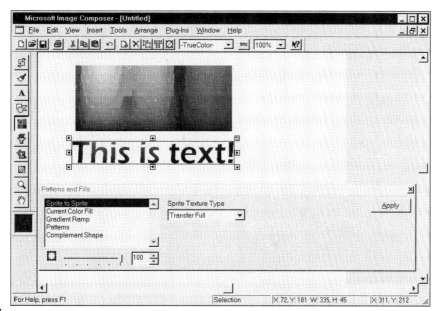

Text after having the rectangle's colors transferred to it

FIGURE 6-17

Using the Paint Tool

The Paint tool, unlike most other bitmapped paint programs, only works within a sprite you have created elsewhere. The Paint tool (or any of the tools in the Paint palette) cannot create its own sprites, it can only color those that already exist.

1. Click on the Paint toolbox tool to open the Paint palette. If your white rectangle is no longer selected, it may have disappeared into the white composition guide. If so, click in the general vicinity of where your rectangle was, and it will reappear. In any case, the rectangle should be selected.

2. Change the current color to a pure red (see step 15 in the previous section), select the Paintbrush tool, click on the fourth brush size in the second row, and paint a line across the top of your rectangle, as shown in Figure 6-18.

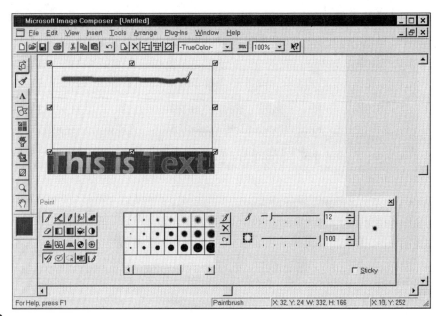

Painting
a line

FIGURE 6-18

3. Change the current color to a bright yellow (Red and Green **255**, Blue **0**), select the Airbrush tool, use the slider or spinner on the right to change the brush size to **40**, and draw another line in your rectangle, a little beneath the first line you drew.

4. Change the color to pure blue, select the Pencil tool, leave the default size, and draw a third line below the first two, so your Image Composer window looks something like Figure 6-19.

TIP: *Hold down SHIFT to get a straight line.*

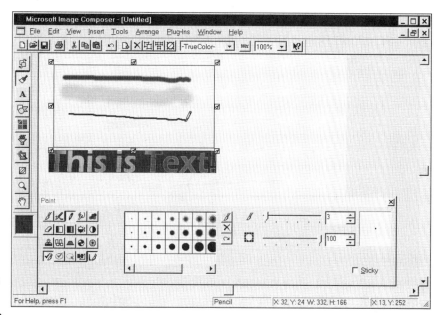

A pencil
line under
the airbrush
line

FIGURE 6-19

 5. Click on the Smear tool, and smear areas of your three lines. Note that the color you start with gets smeared into the other color(s). Your results should look something like this:

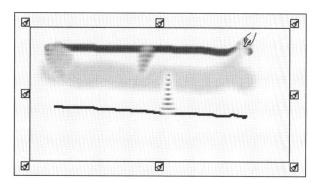

6. Click on the Eraser tool, and erase some of the lines and smears that you created earlier. (You can hold down SHIFT to get a straight erasure.) Here is how my results look (compare with the preceding illustration of the smeared lines):

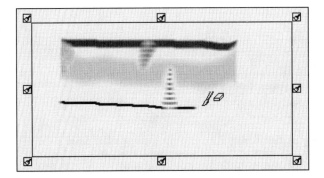

There are several other Paint and toolbox tools that are beyond the scope of this book, but use the examples of experimentation that you have seen here to try these for yourself. I think that you'll agree that the Microsoft Image Composer is a comprehensive tool for creating graphics that you can use in your web pages.

Adding and Managing Hyperlinks and Hotspots

237

W hen you open a web page in a browser, you have access to only the single page in the address given to the browser (FrontPage assumes a web page name of default.htm if no other address is given). There is no way to get to another page without giving the browser its address, unless there is a hyperlink on the first page that takes you to the other page.

A *hyperlink* or *link* is an object, either text or graphic, that when you click on it, tells the browser to move to a bookmark on the same page or to open another page. The hyperlink, when clicked upon, gives the browser an address called a uniform resource locator (URL). The browser then opens the page at that address. The page can be part of the current web, part of another web at the same site, or any web at any site anywhere on the Internet, anywhere in the world—unless your intranet limits you to its domain.

A hyperlink is an essential part of a web page. It is the element that allows it to be interconnected with other pages, producing the "web." Hyperlinks are also why the language behind web pages, HTML, is called *hyper*text markup language. Hyperlinks provide the first and most important level of interactivity in a web page: they give users a choice of where to go when they are done with the current page.

When a hyperlink is viewed in a browser, it is normally a different color than the surrounding text, and it is usually underlined (the person controlling the browser can determine what color a hyperlink is and whether it is underlined). Also, when you move the mouse pointer over a hyperlink, the pointer normally turns into a pointing hand, and either the full or partial URL related to that link is displayed in the status bar at the bottom of the window, as you can see here (with a partial URL to the Home page—a full URL would show the full path, http://marty/FantasyTravel/Default.htm in my case):

In this chapter you will see how to add hyperlinks to text and graphics, how to assign areas of a graphic—or hotspots—to a hyperlink, and how to manage the hyperlinks in a web page.

Adding Hyperlinks to Text and Graphics

Hyperlinks can be assigned to anything you enter on a web page. Any piece of text—be it a word, a phrase, or a paragraph—or any graphic, from a bullet to a large image, can be assigned a link. While there are many similarities, there are some differences, so let's look separately at assigning hyperlinks to text and to graphics.

Assigning Hyperlinks to Text

Within a web, hyperlinks provide the principal means of getting from one page to another and back again. Begin by assigning hyperlinks for that purpose:

1. If it isn't already loaded, start the FrontPage Explorer. In the FrontPage Explorer, open the Fantasy Travel web that you created in Chapter 5, and then open the three pages, one after the other, in the FrontPage Editor.

2. In the FrontPage Editor display the Home page, and then scroll the page so you can see the Available Travel Options.

3. Drag across the word "CRUISES" in the second line to select that word. You'll make this word a link to the Second Level page displaying a list of cruises.

4. Click on the Create or Edit Hyperlink button in the toolbar. Alternatively, you can choose Hyperlink from the Edit menu. In either case the Create Hyperlink dialog box will open. If it is not already selected, click on the Open Pages tab to display it, as you can see in Figure 7-1.

5. The Second Level page is the one that you want to link to, so double-click on it. The Create Hyperlink dialog box will close. When you return to the Home page, you'll see that the word "CRUISES" has changed. If you move the highlight off it, you'll see that it has changed color and is underlined (unless someone changed your FrontPage Editor defaults in the Page Properties dialog box) like this:

```
1. AIR TRAVEL: Domestic, Canada,
2. CRUISES: Alaska, Panama Canal,
3. TOURS: Domestic, Canada, Europ
```

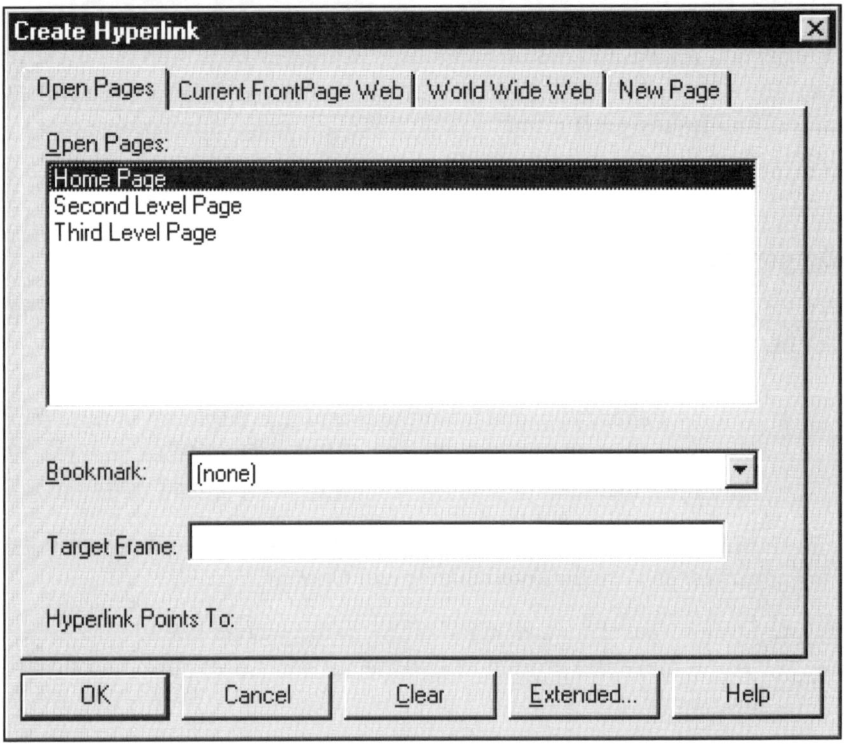

Create Hyperlink   ☒

| Open Pages | Current FrontPage Web | World Wide Web | New Page |

Open Pages:

| Home Page |
| Second Level Page |
| Third Level Page |

Bookmark: [(none)]   ▼

Target Frame:

Hyperlink Points To:

| OK | Cancel | Clear | Extended... | Help |

The Create
Hyperlink
dialog box

FIGURE 7-1

6. Right-click on CRUISES and choose Hyperlink Properties to again open the hyperlink dialog box, now called Edit Hyperlink. Click on the Current FrontPage Web tab, and you'll see that the page name second.htm has been assigned to this link. Click on Cancel to close the dialog box.

7. Click on Save in the toolbar to save the Home page.

8. Right-click on CRUISES again and choose Follow Hyperlink to see where it will take you. You should end up on the Second Level page. (If you didn't, you somehow did not select the correct page in step 5.)

NOTE: *When you choose a page as a link, you are not taken to any particular part of the page. The page is just opened. If you are opening the page for the first time in a session, then you'll be taken to the top of the page. If you have previously opened the page in the current session and scrolled down it, then when you return, you'll be taken to wherever you scrolled. This may or may not be what you want. You can control where you go on a page through bookmarks, which are discussed in "Establishing Bookmarks" later in this chapter.*

Activating a Navbar

Once you are on the second page, you need a way to return to the Home page (ignore for the moment that there is a Back button and a Window menu). To do that, activate the navbar at the top of the page with these steps:

1. Drag across the word "Home" in the navbar, and click on the Create Or Edit Hyperlink button in the toolbar. (From now on this will just be called the "Link" button.)

2. Double-click on Home Page to establish that as the destination of the link.

3. Since you'll copy the navbar to other pages, drag across Cruises in the navbar, and click on the Link button again. FrontPage won't allow you to use the same technique you used with the Home page to select the page you're on.

4. Click on the CurrentFrontPage Web tab, click on Browse, and then double-click on second.htm to establish that as the destination of the Cruises link. Click on OK to close the dialog box. Since you have not established pages for the other elements of the navbar, Home and Cruises are the only two you can activate at this time, and your navbar should look like this:

> *FANTASY TRAVEL* ↵
>
> **Contact Julie Bergan at 555-1234 (julieb) or John Donald**
>
> | **Home** | **Air Travel** | **Cruises** | **Tours** | **Hotels** | **Auto** | **Rail** |

Establishing Bookmarks

Since some web pages can be quite long and you may want to direct exactly where on a page a link will take the user, you need to identify a spot on a page where a link will end up. This is done with the use of bookmarks. *Bookmarks* are objects (text or graphics) that have been selected as destinations for a link. Follow these steps to create a bookmark:

 TIP: *You must identify the bookmark before you establish the link, unless you want to go back and edit the link after it is established.*

1. While still on the Second Level page, drag across the heading "ALASKA" just under the graphic of a cruise ship.

2. Open the Edit menu and choose Bookmark. The Bookmark dialog box will open, as shown here:

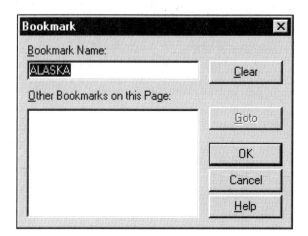

3. Click on OK to make the word "ALASKA" a bookmark. You'll see a dashed line appear under "ALASKA."

4. Drag across the heading "SOUTH PACIFIC," open the Edit menu, choose Bookmark, and click on OK in the Bookmark dialog box. A dashed line will appear under the selected words.

Selecting the bookmarks is only half the procedure; you must also establish the links to the bookmarks. Before going back to the Home page to do that, establish the link to the Third Level page.

Linking to the Third Level Page

The Third Level page is a detailed description of one South Pacific cruise listed on the Second Level page. Therefore, set the line that lists the cruise as the link to the page that describes it, using these steps:

1. With the Second Level page displayed, scroll the page so you can see the list of cruises under the South Pacific heading.

2. Drag across the line that begins "Princess Cruises, Pacific Princess."

3. Click on the Link button in the toolbar to open the Create Hyperlink dialog box, and then double-click on Third Level Page. Your Second Level page with the activated navbar, the two bookmarks, and the link to the third page should look like Figure 7-2.

4. You need to copy the navbar to the Third Level page, so before trying the new link, select the navbar, right-click on it, and choose Copy to copy it to the Clipboard.

5. Click on Save in the toolbar to save the second page.

6. Right-click on the Princess Cruises link you established in step 3 and choose Follow Hyperlink. Your Third Level page should open.

7. Select the navbar on the third page, and click on the Paste button in the toolbar. The navbar with the links will replace the original one, as you can see in Figure 7-3.

8. Click on Save in the toolbar to save the third page.

9. Right-click on the word "Home" in the navbar to open the context menu, and choose Follow Hyperlink to return to the Home page.

You have now followed the links you established from the first to the second page, from the second to the third page, and from the third page back to the first. You can see that they provide a good means of navigating a web. Later in the chapter you'll try them out in a browser, where all you'll need to do is click on them.

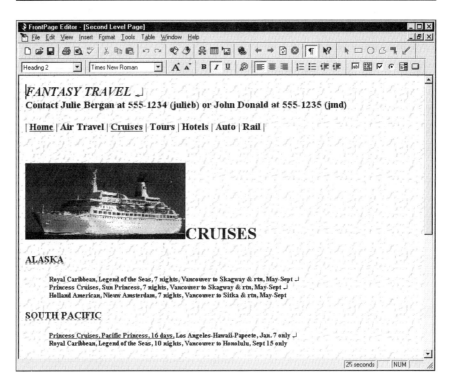

Second
Level page
with links
and
bookmarks

■ **FIGURE 7-2**

Using Bookmarks in Links

On the Home page use the two bookmarks you set to create two detail links within the Cruises travel options:

1. On the Home page, scroll the page so you can see the numbered list of travel options.

2. Drag across the word "Alaska" in the list of cruise destinations, as you can see in the following illustration:

> 1. AIR TRAVEL: Domestic, Canada,
> 2. CRUISES: Alaska Panama Canal,
> 3. TOURS: Domestic, Canada, Europ

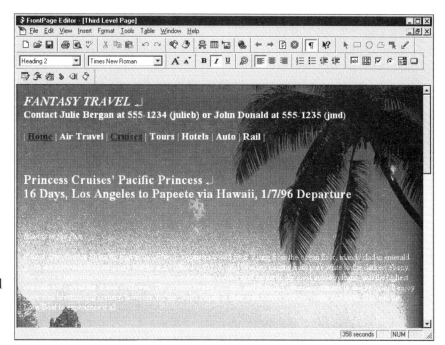

Third Level page with activated navbar

■ **FIGURE 7-3**

3. Click on the Link button in the toolbar to open the Create Hyperlink dialog box.

4. Click on Second Level Page under Open Pages, and then click on the down arrow to the right of the Bookmark drop-down menu. Your two bookmarks will appear, as shown in Figure 7-4.

5. Click on ALASKA to select that bookmark, and then click on OK to close the dialog box and establish the link.

6. Drag across the words "So. Pacific" (in the same lines as the ALASKA you selected in the last step), click on the Link button, select Second Level Page, open the bookmarks, and click on SOUTH PACIFIC. The URL in the bottom of the Create Hyperlink dialog box now includes the bookmark, like this:

Hyperlink Points To: second.htm#SOUTH PACIFIC

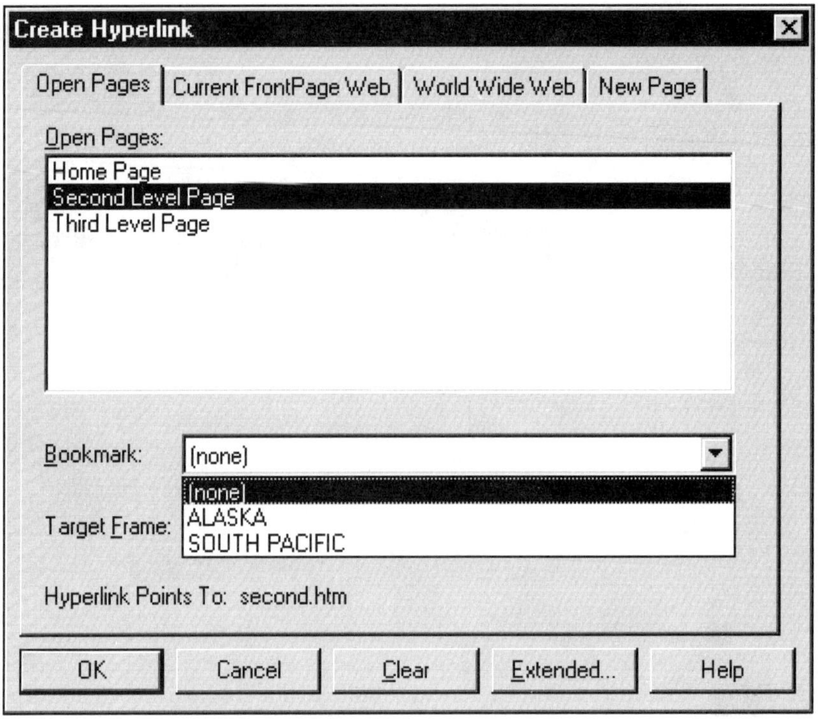

Selecting a
bookmark
to use in a
link

FIGURE 7-4

7. Click on OK to close the dialog box and to set the link.

Setting Links to Other Than Web Sites

All of the links that you have created so far have been to other pages within this single web. Later in this chapter you'll make a link to another web site and web. FrontPage, though, allows you to make a link to other than a web site. The types of links are shown in Table 7-1.

A link to an e-mail address using the mailto link is commonly found in the footer on a web page. This allows the user to easily contact the webmaster or the page's creator by using e-mail. FrontPage will create a mailto link when you enter text that looks like an e-mail address (two text strings, without spaces, separated by the @ character). In the footer for each page in your Fantasy Travel web is the e-mail address webmaster@fantasytravel.com. FrontPage has created the mailto link, as you can with these steps:

Type of Link	How It Is Used
File	To open a file on a local hard disk
Ftp	To download a file on the Internet
Gopher	To perform a Gopher search (based on selections from a series of menus) on the Internet
Http	To open another web (this is the default)
Https	To open another web using Secure Sockets Layer (see Chapter 14)
Mailto	To send e-mail
News	To access information on an Internet news server
Telnet	To connect to and remotely use another computer
Wais	To perform a WAIS (wide area information service) search (looking for one or more words in text) on the Internet

Types of
Internet
Links

TABLE 7-1

7

1. Scroll to the bottom of the Home page in the FrontPage Editor, so you can see the copyright and other information in the footer.

2. Right-click on "webmaster@fantasytravel.com," and then select Hyperlink Properties.

3. On the World Wide Web tab, shown in Figure 7-5, you can see that the URL for the hyperlink is "mailto:webmaster@fantasytravel.com."

4. Click on the down arrow in the Hyperlink Type drop-down menu to see the list of hyperlink types. To create a hyperlink, you select the link type and then enter the URL that is the target of the link.

5. Click on OK to close the Edit Hyperlink dialog box, and then click on the Save button in the toolbar to save the Home page.

You now have a number of links, so it is time to see if they work.

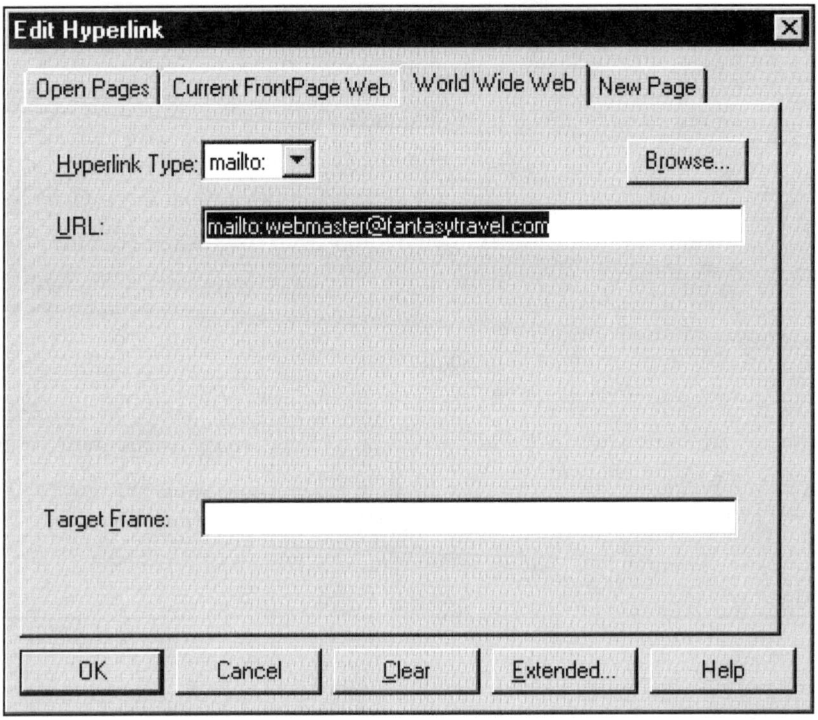

Mailto
hyperlink
in Edit
Hyperlink
dialog box

FIGURE 7-5

Testing Your Links in a Browser

The only way to know if your links are really working is to try them in a browser:

1. If you didn't save each of the three pages in the preceding steps, do that now.

2. Your Home page should still be displayed in the FrontPage Editor. Select Preview In Browser from the File menu.

3. If your web browser is already open, you can enter the address or URL for your Fantasy Travel web in the address text box. The address should be in the form *servername/webname/.* In the FrontPage Editor you can find this in the Page Properties dialog box for any page in a web (right-click on the page and choose Page Properties). In the FrontPage Explorer it's in the Properties dialog box (right-click on the page and choose Properties). For example, here is the URL for the Home page in its Page Properties dialog box opened from the FrontPage Editor:

| Location: | http://marty/FantasyTravel/Default.htm |
| Title: | Home Page |

 NOTE: *If you include a page filename in the URL when you open a browser, you will open that page, which may not be the home page. You do not need to include the page filename if you want to open a home page.*

 TIP: *You can drag across the URL in the FrontPage Page Properties dialog box, press CTRL-C to copy it to the clipboard, open a browser, click in the address box, and press CTRL-V to paste the URL there.*

4. If you have previously opened the Fantasy Travel web in your browser, click on the Refresh button in the browser's toolbar to make sure you are using the latest files.

5. Scroll down the page until you can see the Available Travel Options. Move the mouse pointer until it is over the word "CRUISES." The mouse pointer will turn into a pointing hand, and the URL for the second page will be shown in the status bar at the bottom of the window, as you can see in Figure 7-6.

6. Click once on CRUISES and your second page will be displayed. Your first hyperlink has now opened the Second Level page.

7. Click on Home in the navbar. Your Home page should again be displayed.

8. If you are not already there, scroll down so you can see the Available Travel Options, and then click on So. Pacific. The South Pacific heading will be positioned at the top of the window, as shown in Figure 7-7.

9. Click on the line beginning "Princess Cruises, Pacific Princess." The Third Level page will open.

10. Click on Cruises in the navbar, and you'll be returned to the Second Level page. Notice how the page is positioned where you left it.

11. Scroll up to the navbar and click on Home. When the Home page opens, it will be positioned where you last left it.

7

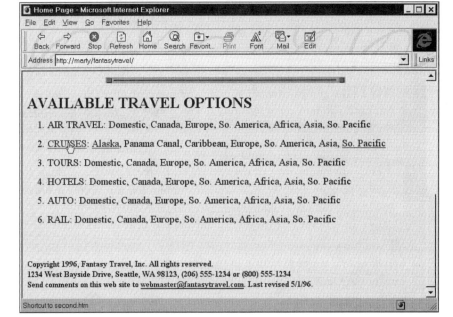

When the mouse pointer is over a hyperlink, its URL is displayed in the status bar

FIGURE 7-6

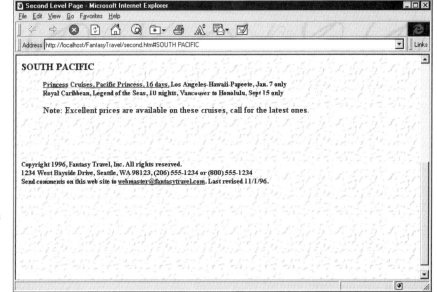

A bookmark in a link will position the bookmark at the top of the window

FIGURE 7-7

12. Scroll to the bottom of the Home page, and click on the webmaster address. Your e-mail system should start and display a new message window with the webmaster address in the To text box, as you can see in Figure 7-8.

13. Close down your e-mail system without trying to send a message, and then close your browser and return to the FrontPage Editor.

All of your links should have worked, providing an excellent navigation system around your web. If you find that a link did not work, right-click on it, click on Hyperlink Properties to open the Edit Hyperlink dialog box, and correct where the link is pointing.

Assigning Hyperlinks to a Graphic

Although text makes for good links, graphics have even greater possibilities. You can assign a single link to a graphic, or you can divide a graphic into sections and make each section a separate link. All of the concepts that you learned about with text links also apply to graphics. You can have links to the existing web, both with and without bookmarks. You can have external links to web sites as well as to other

7

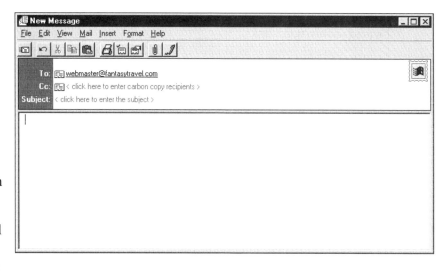

Clicking on a mailto link starts your e-mail system

FIGURE 7-8

types of Internet sites. You can make either a single graphic that has been divided or multiple graphics into a navbar. You can test graphic links in your browser.

Making a Graphic a Single Link

Making a graphic a single link is very much like what you did with a piece of text. To do this for a graphic:

1. In the FrontPage Editor, open the Second Level page. Scroll the page down, if necessary, so you can see the picture of the ship.

2. Click on the picture so it is selected with little boxes in the four corners and the middle of each side, like this:

3. Click on the Link button in the toolbar to open the Create Hyperlink dialog box, and then double-click on Third Level Page to establish that as the destination of the link.

Now when you move the mouse pointer over the graphic, you'll see "third.htm," the address for the third page, in the status bar.

Linking a Graphic to an External Web

Linking a graphic or text to an external web requires nothing more than specifying the external web's URL in the link:

1. Scroll the Second Level page down so the insertion point is on the blank line just above the footer.

2. Insert a horizontal line (you can use the FrontPage Editor–created line from the Insert menu, as is done here, or you can place a graphics line).

3. If a blank line appears above the horizontal line, delete it. If necessary, add a blank line below the horizontal line.

4. On the next line, type **OUTSIDE SOURCES**, format it as a Heading 2, press ENTER, and type

    Check these additional sources for cruise information:

    Format it as a Heading 4, and press ENTER.

5. Insert two or three small images that can be used for links and center them, as shown in Figure 7-9. (You can use the clip art on the FrontPage CD-ROM for this purpose.)

6. Click on one of your images to select it, and then click on the Link button to open the Create Hyperlink dialog box.

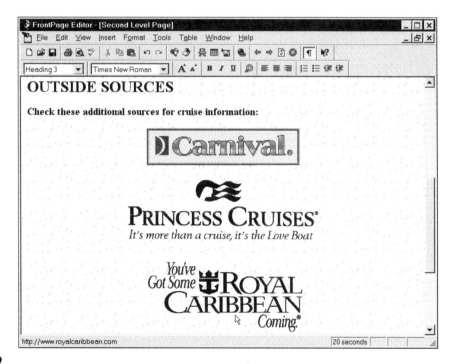

Graphics set up for external links

FIGURE 7-9

7. Click on the World Wide Web tab, make sure that http is chosen as the Hyperlink Type, and then click in the URL text box to the right of the "http://".

8. Type **www.royalcaribbean.com/** and click on OK. You should see the URL in the status bar when you move the mouse pointer over the graphic.

9. Click on Save to save the second page, and answer Yes to All to save all three images.

 TIP: *If you open the World Wide Web site you want to link to in your browser before opening the Create Hyperlink dialog box, the URL will be automatically copied to the URL text box in the Create Hyperlink dialog box.*

Adding Hotspots to Graphics

FrontPage has a feature that allows you to divide a graphic into sections that can be rectangles, circles, or polygons, and to assign each of those sections a different link. Each linked, or clickable, section is called a *hotspot*. When FrontPage generates the actual web that is downloaded by the user, it creates an *image map* of the graphic and all of its hotspots. To create a graphic with hotspots:

1. Open the Home page of the Fantasy Travel web in the FrontPage Editor and, if necessary, scroll down the page until you see the Available Travel Options.

2. Drag across the words "AIR TRAVEL," and click on the Link button in the toolbar.

3. Click on the New Page tab. This will create a new page in the current web and link it to the selected object. A suggested page name is generated out of the link object. Accept that page name, type **air.htm** as the URL, accept the option to immediately edit the new page, and, with your dialog box looking like Figure 7-10, click on OK.

4. The New Page dialog box will open, asking which template or wizard you want to use on the new page. Accept the Normal Page template and click on OK. A blank page will open in the FrontPage Editor.

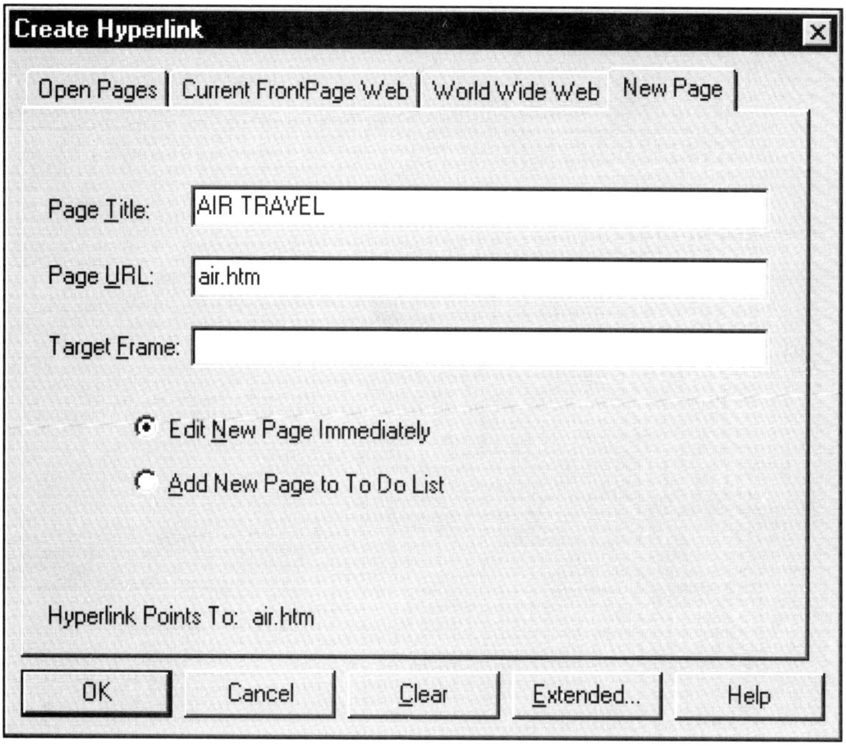

Create Hyperlink

Open Pages | Current FrontPage Web | World Wide Web | New Page |

Page Title: |AIR TRAVEL

Page URL: |air.htm

Target Frame: |

(•) Edit New Page Immediately

( ) Add New Page to To Do List

Hyperlink Points To: air.htm

| OK | Cancel | Clear | Extended... | Help |

Adding a
new page
while
creating a
link

FIGURE 7-10

5. Separately, you can copy the header and footer for the page. For now, enter several blank lines to leave room for the header, and then type

Click on the area of the world for which you want air fares.
(including the period), format it as Heading 3, and then press ENTER.

6. From a clip-art collection, insert a world map on the page and center it, as shown in Figure 7-11.

7. Select your world map and then use the tools in the upper right of the toolbar to draw the hotspots on the map. For example, select the Rectangle tool and draw a rectangle around the United States. When you

complete the rectangle and release the mouse button, the Create Hyperlink dialog box will open. You have all the normal choices for a new link including an existing page, with or without a bookmark, any other site on the Internet, or a new page.

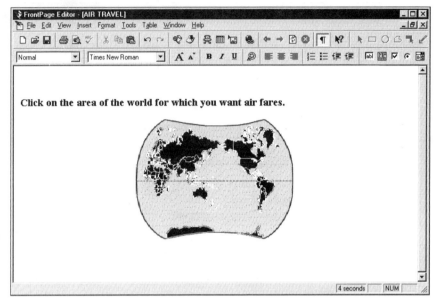

A new page
created
with a
world map

■ **FIGURE 7-11**

8. When you have completed drawing the shapes you want over the various
areas of your map, you'll see all of the shapes on your map. The shapes
will not be visible in a browser. When you move the mouse pointer over
one of the areas, you'll see the URL in the status bar, as you can see here:

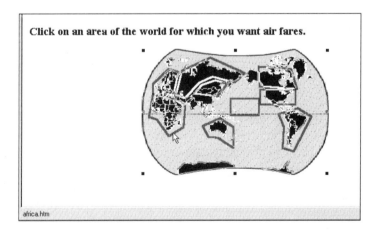

9. Right-click on an area of the map that you have not drawn a hotspot over, choose Image Properties, and in the Default Hyperlink section's Location text box, enter the link that you want used if someone clicks outside of a hotspot, like this:

10. To see the hotspots uncluttered by the map, click on the Highlight Hotspots button. The map will disappear, leaving only the shapes you drew, as you can see here:

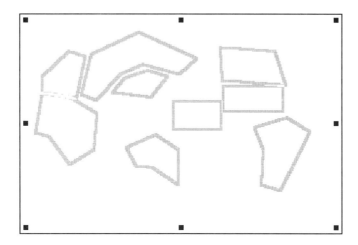

11. Turn off Highlight Hotspots, save your new Air Travel page, save the associated image, return to your Home page, and save it.

NOTE: *An image map may be processed either on the client's computer by encoding the URL for each hotspot into the image map, or on the server, by using the FrontPage Server Extensions. This decision applies to an entire web, affecting all of the image maps it contains. While the web is open in the FrontPage Explorer, open the Tools menu, choose Web Settings, click on the Advanced tab, and make sure that Generate Client-Side Image Maps is checked (it's the default) to have the image maps self-contained in the web.*

Testing Your Graphic Links in a Browser

Once again it is prudent to open your browser and see how your links are working:

1. Open your browser with the Fantasy Travel Home page displayed, and click on the Refresh button in the toolbar to make sure you are looking at the most recent copy of your web.

2. Scroll down the Home page until you can see Available Travel Options, and then click on AIR TRAVEL. Your new Air Travel page will open and display the map you placed there.

3. Move the mouse pointer around the map to see the various hotspots you created and their URLs in the status bar. Click on several to see that they work, and then use Back to return to the Home page.

4. Click on CRUISES to open the second page, click on the image of the ship, and your third page should open (click on Refresh if this doesn't work).

5. Click on Cruises in the navbar to return to the second page.

6. Scroll down the page until you can see the two or three graphics you added, one of which you assigned a link to an external web.

7. If you are connected to the Internet and entered the Royal Caribbean URL, click on it, and the Royal Caribbean web will open as you can see in Figure 7-12. You have been transported out of your web and to the Royal Caribbean web in Miami, Florida.

8. Close your browser. If you have any problems, edit the links to see what the trouble is. When all your links are working, close the FrontPage Editor and return to the FrontPage Explorer.

Managing Hyperlinks

The Fantasy Travel web displayed in your FrontPage Explorer now looks much different than it did when you started this chapter. All of your links are now displayed, as you can see in Figure 7-13. As a result, the FrontPage Explorer becomes an

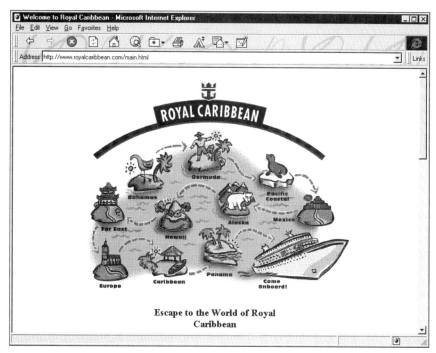

Royal
Caribbean
external
web
opened
from the
Fantasy
Travel web

FIGURE 7-12

7

excellent tool for managing your links. Besides the obvious visual checking that you can do in FrontPage Explorer, it also has two commands in the Tools menu that help you in link management: Verify Links makes sure that each of the links in fact leads somewhere, and Recalculate Links updates the display of all links as well as the server databases used by the Include and Search bots. To check out your links:

1. In the FrontPage Explorer, open the Tools menu and click on Verify Hyperlinks. Each of your internal links is checked and flagged if broken. Your external links also are listed in the Verify Hyperlinks dialog box, as shown in Figure 7-14.

2. Click on Verify and your external links will be checked. (If you are not currently connected to the Internet, this link will also register as broken.)

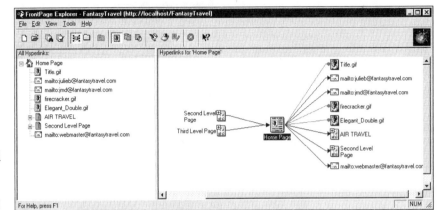

FrontPage
Explorer
showing all
the links
that have
been added

■ **FIGURE 7-13**

3. Select a broken link and click on Edit Link. The Edit Link dialog box will open, as shown next, allowing you to replace the current link with a new one. You can change all pages with this link, or only selected ones.

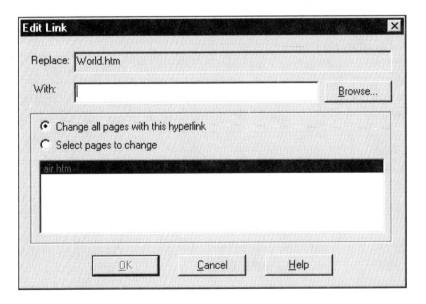

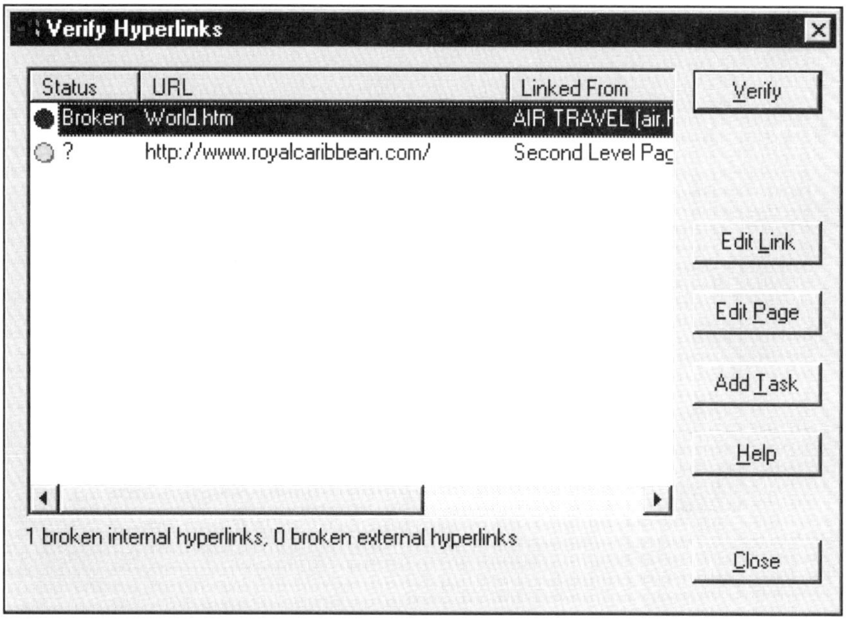

Verify
Hyperlinks
dialog box
listing the
broken and
external
links

FIGURE 7-14

4. Close both the Edit Link and Verify Hyperlinks dialog boxes.

5. Select Recalculate Links from the FrontPage Explorer Tools menu. You are given a warning that the process runs on the web server and will take several minutes. Click on Yes to proceed. If you are using the FrontPage Personal Web Server, your Web Server task on the taskbar will indicate that it is busy for a few seconds; if you are using the Microsoft Personal Web Server, messages about updating the hyperlinks will appear in the Explorer's status bar, and then your web will be redisplayed in the FrontPage Explorer.

 NOTE: *When you have broken a link, the icon for the linked page is broken in the Link view of the FrontPage Explorer, like this:*

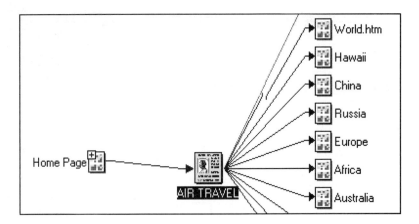

You have seen in this chapter how easy it is to establish links in FrontPage both with text and with graphics, both within a web and externally, and how you can manage those links with some powerful commands in the FrontPage Explorer. Go on now and look at the great tools FrontPage provides to add tables and frames to your webs.

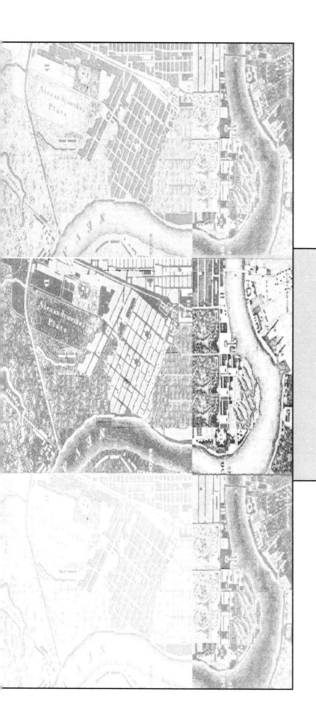

Using Tables and Frames

S o far in this book, you have used the full width of a web page for placing all text and graphics. Good layout designs can be accomplished this way, but it does not allow for text or graphics to be placed in independent columns, and the only way to align text within a line (other than at the ends) is to add spaces with the Formatted paragraph style. FrontPage has two features that allow you to break up some or all of a page into sections that can contain text or graphics. These two features are tables and frames.

Designing with Tables

Tables allow you to divide a portion of a page into rows and columns that create *cells* by their intersection. Tables can be used to systematically arrange information in rows and columns, or they can be used to simply lay out text and graphics on a page. In web design, tables are probably the most important tool for creative page layout. Just a few of the ways that you can use tables are as follows:

- Tabular data display, with and without cell borders

- Side-by-side columns of text

- Aligning labels and boxes for forms

- Text on one side, graphics on the other

- Placing borders around text or graphics

- Placing graphics on both sides of text or vice versa

- Wrapping text around a graphic

When you create a table, you can determine the number of rows and columns in the table, the horizontal percentage of a page that will be used by the table, the percentage of the table's width in each column, and whether the table has a caption. After a table has been created, you can add or remove rows and/or columns, you can combine adjacent cells, and you can add to or remove from a cell or groups of cells any formatting available to the table's contents. Within the percentage limits set for the table and column, a cell will automatically expand both horizontally and vertically to contain the information placed in it.

TIP: *Although you can create a table based on a percentage of the screen, with columns as a percentage of the table, there are often problems getting the table to display the way you want to. If you use fixed pixel widths based on the minimum 640×480 screen, you'll be able to create a more consistent look.*

Displaying Tabular Data in a Table

The classic table, such as you might create in a spreadsheet application, segments text into rows and columns. To build such a table:

1. If it's not already loaded, start the FrontPage Explorer.

2. In the FrontPage Explorer, select Create A New FrontPage Web From A Wizard Or Template in the Getting Started With FrontPage dialog box and click on OK, or open the File menu and choose New FrontPage Web. Click on OK to accept the Normal Web template. Type **Wine** for the Name of New FrontPage Web, and click on OK.

3. Double-click on the Home Page in the right pane to open the FrontPage Editor.

4. Press ENTER to move down the page and leave room at the top.

5. Choose Insert Table from the Table menu. The Insert Table dialog box will open, as shown in Figure 8-1. These are the default values. If your dialog box has different values in it, change them to match the values here; click on OK, select the resulting table from the table menu and delete it; and then reopen the Insert Table dialog box.

6. In the dialog box, take a look at the options available when you create a table; they are described in Table 8-1. Then click on Cancel.

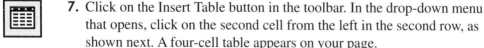

7. Click on the Insert Table button in the toolbar. In the drop-down menu that opens, click on the second cell from the left in the second row, as shown next. A four-cell table appears on your page.

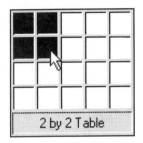

The Insert Table button on the toolbar offers a quick method for creating a table using the defaults, while the Insert Table option in the Table menu allows you to set the properties for the table when it is created.

Insert Table
dialog box

■ **FIGURE 8-1**

TIP: *You can create a table with more rows or columns than shown in the Insert Table drop-down menu by dragging past the edge of the menu. The box will expand to display the number of rows and/or columns you select.*

Option	Description
Rows	Specifies the number of rows in the table.
Columns	Specifies the number of columns in the table.
Alignment	Aligns the table on the left, center, or right of the page. Default alignment is the same as left alignment. The paragraph alignment buttons on the Formatting toolbar affect the content of a cell, but not the table itself.
Border Size	Sets the number of pixels in the border. A 0 pixel border will not appear in a browser, but you'll see a dotted line in the FrontPage Editor when the Paragraph button in the toolbar is enabled. The default is 0.
Cell Padding	Sets the number of pixels between the inside edges of a cell and the cell contents on all four sides. The default is 1.
Cell Spacing	Sets the number of pixels between adjacent cells. The default is 2.
Width	Sets the width to be a fixed number of pixels or a percentage of the window size, if Specify Width is selected. Otherwise, the table width is the sum of the cells, which are individually sized to contain their contents within the size of the window. If the percentage method is selected, each cell is given an equal percentage of the table.

Table
Properties

TABLE 8-1

8

Working with Table Properties

Table properties affect all of the cells in a table and establish how the overall table will look. To see that for yourself:

1. In the new table that was just created, type **1** in the upper-left cell, press TAB to move to the cell on the right, and type

   This is a longer statement

   Press TAB again to move to the left cell in the second row, type **2**, press TAB once more, and type

   This is a statement

   Your table should look like the one shown next. Each column in the table is as wide as the cell in that column with the longest content.

1	This is a longer statement
2	This is a statement

2. Press RIGHT ARROW to move out of the table, and then press ENTER to leave a blank line.

TIP: *Pressing TAB in the last cell of a table will insert a new row at the bottom of the table.*

3. Choose Insert Table in the Table menu, click on Specify Width at the bottom of the dialog box to select it, and then click on OK. A second, much larger table appears.

4. Type **1**, press TAB, and type

   This is a longer statement

   The table takes up almost 100 percent of the window's width, and the two cells split that width, as shown in Figure 8-2.

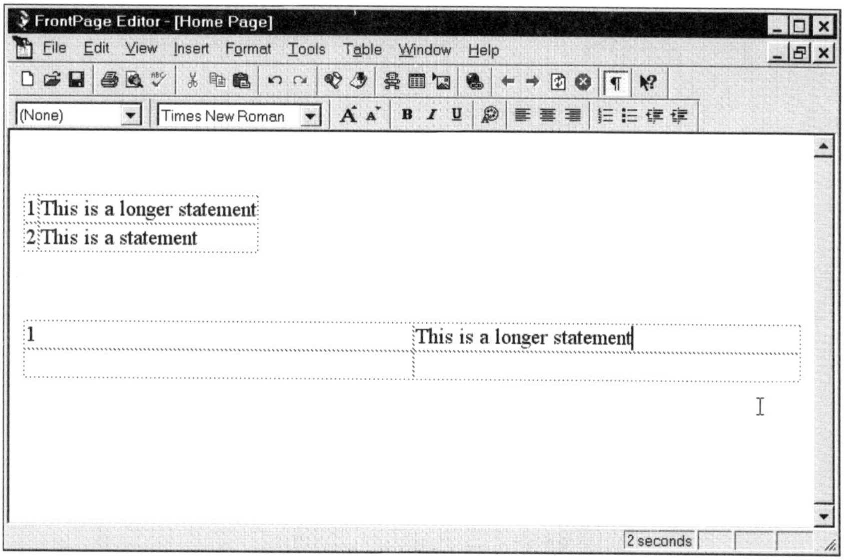

Tables with
and without
a specified
width

FIGURE 8-2

5. Right-click in the first table to open the context menu shown here. You
can see that it has both Table and Cell Properties options. Choose Table
Properties, opening the dialog box shown in Figure 8-3. Like the dialog
box opened with the Insert Table option in the Table menu it allows you to
set the table's Alignment, Border Size, Cell Padding, and Cell Spacing.
You can also choose a background image or color for the table, and colors
for the table's border. It does not allow you to specify the number of rows
and columns.

8

Table Properties ☒

Layout
Alignment: (default) ▼
Border Size: 0 ⬍
Cell Padding: 1 ⬍
Cell Spacing: 2 ⬍

Minimum Width
☐ Specify Width: 100
○ in Pixels
◉ in Percent

OK
Cancel
Apply
Extended...
Help

Custom Background
☐ Use Background Image
[   ] Browse...   Properties...
Background Color: ■ Default ▼

Custom Colors
Border: ■ Default ▼
Light Border: ■ Default ▼
Dark Border: ■ Default ▼

Table
Properties
dialog box

FIGURE 8-3

NOTE: *If you turn off the Specify Width option in the Table Properties dialog box opened from an existing table, not much happens, either initially or as you enter cell content. You can change and readily see the effect of all the layout options such as Border Size and Cell Padding.*

6. Change Border Size to **5**, Cell Padding to **6**, Cell Spacing to **8,** and click on OK. Your table should look like this:

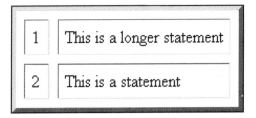

7. Right-click on the upper-right cell in the lower table and select Cell Properties. The Cell Properties dialog box will open, as you can see in Figure 8-4. Take a moment and look at the options it contains. They are described in Table 8-2.

Applying Cell Properties

Cell properties apply to just the one or more selected cells in a table, as shown in the following steps.

NOTE: *If you change the cell width, you should do so for an entire column, and you should make sure that the sum of the cell widths in a row does not exceed 100 percent, or you will get unpredictable results.*

1. In the Cell Properties dialog box, change Horizontal Alignment to Center, Vertical Alignment to Top, and click on OK. You should see the contents of the cell you selected change accordingly.

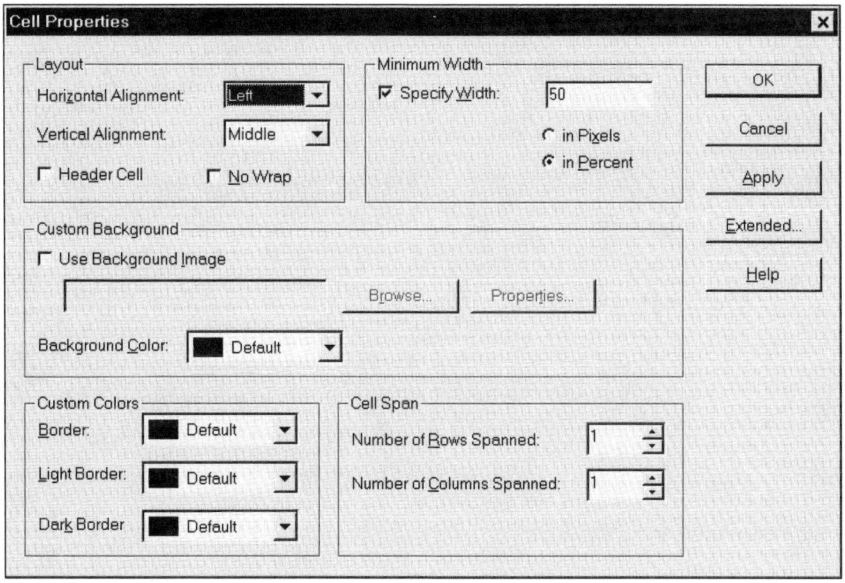

Cell
Properties
dialog box

FIGURE 8-4

Option	Description
Horizontal Alignment	Horizontally aligns the contents of the cell. It can be Left, Center, or Right. Left is the default.
Vertical Alignment	Vertically aligns the contents of the cell. It can be Top, Middle, or Bottom. Middle is the default.
Header Cell	Identifies the cell as the label for a row or column and makes the text in the cell bold. (You can also do this with the paragraph or character formatting options.)
No Wrap	Indicates that the web browser should not wrap the text in the cell; otherwise the text will be wrapped if the browser window is too narrow to display the text.
Minimum Width	Sets the width to be a fixed number of pixels or a percentage of the table size, if Specify Width is selected. Otherwise, the cell width is automatically sized to hold its contents.
Custom Background	Sets the background for a cell. This can be either an image, for which you can browse and set its properties, or a background color.
Custom Colors	Sets the color used for the border, which can consist of one or two colors. Use the Border field to specify a single-color border, and use any two of the three fields to specify a two-color border, which will have a three-dimensional effect.
Cell Span	Joins adjacent cells to make a single larger cell.

Cell Properties

TABLE 8-2

NOTE: *Cell padding and spacing may prevent much movement, especially vertically, in a cell when you change the alignment.*

2. Select the left column of cells in the lower table by pointing on the top border of the table and clicking when the pointer changes to a small arrow pointing downward; open the Cell Properties dialog box, uncheck Specify Width, and click on OK. The width of the first column will collapse, as you can see next. (The top-right cell in this illustration had both its vertical and horizontal alignment changed in step 1.)

TIP: *To select either a row or a column, move the mouse pointer to the outer edge of the table—the left edge for a row, the top edge for a column—until the mouse pointer changes to a heavy arrow, and click. If you drag the heavy arrow, you can select multiple rows or columns.*

8

3. Select the bottom row in the second table, right-click in that row, choose Cell Properties, change the Number Of Columns Spanned to **2**, and click on OK. Your bottom table should look like the table shown next. The leftmost cell does span the two upper cells, but you have an extra cell on the right.

1	This is a longer statement	

4. Press CTRL-Z or choose Undo Edit Properties from the Edit menu to undo step 3. In a moment you'll see another way to do this that is probably more what you want.

5. Select the top row of the second table, open the Cell Properties dialog box, increase the Number Of Rows Spanned to **2**, and click on OK. The top two cells come down and push the bottom two to the right, like this:

1	This is a longer statement	

6. Click on the Undo button in the toolbar, click in the top left cell, open the Cell Properties dialog box, click on Specify Width and In Pixels, type **40** for the width, and click on OK. Both cells in the first column increase, as you can see in the following illustration.

1		This is a longer statement

7. Click on Undo, click in the bottom right cell, and open the Table menu, which is shown here. Look at the options in this menu, which are described in Table 8-3.

Insert Table...
Insert Rows or Columns...
Insert Cell
Insert Caption
Merge Cells
Split Cells...
Select Cell
Select Row
Select Column
Select Table
Caption Properties...
Cell Properties...
Table Properties...

Option	Description
Insert Table	Opens the Insert Table dialog box, where you can select the properties of a table to place at the current insertion point. If the insertion point is in a cell of another table, a second table is placed in that cell.
Insert Rows Or Columns	Opens the Insert Rows Or Columns dialog box, where you can select the number of rows or columns to be inserted above, below, to the left, or to the right of the current selection.
Insert Cell	Inserts a new cell to the left of a selected cell, pushing any cells on the right farther to the right.
Insert Caption	Inserts a blank line, with an insertion point for typing text, immediately above the active table. This line is aligned with and attached to the table. If you select or delete the table, the caption is also selected or deleted. The initial alignment is for the caption to be centered on the table, but it can also be left or right aligned on the table.
Merge Cells	Joins two or more selected cells in a row or column—including an entire row or column—into a single cell that spans the area originally occupied by the cells that were merged.
Split Cells	Opens the Split Cells dialog box, where you can split the selected cell into multiple rows or multiple columns.
Select Cell, Row, Column, or Table	Selects a particular area so that it can be merged, split, or deleted. Use of the Table menu's Select Cell option is the only way to select a cell, so the cell itself, not just its contents, can be copied or cut.
Caption, Cell, or Table Properties	Opens the Caption Properties, Cell Properties, or Table Properties dialog box.

8

Table Menu
Options

TABLE 8-3

TIP: *To select multiple cells not in a row or column, select the first cell by use of the Table menu Select Cell option, and then press and hold SHIFT while clicking on the additional cells.*

Employing the Table Menu Options

Tables is the only FrontPage feature to have its own menu, and well it should. The Table menu provides some important options for working with tables. To see for yourself:

1. In the Table menu, choose Insert Table, accept the existing settings in the Insert Table dialog box, and click on OK. You should now have a 2×2 table in the cell of your original table, as shown here:

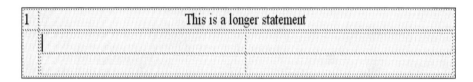

2. Click on Undo and click in the upper-left cell in the same table. Open the Table menu and choose Insert Rows Or Columns. The Insert Rows Or Columns dialog box will open:

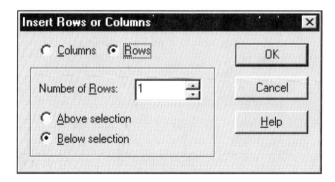

3. Accept the default Rows, 1, and Below Selection options and click on OK. A new row appears in the middle of the table.

4. Reopen the Table menu and again select Insert Rows Or Columns. Click on Columns, Left of selection, and then on OK. A new column appears on the left so that your table now looks like this:

1	This is a longer statement

5. Open the Table menu and choose Insert Cell. A new cell appears in the table, pushing the right cell in the row out to the right. The insertion point also moves to that cell.

6. From the Table menu, choose Select Cell, and then press DEL. The new cell disappears.

 NOTE: *The only way to delete a cell is to first select it in the Table menu and then press DEL.*

7. Choose Insert Caption from the Table menu. An insertion point appears above and centered on the table. Type

This is a Caption

8. Select the bottom row of the second table. Then, from the Table menu, choose Merge Cells. The bottom row now only contains a single cell, as shown next.

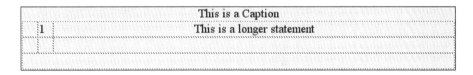

	This is a Caption
1	This is a longer statement

9. Click in the upper-right cell of the second table, and then choose Split Cells in the Table menu. The Split Cells dialog box will open, like this:

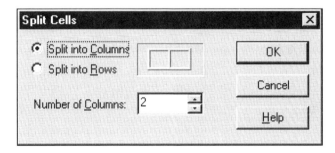

10. Accept the defaults, and click on OK. Your original cell is now split into two.

11. From the Table menu, choose Select Table, and then press DEL. Your table disappears. Click on Undo to bring it back.

 TIP: *Tables can be selected in the Table menu and by double-clicking in the left margin of the page opposite the table.*

Through the above exercises you can see the incredible flexibility in FrontPage's table capability. And it is all WYSIWYG; you instantly see the table you are building very much as it will appear in a browser. Next, build a real table and then look at all three of your tables in a browser.

Building a Tabular Table

This web was called "Wine" earlier in the chapter because you are about to build a table of wines as might be prepared by a winery. To do that:

1. Click below the second table, press ENTER to leave a blank line, and then select Insert Table from the Table menu.

2. Enter **7** rows, **5** columns; choose Center alignment; enter a border size of **2**; a cell padding of **2**; turn off Specify Width if it is selected; and click on OK. In the resulting table, type the following information including the first row headings (the left column is either blank or has one or two asterisks):

	Name	Type	Taste	Year
	Sauvignon Blanc	**Dry white**	**Crisp, balanced**	**1993**
*	**Fumé Blanc**	**Dry white**	**Medium-bodied**	**1993**
**	**La Caille de Fumé**	**Dry white**	**Medium-bodied**	**1992**
	White Riesling	**Medium-sweet white**	**Light, fruity**	**1993**
**	**Merlot**	**Medium-weight red**	**Full-bodied**	**1991**
*	**Cabernet Sauvignon**	**Medium-weight red**	**Full-bodied**	**1990**

TIP: *To get the "é" in Fumé, choose Symbol in the Insert menu, select the "é" character, click on Insert, and then click on Close.*

3. When you are done typing, your table should look like the one shown in Figure 8-5. Look at your table and ask yourself how it can be improved.

4. Right-click on the table and choose Table Properties. Decrease the border size to **1**, increase the cell padding to **4**, and click on OK.

5. Select the top row, right-click on a cell in the first row, open the Cell Properties dialog box, click on Header Cell, and click on OK.

6. From the Table menu, choose Insert Caption. Click on the Bold button and on the Increase Text Size button, both in the Formatting toolbar, and then type

   Fair Mountain Wines Currently Available

7. Select the first row of the table, and then open the Cell Properties dialog box. Select Aqua from the Background Color drop-down menu and click on OK.

8

FrontPage Editor - [Home Page]

File Edit View Insert Format Tools Table Window Help

(None) | Times New Roman

	Name	Type	Taste	Year
	Sauvignon Blanc	Dry white	Crisp, balanced	1993
*	Fumé Blanc	Dry white	Medium-bodied	1993
**	La Caille de Fumé	Dry white	Medium-bodied	1992
	White Riesling	Medium-sweet white	Light, fruity	1993
**	Merlot	Medium-weight red	Full-bodied	1991
*	Cabernet Sauvignon	Medium-weight red	Full-bodied	1990

2 seconds

Wine table before improvements

FIGURE 8-5

8. Select the remaining rows of the table, and then open the Cell Properties dialog box again. Select Yellow from the Background Color drop-down menu and click on OK. When you are done, your table should look like the one in Figure 8-6. You may have further ideas about how to improve the table. Try them out. You can always click on Undo if you don't like a change.

9. Click on the Save button to save the tables you have built. Close your Wine web in both the FrontPage Editor and FrontPage Explorer.

10. Open Microsoft Internet Explorer 3.0 or later, and enter your server name and **wine**. Your three tables should look like Figure 8-7. Close the Internet Explorer when you are done.

11. Open Netscape Navigator 3.0 or later, and enter your server name and **wine**. The tables will look like Figure 8-8. Close the Navigator when you are done.

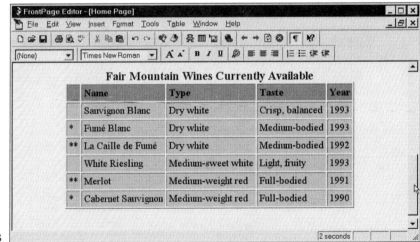

Wine table after improvements

FIGURE 8-6

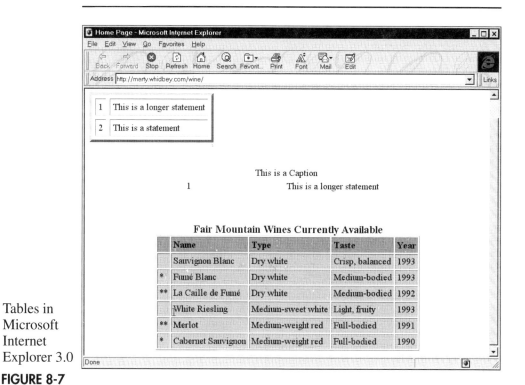

Tables in
Microsoft
Internet
Explorer 3.0

FIGURE 8-7

12. If you have some other browser, like NCSA Mosaic, open it and view
your tables page. The tables in NCSA Mosaic will look like Figure 8-9.
Close your other browser when you are done.

As you can see, there is a considerable difference in how various browsers
display tables—if they even can. You need to decide how these differences affect
you. In the Internet arena, Netscape and Microsoft have the lion's share, with
Netscape's share over twice that of Microsoft.

Using a Table to Enhance a Layout
While tabular tables are the classical way that you think of tables, in web page design,
tables are extensively used to lay out a page. Seldom are you aware that there is a

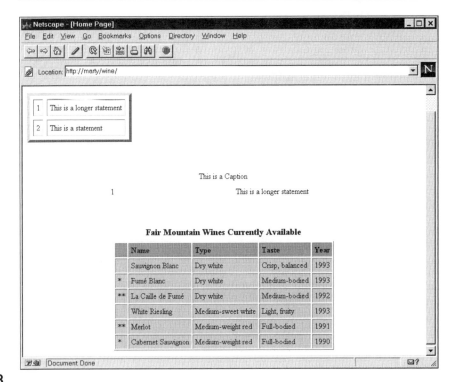

Tables in
Netscape
Navigator
3.0

FIGURE 8-8

table behind the layout. To use the third page of your Fantasy Travel web and look
at some layout ideas:

1. In the FrontPage Editor, open as a file the third page of your Fantasy
   Travel web. You don't have to open the web itself, just the page. If
   you installed FrontPage in the default directories, the page will be at
   C:\WebShare\Wwwroot\FantasyTravel\third.htm.

2. So that you don't affect the original page, resave the page as a file in a
   different directory and name it **New3.htm**.

3. To prepare the page for tables, open the Page Properties dialog box
   (right-click on the page and select Page Properties), turn off the
   Background Image option, set the Text color to Default, and then
   click on OK.

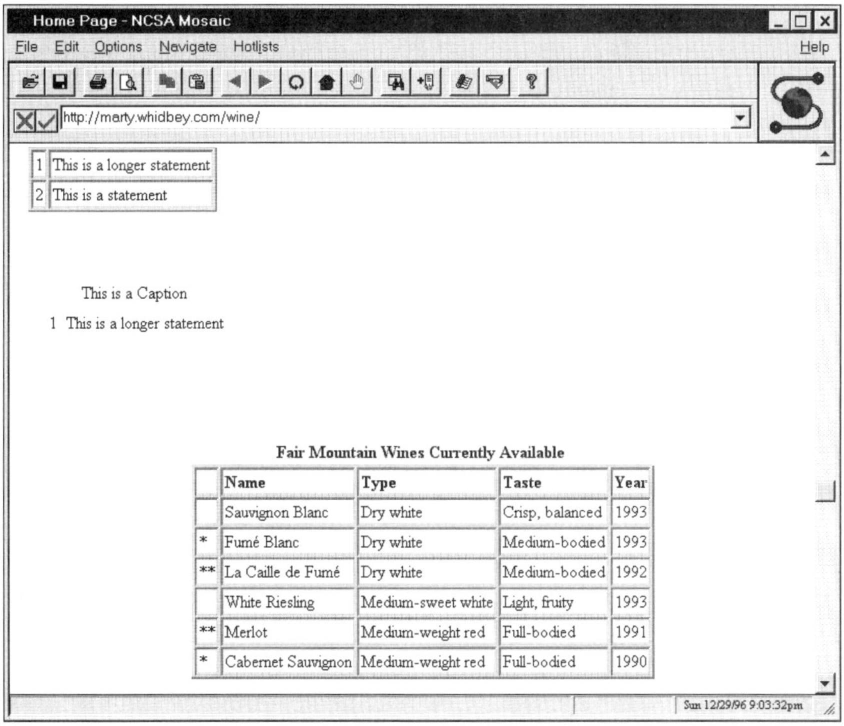

Tables in
NCSA
Mosaic
2.1.1

FIGURE 8-9

4. Click at the top left of the page, open the Table menu, click on Insert Table; change Rows to **1** and Border Size, Cell Padding, and Cell Spacing, all to **0**; check Specify Width and assure that 100 and in Percent is set; and then click on OK.

5. Cut and paste the words "Fantasy Travel" into the left cell (do not include the new-line marker) and the contact information into the right cell. Then drag across the words "Fantasy Travel" and change the font to Size 6 (24 pt), Bold, and Italic.

6. Place the insertion point before the "or" in the contact information, and enter a new line by pressing SHIFT-ENTER. Then select the contact information and click on the Decrease Text Size button in the toolbar.

7. Delete the new line below the table and insert another table of a single row, seven columns, a border of **1**, and select Specify Width 100 percent. Cut and paste the seven navbar entries into the table, and then delete the remaining vertical lines and blank line.

8. Select the row, change the font to Size 4 (14 pt) and Bold, and then change the cell horizontal alignment to Center. When you are done, your title and navbar should look like this:

FANTASY TRAVEL	Contact Julie Bergan at 555-1234 (julieb) ⤶ or John Donald at 555-1235 (jmd)

Home	Air Travel	Cruises	Tours	Hotels	Auto	Rail

9. Move the insertion point down to the blank line below the navbar. Insert a single-cell table (1 row and 1 column), with a border of **3**, a cell padding of **5**, and a width of 100 percent. Cut and paste the two-line title of the cruise into the new table, delete the original line the title was on, and reformat the text in the table to Size 5 (18pt) and Bold.

10. Move the insertion point down to the line below the last table, and insert a fourth table with one row, two columns, a border of **0**, a width of 100 percent, and all the other options at their defaults. Cut and paste the "Islands in the Sun" and its following paragraph into the right cell. The font size is 4 (14pt) and the title line is Bold Italic. Press SHIFT-ENTER after the title line, and delete the resulting blank line.

11. Size a graphic outside of FrontPage in, for example, Microsoft Image Composer, so it fits in about one-third of a page (the graphic used here was about 250×350 pixels). Then place it in the left cell. Adjust the Cell Properties so the horizontal alignment is Center, the vertical alignment is Top, and the specified width is 33 percent. Delete any extra lines between the tables. When you are done, this part of your page should look like Figure 8-10.

12. Save your new third page, and close both the FrontPage Editor and FrontPage Explorer.

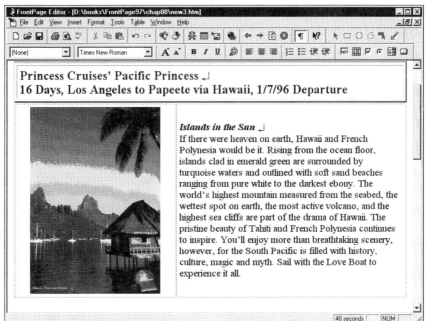

Table used
to separate
text and
graphics

FIGURE 8-10

13. Look at the new third page in different browsers. You'll notice that some of the text may wrap differently—for example, you may find that "Fantasy Travel" is on two lines. Different browsers will also put different spacing between the tables. In Figure 8-11 there is no extra space between the tables. Also look at this at different screen resolutions. By use of percentages everywhere except for the graphic, and with the graphic sized to about one-third of the width of the minimum 640×480 screen, this page should work well in all browsers that handle tables.

TIP: *You can use a new line or a paragraph between tables to increase the space between them.*

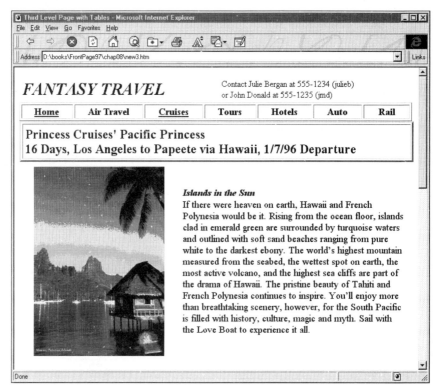

Fantasy
Travel page
3 in a
browser

FIGURE 8-11

You may have some other ideas of how to apply tables to this page. Try them. Play with your ideas until you have the look you want—that is how good designs are created. FrontPage's table capability gives you an extremely powerful tool to create what you want.

Laying Out with Frames

While both frames and tables divide up a page into sections, they do so very differently with very different results. *Tables* are typically a smaller section of a page that has been divided, while *frames* are actually several pages that have each been allocated a section of the viewing window. In FrontPage, frames can only be built by use of the Frames Wizard in the FrontPage Editor. The Frames Wizard establishes a structure of blank pages and the HTML to view them in frames within a single window. This structure of pages along with the HTML is called a *frameset*. Each frame is a full page when you view it in the FrontPage Editor. You do not get a WYSIWYG view of the finished frame, nor is your editing limited to the portion of the page normally viewable in the frame, although frames are scrollable. The only way to view the final result is to open the web in Netscape's Navigator 2.0 or later, or Microsoft's Internet Explorer 3.0 or later.

Explore FrontPage's frames capability by rebuilding the Fantasy Travel home page with frames:

1. In the FrontPage Explorer, create a new web, select the Normal Web template, name it **Frames**, and double-click on the Home Page to open the FrontPage Editor.

2. Select Save As from the File menu. In the Save As dialog box name the page **No Frames** with a filename of noframes.htm and click on OK.

3. In the FrontPage Editor select New in the File menu to open the New Page dialog box, and double-click on Frames Wizard.

4. The Frames Wizard opens and asks you to choose between using a template and creating a custom grid. Accept the default of using a template, and click on Next.

5. The Frames Wizard—Pick Template Layout appears asking you to choose a layout. Look at each of the choices. They offer most of the ways a page can be laid out. When you are ready, select Navigation Bars With Internal Table Of Contents, as shown in Figure 8-12, and then click on Next.

6. You are asked for the alternate page URL to use if your frame page is viewed with a browser that doesn't support frames. This is important, because not all browsers support frames. For this exercise, click on Browse, select noframes.htm (your original blank page you started this web with), click on OK, and then click on Next.

7. Accept the default title, enter **default.htm** as the URL, and click on Finish. The original blank home page appears, giving you no indication that the Frames Wizard did anything. You'll see in a minute that it did.

8. The blank page that you are looking at will be what is seen if a user's browser cannot display frames. Therefore you want this page to display the original Fantasy Travel home page. To copy it here, open the Insert menu, choose File, and select the Fantasy Travel Default.htm page (if you used the default directories when installing FrontPage, the path to this file is C:\WebShare\Wwwroot\FantasyTravel\Default.htm).

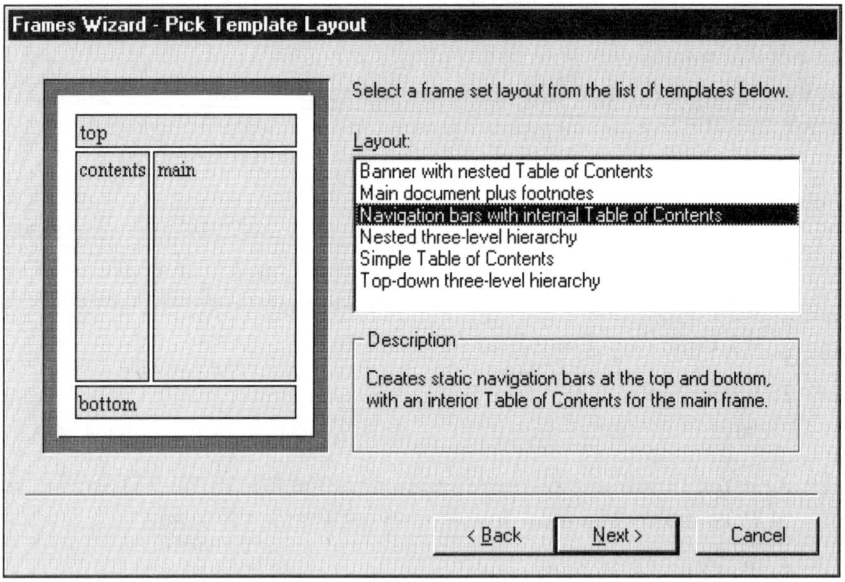

┌───┐
│ **Frames Wizard - Pick Template Layout**   │
│   │
│ ┌──────────────────┐ Select a frame set layout from the   │
│ │ ┌──────────────┐ │ list of templates below.   │
│ │ │ top   │ │   │
│ │ ├──────┬───────┤ │ Layout: │
│ │ │cont- │main   │ │ Banner with nested Table of Contents   │
│ │ │ents │   │ │ Main document plus footnotes   │
│ │ │   │   │ │ Navigation bars with internal Table of │
│ │ │   │   │ │ Contents   │
│ │ │   │   │ │ Nested three-level hierarchy   │
│ │ │   │   │ │ Simple Table of Contents   │
│ │ │   │   │ │ Top-down three-level hierarchy   │
│ │ ├──────┴───────┤ │   │
│ │ │ bottom   │ │ ┌─ Description ──────────────────────┐ │
│ │ └──────────────┘ │ │ Creates static navigation bars at   │ │
│ └──────────────────┘ │ the top and bottom, with an   │ │
│   │ interior Table of Contents for the │ │
│   │ main frame.   │ │
│   └─────────────────────────────────────┘ │
│   │
│   < Back   Next >   Cancel   │
└───┘

Choosing the frame template

FIGURE 8-12

9. Save this page. You will be asked if you want to save the graphics to the current web. Click on Yes To All.

10. Open the FrontPage Explorer. In Hyperlink view, select "Frameset 1" in the left pane to open it in the right pane, as you can see in Figure 8-13. Frameset 1 refers to the four frames in the frame design that was chosen, plus it references the No Frames Page.

11. Double-click on Frameset 1 in the right pane. The FrontPage Editor does not open; rather, the Frames Wizard—Edit Frameset Grid dialog box opens. In this and subsequent dialog boxes, you get a chance to edit all of the characteristics that were automatically applied when the frameset was created.

In this first dialog box you can change the grid you want to use in the frameset. (Each cell in the grid will become a frame.) You can change the overall structure,

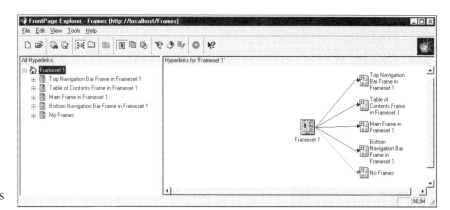

Frameset 1
with its
four frames

FIGURE 8-13

select a particular cell (by holding down SHIFT while clicking on it) and split it, select two cells and merge them, or drag the borders to change the size of any of the cells, as shown in Figure 8-14.

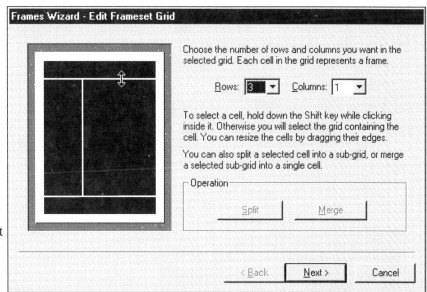

Frames
Wizard—Edit
Frameset
Grid dialog
box

FIGURE 8-14

8

12. Keep the original grid layout and click on Next. The Edit Frame Attributes dialog box, where you can change the names, URLs, and appearance of each frame, will open. Accept the original settings and click on Next.

13. The third dialog box, Choose Alternate Content, allows you to change the URL that is chosen if the user cannot display frames. Click on Next without making a change. Finally, you can change the name and URL of the frameset. Click on Cancel to close the Frames Wizard.

14. Double-click on the Top Navigation Bar Frame in Frameset 1 in the right pane of the FrontPage Explorer. The page representing the Top Navigation Bar Frame will open in the FrontPage Editor. On the page are some comments about how the page and its resulting frame are expected to be used. The most important of these comments is that the *target frame* for this page is the contents frame on the left of the middle section. You can change this target frame in the Page Properties dialog box.

15. The purple (using default colors) comments in the initial Top Navigation Bar Frame page will not be seen in a browser, but the top text in black needs to be replaced. Select it now and press DEL. Then open the Home Page with the original Fantasy Travel home page material in it. Copy the top four lines, down through the contact information, to the new frame page. Add a blank line to separate the title from the comments, and if necessary, delete any blank lines at the top of the page. Your Top Navigation Bar Frame page should now look like Figure 8-15. Save it when it does.

16. Return to the FrontPage Explorer, and open the Table Of Contents Frame in the FrontPage Editor. Note that the target frame for this page is the Main frame. Delete the top three lines on this page, and copy and paste the Available Travel Options from the Home Page to the Table Of Contents Frame page.

17. In the Table Of Contents Frame page, delete the word "Available" and then edit the remainder of the material so that it fits into a narrow column on the left, as shown in Figure 8-16 (very little reformatting is necessary, because the text will wrap to fit the frame width). Save this page when you are done.

Completed
Top
Navigation
Bar Frame
page

FIGURE 8-15

18. In the FrontPage Explorer, open the Main Frame in the FrontPage Editor, and replace the top three lines with the Current Specials information on the Home page. This does not need any editing, so simply save it.

19. As you did with the previous frames, open the Bottom Navigation Bar Frame in the FrontPage Editor, and copy the material at the bottom of Home Page to it. (If the text loses its format, reformat it as Heading 5.) Save this new page. Close the FrontPage Editor, and see what you have.

20. Open a browser that supports frames and bring up *servername*/frames/. After only minor adjustment of the scroll bars, your set of frames should look like those shown in Figure 8-16 (this figure was taken at a screen resolution of 1024×768; at lower resolutions, you'll see less of each of the frames).

21. Considering that you used the frame's default sizing, the result is pretty good. You might want to make the top frame larger and the contents frame narrower. In Netscape Navigator or Internet Explorer you can drag the vertical frame borders to see how it will look, and then go back to the FrontPage Explorer, open the New Frameset Frames Wizard—Edit Frameset Grid as you did earlier, and drag the grid where you want it.

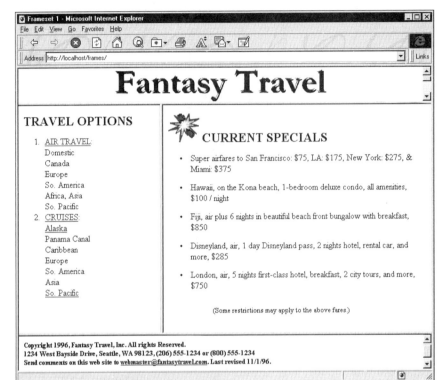

The Fantasy Travel home page using frames

FIGURE 8-16

22. If you have a browser that doesn't support frames (such as NCSA Mosaic 2.1.1 or Internet Explorer 2.0), you can see that the No Frames page will be displayed instead of the Frameset 1 page by opening *servername/* frames/ in the browser.

23. Close your browsers, make any final adjustments to your frameset, save it, and close FrontPage.

TIP: *If you use frames in your web sites, it's a good idea to inform users with browsers that don't support frames that they are missing something. Having a line such as "Your Web browser does not support frames" along with links to Microsoft's Internet Explorer and Netscape's Navigator download sites on your alternate page helps the user get the most from your web site.*

Frames provide some powerful layout capabilities, especially the ability of a frame to scroll and the target frame concept. Based on the default target frames, anything that you open by clicking on a link in the top frame will appear in the contents frame, and contents frame links will appear in the main frame instead of on a separate page. This means that instead of appearing on separate pages as they did in the original Fantasy Travel web, the second and third pages, if they were properly linked, would appear in the main frame on the home page. You would not have to worry about the common title and the common footer on each page.

Tables and frames provide real depth to your ability to create sophisticated, state-of-the-art web pages in FrontPage. And you can do it very easily and, at least with tables, with true WYSIWYG ability to see the final results.

8

FrontPage on the Web

Winnov, Ltd

URL: *http://www.winnov.com*
Webmaster: Robert Scoble
E-mail: *scoble@msn.com*

1150 Kifer Road, Suite 201,
Sunnyvale, CA 94086
(408) 733-9500
(408) 733-5922 (Fax)

Web Site

The Winnov web site is a winner of both the Microsoft Activate the Internet contest
and the Microsoft Great Web Sites Contest. The Home page, shown in Figure 1, uses

Winnov's
Home page

FIGURE 1

FrontPage on the Web (cont.)

a borderless frame to place a navigation column on the left with an ActiveX control that produces a vertical marquee that continuously scrolls accolades for the products. The HTML for the navbar and marquee is shown in Listing 1. In the right frame of the Home page the top rectangular graphic is actually an automated GIF; the right section displays several messages.

Listing 1
tical navbar
nd marquee
HTML

```
<table width="100">
  <tr><td valign="top" rowspan="2" width="150"> <p><center></p>
    <p align="left"><map name="FrontPageMap">
    <area shape="RECT" coords="4, 198, 98, 217" href="contframe.htm">
    <area shape="RECT" coords="2, 179, 98, 202" href="emailf.htm">
    <area shape="RECT" coords="0, 154, 98, 180" href="profilef.htm">
    <area shape="RECT" coords="1, 130, 98, 154" href="supportf.htm">
    <area shape="RECT" coords="2, 105, 98, 130" href="whatsnewf.htm">
    <area shape="RECT" coords="0, 80, 98, 103" href="orderf.htm">
    <area shape="RECT" coords="1, 54, 98, 79" href="applicatf.htm">
    <area shape="RECT" coords="2, 31, 98, 52" href="productsf.htm"></map>
    <a href="win2web/_vti_bin/shtml.exe/navframe.htm/map">
    <img align="bottom" src="images/button.gif" width="99"
    alt="Winnov is the leader in Internet Videoconferencing tools and devices"
    ismap usemap="#FrontPageMap" height="218" border="0"></a></p>
  <object align="LEFT" classid="clsid:1a4da620-6217-11cf-be62-0080c72edd2d"
    width="110" height="350" border="0" hspace="0" id="marquee">
    <param name="ScrollStyleX" value="Circular">
    <param name="ScrollStyleY" value="Circular">
    <param name="szURL" value="marquee.htm">
    <param name="ScrollDelay" value="10">
    <param name="LoopsX" value="-1">
    <param name="LoopsY" value="-1">
    <param name="ScrollPixelsX" value="0">
    <param name="ScrollPixelsY" value="-2">
    <param name="DrawImmediately" value="1">
    <param name="Whitespace" value="0">
```

8

FrontPage on the Web (cont.)

```
        <param name="PageFlippingOn" value="1">
        <param name="Zoom" value="100">
        <param name="WidthOfPage" value="140">
    <img src="images/replace.gif" width="109" height="307"
        alt="If you had Microsoft's browser, this would be cooler.">
        </object></center> </td></tr>
</table>
```

The second page provides a list of products in a table, as you can see in Figure 2. This and all the remaining pages were created using a style sheet, which is shown

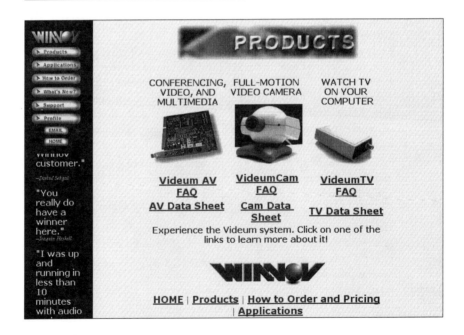

Winnov
product
array

■ FIGURE 2

FrontPage on the Web (cont.)

in Listing 2. The individual product pages, shown in Figure 3, have a secondary navigation bar at the top that is presented in a table.

Listing 2
Style sheet
HTML

```
<style><!--    BODY 7 {font: 9pt Verdana; color: 336699}
   A:link {font: 11pt Verdana;  color: #990000; font-weight:bold}
   A:visited {font: 11pt Verdana; color: #990000; font-weight:bold}
   STRONG {font: 10pt Verdana; color: 003300}
   BIG {font: 10pt Verdana; background: 003300}
   H1 {font: 24pt Verdana; color: 003300}
   EM {font: 14pt Verdana; color: #990000}
   I {font: 11pt Verdana; color: 003366}
   B {font: 16pt Verdana; color: 003300}
   H5 {font: 8pt Verdana; color: 003300}
   H6 {font:8pt Verdana; color:#FFFFFF}--></style>
```

Individual
product
data sheet

FIGURE 3

FrontPage on the Web (cont.)

Webmaster Q & A

WHY FRONTPAGE?   I tried Netscape Gold, Adobe Sitemill, and a few other commercial tools. FrontPage did the most of any of the tools, was among the least expensive, and came from Microsoft, which I knew would be pushing Web-based technology harder than anyone. I wanted to choose a tool that would be powerful in the future, because I had already seen how difficult it was to switch to a different tool. Also, FrontPage felt a lot like Microsoft's Office product, which meant that other users would be able to pick it up very quickly.

LIKES AND DISLIKES   FrontPage allowed me to get the site done without hiring any extra help, and also while working on other things. (I'm not just a webmaster here.) Without FrontPage, I would never have been able to put together and maintain as nice a site as this one is. On the other side, FrontPage 97 actually doesn't push the technology hard enough. There's no cascading style sheet support. It doesn't support borderless frames. It doesn't have a debugger for JavaScript or VBScript. These are all technologies that Microsoft is supporting and pushing with its browser, so I was disappointed at the level of support for these new technologies in FrontPage 97.

NEATEST FEATURES OF THIS SITE   I'm particularly proud of my ActiveX control on the Home page and my borderless frames (which were both added by hand, because FrontPage doesn't really support those two things, but FrontPage97 does give you the ability to manually edit your HTML code).

TIPS   Play with it. Play with it. Play with it. You'll discover all sorts of clever things (like you can drag-and-drop tables directly from Word or Excel, or that when you type an e-mail address, it'll convert it to a link automatically). Also, join one of the Microsoft FrontPage newsgroups; I've gotten a lot of invaluable tips there.

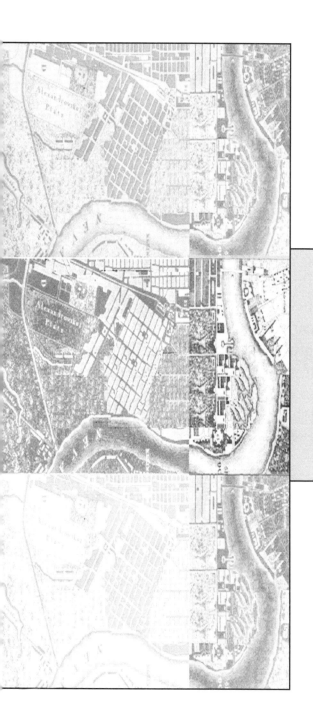

Working with Forms

In Chapters 5 through 8, the focus has been on how to present text and graphic information to users of your web. In this chapter, the tables will be turned—you'll learn how to get information back from users. *Forms* are the obvious mechanism for collecting user input and are the focus of this chapter. *WebBots,* the focus of Chapter 10, also provide means for user input and are instrumental in the use of forms. Both forms and WebBots have classically (meaning "last year," in terms of the Web) required either programming or the use of canned programs on a web server. FrontPage has replaced this with its Server Extensions and WebBots, which save you from any programming or from using canned programs with their arcane HTML calls. FrontPage then goes further by giving you powerful tools to perform these functions in a WYSIWYG environment. See for yourself, starting with using forms.

Using Forms

Forms in a web are very similar to those on paper, as you saw in Chapter 2. You are given boxes to fill in, options to select, and choices to make. The advantages of computer forms over paper forms are that computer forms can be easily modified, you don't have to decipher someone's handwriting, and the data starts out in computer form, so it does not have to be retyped into a computer. As with paper forms, though, the design of a form is very important if you want the user to fill it out willingly and properly. The three cardinal rules of forms are

- Keep it simple
- Keep it short
- Make it very clear what the user is supposed to do

FrontPage provides a comprehensive Form Page Wizard to lead you through the development of a form. In addition, FrontPage has a complete set of tools both in the toolbar and in the Insert menu to allow you to create any form you can dream up. You'll work with both of these in this chapter, beginning with the Form Page Wizard.

Creating Forms with the Form Page Wizard

To create a form, you need to figure out what questions to ask and what fields are necessary for the user to answer them. Go through that process with the idea of creating a questionnaire for prospective project team members. First use the Form Page Wizard to generate the form, then examine and modify the results.

Generating the Form

Like the other wizards you have seen, the Form Page Wizard asks you a series of questions, which it then uses to build a form. To work with the Form Page Wizard:

1. If necessary, start the FrontPage Explorer.

2. In the FrontPage Explorer create a new web based on the Normal Web template and name it **Forms**. When the Home Page appears, double-click on it to open the FrontPage Editor.

3. In the FrontPage Editor choose New from the File menu, select Form Page Wizard, and click on OK. The Form Page Wizard's introductory dialog box will appear telling you about web forms, what the wizard will do, and what you can do with the result. Click on Next after reading this.

4. You are asked for the Page URL or filename and Page Title. Type **project.htm** for the URL and **Project Team Questionnaire** for the Page Title. Click on Next when you are done.

5. The Form Page Wizard dialog box that opens will eventually show the questions that you are asking on your form. Currently it is blank. Click on Add to select the first question.

6. In the next dialog box (shown in Figure 9-1) there is a list of types of questions at the top. Click on Contact Information. As you can see in Figure 9-1, a description of the fields that will be placed on the form appears in the middle of the dialog box, and the actual question is displayed at the bottom, where you can change it as you want. Accept the default and click on Next.

Form Page Wizard ☒

Select the type of input to collect for this question:

contact information ▲
account information
product information
ordering information
personal information ▼

┌─ Description ─────────────────────┐
│ Ask users for their name, affiliation, │
│ addresses and phone numbers. │
└───────────────────────────────────┘

Edit the prompt for this question:

Please provide the following contact information:

[Question 1 of 1]

▐▐▐▐▐▐▐▐▐▐▐▐▐▐▐▐▐

| Cancel | < Back | Next > | Finish |

Choosing the type of questions to be on the form

FIGURE 9-1

7. You are then asked to select the specific fields that you want on the form for your first question (see Figure 9-2). All of these are related to an individual contact. For the Name entry you can use one, two, or three fields. Click on First, Last, which is the two-field choice. Also click on Postal Address and Home Phone, and then click on Next, leaving the suggested name for the group of variables (Contact) as is.

8. You are returned to the list of questions, which now shows the contact information question you just selected. Use steps 5 through 7 to include questions dealing with Account Information and Personal Information, and keep the suggested defaults, except that you don't want to repeat the Name field in Personal Information (do keep Username in Account Information).

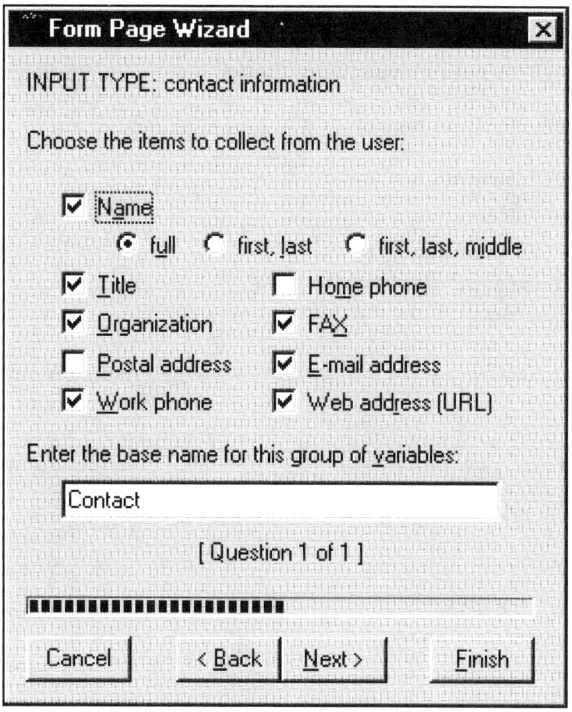

Selecting
the specific
fields to
use for
gathering
contact
information

FIGURE 9-2

NOTE: *After you are done using the Form Page Wizard, you can add to, change, and delete what the wizard has produced.*

9. Click on Add, select the One Of Several Options question, change the prompt to

Choose the city you want to be located in:

click on Next, and enter **New York**, **Dallas**, and **San Francisco** as three separate labels on three lines in the upper list box. Then click on radio buttons, enter the word **Location** as the variable name, and click on Next.

10. Click on Add, select the Any Of Several Options question, change the prompt to

    Select two areas you want to be associated with:

    click on Next, and enter

    Initial design
    Detail plan
    Project management
    Plan implementation
    Evaluation

    on five separate lines. Enter **Preferred areas** as the name for the group, and click on Next.

11. Click on Add, select the Date question, change the prompt to

    Enter the date you are available:

    click on Next, leave the default top date format, enter **Availability** for the variable name, and click on Next.

12. Click on Add, select the Paragraph question, change the prompt to

    Why do you want to be on this project?

    click on Next, enter **Why** as the variable name, and click on Next. When you are done, your list of questions will look like the one in Figure 9-3.

13. Look at your list of questions. Do you want to change any of them or reposition them in the list? While you can change the finished product, it is easier to change it now, before the form is generated. Click on No. 6, the availability date. Click twice on Move Up to move the date ahead of the city question. Click on any question you want to edit and click on Modify. When you are done editing and are returned to the list of questions, click on Next to continue with the form creation.

14. You are asked how the list of questions should be presented. Leave the defaults of: a normal paragraph, no Table Of Contents, and use tables to align form fields; then click on Next.

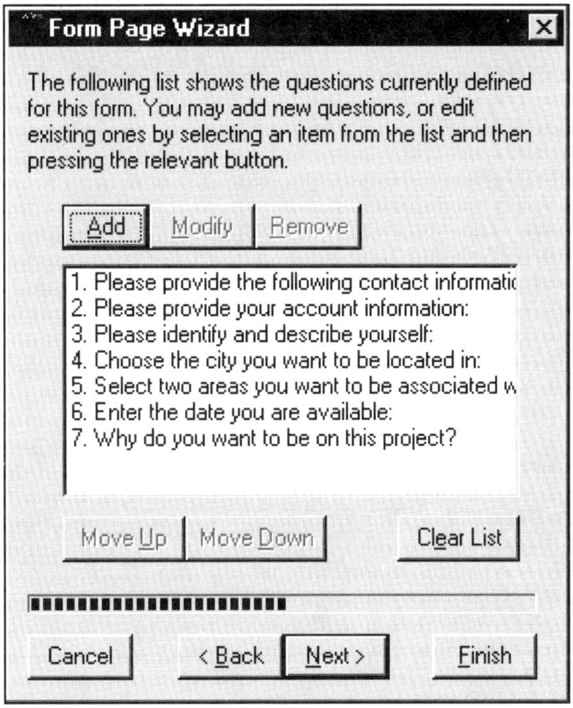

Form Page Wizard ×

The following list shows the questions currently defined for this form. You may add new questions, or edit existing ones by selecting an item from the list and then pressing the relevant button.

[Add] [Modify] [Remove]

1. Please provide the following contact informatic
2. Please provide your account information:
3. Please identify and describe yourself:
4. Choose the city you want to be located in:
5. Select two areas you want to be associated w
6. Enter the date you are available:
7. Why do you want to be on this project?

[Move Up] [Move Down]   [Clear List]

▌▌▌▌▌▌▌▌▌▌▌▌▌▌▌▌▌▌▌▌▌▌▌▌

[Cancel] [< Back] [Next >]   [Finish]

Final list of selected questions

FIGURE 9-3

9

15. You are asked how you want to save the results of the questionnaire. Choose text file, enter the filename of **memans**, click on Next, and then click on Finish to generate the form page, which appears as shown in Figure 9-4. Scroll down the form in the FrontPage Editor to see all the types of form fields created.

16. Save your form either by clicking on Save in the toolbar or opening the File menu and choosing Save, and then clicking on OK to use the Page Title and filename you gave it earlier.

TIP: *If you want to transfer the results of a web form to a database or spreadsheet, it is best to use a text file to collect the information. You can choose a comma-, tab-, or space-delimited file (tab probably being the best), which is fairly easy to import into most products.*

FrontPage Editor - [Project Team Questionnaire]

File Edit View Insert Format Tools Table Window Help

Heading 1 ▼ Times New Roman ▼ A A B I U ▨ ≡ ≡ ≡ ⌸ ⌸ 倖 倖

Project Team Questionnaire

This is an explanation of the purpose of the form ...

Please provide the following contact information:

First name	
Last name	
Title	
Organization	
Street address	
Address (cont.)	
City	
State/Province	
Zip/Postal code	
Country	
Work Phone	
Home Phone	
FAX	
E-mail	
URL	

3 seconds

The form
as
generated
by the
wizard

■ FIGURE 9-4

Forms can be formatted by use of either a table or the Formatted paragraph style. The Formatted style was often used in the past for two reasons: it is the only paragraph style that can display more than one consecutive space, and many browsers did not support tables. Most browsers now support tables, and this is the preferred method for aligning forms. Using tables greatly simplifies aligning the labels and fields in a form and it allows you to use any font.

Reviewing and Editing a Form

As with most documents that you create, you'll want to go through your form in detail and make any necessary changes. In the real world, you would need to replace the introductory paragraph with an explanation of the form. This should tell users how the form will be used and why they should fill it out. In this case you might use something like "This form will be used to qualify prospective members of the Project Team. If you are interested in being a member, please fill out this form."

You can customize many areas of the form. The things that you can do are discussed in the following sections.

CHANGING THE FIELD'S LABEL OR TEXT   Change the label or text on the left of each field by simply typing over or adding to the existing text. This may change the width of the table column. For example, add **& middle** to the first label, and you'll get the column width change shown here:

Please provide the following contact information:	
First & middle name	
Last name	
Title	

Click on Undo to restore your form.

TIP: *If you use the Formatted paragraph style to format your form, changing the label for one field may cause you to adjust other fields to restore the form's alignment. If you use a table to format the form, the realignment will occur automatically.*

CHANGING THE FIELD'S ALIGNMENT   Change the alignment by opening the Cell Properties dialog box for the cell and changing the horizontal or vertical alignment. You can select the entire column to change the alignment for all the labels or fields at one time. If you are using the Formatted paragraph style, you change the alignment by adding or deleting spaces.

CAUTION: *If you use the Formatted style and change the paragraph style on the form fields from Formatted to any other style, you'll lose all the leading spaces that produce the original field alignment. This can easily happen by backspacing up to the first paragraph. If this happens to you, click on Undo to quickly recover.*

DELETING A FIELD   If you want to delete a field and its label, select the table row and press DEL. You can also select either the label or field individually and press DEL. This leaves the table row available for replacing the label or field. Delete an entire section by selecting the question, labels, and fields, and pressing DEL.

CHANGING A FIELD'S PROPERTIES   Right-clicking on a field (not its label) and selecting Form Field Properties opens the field's Properties dialog box, shown next:

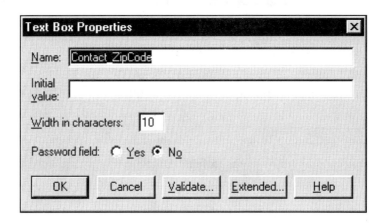

Here you can

- Change the field's name

- Establish an initial value, such as a state abbreviation, if most people filling out a form are from one state

- Determine if the field contains a password so its contents can be encrypted

- Set the width of the text box, which can also be changed by dragging the end of a field, as shown here:

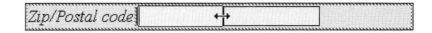

Changing the width of a text box does not affect the maximum number of characters the field can contain. To do that, you use the Form Field Validation dialog box. Right-click on a form field and select Form Field Validation. For a text field the Text Box Validation dialog box shown in Figure 9-5 is displayed. The Max

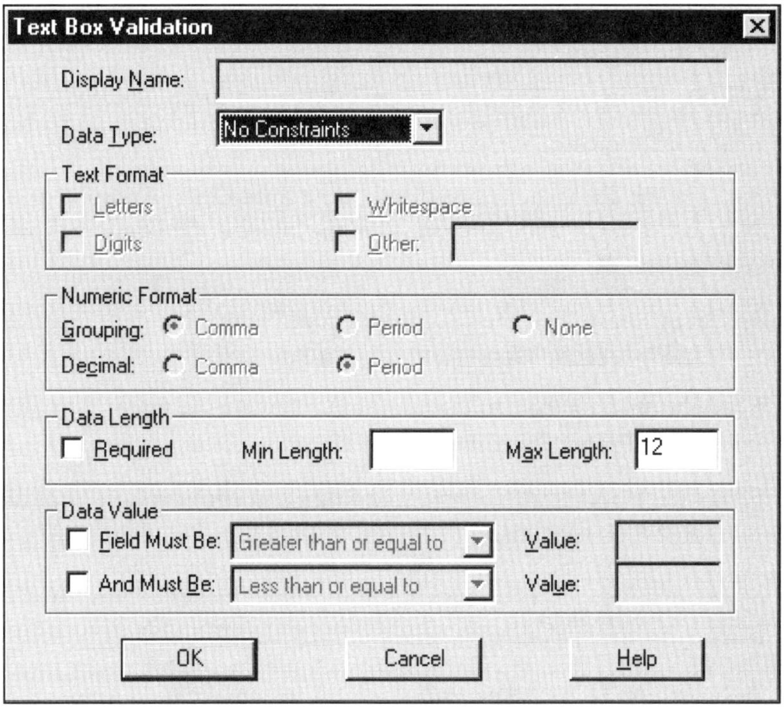

Text Box
Validation
dialog box

FIGURE 9-5

Length text box displays the maximum number of characters the field will accept, regardless of the width of the field. If the maximum length is greater than the width, the text will scroll in the text box until the maximum length is reached. The other options in the Validation dialog box will be covered in the section "Validating a Form." For now, close any open dialog boxes.

> **TIP:**   *Even if you set the field width and maximum length to the same number, all the text might not fit in the text box without scrolling. This is because the width of a character as determined by the HTML is not always the same as a character displayed on the screen. Test your form fields in a browser by entering the maximum number of characters and setting the width accordingly.*

CHANGING THE FIELD'S PLACEMENT   The table created with the Form Page Wizard has two columns, each with one label and one field on each of its lines. You may want to have more than one field on a line, such as the State and Zip fields. To do that, you need to split a single cell into multiple cells, like this:

1. Reduce the width of the State/Province field (not the label) to about a third of its original size by selecting it and dragging the right selection handle to the left.

2. With the cursor in the same cell, select the cell by choosing Select Cell in the Table menu.

3. Open the Table menu again and select Split Cells. Accept the default Split Into Columns, and then enter **3** in the Number Of Columns spinner and click on OK.

4. Cut and paste first the "Zip/Postal code" label, and then separately the "Zip/Postal code" form field into the new cells.

5. Right-click on the cell containing the "Zip/Postal code" label, and open the Cell Properties dialog box.

6. Set the Horizontal Alignment to Right and click on OK. Your form fields should look like this:

State/Province [   ]   Zip/Postal code [   ]

7. Select the vacated row and press DEL to remove it.

VALIDATING A FORM   Fields in a form often need to be limited to specific types of information, such as allowing only numbers (no letters) or requiring that a field not be left blank. Form validation has traditionally been done on the web server by the form handler (*server-side validation*). This has the disadvantage of requiring the form to be sent to the server, validated, and then sent back to the user if the validation fails. Besides the time involved, server-side validation places a greater demand on the web server's resources. If your web site is receiving a large number of hits each day, this can slow down the server. Validating a form before it's sent (*client-side validation*) has the advantages of speeding up the process and placing less demand on the web server.

NOTE: *Client-side validation is performed by the Web browser. FrontPage generates a JavaScript or VBScript script (see Chapter 15) that is run by the browser to validate the form. JavaScript (the default) is supported by both Netscape and Microsoft, while VBScript is supported mainly by Microsoft. Some browsers do not support either scripting language. If the browser being used does not support the scripting language used, the client-side validation is ignored. This is another reason to encourage visitors to your web sites to upgrade to the latest versions of either Netscape Navigator or Microsoft Internet Explorer.*

Validation criteria for one-line and scrolling text boxes are set by use of the Text Box Validation dialog box that you saw in Figure 9-5. The options are explained in Table 9-1.

Radio buttons are validated by use of the Radio Button Validation dialog box, shown next, which allows you to make the field required and to set a display name for error messages.

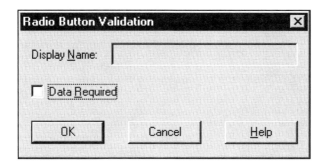

Drop-down menus have an additional validation option: Disallow First Item. When this is selected, the first item in the drop-down menu cannot be chosen. This allows you to place an instruction or comment, rather than an option, as the first item in the drop-down menu.

You can validate all the fields in a form except check boxes and push buttons by right-clicking on them and selecting Form Field Validation. A dialog box is displayed for each form field that fails the validation criteria, such as the dialog box shown here, which was generated by making the First Name field required and then submitting the form with the field left blank. In this case, the Display Name field in the Text Box Validation dialog box was set to "First name." If the

Option	Description
Display Name	Displays this name when an error message is generated. If no name is entered, the contents of the Name field in the form field's Properties dialog box is displayed.
Data Type	Sets the type of data that will be accepted: No Constraints (any characters), Text (alphanumeric characters), Integer (numbers, including "," and "-", without decimals), or Number (numbers with decimal places).
Text Format	Sets the acceptable format for the form field data: Letters, Digits (numbers), Whitespace (spaces, tabs, returns, and new-line characters), and Other. If Other is selected, you type the characters (such as hyphens or commas) that will be accepted in the text box.
Numeric Format	Sets both the Grouping and Decimal numeric punctuation characters. Grouping characters can be Comma (1,234), Period (12.34), or None (1234). Decimal sets the character used as a decimal point: either a comma or a period. You cannot use the same character for both Grouping and Decimal.
Data Length	Sets the acceptable length of the data. Required means that the field cannot be left blank. Min Length and Max Length set the minimum and maximum number of characters that can be entered, respectively.
Data Value	Sets a test for the data entered. The value entered in the Value text box is used for the comparison. You can set two tests for each field: Less than, Greater than, Less than or equal to, Greater than or equal to, Equal to, or Not equal to.

Text Box
Validation
Dialog Box
Options

TABLE 9-1

DisplayName field had been left blank, the error message would have displayed the form field name, "Contact_FirstName."

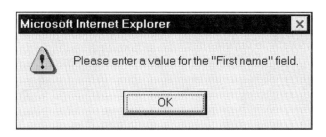

Make the First and Last Name fields required with these steps:

1. Right-click on the First Name form field, and select Form Field Validation from the context menu.

2. In the Text Box Validation dialog box select Required, enter **First name** as the Display Name, and click on OK.

3. Repeat steps 1 and 2 for the Last Name form field, using **Last name** as the Display Name.

CHANGING THE FORM'S PROPERTIES   A *form* is a group of fields enclosed within a dashed border on a page. From the context menu of any field in the form, click on Form Properties to open the Form Properties dialog box shown in Figure 9-6. This allows you to set the following properties.

- The Form Handler, which will return the contents of a form to you. You have a choice of a custom CGI script that you create, an Internet Database Connector, the Discussion or Registration bots for those types of web forms, and the Save Results bot, which is the default (and what you should use most of the time).

- The Form Name.

- The Target Frame in which you want the form to appear.

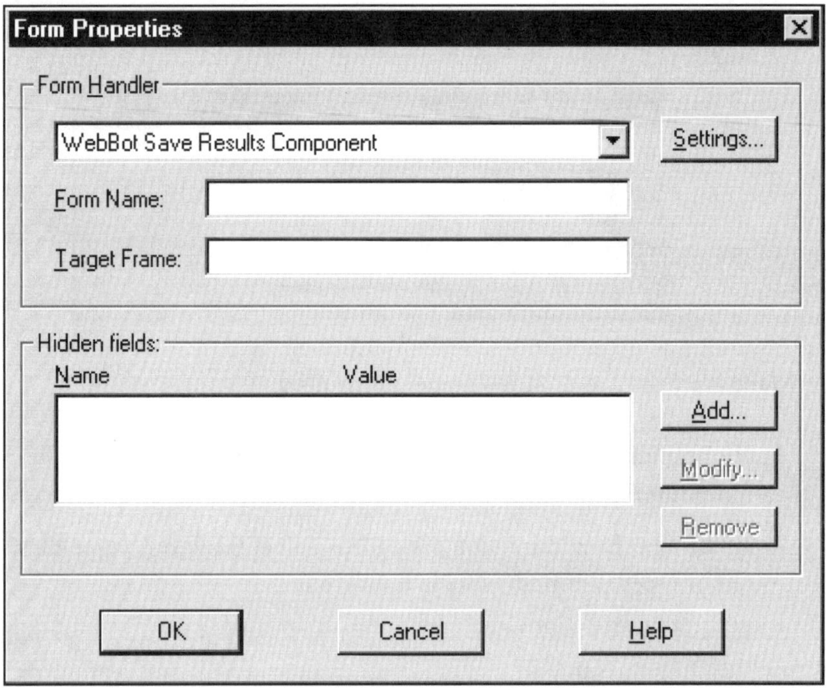

Form
Properties
dialog box

FIGURE 9-6

■ The Hidden Fields that you want to appear in the data collected from the form, but not on the form itself. Through the Add, Modify, and Remove buttons, you can add a field name and a value that appear in the data. For example, if you use the same form on several web pages, you could add a field named "Source" that identifies where this set of data originated, like this:

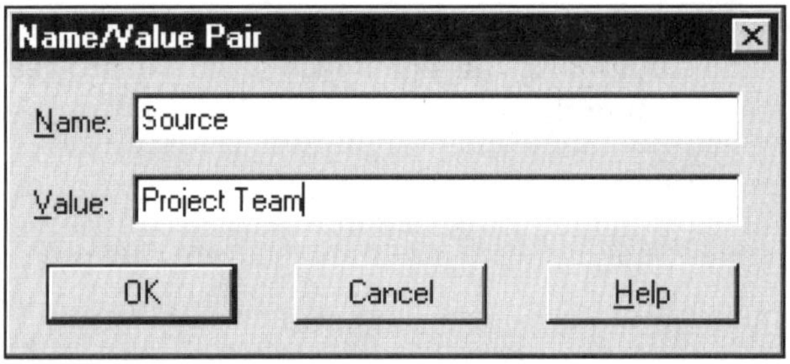

■ The Settings for the form handler. By clicking on the Settings button, you open the Settings For Saving Results Of Form dialog box, shown in Figure 9-7. Here you can change the name and format of the results file, include (or exclude) the field names, add additional fields and data, and establish the URL for a confirmation page to be sent on the receipt of a form. In the Advanced tab you can set up a second file to save the results with its format and the selection of fields to be included.

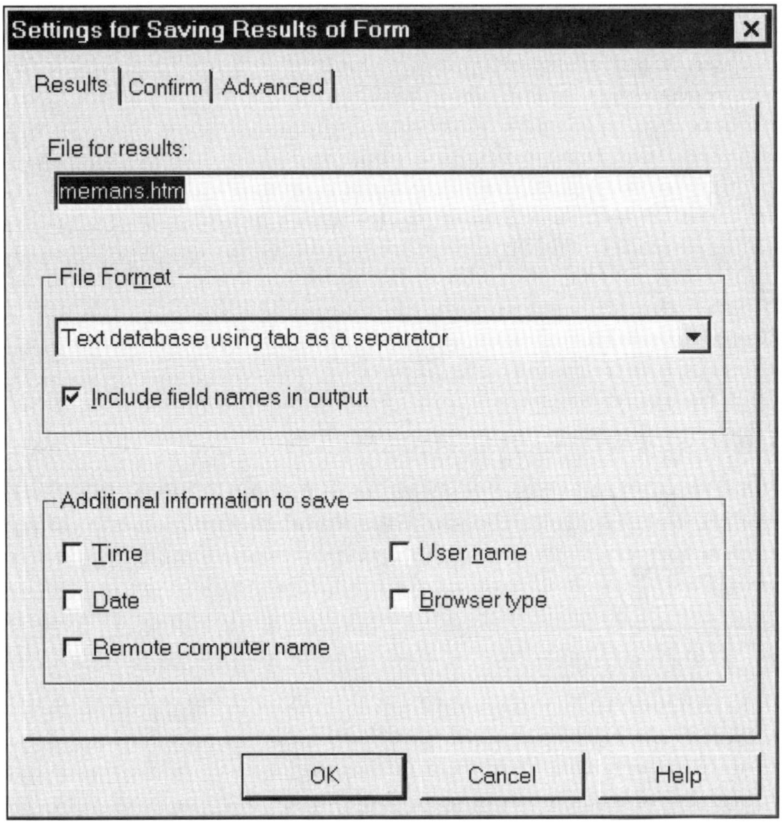

Settings for Saving Results of Form ✕

Results | Confirm | Advanced

File for results:

memans.htm

┌─ File Format ─────────────────────────────────┐
│ Text database using tab as a separator ▼ │
│ ☑ Include field names in output │
└──┘

┌─ Additional information to save ──────────────┐
│ ☐ Time ☐ User name │
│ ☐ Date ☐ Browser type │
│ ☐ Remote computer name │
└──┘

OK   Cancel   Help

Settings
For Saving
Results Of
Form
dialog box

FIGURE 9-7

The lower part of the form in Figure 9-4 contains different types of fields, as shown in Figure 9-8. Each of these fields has slight variations in its Properties dialog box. Open each of these in turn and look at their differences. Note the following features:

- The group of radio buttons is a single field, and the value is the button selected.

- Each of the check boxes is its own field, and the value is "on" if a box is selected.

- In the scrolling text box, you can select the number of lines as well as the width. The total content, though, can be far greater than you might think by looking at the width and number of lines (5 lines of 35 characters, or 175 characters), since each line can contain up to 256 characters.

- You can change the label on the push buttons, but the only functions that can be performed are submitting a form and resetting it (erasing any entries made and not submitting it).

Given the considerable customization that can be done to a wizard-created form, if your form looks anything like a form the wizard can build, it will probably save you time to use the wizard. The wizard also makes the necessary settings for the Save Results bot that you otherwise would have to remember to do. Next you'll see what it is like to build a form from scratch. Before going to that, save your project form one more time.

Building Forms from Scratch

As good as the Form Page Wizard is, there will always be the need for forms that are different enough from the standards that it is worthwhile building them from

scratch. Now that you're familiar with wizard-created forms, take on the building of a form from scratch and see the differences in the following exercise using the

Forms toolbar. (Here you will build a request for literature, which could be built with a wizard, but the design calls for it to be laid out with Formatted text quite differently from what the wizard would do.)

1. With the Project Team Questionnaire still open in the FrontPage Editor, click on the New Page button to open a blank page.

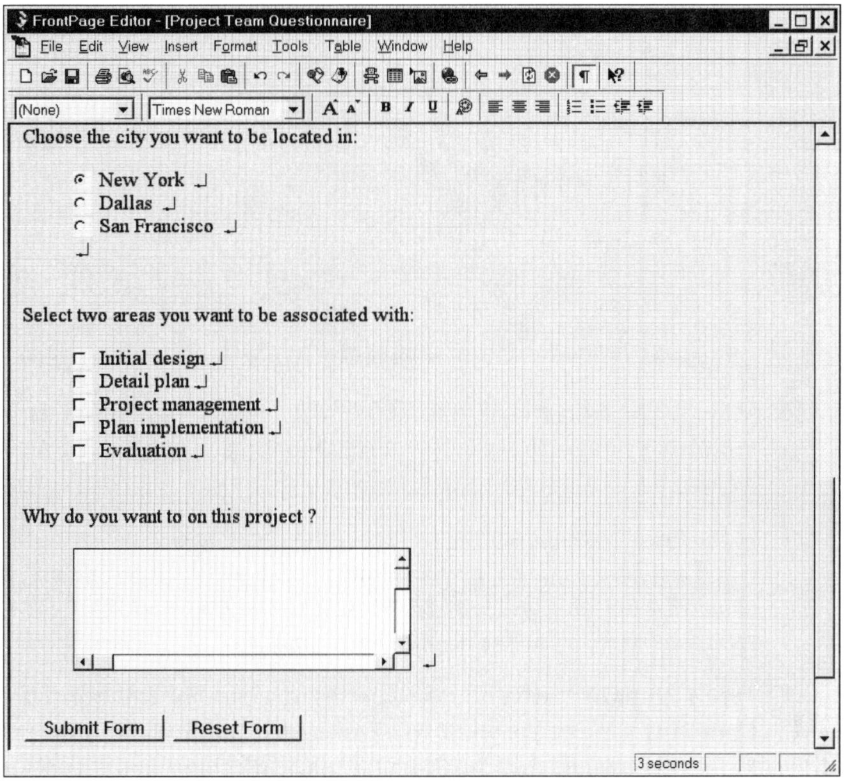

FrontPage Editor - [Project Team Questionnaire]

File Edit View Insert Format Tools Table Window Help

(None)   Times New Roman

Choose the city you want to be located in:

       ⊙ New York ↵
       ○ Dallas ↵
       ○ San Francisco ↵
       ↵

Select two areas you want to be associated with:

       ☐ Initial design ↵
       ☐ Detail plan ↵
       ☐ Project management ↵
       ☐ Plan implementation ↵
       ☐ Evaluation ↵

Why do you want to on this project ?

      [text area] ↵

Submit Form   Reset Form

3 seconds

Different types of fields in the lower part of the form

FIGURE 9-8

2. Open the Page Properties dialog box from the File menu, and type **Literature Request** for the title. Click on OK to close the dialog box.

3. At the top of the New page type **LITERATURE REQUEST**, center it, and format it as Heading 1.

4. Insert a horizontal line under the title by use of the Horizontal Line option in the Insert menu.

5. On the first line below the horizontal line, select the One-Line Text Box tool from the Forms toolbar. A text box will appear within the dashed line representing a form. From the context menu, select Form Field Properties to open the Text Box Properties dialog box, type **First** for the name, change the width to **25**, leave the other defaults as shown next, and click OK.

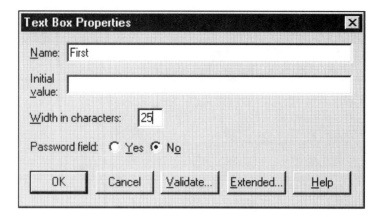

6. Move the insertion point to the left of the new text box, select the Formatted paragraph style, type **First Name:**, and leave a space before the text box.

7. Move the insertion point to the right of the text box, leave two spaces, type **Last Name:**, leave a space, and insert a second one-line text box named **Last** with a width of **25**. Press RIGHT ARROW and then SHIFT-ENTER to start a new line within the form.

8. Type **Company:**, leave four spaces, insert a one-line text box named **Company**, change the width to **65** characters, click on OK, and press RIGHT ARROW and then SHIFT-ENTER. (The 65 characters makes the second line equal to the first line on *my screen;* yours may be different. You can change this if you want.)

9. Type **Address:**, leave four spaces, insert a one-line text box named **Address1** with a width of **25**, and click on OK.

10. Press RIGHT ARROW, leave two spaces, type **Address 2:**, leave a space, insert a one-line text box named **Address2** with a width of **25**, click on OK, and press RIGHT ARROW and then SHIFT-ENTER.

11. Type **City:**, leave seven spaces, insert a one-line text box named **City** with a width of **25**, press RIGHT ARROW, leave two spaces, type **State:**, leave a space, insert a one-line text box named **State** with an initial value of **WA**, change the width to **9** characters, press RIGHT ARROW, leave two spaces, type **Zip:**, leave a space, insert a one-line text box named **Zip** with a width of **12** characters, and press RIGHT ARROW and then SHIFT-ENTER.

12. Type **Phone:**, leave six spaces, insert a one-line text box named **Phone** with a width of **25**, press RIGHT ARROW, leave two spaces, type **E-mail:**, leave four spaces, insert a one-line text box named **Email** with a width of **25**, and press RIGHT ARROW and then SHIFT-ENTER.

13. Click on the Check Box button in the Forms toolbar, give it a name of **Literature**, accept the defaults shown next, and click on OK. Press RIGHT ARROW, but do not enter a space, and then type

> **Click here if you wish literature.**

(include the period). Leave three spaces. (The number of spaces you need in order to make the right end line up may be different.)

Check Box Properties

Name: Literature

Value: ON

Initial State: ○ Checked   ● Not checked

[OK]   [Cancel]   [Extended...]   [Help]

14. Type **Which products?**, leave a space, click on the Drop-Down Menu button in the Forms toolbar, type **Lit_Products** for the name, and click on Add to open the Add Choice dialog box. Type **Portable model**, and click on Selected as the initial state, as shown here:

Add Choice

Choice:
Portable model

☐ Specify Value:
Portable model

Initial State
● Selected
○ Not selected

[OK]   [Cancel]   [Help]

9

15. Click on OK and then click on Add twice more to add the choices of **Desktop model** and **Floor model**. In both cases leave the initial state as not selected. In the Drop-Down Menu Properties dialog box, click on Yes to allow multiple selections, so that your dialog box looks like Figure 9-9.

16. Click on OK. Select both the "Which products?" label and the drop-down menu box, and press CTRL-C to copy them to the Clipboard. You'll use this twice again. Move the insertion point to the end of the line and press SHIFT-ENTER.

17. Insert a check box named **Use**, accept the defaults, and click on OK. Immediately type

    Click here if you use our products.

    leave two spaces, and press CTRL-V to paste in your "Which products?" label and drop-down menu. Right-click on the drop-down menu, choose Form Field Properties, change the name to **Use_Products**, and click on OK. Move the insertion point to the end of the line and press SHIFT-ENTER.

Drop-Down Menu Properties

Name: Lit_Products

Choice	Selected	Value
Portable model	Yes	Portable model
Desktop model	No	Desktop model
Floor model	No	Floor model

Add...
Modify...
Remove
Move Up
Move Down

Height: 1   Allow multiple selections: ⦿ Yes ○ No

OK   Cancel   Validate...   Extended...   Help

Drop-down Menu Properties dialog box

FIGURE 9-9

18. Insert a check box named **Plan**, accept the defaults, and click on OK. Press RIGHT ARROW, and immediately type

> **Click here if planning our products.**

leave a space and press CTRL-V to paste in your "Which products?" label and drop-down menu. Right-click on the drop-down menu, choose Properties, change the name to **Plan_Products**, and click on OK. Move the insertion point to the end of the line and press SHIFT-ENTER.

19. On the new line, type

> **What is your company size?**

leave four spaces, and click on the Radio Button button in the Forms toolbar. In the Radio Button Properties dialog box, enter a group name of **Size**, a value of **Less than 50**, as shown next, and then click on OK.

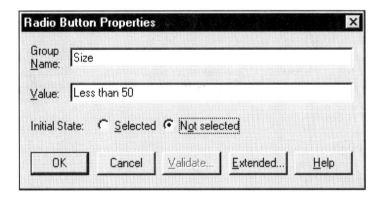

20. Press RIGHT ARROW, and immediately type

> **Less than 50**

leave four spaces, insert a radio button with a group name of **Size** and a value of **50 to 500**, press RIGHT ARROW, immediately type

> **50 to 500**

leave four spaces, insert a third radio button with a group name of **Size** and value of **Over 500**, press RIGHT ARROW, type

> **Over 500**

and press SHIFT-ENTER.

21. Type

Please give us any comments you wish:

click on the Scrolling Text Box button in the Forms toolbar, type a
name of **Comments** in the Scrolling Text Box Properties dialog box,
enter a width of **34**, click on OK, press RIGHT ARROW, and press
SHIFT-ENTER twice.

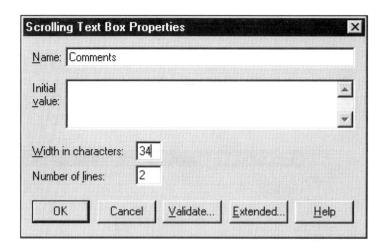

22. Click on the Push Button button in the Forms toolbar. In the Push Button
Properties dialog box, type a name of **Submit**, and a Value/Label of
Submit Form. Make sure the Button Type is Submit, as shown next, and
click on OK.

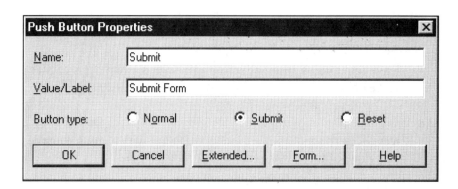

23. Press RIGHT ARROW, leave four spaces, insert a second push button named **Reset** and a Value/Label of **Reset Form**, select a Button Type of Reset, click on OK, save your form, and you're done! The result should look like Figure 9-10.

24. Well, almost done. You still need a handler to process the input from the form. Right-click on the form and choose Form Properties. In the Form Properties dialog box, select WebBot Save Results Component for the Form Handler, and click on Settings.

25. In the Settings For Saving Results Of Form dialog box, type **Literate.txt** for the filename, select Text Database Using Tab As A Separator for the file format, turn off Include Field Names In Output, select Date And User Name For Additional Information, and click on OK twice to get back to your form. Now you are done, so save your form once more.

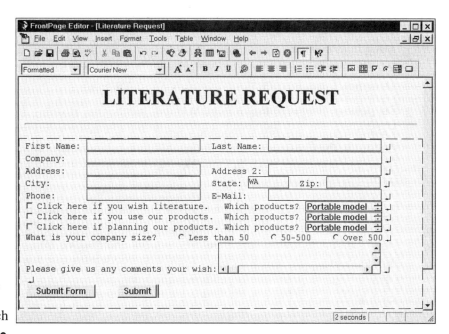

Completed form built from scratch

FIGURE 9-10

NOTE: *Much of the spacing and wording in this form was done interactively—in other words, by use of the "try it and see what it looks like" approach. The beauty of a WYSIWYG form editor is that you can immediately see what the form you're building looks like and change it if needed.*

Part of the purpose of this "from scratch" example is to see what the Form Page Wizard does for you. You must admit it's a lot. The wizard saves you the hassle of naming, spacing, and layout, let alone the setup of the Save Results bot. There aren't many situations where "from scratch" will pay off.

Handling Form Input

The next step is to look at your forms in a browser. The web called Forms should still be active on your screen and should have three pages: a blank Normal Page called Home Page, a Project Team Questionnaire page built with the Form Page Wizard, and a Literature Request form built from scratch. To use the web, you'll need to put some links on the Home Page to the two forms. To do that, and then try out the forms in a browser:

1. From the FrontPage Editor, open the Window menu and choose Home Page. At the top of the page type **FORMS EXAMPLES**, format it as Heading 1, and press ENTER.

2. On the next line, type **Form Page Wizard**, format it as Heading 4, select the three words you just typed, and click on the Create Or Edit Hyperlink button. In the Create Hyperlink dialog box Open Pages tab, select Project Team Questionnaire, and click on OK. Move the insertion point to the end of the line and press ENTER twice.

3. Type **Custom Form**, format it as Heading 4, select the words, and click on the Create Or Edit Hyperlink button. In the Create Hyperlink dialog box Open Pages tab, select Literature Request, and click on OK. Your Home Page should now look like Figure 9-11. Save this page, put a "Home" link back to the Home Page at the bottom of each form, save each of them, and close the FrontPage Editor.

4. Open your favorite browser and display the Forms web. Select the Form Page Wizard to open the Project Team Questionnaire, and submit it without filling in the First Name field. Immediately an error message is displayed, as shown here:

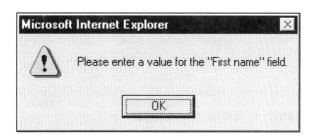

5. Fill out the form and submit it again. Almost immediately you'll see another benefit of FrontPage—an automatic confirmation form is created for you and is used here to confirm your input, as you can see in Figure 9-12. Click on Return To Home Page at the bottom of the confirmation page.

6. Use the Home Page link to get back to the Home Page, and then select Custom Form to open the Literature Request form. Fill it out and click on Submit Form. Again you'll see the automatic confirmation report. Click on Return To The Form, and then close your browser.

NOTE: *The "beautiful" symmetry of the form in the FrontPage Editor has not carried over to the browser, as shown in Figure 9-13. If you look at the form in different browsers, you'll notice different spacing. The user can also change the spacing by selecting different fonts in the browser.*

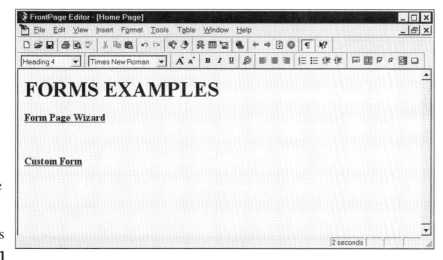

Home Page with hyperlinks to the forms

FIGURE 9-11

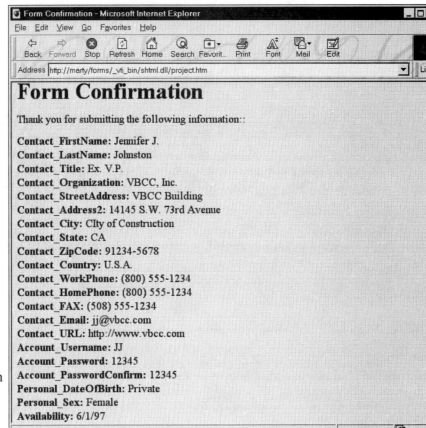

Automatic confirmation page created by FrontPage

FIGURE 9-12

NOTE: *When you use the default settings in Microsoft's Internet Explorer, as was done in Figure 9-13, the text is almost unreadable. Also, when the size of a drop-down menu in a form is set to 1 (as it is in this example) only one line should be displayed. In Internet Explorer all the lines are displayed; in Netscape Navigator only one line is displayed. When Allow Multiple Selections is selected, the list is displayed as a scrolling list box in Navigator. When only a single selection is allowed, it's displayed as a drop-down menu in both browsers.*

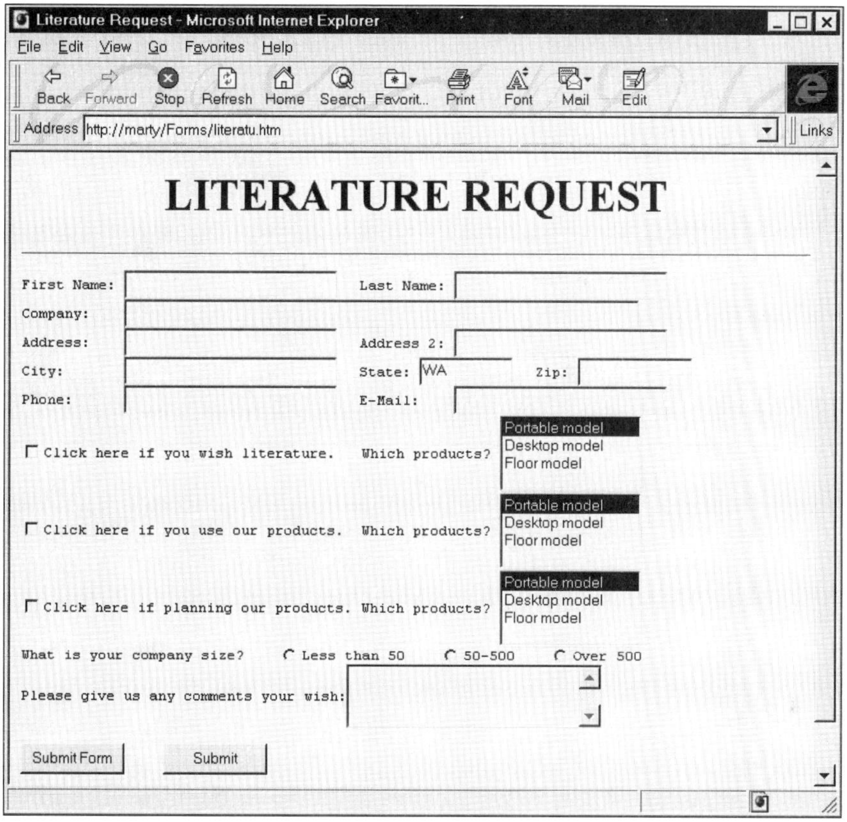

Literature
Request
form loses
its
symmetry
in a browser

FIGURE 9-13

7. Open the file that was created by the WebBot Save Results Component from the Project Team Questionnaire. If you used the default directories when you installed FrontPage, this should be located at C:\Webshare\ Wwwroot\Forms\Memans.txt. Use the Windows Explorer or My Computer to locate it, and then double-click on it to open it in the Notepad. What you see should look like this:

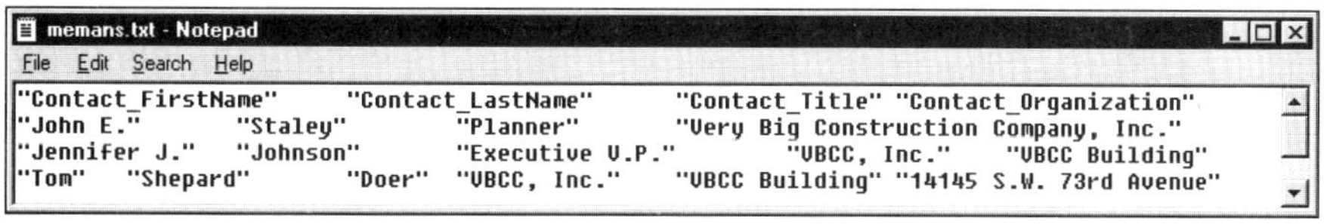

The Project
Questionnaire
data in
Microsoft
Access
and in
Microsoft
Excel

Memans : Table

ID	Contact_FirstName	Contact_LastName	Contact_Title	Contact_Organization	Fiel
1	John E.	Staley	Planner	Very Big Construction Company, Inc.	
2	Jennifer J.	Johnson	Executive V.P.	VBCC, Inc.	VBCC B
3	Tom	Shepard	Doer	VBCC, Inc.	VBCC B
4					

Record: 1 of 4

memans.txt

	A	B	C	D	E
1	Contact_FirstName	Contact_LastName	Contact_Title	Contact_Organization	
2	John E.	Staley	Planner	Very Big Construction Company, Inc.	
3	Jennifer J.	Johnson	Executive V.P.	VBCC, Inc.	VBCC Building
4	Tom	Shepard	Doer	VBCC, Inc.	VBCC Building

\memans

FIGURE 9-14

8. You can also open the files saved from either form in a database program or in a spreadsheet. Figure 9-14 shows the Project Team Questionnaire data in Microsoft Access and Microsoft Excel.

9. Close Notepad and any applications other than FrontPage that you have open. In the FrontPage Explorer close your Forms web.

As you can see, FrontPage not only provides significant power for creating a form, but it also does a lot to get the data collected on the form back to you. Also, in the data collection area, a form created with the Form Page Wizard does not have an advantage over a properly set up custom form.

 NOTE: See the Needham Online and the Bar Net FrontPage on the Web sections of this book to see examples of Web forms and the HTML they generate.

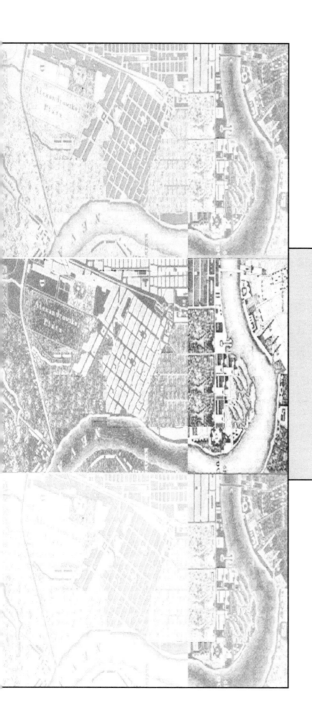

10

Using WebBots

A s you have read in earlier chapters, a WebBot or "bot" is a way you can add automation to your web, often to provide interactivity with the user. Some WebBots are buried in other features, such as the Save Results bot you used in Chapter 9, while others are stand-alone tools that you can use directly. The stand-alone bots, shown in the following illustration of the Insert WebBot Component dialog box, are the subject of this chapter (they are also listed in Chapter 2's Table 2-7). There are two additional WebBots you can use that are opened from the Insert menu, rather than from the Insert WebBot Component dialog box. These are the Comment bot, opened with the Comment option in the Insert menu, and the HTML Markup bot, opened with the HTML Markup option in the Insert menu. The HTML Markup bot allows you to include an HTML command that is not otherwise supported directly on a web page. This bot will be discussed in Chapter 12.

Insert WebBot Component   ☒

Select a component:

Confirmation Field	OK
Include	
Scheduled Image	Cancel
Scheduled Include	
Search	Help
Substitution	
Table of Contents	
Timestamp	

Incorporating WebBots in Your Webs

See how you can incorporate WebBots in your own webs by trying out several of the stand-alone bots in the following sections. Begin by opening a new Normal Web named **Bots** and then opening its Home page in the FrontPage Editor.

Comment Bot

The Comment bot allows you to insert notes that you want to be visible while the web is in the FrontPage Editor, but invisible or hidden while the web is being viewed in a browser. To see how that works:

1. On a blank page in the FrontPage Editor, type

   This is normal text.

   (include the period), and press ENTER.

2. From the Insert menu choose Comment. The Comment dialog box opens, as shown next. Here you can type any text you want to see in the FrontPage Editor but not in a browser.

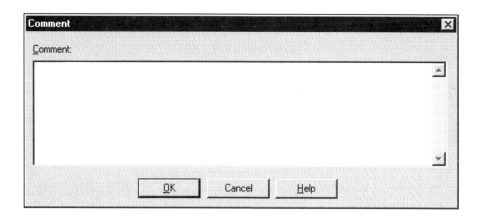

3. Type

   This is comment text that should not be visible in a browser.

 (include the period), and then click on OK. The comment text will appear in the FrontPage Editor as shown next. If you move the mouse pointer over it, you'll see the WebBot icon (shown here in the margin).

This is normal text.

Comment: This is comment text that should not be visible in a browser.

---

4. Save your web page, open it in a browser, and all you'll see is the normal first line.

5. Minimize your browser, close the open page in the FrontPage Editor, and return to the FrontPage Explorer, where you should close the Bots web.

Confirmation Field Bot

The Confirmation Field bot allows you to build a confirmation page that echoes the contents of a web form that has been submitted. Such a page would replace the automatic confirmation form you saw in Chapter 9. To build a confirmation page for your Literature Request form:

1. In the FrontPage Explorer open the Forms web you created in Chapter 9, and then open the Literature Request form in the FrontPage Editor.

2. In the FrontPage Editor create a new Normal page. On the new page you'll create a brief confirmation letter. Begin by putting a heading on the page like

Great Products Company

formatting it as Heading 1, centering it, and then pressing ENTER.

3. Click on the Align Left button; then on the left margin type **To:** and press SHIFT-ENTER.

4. From the Insert menu choose WebBot Component, and double-click on Confirmation Field. In the WebBot Confirmation Field Component Properties dialog box type **First**, as shown next, and then click on OK.

WebBot Confirmation Field Component Properties	✕

Name of Form Field to Confirm:

First

OK	Cancel	Help

5. Leave a space, again open the WebBot Confirmation Field Component Properties dialog box, type **Last**, click on OK, and press SHIFT-ENTER for a new line.

NOTE: *There is no easy way to get a list of field names—you need to either remember them or write them down as you are creating a form, or open the Properties dialog box for each field. A suggestion has been made to Microsoft that a "Browse" feature be added to the WebBot Confirmation Field Component Properties dialog box.*

6. Repeat step 4 to enter confirmation fields for **Company**, **Address1**, and **Address2** all on separate lines ending with SHIFT-ENTER.

7. Again repeat step 4 to enter confirmation fields for **City**, **State**, and **Zip** all on one line, with a comma and a space between "City" and "State," and a space between "State" and "Zip."

8. Type the body and ending of the letter, something similar to that shown in Figure 10-1. Follow this with a link that says **Return to the form** and points to the Literature Request form. When you are done, save the confirmation letter with a page title of **Literature Request Confirmation** and a URL of **Litreqcf.htm**.

10

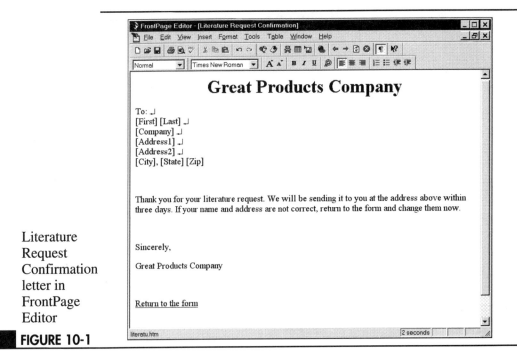

Literature
Request
Confirmation
letter in
FrontPage
Editor

FIGURE 10-1

9. Open the Literature Request form, right-click in the form, choose Form
Properties, click on Settings, and then on the Confirm tab. Click on
Browse, and double-click on Literature Request Confirmation. Your
Settings For Saving Results Of Form dialog box should be similar to the
one shown next. Click on OK twice. Save the Literature Request form
and close the FrontPage Editor.

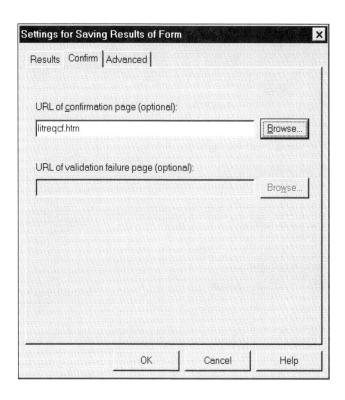

10. In your browser open the Forms web, click on Custom Form, fill out the form, click on Submit Form, and you'll see a confirmation letter similar to the one shown in Figure 10-2.

11. Close your browser and your Forms web.

For more on confirmation forms, see the "Confirmation Form Template" section of Chapter 4.

Filled out
confirmation
letter in
browser

FIGURE 10-2

Include and Scheduled Include Bots

The Include bot allows you to include one web page on another. For example, if you wanted an identical header on every page, as you did in the Fantasy Travel web, you could put the header on a web page and then include that page on all others in the web. The Scheduled Include bot allows you to include one page on another for a given period of time. When that time expires, the included page is no longer included. To try this:

1. In the FrontPage Explorer, open the Bots web and double-click on the Home page to open the FrontPage Editor.

2. Click on the New button to create a new page. At the top of the page type

   This is a page heading, it should be on all pages.

   (include the period) and format it as Heading 2. Save this page with the page title **Included Header** and the Page URL of **Inchead.htm**.

3. Return to the Home page, place the insertion point at the top of the page, choose WebBot Component from the Insert menu, and double-click on Include to open the WebBot Include Component Properties dialog box.

4. Click on Browse to get a list of pages in the current web, double-click on the Included Header page, and then click on OK to return to the web page. You should see the heading appear on this page and the WebBot icon appear when you move the mouse pointer over it, as you can see here:

This is a page heading, it should be on all pages.

This is normal text.

Comment: This is comment text that should not be visible in a browser.

The real beauty of using the Include bot is that not only are you saved from retyping or copying the heading onto each page, but also changes you make need only be typed once. The Scheduled Include bot works similarly to the Include bot, except that it has a start and stop date and time, as will be demonstrated next with the Scheduled Image bot.

Scheduled Image Bot

The Scheduled Image bot allows you to display an image on a page for a fixed period of time. When the time expires, the image disappears. To see how this works:

1. On the Home page of the Bots web in the FrontPage Editor move the insertion point below the annotation line.

2. From the Insert menu choose Image. In the Image dialog box select the Clip Art tab, and then choose Icons from the Category drop-down menu.

3. Scroll to the bottom of the Contents display box and double-click on the Warning.gif.

4. Save your page in the FrontPage Editor. Click on Yes in the Save Image To FrontPage Web dialog box.

5. Delete the image you just placed and open the Insert menu, choose WebBot Component, and double-click on Scheduled Image. The Scheduled Image WebBot Component Properties dialog box will open:

10

```
┌─────────────────────────────────────────────────────────────────────┐
│ Scheduled Image WebBot Component Properties                     [X]   │
├─────────────────────────────────────────────────────────────────────┤
│ Image to include:                                          ┌────────┐ │
│ ┌──────────────────────────────────────────┐ ┌─────────┐  │   OK   │ │
│ │                                          │ │ Browse..│  └────────┘ │
│ └──────────────────────────────────────────┘ └─────────┘  ┌────────┐ │
│ ┌─Starting date and time──────────────────────────────┐   │ Cancel │ │
│ │  Year:       Month:      Day:       Time:            │   └────────┘ │
│ │  ┌─────┬─┐  ┌─────┬─┐  ┌─────┬─┐  ┌──────────┬─┐     │   ┌────────┐ │
│ │  │1996 │▼│  │Nov  │▼│  │05   │▼│  │10:00:12AM│▲│     │   │  Help  │ │
│ │  └─────┴─┘  └─────┴─┘  └─────┴─┘  └──────────┴▼┘     │   └────────┘ │
│ │  Tuesday, November 05, 1996                          │              │
│ └──────────────────────────────────────────────────────┘              │
│ ┌─Ending date and time────────────────────────────────┐               │
│ │  Year:       Month:      Day:       Time:            │               │
│ │  ┌─────┬─┐  ┌─────┬─┐  ┌─────┬─┐  ┌──────────┬─┐     │               │
│ │  │1996 │▼│  │Dec  │▼│  │05   │▼│  │10:00:12AM│▲│     │               │
│ │  └─────┴─┘  └─────┴─┘  └─────┴─┘  └──────────┴▼┘     │               │
│ │  Thursday, December 05, 1996                         │               │
│ └──────────────────────────────────────────────────────┘              │
│ Optional Image to include before or                                    │
│ after the given dates:                                                 │
│ ┌──────────────────────────────────────────┐ ┌─────────┐             │
│ │                                          │ │ Browse..│             │
│ └──────────────────────────────────────────┘ └─────────┘             │
└─────────────────────────────────────────────────────────────────────┘
```

TIP: *The preceding steps are only one way to get the graphic into the web. You could also copy the file from the clip-art directory (C:\Program Files\Microsoft FrontPage\Clipart\Icons) to the web (C:\Webshare\ Wwwroot\Bots\) using the Windows Explorer, or by selecting the Other Location tab in the Images dialog box and using the Browse button to select the file.*

6. Click on Browse next to the Image To Include text box, and then double-click on the Warning.gif file (this is the icon you just saved to your web).

7. Set the ending time for a couple of minutes past the current time by clicking on the minutes in the Time spinner and clicking on the up arrow. (The default is to display the image for one month.) Click on OK. You should see the image appear in the FrontPage Editor.

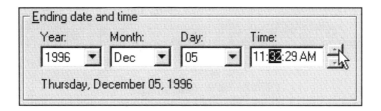

8. Save your web page and open your browser and the Bots web. If necessary, click on the Refresh button in the Standard toolbar; you should see your Warning icon, like this:

This is a page heading, it should be on all pages.

This is normal text.

---

9. After the time has expired, go back to the FrontPage Editor displaying the Bots Home Page, and click on the Refresh button. The Warning icon will be replaced with the message "*[Expired Scheduled Image]*." If you save this page again, return to your browser, and refresh it, the icon will also disappear from there.

10. Minimize your browser.

Search Bot

The Search bot creates a form in which users can enter any text that they want to search for in the current web. After users enter such text and click on the Search button, the Search bot carries out the search and returns the locations where the text was found. To look at how this is done:

1. At the bottom of the Home page of the Bots web open the Insert menu, choose WebBot Component, and double-click on Search. The WebBot Search Component Properties dialog box will open, as shown in Figure 10-3.

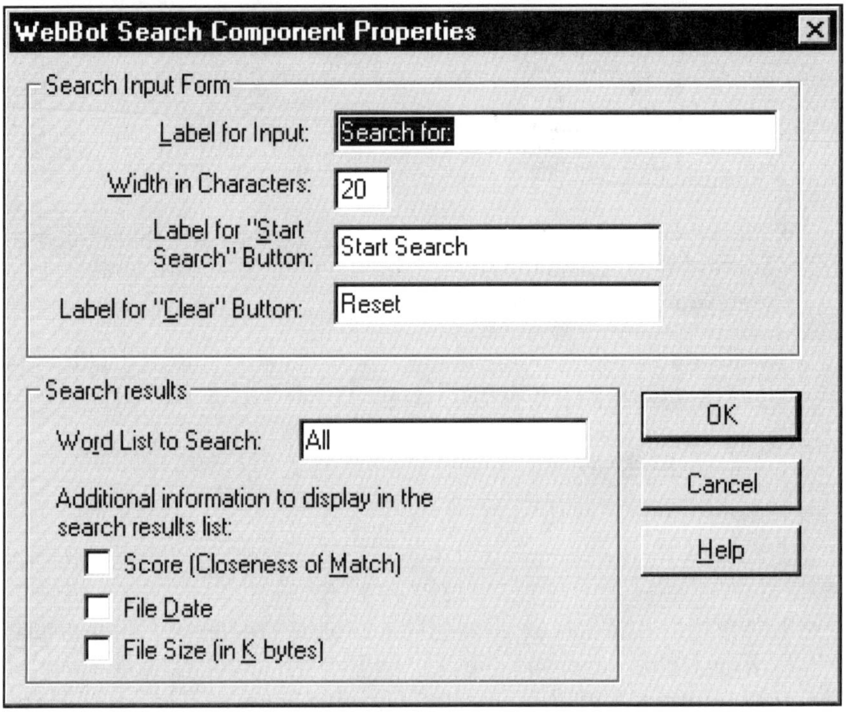

WebBot Search Component Properties   ✕

┌─ Search Input Form ──────────────────────────────┐

               Label for Input: `Search for:`

      Width in Characters: `20`

       Label for "Start
       Search" Button: `Start Search`

  Label for "Clear" Button: `Reset`

└──┘

┌─ Search results ─────────────────────────────┐

  Word List to Search: `All`   **OK**

  Additional information to display in the   **Cancel**
  search results list:
    ☐ Score (Closeness of Match)   **Help**
    ☐ File Date
    ☐ File Size (in K bytes)

└──┘

WebBot
Search
Component
Properties
dialog box

■ FIGURE 10-3

2. Accept the defaults in this dialog box and click on OK. The search form will appear on the Home page.

3. Save the web page, open your browser, refresh the page, and the search form will appear here.

4. In the Search For text box type **home** and click on Start Search. In a moment, you will get the results, which should look like this:

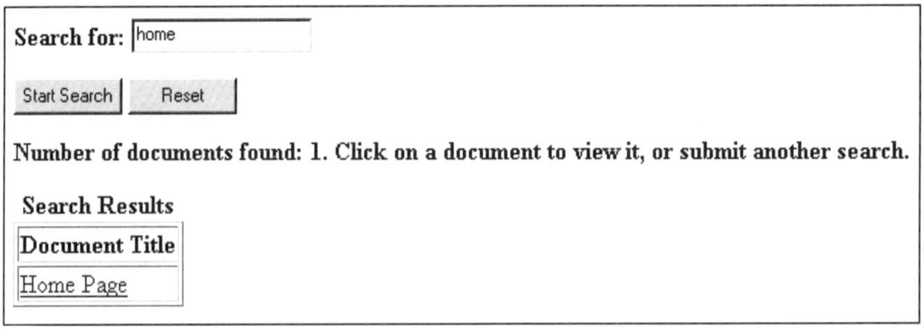

Search for: `home`

`Start Search` `Reset`

Number of documents found: 1. Click on a document to view it, or submit another search.

Search Results

Document Title

Home Page

---

5. Minimize your browser and return to the FrontPage Editor.

TIP: *If you want a page not to be found by the Search bot (like style pages and included pages), place the pages in the _private directory of the current web; that directory is not searched. If you're using FrontPage's default directory structure and the Forms web you created earlier in the chapter, the full path to the private directory for that web is C:\WebShare\Wwwroot\Forms_private. (It's C:\FrontPage Webs\Content \Forms_private if you're using the FrontPage Personal Web Server.)*

NOTE: *The Bar Net FrontPage on the Web secrion shows an example of the FrontPage Search bot.*

Substitution Bot

The Substitution bot replaces a value on a web page with a configuration variable when the page is viewed by the user. A *configuration variable* contains specific information about either the current page or the current web. There are four predefined configuration variables, as shown in Table 10-1, and you can define additional ones in the Web Settings dialog box Parameters tab opened from the Tools menu in the FrontPage Explorer. You can see how this works with the following instructions:

1. Open the FrontPage Explorer while it is still displaying the Bots web, and then from the Edit menu, click on Properties. The page's Properties dialog box will open with the General tab showing, as you can see in Figure 10-4.

10

Variable	Description
Author	The name that is in the Created By field of the FrontPage Explorer's Properties dialog box
ModifiedBy	The name of the person who most recently changed the page, contained in the Modified By field of the FrontPage Explorer's Properties dialog box
Description	The contents of the Comments field of the FrontPage Explorer's Properties dialog box
Page-URL	The filename in the Location field of the FrontPage Explorer's Properties dialog box

Configuration Variables

TABLE 10-1

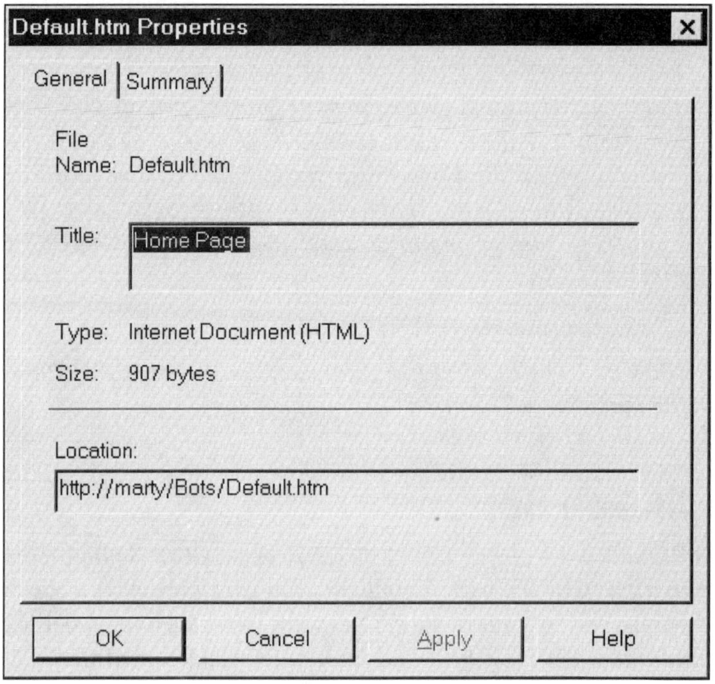

Default.htm Properties ☒

General │ Summary │

File
Name: Default.htm

Title: │Home Page│

Type: Internet Document (HTML)

Size: 907 bytes

Location:
│http://marty/Bots/Default.htm│

| OK | Cancel | Apply | Help |

General tab
of the
current
page's
Properties
dialog box

FIGURE 10-4

---

2. If it isn't already open, click on the General tab of the web's Properties
dialog box so you can see the Location field. Click on the Summary tab to
see the Created By and Modified By fields, and to both see and change
the Comments field, as shown in Figure 10-5.

3. In the Comments field type

   This is a great web!

   click on OK to close the Properties dialog box, and then double-click on
   the Home page to reopen the FrontPage Editor.

4. At the bottom of the Home page in the FrontPage Editor type

   This page was last modified by

   leave a space, choose WebBot Component from the Insert menu, and
   double-click on Substitution. The WebBot Substitution Component
   Properties dialog box will open.

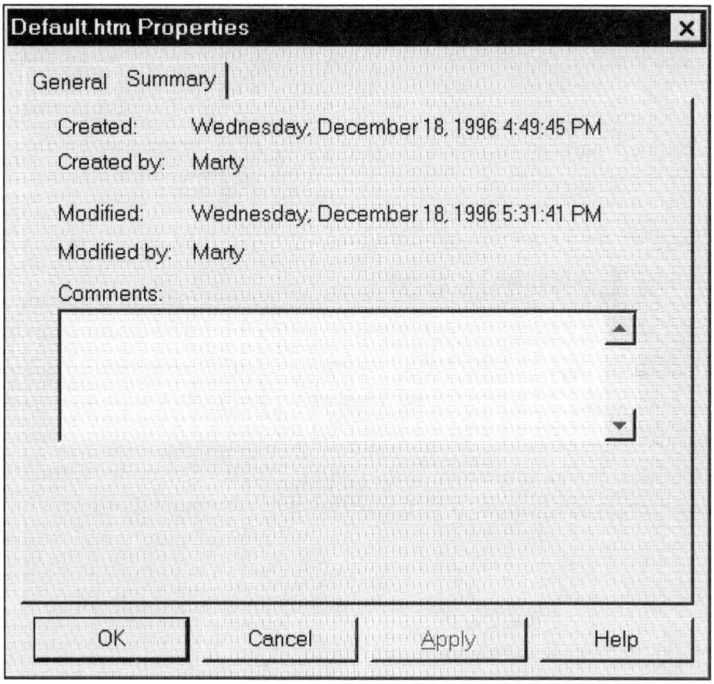
Default.htm Properties
General
Summary
Created: Wednesday, December 18, 1996 4:49:45 PM
Created by: Marty
Modified: Wednesday, December 18, 1996 5:31:41 PM
Modified by: Marty
Comments:
OK
Cancel
Apply
Help

Summary tab of the current page's Properties dialog box

FIGURE 10-5

5. Click on the down arrow to see the list of variables shown next. Click on ModifiedBy and then on OK. You'll see the name of the person who last modified the page appear on the Home page in the FrontPage Editor.

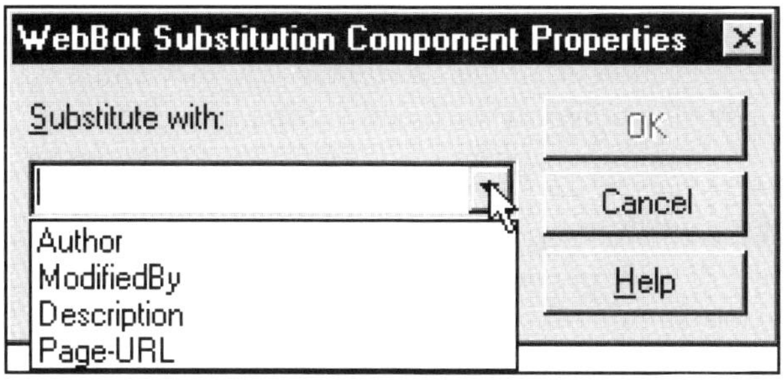
WebBot Substitution Component Properties
Substitute with:
OK
Cancel
Help
Author
ModifiedBy
Description
Page-URL

6. Leave a space and then type

   who left these comments:

leave a space, and from the WebBot Substitution Component Properties dialog box choose Description. The comments you left should appear, as you can see here:

> This page was last modified by Marty who left these comments: This is a great web!

Table of Contents Bot

The Table of Contents bot creates and maintains a table of contents for a web, with links to all the pages in the web. Whenever the web's contents are changed and resaved, the table of contents is updated. The Table of Contents bot builds the structure of the Table of Contents based on the links that are on each page. For example, if the home page has three pages directly linked to it and the second page has two other pages linked to it, the following structure would be built:

Home Page

    First Page
    Second Page

        Linked Page One
        Linked Page Two

    Third Page

If there are pages in the web that are not linked to other pages, they are listed at the end of the table of contents.

Chapters 3 and 4 discuss and have several examples of the Table of Contents bot as used in web and page wizards and templates. See the "Using the Corporate Presence Wizard" section in Chapter 3 and the "Table of Contents Template" section in Chapter 4, as well as Figures 4-16 and 4-17.

NOTE: *When you add the Table of Contents bot to a page, you do not see the full table of contents. It is only when you open the page in a browser that the full table is displayed. See Figures 4-16 and 4-17.*

When you select the Table of Contents bot from the Insert WebBot Component dialog box, opened from the Insert menu's WebBot Component option, the WebBot Table Of Contents Component Properties dialog box will open, as shown here:

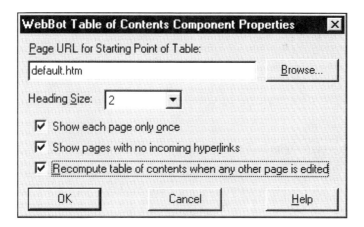

The options in this dialog box are as follows:

- **Page URL For Starting Point Of Table** should be the home page of the web, unless you want a subsidiary table of contents for a section of a web.

- **Heading Size** is the size of the top entry in the table. Each subsidiary entry is one size smaller.

- **Show Each Page Only Once** prevents a page that has links from several pages from being listed under each page.

- **Show Pages With No Incoming Hyperlinks** allows unlinked pages to be listed.

- **Recompute Table Of Contents When Any Other Page Is Edited** forces the table to be rebuilt if any page in the web is changed. Since this can take a significant amount of time, you may not want to do this. A table of contents is also rebuilt every time the page it is on is saved, which should normally be adequate.

 TIP: *Using the Table of Contents bot can be a good way to initially establish a link from the home page to all the other pages in the web.*

A good example of using the Table of Contents bot requires a web with a number of pages and several levels. Since such an example was described in Chapter 4 in the "Table of Contents Template" section, an example will not be repeated here.

Timestamp Bot

The Timestamp bot automatically puts the date, and optionally the time, that a page was last modified on the page. To try it:

1. At the bottom of the home page of the Bots web in the FrontPage Editor type

   This page was last modified on

   leave a space, and then using the WebBot Component option in the Insert menu, double-click on Timestamp. The WebBot Timestamp Component Properties dialog box will open like this:

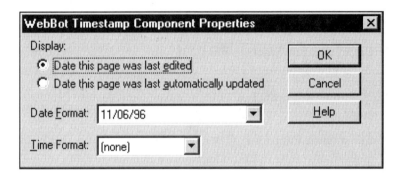

 NOTE: *In the WebBot Timestamp Component Properties dialog box, "Date this page was last edited" refers to the last time the page was saved. "Date this page was last automatically updated" refers to either the last date the page was saved or the last date an included page was saved, whichever is the most recent.*

2. Accept the defaults and click on OK. The date appears, as you can see next.

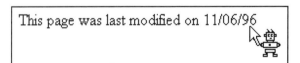

3. Save the Home Page and close the FrontPage Editor, FrontPage Explorer, and your browser.

Forms and WebBots represent a high level of sophistication that gives you significant power to build the web you want. Much of the "gee wiz" that you saw in the wizards and templates in Chapters 3 and 4 came from these tools.

10

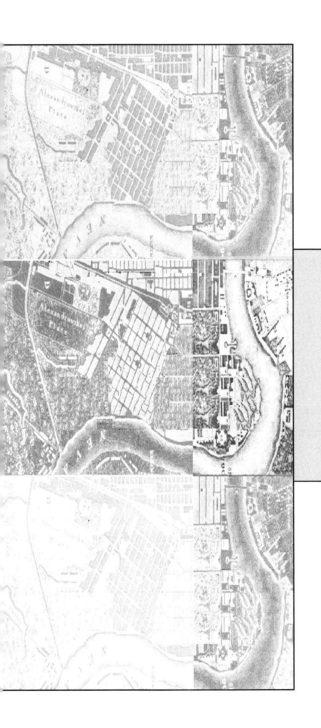

Importing and Integrating Office and Other Files

You will probably want to augment your FrontPage web with files imported from other applications—if for no other reason than because the files already exist in the other format. This is especially true with multimedia files, since FrontPage does not have the capability to create multimedia files. FrontPage has several ways of working with information created outside of it, including importing information onto an existing page, importing information onto a new page, and attaching or linking to a non-FrontPage file from a web. Let's look at this first from the standpoint of Microsoft Office 97 and other productivity application files and then in terms of multimedia files.

In the next several sections of this chapter, if you are working with Microsoft Office 95 products, you will need to have downloaded and installed several programs that Microsoft provides for free on its web site. These products allow you to create HTML web files which you can use directly on the Web and import into FrontPage. (This capability is built into Office 97 applications.) The products that are needed here are Microsoft Word Internet Assistant, Microsoft Excel Internet Assistant, Microsoft PowerPoint Internet Assistant, and the PowerPoint Animation Player for ActiveX. If you connect to http://www.microsoft.com/msdownload/, you'll find links to all of the pages from which these can be downloaded. For each product you'll find instructions for downloading and installation. After you have downloaded the files, you'll see readme files that give you additional pointers. To help you further, Microsoft has posted online tutorials on using the Internet Assistants linked to the home page for each.

Importing Microsoft Office and Other Productivity Files

FrontPage 97 is part of Microsoft's Office 97 family, and thus is tightly integrated, although not bundled, with the other Office products. If you use the Office products Word, Excel, PowerPoint, and Access, you can see a definite similarity to the menus, toolbars, and behavior of FrontPage. Of equal or even greater importance, though, is how easy it is to bring files created in the Office products into FrontPage. Here you'll look at several Office products and see how you can import information they create into FrontPage. If you use other productivity applications, such as those from Corel WordPerfect or Lotus, you will find that they are not as tightly integrated as the Office applications, but you can still easily import these files into FrontPage.

Using Text from Microsoft Word and Other Word Processors

FrontPage can bring into a web externally created text, especially Microsoft Word text, in a number of ways. Among these are

- Pasting text from the Clipboard onto an existing page in the FrontPage Editor.

- Inserting a file on an existing page from within the FrontPage Editor. The file can be in any of the file formats listed in Table 11-1.

- Opening a file onto a new page from within the FrontPage Editor. The file can be in any of the file formats listed in Table 11-1.

- Importing a file onto a new page(s) in either HTML format or its native format, if that format has been associated with its native editor in the FrontPage Explorer (Microsoft Word's DOC format has been).

- Dragging and dropping into either the FrontPage Explorer or FrontPage Editor.

To see how these methods differ, you'll need a text document from Microsoft Word or another word processing application to use as an example.

Creating a Text Document

11

The document that you want to create should include different character and paragraph formats. It should also be saved in several file formats. To do that:

1. Open a new document in Microsoft Word or your word processor.

2. Type a document with several fonts, several type sizes, several character styles (bold, italic, and underline), several paragraph styles (centered, right aligned, and a numbered list), and a table, such as the document shown in Figure 11-1.

File Format	Extensions
HyperText Markup Language	.HTM, .HTML
Preprocessed HTML	.HTX, .ASP
Rich Text Format	.RTF
Text Files	.TXT
Hypertext Templates	.HTT
Windows Write	.WRI
Word 6.0/95 for Windows & Macintosh	.DOC
Word 2.x for Windows	.DOC
Word 4.0 – 5.1 for Macintosh	.MCW
WordPerfect 5.x	.DOC
WordPerfect 6.x	.DOC, .WPD
Microsoft Excel Worksheet	.XLS, .XLW
Word 3.x – 5.x for MS-DOS	.DOC
Word 6.0 for MS-DOS	.DOC
RFT-DCA	.RFT
Works 3.0 for Windows	.WPS
Works 4.0 for Windows	.WPS
WordStar for Windows 1.0 – 2.0	.WSP
WordStar 3.3 – 7.0	.WS*
Word (Asian Versions) 6.0/95	.DOC
Word 97	.DOC
Recover Text from any File	.*
HTML Document	.HTML, .HTM, .HTX, .ASP

File Formats That Can Be Inserted into the FrontPage Editor

■ **TABLE 11-1**

3. Select all of the text you entered (CTRL-A in Word), and copy it to the Windows Clipboard by pressing CTRL-C in most applications.

4. Save the document in its native format. If that format is not Microsoft Word for Windows 97 and you can save the document in Word version 6 or 7 format, do so.

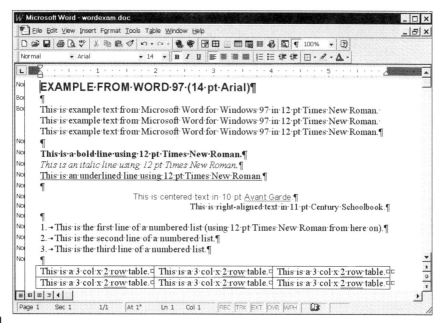

Example document in Microsoft Word 97

FIGURE 11-1

5. Save the document in the RTF format, then the HTML format, and finally in the plain TXT Only format (be sure to save the file in the order given, or you may lose formatting that would otherwise be there).

6. Close Microsoft Word or your word processor.

Pasting Text from the Clipboard

Probably the easiest way to bring in a small amount of text from almost any Windows application is through the use of the Windows Clipboard. To see how it works with FrontPage:

1. Start the FrontPage Explorer.

2. Create a new web by using the Normal Web template, name it **Import**, and double-click on its home page to open the FrontPage Editor.

3. In the FrontPage Editor, click on the page to place the insertion point, and then press CTRL-V to paste the contents of the Clipboard there. Your result should look like Figure 11-2.

4. Press CTRL-A to select all of the text, and press DEL to get rid of it.

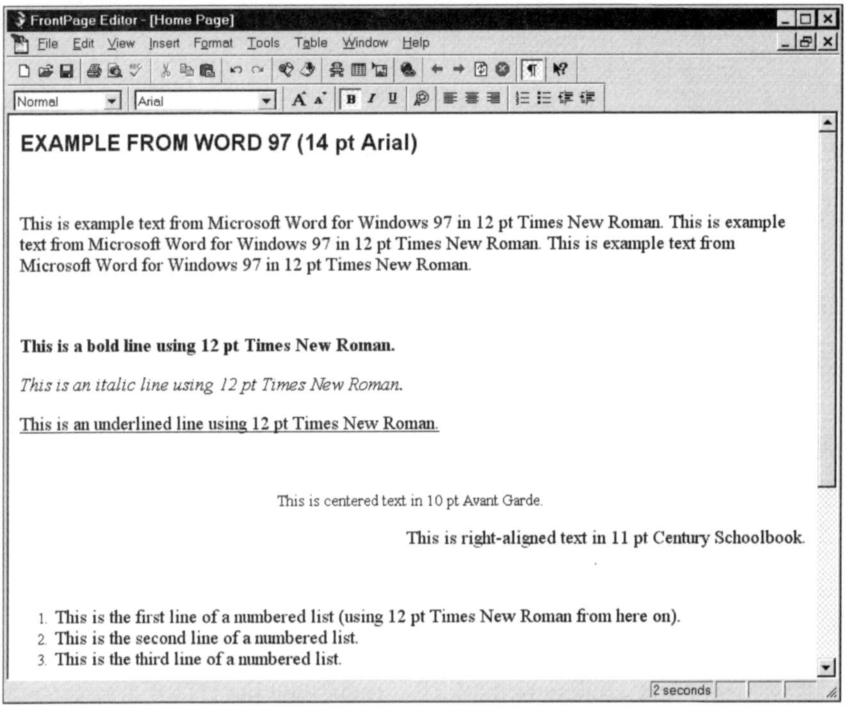

Text brought in on the Clipboard retains its formatting

FIGURE 11-2

As you can see, all the formatting is retained when you bring text into FrontPage from the Windows Clipboard. A 1-point border has been added to the table, which you may or may not want.

NOTE: *FrontPage and some browsers support the use of fonts other than the default Times New Roman. However, the font used must be installed on the user's computer to be displayed correctly, even if the browser supports the use of other fonts. More information about using fonts on the Web can be found at http://www.microsoft.com/truetype/.*

Inserting a File onto an Existing Page

You can insert a file onto an existing page by using any of the supported formats. You'll look at the Word .DOC, HTML, .RTF, and .TXT files next. The steps are similar for all the supported formats.

BRINGING IN .TXT FILES The Text (.TXT) option of inserting a file has several alternatives. To try these alternatives:

1. On the blank page in the FrontPage Editor, open the Insert menu and choose File. The Select A File dialog box will open.

2. Click on the down arrow in the Files Of Type drop-down menu. Here you can see some of the types of files you can bring into FrontPage:

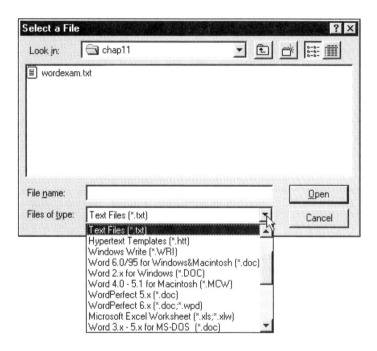

3. Click on Text Files, select the directory and file where you saved the .TXT file, and click on Open.

4. In the Convert Text dialog box, click on Formatted Paragraphs, and then click on OK. The text comes in using the FrontPage Formatted paragraph style, but all of the formatting from Microsoft Word is gone, as you can see in Figure 11-3.

   If you were to use the One Formatted Paragraph option, you would have no paragraph breaks, only new-line (SHIFT-ENTER) breaks throughout. With the Formatted paragraphs option, you get paragraph breaks wherever you had a blank line or two paragraph breaks in the original text.

11

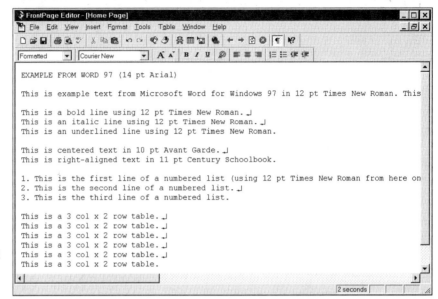

A text file
inserted in
TXT
format with
formatted
paragraphs

FIGURE 11-3

---

5. Click on Undo, open the Insert menu, choose File, select Text Files, and double-click on your .TXT file. Select Normal Paragraphs With Line Breaks and click on OK. The text comes in using FrontPage's Normal style, but again has no other formatting.

    If you were to use the Normal paragraphs option, the only paragraph breaks you would get are where you had blank paragraphs in the original (or two paragraph marks together).

TIP: *Notice that when you inserted the .TXT file with Formatted paragraphs, the first paragraph is one line, that is, without word wrap. With the Normal Paragraphs With Line Breaks option the text is wrapped to the width of the FrontPage Editor.*

6. Click on Undo.

The text format does not give you much, unless you want to bring in some plain text in FrontPage's Formatted paragraph style.

INSERTING A .DOC FILE   As you saw in Table 11-1, many word processors use the .DOC extension for their files. In this example a Word 97 file is used. The steps will be similar for any of the word processors supported by FrontPage.

1. With a blank page in FrontPage Editor, open the Insert menu, choose File, and select the correct file type for your word processor file.

2. Double-click on the Microsoft Word example that you saved with the DOC format. The file will appear on the open page, as shown in Figure 11-4. Note, the numbers are missing on the numbered list.

3. At the right end of the heading that begins "EXAMPLE FROM WORD," type **-INSERTED DOC** to distinguish this page from others that you will create.

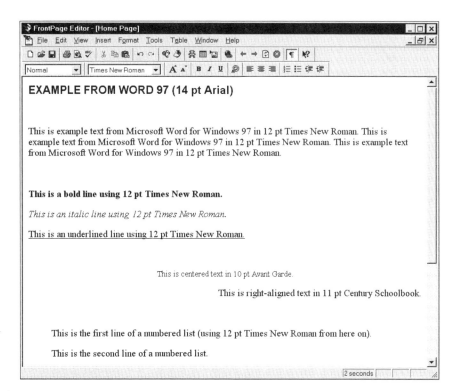

A text file inserted in Word 97 DOC format

FIGURE 11-4

4. Open the File menu and choose Save As. Type **Inserted Word DOC File** for the Page Title, type **Worddoc.htm** as the File Path within your FrontPage web, and click on OK.

An inserted .DOC file retains some, but not all of the formatting in the original document. There are two differences between the original and this HTML version—the lack of numbers on the numbered list, and the 11-point right-aligned line is 12 points. The latter is because there is no standard HTML size of 11 points; the closest standard sizes are 10 or 12 points; the former is just a bug.

INSERTING AN HTML FILE   An HMTL file (with a file extension of .HTM or .HTML) is the normal format of all text files on the Web, including FrontPage text files. For that reason it is the default when you insert a new file. The HTML files come into FrontPage nicely, as you can see.

TIP: *As was mentioned at the beginning of the chapter, some applications, specifically Microsoft Word, Excel, PowerPoint, Schedule+, and Access for Windows 95, have free add-ins that you can download from http://www.microsoft.com/msdownload that will allow you to create HTML files directly. Office 97 applications support HTML files directly.*

1. Open a new Normal Page in FrontPage Editor, open the Insert menu, choose File, and change the file type to HTML.

2. Double-click on the Microsoft Word example that you saved with the HTML format. The file will appear on the open page, as shown in Figure 11-5.

3. At the right end of the heading that begins "EXAMPLE FROM WORD," type **-INSERTED HTML** to distinguish this page from others that you will create.

4. Open the File menu and choose Save As. Type **Inserted Word HTML File** for the Page Title, type **Wordhtml.htm** as the File Path within your FrontPage web, and click on OK.

The HTML format retains the formatting present in the original document.

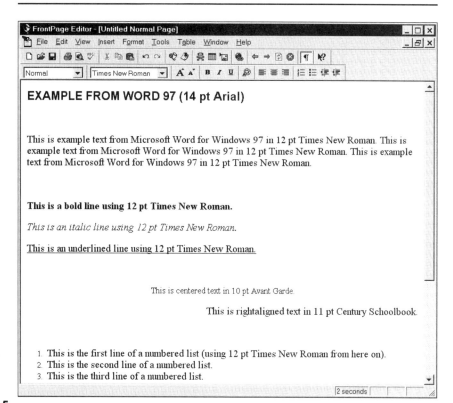

A text file inserted in HTML format

FIGURE 11-5

INSERTING AN .RTF FILE   The RTF file format was created to communicate the majority of text formatting. Many applications, not just word processing programs, have the ability to export files in RTF. To see how well FrontPage handles these files:

1. From the FrontPage Editor, click on the New button in the Standard toolbar to open a new page using the Normal template.

2. Open the Select A File dialog box by clicking on File from the Insert menu, choose Rich Text Format as the file type, and double-click on the RTF version of your Microsoft Word file. The file will appear on the new page, as you can see in Figure 11-6.

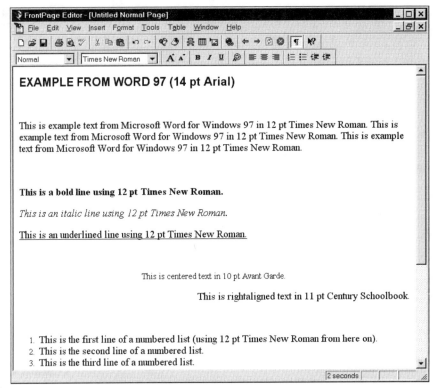

A file
inserted in
RTF format

FIGURE 11-6

3. At the right end of the heading at the top, type **-INSERTED RTF**, select
Save As from the File menu, type **Inserted Word RTF File** for the Page
Title, type **Wordrtf.htm** for the File Path within your FrontPage web, and
click on OK.

The results of the RTF import are very good.

Opening a File onto a New Page

The second way you can bring text files into a FrontPage web is through the
FrontPage Editor's File menu Open File command. This yields the Open File dialog
box, shown in Figure 11-7, from which you can again select any of the supported
file types. To explore this method:

1. From the FrontPage Editor open the File menu, choose Open, click on the
Other Location tab, select From File, and click on the Browse button.

Open File   ×

Current FrontPage Web | Other Location |

Look in: | http://marty/Import   ▼ | 🔼 | ☷ | ▥ |

Name	Title
🗀 _private	
🗀 images	
📄 Default.htm	Home Page
📄 Worddoc.htm	Inserted Word DOC File
📄 Wordhtml.htm	Inserted Word HTML File
📄 Wordrtf.htm	Inserted Word RTF File

| OK | Cancel | Help |

Open File
dialog box

◼ FIGURE 11-7

2. In the second Open File dialog box that is displayed select the Text Files type, and double-click on the TXT version of your Word file.

3. As you saw when you inserted a text file, the Convert Text dialog box opens, asking you the format to convert the text to. Click on Normal Paragraphs With Line Breaks and click on OK. The page that opens is exactly like the one you saw when you inserted a text file in this format, as shown in Figure 11-8.

4. In the Heading, type **-OPENED TEXT**, select Save As from the File menu, type **Opened Word Text File** for the Page title, Type **Opentext.htm** for the File Path within your FrontPage web, and click on OK.

11

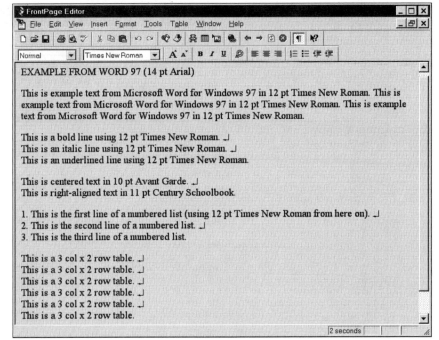

Opened
Word text
file with
Normal
paragraphs
and line
breaks

■ **FIGURE 11-8**

5. From the File menu choose Open, click on the Other Location tab, select
   From File, and click on the Browse button.

6. In the Open File dialog box that is displayed select the HTML Document
   file type, and double-click on the HTML version of your Word file. The
   file will come in on a new page, just as it did earlier (as shown in Figure
   11-5), except that it has a gray background.

7. Type **-OPENED HTML** in the heading, select Save As from the
   File menu, type **Opened Word HTML File** for the Page Title,
   type **Openhtml.htm** for the File Path within your FrontPage web, and
   click on OK.

8. Choose Open from the File menu, click on the Other Location tab, select From File, and click on the Browse button.

9. In the Open File dialog box that is displayed select the Rich Text Format file type, and double-click on the RTF version of your Word file. The file will come in on a new page, just as it did earlier (as shown in Figure 11-6), except that it has a gray background.

10. Type **-OPENED RTF** in the heading, select Save As from the File menu, type **Opened Word RTF File** for the Page Title, type **Openrtf.htm** for the File Path within your FrontPage web, and click on OK.

11. From the File menu choose Open, click on the Other Location tab, select From File, and click on the Browse button.

12. In the Open File dialog box that is displayed select the DOC file type for your word processor, and double-click on the DOC version of your Word file. The file will come in on a new page, just as it did earlier (as shown in Figure 11-4).

13. Type **-OPENED DOC** in the heading, select Save As from the File menu, type **Opened Word DOC File** for the Page Title, type **Opendoc.htm** for the File Path within your FrontPage web, and click on OK.

You can see that the Open command produces the same results as Insert File, except that it creates a new page each time a file is brought in.

Importing a File onto a New Page

The third method for bringing text files into FrontPage is to use the FrontPage Explorer's Import command in the File menu. Try that next:

1. Open the FrontPage Explorer and then from its File menu choose Import. The Import File To FrontPage Web dialog box opens.

2. Click on Add File and the Add File To Import List dialog box opens. Click on the down arrow in its Files Of Type drop-down menu. Notice that you do not have all the choices here that you had in the FrontPage Editor Insert and Open methods, as you can see in Figure 11-9.

11

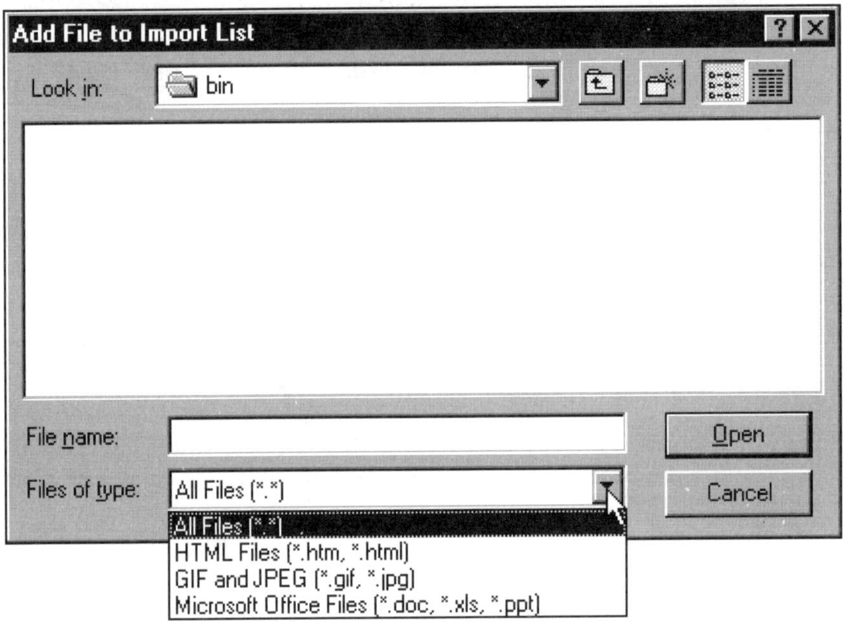

Add File to Import List   ? ✕

Look in: 📁 bin   ▼   🔼 📁 ⬛ ⬛

File name: _____   Open

Files of type: All Files (*.*)   ▼   Cancel

All Files (*.*)
HTML Files (*.htm, *.html)
GIF and JPEG (*.gif, *.jpg)
Microsoft Office Files (*.doc, *.xls, *.ppt)

File types
available
when
importing a
file

FIGURE 11-9

3. Choose HTML Files as the file type, select the directory and filename of the HTML version of your Word file, and then click on Open. The file is added to the Import File To FrontPage Web dialog box.

4. Click on Add File again, select All Files as the type, and then double-click on the DOC version, the native Word for Windows format of your Word file.

5. With your Import File To FrontPage Web dialog box looking like the one shown next, click on OK.

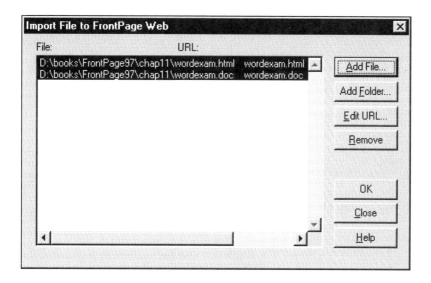

6. Back in the FrontPage Explorer you will see two new pages—one is the DOC file (wordexam.doc), which has the Word icon, and the other is an HTML file with a plain document icon. Both files have your heading or first line of text as its page label, like this:

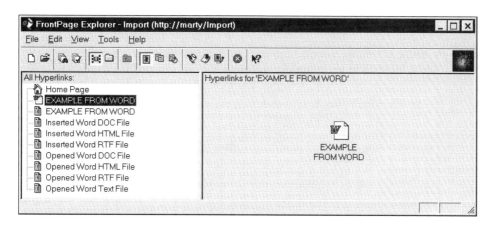

IMPORTING HTML FILES The FrontPage Explorer gives you two ways to import text files—in HTML format and in the native format of the original document. Take a quick look at the HTML file now:

1. Select the HTML file—the one that does *not* have the Word icon—and double-click on it in the Hyperlink pane to open the file in the FrontPage Editor. Again you'll see the same HTML page you have seen twice before and in Figure 11-5.

2. Type **-IMPORTED HTML** in the heading, select Save As from the File menu, type **Imported Word HTML File** for the Page Title, type **Impthtml.htm** for the File Path within your FrontPage web, and click on OK.

3. Return to the FrontPage Explorer, and notice that in renaming your imported page, you actually created an additional page. To correct this, delete the original imported HTML file (the "EXAMPLE FROM WORD" with a plain document icon), and click on Yes to confirm the deletion.

IMPORTING FILES IN THEIR NATIVE FORMAT The ability to import a file in its native format is very important, but it, of course, has limitations. You'll see how this works with the Microsoft Word file next. Later, in the "Bringing Files from Other Productivity Applications" section, you'll see how this works with other applications.

1. Click on the file with the Word icon in the All Hyperlinks pane of the FrontPage Explorer, and double-click on the same file in the Hyperlink pane. Microsoft Word will load, and the file will be displayed and ready to edit as you saw in Figure 11-1.

    Instead of opening the FrontPage Editor, the .DOC extension has been associated with Microsoft Word, and that application is opened to edit the file. While this association comes from your Windows Registry, other associations are maintained in FrontPage.

2. Close Microsoft Word, open the FrontPage Explorer's Tools menu, and click on Options. In the Options dialog box click on the Configure Editors tab, shown here. This dialog box associates a file extension with the application that the FrontPage Explorer will open to edit the file.

Options   [X]

General | Proxies | Configure Editors |

Type: Editor:

mic	ImageComposer (C:\Program Files\Micros
bmp	ImageComposer (C:\Program Files\Micros
dib	ImageComposer (C:\Program Files\Micros
gif	ImageComposer (C:\Program Files\Micros
jpg	ImageComposer (C:\Program Files\Micros
tif	ImageComposer (C:\Program Files\Micros
acc	ImageComposer (C:\Program Files\Micros
tga	ImageComposer (C:\Program Files\Micros
htm	FrontPage Editor (C:\Program Files\Micros
html	FrontPage Editor (C:\Program Files\Micros
htx	FrontPage Editor (C:\Program Files\Micros
asp	FrontPage Editor (C:\Program Files\Micros
frm	FrontPage Frames Wizard (C:\Program File
idc	FrontPage Database Connection Wizard (C

Add...
Modify...
Remove

OK   Cancel   Help

3. Click on Add. The Add Editor Association dialog box will open. Enter a
new file association that makes sense for you. To add an association
between CorelDRAW and .CDR, I'll type **cdr** as the File Type, press TAB,
type **CorelDRAW** for the Editor Name, press TAB again, and then click
on Browse and locate the CorelDRAW application as you can see in the
following illustration. Click on OK. If you don't have CorelDRAW, pick
some other application that you do have and put it on instead.

Add Editor Association   [X]

File Type: | cdr |

Editor Name: | CorelDRAW |

Command: | C:\COREL\PROGRAMS\coreldrw.exe | Browse...

OK   Cancel   Help

11

4. Your new application will appear in the Configure Editors tab of the Options dialog box. Click on OK to close it.

CAUTION: *There is one catch to using a file in its native format in a web—you are assuming that users have the application on their computer so they can view the file. This is made easier for Microsoft Office products, because Microsoft offers free viewers on its web site (http://www.microsoft.com/msdownload) that can be used with Microsoft Internet Explorer.*

Drag and Drop

Another way to bring files into FrontPage is to drag and drop a file into either the FrontPage Explorer or the FrontPage Editor. Start by dragging and dropping a file into the FrontPage Explorer:

1. Open the Windows Explorer and select the directory that contains your text files.

2. Select Folder view in the FrontPage Explorer, and then arrange the Windows Explorer window and the FrontPage Explorer window so that both are visible on your screen, as shown in Figure 11-10.

3. Select the wordexam.txt file in the Windows Explorer, and then drag it onto the left pane of the FrontPage Explorer, on top of the Import folder. The pointer changes to an arrow with a plus sign, indicating the selected file will be copied to the new location, as shown next. Release the mouse button to copy the file to the selected folder.

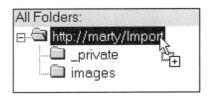

NOTE: *In FrontPage Explorer's Folder view you can drop the file into the selected folder. In Hyperlink view the file is copied to the web root (http://marty/Import in this example).*

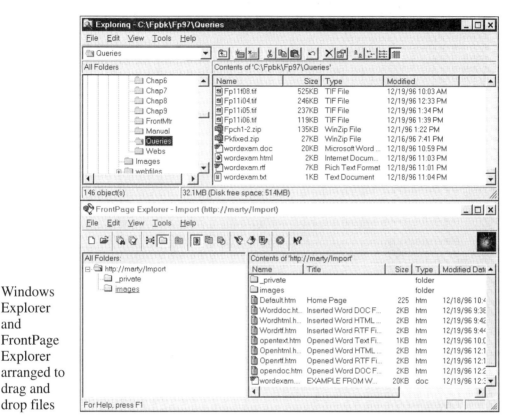

Windows
Explorer
and
FrontPage
Explorer
arranged to
drag and
drop files

FIGURE 11-10

4. Double-click on the wordexam.txt file in the FrontPage Explorer
and it opens in Notepad. Close Notepad without changing the file
before proceeding.

Dragging and dropping a file onto the FrontPage Explorer has the same result
as importing a file using the Import option on the File menu.

NOTE: *Dropping an HTML file onto the FrontPage Explorer imports
only the HTML page; any images on the page are not imported and must
be imported separately.*

DRAG AND DROP IN THE FRONTPAGE EDITOR   You can also use drag and drop to insert files into the FrontPage Editor. The result is the same as selecting File from the FrontPage Editor Import menu, as you'll see next:

1. Arrange your screen so that both the Windows Explorer and FrontPage Editor windows are visible.

2. Click on the New button in the FrontPage Editor toolbar to open a new page.

3. In the Windows Explorer select the wordexam.doc file, and drag it onto the new page in the FrontPage Editor.

4. Type **–DROPPED DOC** in the heading, select Save As from the File menu, type **Dropped Word DOC File** for the Page Title, type **Dropdoc.htm** for the File Path within your FrontPage web, and click on OK.

Bringing Files from Other Productivity Applications

Using HTML, RTF, or a file in its native format if you think the user can open it, you can bring files from many applications into FrontPage. Recently a number of applications have made add-ins available that convert their files to HTML or otherwise allow publishing them on the Internet. Microsoft has made add-ins, called Internet Assistants, available for Word, Excel, PowerPoint, Access, and Schedule+ applications that are part of Office 95 and are built into Office 97. In addition, Microsoft has made available the PowerPoint Animation Player and Publisher, which provide the means to create and deliver a PowerPoint animated presentation, complete with sound, on the Web. While the PowerPoint Player and Publisher come together as one product, they are two separate programs. One, the Animation Player, is an add-on for your browser. The other, the Animation Publisher, is an add-on for PowerPoint. As mentioned earlier, all of the Microsoft add-ins are available for free if you download them from http://www.microsoft.com/msdownload. Now you'll see how this works with Microsoft Excel and PowerPoint files.

Using Microsoft Excel Files

In Microsoft Excel, like most spreadsheet applications, you can create both tabular information and charts or graphs, as shown in Figure 11-11. When you bring this

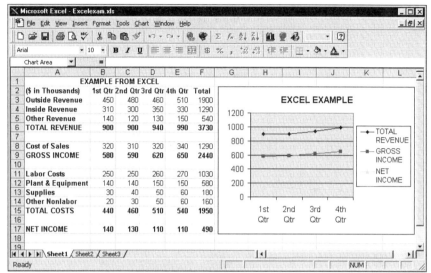

Excel example with both tabular and chart data

FIGURE 11-11

into FrontPage, you must either use the native format—which handles both types of data—and hope the user has the product or the viewer, or you must handle the two data types separately. Try this with Excel (if you don't have Excel, see if your application has the same capability).

1. In Microsoft Excel or your spreadsheet application, create the tabular and chart example shown in Figure 11-11 or use similar information you already have. Save this both in its native format and in TXT format (if your spreadsheet can also directly save the file in RTF, do so; Excel can't).

2. In Excel select a range on the spreadsheet that you want to bring into FrontPage; then from the File menu choose Save As HTML. The first step of the Internet Assistant Wizard will open as shown in Figure 11-12. In the wizard you can save multiple selections and charts as one HTML file. In the example here the tabular data and the chart will be saved as one file.

3. Click on Next. You can choose to create an independent HTML file with a header, body table, and a footer, or just to insert the table in an existing HTML file. Choose the independent HTML file and click on Next.

11

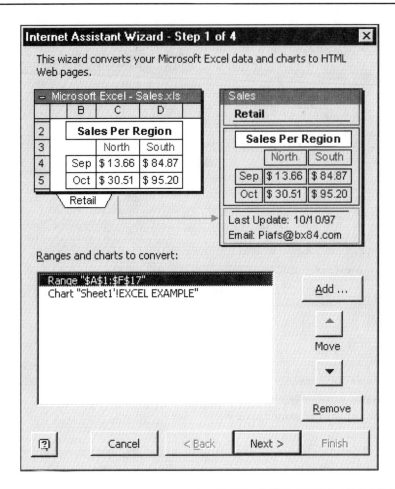

Excel
Internet
Assistant
Wizard –
Step 1

FIGURE 11-12

4. Enter **Excel HTML Example** for the title, **Excel Example** for the header, and complete any remaining empty fields in the footer (Last Update On, By, and Email); select both of the separating lines; and then click on Next. Enter the path and filename to use, and click on Finish.

5. In the FrontPage Explorer, click on Import from the File menu to open the Import File ToFrontPage Web dialog box, click on Add File, select the Excel HTML file, click on Open, click on Add File again, choose All Files as the file type, and double-click on the Excel file in its native format. Click on OK now to complete the process.

6. Open the HTML file in the FrontPage Editor, and you'll see the table with several icons representing HTML comments as shown in Figure 11-13. HTML comments will be covered in Chapter 12.

7. Scroll down the HTML page in the FrontPage Editor. Below the table is an icon representing a graphic with a broken link. When you saved your Excel file as an HTML file, the chart was converted to a GIF image file and linked to the HTML page. When the HTML page was imported into the FrontPage Explorer, the graphic was not imported with it.

8. Right-click on the graphic icon, and select Image Properties from the context menu. In the Image Properties dialog box, click on the Image Source Browse button, locate and select the image file, click on Open, and then click on OK. The chart will replace the broken link graphic icon.

9. Close the FrontPage Editor, saving the changes to the Excel HTML Example as well as saving the .GIF file. Click on the native Excel file, and then double-click on it in Hyperlink view. Excel will open and display the file as Word did. Close Excel.

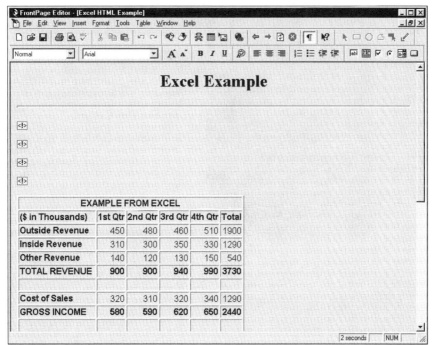

Excel
HTML
example in
the
FrontPage
Editor

FIGURE 11-13

You can also use the methods of bringing files into the FrontPage Editor discussed earlier in this chapter to bring all or part of your spreadsheet into FrontPage. Both spreadsheet tabular and chart data can be copied to the Clipboard and pasted onto a web page, the files can be dragged and dropped onto a web page, and you can use the FrontPage Editor Insert menu File option. However, saving the spreadsheet as an HTML file in Excel first will produce the best results.

Bringing in PowerPoint Files

PowerPoint gives you three choices for getting the files on the Internet: in native format, in HTML, and in PowerPoint Animation. To look at each of these:

1. Load PowerPoint and then either create a new presentation, use an existing presentation, or use the AutoContent Wizard to create a quick example presentation, as I have done for this example.

2. Save the presentation in its native format, and then open the File menu and choose Save As HTML. The Save As HTML Wizard will open as shown here:

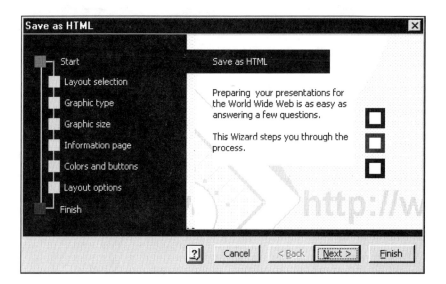

3. Click on Next, select New Layout, and click on Next again.

4. Accept the default Standard for the page style and click on Next.

5. Select GIF and click on Next.

6. Select a monitor resolution of 640×480, then select $\frac{3}{4}$ width of screen from the Width Of Graphics drop-down menu, and click on Next.

7. The Information page options are displayed. In addition to entering your e-mail address, home page, and comments, you can also have buttons for downloading the original PowerPoint file and the latest version of Microsoft Internet Explorer. Enter the information you want displayed on your PowerPoint home page.

8. Click on Next and accept the default Use Browser Colors. Click on Next again.

9. Select the button style of your choice, click on Next, and then select the layout options you want. Click on Next.

10. In the final wizard dialog box specify the location for the HTML folder PowerPoint will create. You can use a temp directory or the same directory where the original presentation is located. Click on Finish.

11. In the Save As HTML dialog box that is displayed you can enter a name to save the settings you just used to create the HTML files. You can use this as a template to create future PowerPoint animations without repeating all the steps you just went through. For now, click on Don't Save.

12. You'll see several message boxes telling you that the presentation is being created and then one that says that the presentation was successfully saved as HTML. Click on OK again to close the final message box.

NOTE: *The Save As HTML command creates a number of files that are placed in their own directory complete with a home page (Index.htm) and a number of graphics. In other words, a complete web is created by this command.*

13. Using the Windows Explorer, open the directory in which you saved the PowerPoint HTML example, and observe the complete web that has been created. Close the Windows Explorer and return to PowerPoint.

14. Open the File menu once more, and choose Save As HTML again.

15. Repeat steps 3 and 4. In the Choose Graphic Type dialog box select PowerPoint Animation, and click on OK.

16. Repeat steps 6 through 9.

17. Select a different directory to save the PowerPoint Animation file; if you use the same directory that you saved the HTML files in, they will be overwritten, since PowerPoint will use the same name for the file.

18. Repeat steps 10 through 12.

19. In the Windows Explorer locate the PowerPoint animation folder, and rename it so you can import both into your FrontPage web.

20. In the FrontPage Explorer, click on Import from the File menu to open the Import File ToFrontPage Web dialog box, click on Add Folder, select the path to the HTML folder, and click on OK.

21. Repeat Step 20 to import the PowerPoint animation folder.

22. Next click on Add File to import the native PowerPoint file, and then click on OK to close the Import File dialog box.

23. In the FrontPage Explorer, click on the PowerPoint Index.htm file in the folder with the HTML presentation, and then open it in the FrontPage Editor (if you can't find it in Hyperlink view, use Folder view). What you get is not very exciting, as you can see in Figure 11-14. But if you right-click on the first link ("Click here to start") and choose Follow Hyperlink, you'll see the first slide in your presentation. Right-click on the right pointing arrow and choose Follow Hyperlink to go to the next slide, or right-click on the double right pointing arrows and choose Follow Hyperlink to go to the last slide. In the right browser this will work beautifully.

24. As you did in step 22, you can open the PowerPoint Animation folder and double-click on Index.htm to open that presentation in the FrontPage Editor. Your screen looks just like Figure 11-14. If you follow the "Click here to start" hyperlink, though, you'll see a different opening slide announcing ActiveX resources, and the "recorder" buttons are gone. You'll see how this works in a browser in a minute.

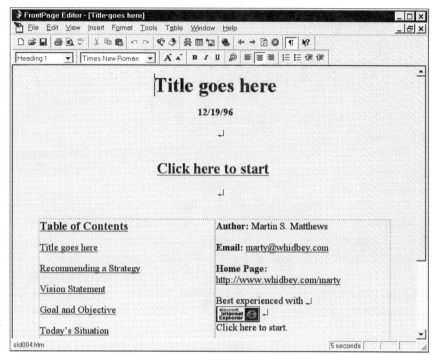

PowerPoint
introductory
page

FIGURE 11-14

25. Close the FrontPage Editor. Next, click and then double-click on the .PPT file to see it opened in the PowerPoint application like the other native files you've seen. Close PowerPoint when you are ready.

All of the Microsoft Office applications, including Access, Schedule+, and Outlook, have an impressive ability to create HTML and other files that are usable in a web and importable with FrontPage. This is a great way to quickly generate web content.

Using Legacy Files on an Intranet

An intranet provides an excellent opportunity to make good use of, or even improve, *legacy* (previously created) files. Manuals and sets of procedures are particularly

good examples of this. Instead of maintaining around the office 20 (or 50 or 500!) sets of company manuals that rarely get used except to settle an argument, maintain one set on your intranet. Here people can use a search capability to quickly find what they are looking for, whenever they want and wherever they are.

Manuals and sets of procedures almost surely exist as word processing files that can be easily transferred to FrontPage. Once you do that, you can add the Table of Contents bot to quickly index the files, the Search bot to search all of the text, and the Include bot to place headers and footers on each page with navbars, time stamps, and contacts.

Company reports and periodicals are also good candidates for your intranet—current editions and previous issues can be searched and read in one easily accessible place.

The simple addition of FrontPage's search capability makes finding information on an intranet so easy, that that could be the primary reason for putting it there. In the same vein, the Table of Contents and Include bots can add significantly improved usability to existing documents. In other words, putting your legacy documents on your intranet with FrontPage not only gives them a new way to be distributed and read, but features like the Search bot, the Table of Contents bot, and the Include bot also make them substantially more usable, and therefore, more likely to be used.

Looking at Imported Files in a Browser

The real test of a web is how it looks in a browser. See for yourself in this next set of steps:

1. Open the very first "Home page" you created for this web in the FrontPage Editor. This should be your Home page with a filename of Default.htm. If you do not find it, use any other page to open the FrontPage Editor and create a new page. In either case title the page **Import Home Page**, formatted with Heading 1 and centered, and insert a Table of Contents bot.

 NOTE: *This is a great demonstration of how the Table of Contents bot can automatically create links to all the .HTM pages. Unfortunately, it will not create links to the .DOC, .XLS, and .PPT files.*

2. Accept the defaults for the bot; this gives you a link to all of the .HTM files (although they won't appear until you get back to the FrontPage Explorer or open the web in a browser). Create links to the .DOC, .XLS, or .PPT files by typing **Link to Word .DOC file** (or Excel .XLS or PowerPoint .PPT), clicking on the Link button, and selecting the link in the current web using the Browse button.

3. Save the Home page with the **Import Home Page** title and the **Default.htm** page URL. Close the FrontPage Editor. You should see all of the links in the FrontPage Explorer, like this:

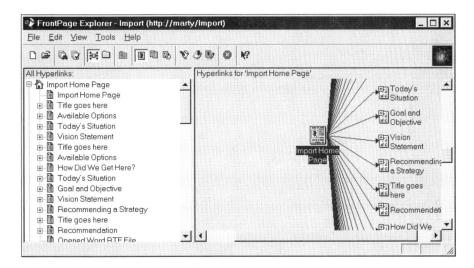

4. Open your browser with a web name of Import. The Import Home Page will appear, as you can see in Figure 11-15.

5. Click on each of the links to view the imported (or opened or inserted) files, using the browser's Back button to return to the Home page. You will not find many surprises.

6. If you have a second browser, open the same web in it, and go through each of the links. Note the differences.

7. The Excel HTML file in both the Internet Explorer and the Navigator comes out reasonably well, as shown in Figure 11-16.

Import
Home Page
with links
to imported
pages

FIGURE 11-15

8. The PowerPoint Animation should work in Netscape Navigator 2.0 and
later if the Animation Player has been properly installed, and it will work
in Microsoft Internet Explorer 3.0 or later. The three native files opened
in Internet Explorer will all load their applications and display the file
with only a virus warning to interrupt the process. In Netscape Navigator,
both the Word and Excel files require that you identify the application
needed to view the file (unless this has already been done). This might be
either the creating application or a viewer. For PowerPoint, the Player that
you installed for the Animation file includes a viewer, so the file opens
directly in the Netscape Navigator.

Excel HTML file in a browser

Excel HTML Example - Microsoft Internet Explorer

File Edit View Go Favorites Help

Back Forward Stop Refresh Home Search Favorit.. Print Font Mail Edit

Address http://marty/import/exclhtml.htm   ▼ Links

Excel Example

EXAMPLE FROM EXCEL					
	1st Qtr	2nd Qtr	3rd Qtr	4th Qtr	Total
Outside Revenue	450	480	460	510	1900
Inside Revenue	310	300	350	330	1290
Other Revenue	140	120	130	150	540
TOTAL REVENUE	900	900	940	990	3730
Cost of Sales	320	310	320	340	1290
GROSS INCOME	580	590	620	650	2440
Labor Costs	250	250	260	270	1030
Plant & Equipment	140	140	150	150	580
Supplies	30	40	50	60	180
Other Nonlabor	20	30	50	60	160
TOTAL COSTS	440	460	510	540	1950

Done

FIGURE 11-16

9. In both browsers open the separate PowerPoint web as a file by identifying the path and then the Index.htm file. In both cases the web looks the same, like the image in Figure 11-17. By clicking on the arrows, you can move through the presentation.

10. Close the one or two browsers you have open.

Importing Multimedia Files

Multimedia is becoming a more significant part of the World Wide Web. In webs you'll see links to .WAV and .AFFI audio files or to .AVI and QuickTime (.MOV) video files.

11

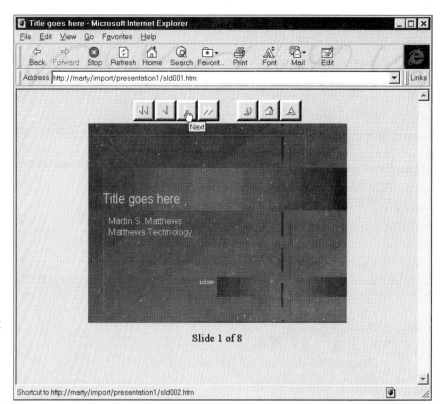

PowerPoint web opened in Internet Explorer

Title goes here - Microsoft Internet Explorer

FIGURE 11-17

These files are first downloaded and then automatically or manually played. There are also streaming products like RealAudio (http://www.realaudio.com) and StreamWorks (http://www.xingtech.com) for both distributing and playing audio and/or video pieces as they are received (instead of waiting for them to be fully transferred).

FrontPage supports the incorporation of the multimedia files listed in Table 11-2. Assuming that your users have the necessary player, they can play back the files by clicking on them in your web. This works well with .WAV and .AVI files if your users have Windows 95, because Windows 95 includes players for these files. Also, the Microsoft Internet Explorer will automatically start the player when these files are clicked (Netscape Navigator 2.0 requires that you identify the player the first time you click on these files).

File Format	Extensions
Video for Windows	.AVI
Wave sound	.WAV
MIDI sequence	.MID
AIFF sound	.AIF, .AFC, .AIFF
AU sound	.AU, .SND

Multimedia Files Supported by FrontPage

TABLE 11-2

TIP: *Remember that sound and especially video files can get quite large and take significant time to download even at 28.8 Kbps.*

You can also insert HTML to play both .AVI and .WAV files automatically when a web page is opened by the user. You'll see how to do this in Chapter 15.

Importing files into a FrontPage web, be they text, tables, presentations, or even multimedia, provides a great deal of ready-made content. When these files are artfully used, they can quickly give a web a lot of depth. As you are building a web site, remember the many existing files that are available. Their use in a web will further leverage their original investment.

11

FrontPage on the Web

The BookBay

URL: *http://www.whidbey.com/bookbay*
Webmaster: Brad Bixby
E-mail: *bookbay@whidbey.com*

1638 E. Main Street
P.O. Box 520
Freeland, WA 98249-0520
(206) 331-5404
(206) 331-5404 (Fax)

Web Site

The BookBay web site was produced by the owner of a small rural bookstore. It is his first effort at web making and was done with the help of the first edition of *Web Publishing with Microsoft FrontPage.* The Home page, shown in Figure 1, uses a number of automated GIFs to give the page some life (the clam, worm, and book pages are all active). The HTML for the bookworm and the table of contents is shown in Listing 1.

Listing 1
Table of
contents HTML

```
<p align=center><font color="#FFFF80"><img src="images/bookworm2.gif"
    align=bottom width=22 height=33></font></p><p align=left>
<a hret="books.htm"><font color-"#FFFF80"><img src-"images/book2.gif"
    align=bottom border=0 width=37 height=30></font></a><font color="#FFFF80">
    </font>
<a href="books.htm"><font color="#FFFF80">Just Browsing?</font></a>
    <font color="#FFFF80"> </font><font color="#FFFF00">Take a look through the
        store.<br></font>
<a href="clubs.htm"><font color="#FFFF00"><img src="images/book2.gif"
    align=bottom border=0 width=37 height=30></font></a><font color="#FFFF00">
    </font>
<a href="clubs.htm"><font color="#FFFF00">Book Clubs</font></a>
    <font color="#FFFF00"> - Book lists from Island Groups and Oprah Winfrey's
        group too!<br></font>
<a href="whidbey.htm"><font color="#FFFF00"><img src="images/book2.gif"
```

FrontPage on the Web (cont.)

```
align=bottom border=0 width=37 height=30></font></a><font
    color="#FFFF00"> </font>
<a href="whidbey.htm"><font color="#FFFF00">Whidbey
    Island</font></a>
  <font color="#FFFF00"> A short history<br></font>
<a href="freeland.htm"><font color="#FFFF00"><img
    src="images/book2.gif" align=bottom border=0 width=37
    height=30></font></a><font color="#FFFF00"> </font>
<a href="whidbey.htm"><font color="#FFFF00">Whidbey Island</font></a>
  <font color="#FFFF00"> A short history<br></font>
<a href="freeland.htm"><font color+"FFFF00"><img scr="images/book2.gif"
<a href="freeland.htm"><font color="#FFFF00">Freeland</font></a>
  align=bottom border=0 width=37 height=30></font></a><font color="#3FFFF00">
    </font>
  <font color="#FFFF00"> The Center for South Whidbey
    Services<br></font>
```

BookBay's
Home page

FIGURE 1

FrontPage on the Web (cont.)

The second page provides a further breakdown in the table of contents, as you can see in Figure 2. Again this page contains a number of automated GIFs, including the eyes in "BookBay," the pages in the book under "BookBay," and the pages of the books used as bullets on the left of the list. Figure 3 shows a page dedicated to the small town in which The BookBay is located.

Webmaster Q & A

WHY FRONTPAGE? The inventory in a retail bookstore changes daily, and I was looking for a "what you see is what you get" (WYSIWYG) web site creation tool that would allow me to update my page rapidly without trial-and-error HTML programming and testing.

LIKES AND DISLIKES Updating my page is done in minutes. And I can be relatively sure that the changes I make will appear on the page correctly and as I expect them. Other than a few exceptions, my design appeared the same in both Netscape

Page 2
of The
BookBay's
web site

FIGURE 2

FrontPage on the Web (cont.)

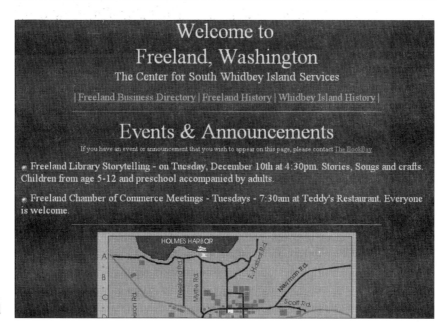

Page
dedicated
to the town
of Freeland

▨ FIGURE 3

Navigator and Microsoft Internet Explorer. When differences did occur, changes could be quickly made. I had some problems with a few GIF files appearing correctly in the FrontPage editor but appearing compressed in width on my web page.

NEATEST FEATURES OF THIS SITE   If other web surfers are like me, they are in and out of a web site in seconds unless there is something to slow them down. Animated GIF files gave my page something to catch the reader's attention and maybe a reason to look further into my web site. Besides, animated GIFs are fun to design and easy to place on the page. Working with the local Chamber of Commerce, I wrote a business directory for our community that was a lot more popular than I anticipated, necessitating constant updates for new business entries. FrontPage allows me to list businesses and provide links to their pages and e-mail addresses quickly and effortlessly. Without links to and from my page, Freeland pages get lost on the web. Every link is a new supply of potential customers and FrontPage makes it easy.

11

FrontPage on the Web (cont.)

TIPS Spend some time, lots of time, on your basic design. Draw a chart of the pages in your web site, and experiment with the different ways your customer might move from page to page. Set up folders or directories to store your graphics. Start with a simple web site and get on line. You can always make it more complex as you learn.

12

Working with HTML

389

Throughout the previous chapters you have read that by using FrontPage you don't have to learn HTML (HyperText Markup Language), the programming language of the Web. You *can* build great web pages without ever learning HTML or even reading this chapter. But this chapter is for those who either want to go further—to put the last bit of flourish on their web page—or who just want to understand the HTML behind their FrontPage-created web. Since, with access to FrontPage, you probably will not have to create many webs from scratch in HTML, this chapter will not provide exhaustive coverage of that topic, nor will it cover every nuance of every HTML tag. Both areas are fully covered by sites on the Web, as listed at the end of this chapter. What this chapter will cover is how to understand the HTML that is generated by a FrontPage web and how to add specific capabilities to a FrontPage web with HTML.

> **NOTE:**   *HTML is an evolving language that's a little out of control. With Netscape and Microsoft adding their own (mutually incompatible) tags, the standards committee is playing catch-up. BGCOLOR (the attribute that controls background color), for example, will respond differently with named colors depending on your browser. Adding to this problem is that both Netscape and Microsoft are rushing ahead with new browsers with many more features. While I have tried to identify what tags work on which products, it is a bit like describing a melting snowball: as soon as you get done describing it, it has changed. The best approach is to use the browsers that you want to write for and test your web on those browsers to make sure it behaves the way you want it to.*

Introducing HTML

HTML is a series of tags that identify the elements in a web page. *Tags* or *markup tags* consist of a tag name enclosed in angle brackets and normally come in pairs. Tags are placed at the beginning and end of an element, with the ending tag name preceded by a slash. For example,

```
<TITLE>This is a title</TITLE>
```

uses the Title tag to identify text that will be placed in the title bar of the browser window. Tags are not case-sensitive, so they can be all uppercase, all lowercase, or a mixture. Tags are placed around text to control its formatting and placement on a page; to identify a hypertext link; to identify a graphic, sound, or video to be loaded; or to identify a particular area of a web page.

In addition to a tag name, a tag may contain one or more *attributes* that modify what the tag does. For example, if you want to center a paragraph on the page, you would use this tag:

```
<P ALIGN=CENTER>This will be a centered paragraph</P>
```

ALIGN=CENTER is an *attribute* for the Paragraph tag.

TIP: *Just because an HTML tag exists doesn't mean that you have to use it. As in most other endeavors, the KISS principle applies to the use of HTML.*

Using Basic Tags

All web pages must contain a basic set of tags. These tags identify the document as being an HTML document and identify the major parts of the document. These are the only tags that must be included in a web page to conform to the HTML standard. The Body tag is also used to identify the page defaults, such as the background color or image and the text color. The basic tags, some of which are shown in Listing 12-1, are described in Table 12-1.

NOTE: *In the listings in this chapter, tags are shown in all capital letters and bold, while attributes are just all capital letters. Also, continuation lines are indented from their parents. These conventions are used solely for readability. Tags and attributes can be any mixture of cases, and there is no need to indent. HTML created by FrontPage is also indented and can be color-coded in the View Or Edit HTML dialog box for readability.*

Listing 12-1
Basic set of
HTML tags

```
<!DOCTYPE HTML PUBLIC "-//IETF//DTD HTML//EN">
<HTML>
<HEAD>
    <META HTTP-EQUIV=" CONTENT="text/html; CHARSET=iso-8859-1">
    <META NAME="GENERATOR" CONTENT="Microsoft FrontPage 2.0">
    <TITLE>Home Page</TITLE>
</HEAD>
<BODY BGCOLOR="blue" TEXT="white">
    <P>This is the text that is the body of this web document</P>
</BODY>
</HTML>
```

NOTE: *In the tables of tags and attributes in this chapter, tags are shown with their angle brackets, and attributes are indented from the left.*

NOTE: *Color names that can be used with BGCOLOR, LINK, TEXT, and VLINK as well as other tags with the Microsoft Internet Explorer 2.0 or later are Black, White, Green, Maroon, Olive, Navy, Purple, Gray, Red, Yellow, Blue, Teal, Lime, Aqua, Fuchsia, and Silver. Netscape Navigator supports 140 named colors including the 16 that Microsoft uses. The color value is a combination of three pairs of hexadecimal numbers, one pair (256 possibilities) each for Red, Green, and Blue. Over 16 million color values can therefore be generated, compared with the 16 or 140 color names. However, most of these colors will not display well in most browsers when used as solid colors. One of the best sources for information on color and web browsers is The DMS Guide to Web Color at http://www.oit.itd.umich.edu/projects/DMS/answers/colorguide/. The site includes palettes that can be used with Adobe Photoshop and Fractal Painter.*

Setting Paragraph Styles

Paragraph styles include basic paragraph definition and alignment; headings; the line break; bulleted, numbered, and definition lists; preformatted (called "formatted" in FrontPage) paragraphs; comments; and horizontal lines or rules. Unless the preformatted style is used, normal line endings, extra spaces of more than one, and tabs are ignored in HTML. Lines simply wrap to fit the space allotted for them, unless you use the Paragraph tag. Listing 12-2 shows examples of paragraph styles. This listing is combined with the tags in Listing 12-1 to produce the web page shown in Figure 12-1. Paragraph styles are described in Table 12-2.

Tag or Attribute	Description
`<!DOCTYPE ...>`	Identifies the document as adhering to the given HTML version. This tag should be the first line in any HTML document.
`<HTML> </HTML>`	Identifies the intervening text as being HTML.
`<HEAD> </HEAD>`	Contains the title and document identifying information. The `<TITLE>` tag is required in the `<HEAD>` tag.
`<TITLE> </TITLE>`	Identifies the title that is placed in the browser's title bar.
`<META ...>`	Assigns content to an element that can be used by a server or browser and cannot otherwise be assigned in HTML; "Microsoft FrontPage 2.0" is assigned to "GENERATOR" in Listing 12-1. Placed within the `<HEAD>` tag.
`<BODY> </BODY>`	Specifies the part of the page that is shown to the user and defines overall page properties.
ALINK	Identifies the color of the active link as either a color name or hexadecimal number representing a color value.
BACKGROUND	Identifies the background image that will be tiled if necessary to fill the window.
BGCOLOR	Identifies the background color that will be used as either a color name or a hexadecimal number representing a color value.
BGPROPERTIES	Specifies that the background will not scroll with the window if `BGPROPERTIES=FIXED`.
LEFTMARGIN	Sets the left margin for the entire page and overrides any default margin (a margin of 0 will be exactly on the left edge).

Basic Set
of HTML
Tags

TABLE 12-1

12

Tag or Attribute	Description
LINK	Identifies the color of links that have not been used as either a color name or a hexadecimal number representing a color value.
TEXT	Identifies the color of text on the page as either a color name or a hexadecimal number representing a color value.
TOPMARGIN	Sets the top margin for the page and overrides any default margin (a margin of 0 will be exactly on the top edge).
VLINK	Identifies the color of links that have been used as either a color name or a hexadecimal number representing a color value.

Basic Set
of HTML
Tags
(*continued*)

TABLE 12-1

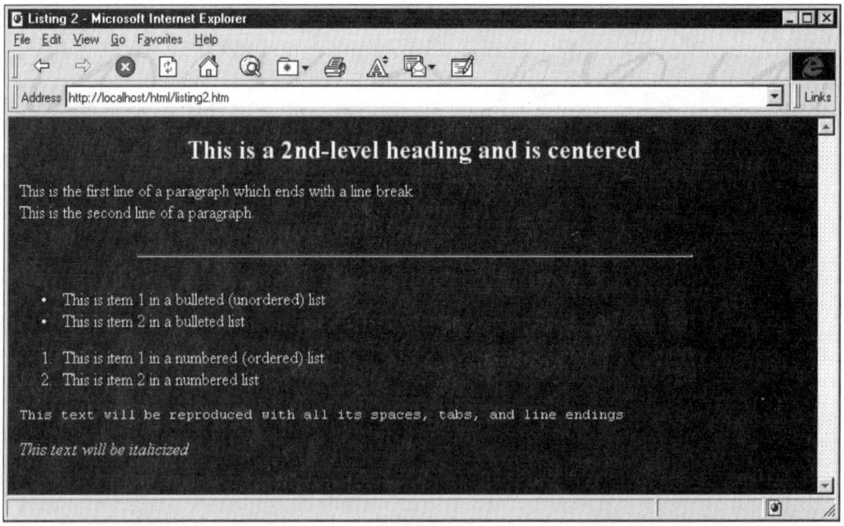

The web
page
resulting
from
placing
Listing
12-2
between
the Body
tags of
Listing 12-1

FIGURE 12-1

TIP: *It is not necessary to have a* </P> *if it would be immediately followed by a* <P>. *All browsers will assume the last paragraph has ended if a new one is started. (Netscape Navigator actually puts in another paragraph when it sees a* </P>.)

NOTE: *You can nest lists within lists and get automatic indenting.*

Listing 12-2
Examples
of using
paragraph
style tags

```
<H2 ALIGN=CENTER>This is a 2nd-level heading and is centered</H2>
<P>
   This is the first line of a paragraph which ends with a line break<BR>
   This is the second line of a paragraph
</P>
<HR SIZE=3 WIDTH=70%>
<UL>
   <LI>This is item 1 in a bulleted (unordered) list
   <LI>This is item 2 in a bulleted list
</UL>
<OL>
   <LI>This is item 1 in a numbered (ordered) list
   <LI>This is item 2 in a numbered list
</OL>
<!-- This is a comment, it is ignored by a browser and not displayed -->
<PRE>This text will be reproduced with all its spaces, tabs, and line
   endings</PRE>
<ADDRESS>This text will be italicized</ADDRESS>
```

Applying Character Styles

Character styles determine how one or more characters will look or behave. There are two forms of character styles. *Logical* character styles are defined by the browser and may be displayed in any way that the browser has established. *Physical* character styles have a strict definition that will be the same in all browsers. Examples of character style tags are shown in Listing 12-3, while Figure 12-2 shows how the Microsoft Internet Explorer 3.0, the Netscape Navigator 3.0, and NCSA Mosaic 2.1.1 display them—note the differences. Table 12-3 describes most character styles.

12

Tag	Description
`<P> </P>`	Identifies the start and end of a paragraph and its alignment with `ALIGN=` and `LEFT, CENTER,` or `RIGHT`.
`<Hn> </Hn>`	Identifies a heading in one of six heading styles (n = 1 to 6) and its alignment with `ALIGN=` and `LEFT, CENTER,` or `RIGHT`.
` `	Forces a line break similar to pressing SHIFT-ENTER in FrontPage.
`<HR>`	Creates a horizontal rule or line where you can specify the alignment, color, shade, size (height), and width across the page.
`<OL> </OL>`	Contains an ordered (numbered) list.
`<UL> </UL>`	Contains an unordered (bulleted) list.
`<LI>`	Identifies an item in either a numbered or bulleted list.
`<DL> </DL>`	Contains a definition list.
`<DT>`	Identifies a term to be defined, displayed on the left of a window.
`<DD>`	Identifies the definition of the term that immediately precedes it, indented from the left.
`<ADDRESS> </ADDRESS>`	Identifies a paragraph of italicized text.
`<BLOCKQUOTE> </BLOCKQUOTE>`	Identifies a paragraph that is indented on both the left and right, as you might do with a quotation.
`<CENTER> </CENTER>`	Centers all text and images contained within it.
`<!-- -->` or `<COMMENT> </COMMENT>`	Identifies a comment that the browser will ignore and not display. `<COMMENT> </COMMENT>` is not used in Netscape Navigator.

Paragraph
Style
HTML Tags

TABLE 12-2

Tag	Description
`<DIV> </DIV>`	Identifies a division of a page for which the alignment is set with `ALIGN=` and `LEFT`, `CENTER`, or `RIGHT`.
`<PRE> </PRE>`	Identifies preformatted text in which all spaces, tabs, and line endings are preserved (called "formatted" in FrontPage). The maximum number of characters in each line can be set with `WIDTH=` (generally 40, 80, or 132).

Paragraph
Style
HTML
Tags
(*continued*)

TABLE 12-2

Character
style tags
displayed
in
Microsoft
Internet
Explorer
3.0,
Netscape
Navigator
3.0, and
NCSA
Mosaic
2.1.1

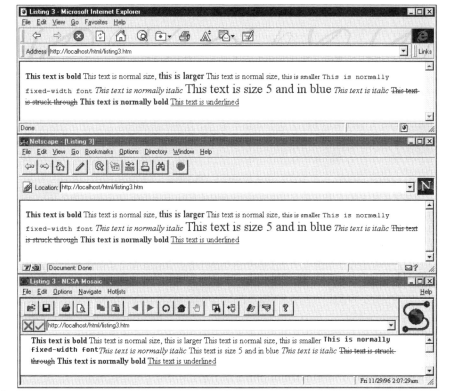

FIGURE 12-2

12

 NOTE: *Figure 12-2 demonstrates that browsers ignore line endings unless they are marked with either <P>, <BR>, or other paragraph styles.*

Listing 12-3
Examples
of using
character
style tags

```
<B>This text is bold</B>
This text is normal size, <BIG>this is larger</BIG>
This text is normal size, <SMALL>this is smaller</SMALL>
<CODE>This is normally fixed-width font</CODE>
<EM>This text is normally italic</EM>
<FONT SIZE=5 COLOR=BLUE>This text is size 5 and in blue</FONT>
<I>This text is italic</I>
<S>This text is struck through</S>
<STRONG>This text is normally bold</STRONG>
<U>This text is underlined</U>
```

Displaying Characters

HTML defines that the less-than, greater-than, and ampersand characters have special meanings and therefore cannot be used as normal text. To use these characters normally, replace them as follows:

Less-than (<)	< or <
Greater-than (>)	> or >
Ampersand (&)	& or &

All other characters that you can type on your keyboard will be displayed as they are typed. In addition, HTML has defined a number of other characters that can be displayed based on entering an *escape sequence* where you want the character displayed. The escape sequence can take either a numeric or a textual format, as was shown with the three special characters immediately above. In either case the escape sequence begins with an ampersand (&) and ends with a semicolon (;). In the numeric format the ampersand is followed by a number sign (#) and a number that represents the character. All characters, be they on the keyboard or otherwise, can be represented with a numeric escape sequence. The textual format has been defined only for some characters and excludes most characters on the keyboard. Additional examples of the two formats are shown in Table 12-4.

Tag	Description
`<B>  </B>`	Applies the Bold physical character style to the enclosed characters
`<BASEFONT>`	Establishes the font size and/or color and/or typeface for a web (color and typeface are not used in Netscape Navigator 3.0)
`<BIG>  </BIG>`	Makes the enclosed characters one size larger
`<BLINK> </BLINK>`	Applies the Blink physical character style to the enclosed characters; not used in Microsoft Internet Explorer 3.0
`<CITE>  </CITE>`	Applies the Citation logical character style to the enclosed characters; normally italic
`<CODE>  </CODE>`	Applies the Code logical character style to the enclosed characters; normally a fixed-width font
`<DFN>  </DFN>`	Applies the Definition logical character style, normally italic, to the enclosed characters
`<EM>  </EM>`	Applies the Emphasis logical character style to the enclosed characters; normally italic
`<FONT>  </FONT>`	Applies the font size and/or color and/or typeface specified to the enclosed characters; if `<BASEFONT>` is used, `<FONT>` size can be relative to the base font size
`<I>  </I>`	Applies the Italic physical character style to the enclosed characters
`<KBD>  </KBD>`	Applies the Keyboard logical character style to the enclosed characters; normally a fixed-width font
`<S>  </S>` or `<STRIKE> </STRIKE>`	Applies the Strikethrough physical character style to the enclosed characters

Character Style HTML Tags

TABLE 12-3

12

Tag	Description
`<SAMP> </SAMP>`	Applies the Sample logical character style to the enclosed characters; normally a fixed-width font
`<SMALL> </SMALL>`	Makes the enclosed characters one size smaller
`<STRONG> </STRONG>`	Applies the Strong logical character style to the enclosed characters; normally bold
`<SUB> </SUB>`	Applies the Subscript physical character style to the enclosed characters
`<SUP> </SUP>`	Applies the Superscript physical character style to the enclosed characters
`<TT> </TT>`	Applies the Typewriter Text physical character style to the enclosed characters; a fixed-width font

Character Style HTML Tags (*continued*)

TABLE 12-3

 NOTE: *Unlike the rest of HTML, escape sequences are case-sensitive—for example, you cannot use < for the less-than symbol.*

Character	Name	Numeric Sequence	Text Sequence
...	Ellipses	`&#133;`	
•	Bullet	`&#149;`	
™	Trademark	`&#153;`	
©	Copyright	`&#169;`	`&copy;`
Æ	AE ligature	`&#198;`	`&aelig;`
ä	a umlaut	`&#228;`	`&auml;`
é	e acute accent	`&#233;`	`&eacute;`
õ	o tilde	`&#245;`	`&otilde;`

Samples of Character Escape Sequences

TABLE 12-4

For complete lists of the escape sequences, see the Microsoft Internet Explorer 3.0 Specification Character Set at http://www.microsoft.com/workshop/author/newhtml/default.htm.

Style Sheets

In addition to applying paragraph and character styles to selected text, you can also apply styles to an entire document or web using *style sheets*. Style sheets are a concept familiar to most users of word processing programs such as Microsoft Word. Simply put, a *style sheet* is a collection of styles or formatting commands (such as font size, paragraph alignment, and text color). Each time you want to have a section of text formatted in a certain way, a style sheet allows you to simply use the name of the style rather than specifying the individual attributes. Style sheets can be part of an HTML document or a separate document referenced by the HTML page.

Style sheets offer several advantages for the web designer. By having all your styles in one place, on a separate style sheet, you can be sure that all the pages in your web use the same styles. For example, if you want the top-level section headings on all your pages to be formatted as Head 1, Arial font, and blue color, you simply define your top-level section heading with those properties in the style sheet. If you want to change the formatting at some point, you only have to change the properties in one place—on the style sheet. It is also faster to format text in a web page when all you have to specify is one property—the name of the style—rather than making multiple selections to select paragraph and font properties individually.

In addition to the paragraph and font formatting properties covered in this chapter, style sheets also allow you to set the height between lines of text (known as *leading* in the print world), and to set top, left, and right margins.

Style sheets are not directly supported by FrontPage. Because of this you need to be somewhat familiar with HTML programming in order to add them to your web pages. A style is a set of properties that can be attached to any HTML tag, such as <H1> (level-1 heading). In effect, you are redefining the standard HTML tags. For example, to have all your level-1 heads display as 18 pt Arial bold in blue, you would define the level-1 head like this:

12

```
H1 {font: 18pt "Arial";

    font-weight: bold;

    color: blue}
```

You can also have classes of styles. For example, if you want some of your level-1 heads to be blue and some red, you could define two styles: H1.blue and H1.red. The HTML for the H1.red style might look like this:

```
H1.red {font: 18pt "Arial";

    font-weight: bold;

    color: red}
```

The style definition for H1.blue would be identical, except that the style name would be H1.blue, and the defined color property would be blue. The HTML to use the red style would then look like this:

```
<H1 CLASS=red>This heading would be in the H1.red style</H1>
```

To use a separate style sheet, you first create the style sheet in a text editor and then create a link to it in each of your web pages. You can create the link using the FrontPage HTML View Or Edit dialog box (select HTML from the View menu). You can also use the HTML Markup command from the Insert menu to embed styles in the body of your pages. In each case the HTML will be inserted as is, without any error checking.

You can learn more about creating and using style sheets on Microsoft's web site (http://www.microsoft.com/workshop/author/howto/css-f.htm).

 NOTE: *At present style sheets are supported only by Internet Explorer 3.0. However, Netscape has announced that style sheets will be supported in the version of Navigator that will come after Navigator 3.0. Style sheets are also part of the draft HTML 3.2 specification. While you may not want to start using style sheets right away, they are definitely part of the future of web design.*

Working with Images and Image Maps

Images are added to a web by use of the Image (`<IMG>`) tag, which specifies the path and filename of the image as well as a number of attributes such as size, positioning, margins, and border. One of the attributes, `ISMAP`, identifies the image as having an image map attached to it. The image map is a separate .MAP file used by the server to relate areas of the image to URLs. To use ISMAP, you must include the Image tag in an Anchor tag (see the next section, "Adding Hyperlinks and Bookmarks"). A couple of examples are given in Listing 12-4 and shown in Figure 12-3. Many of the Image attributes are described in Table 12-5.

NOTE: *The   in Listing 12-4 is a nonbreaking space and is used with the Paragraph tags to create a blank line (paragraph) that HTML will not get rid of.*

Listing 12-4
Examples of using the Image tag

```
<P><IMG SRC="hibiscus.jpg" ALT="A picture of a hibiscus"
    ALIGN="bottom" BORDER="2" HSPACE="3" WIDTH="166"
        HEIGHT="190">
    This is a picture of a hibiscus ...</P>
<P> </P>
<P ALIGN="center"><IMG SRC="undercon.gif" ALT="Under
        Construction"
    ALIGN="top" WIDTH="40" HEIGHT="38">This image is
        centered...</P>
```

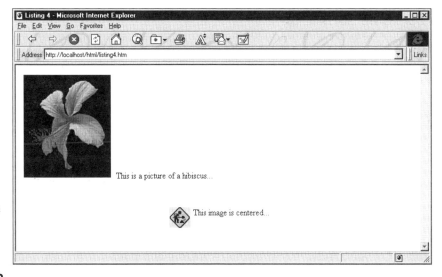

Examples
of using the
Image tag
in Listing
12-4

FIGURE 12-3

12

Attribute	Description
ALIGN	Positions text at the TOP, MIDDLE, or BOTTOM of the image, or positions the image on the LEFT or RIGHT of the text
ALT	Identifies alternative text that is displayed if the image cannot be displayed
BORDER	Specifies that a border of so many pixels be drawn around the image
HEIGHT	Specifies the height, in pixels, of the image
HSPACE	Specifies the blank space on the left and right of the image
ISMAP	Indicates that the image has an image map
SRC	Identifies the path and filename or URL of the image
USEMAP	Identifies the name of the image map that is to be used
VSPACE	Specifies the blank space on the top and bottom of the image
WIDTH	Specifies the width, in pixels, of the image

Image Tag
Attributes
TABLE 12-5

NOTE: *Netscape Navigator will automatically scale the other dimension based on the current aspect ratio of the image if just one of the dimensions (HEIGHT or WIDTH) is given.*

TIP: *Specifying the HEIGHT and the WIDTH speeds up loading, because a quick placeholder will be drawn for the image, allowing the text to continue to be loaded while the image is drawn. Without these dimensions, the loading of the text must wait for the image to be drawn and thereby determine where the remaining text will go.*

Adding Hyperlinks and Bookmarks

Hyperlinks provide the ability to click on an object and transfer what is displayed by the browser (the focus) to an address associated with the object. HTML implements hyperlinks with the Anchor tag (<A> </A>), which specifies that the

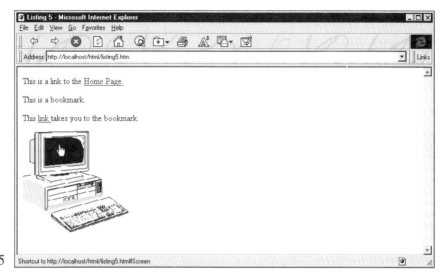

Hyperlinks
and
bookmarks
defined in
Listing 12-5

FIGURE 12-4

text or graphic that it contains is a hyperlink or a bookmark or both. If the tag is a *hyperlink* and the contents are selected, then the focus is moved to either another location in the current page or web, or to another web. If the tag is a *bookmark*, then another Anchor tag may reference it and potentially transfer the focus to it.

An image used as just described assumes that the entire image is the hyperlink. An image may also be broken into sections, where each section is a link or a *hotspot*. To break an image into multiple links requires an *image map* that is implemented with the Map tag. The Map tag contains Area tags that define the shape of a specific area of the image and the link that it is pointing to.

Listing 12-5 provides some examples of the Anchor, Map, and Area tags, which are shown in Figure 12-4. Table 12-6 describes these tags and their attributes.

Listing 12-5
Examples of
hyperlinks and
bookmarks

```
<P>This is a link to the <A HREF="default.htm">Home
    Page.</A></P>
<P><A NAME="This ">This </A>is a bookmark.</P>
<P>This <A HREF="#This ">link </A>takes you to the bookmark.</P>
<P><MAP NAME="ComputerMap">
    <AREA SHAPE="POLYGON" COORDS="163, 121, 197,
        145, 91, 183, 55, 157" HREF="#Keyboard">
    <AREA SHAPE="POLYGON" COORDS="6, 90, 147, 87,
```

12

```
      148, 115, 46, 145, 2, 124" HREF="#Processor">
   <AREA SHAPE="RECT" COORDS="30, 6, 124, 70"
      HREF="#Screen"></MAP>
 <A HREF="computer.map">
   <IMG ALIGN="bottom" SRC="computer.gif" WIDTH="200" ISMAP
   USEMAP="#ComputerMap" HEIGHT="186"></A></P>
```

 NOTE: *The SHAPE attribute of the Area tag may be left out, and a rectangular shape will be assumed.*

Tag or Attribute	Description
<A> </A>	Specifies the definition of a hyperlink.
HREF	Identifies the destination URL, which can be a bookmark, page, or web.
NAME	Identifies the bookmark at this location.
TARGET	Identifies a specific frame in the link destination.
TITLE	Identifies a name for a link that is displayed when the mouse passes over the link; otherwise the link address is displayed.
<MAP> </MAP>	Specifies the definition of an image map.
NAME	Identifies the name of the image map.
<AREA> </AREA>	Specifies the definition of one image area.
SHAPE	Identifies the type of shape being defined to be CIRC, CIRCLE, POLY, POLYGON, RECT, or RECTANGLE.
COORDS	Identifies the coordinates of the shape being defined using X and Y positions in terms of image pixels for each point.
HREF	Identifies the bookmark or URL to which the focus is transferred.
NOHREF	Indicates that a given area causes no action to take place.

Anchor Tag
Attributes

TABLE 12-6

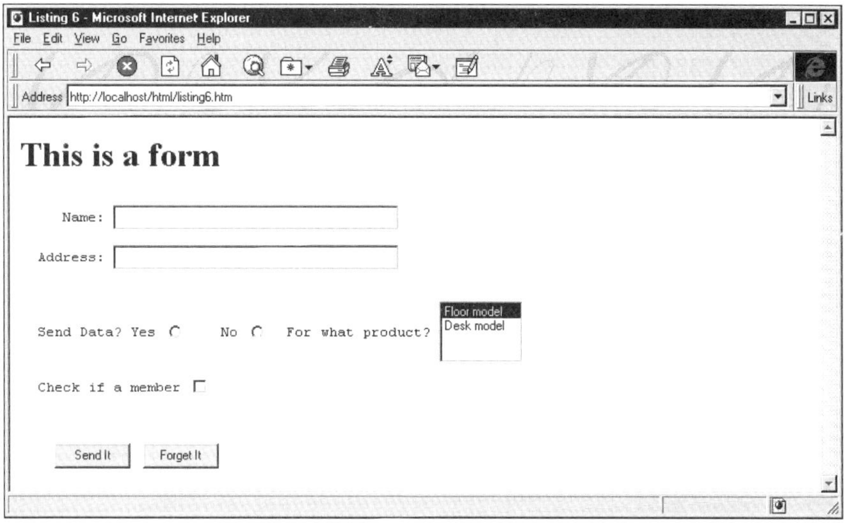

Form
created
with
Listing 12-6

FIGURE 12-5

Defining Forms

A form in HTML is defined by the input fields that it contains. Each input field is defined by its type, name, and potentially a default value. There are a number of field types around which you can wrap text and formatting to get virtually any form you want to define. One example is shown in Listing 12-6 and displayed in Figure 12-5. Table 12-7 describes the tags and attributes related to forms.

NOTE: *The Microsoft Internet Explorer does not correctly display the* `<SELECT NAME="Product" MULTIPLE SIZE="1">` *instruction, as shown in Figure 12-5. The* `SIZE="1"` *says that only one of the multiple entries should be displayed, but the figure shows both "Floor model" and "Desk model." Netscape Navigator will correctly display this.*

12

Listing 12-6
Example of
a form

```
<H1>This is a form</H1>
<FORM ACTION="saveresults" METHOD="post">
<PRE>
   Name: <INPUT TYPE=TEXT SIZE=50 MAXLENGTH=256 NAME="Name"><BR>
   Address: <INPUT TYPE=TEXT SIZE=50 MAXLENGTH=256
```

```
        NAME="Address"><BR><BR>
  Send Data? Yes <INPUT TYPE=RADIO NAME="Send" Value="Yes">
    No <INPUT TYPE=RADIO NAME="Send" Value="No">
  For what product? <SELECT NAME="Product" MULTIPLE SIZE="1">
    <OPTION VALUE="Floor" SELECTED>Floor model
    <OPTION VALUE="Desk">Desk model</SELECT><BR>
  Check if a member <INPUT TYPE=CHECKBOX NAME="Member"
       Value="TRUE">
    <BR><BR>
    <INPUT TYPE=SUBMIT VALUE="Send It"> <INPUT TYPE=RESET
      VALUE="Forget It">
</PRE></FORM>
```

Tag or Attribute	Description
`<FORM>` `</FORM>`	Specifies the definition of a form
`<INPUT>`	Identifies one input field
TYPE	Specifies the field type to be CHECKBOX, HIDDEN, IMAGE, PASSWORD, RADIO, RESET, SUBMIT, TEXT, or TEXTAREA
NAME	Specifies the name of the field
VALUE	Specifies the default value of the field
ALIGN	If TYPE=IMAGE, positions text at TOP, BOTTOM, or CENTER of image
CHECKED	If TYPE=CHECKBOX or RADIO, determines if by default they are selected (TRUE) or not (FALSE)
MAXLENGTH	Specifies the maximum number of characters that can be entered in a text field
SIZE	Specifies the width of a text field in characters, or the width and height in characters and lines of a text area
SRC	Specifies the URL of an image if TYPE=IMAGE

Form Tags and Attributes

TABLE 12-7

Tag or Attribute	Description
<SELECT> </SELECT>	Specifies the definition of a drop-down menu
NAME	Specifies the name of a menu
MULTIPLE	Specifies that multiple items can be selected in a menu
SIZE	Specifies the height of the menu
<OPTION>	Identifies one option in a menu
SELECTED	Specifies that this option is the default
VALUE	Specifies the value if the option is selected

Form Tags and Attributes (*continued*)

TABLE 12-7

Creating Tables

HTML provides a very rich set of tags to define a table, its cells, borders, and other properties. As rich as the original HTML table specification was, there are many extensions to it by both Microsoft and Netscape. Since these extensions are not consistent between the two companies, they need to be used with caution. Listing 12-7 provides an example of the HTML for creating the simple table shown in Figure 12-6. Table 12-8 shows the principal table tags and their attributes.

Listing 12-7
Table example

```
<H2>A New Table</H2>
<TABLE BORDER=2 CELLPADDING=3 CELLSPACING=4 WIDTH=100%>
  <CAPTION ALIGN=CENTER>THIS IS THE TABLE CAPTION</CAPTION>
  <TR><TH ALIGN=LEFT WIDTH=25%>Cell 1, a header</TH>
    <TD COLSPAN=2 WIDTH=25%>Cell 2, This cell spans two
        columns</TD>
    <TD WIDTH=10%>Cell 3</TD>
    <TD WIDTH=10%>Cell 4</TD></TR>
  <TR><TD WIDTH=25%>Cell 5, 25%</TD>
    <TD WIDTH=25%>Cell 6, 25%</TD>
    <TD WIDTH=25%>Cell 7, 25%</TD>
    <TD WIDTH=10%>10%</TD></TR>
  <TR><TD ROWSPAN=2 WIDTH=25%>Cells 9/13, These cells were
        merged</TD>
    <TD WIDTH=25%>Cell 10</TD>
```

12

```
  <TD WIDTH=25%>Cell 11</TD>
  <TD WIDTH=10%>Cell 12</TD></TR>
<TR><TD WIDTH=25%>Cell 14</TD>
  <TD WIDTH=25%>Cell 15</TD>
  <TD WIDTH=10%>Cell 16</TD></TR>
</TABLE>
```

NOTE: *A table without the BORDER attribute will not have a border, but will take up the same space as if it had a border of 1. Therefore, specifying a border of zero (0) will take up less space.*

Incorporating Frames

HTML frames allow the definition of individual panes or *frames* within a browser window. Each frame contains a separate page that can be scrolled independently of the other frames. HTML defines frames in terms of *frame pages*, which contain Frameset tags, which in turn contain Frame tags. In a frame page, the *Frameset tag* replaces the Body tag and provides the overall structure of the frames to be created

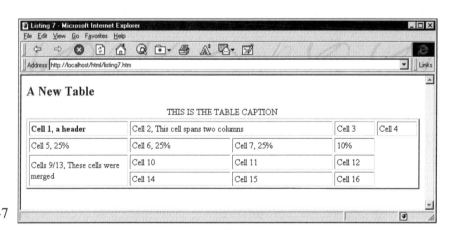

Table created with Listing 12-7

FIGURE 12-6

Tag or Attribute	Description
`<TABLE> </TABLE>`	Specifies definition of a table.
`ALIGN`	Specifies that the table will be aligned on the `LEFT` or `RIGHT` of the page, allowing text to flow around it.
`BACKGROUND`	Specifies that a URL containing an image be used as a background; not used in Netscape Navigator 3.0.
`BGCOLOR`	Specifies a background color for an entire table.
`BORDER`	Specifies the size, in pixels, of a border to be drawn around all cells in a table.
`BORDERCOLOR`	Specifies a border color if a border is present; not used in Netscape Navigator 3.0.
`BORDERCOLORLIGHT`	Specifies the lighter of 3-D border colors if a border is present; not used in Netscape Navigator 3.0.
`BORDERCOLORDARK`	Specifies the darker of 3-D border colors if a border is present; not used in Netscape Navigator 3.0.
`CELLSPACING`	Specifies the amount of space, in pixels, between cells; a default of 2 is used when not specified.
`CELLPADDING`	Specifies the amount of space, in pixels, between the cell wall and its contents on all sides; a default of 1 is used when not specified.

Table Tags
and
Attributes

TABLE 12-8

12

Tag or Attribute	Description
FRAME	Specifies which of the outside borders of a table are displayed—VOID (none), ABOVE (only the top), BELOW (only the bottom), HSIDES (horizontal sides), VSIDES (vertical sides), LHS (left hand side), RHS (right hand side), BOX (all)—not used in Netscape Navigator 3.0.
HEIGHT	Specifies the height of a table as either a certain number of pixels or a percentage of the window.
RULES	Specifies which of the inside borders of a table are displayed—NONE, BASIC (horizontal rules between the heading, body, and footer sections), ROWS, COLS, ALL—not used in Netscape Navigator 3.0.
VALIGN	Specifies that the text in the table can be aligned with the TOP or BOTTOM of the cells; if not specified, text is center aligned—not used in Netscape Navigator 3.0.
WIDTH	Specifies the width of a table as either a certain number of pixels or a percentage of the window.
<TR> </TR>	Identifies the cells in a single row of a table.
ALIGN	Specifies that the text in the cells of this row is aligned on the LEFT, CENTER, or RIGHT of each cell. BACKGROUND, BGCOLOR, BORDERCOLOR, BORDERCOLORLIGHT, BORDERCOLORDARK, and VALIGN are the same as described for <TABLE>.

Table Tags and Attributes *(continued)*

TABLE 12-8

Tag or Attribute	Description
`<TD> </TD>`	Identifies a single data cell in a table.
ALIGN	Specifies that the text in this cell is aligned on the `LEFT`, `CENTER`, or `RIGHT` of the cell. `BACKGROUND`, `BGCOLOR`, `BORDERCOLOR`, `BORDERCOLORLIGHT`, `BORDERCOLORDARK`, `HEIGHT`, `WIDTH`, and `VALIGN` are the same as described for `<TABLE>`.
COLSPAN	Specifies the number of columns a cell should span.
ROWSPAN	Specifies the number of rows a cell should span.
NOWRAP	Specifies that the text in the table cannot be wrapped to fit a smaller cell, forcing the cell to enlarge.
`<TH> </TH>`	Identifies a single header cell in a table (uses the same attributes as `<TD>`).
`<CAPTION> </CAPTION>`	Identifies the caption for a table.
ALIGN	Specifies that the caption is aligned to the `LEFT`, `CENTER`, or `RIGHT` of the table.
VALIGN	Specifies that the caption should appear at the `TOP` or `BOTTOM` of the table; not used in Netscape Navigator 3.0.

Table Tags and Attributes (*continued*)

TABLE 12-8

in a browser window. Similarly, the Frame tag is used to define the structure of a single frame. Figure 12-7 shows a simple frame page that was created with the tags displayed in Listing 12-8. (The banner, contents, and main pages are separately defined to contain the information you see.) The tags and attributes related to frames are described in Table 12-9.

12

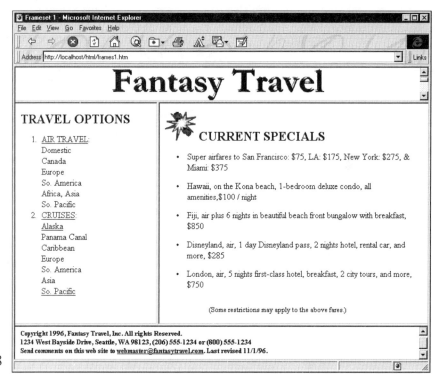

A frame
page
produced
with
Listing 12-8

FIGURE 12-7

Internet Explorer 3.0 has introduced *floating frames*. These are individual frames that can be placed anywhere in a standard HTML document. If the browser does not support floating frames, the HTML within the `<IFRAME></IFRAME>` tags is displayed on the page in the usual manner.

 NOTE: *No tags that would be within a Body tag can precede the first Frameset tag, although Frameset tags can be contained within another Frameset tag.*

Listing 12-8
A frame
page with
Frameset
and
Frame tags

```
<HTML>
<HEAD>
<TITLE>Frameset 1</TITLE>
</HEAD>
<FRAMESET ROWS="12%,*,12%">
```

```
<FRAME SRC="frtop.htm" NAME="top" NORESIZE>
<FRAMESET COLS="35%,65%">
    <FRAME SRC="frconten.htm" NAME="contents">
    <FRAME SRC="frmain.htm" NAME="main">
</FRAMESET>
<FRAME SRC="frbottom.htm" NAME="bottom" NORESIZE>
<NOFRAMES>
<BODY>
<P>This web page uses frames, but your browser doesn't
    support them.</P>
</BODY>
</NOFRAMES>
</FRAMESET>
</HTML>
```

 NOTE: *If FRAMEBORDER and FRAMESPACING are specified in the Frameset tag, they will automatically apply to all the Frame tags contained within it and only need to be specified for the Frame where a change is desired.*

 NOTE: *The Target attribute, which you have seen with other tags, is used to load pages into specific frames.*

Within the ROWS and COLS attributes are a list of values separated by commas, one for each horizontal frame ("row") or vertical frame ("column") in the frameset. These values can be

- The absolute width of a column or height of a row, in pixels. For example,

    COLS="200, 100, 300"

    sets up three columns that, from left to right, are 200, 100, and 300 pixels wide, respectively.

- A percentage of the window's width for a column or the window's height for a row. For example,

    ROWS="15%, 85%"

12

sets up two rows, one taking 15 percent of the window and the other, 85 percent.

■ A relative value to the other rows or columns. For example,

```
COLS="*, 2*"
```

sets up two columns, the right one getting twice as much space as the left one (this is the same as using **"33%, 67%"**)

■ Any combination of absolute, percentage, and relative. For example,

```
ROWS="100, 65%, *"
```

sets up three rows: the top is 100 pixels high, the middle is 65 percent of the window, and the bottom gets the remaining space.

Tag or Attribute	Description
<FRAMESET> </FRAMESET>	Specifies the definition of a set of frames
COLS	Identifies the number of vertical frames (columns) in the frameset and their absolute or relative size (see comments on this attribute)
ROWS	Identifies the number of horizontal frames (rows) in the frameset and their absolute or relative size (see comments on this attribute)
FRAMEBORDER	Turns on (FRAMEBORDER="Yes" or "1") or off (="No" or "0") the border around a frame
FRAMESPACING	Identifies extra space, in pixels, inserted between frames; not used in Netscape Navigator 3.0

Frame Tags and Attributes

▌ TABLE 12-9

Tag or Attribute	Description
BORDERCOLOR	Specifies the color of the frame border; not used in Internet Explorer 3.0
<FRAME> </FRAME>	Specifies the definition of a single frame
FRAMEBORDER	Turns on (FRAMEBORDER="Yes" or "1") or off (="No" or "0") the border around a frame
FRAMESPACING	Identifies extra space, in pixels, inserted between frames
MARGINWIDTH	Identifies the size, in pixels, of the left and right margin in a frame
MARGINHEIGHT	Identifies the size, in pixels, of the top and bottom margins in a frame
NAME	Identifies the name of the frame so it can be referred to by TARGET attributes
NORESIZE	Prevents the frame from being resized by the user
SCROLLING	Turns the appearance of scroll bars on or off with SCROLLING="Yes"/"No"/"Auto"; Auto is the default
SRC	Identifies the URL of the web page that will occupy the frame
BORDERCOLOR	Specifies the color of the frame border; not used in Internet Explorer 3.0
<NOFRAMES> </NOFRAMES>	Specifies HTML that will be displayed by browsers that cannot display frames, but ignored by browsers with frame capability
<IFRAME> </IFRAME>	Specifies the definition of a floating frame; WIDTH, HEIGHT, HSPACE, VSPACE, and ALIGN are the same as described for <IMG>

Frame Tags and Attributes (*continued*)

TABLE 12-9

12

CAUTION: *Using absolute pixel values with the ROWS and COLS attributes can result in some weird-looking frames, due to the many differences in screen sizes and resolutions.*

Using Multimedia

Multimedia is the inclusion of audio, video, and animation pieces in a web. As you read in Chapter 11, you can simply offer a user a multimedia file to be downloaded by clicking on its link, and then, depending on the availability of players, the file can be automatically or manually played. If you want to make multimedia an automatic part of a web (called "inline" audio or video)—for example, to automatically play an audio piece when a web opens—you must use some of the newest extensions to HTML. These include the <BGSOUND> tag for playing inline audio and the DYNSRC attribute for the Image tag to play inline audio-video. Also <MARQUEE>, which is a scrolling bar of text across the window, is included here as a form of animation. These HTML extensions are *only* supported by Microsoft Internet Explorer 2.0 or later, and to a lesser extent NCSA Mosaic. Netscape Navigator 3.0 supports the <EMBED> tag, which allows you to include audio and video files which are supported by one of the Netscape plug-ins. Netscape plug-ins for standard audio and video files are included with Navigator 3.0, and more can be found on the Netscape web site (http://home.netscape.com). Listing 12-9 provides some examples of using multimedia, and Table 12-10 describes the related tags.

Listing 12-9
Examples of
the HTML
to use
multimedia

```
<BGSOUND SRC="all.wav" LOOP=2>
<IMG SRC="hibiscus.jpg" DYNSRC="goodtime.avi" CONTROLS
    START=MOUSEOVER>
<MARQUEE BEHAVIOR=SLIDE, DIRECTION=RIGHT>The marquee will
    scroll this
  text</MARQUEE>
```

NOTE: *The Image tag attributes in Table 12-10 are in addition to all the regular Image tag attributes listed in Table 12-5, which can all be used with video and animation clips.*

Understanding FrontPage-Generated HTML

Many of the example listings in the "Introducing HTML" section have been created with FrontPage and only slightly modified to fit the needs of the section. Look at

Tag or Attribute	Description
\<BGSOUND>	Specifies a sound to be played automatically as a page is loaded.
SRC	Identifies the URL of the .WAV, .AU, or .MID file that will be played as soon as it is downloaded.
LOOP	Identifies the number of times the sound will play; if LOOP=-1 or INFINITE, the sound will play until the page is closed.
\<IMG>	Specifies a video or animation clip is to be played.
DYNSRC	Identifies the URL of the inline video .AVI file to be played.
START	Identifies when the file should start playing (START=FILEOPEN or MOUSEOVER); FILEOPEN is the default, and MOUSEOVER means the file will start playing when the mouse is moved over the alternative image.
CONTROLS	Specifies that the video player control panel should be displayed.
LOOP	Identifies the number of times the video will play; if LOOP=-1 or INFINITE, the sound will play until the page is closed.
LOOPDELAY	Identifies how long to wait, in milliseconds, between repetitions in a loop.
SRC	Identifies the image to display if the browser cannot play the video.
\<MARQUEE> \</MARQUEE>	Specifies the definition of a scrolling bar of text across the browser window.

Multimedia
Tags and
Attributes

TABLE 12-10

12

Tag or Attribute	Description
ALIGN	Identifies the alignment of the text in the marquee to be at its TOP, MIDDLE, or BOTTOM.
BEHAVIOR	Identifies how the text should behave—BEHAVIOR=SCROLL means the text will continuously scroll from one side to the other; =SLIDE means it will move from one side to the other and stop; =ALTERNATE means the text will continuously bounce from one side to the other; SCROLL is the default
BGCOLOR	Identifies the background color.
DIRECTION	Identifies the direction that the text will scroll (=LEFT or =RIGHT); LEFT is the default
HEIGHT	Identifies the height of the marquee in either pixels or percentage of the window
HSPACE	Identifies the right and left margins of the marquee in pixels
LOOP	Identifies the number of times that the text will loop; if LOOP=-1 or INFINITE, the sound will play until the page is closed
SCROLLAMOUNT	Identifies the number of pixels between successive loops of text
SCROLLDELAY	Identifies the number of milliseconds between successive loops

Multimedia Tags and Attributes (*continued*)

TABLE 12-10

Tag or Attribute	Description
VSPACE	Identifies the top and bottom margins of the marquee
WIDTH	Identifies the width of the marquee, either in pixels or as a percentage of the window
<EMBED>	Specifies a sound or video file to be played by the appropriate plug-in; SRC, WIDTH, HEIGHT, BORDER, HSPACE, and VSPACE are the same as for <IMG>

Multimedia Tags and Attributes (*continued*)

TABLE 12-10

three more examples in increasing complexity and get a feeling for the HTML generated by FrontPage. First, though, explore the ways of looking at FrontPage's HTML.

How to Look at FrontPage HTML

You have at least three ways to look at the HTML generated by FrontPage. Two of these are in the FrontPage Editor. The third is in your browser. If you have more than one browser, you can look at the HTML in each. Use the following steps to see the differences among the views:

1. Load the FrontPage Explorer if it's not already loaded. Create a new web with the Normal template, name it **SimpleHTML**, and open it in the FrontPage Editor.

2. Enter a heading, a couple of short paragraphs with some formatting, and place an image with text after it, as shown in Figure 12-8. Save the page.

3. Open the View menu and choose HTML. The View Or Edit HTML dialog box will open, as you can see next. Notice that there are two option buttons and a check box in the lower left of the window: Original, Current, and Show Color Coding. Current and Show Color Coding should be selected.

12

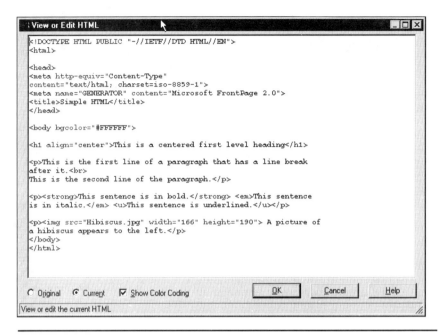

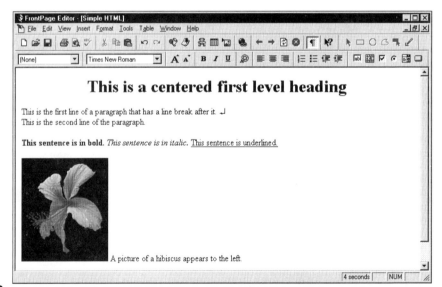

A simple
web page

FIGURE 12-8

4. Click on Original and you should see no differences if you have made no changes since saving the page in step 2.

5. Close the window, make some small change to your web page like centering the image, and *without saving* the page, reopen the View Or Edit HTML window. In Current view you should see the change you just made, like this:

```
<p align="center"><img src="Hibiscus.jpg" width="166"
height="190"> A picture of a hibiscus appears to the left.</p>
</body>
</html>
```

6. Click on Original and you should see the HTML the way it was *prior* to your change, as shown in the illustration following step 3. Go back and forth between Original and Current, and the change will be very obvious, because only the changes will move on the screen.

 NOTE: *The Original and Current views are important, because they allow you to see the effect on the HTML of the changes you make in FrontPage.*

7. Close the HTML window, save your changes, and reopen the HTML window. Now you won't see any differences between Original and Current.

8. Close the HTML window and open the SimpleHTML web in Microsoft Internet Explorer if you have it. Open the View menu and choose Source. The Windows Notepad will open and display the HTML behind the SimpleHTML web page, as you can see in the following:

```
simple.htm - Notepad                                              _ □ ×
File  Edit  Search  Help
<!DOCTYPE HTML PUBLIC "-//IETF//DTD HTML//EN">
<html>

<head>
<meta http-equiv="Content-Type"
content="text/html; charset=iso-8859-1">
<meta name="GENERATOR" content="Microsoft FrontPage 2.0">
<title>Simple HTML</title>
</head>

<body bgcolor="#FFFFFF">

<h1 align="center">This is a centered first level heading</h1>

<p>This is the first line of a paragraph that has a line break
after it.<br>
This is the second line of the paragraph.</p>

<p><strong>This sentence is in bold.</strong> <em>This sentence
is in italic.</em> <u>This sentence is underlined.</u></p>

<p align="center"><img src="Hibiscus.jpg" width="166"
height="190"> A picture of a hibiscus appears to the left.</p>
</body>
</html>
```

9. Close Notepad and Internet Explorer, and open Netscape Navigator if you have it. Open the View menu and choose Document Source. A Netscape window will open as shown next. Onscreen you can see that tags are one color, attributes another, and text a third.

```
Netscape - [Source of: http://localhost/simplehtml/simple.htm]      _ □ ×
<!DOCTYPE HTML PUBLIC "-//IETF//DTD HTML//EN">
<html>

<head>
<meta http-equiv="Content-Type"
content="text/html; charset=iso-8859-1">
<meta name="GENERATOR" content="Microsoft FrontPage 2.0">
<title>Simple HTML</title>
</head>

<body bgcolor="#FFFFFF">

<h1 align="center">This is a centered first level heading</h1>

<p>This is the first line of a paragraph that has a line break
after it.<br>
This is the second line of the paragraph.</p>

<p><strong>This sentence is in bold.</strong> <em>This sentence
is in italic.</em> <u>This sentence is underlined.</u></p>

<p align="center"><img src="Hibiscus.jpg" width="166"
height="190"> A picture of a hibiscus appears to the left.</p>
</body>
</html>
```

10. Close the Netscape window and Navigator, and reopen the FrontPage Editor window.

In the three or four views in which you have just seen the Simple HTML example, there are no major differences, although you will see some as the examples become more complex. In this example it just depends on your preference and what you want to do with what you are looking at. If you just want to look, Netscape and FrontPage offer the advantage of having different colors for the different HTML components, which Microsoft Internet Explorer does not. If you want to directly change the HTML, opening the FrontPage View Or Edit HTML dialog box or Microsoft Internet Explorer's Notepad editor allows you to do that. In all three views you can select and copy the HTML to the Windows Clipboard, copy it to another editor, and then easily move the HTML from both FrontPage and Navigator to, for example, Notepad.

In the next several sections of this chapter, you will try all three methods (if you have both browsers), and by the end of the chapter you'll be able to decide which you like best.

Looking at a Simple HTML Example

Take a closer look at the tags and attributes that were created by FrontPage in the Simple HTML example. Listing 12-10 shows the HTML for this example. It was copied to the Clipboard and then pasted in the manuscript for this book. The tags and attributes were put in uppercase letters, the tags were made bold, and tags contained in other tags or lines that were a continuation of the previous line were indented. Otherwise this listing has not changed from that generated by FrontPage.

ing 12-10
ple HTML
example

```
<!DOCTYPE HTML PUBLIC "-//IETF//DTD HTML//EN">
<HTML>
<HEAD>
<META HTTP-EQUIV="Content-Type" CONTENT="text/html; charset=iso-8859-1">
<META NAME="GENERATOR" CONTENT="Microsoft FrontPage 2.0">
<TITLE>Simple HTML</TITLE>
</HEAD>
<BODY BGCOLOR="#FFFFFF">
    <H1 ALIGN="CENTER">This is a centered first level heading</H1>
    <P>This is the first line of a paragraph that has a line break after it.<BR>
    This is the second line of the paragraph.</P>
    <P><STRONG>This sentence is in bold.</STRONG>
    <EM>This sentence is in italic.</EM>
    <U>This sentence is underlined.</U></P>

    <P ALIGN="CENTER"><IMG SRC="Hibiscus.jpg" WIDTH="166" HEIGHT="190">
        A picture of a hibiscus appears to the left.</P>

</BODY>
</HTML>
```

12

There are no surprises in Listing 12-10. All of the tags and attributes were discussed in the "Introducing HTML" section earlier in the chapter. There are, however, several interesting items to note. Among these are

- In the Doctype statement, FrontPage doesn't say what version of HTML it is using, even though that is a major part of the reason to have the statement.

- FrontPage uses the new `ALIGN=CENTER` attributes of Heading and Paragraph tags instead of embedding the tags in a Center tag.

- The Strong and Emphasis tags are used in place of the Bold and Italic tags.

- The `HEIGHT` and `WIDTH` attributes are added to the Image tag to establish the area to be occupied by the image and allow the following text to be displayed while the image is loaded.

Looking at Fantasy Travel HTML

For a second example, close your Simple HTML example and open the Fantasy Travel Home Page you created in Chapters 5 and 7. The beginning of the web page is shown in Figure 12-9, and the HTML that creates it is provided in Listing 12-11 (to reduce the bulk and repetition, the middle three items in the bulleted list and the middle four items in the numbered list were removed, as were two lines of text and a Break tag in the contact section and a line of text and a Break tag at the bottom).

Listing 12-11
Fantasy Travel
Home Page

```
<!DOCTYPE HTML PUBLIC "-//IETF//DTD HTML//EN">
<HTML>
<HEAD>
    <META HTTP-EQUIV="Content-Type" CONTENT="text/html; charset=iso-8859-1">
    <META NAME="GENERATOR" CONTENT="Microsoft FrontPage 2.0">
    <TITLE>Home Page</TITLE>
</HEAD>
<BODY BGCOLOR="#F9E1A4">
    <H1 ALIGN="CENTER"><EM><IMG SRC="Title.gif" WIDTH="404" HEIGHT="62"><BR>
&quot;The Exciting Way To Go!&quot;</EM></H1>
    <P ALIGN="CENTER">For the latest fares, contact Julie Bergan at 555-1234 or
        John Donald at 555-1235 <BR> or through e-mail at <A
HREF="mailto:julieb@fantasytravel.com">julieb@fantasytravel.com</A> or <A
HREF="mailto:jmd@fantasytravel.com">jmd@fantasytravel.com</A></P>
    <HR>
```

```
   <H2 ALIGN="LEFT"><IMG SRC="firecracker.gif" WIDTH="59" HEIGHT="53">CURRENT
SPECIALS</H2>
   <UL>
     <LI><P ALIGN="LEFT">Super airfares to San Francisco: $75, LA: $175, New
York: $275, &amp; Miami: $375</P></LI>
     <LI><P ALIGN="LEFT">London, air, 5 nights first-class hotel, breakfast, 2
city tours, and more, $750</P></LI>
   </UL>
   <BLOCKQUOTE><BLOCKQUOTE>
     <P ALIGN="LEFT"><FONT size="2">(Some restrictions may apply to the above
fares.)</FONT></P>
   </BLOCKQUOTE></BLOCKQUOTE>
   <P ALIGN="CENTER"><FONT SIZE="2"><IMG SRC="Elegant_Double.gif" WIDTH="536"
HEIGHT="5"></FONT></P>
   <H2>AVAILABLE TRAVEL OPTIONS</H2>
   <OL>
     <LI><A HREF="air.htm">AIR TRAVEL</A>: Domestic, Canada, Europe, So. America,
Africa, Asia, So. Pacific</LI>
     <LI>RAIL: Domestic, Canada, Europe, So. America, Africa, Asia, So.
Pacific</LI>
   </OL>
   <P> </P>
   <H5>Send comments on this web site to <A
HREF="mailto:webmaster@fantasytravel.com">webmaster@fantasytravel.com</A>. Last
revised 11/1/96.</H5>
</BODY>
</HTML>
```

There is not much difference whether you look at the Fantasy Travel Home Page HTML in FrontPage's View Or Edit HTML window, or in either Microsoft Internet Explorer or Netscape Navigator. All three look like Listing 12-11 (with more or less formatting). Several items to observe in them are

■ The use of the color value for the custom color you created. Without FrontPage to figure this out for you, you would have had to either be satisfied with one of the 16 color names, or get and work with one of the unwieldy color charts.

■ The replacement of the quote (") character in your text with """ because the quote is considered a reserved character. You can use it in text, unlike the other reserved characters.

12

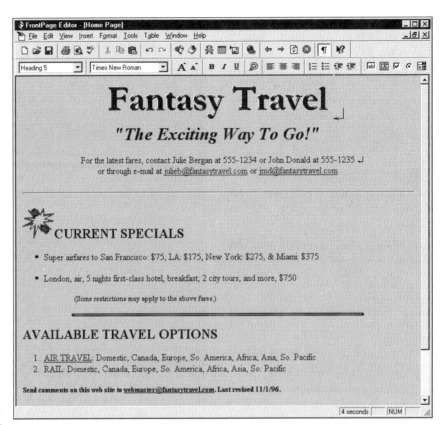

Fantasy
Travel
Home Page

FIGURE 12-9

- The pair of Blockquote tags used to double indent the "Some restrictions" paragraph. While this looks awkward, it works—looks don't count.

Looking at the Corporate Presence HTML

The Corporate Presence Wizard (and the web it creates, shown in Figure 12-10) is FrontPage's tour de force. It uses most of the features available in FrontPage, including many of the WebBots. As a result the HTML looks very different depending on whether you look at it in the FrontPage View Or Edit HTML window, shown in Listing 12-12, or in a browser where the web looks like Figure 12-11 and is based on the HTML shown in Listing 12-13. This difference is primarily caused by the bots used by the FrontPage Personal Web Server or FrontPage Server

Extensions (which are used with the Microsoft Personal Web Server). In a server the HTML in the first listing is used to generate the HTML in the second listing. In Listings 12-12 and 12-13, significant repetition—for example, in the navbars—has been removed for brevity.

ing 12-12
Corporate
sence web
me Page in
FrontPage
Editor

```
<HTML>
<HEAD>
   <META HTTP-EQUIV="Content-Type" CONTENT="text/html; charset=iso-8859-1">
   <META NAME="FORMATTER" CONTENT="Microsoft FrontPage 2.0">
   <META NAME="GENERATOR" CONTENT="Microsoft FrontPage 2.0">
<TITLE>ACME Home Page</TITLE>
</HEAD>
<BODY STYLESRC="_private/style.htm">
   <!-- WEBBOT BOT="Include" STARTSPAN TAG="BODY" U-INCLUDE="_private/logo.htm" -->
   <P><IMG SRC="images/logo.gif" ALT="[Company Logo Image]" WIDTH="120"
         HEIGHT="24"> Comment: -- replace with your logo image</P>
   <!-- WEBBOT BOT="Include" I-CHECKSUM="39927" ENDSPAN -->
   <P><IMG SRC="images/hhome.gif" ALT="[Banner Image]" WIDTH="472"
         HEIGHT="48"> </P>
   <!-- WEBBOT BOT="Include" STARTSPAN TAG="BODY" U-INCLUDE="_private/
         navbar.htm" -->
   <P><A HREF="Default.htm"><IMG SRC="images/bhome.gif" ALT="[Home]" BORDER="0"
         WIDTH="59" HEIGHT="15"></A>
   <!-- WEBBOT BOT="Include" I-CHECKSUM="64747" endspan -->
   <P><!-- WEBBOT BOT="PurpleText" PREVIEW="Write an introductory... " --></P>
   <P><IMG SRC="images/div.gif" ALT="[Dividing Line Image]" WIDTH="471"
         HEIGHT="6"> </P>
   <H2>Our Mission</H2>
   <P><!-- WEBBOT BOT="PurpleText" PREVIEW="Write one or two short sentences..."
         --> </P>
   <P><IMG SRC="images/div.gif" ALT="[Dividing Line Image]" WIDTH="471"
         HEIGHT="6"> </P>
   <H2>Contact Information</H2>
   <P><!-- WEBBOT BOT="PurpleText" PREVIEW="Tell readers... " --</P>
   <DL>
     <DT><STRONG>Telephone</STRONG> </DT>
       <DD><!-- WEBBOT BOT="Substitution" STARTSPAN S-VARIABLE="CompanyPhone"
         -->617-555-1212
       <!-- WEBBOT BOT="Substitution" I-CHECKSUM="13173" ENDSPAN --></DD>
     <DT><STRONG>Electronic mail</STRONG> </DT>
```

12

```
            <DD>General Information: <a href="mailto:info@yourcompany.com">
         <!--WEBBOT BOT="Substitution" STARTSPAN S-VARIABLE="CompanyEmail"
            -->info@yourcompany.com
         <!--WEBBOT BOT="Substitution" I-CHECKSUM="59209" ENDSPAN --></A><BR>
         Sales: <BR>
         Customer Support: <BR>
         Webmaster: <A HREF="mailto:webmaster@yourcompany.com"><!-- WEBBOT
            BOT="Substitution" STARTSPAN S-VARIABLE="CompanyWebmaster"
               -->webmaster@yourcompany.com
         <!-- WEBBOT BOT="Substitution" I-CHECKSUM="14973" ENDSPAN --></A></DD>
      </DL>
      <H5>Send mail to <A><!--WEBBOT BOT="Substitution" STARTSPAN S-
         VARIABLE="CompanyWebmaster" -->webmaster@yourcompany.com
      <!-->WEBBOT BOT="Substitution" I-CHECKSUM="14973" ENDSPAN --></A> with
         questions or comments about this web site.<BR>
      Last modified: <!--WEBBOT BOT="TimeStamp" STARTSPAN S-TYPE="EDITED" S-
         FORMAT="%B %d, %Y" -->November 29, 1996
      <!--WEBBOT BOT="TimeStamp" I-CHECKSUM="41306" ENDSPAN --> </H5>
   </BODY>
</HTML>
```

Listing 12-13
Corporate
Presence Web
Home Page in a
browser

```
<HTML>
<HEAD>
   <META HTTP-EQUIV="Content-Type" CONTENT="text/html; charset=iso-8859-1">
   <META NAME="GENERATOR" CONTENT="Microsoft FrontPage 2.0">
   <TITLE>ACME Home Page</TITLE>
   <META NAME="FORMATTER" CONTENT="Microsoft FrontPage 2.0">
</HEAD>
<BODY BACKGROUND="images/brntxtr1.jpg" BGCOLOR="#c5af8b">
   <P><IMG SRC="images/logo.gif" ALT="[Company Logo Image]" BORDER="0"
WIDTH="120" HEIGHT="24"> </P>
   <P><IMG SRC="images/hhome.gif" ALT="[Banner Image]" WIDTH="472"
      HEIGHT="48"> </P>
   <P> <A HREF="Default.htm"><IMG SRC="images/bhome.gif" ALT="[Home]" BORDER="0"
      WIDTH="59" HEIGHT="15"></A>
   <A HREF="search.htm"><IMG SRC="images/bsrch.gif" ALT="[Search]" BORDER="0"
      WIDTH="57" HEIGHT="15"></A> </P>
   <P><IMG SRC="images/div.gif" ALT="[Dividing Line Image]" WIDTH="471"
HEIGHT="6"> </P>
   <H2>Our Mission</H2>
```

```
    <P><IMG SRC="images/div.gif" alt="[Dividing Line Image]" WIDTH="471"
HEIGHT="6"> </P>
   <H2>Contact Information</H2>
   <DL>
     <DT><STRONG>Telephone</STRONG> </DT>
       <DD>617-555-1212</DD>
     <DT><STRONG>Electronic mail</STRONG> </DT>
       <DD>General Information: <A
          HREF="mailto:info@yourcompany.com">info@yourcompany.com</A><BR>
       Webmaster: <A
HREF="mailto:webmaster@yourcompany.com">webmaster@yourcompany.com</A></DD>
   </DL>
   <H5>Send mail to <A
HREF="mailto:webmaster@yourcompany.com">webmaster@yourcompany.com</A> with
     questions or comments about this web site.<BR>
     Last modified: November 29, 1996 </H5>
</BODY>
</HTML>
```

The primary observation to make regarding Listings 12-12 and 12-13 is how the WebBots in Listing 12-12 translate to straight HTML in Listing 12-13. Some of the major points are

- The internal FrontPage HTML in Listing 12-12 uses a unique-to-FrontPage STYLESRC attribute to attach a background image and color as well as a logo to each page in the web. This concept of a style sheet is being discussed as a part of the HTML 3.2 specification and will become part of the standard.

- The Include bot for the navbar in Listing 12-12 is exploded into six Anchor tags, only two of which were kept in Listing 12-13.

- The "PurpleText" Annotation bots, which were sprinkled throughout the original FrontPage listing (although only two remain in Listing 12-12), are nowhere to be seen in the browser listing, as is intended. They provide text that the author only wants visible while authoring—not in the browser.

- The Substitution bots also provide a useful and observable function by being a single source of information, like the company phone number, that can be used throughout the web.

12

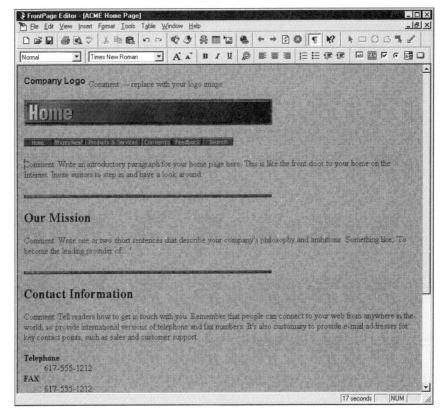

Corporate
Presence
web Home
Page in the
FrontPage
Editor

FIGURE 12-10

If there is one feeling that you should come away with after looking at the HTML generated by FrontPage, it is a much greater appreciation for FrontPage and what it saves you in creating web pages. Just the amount of reduced typing is mind boggling, but more important are all the automatic features, where you simply don't have to worry about some minutiae that is important to the browser, but to no one else. For example:

- The hexadecimal triplet for the custom color you came up with
- The height and width of your images
- The particular font size for a piece of text
- Making sure you have all the ending tags for all your beginning tags
- Translating some characters into their escape sequence

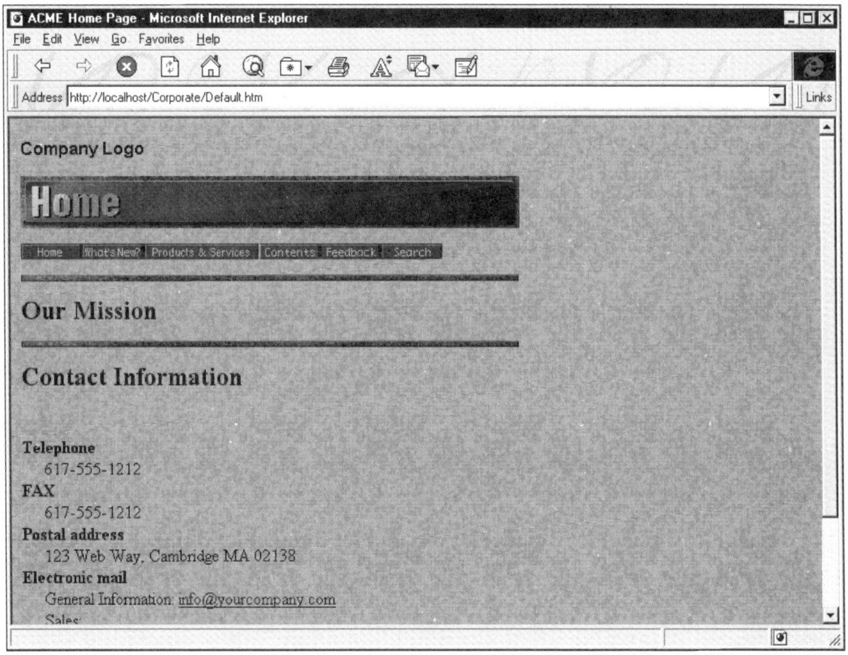

Corporate
Presence
web Home
Page in a
browser

FIGURE 12-11

Adding Capability to a FrontPage Web with HTML

Besides understanding the HTML that FrontPage generates, the other reason to learn
about HTML is to be able to augment FrontPage when it doesn't provide an
HTML-supported function. First look at how you'd add HTML to FrontPage, and
then look at two examples of added features: one to add a floating frame, and the
other to modify a table.

How to Add HTML to FrontPage

There are three ways to add HTML to FrontPage:

- Directly edit the HTML produced by FrontPage and resave it. This
  technique should be strongly discouraged, because it potentially removes
  the ability to maintain the web with FrontPage, and there are two other
  ways to add HTML within FrontPage.

■ Use the Extended Attributes dialog box, shown next, which is available from most properties dialog boxes by clicking on the Extended button.

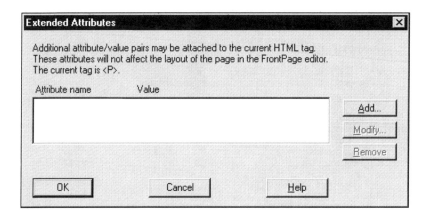

■ Use the HTML Markup bot, which is available anywhere on a page from the Insert menu HTML Markup option.

In the two examples that follow you'll use the latter two approaches to adding HTML, and you can decide which you like best. As a general rule, the Extended Attributes dialog box is more finely tuned to precisely place an added tag or attribute within the generated HTML. The HTML Markup bot allows you to encapsulate the HTML you are adding and keep it separate from the FrontPage-generated and -checked HTML.

Adding HTML to Display a Floating Frame

To use the HTML Markup bot to add a floating frame to your Simple HTML web page:

1. Open a blank page in the FrontPage Editor, move the insertion point to the upper-left corner, and type **This hibiscus is in a floating frame:**.

2. Format it as Heading 1 and move the cursor to the next line.

3. Open the Insert menu and choose HTML Markup.

4. In the text window type

```
<IFRAME NAME="hibiscus" WIDTH="166" HEIGHT="190"
SRC="hibiscus.jpg">If this browser supported
floating frames you would see a
hibiscus.</IFRAME>
```

so your dialog box looks like that shown next.

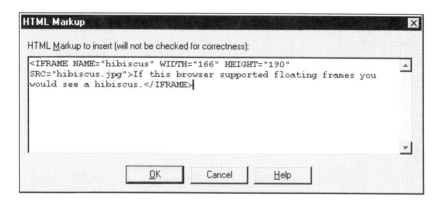

5. Click on OK to close the dialog box, save the page, and then open it in the Microsoft Internet Explorer (Netscape Navigator 3.0 does not support floating frames). You should see the image of the hibiscus (or whatever image you used) in a floating frame, as shown in Figure 12-12. In a browser that does not support floating frames the text "If this browser supported floating frames you would see a hibiscus." is displayed.

6. Close your browser and the FrontPage Editor. Also close the Simple HTML web in the FrontPage Explorer.

Inserting HTML to Modify a Table

Next use the Extended Attributes dialog box to remove the borders of any simple table. For illustration purposes the table created earlier in this chapter and shown in Figure 12-6 is used, but you can use any table with these steps:

1. From the FrontPage Explorer either create a new web, or open an existing web with a table in it. In either case, open the FrontPage Editor.

2. If necessary, create a simple 4×4 table with some simple text in each cell (like "Cell 1," "Cell 2," and so on).

12

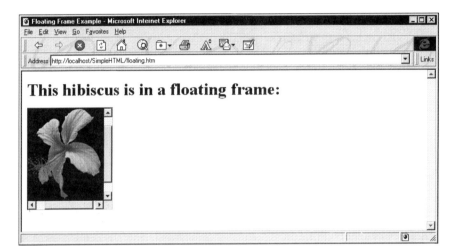

Web page
with
floating
frame in
Internet
Explorer

FIGURE 12-12

3. Right-click on the table and choose Table Properties. In the Table
Properties dialog box, click on Extended. The Extended Attributes
dialog box that you saw earlier will open. Notice that the current tag is
identified as <TABLE>.

4. Click on Add to open the Name/Value Pair dialog box, click in the Name
text box, type **frame**, press TAB, type **void** for the Value, and click on OK.
The Extended Attributes dialog box, it should look like this:

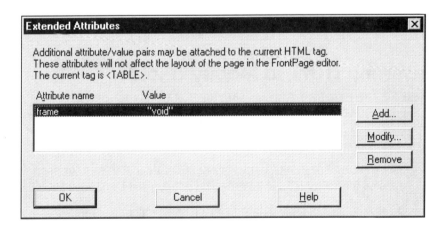

5. Click on OK twice more, save your page, and then open it in a browser. Your result should resemble the table in Figure 12-13.

6. Close your browser, FrontPage Editor, and FrontPage Explorer.

With the two examples here and the HTML reference earlier in the chapter, you can see how easy it is to add significant capability to your FrontPage webs.

HTML Authoring Resources

There are a number of excellent resources on HTML authoring available on the Web. The following is a list of the ones that are most important.

NOTE: *URLs change very quickly. While every effort was made to get the following URLs correct when this book went to print, they probably will have changed by the time this book reaches the bookstores. If you are having trouble with a URL, drop off right-hand segments, delineated by slashes, until it works. Microsoft's site is changing faster than anybody's, so if one of their URLs isn't working, don't be surprised. The best work-around is to go to http://www.microsoft.com and work forward.*

Table with no outside borders

FIGURE 12-13

A Beginner's Guide to HTML by NCSA (the National Center for Supercomputing Applications at the University of Illinois, original creators of Mosaic, the first of the web browsers from which Netscape Navigator, Microsoft Internet Explorer, and others have descended), last updated October 1996, available at:

http://www.ncsa.uiuc.edu/General/Internet/WWW/HTMLPrimer.html

Composing Good HTML by Eric Tilton, last updated December 8, 1995, available at:

http://www.cs.cmu.edu/~tilt/cgh/

Style Guide for Online Hypertext by Tim Berners-Lee (the originator of the World Wide Web), last updated May 1995, available at:

http://www.w3.org/hypertext/WWW/Provider/Style/All.html

Web Etiquette by Tim Berners-Lee, last updated May 1995, available at:

http://www.w3.org/hypertext/WWW/Provider/Style/Etiquette

Style Guide for Online Hypertext by Alan Richmond (NASA GSFC), available at:

http://guinan.gsfc.nasa.gov/Style.html

Elements of HTML Style by Jonathan Cohen, available at:

http://www.book.uci.edu/Staff/StyleGuide.html

Microsoft offers a number of documents that provide support of HTML authoring for the Internet Explorer. These can be found at:

http://microsoft.com/workshop/

Another excellent resource is the Internet Development Toolbox, at:

http://microsoft.com/inetdev/

Netscape's HTML resources for use with the Navigator include a number of documents, some also referenced here, indexed at:

http://home.netscape.com/assist/net_sites/index.html

World Wide Web Consortium's (W3C) **HTML 3.0 Specification** available at:

http://www.w3.org/hypertext/WWW/MarkUp/html3/CoverPage.html

World Wide Web Consortium's (W3C) **HTML 3.2** overview available at:

http://www.w3.org/hypertext/WWW/MarkUp/Wilbur/

One of the most valuable free HTML references on the Internet is **The HTML Reference Library** by Stephen Le Hunte. This is a very extensive Windows 3.1, or alternatively, Windows 95, Help System for HTML. It is a gold mine of information and is available for download from:

http://subnet.virtual-pc.com/~le387818/

This site is mirrored for North American users at:

http://www.terminalp.com/htmlib/

You may also be placed on a mailing list to be notified of updates to the library by sending an e-mail request to

cmlehune@swan.ac.uk.

12

There are also a number of other good books on the Web and HTML authoring. Among them are

The World Wide Web Complete Reference by Rick Stout, published 1996 by Osborne/McGraw-Hill.

Beyond HTML by Richard Karpinski, published 1996 by Osborne/McGraw-Hill.

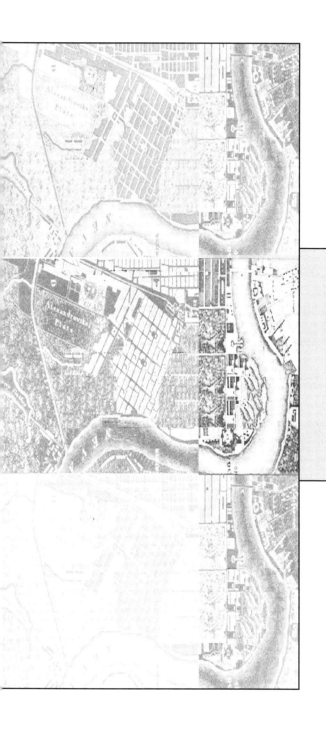

13

Working with Databases

U p to this point you have learned how to create web sites that contain information that is basically static. You define the content that the user sees on each web page. WebBots, such as the Include bot, allow you a certain amount of freedom to create web pages with content that changes, but integrating databases into your webs allows you much greater freedom to customize your web pages. By integrating databases into your webs, you allow the user to select the precise information that is displayed on a web page.

The focus of this chapter is to provide you with an understanding of databases and how to add them to your webs using FrontPage. Each of these subjects really requires a book of its own. The information here will give you an overview of how the pieces fit together and show you how to get started using databases with your webs. The first step is to understand what a database is.

NOTE: *The tools provided with FrontPage for integrating databases into webs are specific to Windows NT servers running Microsoft Internet Information Server. The MSPWS included with FrontPage also supports these tools, so you will be able to run the examples provided in this chapter on your local computer. To actually place your database-enhanced webs on the Internet, your host will need to be running Internet Information Server and support either Microsoft Access or Microsoft SQL Server databases. The examples in this chapter were created by use of Microsoft Access 97.*

Understanding Databases on the Web

A *database* is an organized collection of information. This can be a simple list of names and telephone numbers, or a complete collection of all the information about a company—its products, salespeople, sales, and inventory. In a database all the information about one item, such as the name and telephone number for one person, is a *record*. Each record is made up of a number of *fields*. In a list of names and telephone numbers, each name is one field, and the telephone number associated with the name is another field in the record. A collection of records is a *table*. A simple *flat-file* database is made up of one table, while a *relational* database has two or more tables with one or more relationships, or *links,* between fields in the tables.

In the database table shown here there are four records, each consisting of five fields. Each row in the table is a record; each column is a field. At the top of each column is the field name for that column. The CustomerID field provides a unique number to identify each record. You may have customers with the same name, or in the same city and state, so you need a way to uniquely identify each customer. There should be at least one field in each record that contains a unique value to identify that record.

CustomerID	Name	Address	City	State
1	Clark's Hardware	1200 Spruce St.	Lake City	WA
2	Tom's Tools	2714 E. Ocean Ave.	Ventura	CA
3	Bulldog Hardware	3609 Bulldog Lane	Athens	GA
4	Downtown Tools	3787 Main St.	West Caldwell	NJ
(AutoNumber)				

⊞ Customers : Table — □ ✕

Record: ◄◄ ◄ [5] ► ►◄ ►✳ of 5

Simple flat-file databases are of limited use. Relational databases, on the other hand, can contain millions of records that can be sorted and organized by use of complex criteria. Relational databases get their name from the fact that relationships are created between fields in two or more tables. Figure 13-1 shows the relationships between the tables in the North Beach Tools database that will be used in this chapter. This is a very simple relational database whose purpose is to introduce you to both relational databases and to integrating a relational database into a web. In real life the database would contain additional tables, and each table would include several more fields. It is, however, adequate for our purposes.

The North Beach Tools database contains four tables, described in Table 13-1. The Orders table has a relationship with fields in each of the other three tables. These are one-to-many relationships, which means that the contents of a field must be unique in one table, but it can appear many times in the other table. In Figure 13-1 this is shown by a *1* next to the field in the table with the unique field and by the symbol for infinity (∞) next to the field in the table that can have many occurrences of the same data. For example, the Customers table contains a unique CustomerID to identify each customer. This is the "one" side of the relationship. The Orders table contains a record for each order the customer places, so there can be a number of records for each customer. This is the "many" side of the relationship. There can also be one-to-one relationships, but these are less common.

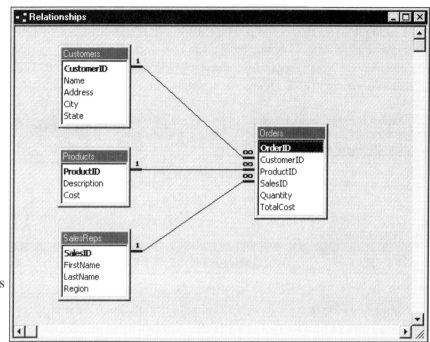

Relationships
in the North
Beach Tools
database

FIGURE 13-1

The benefit of a relational database is that by linking a unique field in one table to a field in another table, all the information in the first table is available to the second table without having to be entered each time. In a simple flat-file database each record in the Orders table would have to contain all the information about the

Table	Description
Customers	Contains the information relating to a single customer
Products	Contains the information describing each product
SalesReps	Contains the information relating to each salesperson
Orders	Contains the information for each order

Tables in
the North
Beach
Tools
Database

TABLE 13-1

customer, the product, and the salesperson, as well as the information about the order itself. In the relational database described here each record in the Orders table only contains the information unique to the order. The information about the customer, product, and salesperson is collected from the appropriate table as needed. This greatly reduces the size and complexity of the database. For example, to record a price change for a product, only one field in one table (the Cost field in the Products table) needs to be changed. From that point on every record in the Orders table will reflect the new price. Relational databases also reduce the size of the total database by avoiding the duplication of information, an important consideration when the database contains thousands or millions of records.

There are two primary database programs that you would use with FrontPage in creating webs. These are Microsoft Access and Microsoft SQL Server. Access (included with Office 97 Professional) is an excellent database for applications where the number of queries is limited. If the database will be queried often (more than a few hundred times a day), or contain thousands of records, Access is not really up to the task. SQL Server, on the other hand, is a robust, full-featured database application that can handle millions of records.

Microsoft Access

For many applications, Access is all the database you will ever need. If you are new to relational databases, it is an excellent place to start. Access contains a number of features, such as wizards, that guide you through the process of creating relational databases. Access is a good choice for a small office intranet. You can also use Access to develop your databases and then upsize them to SQL Server. Microsoft provides free tools to do this in the Free Software section of their Access Developer's Forum at http://www.microsoft.com/accessdev/. Access 97 is used in this chapter to develop the database that will be used in the examples.

TIP: *Two excellent resources for learning more about Access are* Access for Windows 95 for Busy People *by Alan Neibauer (Osborne/McGraw-Hill, 1996) and* Microsoft Access Answers *by Mary Campbell (Osborne/McGraw-Hill, 1994).*

13

Microsoft SQL Server

SQL Server is a *Structured Query Language* (SQL) database. SQL (pronounced "sequel" or "S-Q-L") is a programming language for creating, managing, and querying large relational databases. SQL Server can easily handle millions of records and tens of thousands of queries per day. For large corporations this is a common scenario. It lacks the graphical user interface that Access has and so requires a higher level of expertise to use effectively. A detailed discussion of SQL Server is beyond the scope of this book, nor is it necessary in order to understand how to integrate databases into your webs.

> **TIP:** *You can learn more about SQL Server and other large relational databases, as well as gain a better understanding of how to design relational databases, from the* LAN Times Guide to SQL *by James R. Groff and Paul N. Weinberg (Osborne/McGraw-Hill, 1994).*

So far in this book all the web files you have created have been HTML files with an .HTM extension. There are two additional types of files you use when working with databases and the Web: Internet Database Connector (.IDC) files and Hypertext Extension (.HTX) files. The .IDC files contain the instructions for querying the database, and the .HTX files are the templates for displaying the results of the database queries. Each type of file is discussed in the following sections.

Internet Database Connector Files

Internet Database Connector files (with an .IDC extension) contain the SQL statements that query the database. A query may be something like "find all the records for customers in Washington" or "find all the orders that have been placed in the last 30 days." Listing 13-1 shows a simple .IDC file that returns all the records in the Products table of the North Beach Tools database. This .IDC file asks the database to "find all the products in the database." Table 13-2 describes the parameters that are required in an .IDC file, and Table 13-3 describes the optional parameters.

Listing 13-1
.IDC file for finding all the records in the Products table

```
Datasource: NBT
Template: allprod.htx
SQLStatement:
+ SELECT products.*
+ FROM products
```

The required parameters for .IDC files will be covered in depth in the section "Creating an .IDC File." SQL statements are explained in the "Structured Query Language Statements" section. .HTX files are described next.

Parameter	Description
Datasource	System Data source Name (DSN) of the database
Template	.HTX file that will display the results generated by the .IDC file
SQL Statement	SQL commands that will be executed on the Datasource

IDC
Required
Parameters
TABLE 13-2

Hypertext Extension Files

After the database is queried by the .IDC file, the results must be formatted as an HTML page that can be displayed by a web browser. This is the function of the .HTX

Parameter	Description
DefaultParameters	Values that will be used by the SQL statement if a value is not sent by the HTML page calling the .IDC file.
Expires	Time in seconds that must pass before the database will be queried by resubmitting the same request; if the specified time has not expired, the previous results will be displayed.
MaxFieldSize	Maximum amount of space allowed per field; the default value is 8192 bytes.
MaxRecords	Maximum number of records that will be returned by a query; the default is to return all the records that match the query criteria.
Password	Password used when a username is required.
RequiredParameters	Parameters that must be sent by the HTML page calling the .IDC file; an error is returned if the parameters are not sent.
Username	Name used to access SQL Server databases that do not have integrated security.

IDC
Optional
Parameters
TABLE 13-3

13

file. An .HTX file can contain any standard HTML as well as a special set of keywords that can only be used in .HTX files, described in Table 13-4. Listing 13-2 shows how these keywords are combined with a HTML table to display the data returned by the SQL query in Listing 13-1. In Listing 13-2 the <%BEGINDETAIL%> and <%ENDDETAIL%> tags enclose the HTML for a single row in the table. When the .HTX file is executed, a row is created for each record returned by the .IDC file. The output of the .IDC file formatted by the .HTX file is shown in a web browser in Figure 13-2.

> **NOTE:** *Unlike the .IDC extension used with Internet Database Connector files, the .HTX extension is not required. You could use the .HTM instead, but it is not recommended. Use of the .HTX extension clearly identifies the file as a Hypertext Extension file used to display the results of a database query.*

Listing 13-2
.HTX file

```
<TABLE border="2" cellpadding="5" cellspacing="3">
    <TR>
        <TD align="center"><strong>Product</strong></TD>
        <TD align="center"><strong>Description</strong></TD>
        <TD align="center"><strong>Cost</strong></TD>
    </TR>
<%BeginDetail%>
    <TR>
        <TD width="33%"><%ProductID%></TD>
        <TD width="33%"><%Description%></TD>
        <TD align="right"><%Cost%></TD>
    </TR>
<%EndDetail%>
</TABLE>
```

Structured Query Language Statements

SQL is the language you use to query and maintain your database. It consists of about 30 commands, but you can accomplish quite a bit with just a few main commands. Table 13-5 describes the major SQL commands that are used to query and maintain a database.

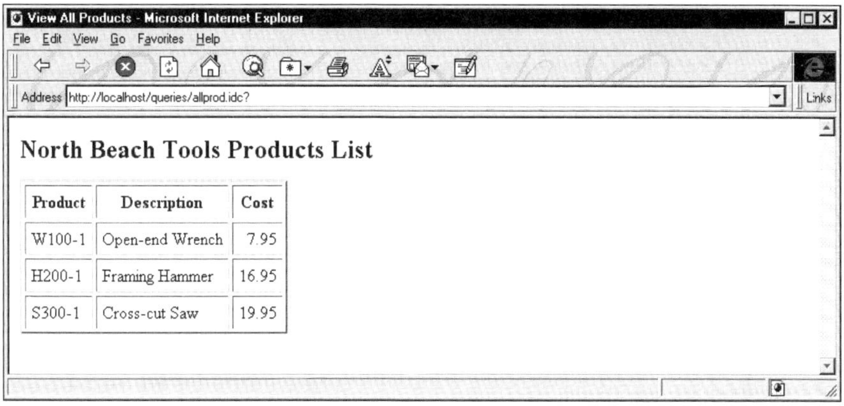

Allprod.idc
displayed
in a web
browser

FIGURE 13-2

Every SQL statement begins with an SQL command followed by a keyword and variable names. For example, in Listing 13-1 the SQL statement is

```
SELECT products.* FROM products
```

The SELECT command defines the operation—to find all the records that meet the defined criteria. In this case there is a single criterion, all the records in the Products table, which is written as

```
products.*
```

In the example here the asterisk wildcard is used to match all the fields in the Products table. The FROM command identifies the table that is the object of the query.

NOTE: *In SQL the syntax* table.field *should always be used to identify a field in a table. The SQL statement could be written as SELECT * FROM* products, *but this is not a good habit.*

You will learn more about SQL statements in the sections on creating .IDC files in FrontPage.

13

Keyword	Description
<%BeginDetail%> <%EndDetail%>	These mark the start and end of the section of the HTML page that will contain the data returned by the SQL query; if no records are returned, the code between the keywords is ignored.
<%If%> <%EndIf%>	These begin and end a section of code that determines what will be displayed if the condition described is True; conditional operators are EQ, LT, GT, and CONTAINS.
<%Else%>	This begins the section of code that will be displayed if the condition described by <%If%> is False.
EQ	Equal to; if A is equal to B, then the condition is True.
LT	Less Than; if A is less than B, then the condition is True.
GT	Greater Than; if A is greater than B, then the condition is True.
CONTAINS	If any part of A is included in B, then the condition is True.
CurrentRecord	Built-in variable that contains the number of times the instructions between the <%BeginDetail%> and <%EndDetail%> tags have been executed.
MaxRecords	Built-in variable that contains the value set by the MaxRecords parameter in the .IDC file, if used.
Parameters	Values defined in the .IDC file and passed to the .HTX file.
HTTP variables	Variables that are passed by the HTTP server and web browser.

Keywords
Used in
.HTX Files

TABLE 13-4

SQL Commands	Description
SELECT	Retrieves from a database the records that meet the specified criteria
INSERT	Creates a new record in the database
DELETE	Removes an existing record
UPDATE	Modifies an existing record
FROM	Identifies the database table that is the object of the query
WHERE	Identifies the criteria for the query

Major SQL Database Statements

TABLE 13-5

Open Database Connectivity (ODBC)

The Open Database Connectivity standard was developed as a way to allow databases to be accessed by different programs—not just the database program that created the data. For example, by using ODBC you can access a database file using Microsoft Word. This is an important feature for organizations that have data in a number of different database formats, as well as for using databases on the Web. In effect, the ODBC driver is an interpreter between the data stored in the database and the program that is querying the data.

To use an ODBC-compliant database on the Web, or with a database program other than the one that created the database itself, the proper ODBC driver must be installed. In the case of web-based databases, the ODBC driver for the database being used must be installed on the web server. To run the examples you will create in this chapter, you will need the Access ODBC driver installed on your computer. This driver, along with ODBC drivers for other popular database programs, can be found on the Office 97 CD-ROM, the Windows 95 CD-ROM, and on Microsoft's web site at http://www.microsoft.com/kb/softlib/.

How the Web Server Handles a Request

When an .IDC file is called by a web browser, a number of things happen before the data is returned and displayed by the browser:

1. The request is sent by the browser to the web server.

13

2. The web server passes the name of the data source and the SQL statement to the ODBC driver.

3. The ODBC driver executes the SQL statement on the specified database.

4. The database returns the results of the SQL statement to the ODBC driver.

5. The ODBC driver passes the query results to the web server.

6. The web server formats the query results with the specified template and sends the file to the web browser.

In addition to the Access ODBC driver used to actually query the database, another program, HTTPODBC.DLL, is used by the web server to process the .IDC and .HTX files. This program is specific to Windows NT and Microsoft Internet Information Server, and to Windows 95 and the MSPWS included with FrontPage 97. This is the reason the examples in this chapter must run on either the IIS web server or the Microsoft Personal Web Server.

Building the Access Database

Now that you've learned the basics of how databases are integrated into webs, it's time to put theory into practice. In this section you will create the Access database that will be used in the examples in this chapter. This is a very simple relational database for a fictional tool company, North Beach Tools. It consists of four tables: Products, Customers, SalesReps, and Orders. Before actually creating the database, you must first create a directory for it. This will be important later when you define it as a system data source. Create the directory with these steps:

1. In the Windows Explorer locate your Wwwroot directory. The default location is C:\Webshare\Wwwroot.

2. Select the Wwwroot directory and then select New Folder from the File menu.

3. Name the new folder **Database**, so that the path to the directory is C:\Webshare\Wwwroot\Database (your path will be different if you didn't use the defaults when you installed MSPWS and the Webshare directory).

Now you're ready to create the Access database. Do that next.

NOTE: *Access 97 can use filenames that include spaces, but you cannot set up a system data source using a filename that includes spaces. You should also avoid spaces in the names of database tables and fields, as these will needlessly complicate your SQL statements.*

1. Start Microsoft Access. In the dialog box shown here select Database Wizard and click on OK.

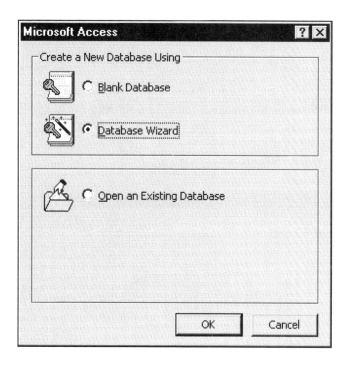

2. In the New dialog box shown next, if they are not already selected, click on the General tab, then the Blank Database icon, and click on OK.

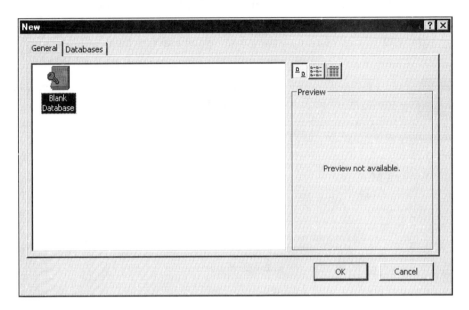

3. In the File New Database dialog box shown next select the path to your database directory (C:\Webshare\Wwwroot\Database if you used the defaults to install the MSPWS) to save your database and name it **NorthBeachTools**. Click on Create.

4. The NorthBeachTools: Database dialog box is displayed, as shown here. In the Tables tab, click on New.

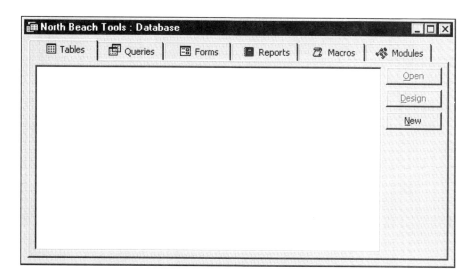

5. The New Table dialog box is displayed (shown next). Select Design View and click on OK. In the Table1 dialog box that opens, shown completed in Figure 13-3, you will enter the information for each field that will be in the table.

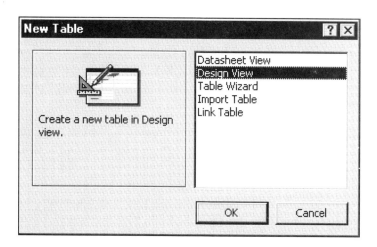

13

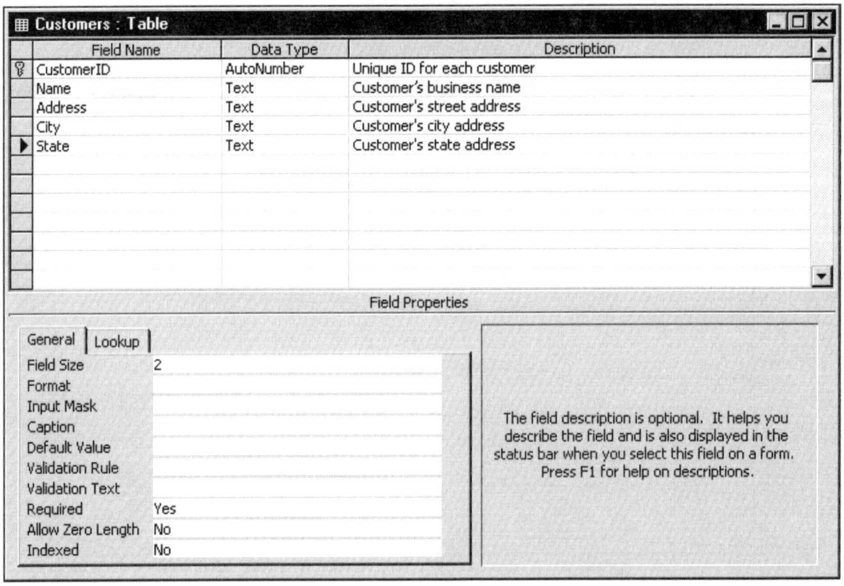

Completed
Table
Design
View
dialog box
for
Customers
table

FIGURE 13-3

6. In the first column in the first row type **CustomerID** for the Field Name and press TAB. In the Data Type column in the first row click on the down arrow, and select AutoNumber from the drop-down menu. Press TAB and type **Unique ID for each customer**.

This field is the *primary key* field for the table. Each table in a relational database should contain a primary key field which is a unique identifier for that record. This is the field you will use to create relationships between the tables in the database.

7. Right-click on the first row; select Primary Key from the context menu.

8. In the second row type **Name** for the Field Name and then press TAB. By default the field will be defined as a Text field.

9. In the General tab at the bottom of the Table1 dialog box, select the displayed value and type **16** in the Field Size text box.

10. Click on the Required text box in the General tab, and then select Yes from the drop-down menu.

11. Click on the Description text box in the second row, type **Customer's business name**, and then press TAB.

12. Type **Address** in the Field Name text box, press TAB, select the displayed value, type **24** in the Field Size text box, and select Yes in the Required field drop-down menu. Type **Customer's street address** in the Description text box. Press TAB.

13. Type **City** in the Field Name text box, press TAB, select the displayed value, type **24** in the Field Size text box, and select Yes in the Required field drop-down menu. Type **Customer's city address** in the Description text box. Press TAB.

14. Type **State** in the Field Name text box, press TAB, type **2** in the Field Size text box, and select Yes in the Required field drop-down menu. Type **Customer's state address** in the Description text box. Your Table1 dialog box should look like Figure 13-3.

15. Save the Customers table by clicking on the Save button on the toolbar. In the Save As dialog box that is displayed type **Customers** for the Table Name and click on OK.

16. Close the Customers table.

You will use similar steps to create the other three tables in the database. Create the Products table next:

1. In the NorthBeachTools: Database dialog box click on New.

2. Select Design View in the New Table dialog box and then click on OK.

3. In the first row of the Table1 dialog box type **ProductID** for the Field Name, press TAB, and select Text. In the General tab select the displayed value, type **8** in the Field Size text box, and select Yes from the Required drop-down menu. In the Description field type **Unique ID for each product**.

4. Right-click on the first row; select Primary Key from the context menu.

5. In the second row type **Description** for the Field Name and then press TAB.

6. In the General tab select the displayed value, type **24** in the Field Size text box, and select Yes from the Required drop-down menu.

7. Type **Description of product** in the Description text box, and then press TAB again.

8. Type **Cost** in the Field Name text box and press TAB.

9. Select Number in the Data Type drop-down menu. In the General tab select Single from the Field Size drop-down menu, Fixed from the Format drop-down menu, 2 from the Decimal Places drop-down menu, and Yes from the Required drop-down menu.

10. In the Description text box in the third row type **Cost of each product**. The finished Products table is shown in Figure 13-4.

11. Click on the Save button on the toolbar, and type **Products** in the Table Name text box in the Save As dialog box.

12. Click on OK and then close the Products table.

Next you will create the table listing the sales representatives for North Beach Tools.

1. In the NorthBeachTools: Database dialog box click on New.

2. Select Design View in the New Table dialog box and then click on OK.

3. In the first row of the Table1 dialog box type **SalesID** for the Field Name, press TAB, select AutoNumber from the Data Type drop-down menu, press TAB again, and type **Unique ID for each sales person**.

4. Right-click on the first row; select Primary Key from the context menu.

5. In the second row type **FirstName** for the Field Name and then press TAB.

6. In the General tab select the displayed value, type **16** in the Field Size text box, and select Yes from the Required drop-down menu.

7. Type **Sales rep's first name** in the Description text box; then press TAB.

8. Type **LastName** in the Field Name text box and press TAB.

9. In the General tab select the displayed value, type **16** in the Field Size text box, and select Yes from the Required drop-down menu.

```
Products : Table                                              _ □ ×
     Field Name          Data Type              Description          ▲
🔑▶ ProductID          Text         Unique ID for each product
    Description         Text         Description of product
    Cost                Number       Cost of each product

                                                                    ▼
                              Field Properties

    General │ Lookup │
    Field Size        8
    Format
    Input Mask
    Caption                             A field name can be up to 64 characters long,
    Default Value                       including spaces.  Press F1 for help on field
    Validation Rule                                      names.
    Validation Text
    Required          Yes
    Allow Zero Length No
    Indexed           Yes (No Duplicates)
```

Products
database
table in
Design view

FIGURE 13-4

10. In the Description text box in the third row type **Sales rep's last name**
    and then press TAB.

11. Type **Region** and then press TAB.

12. In the General tab select the displayed value, type **16** in the Field Size text
    box, and select Yes from the Required drop-down menu.

13. Type **Sales rep's sales region** in the Description text box. Figure 13-5
    shows the finished SalesReps table.

14. Click on the Save button on the toolbar, and type **SalesReps** in the Table
    Name text box in the Save As dialog box.

15. Click on OK and then close the SalesReps table.

The last table to create is the Orders table. Do that now:

1. In the NorthBeachTools: Database dialog box click on New.

13

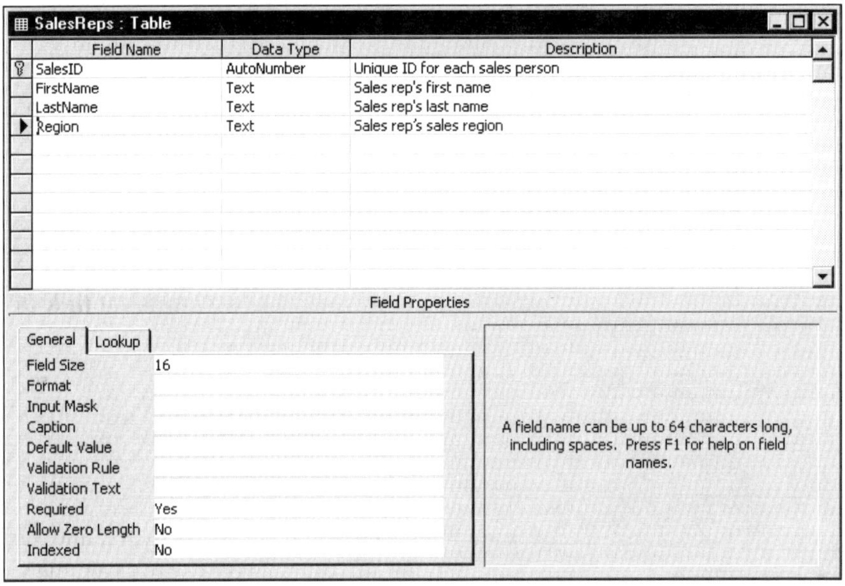

SalesReps
database
table in
Design view

FIGURE 13-5

2. Select Design View in the New Table dialog box and then click on OK.

3. In the first row of the Table1 dialog box type **OrderID** for the Field Name, press TAB, select AutoNumber from the Data Type drop-down menu, press TAB again, and type **Unique ID for each order**.

4. Right-click on the first row, and select Primary Key from the context menu.

5. In the second row type **CustomerID** for the Field Name and then press TAB.

6. Select Number from the Data Type drop-down menu.

7. In the General tab verify Long Integer is selected from the Field Size drop-down menu, Yes from the Required drop-down menu, and verify Yes (Duplicates OK) is selected from the Indexed drop-down menu.

8. Type **Relational link to Customer table** in the Description text box and then press TAB.

9. Type **ProductID** in the Field Name text box and press TAB.

10. Accept the defaults in the General tab by pressing TAB.

11. In the Description text box in the third row type **Relational link to Products table** and then press TAB.

12. Type **SalesID** in the Field Name text box and press TAB.

13. Select Number from the Data Type drop-down menu.

14. In the General tab verify Long Integer is selected from the Field Size drop-down menu, Yes from the Required drop-down menu, and verify Yes (Duplicates OK) is selected from the Indexed drop-down menu.

15. In the Description text box in the fourth row type **Relational link to SalesReps table** and then press TAB.

16. Type **Quantity** and then press TAB.

17. Select Number from the Data Type drop-down menu. In the General tab select Yes from the Required drop-down menu.

18. Type **Quantity of product ordered** in the Description text box and then press TAB.

19. Type **TotalCost**, press TAB, and select Currency from the Data Type drop-down menu.

20. In the General tab select 2 from the Decimal Places drop-down menu and Yes from the Required drop-down menu.

21. Type **Total cost of order** in the Description text box. The completed Orders table is shown in Figure 13-6.

13

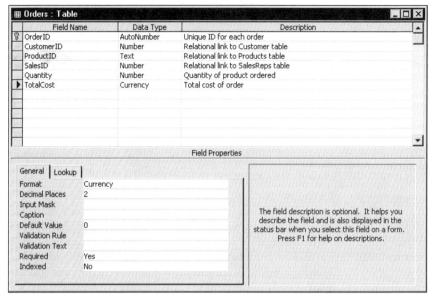

Completed
Orders
table in
Design view

FIGURE 13-6

22. Click on the Save button on the toolbar, and type **Orders** in the Table Name text box in the Save As dialog box.

23. Click on OK and then close the Orders table.

The next step in building the database is to create the relationships between the fields.

Creating Database Relationships

Creating the relationships between the fields in the various tables of the database is a straightforward process in Access, as you will see next:

1. In Access, open the Tools menu and select Relationships. The Show Table dialog box, shown here, will be displayed:

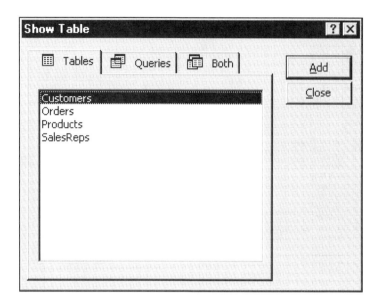

2. Select the four tables in the database (hold down SHIFT while clicking on each of them), click on Add, and then click on Close. The four tables will be displayed in the Relationships dialog box.

3. Drag the Products and SalesReps tables so that they are lined up below the Customers table, and then drag the Orders table so it is to the right of the Products table, as shown in Figure 13-7.

4. In the Customers table, click on CustomerID, drag it on top of CustomerID in the Orders table, and then release the mouse button. The Relationships dialog box shown next is displayed.

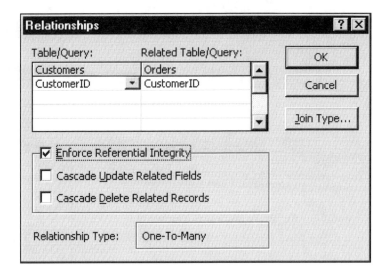

5. Select the Enforce Referential Integrity check box and click on Create. A line connecting the two fields is drawn to indicate the relationship between the fields.

6. Repeat steps 4 and 5 for the ProductID field in the Products table and Orders table, and the SalesID field in the SalesReps table and Orders table. Your finished Relationships dialog box should look like Figure 13-8.

7. Close the Relationships window and click on Yes to save the changes to the Relationships layout.

This will bring the North Beach Tools database to the point where you can almost begin using it with FrontPage. One more step needs to be taken first—adding records to it.

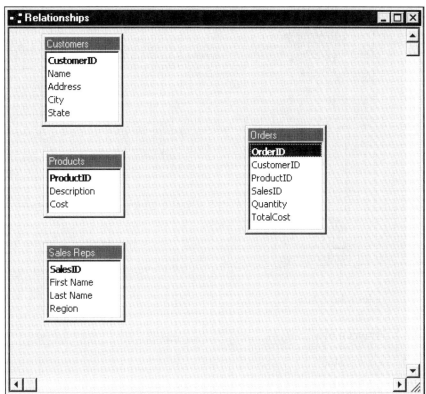

Tables in Relationships dialog box

FIGURE 13-7

Adding Records to the Database

Now that your database is set up, you need to add some data to it. Do that now with these steps:

1. Double-click on the Customers table in the Tables tab of the NorthBeach Tools: Database dialog box. The Customers table will open in Datasheet view as shown next.

13

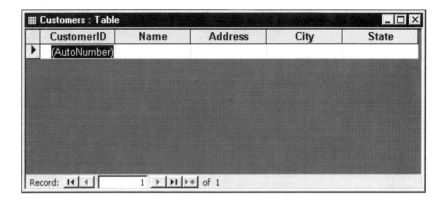

2. Press TAB. In the Name text box type **Clark's Hardware**, press TAB, type **1200 Spruce St.** in the Address text box, press TAB again, and type **Lake City** in the City text box. Press TAB once more, type **WA** in the State text box, and then press TAB twice.

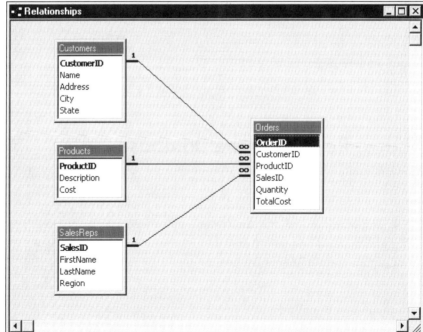

Relationships dialog box with relations between tables set

FIGURE 13-8

3. Type **Tom's Tools**, press TAB, type **2714 E. Ocean Ave.**, press TAB, type **Ventura**, press TAB, and type **CA**. Press TAB twice.

4. Type **Bulldog Hardware**, press TAB, type **3609 Bulldog Lane**, press TAB, type **Athens**, press TAB, and type **GA**. Press TAB twice.

5. Type **Downtown Tools**, press TAB, type **3787 Main St.**, press TAB, type **West Caldwell**, press TAB, and type **NJ**.

The finished Customers table should look similar to the one shown here. Next create the records for the SalesReps table with these steps:

CustomerID	Name	Address	City	State
1	Clark's Hardware	1200 Spruce St.	Lake City	WA
2	Tom's Tools	2714 E. Ocean Ave.	Ventura	CA
3	Bulldog Hardware	3609 Bulldog Lane	Athens	GA
4	Downtown Tools	3787 Main St.	West Caldwell	NJ
(AutoNumber)				

Record: |◄| |◄| 5 |►| |►I| |►*| of 5

NOTE: *You can drag the dividing lines between the column headers to change the width of a column.*

1. Close the Customers table and then open the SalesReps table in Datasheet view.

2. Press TAB. In the FirstName text box type **Allen**, press TAB, type **Johnson** in the LastName text box, press TAB, type **Northwest** in the Region text box, and then press TAB twice.

3. Type **Beverly**, press TAB, type **Bowman**, press TAB, type **Southwest**, and press TAB twice.

13

4. Type **Dylan**, press TAB, type **Sherman**, press TAB again, then type **Southeast**, and press TAB twice.

5. Type **Linda**, press TAB, type **Marshall**, press TAB again, and type **Northeast**. Save the completed SalesReps table.

The completed SalesReps table should look similar to the one shown next. Then create the records for the Products table with these steps:

SalesID	FirstName	LastName	Region
1	Allen	Johnson	Northwest
2	Beverly	Bowman	Southwest
3	Dylan	Sherman	Southeast
4	Linda	Marshall	Northeast
(AutoNumber)			

SalesReps : Table

Record: 4 of 4

1. Close the SalesReps table, and then open the Products table in Datasheet view.

2. In the ProductID text box type **W100-1**, press TAB, type **Open-end Wrench** in the Description text box, press TAB again, type **7.95** in the Cost text box, and then press TAB.

3. Type **H200-1**, press TAB, type **Framing Hammer**, press TAB, type **16.95**, and press TAB.

4. Type **S300-1**, press TAB, type **Cross-cut Saw**, press TAB again, and type **19.95**. Save the completed Products table.

The completed Products table should look similar to the one shown next. That completes the steps for creating the North Beach Tools database. The next step is to make the database available to your web. You do this by creating a System Data Source Name (DSN) as you will see in the next section.

⊞ Products : Table		_ □ ✕
ProductID	**Description**	**Cost**
W100-1	Open-end Wrench	7.95
H200-1	Framing Hammer	16.95
S300-1	Cross-cut Saw	19.95
		0.00

Record: ⏮ ◀   4   ▶ ⏭ ▶✳ of 4

5. Close the Products table and the North Beach Tools database.

Defining a System Data Source Name

A System Data Source Name (System DSN) allows anyone with the correct permissions to use the database. This is necessary to allow users accessing a database over the Internet to use it. Define the System DSN with these steps:

1. Open the Windows Start menu and point on Settings. In the flyout menu select Control Panel.

2. In the Control Panel double-click on the 32bit ODBC icon. The ODBC Data Source Administrator dialog box is displayed as shown in Figure 13-9.

32bit ODBC

The ODBC Data Source Administrator dialog box is used to set User, System, and File Data Source Names, and to display information about the installed ODBC drivers. A *User DSN* is local to the computer and can only be used by the current user. A *File DSN* is a data source that can be shared by all users who have the appropriate ODBC driver installed and can be shared across a network.

3. Select the System DSN tab and then click on Add. The Create New Data Source dialog box shown next is displayed.

13

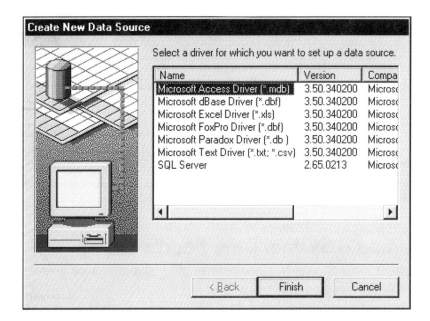

4. Select the Microsoft Access Driver and click on Finish. The ODBC Microsoft Access 97 Setup dialog box, shown next, is displayed.

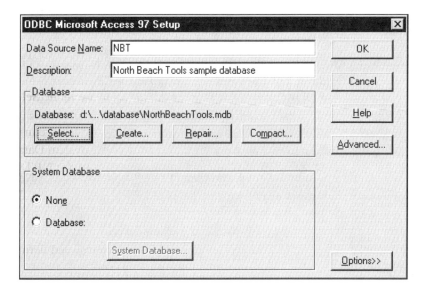

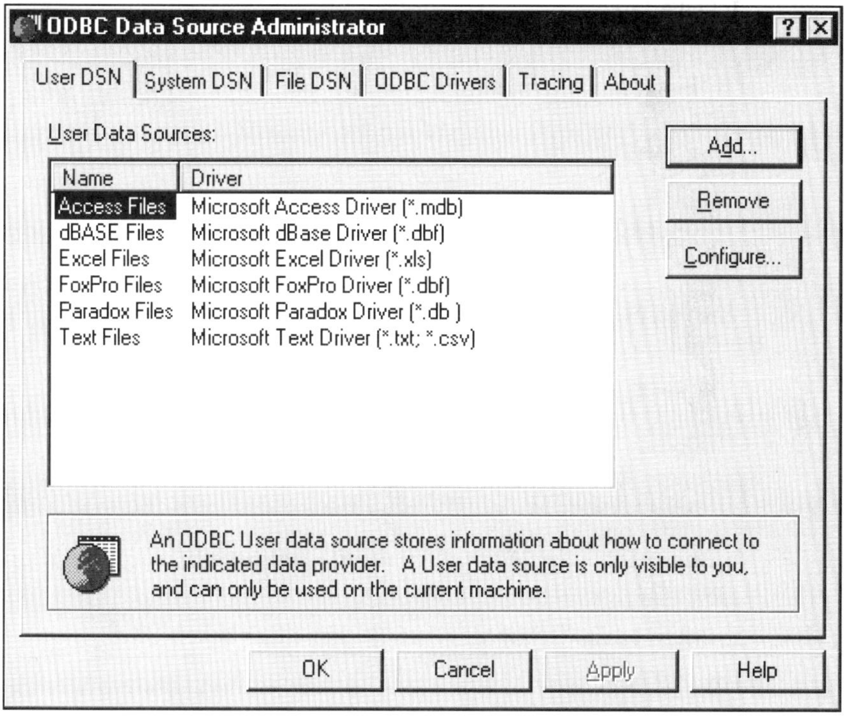

The ODBC
Data Source
Administrator
dialog box

FIGURE 13-9

5. Type **NBT** in the Data Source Name text box, press TAB, and type **North Beach Tools sample database** in the Description text box.

6. Click on the Select button, locate your sample database in the Select Database dialog box (the default path is C:\Webshare\Wwwroot\ Database\NorthBeachTools.mdb), and click on OK twice to return to the ODBC Data Source Administrator dialog box. In the System Data Sources list box on the System DSN tab you should see the NBT data source you have defined.

7. Click on OK.

Now that you have created the North Beach Tools database and defined it as a system data source, you're ready to integrate it into a FrontPage web.

13

Creating Database Webs with FrontPage

Creating a database to integrate into a web is only half the process. Next you will create a FrontPage web that includes HTML, .IDC, and .HTX files. This web will allow you to select and modify records in the database.

1. Open the FrontPage Explorer if it isn't already open.

2. Create a new Normal Web. Name the web **NBT**.

3. Select Web Settings from the FrontPage Explorer Tools menu to display the FrontPage Web Settings dialog box shown in Figure 13-10.

FrontPage Web Settings ☒

| Parameters | Configuration | Advanced | Language |

Web _N_ame: | NBT |

Web _T_itle: | North Beach Tools |

Web Server: http://localhost

FrontPage Server
Extensions Version: 2.0.2.1104

Server Version: Microsoft-PWS-95/2.0

IP Address: 127.0.0.1

Proxy Server:

[OK] [Cancel] [_A_pply] [Help]

FrontPage
Web
Settings
dialog box

FIGURE 13-10

4. In the Web Title text box select the displayed name, type **North Beach Tools,** and then click on OK. This is to give the web a more descriptive name that will appear in the FrontPage Explorer title bar.

5. In the FrontPage Explorer, double-click on the Home page to open it in the FrontPage Editor.

6. Right-click on the Home page in the FrontPage Editor, and select Page Properties in the context menu.

7. In the Page Properties dialog box type **North Beach Tools Home Page** in the Title text box on the General tab, and then click on OK.

8. At the top of the Home page in the FrontPage Editor type **North Beach Tools**, and format it as Heading 1.

9. Press ENTER, type **Products**, and then format it as Heading 2.

10. Move the cursor to the next line, and click on the Bulleted List toolbar button.

11. Type **View All Products** and press ENTER.

12. Type **Find A Product** and press ENTER.

13. Type **Add A Product** and press ENTER.

14. Type **Delete A Product** and press ENTER.

15. Click on the Bulleted List toolbar button to end the bulleted list.

16. Type **People**, format it as Heading 2, and then press ENTER.

17. Click on the Bulleted List toolbar button and type **Sales Representatives**.

18. Press ENTER and type **Customers**.

19. Use the DOWN ARROW key to move to the next line.

20. Choose Horizontal Line from the Insert menu, right-click on the line, and select Horizontal Line Properties from the Context menu.

21. In the Horizontal Line Properties dialog box set the Width to **80** percent, the Size to **6** pixels, and click on OK.

22. Move the cursor to the first line below the horizontal line, and select Symbol from the Insert menu.

13

23. Click on the copyright symbol, as shown here, click on Insert, and then click on Close.

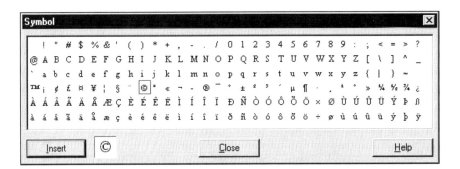

24. Type **1997 North Beach Tools** (leave a space between the copyright symbol and the date), and format it as Heading 5.

25. Your Home page should be similar to Figure 13-11. Save your North Beach Tools Home page.

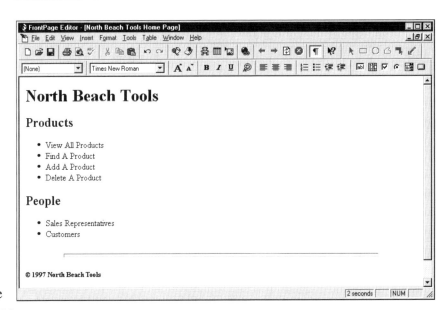

North
Beach
Tools
Home page

FIGURE 13-11

Creating an .IDC File

Now you're ready to create your first Internet Database Connector file. This will be a simple SQL query to display all the products in the Products table of the North Beach Tools database. The .IDC file will be called by a hyperlink from the first item in the Products bulleted list, View All Products. The .IDC files are called either by hyperlinks or from a form. You will see how to use forms in the following sections.

Creating a Directory for Executable Scripts

There's one more thing to do before you create the .IDC file. That is to create a directory where executable scripts can be stored. With MSPWS or Internet Information Server the Scripts directory is normally used to store executable files for your webs. This directory has Execute permission but not Read permission. This allows anonymous users, such as anyone accessing the files over the Internet, to execute the files without being able to read or change the files. This is an important security consideration for the webmaster. Leaving the door open for users to place executable files on your web server is an invitation to disaster.

You could place the .IDC files you will create in the next section in your Scripts directory (which is set up by default when you installed the MSPWS), but it is better to store only scripts there that are used by more than one web on your server. For executable files that are going to be used by one web it is convenient to place those files in the same web. Creating a directory for scripts is a two-step process: first you create the directory, then you give it the proper permissions, using the MSPWS Administration tools. First create the directory in the NBT web:

1. In the FrontPage Explorer, change to Folder view, and select New Folder from the File menu.

2. Rename the folder **Queries** by selecting the folder and then choosing Rename from the Edit menu. Press ENTER.

3. Click on the Start button on the Windows 95 taskbar, point on Settings in the Start menu, and select Control Panel from the flyout menu.

Personal Web Server

4. In the Control Panel double-click on the Personal Web Server icon. The Personal Web Server Properties dialog box shown in Figure 13-12 is displayed.

13

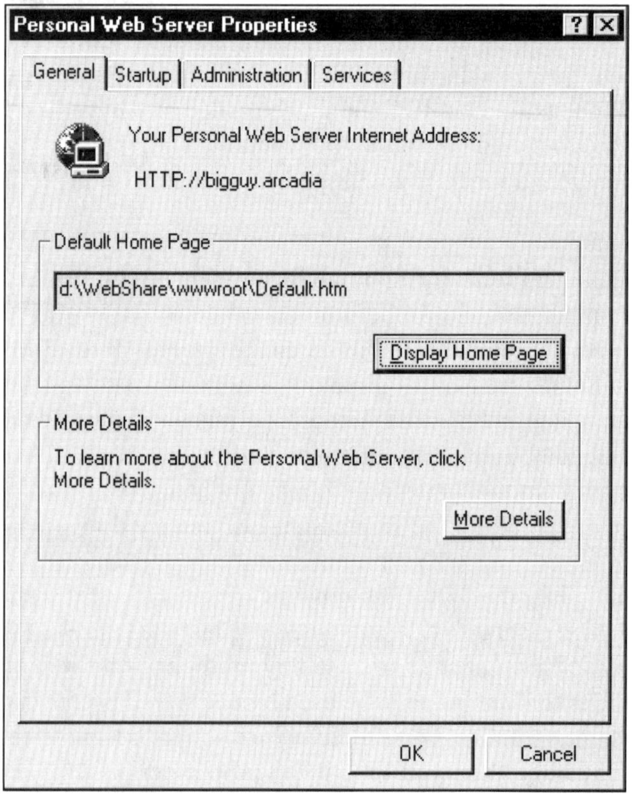

Personal
Web Server
Properties
dialog box

FIGURE 13-12

5. Select the Administration tab and click on the Administration button. The administration tool is an HTML-based application. Your web browser will open (if it's not open already) and load the first page of the MSPWS administration web, as shown in Figure 13-13.

6. Click on the WWW Administration hyperlink. Figure 13-14 shows the Internet services Administrator – WWW web page that is displayed.

7. Click on the Directories tab to display the WWW Administrator – Directory web page shown in Figure 13-15. Here you will see a list of the virtual directories for all your webs. These were created by FrontPage when you created the webs.

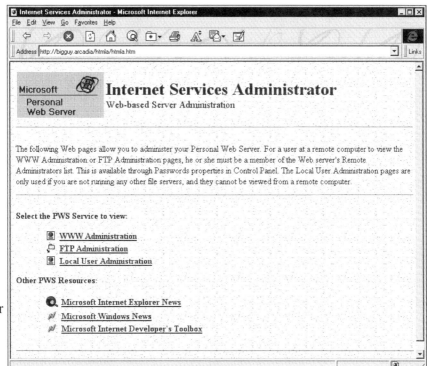

Internet
Services
Administrator
for the
MSPWS
web page

FIGURE 13-13

8. Move to the bottom of the web page by pressing CTRL-END.

9. Click on the Add hyperlink in the Action column at the far right of the page. The WWW Administrator – Directory Add web page shown in Figure 13-16 will be displayed.

10. Click on the Browse button, and locate your Queries directory in the NBT web, or type the path in the Directory text box. If you're not sure of the path, use the Browse button. In Figure 13-16 the Webshare directory is located on the D drive; the default installation will put it on the C drive.

11. In the Directory Alias text box type **/NBT/Queries**, deselect the Read check box, and select the Execute check box. Click on OK.

13

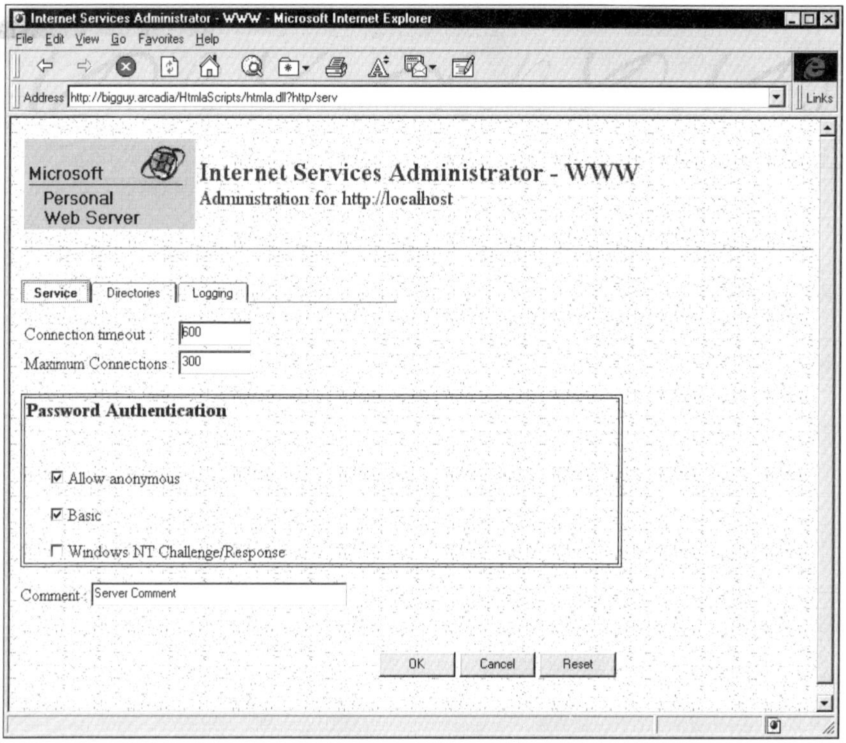

Internet
Services
Administrator
– WWW
web page

FIGURE 13-14

12. When the web browser returns to the WWW Administrator – Directory web page, close your browser.

13. Click on Cancel in the Personal Web Server Properties dialog box to close it.

Now you're ready to create your first .IDC file.

Creating the Allprod.idc .IDC File

To create an .IDC file, you use the Database Connector Wizard, as you will see next:

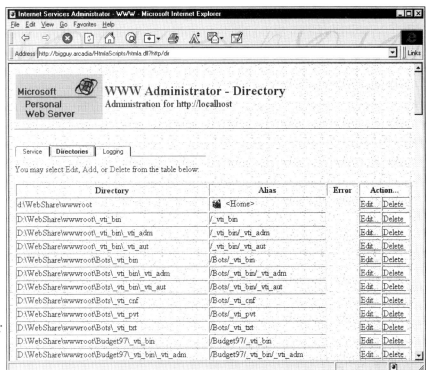

WWW
Administrator
– Directory
web page

FIGURE 13-15

1. In the FrontPage Editor select New from the File menu.

2. In the New Page dialog box click on Database Connector Wizard and click on OK. The Internet Database Connector Wizard dialog box shown in Figure 13-17 is displayed.

3. In the ODBC Data Source text box type **NBT**, the name you used when you created the system data source.

4. In the Query Results Template text box type **Allprod.htx**. This will be the name of the template you will create in the section to display the results of the query. Click on Next.

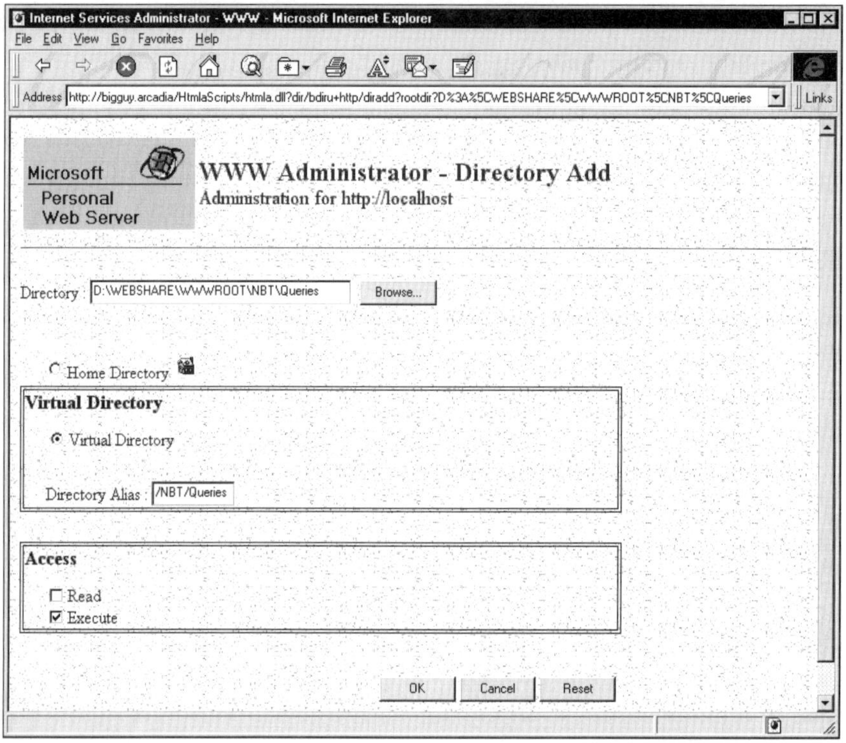

WWW
Administrator
– Directory
Add web
page

FIGURE 13-16

---

5. In the text box type **SELECT products.* FROM products**. (Do not type the period at the end of the sentence.)

6. Click on Finish. The Current Web dialog box shown here will be displayed.

Current Web

Look in: | http://localhost/NBT

Name	Title
_private	
images	
Queries	

Save As

Choose a folder where executable scripts can be stored.

OK
Cancel
Help

7. Select the Queries directory, type **Allprod.idc** in the Save As text box, and then click on OK.

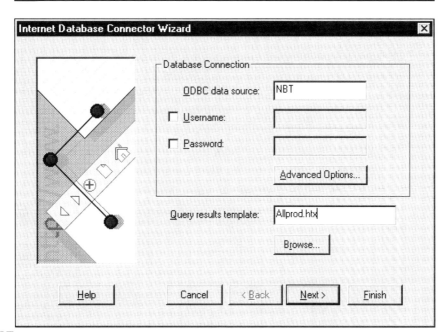

Internet Database Connector Wizard

Database Connection

ODBC data source: NBT

☐ Username:

☐ Password:

Advanced Options...

Query results template: Allprod.htx

Browse...

Help   Cancel   < Back   Next >   Finish

Internet
Database
Connector
Wizard
dialog box

13

■ FIGURE 13-17

Next you will create the HTX template that will be used to display the results of an SQL query in the Allprod.idc file.

Creating a Hypertext Extension File

As you learned earlier in this chapter, an .HTX file contains both standard HTML tags as well as certain tags that are specific to .HTX files. You will use the Database command on the Edit menu to enter these commands in your .HTX file. Do that now with these steps:

1. In the FrontPage Editor select New from the File menu.

2. In the New Page dialog box double-click on Database Results. A new page is displayed with a FrontPage comment describing the purpose of the page.

3. In the first line beneath the comment type **North Beach Tools Product Line**, and format it as Heading 2.

4. Press ENTER and then insert a two-row by three-column table using either the Table menu or the Insert Table button in the toolbar.

5. Right-click on the table, and select Table Properties on the context menu.

6. In the Table Properties dialog box set the Border Size to **2**, and, if it isn't already, deselect the Specify Width check box. Click on OK.

7. Select the bottom row of the table, and then select Database from the Edit menu. In the flyout menu select Detail Section. Your page should like the one shown in Figure 13-18. The brackets on each side of the bottom row of the table indicate the beginning and end of the detail section, where the .HTX-specific tags must be placed.

8. Click on the first cell in the bottom row of the table. From the Edit menu select Database, and then select Database Column Value. The Database Column Name dialog box shown next is displayed.

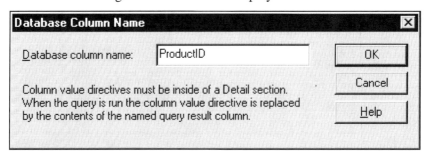

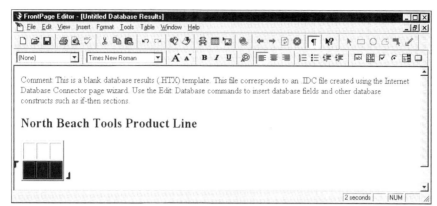

.HTX page
in the
FrontPage
Editor

FIGURE 13-18

NOTE: *With SQL, field names are usually referred to as "column values."*

9. Type **ProductID** in the Database Column Name text box and click on OK.

TIP: *FrontPage does not have a Browse feature for locating the names of fields in your database. It's a good idea to keep a list handy for when you are creating the .IDC and .HTX files.*

10. Click on the middle cell of the bottom row of the table. From the Edit menu select Database, and then select Database Column Value. Type **Description** in the Database Column Name text box and click on OK.

11. Press TAB, select Database Column Value from the Database flyout in the Edit menu, and then type **Cost** in the Database Column Name text box. Click on OK.

12. Right-click on the last cell in the bottom row of the table, and select Cell Properties from the context menu.

13. In the Cell Properties dialog box select Right from the Horizontal Alignment drop-down menu. Click on OK.

13

14. Select the first row of the table; then click on the Bold and Center
toolbar buttons.

15. Click on the first cell in the first row of the table, type **Product ID**, and
then press TAB.

16. Type **Description**, press TAB, and type **Cost**. Your table should now look
similar to the one shown next.

Product ID	Description	Cost
<%ProductID%>	<%Description%>	<%Cost%>

17. Click on the Save toolbar button. In the Save As dialog box accept
the Page Title of North Beach Tools Product Line, and type
Queries/Allprod.htx for the File Path within your FrontPage web.
Click on OK.

All that remains before you can test your .IDC and .HTX files is to create a
hyperlink from the Home page to the Allprod.idc file. Do that now:

1. Open the North Beach Tools Home page in the FrontPage Editor.

2. Select the View All Products text in the Products bulleted list, and then
click on the Create Or Edit Hyperlink toolbar button.

3. In the Create Hyperlink dialog box select the Current FrontPage Web tab,
and then click on the Browse button.

4. Open the Queries folder in the Current Web dialog box and select
Allprod.idc. Click on OK.

5. In the Page text box on the Current Web tab of the Edit Hyperlink dialog
box type a question mark (**?**) after Allprod.idc. You cannot have any
spaces between the .IDC filename and the question mark. When an .IDC
file is called by a hyperlink, the filename must always have a question
mark at the end.

6. Click on OK and then save your Home page. Now you are ready to test
your .IDC and .HTX files in a web browser.

7. Open the North Beach Tools Home page in your browser, and click on the View All Products hyperlink. Figure 13-19 shows the results returned by the Allprod.idc file, formatted by the Allprod.htx template.

This example has used a very simple SQL statement to return all the records in a table. In the next example you will create an .IDC file that returns only the records that meet certain criteria.

Finding Specific Products

While returning all the records in a database table can be useful, many databases contain too many records to be manageable this way. In that case you want to be able to limit the records returned. You can do this by adding a WHERE statement to the SQL query you created in the previous example. In this next example you will use a form to call the .IDC file. In the form you specify the criterion that will be passed to the .IDC file and used to filter the database records. Begin now with these steps:

1. Open a new Normal page in the FrontPage Editor.

2. At the top of the page type **Selected North Beach Tools**, and format it as Heading 2.

Results returned by the Allprod Internet Database Connector file

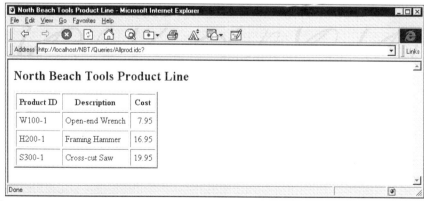

FIGURE 13-19

13

3. Move the cursor to the next line, display your Forms toolbar if it is not visible, and click on the One-line Text Box toolbar button.

4. Move the cursor to the right of the text box, and type **Enter a keyword:** (include the colon and leave a space between the text and the text box).

5. Move the cursor to the left of the text box, and click on the Push Button toolbar button.

6. Right-click on the form and select Form Properties from the Context menu.

7. In the Form Properties dialog box select Internet Database Connector from the Form Handler drop-down menu.

8. Click on the Settings button, type **Queries/Selectprod.idc** in the Internet Database Connector File text box, and then click on the Edit button to open the Internet Database Connector Wizard.

9. In the ODBC data source text box type **NBT**.

10. Type **Selectprod.htx** in the Query Results Template text box and then click on Next.

11. In the SQL Query text box type **SELECT products.* FROM products**, press ENTER, and then type **WHERE'%%%Description%%%' LIKE product.description;** (include the semicolon at the end). The extra percent signs (%%) around the Description variable act as wildcards. This search will return every record that contains the text string entered in the form.

 TIP: *Syntax is very important in writing SQL statements. Be sure to enter the text exactly as shown in the examples.*

12. Click on Finish, then on OK twice.

13. Right-click on the text box in the form, and select Form Field Properties from the context menu.

14. In the Text Box Properties dialog box type **Description** in the Name text box and press ENTER.

15. Save the page with the Page Title **Selected North Beach Tools** and the filename **Selected.htm**.

Next you will create the .HTX file that will display the results of the query. Since it's always possible that a search will fail to find any matching records in the database, this .HTX file will include an If-Then conditional statement. If no records are found, a message will be displayed suggesting the user try a different keyword. If at least one record is found, the records will be displayed. Create the .HTX file with these steps:

1. Select New from the File menu, and then double-click on Database Results in the New Page dialog box.

2. Delete the FrontPage comment from the new page, type **Selected North Beach Tools**, and format it as Heading 2. Press ENTER.

3. Open the Edit menu, select Database, and then choose Detail Section.

4. Place the cursor between the Detail icons, and type **The following products were found:**. Format it as Heading 3 and then press ENTER.

5. Click on the Bulleted List toolbar button, and then select Database Column Value from the Database flyout on the Edit menu.

6. Type **Description** in the Database Column Value dialog box and press ENTER.

7. Select the <%Description%> variable you just entered, and click on the Text Color toolbar button.

8. In the Color dialog box select a blue square and click on OK. Click on the Bold toolbar button.

9. Move the cursor to the line below the ending Detail icon.

10. From the Database flyout menu select If-Then Conditional Section. The If-Then Conditional Section dialog box shown next is displayed.

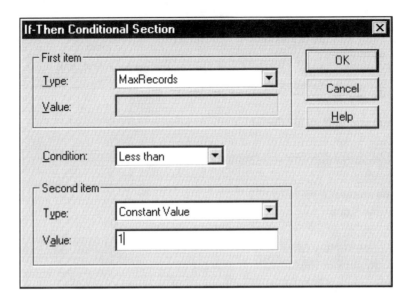

11. Select CurrentRecord from the First Item Type drop-down menu, and then verify Equals is selected in the Condition drop-down menu.

12. Verify Constant Value is selected from the Second Item Type drop-down menu, type **0** in the Second Item Value text box, and click on OK.

    A small diamond and a triangle will appear on the page. These represent the If and EndIf tags.

13. Place the cursor between the diamond and triangle icons and type **No matches were found. Please try a different keyword.** Format the text as Heading 3. Your .HTX page should look like Figure 13-20.

14. Save your .HTX file with a Page Title of **Selected North Beach Tools** and a filename of **Queries/Selectprod.htx**.

15. Open the Home page in the FrontPage Editor and select Find A Product. Click on the Create Or Edit Hyperlink toolbar button, and type **Selected.htm** in the Page text box on the Current FrontPage Web tab. Press ENTER.

16. Save your Home page and then open it in your web browser.

17. Click on the Find A Product hyperlink.

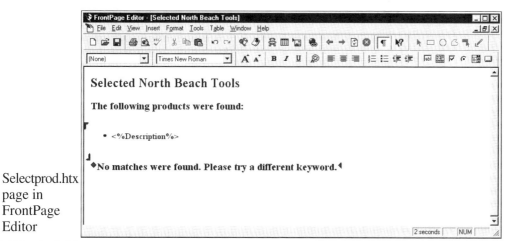

Selectprod.htx page in FrontPage Editor

FIGURE 13-20

18. When the Selected.htm page is loaded, type **a** in the Form text box and click on Submit. Two items should be returned: Framing Hammer and Cross-cut Saw, as shown in Figure 13-21.

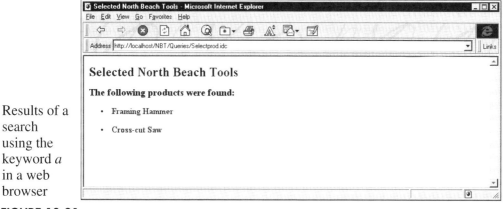

Results of a search using the keyword *a* in a web browser

FIGURE 13-21

13

19. Click on your browser's Back button, type **drill** in the Form text box, and then press ENTER. No matches will be found, and your browser will display the "No matches found" message, as shown in Figure 13-22.

In the next exercise you will add a new record to the database.

Adding a Product to the Database

One useful feature of integrating databases into your webs is the ability to remotely add records to a database. On an intranet this can be an effective way to allow multiple users, such as customer service representatives, to update a single database. It is also useful for a web application such as a guest book. In this next exercise you will create an .IDC file and the related HTML and .HTX files to add a product to your database.

1. Open a new Normal page in the FrontPage Editor.

2. At the top of the page type **North Beach Tools**, format it as Heading 2, and then press ENTER.

3. Type **Add a product to the database:** and format it as Heading 3.

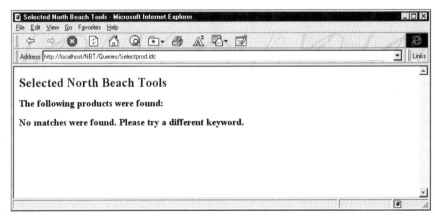

Results of a
search with
no matches
in a web
browser

FIGURE 13-22

4. Move the cursor to the next line, and click on the Push Button toolbar button.

5. Move the cursor to the left of the button, and select Insert Table from the Table menu.

6. In the Insert Table dialog box select 3 rows and 2 columns, and then, if it isn't already, deselect the Specify Width check box. Click on OK.

7. Select the left column of the table, and click on the Align Right toolbar button.

8. Click in the first cell in the first row of the table, type **Product ID**, and then format it as bold.

9. Press TAB twice, type **Description**, and then format it as bold.

10. Move the cursor to the bottom cell in the first column, type **Cost**, and then format it as bold.

11. Click on the rightmost cell in the first row, and click on the One-line Text Box toolbar button.

12. Right-click on the text box. In the Text Properties dialog box type **ProductID** for the Description and **8** in the Width In Characters text box. Press ENTER.

13. Move the cursor to the rightmost cell in the second row, and then click on the One-line Text Box toolbar button again.

14. Right-click on the text box. Click on Form Field Properties, and in the Text Box Properties dialog box type **Description** for the Name and **24** in the Width In Characters text box. Press ENTER.

15. Move the cursor to the rightmost cell in the third row, and click on the One-line Text Box toolbar button.

16. Right-click on the text box. Click on Form Field Properties, and in the Text Box Properties dialog box type **Cost** for the Name and **8** in the Width In Characters text box. Press ENTER.

17. Right-click on the form, and select Form Properties from the context menu.

13

18. In the Form Properties dialog box select Internet Database Connector from the Form Handler drop-down menu and then click on Settings.

19. In the Settings For Database Connector dialog box type **Queries/Addprod.idc** and press ENTER.

20. An error message, shown here, will be displayed. Click on Yes—you will create the file in the set of instructions. Click on OK.

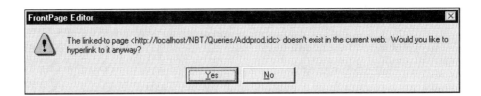

21. Click on the Save toolbar button. In the Save As dialog box type **Add A Product** in the Page Title text box and **Addprod.htm** for the filename. Press ENTER. Your page should be similar to Figure 13-23.

22. Open the North Beach Tools Home page in the FrontPage Editor, and select Add A Product in the bulleted list.

Completed Add A Product page in the FrontPage Editor

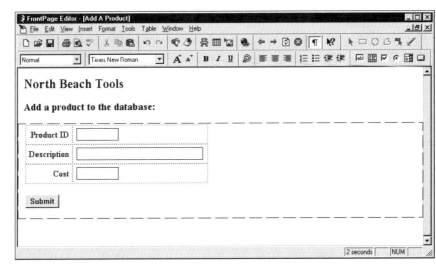

FIGURE 13-23

23. Click on the Create Or Edit Hypertext Link toolbar button. In the Create Hyperlink dialog box create a link to the Addprod.htm page you just created.

24. Save the Home page.

Create the .IDC file to go with the Add A Product page with these steps:

1. Open the File menu and select New. In the New Page dialog box double-click on Database Connector Wizard.

2. Type **NBT** for the ODBC Data Source and **Addprod.htx** for the Query Results Template. Click on Next.

3. In the SQL Query text box type **INSERT INTO products (ProductId, Description, Cost)**, press ENTER, and then type **VALUES ('%ProductId%', '%Description%', '%Cost%');**

4. Click on Finish. Save the file in the Queries folder with the name **Addprod.idc**.

Now create the .HTX template for the .IDC file. This template will confirm that the record has been entered in the database.

1. Open the File menu and select New. In the New Page dialog box double-click on Database Results.

2. Delete the FrontPage comment, type **North Beach Tools**, and then format it as Heading 1.

3. On the next line type **The following information has been added to the database:** and format it as Heading 3.

4. Move the cursor down one line, and insert a three-row by two-column table.

5. Select the left column and click on the Align Right and Bold toolbar buttons.

6. In the left cell in the first row type **Product ID:** and then press TAB.

13

7. From the Edit menu, select Database, then IDC Parameter Value. This the value for the parameter that was entered into the form. Notice that when the variable is entered in the table, the prefix "idc." has been added. This differentiates it from a value that is read from the database. Also, IDC parameters are not placed inside a detail section.

8. In the IDC Parameter Value dialog box type **ProductID** and press ENTER.

9. In the left cell in the second row type **Description:** and then press TAB.

10. From the Edit menu, select Database, then IDC Parameter Value. In the IDC Parameter Value dialog box type **Description** and press ENTER.

11. In the left cell in the third row type **Cost:** and then press TAB.

12. From the Edit menu, select Database, then IDC Parameter Value. In the IDC Parameter Value dialog box type **Cost** and press ENTER.

13. Save the page with the Page Title **Add A Product Confirmation** and a filename of **Queries/Addprod.htx**.

The finished Addprod.htx page is shown in Figure 13-24.

Test the page by opening the North Beach Tools Home page in your browser and clicking on the Add A Product hyperlink. When the Add A Product page is loaded,

Completed
Add A
Product
.HTX page
in the
FrontPage
Editor

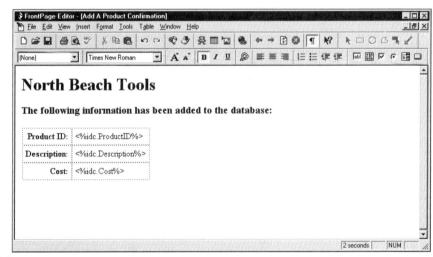

FIGURE 13-24

enter a product ID, description, and cost for a tool, and click on Submit. Figure 13-25 shows the Add A Product Confirmation page.

This is a good time to find out what happens if the data submitted to a database doesn't meet the rules specified by the database. Each field in the Products table is required. Submitting a blank field or a field that is too long will produce an error message similar to the one shown in Figure 13-26. In Chapter 15 you will learn how to use JavaScript and VBScript (generated by FrontPage or by you) to check forms before the data is sent to the server. This allows you to create much more descriptive error messages than the one shown in the figure.

Deleting a Record

Part of database maintenance is deleting old records. In a relational database this might not be done very often because some tables will have links to the data that is being deleted. For example, North Beach Tools may decide to stop selling a particular saw. If the record for the saw is deleted from the Products table, the information about the saw will no longer be available to the Orders table. When a particular file is deleted, you can set a relational database to delete all records linked to that file. There are times when you will want to delete records. In this example you will see how to do that:

1. Open a new Normal page in the FrontPage Editor.

2. Type **North Beach Tools** at the top of the page, and format it as Heading 2. Press ENTER.

3. Click on the One-line Text Box toolbar button, and then move the cursor to the right of the text box.

4. Type **Enter product ID of record to delete:** (include a space).

5. Move the cursor to the left of the text box, and click on the Push Button toolbar button.

6. Right-click on the text box, and select Form Field Properties from the context menu.

7. In the Text Box Properties dialog box type **ProductID** in the Name text box and **8** in the Width In Characters text box. Press ENTER.

8. Right-click on the form and select Form Properties from the context menu.

13

Add A
Product
Confirmation
page in a
web
browser

FIGURE 13-25

9. In the Form Properties dialog box select Internet Database Connector from the Form Handler drop-down menu. Click on Settings.

10. In the Settings For Internet Database Connector dialog box type **Delprod.idc** and click on Edit.

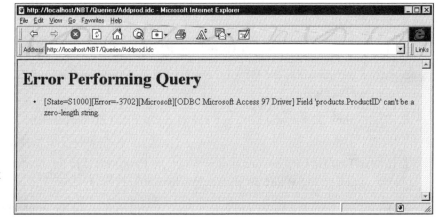

Error
message
produced
by leaving
the Product
ID field
blank

FIGURE 13-26

11. Type **NBT** for the ODBC data source and **Delprod.htx** for the Query results template. Click on Next.

12. Type **DELETE products.* FROM products**, press ENTER, and then type **WHERE products.productid = '%productid%'**

13. Click on Finish and then click on OK twice.

14. Save your page with the Page Title **Delete A Product** and the filename **Delprod.htm**.

15. Open the Home page in the FrontPage Editor, and select Delete A Product in the bulleted list.

16. Click on the Create Or Edit Hyperlink toolbar button, and create a link to the Delprod.htm page.

17. Save the Home page.

18. Open the File menu and select New. In the New Page dialog box double-click on Database Results.

19. Delete the FrontPage comments. At the top of the new page type **North Beach Tools**, and format it as Heading 2.

20. Press ENTER and type **Product Number has been deleted from the database.**

21. Place the cursor between *Number* and *has*, and then select IDC Parameter Value from the Database flyout on the Edit menu.

22. Type **ProductID** in the IDC Parameter Value dialog box and press ENTER.

23. Make sure there is a space on each side of the variable, select it, and click on the Bold toolbar button.

24. Save the page with the Page Title **Delete Record Confirmation** and a filename of **Queries/Delprod.htx**.

You can test your page by adding records with the Add A Product web page and then deleting them with the Delete A Product web page. In between you can open the database in Access and see the changes being made by the Internet Database Connector.

NOTE: *If the North Beach Tools database is open in Access, your web pages will not be able to read or modify it. Access is not a multiuser database; when the database is open in Access, it is locked from any other changes.*

The examples in this chapter have barely scratched the surface of what you can do with SQL databases and the Web. It has been an introduction to give you some ideas about the possibilities of integrating databases into your webs. The tools FrontPage provides streamline the task of creating .IDC and .HTX files, but a thorough knowledge of SQL programming and relational database theory are still essential. Both of these subjects are beyond the scope of this book. If you don't have these skills yourself, consider finding a good relational database programmer who can help make your ideas a reality. More and more, the creation of world-class web sites is becoming a team effort.

Security on
the Web

499

There has been a lot of discussion in the media regarding security risks on the Web. You've probably heard stories about how someone has done something to compromise someone else's security on the Internet or has gotten through to a private intranet. These stories appear infrequently for two reasons: the occurrences are rare, and people don't like to report that their security has been compromised. The vast majority of stories are about university or private research efforts that, with much work and a lot of computer power, have broken through the security in some obscure area of a given Internet program. A lot of hoopla is made of the weakness found, the manufacturer rushes to fix it, and few if any people ever experience a loss or misuse of their Internet information. The reason for the negligible impact, much more effective than any security system, is the sheer volume of transactions on the Web. Only a tiny percentage of those transactions has value to others. Probably less than 1/100th of 1 percent of all the Internet transactions has any potential to be misused.

Security *is* an issue—this chapter wouldn't exist if it weren't—but it also needs to be placed in the proper perspective. *Today,* given the nature of the vast majority of what takes place over the Internet, security is not a major consideration for most people. In the future, as more and more commerce takes place on the Web, and as it is used regularly for confidential and financial transactions, then security will become a much larger concern. It is toward this future need that this chapter is directed.

 **NOTE:** *Security is important not so much for what is happening on the Internet today as for what will be happening on the Internet in the near future.*

Areas Where Security Is Needed

Look at all the activity on either the Internet or intranets now, and more importantly, consider what will be taking place in the future, and ask yourself in what areas security is an issue. The Internet, which grossly simplified looks something like Figure 14-1, has millions of users connected to hundreds of interconnected computers. Added to this are a small but growing number of intranets connected to the Internet. As information is transferred between two users on the Internet, it is routed through a large number of intermediary computers under the independent control of many different entities. There is no way to control where the information may be routed or to limit who controls the computers it is routed through. Also, for the modest price of an Internet account, anyone can get on the Internet and do what they wish. Consider what is happening on the Internet:

- E-mail is being sent, routed, and received. It can contain anything from "Hi, how are you?" to very sensitive trade secrets.

- Web sites are being accessed to read, print, or download their information. On the majority of sites access is unlimited and free, but on others access is limited (by a password or other means) for various reasons.

- In a growing number of web sites, goods and services are being sold with payment by credit card or other payment forms.

- Newsgroups are being read and contributed to, again generally with unlimited access, although occasionally it is password controlled.

- Direct real-time audio and video communications, which today is a small part of the Internet traffic, will grow as the bandwidth of the Internet expands. For the most part the communication is not sensitive in nature, but someone could want it to be.

- Telnet, Gopher, and other classical Internet services are continuing at a decreasing pace.

- Web servers are being maintained; web pages are being added, revised, and removed; user IDs and passwords are being changed; and CGI and Perl scripts are being worked on.

- Increasingly, people on intranets are gaining access to the Internet. To a more limited and slower-growing extent, people on the Internet are gaining limited access to intranets.

14

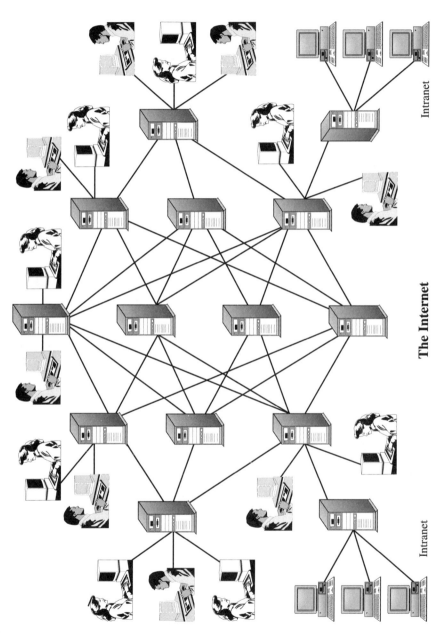

Intranet

The Internet

Intranet

The Internet

FIGURE 14-1

Where are the risks in this Internet activity? There are, of course, many, but among them are

- Interception and misuse or misdirection of e-mail

- Creation and sending of e-mail from someone other than who it appears to be from

- Accessing a controlled-access web site without the appropriate permission

- Interception and misuse of credit card or other financial information during an Internet business transaction

- Misrepresentation on the part of a buyer or seller in an Internet business transaction

- Gaining unauthorized access to the administrative functions of a web server to misuse the user IDs and passwords, or to otherwise upset the operation of the server

- Gaining unauthorized access to a web server and changing web pages or CGI or Perl scripts

- Gaining unauthorized access to an intranet for whatever reason

The primary security goals, then, are just three:

- Limiting access to web pages, web servers, and intranets to only those with proper authorization

- Securing the transmission of information, be it sensitive e-mail, credit card data, or financial information

- Authenticating the sender, the receiver, and the data transferred

Controlling Access

Controlling access has at least two different connotations:

- Limiting access to all or part of a web site to only a certain group, such as subscribers to an electronic publication or administrators on the web site

- Securing an intranet site from being accessed via the Internet by setting up a computer called a *firewall*, which controls entry to and possibly exit from the intranet

14

Limiting Access to a Web Site

Limiting access to a web site means that you have a specific list of people to whom you have granted some type of permission to access your site. When you install FrontPage on your computer, you (really your computer) are automatically given permission to access the web pages that you create. Also a default *root web* (containing your home page) is automatically created, and *the world* (everyone) is given permission to access it. By default, all the web pages that you create are given the same permission as the root web, meaning that if you do nothing, everybody has permission to access all the pages you build.

FrontPage has established three levels of permissions:

■ **Browse this web**, which allows the user to look at, read, and navigate the web site

■ **Author and browse this web**, which allows the user to change as well as browse the site

■ **Administer, author, and browse this web**, which allows the user to set permissions as well as author the web site

To change the permissions on a web, you must load that web, and then use the Permissions option in the Tools menu. Do that now and see how permissions can be set.

> **NOTE:** *If you are on a LAN and have file- and printer-sharing both active, you'll not be able to set your web permissions as discussed in the following steps. To correct this, you must open the Control Panel, double-click on the Network icon, click the File And Print Sharing button just below the middle of the dialog box, uncheck the two check boxes for File and Printer Sharing, respectively, and click on OK twice to close the various dialog boxes. (You may be asked to insert your Windows 95 CD to get some needed files.)*

1. Load the FrontPage Explorer and then open the Fantasy Travel web that you created earlier in this book.

2. With the Fantasy Travel web displayed, open the Tools menu and choose Permissions. The Permissions dialog box will appear, as you can see in Figure 14-2.

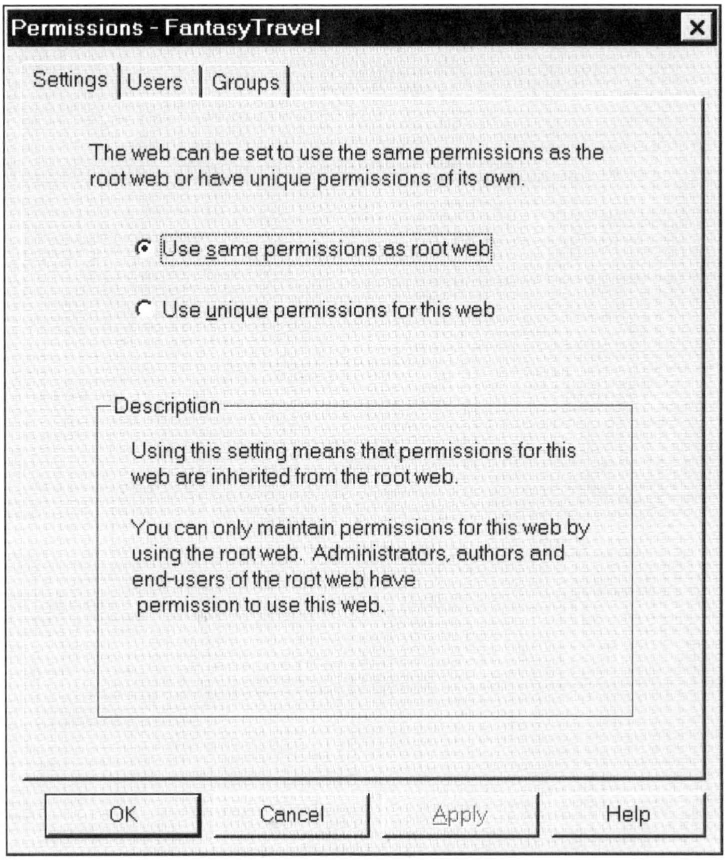

Permissions dialog box

FIGURE 14-2

The default is Use Same Permissions As Root Web, which means that to change the permissions, you must change them for the root web.

3. First click on the Users tab, where you should see a blank list of users. If you click on the Groups tab, you'll see that The world has been granted all possible permissions, as shown in Figure 14-3.

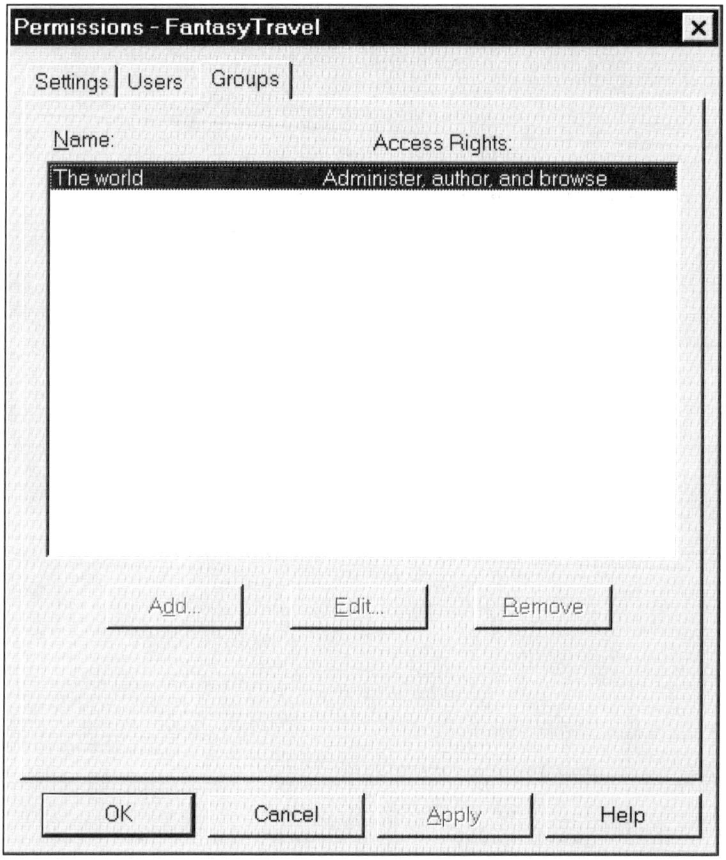

Permissions – FantasyTravel ✕

Settings | Users | Groups |

Name: Access Rights:

The world   Administer, author, and browse

Add...   Edit...   Remove

OK   Cancel   Apply   Help

The world
granted all
permissions

FIGURE 14-3

4. Return to the Settings tab, click on Use Unique Permissions For This Web, and click on Apply (if you don't click on Apply, you won't be able to open the Users and Groups tabs).

5. Click on the Users tab. You'll see that you and the rest of the world have all permissions, as shown here:

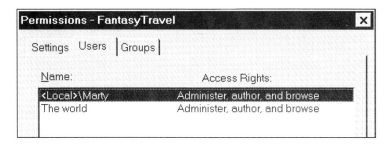

6. Click on The World in the list, and then click on Edit. (If Edit is dimmed, click on OK to close the dialog box, and then reopen it.) In the Edit Users dialog box, click on Browse This Web, like this:

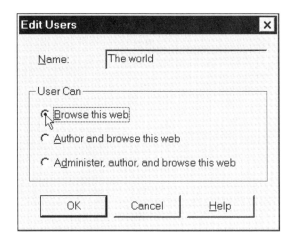

7. Click on OK to return to the Users tab of the Permissions dialog box.

8. Click on Add to open the Add Users dialog box. If you have a list of names on the left, double-click on one that you want to have some level of permission with this web. If you do not have a list of names, click in the empty Add Names list on the right, and type a name of a person (or computer) on your network that you want to have some permission with this web.

9. Click on the permission level you want for this person, as shown in Figure 14-4. (Given that The world has browse permission, the person you're adding should have a higher-level permission.)

14

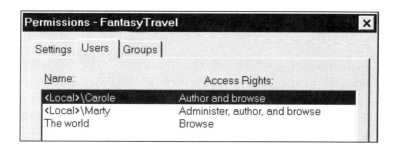

Adding a
user

FIGURE 14-4

10. Click on OK. Your User tab should now look like this:

11. Click on Groups to open an empty tab. Click on Add. Again you can
double-click on an entry on the list on the left or type a new group on the
right. Select the permission level desired, and then click on OK to close

the Add Group dialog box. Then click on OK again to close the Permissions dialog box.

SETTING UP USERS AND GROUPS You can set up users, groups, and members of groups in your web server. For example, in the Microsoft Personal Web Server (MSPWS) you would use the following steps:

1. Given that the MSPWS is running (if not, start it now), double-click on its icon on the right of the taskbar at the bottom of the Windows 95 screen. The Personal Web Server Properties dialog box will open as you can see in Figure 14-5.

2. Click on the Administration tab and then on the Administration button. Your default browser will load and open the Internet Services Administrator, which is shown in Figure 14-6.

3. Click on Local User Administration, and that page will open with the Users tab active, shown next (you may not have any users displayed even if you are on a network, but you'll add some in the next few steps).

Microsoft
Personal
Web Server

Internet Local User Administrator
Administration for
http://marty

| Users | Groups | User/Group |

User List:

Marty
Carole
Ruth
Michael

Properties... | New User... | Remove

14

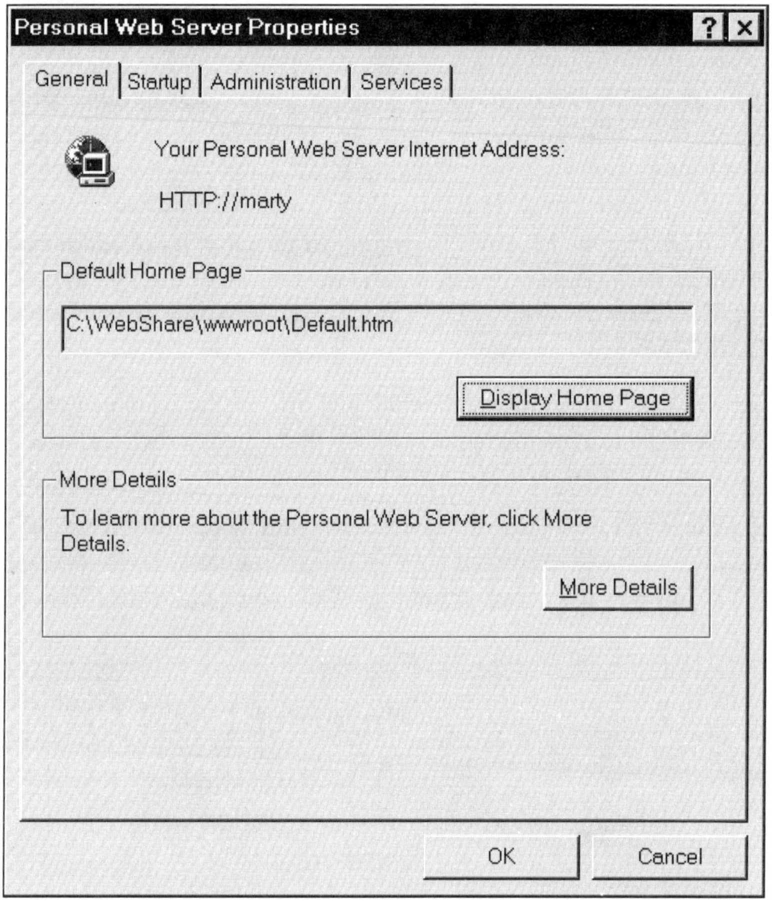

Microsoft
Personal
Web Server
Properties
dialog box

FIGURE 14-5

4. Click on the New User button to open a page where you can enter a user
name and password. Type any name, and then enter and confirm a
password, as you can see next. You must enter a password—you cannot
leave it blank.

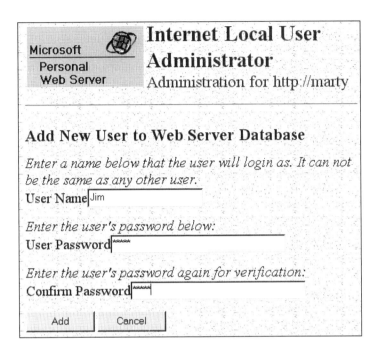

5. Click on Add. You'll be told that you are about to send several lines of text over the Internet and asked if you want to continue (unless you have turned this off). We'll come back to this message later in this chapter, but for now click on Yes. The new name that you entered should appear in your user list. Enter several
more names.

6. Click on the Groups tab, where there is a list of the groups that have been set up on your server.

7. Click on New Group, enter a group name, and click on Add. Again you are informed about sending information over the Internet. Click on Yes.

8. Click on the User/Group tab, select your new group in the Group List, select a user in the User List that you want in the group, and click on Add User To Group, as shown in Figure 14-7.

14

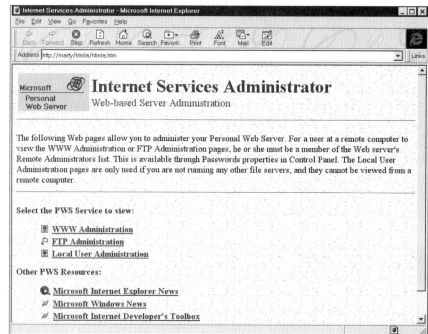

Personal Web
Server
Administrator

FIGURE 14-6

9. Click on the Groups tab, select your new group, and click on Properties. You'll see a list of the users in the group. Click on OK, click on Back To Main Menu, and close your web browser. Also, close the Microsoft Personal Web Server dialog box that you opened and the web that is still displayed.

Controlling Access to a Web Server

The permissions that you set for the web pages that you are creating are used by the FrontPage Server Extensions on the web server to implement the access controls that you want. If your Internet service provider (ISP) has not implemented the FrontPage Server Extensions, then you must work with your ISP to set up the access controls that you want by using the services that are available on the ISP's web server. Most web servers have a multiple-level permission scheme set up by user and/or group that will allow you to implement an access scheme similar to

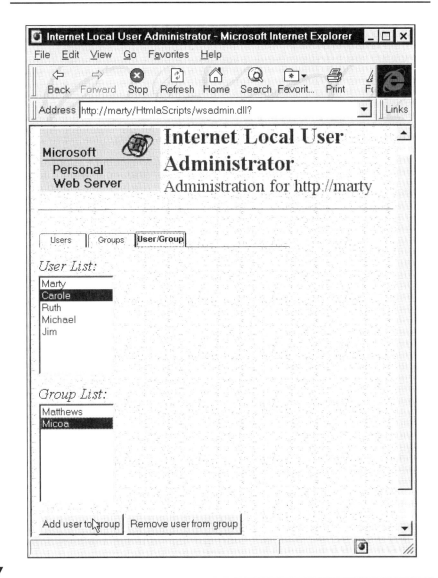

Adding
users to a
group

■ FIGURE 14-7

FrontPage's Browser, Author, Administrator scheme. In fact, most servers go far
beyond this.

Microsoft's Internet Information Server (IIS) running on a Windows NT 4.0
server provides four security mechanisms, each of which can give you one or more

14

levels of access, as you can see in Figure 14-8. These four mechanisms, which can be implemented in any combination by IIS, are

- Internet Protocol (IP) address control

- User account control

- Virtual directory control

- Windows NT File System (NTFS) control

IP ADDRESS CONTROL   The IP address control checks the *source* IP address (where the data is from) on every packet of data received by the server and compares it against a list of IP addresses that contain predefined actions to be applied to packets with that address. The packet is then handled in accordance with the predefined actions. IP address control is useful for either blocking or accepting major groups of users, like everyone from a particular company or organization within a company. This is the principal mechanism used by firewalls (discussed later in this chapter). The major limitation in IP address control is that you cannot identify particular directories that can be accessed by a given IP address.

USER ACCOUNT CONTROL   A standard part of Windows NT security is user account control that requests a user ID and password when accessing the server or specially designated directories. Such access can be over a LAN or over the Internet, so part of the IIS security that is implemented can include the Windows NT user account control. To make user account control simpler, define an anonymous account allowing access to nonsensitive directories with limited privileges—normally read-only—for anyone who makes it through the IP address control. For additional access and privileges, users are asked to enter their user ID and password. These are checked for validity by use of either *Basic* or *Windows NT Challenge/Response* user authentication. The difference between these two authentication schemes is in the way that the ID and password are returned to the server. In the Basic scheme, the user ID and password are simply encoded in a manner that is not terribly hard to decode by someone intercepting it on the Internet. The Windows NT Challenge/Response scheme never requires that the password be transmitted, but rather uses a cryptographic challenge sequence to authenticate it. The Windows NT Challenge/Response scheme only works on Microsoft Internet Explorer 2.0 and above.

VIRTUAL DIRECTORY CONTROL   With IIS you can define an alias for a directory path on the server and then use that path in a URL (the uniform resource locator,

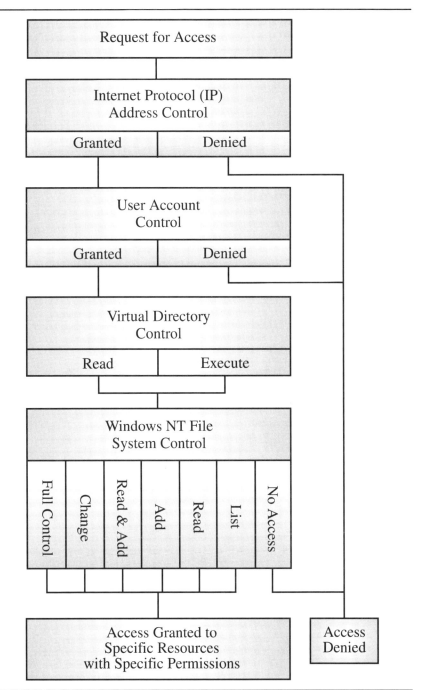

IIS /
Windows
NT 4.0
access
control

FIGURE 14-8

which is an address on the Internet). This alias is called a *virtual directory*. For example, the default path for a web site called TRAVEL on a server named SERVER is C:\Winnt\System32\Inetsrv\Wwwroot\Travel. If you define the alias for this path to be /Travel, then the URL for the web site would be http://server/travel.

When you define an alias, you can give it one of two access privileges, Read or Execute, used for the defined path and all files and folders within it. The Read privilege allows the user to read and download the contents. The Execute privilege only allows the user to execute the contents—not read or download them. The Execute privilege is used for CGI scripts and other applications.

WINDOWS NT FILE SYSTEM (NTFS) CONTROL   The Windows NT File System (NTFS) control is what associates a user account (name and password) with specific directories, files, and folders, as well as other server resources. This association is accomplished through the Access Control List (ACL) for each server resource. The ACL for a particular resource, say, a directory, will have a list of users and groups of users and one of seven levels of permissions, as you can see in Figure 14-9. The permissions and their description are shown in Table 14-1. By default all users ("Everyone") have full control of all directories, files, and folders.

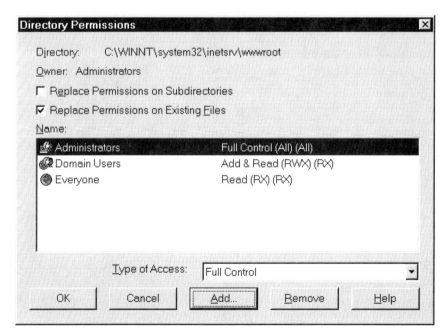

NTFS Access Control List (ACL) for a directory

FIGURE 14-9

Permission Level	Description
No Access	Prevents any access to the directory and its files.
List	Allows the listing of filenames and subdirectory names and the changing of the subdirectories. Prevents access to file contents.
Read	Allows listing filenames and subdirectory names, changing subdirectories, viewing data files, and running applications.
Add	Allows adding files and subdirectories to directories, but does not allow viewing data files or running applications.
Add & Read	Allows listing filenames and subdirectory names, changing subdirectories, viewing data files, and running applications, as well as adding files and subdirectories to directories.
Change	Adds and reads permissions, changes data in files, and deletes the directory and its files.
Full Control	Changes permissions, changes permissions for the directory and its files, and takes ownership of the directory and its files.

Description of Permission Levels

TABLE 14-1

Limiting Access to an Intranet Site

One type of access control that is not handled by FrontPage is limiting access to an intranet web site. This is the situation where you have an intranet that you want to connect to the Internet. It may be that you want to just allow your intranet users access to the Internet. Alternatively, you may want to allow people on the Internet, for example, your own employees who are traveling, to get onto your intranet. This is done with several schemes, but the most common is a firewall, which is a separate computer through which all traffic to and from the Internet must pass, as shown in Figure 14-10. At the simplest level, a firewall works by *packet filtering,* which checks each packet of information that is transferred, either outbound or inbound, through the firewall and makes sure that its IP address is acceptable.

To add a further level of protection and in some cases speed up this process, the firewall computer may be set up as a *proxy server.* A proxy server, which is simply

14

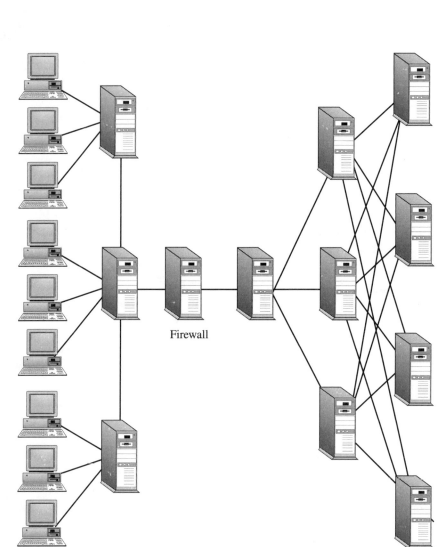

Firewall

A firewall
between an
intranet and
the Internet

An Intranet

The Internet

FIGURE 14-10

software running in a computer acting as a firewall, acts as a relay station between your intranet and the Internet. It acts like an "air gap" between the two. Requests to servers on either side of the firewall are made to the proxy server, which examines them, and if they are appropriate, sends a proxy on to the addressed server to fulfill the request.

To find out more about firewalls, packet filtering, and proxy servers, see two excellent books by Tom Sheldon entitled *The Windows NT Security Handbook* and *The Windows NT Web Server Handbook,* both published by Osborne/McGraw-Hill in 1996. Also see the bibliography at the end of this chapter.

Securing Transmission

Transmission security means the *encryption* or concealment of the information being transmitted so it cannot be read and misused without the ability to *decrypt* or reveal it. Encrypting of information is probably as old as the human race and has really blossomed with the advent of computers. Data encryption has become so sophisticated that the U.S. government, worried that they won't be able to decrypt the data (can you imagine that!), won't allow the technology to be exported (although it is freely available on the Internet at http://www.pgp.com). Several encryption schemes for securing Internet transmissions are in use. They are private key encryption and public key encryption—and combinations of the two.

Private Key Encryption

Private key encryption or *symmetric cryptography* is relatively old and uses a single key to both encrypt and decrypt a message. This means that the key itself must be transferred from sender to receiver. If this is done over the phone, the Internet, or even a courier service, all someone needs to do is get hold of the key, and he or she can decrypt the message. Private key encryption, though, has a major benefit in that it is much faster (as much as 1,000 times faster) than the alternative. Private key schemes are therefore valuable in situations where you do not have to transfer the key or can do so with security—for example, personal use such as encrypting the contents of a disk or sending information to someone that you first met face to face. There are several private key encryption schemes being used with the Internet, including the U.S. government's Data Encryption Standard (DES) and the private RC2 (*Rivest Cipher* or *Ron's Code* [for Ron Rivest] *2*), and RC4 from RSA Laboratories.

Public Key Encryption

Public key encryption or *asymmetric cryptography* was developed in the mid-1970s and uses a pair of keys—a public key and a private key. The public key is publicly known and transferred, and is used to encrypt a message. The private key never leaves its creator and is used to decrypt the message. For two people to use this technique, each generates both a public and a private key, and then they openly exchange public keys, not caring who gets a copy of it. They encrypt their messages to each other using the other person's public key, and then send the message. The message can only be decrypted and read by using the private key held by the recipient. The public and private keys use a mathematical algorithm that relates them to the encrypted message. By use of other mathematical algorithms it is fairly easy to generate key pairs, but with only the public key, it is extremely difficult to generate the private key. Public key encryption is best in open environments where the sender and recipient do not know each other. Most public key encryption uses the Rivest-Shamir-Aldman (RSA) Public Key Cryptosystem, called *RSA* for short, developed and supported by RSA Laboratories.

 NOTE: *You can encrypt your e-mail using the Pretty Good Privacy (PGP) freeware that uses RSA public key encryption and is available from the URL mentioned earlier (http://www.pgp.com).*

Combined Public and Private Key Encryption with SSL

Most encryption on the Internet actually is a combination of public and private key encryption. The most common combination was developed by Netscape to go between HTTP and TCP/IP and is called Secure Sockets Layer (SSL). It provides a highly secure as well as fast means of both encryption and authentication (see "Authenticating People, Servers, and Data" later in this chapter).

Recall that private key encryption is very fast, but has the problem of transferring the key. And public key encryption is very secure, but slow. If you were to begin a secure transmission by using a public key to encrypt and send a private key, you could then securely use the private key to quickly send any amount of data you wanted. This is how SSL works. It uses an RSA public key to send a randomly chosen private key for either a DES or RC4 encryption, and in so doing sets up a "secure socket" through which any amount of data can be quickly encrypted, sent, and decrypted. After the SSL *header* has transferred the private key, then all information transferred in both directions during a given session—including the URL, any request for a user ID and password, all HTTP web information, and any data entered on a form—is automatically encrypted by the sender and automatically decrypted by the recipient.

There are several versions of SSL, with SSL version 2 being the one in common use as this is written (fall 1996), and SSL version 3 available on the newer servers and browsers. SSL 3 is both more secure and offers improved authentication. Microsoft also has its own improvement of SSL 2 called Personal Communications Technology (PCT). Both SSL 3 and PCT have been proposed to the World Wide Web standards committee (W3C) as security standards.

Implementing SSL

You may be thinking that SSL sounds great, but it also sounds complex to use. In fact, it's easy to use. You need a web server that supports SSL, such as the Netscape Commerce Server or the Microsoft IIS, plus a supporting web browser such as Netscape Navigator 3.0 or Microsoft Internet Explorer 3.0. From the browser, you simply need to begin the URL you want with "https://" in place of "http://". SSL will then kick in, and without you even being aware that it's happening, the browser and server will decide whether to use DCS or RC4, use RSA to transfer a private key, and then use that key and chosen private key encryption scheme to encrypt and decrypt all the rest of the data during that session. The only thing that you see is a message saying you are about to begin to use a secure connection, like this:

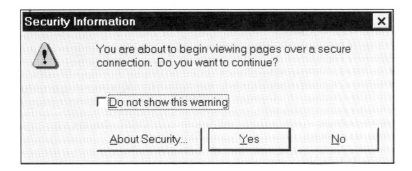

NOTE: *Even though the combination of public and private encryption is relatively fast, it is still significantly slower than no encryption. For that reason it is recommended that you only use SSL when you send sensitive information such as financial or credit card data.*

14

FrontPage and SSL

FrontPage 97 implements SSL 2 in several ways. Most importantly, FrontPage 97 automatically and, without you doing anything, uses SSL for all communications between the FrontPage 97 client and the FrontPage 97 Server Extensions. This provides protection when you are transferring a web page to the server and when you are doing remote web authoring. You can also identify whether a particular web is expected to use SSL, by using the dialog box where you specify the name of the server and the name of the web, like this:

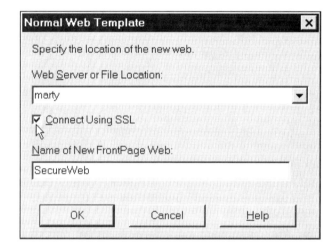

The purpose of specifying whether a particular web is expected to use SSL is to check the proposed server to determine if it can support SSL. This is done is by looking at the port the server is using to communicate with FrontPage. If the port is 443, then the server is using SSL. If the port is something else, then there is a very good chance that SSL is not being used, and you will get an error message, as you can see here:

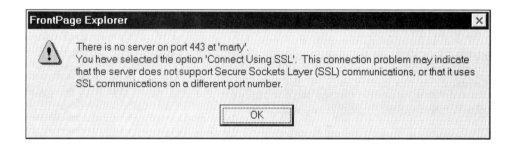

 NOTE: *As this is written, the Microsoft Personal Web Server does not support SSL, although it is rumored that it will. Check it out by trying to create a secure web page on it, and see if you get the preceding message.*

Authenticating People, Servers, and Data

SSL is designed to do double duty. Not only does it provide a secure method of data transmission, but it also provides the authentication of the data and the server, and with SSL 3 it will provide authentication of the user. Authentication is important for three reasons:

- To make sure that senders are who they say they are, and to prevent them from denying that they are the sender. This is authentication of the client or sender.

- To make sure that recipients are who they say they are, and to assure that they received the information. This is authentication of the server or recipient.

- To make sure that the data being sent has not been modified before it was received. This is authentication of the data.

SSL addresses each of these areas of authentication with the following steps:

1. A *message digest* is generated for the data being sent by use of a sophisticated algorithm that is very sensitive to changes in the data. This is equivalent to computing a checksum or a cyclical redundancy check (CRC) for a large number.

2. The message digest is encrypted with the sender's private RSA key to produce a *digital signature.*

3. The recipient uses the sender's public key to decrypt the digital signature that came with the data exposing the message digest. If the public key works, then the sender is who she said she was and in fact sent the data.

4. The recipient then recomputes a new message digest using the data that was received. If the two message digests are the same, then the data has not been altered in transit.

5. The recipient next encrypts the new message digest using the recipient's private RSA key to create a new digital signature and sends it to the original sender.

6. The original sender uses the recipient's public key to decrypt the second digital signature. If the public key works, then the recipient is as claimed, and if the two message digests are the same, then the original data was received by the recipient.

This sounds complicated, but if you are using SSL, it is all done automatically, and you only know if there is a problem. There is one flaw in this security scheme—how can either the sender or the recipient be sure they have the public key of the other and not of someone masquerading as the other person? In this situation the false person would be able to use the private key that went with the false public key to decrypt and misuse the data. To counter this flaw, a public key can be enclosed in a *certificate*. A certificate uses the private key of a *certifying authority* to encrypt both a message digest of the human-readable name of the sender and the sender's public key. Then by using the public key of the certifying authority, you can get the public key along with the name of the owner. Of course, you must trust that the public key of the certifying authority is legitimate! A prominent certifying authority is VeriSign, Inc. at http://www.verisign.com/.

Bibliography

There are mountains of information on Internet and intranet security issues (I know, I tried to read and understand a small portion of this information to write this chapter). Here are two books and several documents available on the Internet. Most of the Internet sites mentioned had many more related documents.

Computer Security Institute, *CSI Manager's Guide to Internet Security,* 1994, http://www.gocsi.com/html/ismg.htm

Dellino, Domenick J., *The Evolution of Security on the Web, An Introduction to CryptoSystems of the Internet,* 6/25/96, http://www.microsoft.com/workshop/admin/adm-sec/websec-f.htm

Library of Congress, *Internet Security, A Library of Congress Internet Resource Page,* 8/7/96, http://lcweb.loc.gov/global/Internet/security.html

National Security Institute, *Connecting to the Internet: Security Considerations,* CSL Bulletin, July 1993, http://www.nsi.org/Library/Compsec/intersec.txt

National Security Institute, *Security Issues in WWW,* http://www.nsi.org/Library/Internet/security.htm

Netscape Communications Corporation, *Netscape Data Security, An Overview of Implementations and Plans from Netscape Communications,* 1996, http://home.mcom.com/newsref/ref/netscape-security.html

Netscape Communications Corporation, *On Internet Security,* 1996, http://home.mcom.com/info/security-doc.html

Redmond, Frank III, *Making Sure Your Server's Secure,* Microsoft Interactive Developer, 11/96, http://www.microsoft.com/mind/1196/iissecurity.htm

RSA Laboratories, Inc., *Answers to Frequently Asked Questions about Today's Cryptography,* Third Edition, 8/1/96, http://www.rsa.com/rsalabs/newfaq/

RSA Laboratories, Inc., *PKCS #1, RSA Encryption Standard,* An RSA Laboratories Technical Note, Version 1.5, 11/1/93, http://www.rsa.com/Pubs/

Rutgers University Network Services, *World Wide Web Security,* 12/4/95, http:/www-ns.rutgers.edu/www-security/index.thml

Rutgers University Network Services, *WWW Security References,* 6/2/95, http:/www-ns.rutgers.edu/www-security/reference.thml

Sheldon, Tom, *The Windows NT Security Handbook,* 1996, Osborne/McGraw-Hill

Sheldon, Tom, *The Windows NT Web Server Handbook,* 1996, Osborne/McGraw-Hill

Stein, Lincoln D., *The World Web Security FAQ,* Version 1.3.0, 11/8/96, http://www.genome.wi.mit.edu/WWW/faqs/www-security-faq.html/

14

FrontPage on the Web

NeedhamOnline

URL: *http://www.needhamonline.com*
Webmasters: Lee and Amy Levitt
E-mail: *lee@needhamonline.com*

> 63 Tudor Road
> Needham, MA 02192
> (617) 455-0545
> (617) 453-0765 (Fax)

Web Site

The NeedhamOnline web site is a winner of the Microsoft Great Web Sites Contest. The Home page, shown in Figure 1, has an animated spinning globe on the left of the title as well as an animated welcome message that moves across a one-cell table to provide a border, as shown in Listing 1. The site provides easy navigation by use of the links in the table shown in the lower part of Figure 1.

Listing 1
Table animation
HTML

```
<table border="5" cellpadding="0" cellspacing="0" width="55%">
  <tr>
    <td width="100%"><font face="Times New Roman">
      <img src="images/animatedwelcometrain.gif"
      alt="Welcome to Needham!" width="416" height="63"></font>
    </td>
  </tr>
</table>
```

One of NeedhamOnline's pages is a guest book, as you can see in Figure 2. Note the book-like background. The guest book was created by use of a form, the HTML for which is shown in Listing 2. NeedhamOnline also includes a form for searching the web site, shown in Figure 3 and in Listing 3, that was built around the Excite search engine. Note that both forms have an ACTION attribute that determines what to do with the form's contents, which is different than the standard FrontPage Save Results bot. In the guest book form the contents are sent back to NeedhamOnline; in the search form they are passed to a script that does the search.

FrontPage on the Web (cont.)

NeedhamOn-
line Home
page

FIGURE 1

Listing 2
Guest book
form HTML

```html
<form action="mailto:feedback@needhamonline.com" method="POST">
  <p>Please provide your name and email address:<br>
    <textarea name="name" rows="1" cols="35"></textarea></p>
  <p>Please provide your comments:<br>
    <textarea name="sitefeedback" rows="4" cols="35"></textarea></p>
  <p>How did you find us? Select as many as are applicable:</p>
  <p><input type="checkbox" name="found1" value="search engine">
    Found this location from a search engine or directory<br>
    such as Infoseek or Lycos<br>
  <input type="checkbox" name="found2" value="saw on provider list">
    Followed a link from another site<br>
  <input type="checkbox" name="found4" value="reference in newsgroup">
    Saw a reference to this site on a newsgroup <br>
  <input type="checkbox" name="found5" value="told by a friend">
```

14

FrontPage on the Web (cont.)

```
    A friend told me about this site <br>
  <input type="checkbox" name="found6" value="just stumbled">
    Just stumbled into it while browsing around<br>
  <input type="checkbox" name="found7" value="other">
    Other <input type="text" size="29" maxlength="256" name="othersource"></p>
<p align="center"><input type="submit" name="submit" value="Sign Guestbook">
  <a href="mailto:sales@amydoodles.com"><input type="reset" name="reset"
    value="Clear All Fields"></a></p>
</form>
```

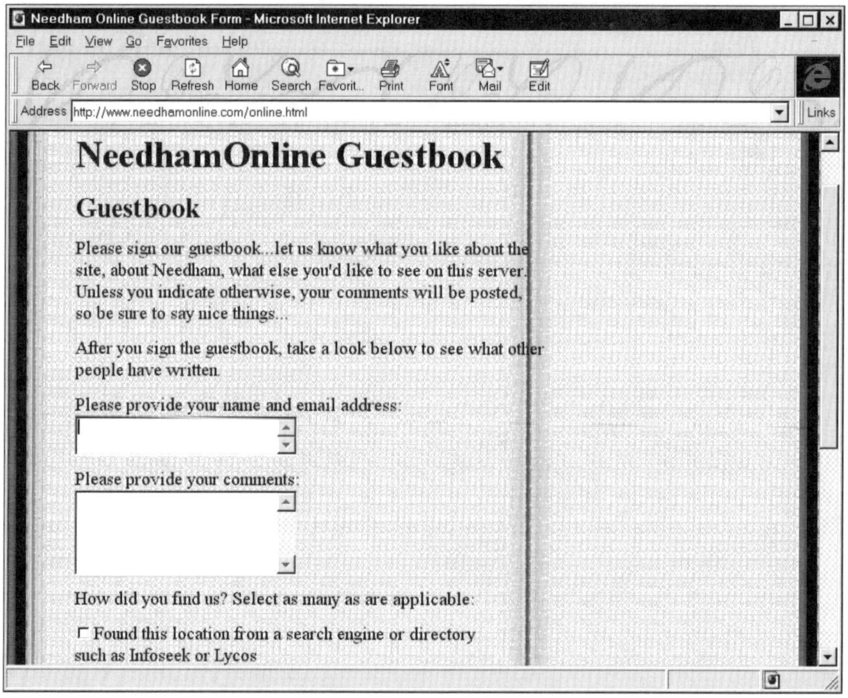

Guest book
page

■ **FIGURE 2**

FrontPage on the Web (cont.)

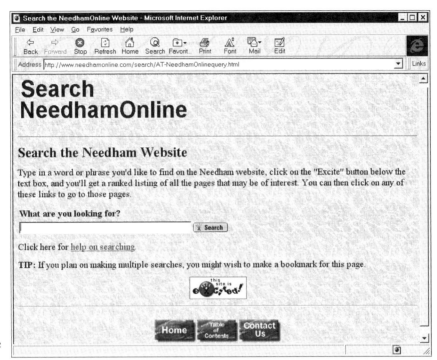

Search page

FIGURE 3

Listing 3
xcite search
ine HTML

```
<FORM ACTION="/scripts/AT-NeedhamOnlinesearch.exe" METHOD=POST>
   <TABLE><TR><TD>
     <b>What are you looking for?</b>
   </TD></TR></TABLE>
   <TABLE><TR><TD><INPUT NAME="search" VALUE="" size=50>
     </TD><TD><INPUT TYPE="image" SRC="pictures/AT-search_button.gif"
       NAME="searchButton" HEIGHT=20 WIDTH=75 ALT="Search" BORDER=0>
   </TD></TR></TABLE>
   <INPUT TYPE="hidden" NAME="sp" VALUE="sp">
</FORM>
```

14

FrontPage on the Web (cont.)

Webmaster Q & A

WHY FRONTPAGE?   I chose FrontPage as my primary web-authoring tool when it still was a Vermeer product, before purchased by Microsoft. In the fall of 1995, very few web-authoring tools on the market provided a reasonable level of abstraction from HTML, and most were rather kludgy or awkward, or both. FrontPage allowed me to focus on cranking out content, and content is what makes a web site good. Flashy graphics often stand in the way of providing valuable content. I wanted to stick to basic page layout plus a very strong focus on providing *useful* information. I believe that is what makes a web page valuable. FrontPage allowed me to do this.

LIKES AND DISLIKES   FrontPage provides a good foundation for building basic sites and then enhancing them over time. The product is quite powerful, although some of this power is rather well hidden. It will read .RTF files quite nicely, allowing relatively quick conversion. Spelling and other writing support is excellent, and the support of tables, formatting, and other basic HTML tricks is excellent.

My biggest complaint is that my ISP does not support the FrontPage Server Extensions, keeping me from using much of the advanced functionality of the package (in the bots, specifically), although by the time this book is published, I may have migrated to another ISP.

The latest version of FrontPage supports background sounds that are usable only with the Internet Explorer. I think FrontPage ought to also support the Netscape Navigator plug-in. To support Netscape, you must save the page and then edit the HTML.

Similarly, FrontPage has problems with animated GIFs. The automatic size tags mess up the actual GIF implementation on the page if the GIF changes position. The animated GIF problem is quite minor once you figure out the problem and go into the HTML and remove the size tags.

NEATEST FEATURES OF THIS SITE   Most recent is a reorganization of the Home page with an invisible table to better present navigation options. FrontPage makes such experimentation extremely quick and simple. I've also used the form definition function to create mailto forms for feedback, and for product ordering on my wife's site (http://www.amydoodles.com). Very powerful and straightforward.

FrontPage on the Web (cont.)

I've spent a lot of time working with tables, in part because FrontPage makes table manipulation so easy. I've also used a variety of fonts, but find that not all users, or browsers, have the additional fonts available to them. FrontPage makes changing fonts and other text attributes quite easy, perhaps too easy for the neophyte publisher (ten different sizes/colors/fonts on a page is not a Good Thing stylistically).

TIPS   Start simple, with a few pages. Have a good site layout in your head, or on paper, or up on the wall, and build your site to make navigation simple. Most good site design is not in the HTML or even the content, but in the overall style, flow, and commonality across the site. Then, of course, comes the content. Flashy graphics do little for sites.

Once you have the layout, build a few pages, starting at the top of the tree. Grow both depth and breadth of the site, and focus on good page layout rather than flash. A few images can be easily inserted, and varying styles can be experimented with. FrontPage does have a lot of power, but don't try to use all of it at once. It's easy to get bogged down in the technology rather than focus on cranking out useful pages. For help with smilies like :-) and acronyms like BTW (for "by the way") on the Internet, check out http://www.magicpub. com/netprimer.

14

15

Activating
Your Webs

The World Wide Web has come a long way since the ability to hyperlink between documents was a revolutionary technology. Today's web browsers support animations, video, and audio files integrated in webs, but even those advances have been overshadowed by Java, ActiveX, JavaScript, and VBScript (Visual Basic Script). These technologies are truly revolutionary and are the future of world-class web sites.

The same technologies are the key to activating your webs. Java applets and ActiveX controls are computer programs that are downloaded to and then executed on your computer by your web browser. JavaScript and VBScript are scripting languages that are used to add *scripts* (a series of instructions) to HTML pages; they are run when the page is loaded by your browser.

In this chapter you will first learn how current web browsers support active features such as *marquees* (text that scrolls across a web page) and how these are different from Java applets and ActiveX controls, and from scripts written in JavaScript or VBScript. Then you will learn how to use these newest web technologies in your own webs. This is the frontier of the World Wide Web.

Active Browser Features

As you've learned in the previous chapters, a web page is a text file containing HTML instructions. Your web browser loads the HTML file and creates the web page displayed in the browser by interpreting the HTML instructions. In Chapter 12 you saw how to add sound and animations to your web pages using some of the newest HTML tags. However, these features only work with web browsers that support these HTML tags. This means that there often needs to be a cycle of browser upgrades before the features are widely supported. Even after browser support is available, not everyone downloads the latest version of his or her favorite browser promptly (particularly as browser downloads have become quite large). This all means that you use these features at your own risk—only a small portion of your audience may see your webs the way you intended.

Java, ActiveX, JavaScript, and VBScript are fundamentally different. If a browser supports these programming languages, as both Netscape Navigator and Microsoft Internet Explorer do to some extent, what you can do on a web page is limited only by your imagination. This frees the web designer from waiting for browser upgrades to begin using the latest web features. The resulting stability is essential as the Web grows. One of the biggest problems in creating webs is the dependence on the user's web browser. Almost every current browser can support the standard HTML features such as displaying tables to one degree or another, but support of multimedia varies greatly. With Netscape and Microsoft offering conflicting HTML tags, the situation will not resolve itself soon.

With Java and ActiveX the problem is simply sidestepped. You can either write your own applets and controls (which requires a good knowledge of computer programming), or download them from a number of sources on the Web. Both JavaScript and VBScript scripts can be generated within FrontPage or written in a text editor and inserted into your FrontPage web pages.

NOTE: *Support for these technologies in current browsers is less than perfect. This situation is rapidly changing, and you can expect that most web users will soon be able to see your activated webs exactly as you intended.*

Adding a Scrolling Marquee

A good example of the differences in how an HTML tag (interpreted by a browser) differs from a Java applet (a stand-alone executable computer program) can be seen by adding a marquee to a web page. This is a new HTML tag currently only supported by Microsoft's Internet Explorer. If you use this feature, it will be lost on anyone using Netscape Navigator, which still has the lion's share of the market. By creating the same effect with a Java applet, you can make it possible for more of the people visiting your web site to see your pages as you intended. To understand the differences, first create a web page with a marquee in FrontPage using the MARQUEE HTML tag with these instructions:

1. Open the FrontPage Explorer if it's not already open, and then create a new Normal web and name it **Active**.

2. Open the Home page in the FrontPage Editor.

3. With the cursor at the top of the page, open the Insert menu and select Marquee. The Marquee Properties dialog box shown next will be displayed.

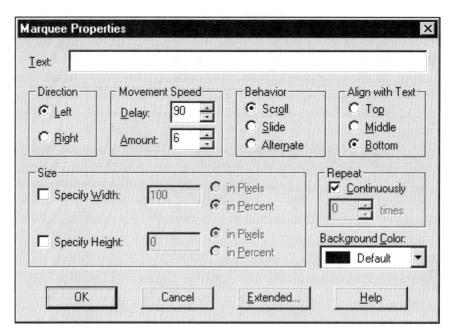

In the Marquee Properties dialog box you specify the text to be displayed; the direction, speed, and type of movement of the text; its alignment; the number of times it repeats; and the width and height of the marquee box.

4. In the Text text box type **Welcome To the World of Active Web Pages**. Accept the defaults and click on OK.

5. In the FrontPage Editor format the text as Heading 2. Your page in the FrontPage Editor should look similar to Figure 15-1.

6. Save your home page with the title **Active Web Home Page** and the filename **default.htm**.

7. Open your Microsoft Internet Explorer web browser, and load the Active Web Home Page. The text you entered previously will scroll from the right side of the page to the left and repeat continuously.

8. Open Netscape Navigator and load the Active Web Home Page into it. The text simply sits at the top of the page, since the MARQUEE tag is not supported by Netscape's browser.

Marquee in
the
FrontPage
Editor

▮ FIGURE 15-1

9. In the FrontPage Editor, right-click on the marquee and select Marquee Properties.

10. In the Marquee Properties dialog box select the Alternate Behavior option button and click on OK. Save the page again.

11. In Internet Explorer click on the Refresh toolbar button. The marquee will now travel back and forth between the left and right margins of the page.

12. Close FrontPage.

As you can see, the MARQUEE tag can add a little life to a web page, but only if it is supported. Since only Internet Explorer currently supports the tag, this is a feature of limited use. In the next section you will learn more about Java and how it can be used to liven up your web sites.

Java

The Java programming language was developed by Sun Microsystems, Inc. and initially released in fall 1995. Netscape was an early licenser of Java. Microsoft soon followed.

Object-Oriented Programming

Java is an *object-oriented* programming language very similar to C++, today's standard programming language. An object-oriented programming language defines an *object* as a process that accepts information, processes it, and then outputs the result of the processing. The format of the input is always clearly defined, as is the output. One object may receive its input from the output of another object. For example, an object may be a simple program that accepts a text string and then converts the text to all capitals. The input is the text string, regardless of case, and the output is the same text string converted to all uppercase. The object is the code that performs the conversion. Java applets are built by combining a number of objects, each performing a relatively simple task, into a computer program that can perform complex operations. This concept is very powerful, as you will learn in the following sections.

NOTE: *Programming your own Java applets is a complex subject, well beyond the scope of this book. An excellent resource for learning more about object-oriented programming and Java is* The Java Handbook *by Patrick Naughton (Osborne/McGraw-Hill, 1996). There are many preprogrammed Java applets available on the Web, so programming your own applet is not necessary for you to add Java applets to your web. The examples in this chapter will use readily available Java applets.*

By its nature, Java offers several features besides object orientation that make it suitable for programming on the Web. It's also safe, robust, interactive, platform independent, and high performance.

Safe

Since Java applets are computer programs that are downloaded and executed on the user's computer, what's to stop the unscrupulous programmer from sending a destructive applet over the Web to wreak havoc on thousands of computers? With the rapid growth of the Internet this has become a leading concern for many, including the creators of Java. Their solution was to strictly limit what a Java applet can do. Java applets cannot access or misuse operating system resources, which leaves little room for vandalism. It is possible, for example, to write an applet that will slow down your computer by monopolizing resources, but this does not cause permanent damage.

Robust

With millions of users around the world connected to the Internet, any program that is written to be used over the Internet must be able to function flawlessly on many different computers with unique configurations. By Java's nature these problems are kept to a minimum. Provided the browser includes support for the Java language, applets can be depended on to function properly.

Interactive

Most web sites today display information passively; that is, the content is defined by the web author and displayed by a browser in much the same way as a page in a magazine is produced. In Chapter 13 you saw how databases could be integrated in webs so that information could be presented dynamically. Java and the other technologies covered in this chapter take the process a step further. As you will see in the examples in this section, Java applets, because they are computer programs running on the user's computer, can accept input from the user, process it, and display the output on a web page. All this can be done locally (on the user's computer) and so leaves the web server free to handle other tasks.

Platform Independent

On the Internet (and intranets), computers running Windows, Apple's Macintosh operating system, and UNIX can all coexist along with a few other minor operating systems. One of the beauties of HTML and the Web is that all these systems can access and display the same web pages. Java extends this platform independence by creating code that does not rely on a specific operating system. Each browser that supports Java applets contains a Java interpreter that handles the interaction between the applet itself and the computer operating system. In this way a single Java applet will function properly on a Windows PC, a Mac, or a UNIX computer. This is a capability with far-reaching implications. Up to this point computer programs have been written to run only on a single operating system. With Java it is now possible to write complex applications that can run on any operating system for which an appropriate browser is available.

High Performance

All the features of Java applets mentioned so far would be of limited use if the applets were not high performance. Almost every computer user has experienced the frustration of slow response times when running some applications. Java's creators made sure that the Java code would work efficiently even on older, slower computers. Also, both Netscape and Microsoft have worked to make the Java interpreters in their web browsers as fast as possible.

The features just described combine to make Java the first of a new generation of programming languages created to work efficiently and flawlessly across the Internet or a company intranet. Now that you have some understanding of just what Java is and can do, it's time to add some applets to your own webs.

Finding Java Applets

Unless you're an experienced C++ programmer, your first Java applets will probably be ones that you download from the World Wide Web. There are a growing number of web sites that have applets available for downloading. The first step, then, is to get onto the Web and find Java applets. A good place to start is Sun Microsystems's Java home page. The following steps will take you there:

NOTE: *Web sites that offer Java applets change often as new applets are added. The descriptions of the web sites in this book reflect their status at the end of 1996, when this book was written.*

TIP: *The current versions of both Netscape Navigator and Internet Explorer support Java, but Netscape does a better job. If an applet functions correctly with Internet Explorer, it should also work with Netscape's Navigator. The reverse is not always true. It is also important to have the latest version of whichever browser you prefer.*

1. Make sure your Internet connection is functioning and open Netscape Navigator.

2. In the Location text box type **java.sun.com/applets/** and press ENTER. In a few moments the web page shown in Figure 15-2 will be displayed in your browser.

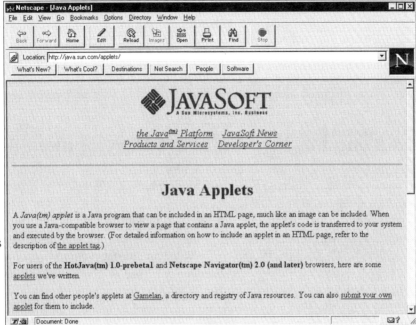

Sun
Microsystems's
JavaSoft
Java Applets
Home Page
in Netscape
Navigator

FIGURE 15-2

TIP: *Web sites change often and URLs sometimes become outdated. If the URLs used in this chapter no longer work when you try them, start from the home page and follow the hyperlinks to the resources described.*

3. On the Java Applets page, click on the "applets" hyperlink in the paragraph that begins with "For users of the HotJava(tm)..." (the second paragraph in Figure 15-2).

4. When the Applets From JavaSoft web page is displayed, scroll down the page to the list of hyperlinks for the Applets To Spice Up A Page section. Find the hyperlink for Scrolling Images (http://java.sun.com/applets/ applets/ScrollingImages/example1.html) and click on it. When the Image Tape web page is finished loading, you will see a series of images scrolling across the top of the page displayed in the browser, similar to

Figure 15-3. In the status bar at the bottom of the browser you can see that the Image Tape applet is running. Clicking on the hyperlink "The source" will display the actual Java source code used to create the Image Tape applet.

Now that you've seen a Java applet in action, it's time to add one to your web page. First, you need to download and install some Java development tools.

Installing the Java Software Development Kit

Java applets are generally distributed as source code that must be compiled before it can be used in your webs. This provides an additional measure of security. Rather than downloading an executable applet that may or may not perform as advertised, you download a text file that is compiled into the executable. This helps ensure the applet will do what it's advertised to do and nothing more. There are several sources for Java toolkits. The Java Development Kit, available from Sun Microsystems' web site (http://java.sun.com/), is the one you will use in the following sections. It includes the source code for a number of sample applets as well as a Java compiler for converting the Java source code into Java applets that can be included in your webs. Another useful toolkit is the Microsoft Software Development Kit (SDK) for Java (http://www.microsoft.com/java/sdk). If you plan on really working with Java, you should download both toolkits. Both contain extensive documentation that will make working with Java much easier.

Java Image Tape web page in Netscape Navigator

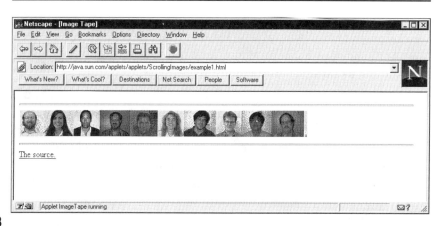

FIGURE 15-3

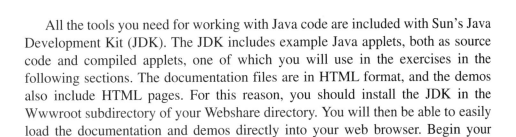

All the tools you need for working with Java code are included with Sun's Java Development Kit (JDK). The JDK includes example Java applets, both as source code and compiled applets, one of which you will use in the exercises in the following sections. The documentation files are in HTML format, and the demos also include HTML pages. For this reason, you should install the JDK in the Wwwroot subdirectory of your Webshare directory. You will then be able to easily load the documentation and demos directly into your web browser. Begin your exploration of Java by downloading the Java Development Kit.

NOTE: *The JDK is a very large download (6.5MB for the SDK and 1.7MB for the documentation), but the tools provided are necessary if you really want to work with Java. The installed files will require about 20MB of disk space.*

1. Create a new directory in your Wwwroot directory (C:\Webshare\ Wwwroot by default) by selecting the Wwwroot directory in the Windows Explorer and selecting New Folder from the File menu. Name the directory **Jdk**.

2. In your web browser go to Sun's JavaSoft Home Page (shown in Figure 15-4) at http://java.sun.com/.

3. Click on the Download The JDK hyperlink. Follow the instructions on the page, and download both the Java Development Kit (jdk1_1-beta2-win32-x86.exe) and document files (jdk1_1-beta2-win32-docs_html.zip) to the Jdk directory. The JDK file is self-extracting, but the documentation files require a compression utility, such as WinZip from Nico Mak Computing, Inc. (http://www.winzip.com), to be extracted.

NOTE: *At the time this was written (the end of 1996) the most recent release of Sun's JDK was Version 1.1 Beta 2. By the time you read this there may be a more recent version. If so, the filenames will have changed.*

4. In Windows Explorer open the Jdk directory where you saved the JDK program file and double-click on it. This will extract several files in your temporary directory including setup.bat.

5. Double-click on the setup.bat file. A DOS window will open displaying the license agreement, as shown next.

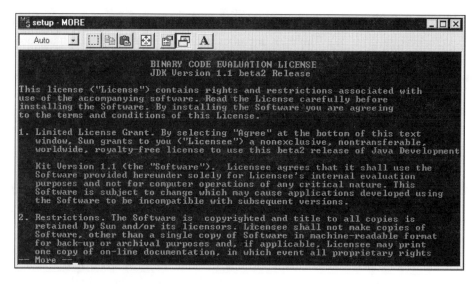

Sun's
JavaSoft
Home Page

FIGURE 15-4

6. After reading the license agreement (press ENTER to see more of it), type **y** and press ENTER if you agree to the terms. (If you do not agree, the software will not be installed.) A subdirectory named Java will be created, and the JDK will be installed there.

7. When the installation is completed (the DOS window title bar will read "Finished - setup"), click on the Close button of the DOS window.

8. In the Windows Explorer, double-click on the documentation file (jdk1_1-beta2-docs_html.zip). If you have installed and associated an application for Zip-compressed files, the application will open.

9. Unzip the files to the Jdk directory. You must unzip the documentation files to the same directory structure as when they were originally compressed. In WinZip you do this by selecting the Use Directory Names check box as shown here:

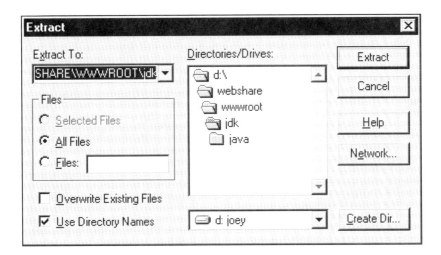

10. To save space on your hard drive, you can now delete the original files. These are all the files in the Jdk directory except the Java and Docs folders; all the JDK files you need are in the Java folder, and the documentation files are in the Docs folder. You may want to save the original compressed JDK and documentation files in case you need to reinstall the files.

Before using the JDK, you need to update your autoexec.bat file. This file is read by Windows 95 at startup and provides information that Windows 95 needs to

function properly. It's important that you enter the new information correctly. Whenever you edit a system file such as your autoexec.bat file, you should first make a backup file.

11. In the Windows Explorer open your C drive. In the Contents pane scroll down the list of folders and files until you find your autoexec.bat file.

12. Click on the file to select it (do not double-click on it). Open the Edit menu and select Copy, and then open the Edit menu again and select Paste. A copy of your autoexec.bat file will be created with the name "Copy of AUTOEXEC.BAT."

13. Click on the Start button on the taskbar, and select Run from the Start menu. The Run dialog box, shown next, will be displayed.

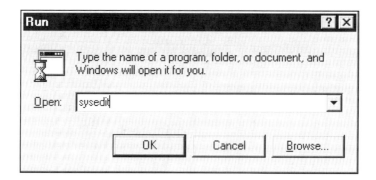

14. Type **sysedit** in the Open text box and press ENTER. The System Configuration Editor will open as shown in Figure 15-5.

15. In the C:\AUTOEXEC.BAT window locate your PATH statement. This is a line that begins with the word *PATH*.

16. At the end of the PATH statement type **;C:\Webshare\Wwwroot\ Jdk\Java\Bin** (include the semicolon). There should be no spaces between the end of the original PATH statement and the semicolon. For example, PATH C:\Windows;C:\Webshare\Wwwroot\Jdk\Java\Bin.

17. Press ENTER and type **SET CLASSPATH=C:\Webshare\ Wwwroot\ Jdk\Java\lib\classes.zip**. (Do not include the final period.)

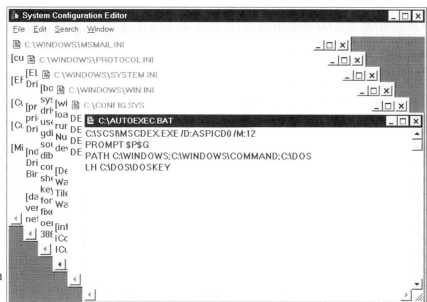

System
Configuration
Editor

FIGURE 15-5

NOTE: *Both your PATH and CLASSPATH statements must correctly point to where you have placed the JDK files. If you installed the files to a path different than the one shown here, use the correct path for your system in the autoexec.bat file.*

18. Select Save from the File menu, and then close the System Configuration Editor.

The autoexec.bat file is read by the system at startup, so you now need to restart your computer. Once that is done, you will be ready to begin working with Java applets.

Working with Java

By now you're probably eager to get started working with Java applets, so jump right in.

1. Open your web browser, type ***servername*/jdk/javaq/docs/index.html** in the Address (or Location with Netscape Navigator) text box, and then press ENTER. The page shown in Figure 15-6 will be displayed. This is the index page for documentation included with the Java Development Kit. You should become familiar with this resource.

2. Click on the Demonstration Applets hyperlink. This will take you to the Demonstration Applets And Applications page, which contains links to the applets included with the JDK.

3. Scroll down the list of applets until you see the TicTacToe hyperlink. Click on it to open the TicTacToe page, shown in Figure 15-7, which contains a Java applet (TicTacToe.class) that will play a game of TicTacToe with you.

JDK
Documentation
Home Page
in browser

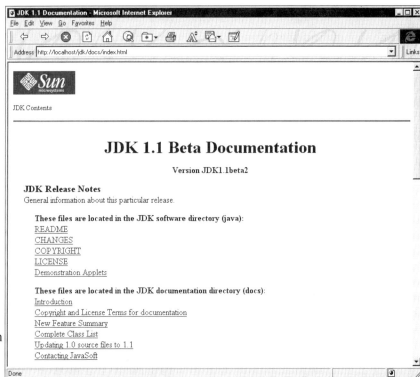

FIGURE 15-6

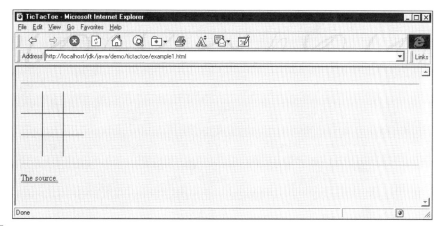

TicTacToe
web page
displayed
in Internet
Explorer

FIGURE 15-7

> **NOTE:** *Java applets have an extension of .CLASS, and Java source code files end in .JAVA.*

4. Click on one of the squares in the grid displayed. In a few moments your *X* will be displayed, followed by the applet's move, like this:

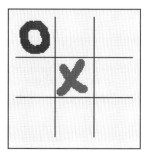

As you can see, Java applets can greatly expand what's possible on a web page. Take a moment to look at the source code for the applet by clicking on the The Source hyperlink. The source code for the TicTacToe applet will be displayed in your browser, as shown in Figure 15-8.

Next you will add this same applet to your own web page.

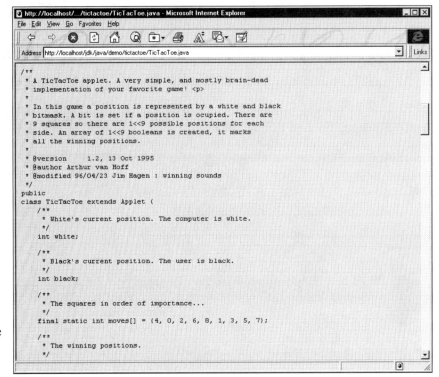

TicTacToe
applet
source code
in a web
browser

FIGURE 15-8

FrontPage and Java

Adding a Java applet to a web page is very similar to inserting a graphic. FrontPage
provides a dialog box that allows you to easily enter the necessary information. First,
you will copy the applet to your FrontPage web, as you will do with these instructions:

1. Open the FrontPage Explorer if it's not already open and open the
   Active web.

2. Click on the Folder View toolbar button if you're not already in
   Folder view.

3. Open the File menu and select Import. In the Import File To FrontPage
   Web dialog box click on Add Folder.

4. In the Browse For Folder dialog box open the location where you installed the JDK demo files (C:\Webshare\Wwwroot\jdk\java\demo by default), select the TicTacToe folder, and click on OK twice.

5. Open the home page in the FrontPage Editor.

6. Move the cursor to the line below the marquee you created earlier.

7. Type **Anyone for a game?** and format it as Heading 3.

8. Display the Advanced toolbar by selecting Advanced from the View menu.

9. Click on the Insert Java Applet toolbar button. The Java Applet Properties dialog box shown in Figure 15-9 will be displayed.

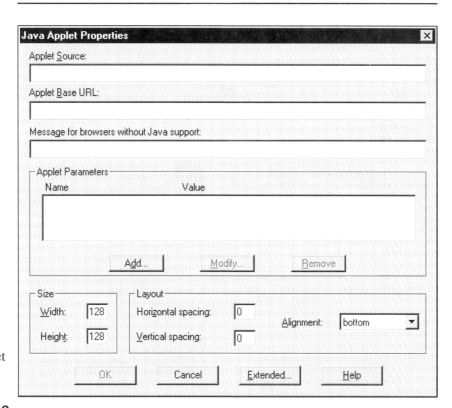

Java Applet
Properties
dialog box

FIGURE 15-9

 NOTE: *Java applets and other types of files can also be inserted by selecting Other Components from the Insert menu.*

10. Type **TicTacToe.class** in the Applet Source text box. Unlike other HTML tags, Java applet names are case-sensitive and must be typed exactly as shown.

11. In the Applet Base URL text box type **TicTacToe**.

12. Type **120** in the Width and Height Size text boxes, type **6** in the Horizontal Spacing text box, and select Top from the Alignment drop-down menu.

13. Click on OK. Your home page in the FrontPage Editor should look similar to Figure 15-10.

14. Open the Home page in your web browser, and play TicTacToe as shown in Figure 15-11 (in the middle of a game).

15. Close your browser.

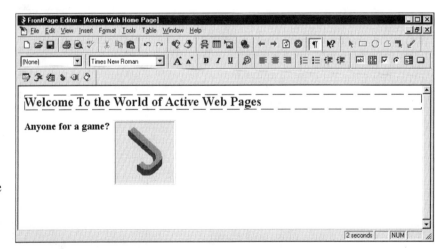

Home page in the FrontPage Editor

FIGURE 15-10

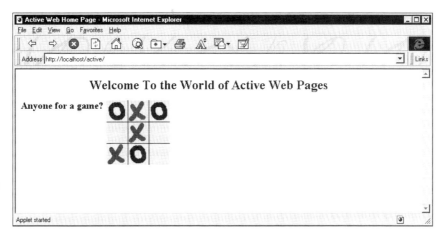

Home page
in Internet
Explorer

FIGURE 15-11

16. In the FrontPage Editor select HTML from the View menu, and take a
look at the HTML used to display the applet, listed here:

```
<APPLET code="TicTacToe.class" codebase="TicTacToe"
align="top" hspace="6" width="120" height="120"></APPLET>
```

The APPLET HTML tag is used to display a Java applet. The attributes of the
tag are described in Table 15-1.

17. Close the View Or Edit HTML dialog box.

Adding a Java applet to a web is actually a simple process, very much like adding
a graphic, as you've just seen. The next step in learning about Java is to see how
Java source code (the text files that contain a series of instructions) are converted to
Java applets (the executable program that is included in your web pages). You will
do that by taking the source code for the TicTacToe applet, TicTacToe.java, and
compiling it into the applet TicTacToe.class.

Compiling Java Applets

While the Java Development Kit contains some precompiled applets as well as
complete HTML pages that demonstrate them, knowing how to compile a Java

Attribute	Description
Code	Name of the applet—required; cannot include the URL of the folder containing the applet
Codebase	URL of the folder containing the applet—required if the applet is not in the same folder as the HTML page calling it
Alt	Specifies the text that should be displayed if the browser can interpret the APPLET tag but cannot run a Java applet
Align	Specifies the alignment of the applet and has the same options as the IMG tag—required
Width, Height	Specifies the applet display area in pixels—required
Vspace, Hspace	Specifies the vertical and horizontal space around the applet display area in pixels; used in the same way as the attributes for the IMG tag
Name	Unique name that identifies the applet instance; allows applets on the same web page to communicate with each other
Param Name, Value	Used to pass a parameter name and value to the applet if the applet has been written to accept parameter values

APPLET Tag Attributes

■ **TABLE 15-1**

applet from source code is a necessary skill for web designers who intend to use Java in their webs. Even if you never intend to write your own applets, you will still need to compile the applets you download from the Web, many of which are available as only Java source code. The process is relatively straightforward, but it does require using the MS-DOS interface included in Windows 95 (commonly referred to as a "DOS window") and a basic knowledge of using MS-DOS command syntax. The following steps will take you through the process:

1. Create a temporary directory on your hard drive for the source code file. Name the directory **Javawork**.

2. Copy the TicTacToe.java file (C:\Webshare\Wwwroot\jdk\java\demo\ TicTacToe\TicTacToe.java if you used the default directory structure) to the Javawork directory.

3. Open WordPad (Start menu, Programs, Accessories, WordPad), and then select Open from the File menu. In the Open dialog box select All Documents (*.*) from the Files Of Type drop-down menu.

NOTE: *Notepad is not suitable for opening or editing the Java source code files included with the JDK. These files contain characters that do not display properly in Notepad.*

4. Open your Javawork directory from the Look In drop-down menu and then the file and folder list, and double-click on TicTacToe.java. The TicTacToe.java source code file will be displayed as shown in Figure 15-12.

```
/**
 * A TicTacToe applet. A very simple, and mostly brain-dead
 * implementation of your favorite game! <p>
 *
 * In this game a position is represented by a white and black
 * bitmask. A bit is set if a position is ocupied. There are
 * 9 squares so there are 1<<9 possible positions for each
 * side. An array of 1<<9 booleans is created, it marks
 * all the winning positions.
 *
 * @version     1.2, 13 Oct 1995
 * @author Arthur van Hoff
 * @modified 96/04/23 Jim Hagen : winning sounds
 */
public
class TicTacToe extends Applet {
    /**
     * White's current position. The computer is white.
     */
    int white;

    /**
     * Black's current position. The user is black.
     */
    int black;

    /**
     * The squares in order of importance...
```

TicTacToe .java source code in WordPad

FIGURE 15-12

The source code includes a number of comments that describe the function of each Java statement in the file. Comments are all the text between the /** and */ markers. For example, in the lines

```
/**
 * White's current position. The computer is white.
 */
int white;
```

the comment (White's current position...) explains that the Java statement int white; is an integer that represents the current grid position of white's move. White is the variable name that contains the integer value. This variable is used to pass the current position of white to other functions in the applet. It is an axiom of programming that one of the best ways to learn a new programming language is to study other people's code. This is equally true of Java. If you are familiar with programming languages such as C++, the Java code will look familiar to you.

5. Close WordPad without changing the file.

6. Open a DOS window, by opening the Start menu, pointing on Programs, and then clicking on MS-DOS Prompt.

7. At the C:WINDOWS> prompt in the DOS window type **cd C:\Javawork** (or use the path where you created the Javawork directory), as shown here, and then press ENTER. CD is the DOS command for Change Directory. This will make the Javawork directory the current directory, and the prompt will read C:\Javawork>.

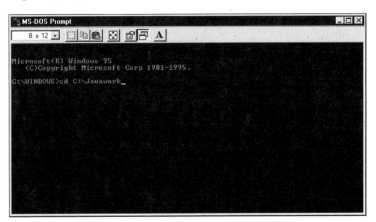

8. Type **dir** and then press ENTER. This is the command to display the contents of the current directory. Your DOS window should display a listing similar to this:

```
MS-DOS Prompt

8 x 12

Microsoft(R) Windows 95
     (C)Copyright Microsoft Corp 1981-1995.

C:\WINDOWS>cd C:\Javawork

C:\Javawork>dir

 Volume in drive C is BIGGUY
 Volume Serial Number is 2089-60DD
 Directory of C:\Javawork

.                <DIR>        12-20-96  4:46a .
..               <DIR>        12-20-96  4:46a ..
TICTAC~1 JAV        7,593     12-06-96 10:27a TicTacToe.java
          1 file(s)           7,593 bytes
          2 dir(s)       94,863,360 bytes free

C:\Javawork>
```

NOTE: *The directory listing displays two names for each file. On the left is the DOS name of the file in 8.3 format, in this case TICTAC~1 JAV, and on the right, the long filename supported by Windows 95, TicTacToe.java.*

9. Compile the TicTacToe.java source file by typing **javac TicTacToe.java** at the C:\Javawork> prompt and pressing ENTER. Javac is the name of Sun's Java compiler. The command you entered instructed it to convert the source file TicTacToe.java into the executable applet TicTacToe.class. Remember that Java names are case-sensitive and must be entered exactly as shown.

10. When the C:\Javawork> prompt reappears in the DOS window, type **dir** and press ENTER. In the listing that is displayed you will see that there are now two files in the Javawork directory—the original source file and TicTacToe.class, the executable applet.

In the preceding steps you used the simplest form of the javac command to generate the applet. There are also a number of options you can use with javac to control the compiling or to generate messages. In the next step you will use the

−verbose option to generate a list of all the steps the compiler is taking to generate the applet. This will overwrite the applet you just created.

> **11.** At the C:\Javawork> prompt type **javac −verbose TicTacToe.java** and press ENTER. As each step is executed by the compiler, a message will be displayed.

A complete listing of the options for the javac compiler can be found in the documentation web pages at *servername*/jdk/docs/tooldocs/win32/javac.html. You can open this page, and find information about the other tools included with the JDK. You open the documentation home page (*servername*/jdk/docs/index.html), then scroll down the page to the JDK Tools heading, and click on the Windows hyperlink. This takes you to the Tools Reference Pages – Windows page, shown in Figure 15-13, which contains a brief description of each tool and a hyperlink to the page where the tool is explained in detail.

> **12.** Close the DOS window by typing **exit** at the C:\Javawork> prompt and pressing ENTER.

This has been only a brief trip through the world of Java. It is a powerful programming language that opens new doors for the web designer. Because Java is a real programming language, it also requires a comprehensive knowledge to be used effectively. If you are a C++ programmer, the transition will be smooth. If Java is your first real programming language, you will have to devote a significant amount of time and energy to learning it. It is a language that will play an ever-increasing role in web design, so your time may be well spent. If you don't want to learn a programming language, you can find a growing number of prebuilt Java applets on the Web. The information in this section has presented the basics you need to download and use applets you find on the Web.

In the next section you will learn about ActiveX, Microsoft's technology that is designed to offer even more advantages to the web designer than Java does.

ActiveX

Java is a new technology. In a sense its designers began with a clean sheet of paper. (An interesting personal history of Java is included in *The Java Handbook* by Patrick Naughton—Osborne/McGraw-Hill, 1996—one of the original team at

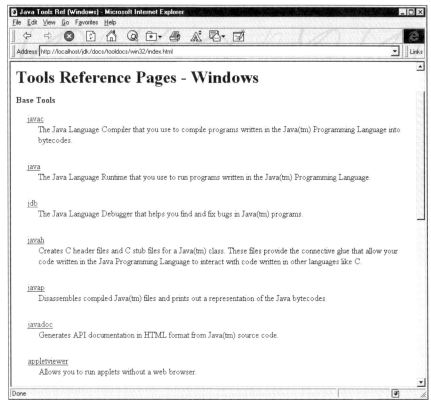

15

JDK Tools
Reference
Pages –
Windows
displayed
in a browser

FIGURE 15-13

Sun that created the language.) ActiveX is more evolutionary, having its roots in Microsoft's OLE (object linking and embedding) technology.

OLE was developed as a method of sharing text and graphics, generally called *objects,* between applications on a computer. If an object was linked between documents, a pointer was created in the receiving document pointing to the object in the original document. When the original object was updated, the linked object was also updated. For example, you could link a spreadsheet to a word processing document. When the data in the spreadsheet changed, it would be reflected in the word processing document. When an object was linked, it actually existed only in the original document. The receiving document only contained a pointer to the original. When an object was embedded, an actual copy was placed in the receiving document.

This method, while it worked fine when both documents were on a single computer, had its shortcomings in a networked environment. This led Microsoft to develop new technologies, such as Component Object Model (COM), Distributed Component Object Model (DCOM), and OLE Control Extensions (OCX).

Essentially, ActiveX is object-oriented programming for the Web. In the section of this chapter on object-oriented programming, the concept of objects was introduced. An object was defined as a process that accepts information, processes it, and then outputs the result. ActiveX brings the same modular concept to a web page, with the addition that an object can also be a data file. This is a greatly simplified explanation of the technology, but it avoids turning this chapter into a programming handbook, rather than a guide for the web designers who want to add the latest features to their FrontPage webs.

TIP: *For those who do want a programming handbook for ActiveX,* ActiveX from the Ground Up, *by John Paul Mueller (Osborne/ McGraw-Hill, 1997) is an excellent choice. It contains a thorough explanation of the evolution of ActiveX from OLE, as well as all you need to know to create your own ActiveX controls.*

The ActiveX equivalent of a Java applet is an ActiveX control. Because ActiveX has evolved from OLE, ActiveX controls can be used with many different programming languages, including all the Microsoft programming and database languages. This means you can use the same control with your Access database as you do with your web page. This is also an area where ActiveX differs from Java.

ActiveX is a very useful technology, but it does have its drawbacks. In particular, it is a Windows 95/NT-based technology. This leaves Mac and UNIX users out of the picture, at least for the present. If and when support is added for these platforms, the code will need to be compiled separately for each. This would lead to maintaining separate web pages for each operating system (unless a method was developed that would identify the operating system and use the appropriate control). Of course, Windows computers make up the majority of the market, and, with corporate intranets, the operating system can be controlled. It also is less secure than Java, which is balanced by the fact it is potentially more powerful.

Netscape offers its Open Network Environment (ONE) as an alternative to ActiveX on an intranet. Netscape ONE is based on existing Internet standards, including Java. Both technologies will probably find a home in the marketplace. Which one you should use will depend on a number of factors, but neither should be rejected out of hand. Since Netscape ONE is based on existing Internet standards (rather than being a new technology itself) and is primarily for intranets, it is not covered in this book. More information about Netscape ONE can be found on Netscape's web site (http://developer.netscape.com/library/one/index.html).

These issues are not new to computing. At every stage of growth in the industry the question of features versus compatibility has arisen. Often, as with ActiveX, compatibility has suffered in order to increase the usefulness of software. These are simply issues you need to consider before using ActiveX with your webs.

Since ActiveX controls are commonly written in C++, this section will not go into writing your own controls. Instead you will use ActiveX controls included with FrontPage and readily available on the Web. If you do want to write your own, you will need the ActiveX SDK from Microsoft (http://microsoft.com/msdownload/activex.htm) and the latest Win32 SDK, which is available only to members of the Microsoft Developers Network (http://microsoft.com/msdn/). Additional information about ActiveX and other Internet technologies can be found on the Microsoft Site Builder Network (http://microsoft.com/sitebuilder/).

The next section will take you right into using ActiveX with your FrontPage webs.

ActiveX and FrontPage

FrontPage comes with a number of ActiveX controls you can add to your webs, as you will see next:

1. Open your Active web in the FrontPage Explorer if it's not open already, and then open the home page in the FrontPage Editor.

2. Move the cursor to the line below your Java applet, and type **Or don't you have the time?**. Format it as Heading 2 and press ENTER.

3. Click on the Insert ActiveX Control toolbar button. The ActiveX Control Properties dialog box shown in Figure 15-14 will be displayed.

4. Select Active Earth Time from the Pick A Control drop-down menu.

5. Type 480 in the Width text box and 280 in the Height text box.

6. In the HTML text box type **<H1>This browser doesn't support ActiveX</H1>** and click on OK. Your home page should look similar to Figure 15-15.

7. Click on the Active Earth Time ActiveX control to select it, and then click on the Center alignment toolbar button. Save your home page.

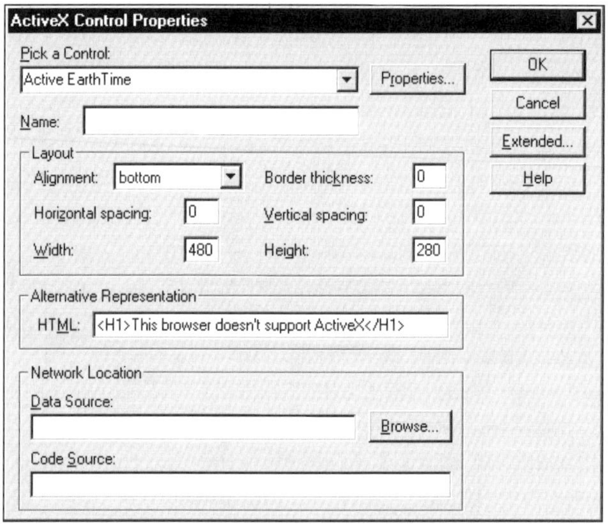

ActiveX
Control
Properties
dialog box

FIGURE 15-14

8. Open the Active Web Home Page in Internet Explorer, as shown in Figure 15-16.

9. Close Internet Explorer and open the home page in Netscape Navigator. Figure 15-17 shows what the page will look like.

The preceding example illustrates one of the problems with ActiveX controls; Netscape Navigator doesn't support them without a separate plug-in. Since Netscape still holds the largest share of the browser market, this currently makes using ActiveX controls in your webs a risky business. However, this situation will change as support for ActiveX grows. On an intranet, if you can control the browsers used, this limitation doesn't apply.

The Active Earth Time ActiveX control is one of a number of ActiveX controls that are included with FrontPage. All the ActiveX controls installed on your system (both those included with FrontPage and those you download and install separately) are displayed in the Pick A Control drop-down menu on the ActiveX Control Properties dialog box. Take a moment now to examine the ActiveX Control Properties dialog box.

The ActiveX Control Properties Dialog Box

The ActiveX Control Properties dialog box, shown in Figure 15-14, allows you to set the properties for the ActiveX controls you use in your webs. The options are

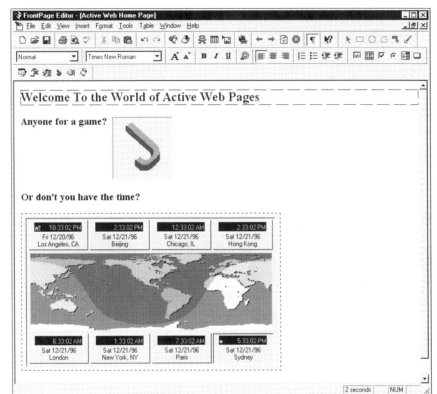

Home page with Active Earth Time ActiveX control inserted in the FrontPage Editor

FIGURE 15-15

- **Pick a Control** provides a drop-down menu listing all the ActiveX controls installed on your system.

- **Properties** opens the Properties dialog box where you can set the properties for the selected ActiveX control such as size, location, and whether it will be visible in the browser.

- **Name** allows you to name the ActiveX control so that it can be referenced by scripts.

- **Layout** contains the options for the appearance of the control on the page. These are the same as those for graphic images.

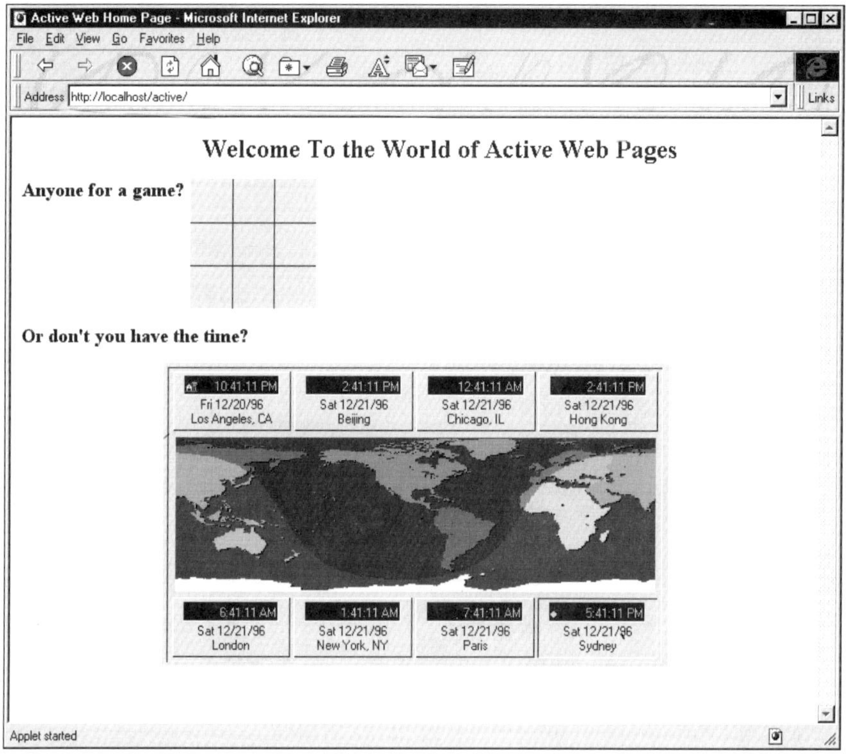

Active Web
Home Page
in Internet
Explorer

FIGURE 15-16

- **Alternative Representation** provides the HTML that will be displayed if the browser doesn't support ActiveX controls. This can be a text message, a graphic, a hyperlink, or any other valid HTML.

- **Network Location** sets the location of the ActiveX control and data for downloading if it doesn't exist on the client computer.

- **Data Source** provides the location for any data the control uses when it runs. This can be a file on the web or a network file.

- **Code Source** provides the location of the ActiveX control on the web or a networked computer if it's not installed on the browser's computer. The control is downloaded from this location when needed.

Active Web
Home Page
in Netscape
Navigator

FIGURE 15-17

The OBJECT Tag

Now take a look at the HTML that was generated to display the ActiveX control by going back to the FrontPage Editor and selecting HTML from the View menu. The HTML that displays the control looks like this:

```
<OBJECT classid="clsid:9590092D-8811-11CF-8075-444553540000" border="0"
width="480" height="280"><H1>This browser doesn't support
ActiveX</H1></OBJECT>
```

The OBJECT tag is used to display an ActiveX control. At present only Internet Explorer supports this tag, but it's reasonably certain that it will become part of the HTML standard in time. This tag has some interesting implications for the web designer. Even though it is currently used only for ActiveX controls, it has the

potential to insert any object, such as a word processing document, Java applet, image, or any valid HTML code, into a web page. FrontPage can do some of these tasks, particularly using WebBots, but in a limited way.

With the OBJECT tag any valid object can be inserted on a web page. With scripting languages such as JavaScript or VBScript (which will be covered in the JavaScript and VBScript sections in this chapter), these objects can be linked. Currently, the OBJECT tag supports only ActiveX controls, but support for Java applets is planned. When support is added for other objects, you will be able to create your own programs combining ActiveX controls, Java applets, data files, or any other valid object, and include them on a web page. The script gathers the input for the objects, controls the flow of data between the objects, and formats the output.

The OBJECT tag and the scripting languages are the tools the web designer will use to place all the pieces in a web page. Many of the current attributes of the tag are described in Table 15-2. Since the tag has not been adopted as part of the HTML standard, it's probable that the attributes will change to some extent over time. In addition to the attributes listed in Table 15-2, the standard IMG tag alignment attributes (such as Align, Border, and so on) are also supported.

 NOTE: *The term* object *is used to describe any of the object types already mentioned, not just ActiveX controls.*

In addition, the PARAM tag is used inside the OBJECT tag to define parameters for the object. The PARAM tag has one attribute—a Name and Value pair. PARAM is an empty tag, meaning there is no closing tag, like

```
<PARAM Name="caption" Value="Click Here">
```

Since object properties are defined by the authors of the object, there is no standard set of properties that is set with the PARAM tag. When you are finished looking at the HTML, close the View Or Edit HTML dialog box.

ActiveX and Netscape Navigator

The previous example illustrated that Netscape Navigator, because it does not support the OBJECT tag, cannot display ActiveX controls. This excludes a large portion of the browser market from viewing your ActiveX-enhanced web pages properly. There is a work-around that, while not perfect, does provide a partial solution.

Attribute	Description
Classid	A unique identifier for the control using the COM class ID numbering scheme.
ID	The value entered in the Name text box of the ActiveX Control Properties dialog box to identify the control for scripting.
Codebase	Identifies the location of the control; it will be downloaded from this location if it's not on the user's machine.
Data	Identifies the location for the data that is used by the control.
Declare	Identifies the control without running it; this allows it to be referenced by other controls or objects, or by scripts.
Name	The name used when the object is part of a form.
Standby	The message that is displayed while the object is being loaded.
Tabindex	The position in the tabbing order for the object when it is included in a series of objects.
Notab	Leaves the object out of the series of objects that can be tabbed.
Title	The text displayed as a title.
Type	The Internet media type of the object.

OBJECT
Tag
Attributes
TABLE 15-2

NCompass Labs, Inc. (http://www.ncompasslabs.com) offers a plug-in for Netscape that will, with some modifications to your HTML, display ActiveX controls in Navigator. Plug-ins are programs that extend the capabilities of Netscape Navigator by adding support for file types not natively supported by Navigator. This allows Navigator to stay current with new Internet file types without requiring constant updates to the browser.

The root of the problem is that while Microsoft developed the OBJECT tag to place objects in a web page, Netscape supports the EMBED tag. This is an example

of what happens when the HTML standards body gets left behind by the marketplace. Both tags are under consideration by the HTML working groups, and it is almost certain that both will be adopted. Internet Explorer supports both tags for compatibility.

To make your ActiveX controls work with Navigator, you need to do two things: install the NCompass Labs ScriptActive plug-in (which has to be done by every user of Netscape in order to view the pages properly), and modify your HTML to include both tags (which only has to be done once). The ScriptActive plug-in includes an optional conversion utility to convert your HTML that contains the OBJECT tag.

> **NOTE:** *NCompass Labs, Inc. also makes a plug-in, DocActive, that integrates Microsoft Office documents with Navigator. By using it, users can open, view, edit, save locally, and print Excel, Word, and PowerPoint documents as well as other types of document object files. They also have their own line of ActiveX controls under the name CaptiveX.*

In the next sections you will see how to modify your HTML to work with both Internet Explorer and Netscape Navigator with the ScriptActive plug-in installed. It is more work and will become unnecessary with time, but for now it is the only real solution to the problem.

Installing the ScriptActive Plug-In

Installing plug-ins for Navigator is a relatively simple process. First, you need to download the plug-in from the NCompass Labs web site, as you will do now:

1. Open your web browser and log onto the NCompass Labs web site (http://www.ncompasslabs.com/products.htm).

2. Scroll down the page, if necessary, until you see the description of the ScriptActive plug-in.

3. Click on the 30 Day Evaluation Copy hyperlink. You will be taken to a page where you register to download the program.

> **NOTE:** *ScriptActive is a commercial product that is available for purchase from NCompass Labs. The evaluation copy you are downloading will expire 30 days after it is installed and is intended to be used to evaluate the product before purchasing. Details for purchasing ScriptActive can be found on the NCompass Labs web site.*

4. Fill out the registration form and click on Submit Report.

5. On the next page, click on the hyperlink to download ScriptActive, and save it to a temporary directory on your hard drive.

NOTE: *At this writing the filename was sa2509er.exe (a self-extracting compressed file), and the file size was 2.8MB. The name and file size may change as newer versions are released.*

6. Close your web browser.

Next you will install the ScriptActive plug-in. Netscape Navigator as well as all other programs must be closed while you do this.

7. In Windows Explorer, open the directory where you have saved the plug-in and double-click on it.

8. A license agreement will be displayed. If you agree to the terms of the license, click on Yes. The setup program will determine the location of your Netscape Navigator files and install the plug-in in the same directory.

9. You will be asked if you also wish to install the NCompass Conversion Utility. Click on Yes.

When the installation is completed, you will need to restart your computer. The plug-in will be installed in the Plugins subdirectory of your Netscape Programs directory. When Navigator is started, the plug-in will be active. A new program group will also be added to your Start menu Programs menu, NCompass, which will contain the NCompass HTML Conversion Utility.

If you reload the Active Web Home Page in Navigator, you will see that the ActiveX control still does not appear, even with the plug-in installed. You must modify the HTML to include the EMBED tag.

Using the HTML Conversion Utility
The NCompass HTML Conversion Utility is simple to use, as you will see next.

1. Click on the Start menu button on the taskbar, point on Programs, then NCompass, and then select NCompass HTML Conversion Utility. The dialog box shown here will be displayed.

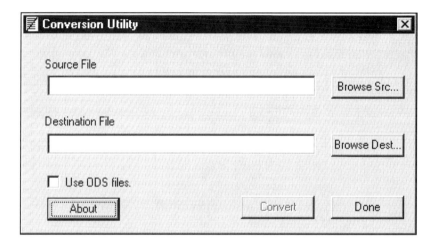

2. Click on the Browse Src button. In the Open dialog box locate the Active Web Home Page (C:\Webshare\Wwwroot\Active\Default.htm) and click on OK.

3. Click on the Browse Dest button. In the File Name text box type **Converted.htm** and click on Save.

4. Click on the Convert button. In a few moments the Conversion Success dialog box shown next should be displayed.

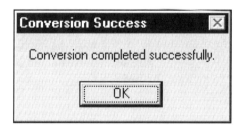

5. Click on OK, then click on Done.

6. In Windows Explorer locate the converted file, and place a copy of it in a temporary directory. (This is to see the changes in the HTML at each stage of the conversion.)

7. Restart FrontPage, again load the Active web, and in the FrontPage Editor click on the Open toolbar button.

8. Select the Other Location tab on the Open File dialog box. Click on Browse and select the Converted.htm file in the Active directory. Click on Open.

9. When the page is opened in the FrontPage Editor, right-click on it and select Page Properties.

10. In the Page Properties dialog box type **Active Web Converted Home Page** in the Title text box and click on OK. Click on the Save toolbar button, and then select Close from the File menu.

11. In the FrontPage Explorer select Import from the File menu (the Active web should still be open).

12. Click on Add File in the Import File To FrontPage Web dialog box, and then select Converted.htm from the Active directory in the Add File To Import List dialog box. Click on Open, then on OK to replace the existing file.

13. When the Confirm Save dialog box, shown next, is displayed, click on Yes. (These steps are needed to update the information FrontPage keeps about each page in a web.)

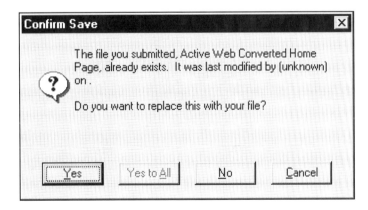

14. Open the Converted.htm page in the FrontPage Editor, and then select HTML from the View menu.

15. Open the copy of Converted.htm you copied to another directory in step 6 in Notepad.

The original HTML generated by FrontPage when you inserted the ActiveX control into the Active Web Home Page, using the OBJECT tag, is shown in Listing 15-1. The converted HTML generated by the NCompass HTML Conversion Utility is shown in Listing 15-2 (this should be visible in Notepad). Listing 15-3 is the HTML as it was generated by FrontPage when the file was imported into the Active web.

Listing 15-1
Original ActiveX

```
<OBJECT Classid="clsid:9590092D-8811-11CF-8075-444553540000"
Align="baseline" Border="0" Width="480" Height="280">
<H1>This browser doesn't support ActiveX</H1>
</OBJECT>
```

Listing 15-2
NCompass
conversion

```
<OBJECT Classid="clsid:9590092D-8811-11CF-8075-444553540000"
Border="0" Width="480" Height="280">
<H1>This browser doesn't support ActiveX</H1>
<EMBED
classid="clsid:9590092D-8811-11CF-8075-444553540000"
border="0" width="480" height="280" TYPE="application/oleobject"
<H1>This browser doesn't support ActiveX</H1>>
</OBJECT>
```

Listing 15-3
FrontPage
conversion

```
<OBJECT Classid="clsid:9590092D-8811-11CF-8075-444553540000"
Align="baseline" Border="0" Width="480" height="280">
</OBJECT>
<EMBED align="baseline" border="0" width="480" height="280"
Classid="clsid:9590092D-8811-11CF-8075-444553540000"
Type="application/oleobject"
<h1>This browser doesn't support ActiveX&gt;
```

Looking at the three versions of the HTML, you can see that the code generated by FrontPage (Listing 15-3) has some problems. In Listing 15-2 the EMBED tag is enclosed by the OBJECT tag, as it should be. In Listing 15-3 the EMBED tag has been placed after the OBJECT tag, and FrontPage has lost the closing Heading 1 tag (</H1>) as well as the closing greater-than symbol (>) for the EMBED tag, replacing it with the escaped text sequence (>). You need to fix these problems before the converted home page will display correctly in Netscape Navigator. The only way to fix this is to use the Insert HTML Markup command to place the correct HTML in the page. If you try to edit the HTML in the View Or Edit HTML dialog box, FrontPage will make the same changes to your edited HTML when it is saved. Insert the correct HTML with these steps:

1. In Notepad select all the HTML between the paragraph tags ( ), including the paragraph tags themselves.

2. Press CTRL-C to copy the text to the Clipboard.

3. In the FrontPage Editor close the View Or Edit HTML dialog box, select the ActiveX control on the Converted.htm page, and press DEL. The cursor should be on the line below the "Or do you have the time?" text.

4. Open the Insert menu and select HTML Markup. In the HTML Markup dialog box paste the text you copied from Notepad by pressing CTRL-V. The result is shown here:

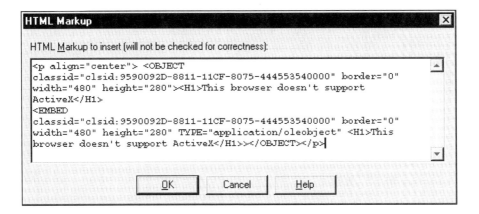

5. Click on OK and then save the Converted.htm page.

6. Open Internet Explorer and load the Converted.htm page (*servername/* Active/Converted.htm). The page really doesn't look any different than before you converted the HTML.

7. Close Internet Explorer, open Netscape Navigator, and then load the Converted.htm page into it.

Figure 15-18 shows what the page will look like in Netscape. Clearly, even with the ScriptActive plug-in the process isn't perfect. The heading "This browser doesn't

Converted
.htm web
page with
ActiveX
control in
Netscape
Navigator

FIGURE 15-18

support ActiveX" appears at the top and bottom of the control, since Netscape doesn't know what else to do with it. This is because Netscape is using the EMBED tag and ignoring the OBJECT tag. Leaving this text out will solve this problem.

The larger problem for the web designer is what to do with ActiveX. Netscape has no desire to help Microsoft establish ActiveX as a viable web technology. You can expect no support for the OBJECT tag until it becomes part of the HTML standard, or until market forces cause Netscape to rethink its position. With careful planning you can make ActiveX controls work with the ScriptActive plug-in, but only on those browsers that have it installed. Realistically, you have two choices: ignore ActiveX, or limit its use to specific pages on your web and provide Netscape-compatible alternatives for those pages. Give serious thought to the latter choice, even though it will increase your workload somewhat. ActiveX is a technology that, while not perfect, offers some real benefits.

In the next sections you will look at the scripting languages for the Web: JavaScript and VBScript. To prepare for them, close Notepad and Netscape Navigator.

Web Scripting Languages

The general difference between scripting languages and programming languages is in how they are treated when executed. Programming languages, like Java and C++, create a *bytecode* file that is executed by the operating system. A bytecode file is a binary (all 0's and 1's) file containing instructions that are directly used by the operating system. Scripts are text files that are interpreted at the time they are executed and converted into the bytecode the system needs. This explanation is a bit simplified. Java applets, for example, are bytecode files compiled from the text source file, but they are still interpreted at run time by the browser's Java interpreter. A good working definition is simply that scripts are text files that you can edit directly, unlike a Java applet or ActiveX control that you can only pass properties to.

JavaScript and VBScript (Visual Basic Script) are the two primary scripting languages used on the Web that are interpreted by the user's system. Other languages, such as Perl (Practical Extraction and Report Language), are executed on the server, requiring the data to make a round-trip over the Internet and using the server's processing time. Because JavaScript and VBScript run on the client (the user's computer), the transit time and server overhead are eliminated. This is an important consideration—it means much faster processing times for the user.

A short time ago these languages were primarily doing simple tasks, such as validating form input (as you'll see in the next section). Their future is much more glorious—they are becoming the glue that will bind Java applets, ActiveX controls, and other types of program and data files into powerful web-based desktop applications.

In the section on ActiveX some of the implications of this trend were discussed. Not content to let Microsoft get all the limelight with ActiveX, Netscape has released LiveConnect, its framework for combining Java applets, JavaScript scripts, and HTML elements into interactive web pages. These are the front lines of the browser wars. A lot of effort is going into developing these technologies, and you can expect to see a number of advances (and a lot of hype) in the coming months. There is a fundamental difference in philosophy between Microsoft and Netscape. Netscape is building its products on the open standards of the Internet, such as Java, while Microsoft is building theirs on technologies they own. An example of this is the difference between Java applets and ActiveX controls. A Java applet will run on any operating system for which a Java-enabled browser is available. ActiveX controls,

on the other hand, will currently only run on Windows machines, a product of their OLE lineage. Part of this difference in philosophy may simply be that Microsoft had the technologies to build on, while Netscape didn't.

Neither technology is the total answer for the web designer. The Web is ready to burst again with an avalanche of products that will allow you to create webs that are completely interactive. Users will be able to see web pages tailored to their needs rather than static presentations of information. Data contained in remote databases or other applications will be accessible, not as raw data the user has to wade through, but as concise presentations that can be manipulated on the user's desktop.

At the center of these developments are the scripting languages. They accept information from the user, control the flow of data between objects, and prepare the output of the processing. Currently, JavaScript has greater support than VBScript, so that's where you'll start.

JavaScript

Like Java, JavaScript was developed by Sun Microsystems Inc., with involvement from the early stages by Netscape. At the time (late 1995) Netscape was developing a prototype scripting language named LiveScript, but chose to abandon the name and combine their efforts with Sun. JavaScript is supported by both the current releases of Netscape Navigator (3.01) and Internet Explorer (3.01), while VBScript is only supported by Internet Explorer.

The best way to understand JavaScript is to look at some code. FrontPage makes this easy to do, as it will generate either JavaScript or VBScript for you. In the next section you will use FrontPage to generate a JavaScript script that will validate a form.

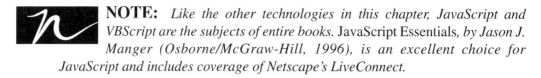

NOTE: *Like the other technologies in this chapter, JavaScript and VBScript are the subjects of entire books.* JavaScript Essentials, *by Jason J. Manger (Osborne/McGraw-Hill, 1996), is an excellent choice for JavaScript and includes coverage of Netscape's LiveConnect.*

Form Validation with JavaScript

Form validation, the process of checking the data in each field of a form to be sure it is of the correct type, used to be done on the server by use of a language such as Perl. This was done through the common gateway interface (CGI). You may be familiar with the term *CGI script* to describe this type of programming. This had the disadvantage of requiring a round-trip over the Internet and using the server's processing time. With client-side form validation the process is speeded up by doing the work on the user's computer, rather than on the server.

With FrontPage you use the Form and Field Properties dialog boxes to define the criteria for validation, and the script is created for you—you don't need to know a thing about either scripting language. These steps will take you through the process:

1. In the FrontPage Editor create a new Normal page. At the top of the page type **JavaScript Form Validation**, and format it as Heading 1.

2. Move the cursor to the next line, and click on the One-Line Text Box button on the Form toolbar.

3. Press HOME to move the cursor to the beginning of the line, and type **Enter some text:** (leave a space after the colon). Format the text as Formatted.

4. Press END to move the cursor to the end of the line and press SHIFT-ENTER.

5. Click on the One-Line Text Box button on the Form toolbar once more and then press HOME.

6. Type **Enter a number:** (leaving two spaces after the colon), press END, and then press ENTER.

7. Click on the Push Button Forms toolbar button.

8. Save the page with the title **JavaScript Form Validation** and the filename **Jsform.htm**.

Your page should look similar to Figure 15-19. Before setting the validation criteria for the form, check which scripting language is set as the default.

9. In the FrontPage Explorer open the Tools menu and select Web Settings.

10. In the FrontPage Web Settings dialog box click on the Advanced tab, as shown in Figure 15-20. JavaScript should be displayed in the Validation Scripts Language drop-down menu. VBScript and None are the other choices.

11. Click on OK and return to the FrontPage Editor.

12. Right-click on the form and select Form Properties.

13. In the Form Properties dialog box select WebBot Save Results Component from the Form Handler drop-down menu.

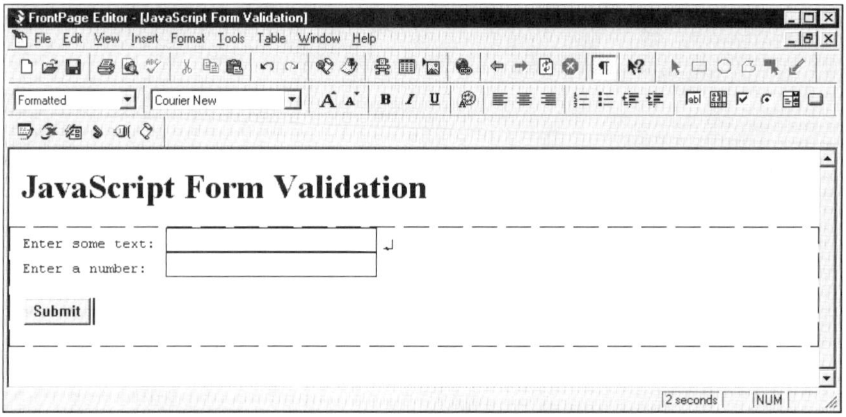

JavaScript
Form
Validation
page

FIGURE 15-19

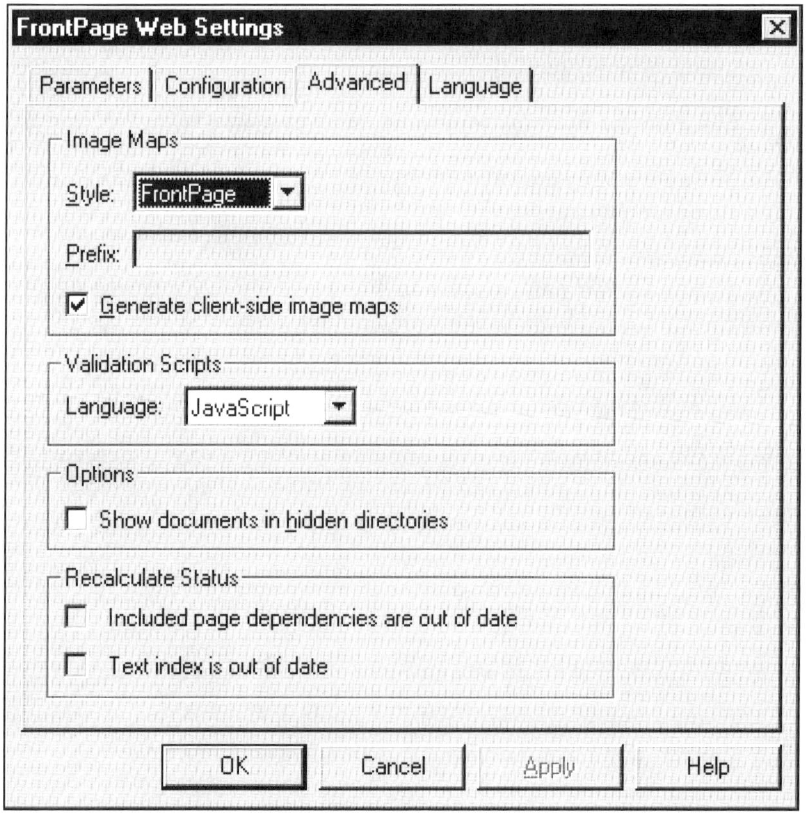

FrontPage
Web
Settings
dialog box
Advanced
tab

FIGURE 15-20

14. Click on Settings, type **Form1** in the File For Results text box on the Settings For Saving Results Of Form dialog box, and then press ENTER.

15. Type **Form1** in the Form Name text box and then click on OK.

16. Right-click on the first one-line text box in the form, and select Form Field Validation from the context menu.

17. In the Text Box Validation dialog box select Text from the Data Type drop-down menu.

18. In the Display Name text box type **Text Field**. This is the name for the field that will be used in the validation error messages.

19. Click on the Letters check box and then click on OK.

20. Right-click on the second one-line text box, and select Form Field Validation from the context menu.

21. Select Integer from the Data Type drop-down menu, and type **Numeric Field** in the Display Name text box.

22. Select the Field Must Be check box, and type **5** in the Value text box.

23. Select the And Must Be check box, and type **10** in the Value text box. Your Text Box Validation dialog box should look like Figure 15-21.

24. Click on OK and then save the page.

25. Open the page in your browser, type **11** in the numeric field, and click on Submit. You should see an error message similar to this:

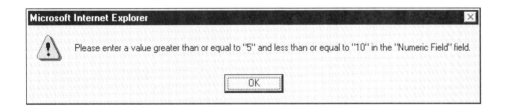

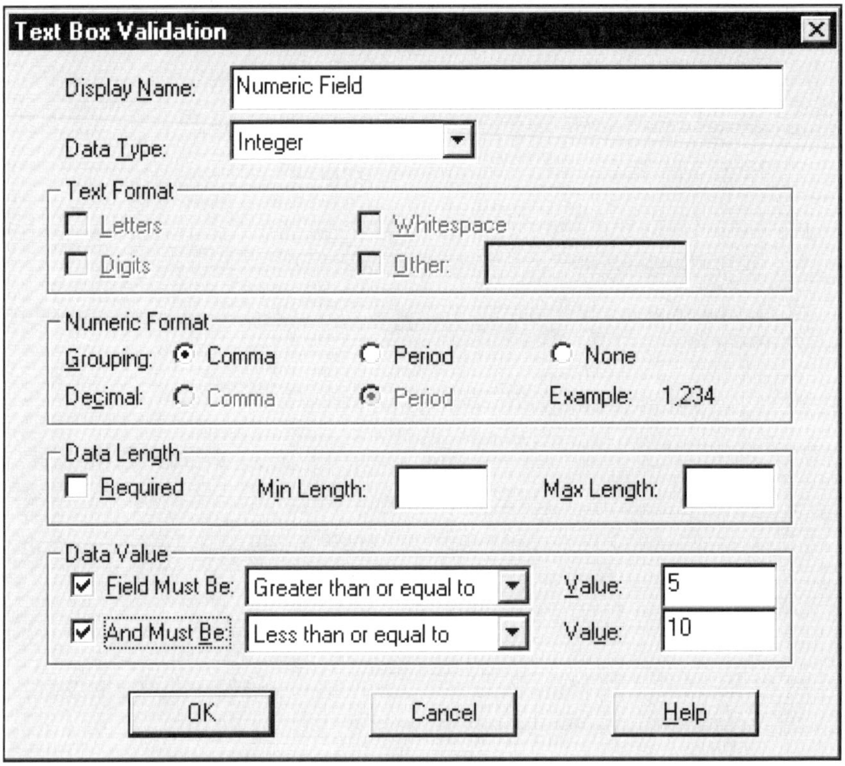

Text Box
Validation
dialog box

FIGURE 15-21

26. Click on OK and then select Source from the View menu in Internet Explorer, or Document Source from the View menu in Netscape Navigator. At the beginning of the HTML listing you will see the JavaScript script that generated the error message. The JavaScript portion of the file is shown in Listing 15-4.

If you've ever done any programming, the JavaScript script in Listing 15-4 will look familiar to you. If you haven't, it may look very strange. The best way to understand what it does is to step through the script and look at each section.

ting 15-4
cript form
validation

```
<script language="JavaScript"><!--
function FrontPage_Form1_Validator(theForm)
{
  var checkOK =
"ABCDEFGHIJKLMNOPQRSTUVWXYZabcdefghijklmnopqrstuvwxyz??????ÀÁÂÃÄÅÆÇÈÉÊËÌÍÎÏ ÐÑÒ
ÓÔÕÖØÙÚÛÜÝÞßàáâãäåæçèéêëìíîïðñòóôõöøùúûüýþ";
  var checkStr = theForm.T1.value;
  var allValid = true;
  for (i = 0;  i < checkStr.length;  I++)
  {
    ch = checkStr.charAt(i);
    for (j = 0;  j < checkOK.length;  j++)
      if (ch == checkOK.charAt(j))
        break;
    if (j == checkOK.length)
    {
      allValid = false;
      break;
    }
  }
  if (!allValid)
  {
    alert("Please enter only letter characters in the \"Text Field\" field.");
    theForm.T1.focus();
    return (false);
  }
  var checkOK = "0123456789-,";
  var checkStr = theForm.T2.value;
  var allValid = true;
  var decPoints = 0;
  var allNum = "";
  for (i = 0;  i < checkStr.length;  i++)
  {
    ch = checkStr.charAt(i);
    for (j = 0;  j < checkOK.length;  j++)
      if (ch == checkOK.charAt(j))
```

```
        break;
    if (j == checkOK.length)
    {
      allValid = false;
      break;
    }
    if (ch != ",")
      allNum += ch;
  }
  if (!allValid)
  {
    alert("Please enter only digit characters in the \"Numeric Field\"
field.");
    theForm.T2.focus();
    return (false);
  }
  var chkVal = allNum;
  var prsVal = parseInt(allNum);
  if (chkVal != "" && !(prsVal >= "5" && prsVal <= "10"))
  {
    alert("Please enter a value greater than or equal to \"5\" and less than
or equal to \"10\" in the \"Numeric Field\" field.");
    theForm.T2.focus();
    return (false);
  }
  return (true);
}
//--></script>
```

The JavaScript Form Validation Script

Don't worry if the JavaScript code looks indecipherable. The function of each section of a program is understandable once you begin to understand the type of shorthand it's written in. In this section you will look at each piece of the code and see what it does and how it fits in with the other pieces to make a complete script.

NOTE: *Programming, like writing in any language, has a lot of room for style, and programmers tend to develop their own styles. There are rules for good programming, such as adding comments to explain each section, that make code easily understood. The JavaScript code in this section was generated by FrontPage using the rules defined by the team that programmed this feature of FrontPage. This is not the only way the script could have been written, but it is a good example of JavaScript scripting.*

In the rest of this section the script has been dissected to explain the purpose of each section of code. In doing so, the formatting has been changed somewhat. Listing 15-4 contains the correct syntax for the script.

```
<script language="JavaScript"><!--
```

The script begins by declaring the programming language using the SCRIPT tag. The entire body of the script is within the opening and closing SCRIPT tags. If the browser doesn't support the scripting language, then the entire script is ignored. The Language attribute is required to inform the browser which language is being used (either JavaScript or VBScript). There is also an optional attribute, Src, which identifies the location of the script (as a URL) if it's not included on the HTML page. This allows you to create a library of scripts that can be used by many web pages without requiring you to include the script on each page. There is also a NOSCRIPT tag that is used to define the HTML that will be displayed if the script isn't supported. It is placed after the script in the HTML document.

After the SCRIPT tag is an opening HTML comment tag (<!--) matched by the closing comment tag (-->) at the end of the script. Without these tags the entire text of the script would be displayed in browsers that don't support the SCRIPT tag.

```
function FrontPage_Form1_Validator(theForm)
```

This next line declares the function name and its arguments in the form `function functionName (arguments)`. In this case the functionName is

`FrontPage_Form1_Validator`, and the single argument is `theForm`. A *function* is a series of JavaScript statements that perform a task and optionally return a value. The function statements are enclosed within the { and } brackets. An *argument* is a value that is passed to the function. What this value can be will depend on the purpose of the function. For example, if the purpose of the function was to multiply two numbers, then the two numbers would be the arguments passed to the function. Since the arguments are represented by variables (which can be considered a container for the value), they could be passed from the web page through a form as variables, which is what is being done in this script. The argument `theForm` refers to the values you enter in the form text boxes and then submit. The script intercepts the values before the form handler and checks them against the rules established by the function. If they meet the criteria, they are passed on to the form handler; if not, then an error message is generated, as you saw earlier, and the form handler never receives the data. Since the form handler will be on the server, this prevents unnecessary traffic and server time.

 NOTE: *Functions cannot be* nested, *that is, a function cannot be defined inside another function.*

```
{ var checkOK = "ABCDEF...";
  var checkStr = theForm.T1.value;
  var allValid = true;
```

These three lines define the variables that are used by the function in the form `var variableName = variableValue`. The first variable, `checkOK`, is a text string consisting of all the acceptable characters that can be returned by the first form field. (The list has been shortened here.) The second, `checkStr`, is the value entered in the first text box, T1. T1 is the default name given to the form field when you created it in FrontPage. If you had given the field a different name, that is the name that would be used in defining the variable. This variable illustrates a JavaScript naming convention—defining an object as a hierarchical string with each level of the hierarchy separated by a period. In this case the hierarchy is the form itself, the field in the form, and the value contained in the field. This is one method by which data is passed between the HTML page and the script. To the script, the form is an object and so can have properties that can be processed. JavaScript can also recognize events, such as a mouse click or placing the mouse pointer over a defined area, and execute a function based on the event. The third variable, allValid, is a flag that will be used later in the script to determine if the data will be passed to the form handler. It is defined as true, meaning that the script is assuming the data entered in the first text box is valid. If the data fails to meet the criteria for the field, the value of the variable will be changed to false, which will trigger the error message.

```
for (i = 0;  i < checkStr.length;  i++)
 { ch = checkStr.charAt(i);
    for (j = 0;  j < checkOK.length;  j++)
  if (ch == checkOK.charAt(j))
      break;
  if (j == checkOK.length)
  { allValid = false;
      break; }}
```

This section of the script is the part that does most of the work. The first line is a For-Next loop. The variables i and j are counters that are used to determine which character in the text string is being evaluated. What's happening is that the text string entered in the text form field is being *parsed,* being looked at one character at a time, and compared with the legal characters defined in the checkOK variable. At each step each counter is incremented by 1 (i++ and j++) until the last character in each string is reached (i < checkStr.length; and j < checkOK .length;). The variable checkStr.length holds the current position of each character that has been entered in the text box. The variable checkOK.length holds the current position of each character in the string of legal characters. When the first loop is started, the character at position i in the input string is compared with the character at position j in the string of legal characters. For the first iteration, each of these is 0 (zero), since that is the first position as far as the computer is concerned. (If the input string were ten characters long, the computer would count them as 0 to 9, not 1 to 10.)

The first character in the input string is loaded into the variable ch, then ch is compared with the first character in checkOK. If the characters don't match (if the character isn't A), j is incremented (j++) and the first character in the input string is compared with the second legal character (B). This continues, with j being incremented each time, until a match is found or the end of the string of legal characters is reached. If a match is found, the loop stops (break;) and i is incremented so that the next character in the input string can be checked. Then the process starts over, with j being reset to zero (j = 0;) so that the entire string of legal characters will be checked.

If no match is found, meaning the character entered in the form field is invalid, the process stops and the value of the variable `allValid` is changed to false. This happens if the end of the string of legal characters is reached without finding a match (`j == checkOK.length`). If the character is determined to be invalid, the steps shown next are executed.

```
if (!allValid)
 { alert("Please enter only letter characters in the \"Text Field\" field.");
   theForm.T1.focus();
   return (false);}
```

The first line in the preceding code tests the value of the variable `allValid`. This line can be read as "If `allValid` is not true, then…" (the exclamation mark, !, is the notation for the logical NOT operator). As you saw in the previous code, `allValid` is defined as true at the beginning of the script, and the value is changed only if an illegal character is encountered. The "then" is defined by the next line, which causes an alert message box to be displayed, as you saw earlier when you entered the number **11** in the numeric text box and clicked on Submit. This is a built-in function of JavaScript, so all you have to do is define the text that will appear in the alert (`"Please enter only letter…"`). The next line contains a very useful JavaScript function, the `focus()` method, written in the form `object.focus()`. What this does is make the form field where the error occurred the selected object. Once you click on OK in the alert message box, your browser will return you to the first form field so you can fix the error. The form field (`theForm.T1`) is the object. Finally, the script returns the value false (`return (false);`). This value can be used by the statement that called the function, or it can be ignored. In this case it will prevent the data from being sent to the form handler.

If all the characters input pass the test, then the first loop ends when the last character in the `checkStr` variable has been checked. The script then begins the test for the data entered in the second text box.

```
var checkOK = "0123456789-,";
var checkStr = theForm.T2.value;
var allValid = true;
```

```
var decPoints = 0;
var allNum = "";
```

Like the test for the first form field, this one also begins by defining the variables.
Then similar loops and tests are started with the new variables.

```
for (i = 0;  i < checkStr.length;  i++)
 { ch = checkStr.charAt(i);
   for (j = 0;  j < checkOK.length;  j++)
     if (ch == checkOK.charAt(j))
       break;
   if (j == checkOK.length)
   { allValid = false;
     break; }
   if (ch != ",")
     allNum += ch;
 }
 if (!allValid)
 {
   alert("Please enter only digit characters in the \"Numeric Field\"
field.");
   theForm.T2.focus();
   return (false);
 }
```

The next test determines if the number entered is within the range specified.

```
var chkVal = allNum;
 var prsVal = parseInt(allNum);
 if (chkVal != "" && !(prsVal >= "5" && prsVal <= "10"))
 { alert("Please enter a value greater than or equal to \"5\" and less than
or equal to \"10\" in the \"Numeric Field\" field.");
   theForm.T2.focus();
   return (false);
 }
```

The work in this section of code is done by the third line. After the second line converts the number string to an integer (`var prsVal = parseInt (allNum);`), three checks are performed: is it a null value (was a value entered), is it equal to or greater than 5, and is it equal to or less than 10. The second line is necessary because the program can interpret a number in two ways: as a text string and as an actual number. This line converts the text to a number so that it can be used for the tests that follow. The `!=` operator is the logical NOT EQUAL, so that the expression could be read as "is the value in the form field not equal to null." The `&&` operator is the logical AND. The third line could be read as "if the number is not equal to null and it's not equal to or greater than 5 and it's not equal to or less than 10, then display the alert error message." Focus would then be returned to the second form field box.

```
 return (true);
}
//--></script>
```

These last two lines clean up and end the script. If both values have passed all the tests, the value true is returned, and the data is sent to the form handler. The last line contains three elements: the `//` is the JavaScript comment tag, which is required at the end of the JavaScript script; the `-->` is the HTML closing comment tag; and finally the HTML `</script>` tag ends the script.

You'll be using the Form Validation page again with VBScript, so leave your current FrontPage and Internet Explorer windows open. You can close Notepad.

VBScript

VBScript is similar to JavaScript. It is based on Microsoft's Visual Basic programming language, which gives Visual Basic programmers a bit of a head start. The problem with VBScript is lack of support among browsers. Currently only Microsoft includes support for VBScript, and it's unlikely that Netscape will add support anytime soon, so your VBScript scripts will have a limited audience. VBScript could be your first choice if you are planning an ActiveX web site (such as an intranet) and so already are targeting users of Internet Explorer. Otherwise it's hard to see why you shouldn't simply go with JavaScript. There are enough differences in the languages to make learning both of them a burden.

You can see some of the differences in the two languages by changing the scripting language in the Advanced tab on the Web Settings dialog box. Do that now with these instructions:

1. In the FrontPage Explorer open the Tools menu and select Web Settings.

2. In the FrontPage Web Settings dialog box click on the Advanced tab, and then select VBScript from the Language drop-down menu. Click on Apply. The FrontPage Explorer dialog box shown next will be displayed.

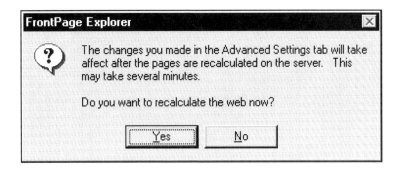

3. Click on Yes. After the Active web is recalculated, click on OK.

4. Reload the Form Validation page in your web browser, and select Source or Document Source from the View menu, depending on which browser you are using.

Listing 15-5 shows the same form validation script as Listing 15-4, except that it is now written in VBScript. The flow of the script is pretty much the same, but the syntax has changed. You should still be able to follow what the script is doing.

isting 15-5
isual Basic
validation

```
<script language="VBScript">
<!--
function FrontPage_Form1_onsubmit()
  Set theForm = document.FrontPage_Form1
  checkOK =
"ABCDEFGHIJKLMNOPQRSTUVWXYZabcdefghijklmnopqrstuvwxyzfŠŒšœŸÀÁÂÃÄÅÆÇÈÉÊËÌÍÎÏÐÑÒ
ÓÔÕÖØÙÚÛÜÝÞßàáâãäåæçèéêëìíîïoñòóôõöøùúûüÿÞ"
  checkStr = theForm.T1.value
  allValid = True
```

```
For i = 1 to len(checkStr)
  ch = Mid(checkStr, i, 1)
  If (InStr(checkOK, ch) = 0) Then
      allValid = False
      Exit For
  End If
Next
If (Not allValid) Then
  MsgBox "Please enter only letter characters in the ""Text Field"" field.
", 0, "Validation Error"
  theForm.T1.focus()
  FrontPage_Form1_onsubmit = False
  Exit Function
End If
checkOK = "0123456789-,"
checkStr = theForm.T2.value
allValid = True
decPoints = 0
allNum = ""
For i = 1 to len(checkStr)
  ch = Mid(checkStr, i, 1)
  If (InStr(checkOK, ch) = 0) Then
      allValid = False
      Exit For
  End If
  If (ch <> ",") Then
    allNum = allNum & ch
  End If
Next
If (Not allValid) Then
  MsgBox "Please enter only digit characters in the ""Numeric Field""
field.", 0, "Validation Error"
  theForm.T2.focus()
  FrontPage_Form1_onsubmit = False
  Exit Function
End If

If ((Not IsNumeric(allNum)) Or (decPoints > 1)) Then
  MsgBox "Please enter a valid number in the ""T2"" field. ", 0, "Validation
Error"
```

```
      theForm.T2.focus()
      FrontPage_Form1_onsubmit = False
      Exit Function
   End If


   prsVal = allNum
   If ((prsVal <> "") And (Not (prsVal >= 5 And prsVal <= 10))) Then
      MsgBox "Please enter a value greater than or equal to ""5"" and less than
or equal to ""10"" in the ""Numeric Field"" field.", 0, "Validation Error"
      theForm.T2.focus()
      FrontPage_Form1_onsubmit = False
      Exit Function
   End If
   FrontPage_Form1_onsubmit = True
End Function
-->
</script>
```

The FrontPage Script Wizard

The examples in the previous sections used scripts generated by the Text Field Validation dialog box. This is a good method if all you want the script to do is validate a form. Both languages are much more useful than that. Writing your own scripts is beyond the scope of this chapter, but you should be aware of the tools FrontPage provides for writing and editing scripts in either language.

The Script Wizard, shown in Figure 15-22, will make the job of writing scripts in FrontPage much easier than the traditional method using a text editor such as Notepad. Open the Script Wizard with these steps:

1. In the FrontPage Editor right-click on the first form field and then select Script Wizard. The Script Wizard dialog box will open.

In List view the upper-left pane displays the events that are contained in the script. The upper-right pane provides a list of actions that can be inserted into the script. At the bottom are the details for the action selected in the Select An Event pane.

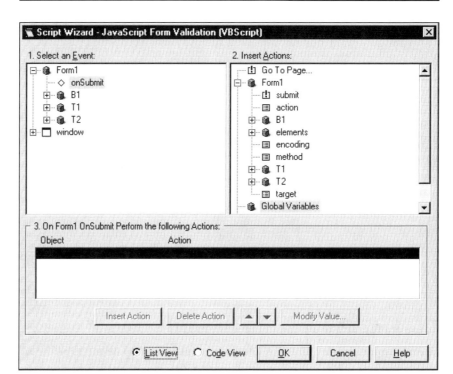

FrontPage
Script
Wizard in
List view

FIGURE 15-22

2. Click on the Code View option button. The Script Wizard dialog box will change, as shown in Figure 15-23. If you select an event, the bottom pane will show the actual code, which you can edit.

3. Close the Script Wizard.

Another tool that will make your life easier is the Microsoft Script Debugger for Internet Explorer 3.01.

The Microsoft Script Debugger

The Microsoft Script Debugger, shown in Figure 15-24, is an add-in for Internet Explorer 3.01 or later. With this tool you can debug scripts written in VBScript and JScript (Microsoft's own version of JavaScript). It allows you to directly edit your scripts and to use standard debugging tools such as *breakpoints*. Breakpoints are

```
Script Wizard - JavaScript Form Validation (VBScript)                    [X]

1. Select an Event:                        2. Insert Actions:
 □ ⊟ ● Form1                                 □ ⊟ ● Form1
        ◇   onSubmit                                 [↑] elementItem
    ⊞ ● B1                                           [↑] submit
    ⊞ ● T1                                           ▤ action
    ⊞ ● T2                                       ⊞ ● B1
 ⊞ □ window                                      ⊞ ● elements
                                                     ▤ encoding
                                                     ▤ method
                                                 ⊞ ● T1
                                                 ⊞ ● T2
                                                     ▤ target
                                                 ● Global Variables

<FORM NAME=Form1 OnSubmit=...>



                                    ○ List View   ● Code View    OK      Cancel    Help
```

FrontPage
Script
Wizard in
Code view

FIGURE 15-23

used to stop or pause a script at a specified point in its execution so that you can examine the state of the variables. You can also step through the script one statement at a time, which is handy for tracking down errors in the script.

You can download the Microsoft Script Debugger from Microsoft's web site (http://www.microsoft.com/workshop/prog/scriptie/), where you will also find examples for using it.

 NOTE: *At the time this was written the Microsoft Script Debugger had just been released as a beta product. Support for Java applets is also planned.*

Each of the technologies covered in this chapter easily could fill a book of its own, and, in fact, each does. The purpose here was to give you an overview of them so that you could make an informed decision about which technologies you want to add to your own webs. At a minimum, a working knowledge of JavaScript will be

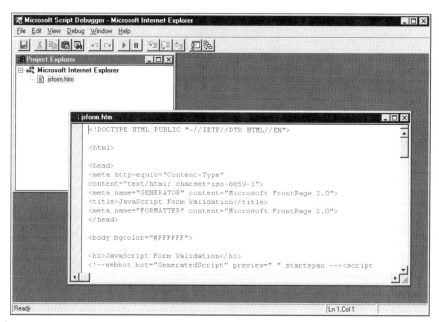

Microsoft
Script
Debugger

FIGURE 15-24

beneficial to web designers. Both Java applets and ActiveX controls require programming that is not for the faint of heart. If you already program in C++, the step up to these new languages will not be difficult. The Sun (http://www.sun.com), Netscape (http://home.netscape.com), and Microsoft (http://www.microsoft.com) web sites all have a variety of programming tools, documentation, and examples to get you started.

The coming months will see these technologies added to a growing number of web sites, as well as advances in the technologies themselves. If you want your webs to stand out in the crowd, these tools are part of your future.

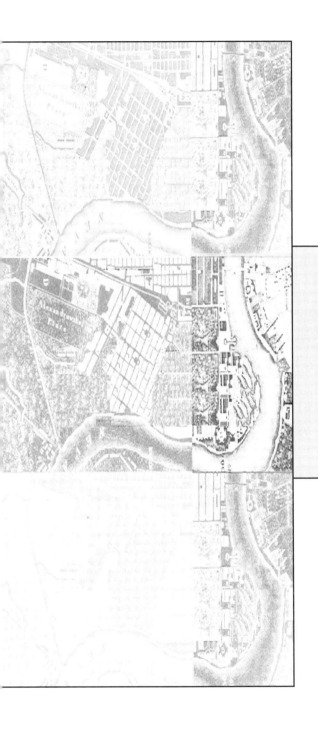

16

Setting Up an Intranet Web Site

Just as the Internet and the World Wide Web are an exploding phenomenon, so are LANs and intranets. As this growth increases, many expect the use of intranets to exceed that of the Internet. The competitive success of a company often depends on internal communication and the ability to quickly share information—two major benefits of intranets. But as with any new technology, there are and will be many opportunities to stumble. How a company implements an intranet may be even more important than the decision to do so.

This chapter will look at intranets—what they are, why they are needed, and how to set them up—both in terms of the hardware and software needed to make them function, and the content they should provide. You will learn about intranets, how they can help your business or organization, and how to create an intranet by using FrontPage. This chapter is meant to be an introduction to a subject on which numerous books will be written.

What Is an Intranet Site?

With the focus on the World Wide Web and connecting to the world over the Internet (a wide area network, or WAN), the fact that the same protocols and technology can be used over a local area network (LAN) can be overlooked. With a LAN and the Microsoft Personal Web Server or to a lesser extent the FrontPage Personal Web Server, you can create your own web to link computers in an office. With the Microsoft Internet Information Server, Windows NT 4.0 server, and a LAN or private WAN, you can set up an intranet within a large office, between buildings, or even among company sites around the world. FrontPage, with the various web servers, offers some real advantages over other means of implementing an intranet.

While the *Internet* is a network that provides access to information outside an organization, an *intranet* is a network that does exactly the same thing within an organization. An intranet may be as simple as two computers networked in a home office, or as complex as a network linking the offices of a global corporation. In the latter case, an intranet could link the computers within the organization, while the Internet could be used to connect the various intranets (or private lines could be used).

Networking computers to share information is, of course, not a new concept. Networked computers can be found in virtually every medium-to-large business and in many smaller ones. When networked, the resources on any computer can be shared by any other computer on the network. With Windows 95, the addition of a network interface card can turn any PC into either a network server or a workstation. For larger networks, specialized software, such Novell's NetWare, has traditionally been required to effectively allow computers to share information.

Classical networking involves the sharing of files and some hardware devices such as printers. More recently it has included the use of e-mail. An intranet with FrontPage and the technology of the Web significantly enhances the functionality of a LAN or a corporate WAN by adding the ability to read and interact with a large set of documents that are easily created and kept up-to-date. Almost as important is the fact that many of these documents already exist as word processing, spreadsheet, and database files. With FrontPage they can be easily converted to interactive web pages.

TIP: *Existing word processing, spreadsheet, and database files can be easily converted for use on an intranet by importing them into FrontPage. In the classic example of the company procedures manuals, the web's ready availability, search tools, and easy maintenance and updating are powerful incentives to have an intranet.*

As was explained in Chapter 1, the Internet and the World Wide Web are built upon three software technologies:

- **TCP/IP** (Transfer Control Protocol/Internet Protocol), which is the underlying technology of the Internet for the exchange of information and the identification of parts of the network

- **HTTP** (HyperText Transfer Protocol), which handles the actual transmission of Web documents

- **HTML** (HyperText Markup Language), which is the programming language of the Web

These same technologies are used to implement an intranet, and they must be added to the networking software that is already in place. HTTP and HTML are used only by the web server and the browser, and do not affect the classical networking software. TCP/IP, on the other hand, directly competes with classical networking

protocols such as IPX/SPX or NetBEUI on Intel-based computers. TCP/IP can be used instead of or in addition to other protocols, and setting it up can be a major pitfall. The objective, of course, is to have the protocols operate in harmony to perform all of the necessary networking functions.

One of the problem areas with classical networking was linking different types of computers, such as PCs or Macintosh, Hewlett-Packard, or UNIX computers. Each operating system (or platform) requires its own specialized software, which isn't always compatible between systems. An intranet built with TCP/IP, HTTP, and HTML doesn't have the compatibility problems of other networking systems. The early support of the federal government ensured the widespread adoption of TCP/IP as a network protocol, and HTTP servers and HTML browsers are available for virtually every platform. For organizations that have acquired a variety of computer hardware, creating an intranet has never been easier. While a simple file-sharing network allows files to be accessed between computers, the three Internet technologies allow much greater interactivity by use of hypertext links, searches, and forms. Some of these features are available with products such as NetWare, but at greater cost and complexity. A FrontPage intranet presents a middle course of power and economy.

NOTE: *For an example of an intranet that uses Microsoft's Office family, visit the Volcano Coffee Company at http://www.microsoft.com/msoffice/ intranet/volcano/index.htm shown in Figure 16-1.*

Why Have an Intranet?

The reasons for an intranet are as varied as the organizations creating it, but the common purposes are to communicate with and involve the members of the organization to improve their effectiveness and collaboration. The communication aspect is obvious. The intranet can replace newsletters, reports, lists of job openings, manuals, procedures, employee guidelines, meeting schedules, details of benefit plans, and lunch menus. Almost anything that is written or graphic and has an

Microsoft's demonstration intranet site

FIGURE 16-1

audience of more than a couple of people is a candidate for the intranet. The benefits of using the intranet are substantial:

- An intranet document can be put up when convenient for the creator, and read when convenient for the reader.

- Readers can keep and conveniently file an intranet document, or they can just read it and discard it, knowing the source document will be there for some time.

■ The documents can be simple text or full multimedia. By including multimedia, documents can be made more inviting to open and read.

■ The communication can be one-way, from the creator to the reader, or it can include forms and discussion groups to let the reader communicate back to the creator.

■ The documents can be easily indexed and searched, making the information they contain easier to find and use.

■ The cost of printing, distributing, and maintaining manuals, procedures, and guidelines is reduced, as are some fax and delivery expenses.

■ Information can be shared over many different computers and work-stations, not just PCs. The Internet protocols and technology have been implemented on most computers, giving them the ability to attach to an intranet.

One of the biggest benefits, though, and the second major reason for using an intranet, is that it facilitates the involvement of more members of the organization in the organization's activities. The reasoning is that if you make it easier to locate, read, excerpt, file, and dispose of documents, more people will use them and acquire the knowledge they contain. If you make it easier to comment on and participate in the creation of something that can be put on an intranet, more people will. If you provide easy access and use of indexing and search capabilities, more archival information will be directly sought by end users. If you add multimedia and color graphics and thereby make a document more fun and interesting, more people will read it. If you allow many different types of computers and workstations to connect to an intranet, more people will be able to participate.

Simply stated, an intranet greatly facilitates the dissemination of information within an organization, and the communication among and the involvement of its members.

What to Put on an Intranet

The decision on what to put on an intranet is one of the most difficult; much depends on the character and philosophy of the organization. How open does your organization want to be, and how much security do you need? What does the company want to do with their intranet? Disseminating relatively simple information, such as newsletters, administrative manuals and procedures, and lunch menus, is not a problem. On the other hand, disseminating financial information, marketing reports, and corporate plans may well be more difficult.

The answers can be found beginning at the top of a company. Here a policy needs to be set on how open the company wants to be with its employees. This broad policy then needs to be translated into specific examples of documents in each of the major areas of the company (marketing, production, finance, and so on) that are allowed on the intranet and those that are not. It is very easy to gloss over this issue in the crush of all the other issues, but unless this is clearly thought through and then delineated, problems can occur.

Once the policy is established, specific documents and their priority have to be identified. This is best done by a committee of users and providers. The users can set out their needs and desires, and the providers can respond with their ability and willingness to satisfy the requests. Either group alone is liable to create an intranet that is not as effective as it might be.

With the committee constituted, they should look at all the documents the company produces that fit within the policy guidelines. For each document, the following questions should be answered:

- How wide an audience does it have?

- How often is it produced, and is that schedule supportable on the intranet?

- Do the layout and graphics lend themselves to the document being easily placed on the intranet?

- Does the addition of intranet features such as searching, forms, and hyperlinks make it a particularly attractive candidate?

- Are there any pressing needs to get the document up on the intranet?

- Is the document going to be revised soon?

Based on the answers to these questions, a prioritized list of documents to go on the intranet should be drawn up, and the documents created and placed on the intranet in their designated order. The review process should be repeated periodically to confirm that the documents on the intranet should stay there and to determine what new documents should be added.

Building a FrontPage Intranet

Building a FrontPage intranet is fairly simple. The first requirement is that you have a local area network (LAN) that supports the TCP/IP protocol. The specifics of setting up such a network are beyond the scope of this book. Two highly recommended sources of information on setting up LANs and networking are Tom Sheldon's *LAN Times Encyclopedia of Networking* and *The Windows NT Web Server Handbook*, which contains an excellent section on intranets (both published by Osborne/McGraw-Hill).

Once your LAN is functioning, you can use FrontPage as the basis for an intranet as small as two computers in the same office, or use it to link a number of computers in several remote locations. The limits on growth for your intranet will be determined by the number of users and the amount of traffic on the LAN. For several computers in an office, you do not need a dedicated server. In other words, the computer running Microsoft or FrontPage Personal Web Server can still be used for other tasks. As the number of users and the network traffic grow, a computer will need to be dedicated to running the FrontPage Personal Web Server. At that point you may also want to switch from Windows 95 to Windows NT for your server operating system.

For larger intranets you should consider using Microsoft's Internet Information Server (IIS) as your HTTP server software. IIS is more powerful than either the Microsoft Personal Web Server or the FrontPage Personal Web Server and is an integral part of Windows NT 4.0. FrontPage and the FrontPage IIS Server Extensions are completely compatible with Windows NT 4.0. *The Windows NT Web Server Handbook* (Osborne/McGraw-Hill, 1996) mentioned previously is an excellent reference for creating an NT and Internet Information Server intranet or Internet Web server.

Installing TCP/IP on Your Network

The first step in building a FrontPage intranet on your local area network is to install the TCP/IP protocol. If you have a connection to the Internet, either through a dial-up or network connection, TCP/IP will already be installed and configured on your computer. If you need to install TCP/IP, follow these steps:

NOTE: *If you are using a dial-up connection for the Internet, you may still need to install TCP/IP for your LAN, so you should go through the next set of steps just to check it out.*

1. Open the Start menu, click on Settings, and then select Control Panel.

Network

2. When the Control Panel opens, double-click on the Network icon.

3. In the Network dialog box select the Configuration tab if it's not already selected. Your Network dialog box should appear similar to Figure 16-2.

16

In Figure 16-2 the NetBEUI protocol is bound to both the network interface card and the Dial-Up Adapter (modem). Multiple protocols can be bound to these cards, so TCP/IP can be added without removing any existing protocols.

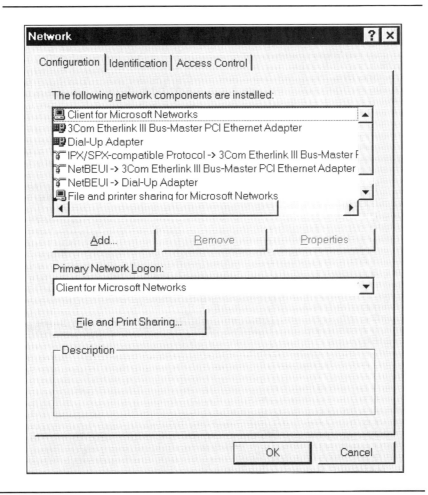

Network dialog box before installing TCP/IP

FIGURE 16-2

4. Click on Add. In the Select Network Component Type dialog box select Protocol and click on Add.

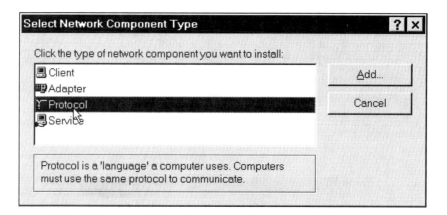

5. In the Select Network Protocol dialog box select Microsoft from the Manufacturers list box, and then select TCP/IP from the Network Protocols list box, as shown in Figure 16-3. Click on OK.

Selecting the TCP/IP network protocol

FIGURE 16-3

In a moment the Network dialog box will be redisplayed, showing that the TCP/IP protocol has been installed and bound to your installed adapters, as you can see in Figure 16-4.

Configuring TCP/IP

You need to configure the TCP/IP protocol for each device it is bound to. For an intranet, the device is your network interface card. For a dial-up connection

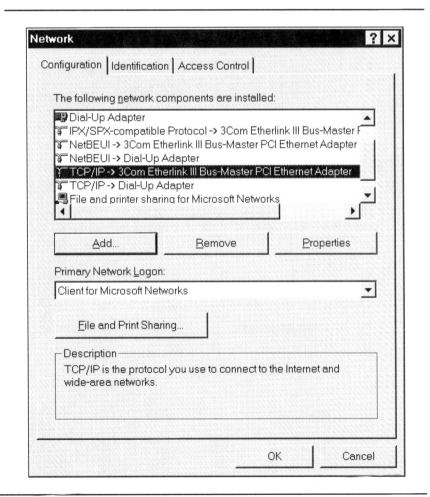

TCP/IP installed on both the network and dial-up adapters

FIGURE 16-4

to the Internet, the device is the dial-up adapter. Configure your network card with these instructions:

1. In the Network dialog box, select the TCP/IP binding to your network card (in Figure 16-4 this is the line that reads "TCP/->3Com Etherlink III," where "3Com Etherlink III" is my network card—yours will probably be different) and click on Properties. Your TCP/IP Properties dialog box will open, as shown in Figure 16-5.

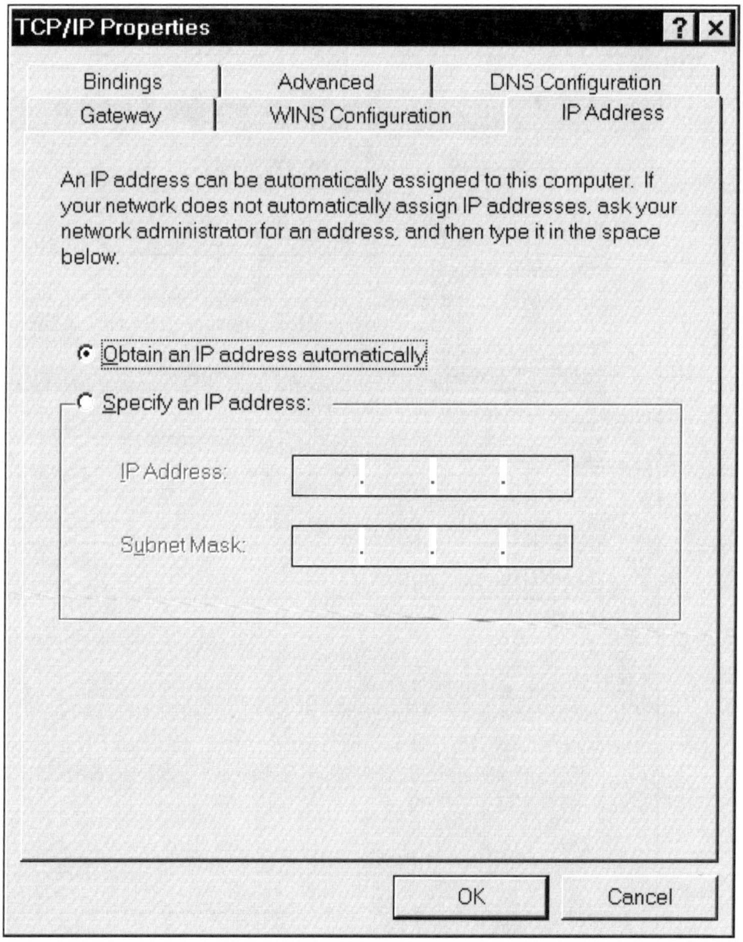

TCP/IP Properties   [?] [X]

Bindings	Advanced	DNS Configuration
Gateway	WINS Configuration	IP Address

An IP address can be automatically assigned to this computer. If your network does not automatically assign IP addresses, ask your network administrator for an address, and then type it in the space below.

   (•) Obtain an IP address automatically

   ( ) Specify an IP address:

      IP Address: [. . .]

      Subnet Mask: [. . .]

         [OK]   [Cancel]

TCP/IP
Properties
dialog box

FIGURE 16-5

2. In the TCP/IP Properties dialog box select the IP Address tab, if it's not already selected.

   The IP (Internet Protocol) address is a group of four numbers that uniquely identify your computer on a TCP/IP network. For a dial-up connection to the Internet, your IP address will usually be assigned automatically by the server, as might be the case with large intranets using dedicated web servers. For small intranets using the Microsoft or FrontPage Personal Web Server, you need to specify an IP address. You should consult your network administrator to learn what IP address you should use. However, on a small TCP/IP network, you can basically make up your own number—10.0.0.1, for example. You could then increment the number for each computer—10.0.0.2 for the next machine, and so on. As long as your computer does not try to use your IP addresses on the Internet (which it won't, if you use the dial-up adapter to connect to the Internet), you will not have a problem. The IP addresses you use for your network card will not affect your settings for your dial-up adapter.

   An IP address is like a phone number. If you set up your own small phone system, you can use any phone numbers you want. But if you then connect your phone system to the outside world, you may have to use the phone numbers assigned by the outside authority. (Three series of numbers, though, 10.0.0.0 through 10.255.255.255, 172.16.0.0 through 172.31.255.255, and 192.168.0.1 through 192.168.255.255, are not supposed to be used on the Internet.)

NOTE: *Do not use an IP address beginning with* 127 *(for example,* 127.0.0.1*), as this is reserved as a localhost, or loopback, address.*

3. Click on Specify An IP Address, click on the left of the IP Address text box, and type your IP address. If any number is fewer than three digits, you'll need to press RIGHT ARROW to move to the next block of numbers. If you don't have a normally assigned IP address, use the 10.0.0.n (n is a number between 1 and 255) set of numbers with 10.0.0.1 being the first. (Type **10**, press RIGHT ARROW, type **0**, press RIGHT ARROW, type **0**, press RIGHT ARROW, and type **1** to get the address shown next.)

> ○ O̲btain an IP address automatically
>
> ● S̲pecify an IP address:
>
>   I̲P Address: **10** . **0** . **0** . **1**|
>
>   S̲ubnet Mask: . . .

4. Click on the left end of the Subnet Mask text box and type **2552552550**. This is the default subnet mask, applicable in almost all circumstances; in most instances it is automatically entered for you. I'm suggesting that you enter it here to cover the few instances where it will hang you up if it is missing.

5. Select the Bindings tab. Client For Microsoft Networks should be selected, and File And Printer Sharing For Microsoft Networks should be selected, as you can see in Figure 16-6. Click on them if they are not.

6. Click on OK twice.

After changing your network settings, you must restart your computer for the changes to take effect. Make sure you save any open documents before restarting.

CAUTION: *For TCP/IP on your dial-up adapter, you do not want to have File And Printer Sharing selected. This is for security. If you are connected to the Internet by use of your dial-up connection, it is possible (although unlikely) for others on the Internet to access your shared resources over the TCP/IP connection. You can still share resources with others on your network by using your LAN adapter.*

Using Your FrontPage Intranet

Once TCP/IP is configured properly on your network, accessing your FrontPage webs from any computer on the network is a simple process. First make sure the

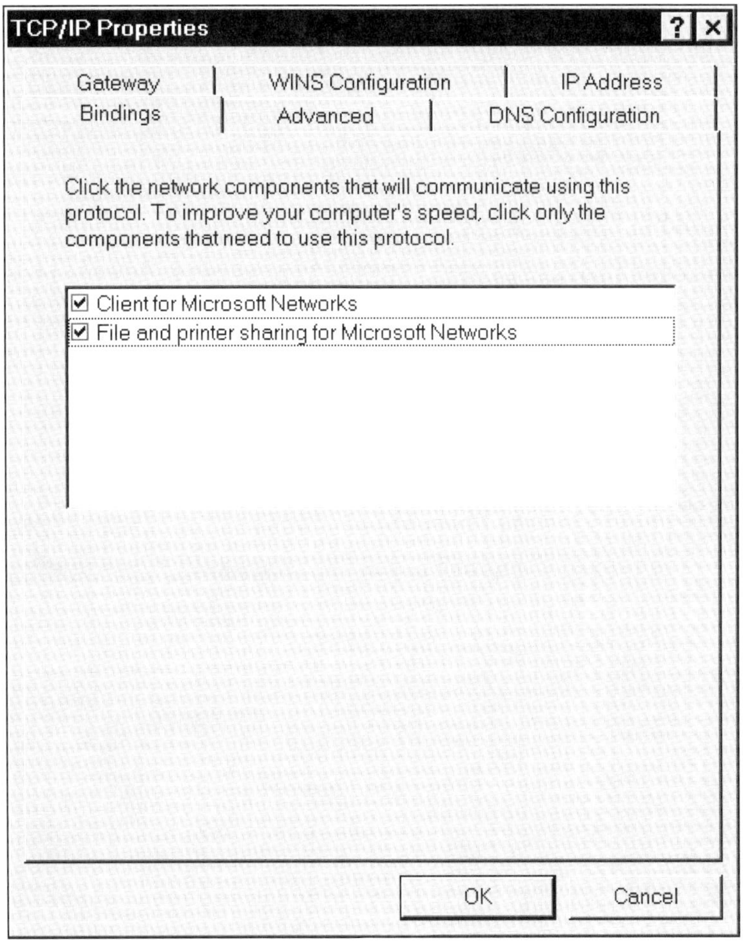

TCP/IP Properties

| Gateway | WINS Configuration | IP Address |
| Bindings | Advanced | DNS Configuration |

Click the network components that will communicate using this protocol. To improve your computer's speed, click only the components that need to use this protocol.

- ☑ Client for Microsoft Networks
- ☑ File and printer sharing for Microsoft Networks

OK   Cancel

Selecting
the
bindings
for TCP/IP

FIGURE 16-6

Microsoft or FrontPage Personal Web Server is running on the computer that will be the server. Then start your web browser on one of the other computers on the network. To access a web, use the URL http://*computername*/*webname* where *computername* is the computer's name running the Microsoft or FrontPage Personal Web Server, and *webname* is the name of the web you want to open.

For example, I have two networked computers named "Marty" and "Marty2" using Windows 95 and Ethernet cards. Here are the steps I went through to bring up a FrontPage intranet:

1. Set up the TCP/IP protocol bound to the LAN adapters on both computers, as described earlier.

2. Restart both computers.

3. Make sure the Microsoft Personal Web Server is running on Marty.

4. Start a browser on Marty2, enter the address **marty/fantasytravel/**, and press ENTER. My Fantasy Travel Home page appears as shown in Figure 16-7.

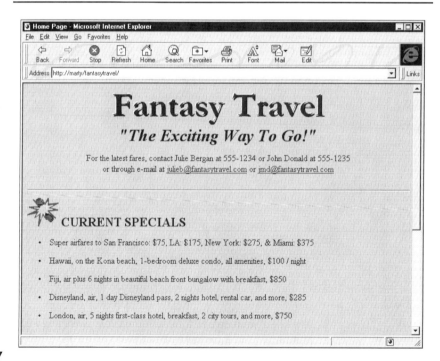

Page received on an intranet

FIGURE 16-7

If your intranet doesn't immediately come up the first time you try, take heart, mine didn't either. Here is a list of troubleshooting questions:

- Does your network otherwise function normally between the two computers you are trying to use with an intranet? If not, you must solve your networking problems before trying to use an intranet. See your network administrator or other technical network reference.

- Has TCP/IP been successfully installed and bound to your LAN adapter (not just to your dial-up adapter)? Reopen your Network control panel to check this.

- Did you restart both computers after installing TCP/IP?

- Is either the Microsoft Personal Web Server or the FrontPage Personal Web Server loaded on the machine where the webs are located? When you address this machine from the second machine, and if you are using the FrontPage Personal Web Server, you should see it in the taskbar momentarily going from "IDLE" to "BUSY." With the Microsoft Personal Web Server you won't see anything on the screen, but your hard disk light will blink.

- Have you entered the correct server name and web name in your browser? You can determine the server name and how well your TCP/IP network is running by loading the program Tcptest.exe in the C:\Program File\ Microsoft FrontPage\bin directory. Click on Start Test, and it will respond with the "Host name," as shown next, which is the server name to use in the address. If you do not get a response similar to that shown here (obviously, your server will be named differently and your IP address may be different), then your TCP/IP network is not functioning properly.

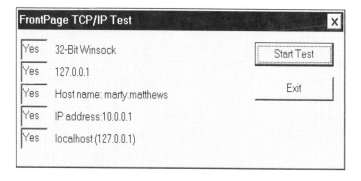

If you take a couple of minutes to make sure that each of the preceding questions is answered in the affirmative, your intranet will almost surely work. I made several errors, including forgetting to restart one of the computers and not spelling the web name correctly.

Putting Information on Your Intranet

In Chapter 11 you read about importing existing, or *legacy* files into FrontPage to create webs both on the Internet and on your intranet with examples of word processing, spreadsheet, and presentation files being used. In Chapter 13 you saw how to access database files in a FrontPage-created web. With the techniques in these chapters, just about all corporate information can be used on an intranet site. Once you have imported the raw material from existing files, you can add any of the interactive features that are available with FrontPage. Among these are

- **Table of Contents bot** to quickly build an index of the material that is brought in

- **Search bot** to add the capability to search the material

- **Include bot** to place headers and footers on each page with navbars, time stamps, and mailto addresses

- **Forms** to solicit responses from the reader

- **Discussion web** associated with the legacy-derived web to promote a discussion about the contents of the legacy web

Most legacy material does not contain much graphics or any multimedia. Consider augmenting your legacy-derived webs with additional graphics and multimedia to make them more interesting to read and/or use.

One obvious question is: given that all the bots, graphics, and multimedia are great, but I don't have time for all that, can I quickly put my legacy documents on the company intranet and have them usable? The answer is yes—most definitely yes if they have a consistently applied style. Look at the few steps it takes to put part of the Chapter 5 manuscript from this book on a web, and the neat results:

1. From the FrontPage Getting Started dialog box, click on With The Import Wizard, and then on OK. Name the web **FrontPageChapter5** and click on OK. The Import Web Wizard dialog box will open.

2. Select the source directory containing the files you want to import and click on Next. Select the files in the directory that you *don't* want and click on Exclude (see next illustration). Click on Next and then on Finish. Your web is created!

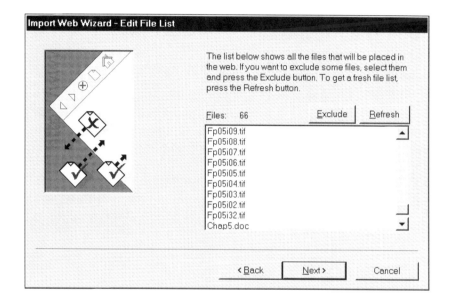

3. Open your browser, type **//servername/FrontPageChapter5/** and you will get a list of files associated with the web, since we didn't specify a Default.htm file ("Directory Browsing Allowed" in the WWW Administrator-Directory page of the Web server administrator).

4. Click on the legacy document name (Chap5.doc in my case), and voilà! your document appears as you can see in Figure 16-8. (If you don't have the index on the side, open the View menu and choose Online Layout, if you are using the Internet Explorer.)

All of your headings are automatically made into a table of contents with hyperlinks to the actual headings in the document, so you have a built-in navigation system without doing anything.

Web Page Version Control with SourceSafe

If you have several or especially if you have many people working on creating material for your web site, you'll need a way to control the various versions of the many pages

Web Publishing with Microsoft FrontPage 97

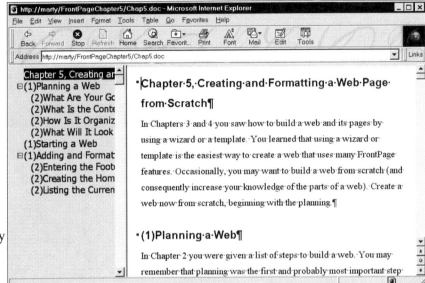

Web
document
with
automatically
created
table of
contents

FIGURE 16-8

you'll end up with. FrontPage 97 has provided help in this area by incorporating links between Microsoft SourceSafe and the FrontPage Server Extensions.

Microsoft SourceSafe is a separate product that you must purchase. It allows you to track various versions with a project orientation, while providing tools for storing, accessing, and organizing files, and mediating among developers. The project orientation allows the system, not the people, to keep track of the relationship between files.

Use of SourceSafe with FrontPage requires that SourceSafe be installed on the server where the FrontPage Server Extensions and the production webs that are in use are kept. If you have SourceSafe installed this way, when you place a web on the server, you'll be asked if you want to make the web a SourceSafe project. If so, when you recalculate the links, the files will be checked into SourceSafe. You can then use SourceSafe from a client workstation using the FrontPage Explorer through three commands in the Edit or context (by right-clicking on the file) menus:

- **Check Out** to edit a file

- **Check In** to return a file that has been edited and have it update SourceSafe accordingly

- **Undo Check Out** to return a file that has not been changed

When you are the first or only person to check out a file, a check mark will appear beside the file name in the FrontPage Explorer. When someone else has checked out a file you are looking at, it will have a padlock beside the name. If you open the FrontPage Editor with a file that someone else has checked out, you'll see "(Read Only)" in the title bar, and you'll be unable to edit the file. If you open the FrontPage Editor with a file that you have not checked out (and no one else has either), you'll see "(Not Checked Out)" in the title bar. In this latter case you can still make changes to the file, but when you go to save the file, FrontPage will check to see if the file has changed since you opened it. If the file has not changed, FrontPage will automatically check it out and back in again in SourceSafe. If the file has been modified, then you will be asked if you want to overwrite the changes.

In some instances, changes you make to a page you have checked out effect pages that others have checked out. These changes fall into two categories: incidental changes and substantive changes. Incidental changes, for example, are like changing an included page used as a header on other pages. In this case FrontPage is not concerned about the pages on which the header is included, and the pages are not checked to see if they are being edited. Substantive changes, like deleting or moving a page referenced by other pages that are checked out, will not be allowed, and an error message will tell you why.

SourceSafe is a powerful tool to help maintain an intranet where multiple people are working on it. It does assume, though, that you are using a separate server with the FrontPage extensions on it.

Security and Firewalls

Anytime you share resources over a network, the possibility exists that someone may access your files without your permission. The risk is greater when one or more computers on an intranet are also connected to the Internet. There are several things you can do to protect yourself and your files. One of the simplest, as mentioned previously, is to disable file and printer sharing for TCP/IP on your dial-up adapter. You can still share files over your LAN, but you have closed access to everyone on the Internet coming in through TCP/IP and your dial-up adapter.

Greater security can be achieved through the use of a firewall and possibly a proxy server as was discussed in Chapter 14. A firewall is a computer that controls the flow of data between an intranet and the Internet by packet filtering.

Packet filtering passes or rejects IP packets based on the IP address that sent the packet. This allows you to configure your firewall to allow access from specific computers outside your intranet that you trust. This method isn't as secure as a proxy server because it's possible for someone to duplicate a trusted IP address.

Use of a proxy server means that every request and response must be examined by the proxy server. This can slow the response of your network, but the proxy server can also cache frequently requested information, thus speeding some responses. If the source of a request is a computer without permission to access your intranet, the proxy server will reject it.

Besides Chapter 14, check out Tom Sheldon's *The Windows NT Security Handbook*, published by Osborne/McGraw-Hill on the subject of intranet security and how to implement it. If your intranet will be accessible to the outside world, you will need to take measures to protect your data. This and the books mentioned earlier in this chapter can provide a good place to start.

Publishing and Promoting Webs on the Internet

B y now in this book, you have created your own webs with FrontPage and possibly have put them on your intranet. Next you can make your efforts available to the millions of people worldwide who have access to the Internet. You do this by first publishing your web on a web server, a computer that is connected to the Internet. Then you promote your web site by using web-based and traditional advertising.

Publishing Your Web Pages

Unless you have your own server connected to the Internet, you will need to find an Internet service provider (ISP) who will rent you space on their web server for your web. Also, to get the full functionality of your web, your ISP should support the FrontPage Server Extensions.

Providing access to the Internet has become a very competitive field, and you should be able to find several ISPs in your area that you can choose from. You can find a local ISP by asking others, by looking in your regional newspapers and other periodicals, and even by looking in a recent phone book. You can also use the Internet. You can begin by using one of the many search engines available, such as AltaVista (http://www.altavista.digital.com). Simply enter a search criterion such as "internet access providers [your state]" (include the quotes). Another Internet site with a list of providers is Yahoo! (http://www.yahoo.com). Finally, Microsoft posts a list of ISPs with FrontPage Server Extensions at http://www.microsoft.com/frontpage/. With a little searching, you should be able to locate several ISPs in your area. It is unnecessary that your ISP be located close to you. Most of your transactions will occur over the Internet, and there are a number of national providers, such as Netcom (http://www.netcom.com) or AT&T's Easy World Wide Web Services (http://www.att.com), both of whom offer the FrontPage Server Extensions as part of their service.

Generally, an ISP will provide dialup access to the Internet, as well as hard disk storage for webs. Many offer space for a personal (noncommercial) web as part of their basic package. The amount of hard disk space allowed for a personal web site varies. In many areas this basic service costs $20 to $30 a month with unlimited Internet access. (These rates are for 14.4-Kbps or 28.8-Kbps modems; rates for ISDN and cable modems are higher.)

Rates for commercial web sites can vary greatly—from $30 to several hundred dollars a month—depending on the ISP, the amount of hard disk storage, and the bandwidth used. *Bandwidth* is the amount of data that is transferred from your web site over the ISP's Internet connection. For example, if your web is 1 megabyte (MB) in size and it was accessed 100 times in the course of a month, you would have used 100MB of bandwidth (or transfer bandwidth) in that month.

Another point to consider is whether you want to have your own domain name. Without your own domain name, your web's URL would begin with the ISP's domain name, such as http://www.*ispname*.com/*yourname*. With your own domain, your URL would be http://www.*yourname*.com. Your own domain is unnecessary for a personal web site, but should be seriously considered for a commercial web. Your ISP can help you set up a domain name for your web site. Alternatively, you can contact InterNIC at http://www.internic.net, and with some information from your ISP and $100, you can register your own domain name. InterNIC has complete instructions at their site. Also, at the InterNIC site you can search for existing domain names to make sure yours is unique.

In deciding upon an ISP, you should be more concerned about the quality of the service than the price. The Internet is a little chaotic—new technologies (particularly in data transmission) are coming into play, and finding people who truly understand and can use these technologies is not always easy. Software doesn't always work as advertised, and keeping everything flowing smoothly sometimes requires a little "spit and baling wire." When evaluating an ISP, look at the design and features of their own web site, and contact others who have their webs on the ISP's server. Choosing the cheapest ISP could be an expensive decision in the long run if they don't provide the services you need, such as the FrontPage Server Extensions.

FrontPage Server Extensions

HTML used to be written by hand, by use of text editors such as Windows Notepad. When you wanted to include a form for the user to fill out, you had to make sure there was an application running on the server that would implement this. There were a number of applications that could do this, so you needed to know the syntax required by the particular application running on your server. If your web page was transferred to another server running a different application, your HTML would probably have to be modified.

With FrontPage those days are over. A great deal of the functionality and usefulness of FrontPage comes from the fact that it includes a standard set of server extensions that can run on virtually any HTTP server platform with any major server

software. This means your FrontPage-created web can be placed on any web server running the FrontPage Server Extensions and will function correctly.

As a content creator, you simply need to know that the FrontPage Server Extensions are installed on your ISP's web server. (When you installed FrontPage on your local computer, the server extensions for the Microsoft Personal Web Server or FrontPage Personal Web Server were also installed.) Then you are assured that any WebBots, forms, or discussion groups you've included in your web will function on your ISP's server.

TIP: *Microsoft maintains a list of ISPs who support the FrontPage Server Extensions at http://www.microsoft.com/frontpage/. Given the vast improvement in creating web content enabled by FrontPage, you should expect this list to grow considerably.*

Installing the FrontPage Server Extensions

If you are maintaining your own web server (as distinct from your FrontPage Personal Web Server), you need to install the FrontPage Server Extensions on it. Alternatively, you may have to work with your ISP to install the FrontPage Server Extensions on their server. (For a variety of reasons, including security, ISPs can be reluctant to install every piece of software a client suggests.) Therefore, the next several paragraphs provide some of the reasoning behind the FrontPage Server Extensions, and an overview of the installation process.

For the most part, the FrontPage Server Extensions use the standard common gateway interface (CGI) found on all web servers. The CGI provides a standard protocol for the transfer and processing of data between a client (a web browser, for example) and a server. On an Internet Information Server, the server extensions are implemented as dynamic link libraries (DLLs). This allows the server extensions to take up less room and to execute faster. In any case, data is transferred to the FrontPage Server Extensions from the web server software. The server extensions then process the data and hand back the output to the server software. For example, in the case of a text search, the search criteria would be passed from the HTTP server to the appropriate FrontPage Server Extension. The database would then be searched using the specified criteria, and the results of the search handed back to the HTTP server. It would then be formatted with the specified HTML and sent back to the client (web browser) that initiated the search.

Adding the FrontPage Server Extensions to an existing web server is a relatively simple process. The first step is to get a copy of the FrontPage Server Extensions for your web server. These are available at no charge from Microsoft's web site (http://www.microsoft.com/frontpage/softlib/fp_97_extensions.htm).

Microsoft currently provides FrontPage Server Extensions 97 (2.0) for the hardware, operating system, and web servers shown in Table 17-1.

As you can see, the FrontPage Server Extensions are available for most web server platforms and HTTP server software.

Installation of the FrontPage Server Extensions varies depending on the platform, but complete instructions are included with the server extension files from Microsoft and are relatively simple. The only time FrontPage has to be installed on the web server running the server extensions is when you're using Windows NT and Microsoft Internet Information Server.

The primary issue with an ISP about installing the FrontPage Server Extensions (besides being one more thing to learn) will be security. When someone accesses a web page on a server, he or she is given certain permissions. Normally these are limited to reading data on the server. The user is usually not allowed to write to the server's hard disk or to change any of the files on the server outside of the user's personal directory. The reason is obvious: if a user is allowed to place a file on a server, that file, through malicious intent or simple ignorance, could wreak havoc on the server. Network administrators protect their servers by restricting the type of access users are allowed (and some people make a hobby of beating the administrator's best efforts).

The FrontPage Server Extensions, like virtually every CGI application and script, need to allow the user to write to a file or directory on the server. The server's security is maintained by cordoning-off these specific areas. Depending on the operating system and HTTP server software, the FrontPage Server Extensions generally require the same permissions as other CGI applications and do not represent an increased security risk.

The last word may simply be that FrontPage fills a tremendous gap in the quality of tools available for creating web content. If you remember the days of creating HTML in a text editor, you know how much more efficiently your time is used with FrontPage (if you don't remember, fire up Notepad and review Chapter 12).

It is possible to re-create the interactive functions of your web on a web server that is not using the FrontPage Server Extensions. Rather than the integrated set of functions that FrontPage Server Extensions provides, the web server may have a number of individual applications and scripts that provide the same functions. It may be, however, that if your ISP can't be convinced to install the FrontPage Server Extensions, you need to find another ISP.

Hardware Used	Operating System Used	Web Server Used
Alpha or PowerPC	Windows NT 4.0 Server	Microsoft Internet Information Server 2.0
Alpha or PowerPC	Window NT 4.0 Workstation	Microsoft Peer Web Services
Intel x86	Windows 95 Windows NT 4.0 Workstation	Microsoft Personal Web Server FrontPage Personal Web Server Netscape FastTrack 2.0 O'Reilly & Associates WebSite
Intel x86	Windows NT 4.0 Server	Microsoft Internet Information Server 2.0 Microsoft Personal Web Server FrontPage Personal Web Server Netscape Commerce Server 1.12 Netscape Communications Server 1.12 Netscape Enterprise 2.0 Netscape FastTrack 2.0 O'Reilly & Associates WebSite
Digital Alpha	Digital UNIX 3.2c, 4.0	Apache 1.5.5, 1.1.1
Intel x86	UNIX-BSD/OS 2.1 or Linux 3.0.3 (Red Hat)	CERN 3.0 NCSA 1.5a, 1.5.2 (not 1.5.1)
HP (PA-RISC)	HP/UX 9.03, 10.01	Netscape Commerce Server 1.12
Silicon Graphics	IRIX 5.3, 6.2 Solaris 2.4, 2.5	Netscape Communications Server 1.12
Sun (SPARC)	or SunOS 4.1.3, 4.1.4	Netscape Enterprise 2.0 Netscape FastTrack 2.0

FrontPage Server Extensions Availability

TABLE 17-1

Posting to a Host with FrontPage Server Extensions

Once your FrontPage web is completed and tested on your Microsoft or FrontPage Personal Web Server, it's ready for the Big Time: the World Wide Web. Hopefully your ISP has the FrontPage Server Extensions installed and has created a directory for your web on the web server. (Posting your web to a server without the FrontPage Server Extensions is covered in the next section.)

To post a FrontPage web to a server with FrontPage Server Extensions, you must first have permission to write files to the server. Your webmaster or server administrator will be able to assign the proper permission to your account. Your webmaster or administrator may have you post your web to a temporary directory as an additional security measure. Once you have the proper permissions and location on the server for your web, you would use these steps to post your web:

1. Start the FrontPage Explorer if necessary.

2. If you use a dialup account to access the Internet, activate your Internet connection.

3. In the FrontPage Explorer open the web you will place on the web server.

4. Open the File menu and select Publish FrontPage Web. The Publish FrontPage Web dialog box will be displayed, as shown here:

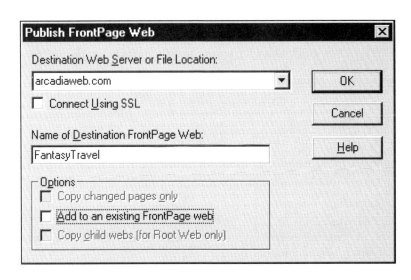

5. Select or type in the name of the destination server in the Destination Web Server or File Location drop-down menu.

6. The current name for the web is displayed in the Name Of Destination FrontPage Web text box. If you want to use a different name for the web, type it there.

7. If you are adding to or replacing pages in an existing web, select the Add To An Existing FrontPage Web check box. With an existing web you can choose to Copy Changed Pages Only by clicking on that option. If you are copying the root web of the server, select the Copy Child Webs (For Root Web Only) check box to have the child webs of the root web copied also.

8. Click on OK. After a few moments the dialog box will disappear and the following sequence of messages will appear in the FrontPage Explorer status bar. Obviously, your server name (arcadiaweb.com, in my case) and the originating computer (marty.matthews, here) will be different than shown:

> **Copying the FantasyTravel web to http://arcadiaweb.com/FantasyTravel**
> **Listing pages in http://marty.matthews**
> **Copying pages *xx*% complete**

When the copying reaches 100 percent, this message will appear telling you your web has been successfully copied:

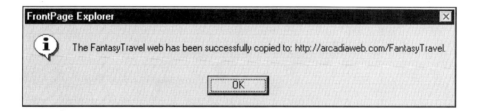

9. Test your web by starting your favorite browser and entering the URL given in the transfer process (http://arcadiaweb.com/FantasyTravel, in my case). Your web should appear as you can see mine did in Figure 17-1.

In most cases posting your web to the server will be this simple. There is, however, the possibility that one or more of the files may not transfer correctly or may become corrupted, particularly if your web contains a number of large files. If you think this has happened, the easiest way to correct the problem is to edit the web

17

Fantasy
Travel web
opened on
my ISP

FIGURE 17-1

on the server just as you would on your computer. To do this, you need to make sure you are first connected to the web server and then specify the server when you open the web in the Open FrontPage Web dialog box. Except for the fact that you are doing it long distance, this is not any different than editing on your own computer.

Deleting a Web on a Server

Another approach to correcting or changing a web on a server is to delete the web from the server and copy it again. To delete your web:

1. In the FrontPage Explorer, with your Internet connection active, open the web by selecting Open FrontPage Web from the File menu.

2. In the Open FrontPage Web dialog box select the correct web server in the Web Server or File Location drop-down menu.

3. Click on the List Webs button, and select the web from the Webs list box.

4. When the web has opened in the FrontPage Explorer, select Delete FrontPage Web from the File menu.

Once the web is deleted, repeat the steps given previously to again copy the web to the web server. If you continue to have problems copying your web to the web server, contact the webmaster or server administrator. It is possible to delete individual files from the web server by using Dial-up Networking and Windows Explorer (provided, once again, you have the correct permissions), but this can confuse FrontPage. FrontPage keeps track of all the components of your web; if you change any of the components outside of FrontPage, then FrontPage may end up looking for files that no longer exist or are in a different place.

If you successfully copy your web to the server but find that some elements don't function correctly, first make sure that the web works correctly on your Personal Web Server. Then contact your webmaster or server administrator and explain the problem. If other webs using the same feature work correctly on the web server, the odds are that the problem is in your web. If the problem is common to other webs on the web server, then the FrontPage Server Extensions might not be installed correctly.

Posting to a Host Without FrontPage Server Extensions

You can also post a web created in FrontPage to a web server that isn't running FrontPage Server Extensions. While any features relying on the server extensions (forms, and so on) will not function, all the standard HTML functions, such as hyperlinks, will be unaffected.

Microsoft provides the FrontPage Web Publishing Wizard as a separate program, which assists you in posting your web to a web server that does not support the FrontPage Server Extensions. The FrontPage Web Publishing Wizard is on the FrontPage 97 with Bonus Pack CD and directions for installing it are in Appendix A. The Web Publishing Wizard can also be downloaded from http://www.microsoft.com/frontpage/. The Web Publishing Wizard copies the web pages you select to the destination web server and notifies you of which pages require the FrontPage Server Extensions to function correctly. The Web Publishing Wizard posts your web pages to an FTP (file transfer protocol) server, rather than a web server. The FTP server usually provides access to the same directories as the ISP's web server, so your web pages can be immediately opened by a web browser. In some cases, the webmaster or server administrator will have to activate your pages once they are uploaded to the FTP server. You will need permission to write to the destination FTP server. Your webmaster or server administrator will be able to assign the proper permission to your account.

The following instructions can be used with the Web Publishing Wizard to post a FrontPage web to a server without the FrontPage Server Extensions. (The first server of steps are exactly like those given earlier for publishing to a host with the FrontPage Server Extensions.)

1. Start the FrontPage Explorer if necessary.

2. If you use dialup networking to access the Internet, activate your Internet connection.

3. In the FrontPage Explorer open the web you will place on the web server.

4. Open the File menu and select Publish FrontPage Web. The Publish FrontPage Web dialog box will be displayed, as you saw earlier in this chapter.

5. Select or type in the name of the destination server in the Destination Web Server or File Location drop-down menu.

6. The current name for the web is displayed in the Name Of Destination FrontPage Web text box. If you want to use a different name for the web, type it there.

7. If you are copying a new web to the server, make sure all the options are unchecked. If you are adding to or replacing pages in an existing web, select the Add To An Existing FrontPage Web check box. With an existing web you can choose to Copy Changed Pages Only by clicking on that option. If you are copying the root web of the server, select the Copy Child Webs (For Root Web Only) check box to have the child webs of the root web copied also.

8. Click on OK. If the web server does not have the FrontPage Server Extensions, the Web Publishing Wizard will open. The first page simply tells you what the wizard will do. Click on Next.

9. You are then asked to select the folder or files you want to publish. Use the Browse Folders button to select it. If you are using Microsoft Personal Web Server, the default is C:\Webshare\Wwwroot\, as you can see in Figure 17-2. If you are using the FrontPage Personal Web Server, the default path is C:\FrontPage Webs\Content\.

10. Click on Next. You are asked to enter a name for the web site that you are creating on the server. This is *not* the server name, but rather a name that you can use instead of the URL. For example, I'm using "Fantasy Travel." If your server is not listed, click on New. Here you can enter a name for your web server and again select it from a list or choose "<Other Internet Provider>." Click on Next.

11. You are asked for the URL to access your web pages on the server. This is assigned by your ISP. You can see what I'm using in Figure 17-3. (If you are connecting to an intranet web server, the URL might look more like Figure 17-4.)

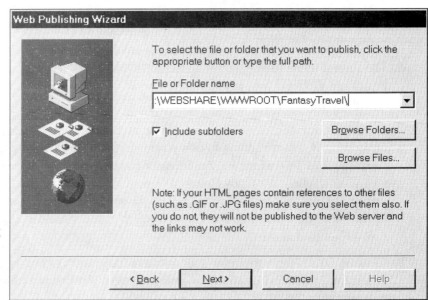

Establishing the path to the web to be published

FIGURE 17-2

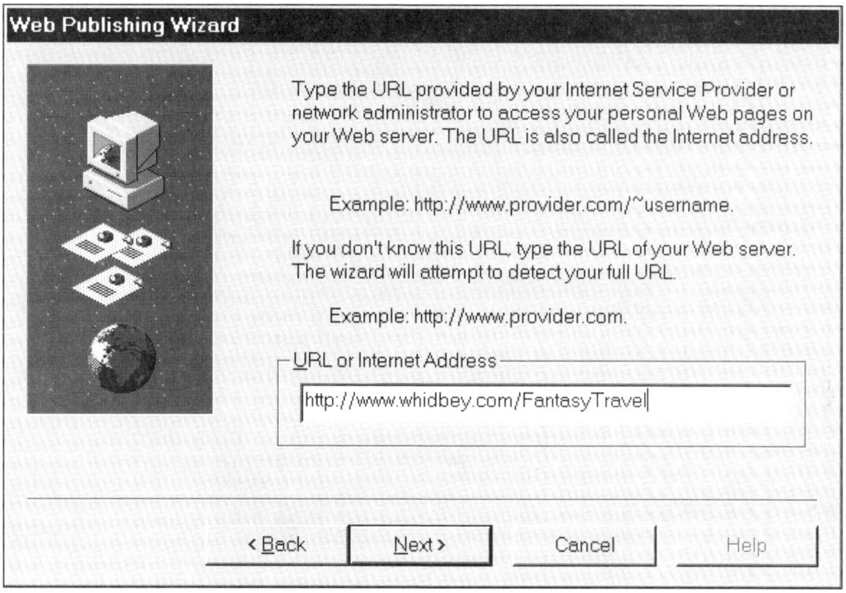

17

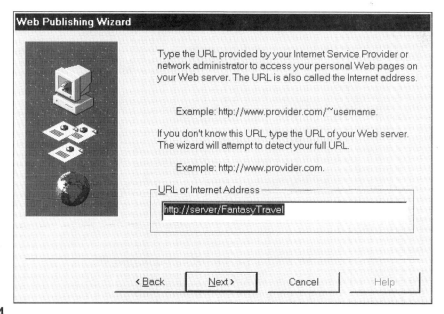

Entering
the Internet
URL for
your web

FIGURE 17-3

Entering an
intranet
URL for
your web

FIGURE 17-4

12. Click on Next. Choose between using a LAN to access an intranet server and Dial-up Networking to access an Internet ISP. You can also create a new dialup connection by clicking on the New Dial-up Connection button. Click on Next.

13. Enter your user name and password that you use with your web server account. Click on Next.

14. The wizard will then try to verify the information you have entered, and if it is correct, your web will be copied to the server. You'll see comments in the FrontPage Explorer status bar, including the percentage complete. When it is done, you'll get a message telling you that the web was successfully copied, like the one shown earlier.

15. If the wizard runs into problems, you will again be asked to select a transfer protocol—either the Internet's FTP (File Transfer Protocol) or Windows file transfer. If you are working with an intranet Windows NT server on a LAN, you can use Windows' file transfer; otherwise you should use FTP. Click on Next.

16. Verify your user name and password again, and click on Next. Verify your FTP server name. For example, mine is whidbey.com. Click on Next

17. You are asked to check, and correct if necessary, the normal file path to the destination on the server where the web will reside and also what the URL is for this site. If you are using an intranet, you'll get a dialog box similar to Figure 17-5. With an Internet connection, this dialog box looks like Figure 17-6.

18. Click on Next. Again the wizard will attempt to verify the information you have entered. This process will continue until either you give up or you are successful. If you continue to run into problems, contact your network/server administrator or ISP, and have them walk you through the answers to the various dialog boxes.

NOTE: *The specific paths in some of the FrontPage Web Publishing Wizard dialog boxes are unique to an ISP or network installation. If after several attempts the copying is not working, you need to contact your ISP or network/server administrator.*

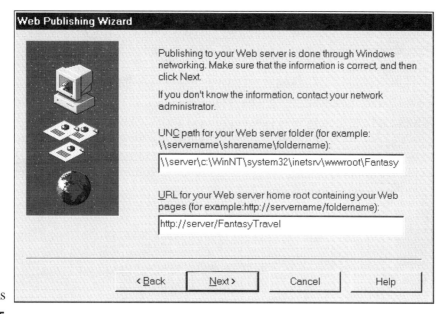

Intranet path confirmations

FIGURE 17-5

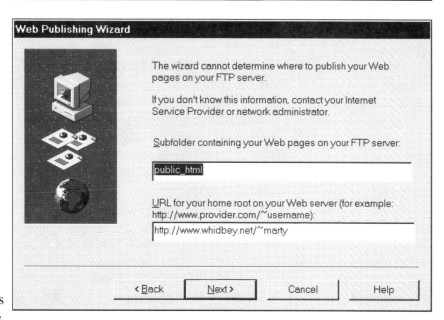

Internet path confirmations

FIGURE 17-6

Once your information has been confirmed and a connection has been made to your web server, the FrontPage Web Publishing Wizard will identify which pages contain elements that require the FrontPage Server Extensions to work correctly. You can then either ignore this fact, or you can go back into the page and make the necessary changes.

Even if the web server that will host your web pages does not have the FrontPage Server Extensions, you may still be able to have the same functionality. For example, most servers will have an application or script for handling form input. You will need to ask your webmaster or server administrator how to access the application and then incorporate it into your web page by editing the HTML. Of course, it would be much easier if the server hosting your web were to support the FrontPage Server Extensions.

 NOTE: *The description of NeedhamOnline in the "FrontPage on the Web" section at the end of Chapter 14 shows how they got forms functionality without the FrontPage Server Extensions.*

Promoting Your Web Site

Once your web site has been posted to a web server, you need to let people know that it is there. If your web site is business related, the first step is to tell your existing customers about it. You might include an announcement with your regular invoicing, for example. You should also include your URL in all your conventional advertising, including your business cards, invoices, statements, purchase orders, drawings, reports, and any other document you produce. It's not uncommon to see URLs on everything from television commercials to billboards.

You also need to make sure you can be found on the Web by anyone looking for the products and services you offer. A number of search engines for the Web have been developed. Some, like Digital's AltaVista, actively search the Web for information. Others, like Yahoo!, which also searches the Web, allow web sites to submit their information to them. Figure 17-7 shows the introduction to the pages used for submitting web sites to Yahoo!. You can also submit your web site to virtually all the search engines. A simple way to reach a number of search engines is to use the Submit It web site (http://www.submit-it.com/), where your single entry is submitted to over 16 search engines for free, or pay a fee (currently $59.95) and submit up to three URLs to be submitted to up to 300 search engines and directories that you select.

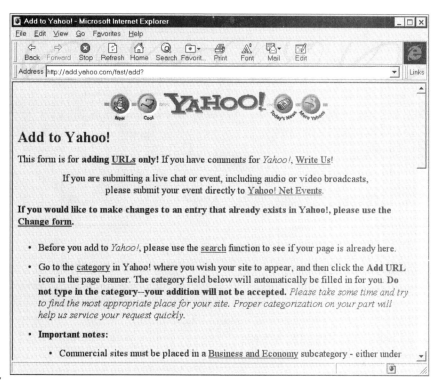

Yahoo! submission area

FIGURE 17-7

Since many search engines are actively searching the Web for sites, it helps to have an introductory paragraph on your home page that gives a concise description of your site. This paragraph should include the keywords that apply to your site.

Table 17-2 gives names and addresses of search engines that you should make sure you are correctly listed on.

Another useful tool for promoting your web site is reciprocal links. These are simply hyperlinks on your web page that point to someone who has a link to your site. Say you sell mountain-climbing equipment. You could search the Web for climbing clubs and other groups with web sites relating to climbing. You then contact the owners of the sites, offering to put a link from your site to theirs if they will return the favor. This way anyone who finds any of the sites you're linked to has a direct link to your site. If you gather enough links on your site, it may become a starting point for people "surfing the Net."

You shouldn't overlook a press release, either. When your web site goes online, or you make a major addition, let the press and publications related to your business

Search Engine	Web Address
AltaVista	http://www.altavista.digital.com/
Excite	http://www.excite.com/
Hot Bot	http://www.hotbot.com/
Infoseek	http://www.infoseek.com/
Lycos	http://lycos.com/
Switchboard	http://www2.switchboard.com/
Web Crawler	http://webcrawler.com/
Yahoo!	http://www.yahoo.com/search.html

Search
Engines
TABLE 17-2

know about it. What you should *not* do is advertise your web site or business in newsgroups, unless the newsgroup is specifically run for that purpose. Say you decide to have a sale on climbing equipment. In your zeal to let the world know, you post a message on a recreational climbing newsgroup. The one result you can count on is that you will be flooded with "flames," (rather pointed e-mail messages) and frankly, you will deserve them.

A surefire way to get your web site widely known is simply to produce an outstanding web site. Today there are over 40 million sites on the World Wide Web. Aim to be in the top 5 percent of that group. In the era of conventional marketing, that goal would have been virtually impossible for a small business, but the web is a new paradigm. Creativity and content count more than advertising budgets. Give people a reason to visit your site by providing content that is unique and useful to them. Then package it in an effective, pleasing design. Take the time to explore the Web and gather ideas for your own site. (Gathering ideas is fine, gathering graphics or other actual content, no matter how easy it is, is a violation of copyright laws.)

The World Wide Web, whether you use it for business or pleasure, is having an effect on society as fundamental as the invention of the printing press. With FrontPage you have the tools to participate in this new world.

FrontPage on the Web

Bar Net

URL: *http://www.bar-net.com*
Webmaster: Chris Witherell
E-mail: *chris@bar-net.com*

470 South 45th Street
Boulder, CO 80303
(303) 499-8221

Web Site

The Bar Net web site is a winner of the Microsoft Great Web Sites Contest. The Home page, shown in Figure 1, uses tables to give the appearance of frames. The stripe (blue) on the left is done with a background image. Then a table is used to put the triangle and "BAR NET" on the left and "The Vitua-Bar…" on the right, as you can see in Listing 1. Another three-column by one-row table is used to produce the first-column vertical navbar by use of line breaks (<BR>); the second-column thin 15-pixel separation between the other two columns; and the third-column blocks of text on the right.

Listing 1
ble HTML

```
<table border="0" width="600">
  <tr><td width="100"><font face="Arial">
     <img src="images/bnbutton.gif" alt="Welcome to Bar Net"
     align="top" width="100" height="50"></font></td>
    <td align="center" width="500"><p align="center">
     <a href="http://www.bar-net.com/bar/"><font face="Arial">
     <img src="images/virtua.gif" alt="The Virtua-Bar" border="0"
     width="250" height="40"></font></a><font face="Arial"><br>
     </font><font size="2" face="Arial"><strong>Wanna go here?
     Better get </strong></font>
     <a href="http://www.microsoft.com/ie/"><font size="2"
     face="Arial"><strong>IE 3.0</strong></font></a>
     <font size="2" face="Arial"><strong>!</strong></font></p>
    </td></tr>
</table>
```

FrontPage on the Web (cont.)

Bar Net
Home page

FIGURE 1

Many of Bar Net's pages use the column-background-and-table approach of the
home page, as shown in the Hosted Sites page, which you can see in Figure 2. Bar
Net also includes a form for searching the web site, shown in Figure 3 and in Listing

FrontPage on the Web (cont.)

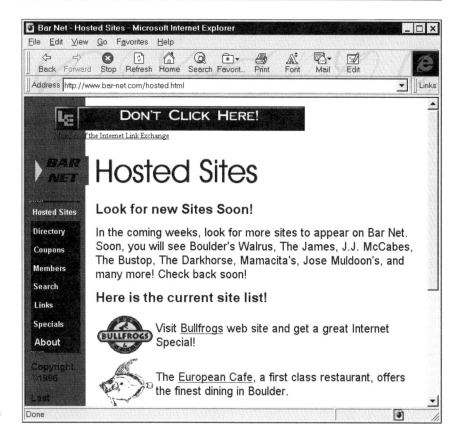

Hosted
Sites page

FIGURE 2

2, which was built around the FrontPage Search WebBot. Compare this with NeedhamOnline's (shown in an earlier "FrontPage on the Web" section) use of an alternative search capability.

FrontPage on the Web (cont.)

Search page

FIGURE 3

Listing 2
Search form
HTML

```
<td valign="top"><!--webbot bot="Search" s-link
    s-fields="TimeStamp,DocumentK," s-index="All"
    s-dsn="default" tag="FORM" s-text="Search for:"
    i-size="20" s-submit="Start Search" s-clear="Clear"
    startspan -->
  <form action="_vti_bin/shtml.exe/search.htm" method="POST">
    <input type="hidden" name="VTI-GROUP" value="0"><p><b>Search
    for: </b><input type="text" name="search" size="20" value></p>
    <p><input type="submit" value="Start Search">
      <input type="reset" value="Clear"></p>
  </form><!--webbot bot="Search" endspan i-checksum="15524" -->
```

FrontPage on the Web (cont.)

Webmaster Q & A

WHY FRONTPAGE?   I initially decided to use FrontPage to help me easily create forms without CGI scripting. Using FrontPage also cut my design time drastically and made the pages I produced more pleasing to the eye.

LIKES AND DISLIKES   I like FrontPage because it does everything for you. I also dislike FrontPage for the same reason! For example, when I try to add an HTML markup to the <HEAD> section, FrontPage does not keep the HTML I have inserted; instead, it checks for "correctness" and then replaces my code with new code. This happens when I try to add my RSAC rating tag. I find it very annoying! I have to open the file in a text editor, like Notepad, and insert the HTML manually, which takes time and can become frustrating.

NEATEST FEATURES OF THIS SITE   Created a standard look to all of the pages using background GIFs, tables, and standard menu buttons. The greatest accomplishment at the site is the Virtua-Bar. This is an ActiveX bar-tending guide that allows the visitor to play games and view hundreds of drink recipes.

TIPS

- Watch what is happening to your HTML behind the scenes. Make sure that FrontPage isn't making corrections to your HTML markups that you don't want.

- Don't use too many marquees or blinking text.

- If you have problems with FrontPage, consult the Microsoft newsgroups; they are helpful.

Installing
FrontPage 97
with Bonus Pack

Installing FrontPage is an easy task, as you'll discover in this appendix. The onscreen instructions are clear, the steps are few, and with the information in this appendix, you will soon have FrontPage ready to use.

As this is written, FrontPage 97 is being primarily sold as a CD with the Microsoft Bonus Pack. If you have a choice, you definitely want the Bonus Pack. As you can see in Figure A-1, in addition to FrontPage, the CD includes

■ **Microsoft Image Composer**, which is a bitmap graphics program for creating and editing images you can put in your web pages

Contents of the FrontPage 97 with Bonus Pack CD

FIGURE A-1

- **Microsoft Personal Web Server**, which allows web pages to be viewed on smaller Windows 95-based LANs

- **Microsoft Internet Explorer 3.0**, which is a web browser program for looking at the web pages you create with FrontPage and other pages on either the Internet or an intranet

- **Microsoft Web Publishing Wizard**, which assists you in placing FrontPage webs on web servers that do not have the FrontPage Server Extensions

This appendix will discuss the installation of these products, which is easier than it sounds.

What You Need to Install FrontPage 97 with Bonus Pack

To install FrontPage 97 with Bonus Pack, you'll need the following software and hardware:

- Windows 95 or Windows NT (version 3.51 with Service Pack 5 or higher)

- A PC with a 486DX-33 or higher, or a Pentium (a Pentium 100 or higher is recommended)

- 8MB of memory for FrontPage under Windows 95 (16MB with Windows NT), 16MB for the Microsoft Personal Web Server, and 16MB for Microsoft Image Composer (16MB or higher is strongly recommended)

- At least 30MB of disk space plus 1MB for the Microsoft Personal Web Server, 1MB for the Microsoft Web Publishing Wizard, 11MB minimum for the Microsoft Image Composer (17MB for a complete installation), and 11MB for the Microsoft Internet Explorer (2MB more with the Internet Mail and News options)

- VGA or higher with 256 or more colors from your video adapter and monitor (Super VGA with True Color and 2MB video memory recommended)

- Microsoft Mouse or compatible pointing device and CD-ROM drive (pressure-sensitive tablet recommended with Microsoft Image Composer)

To access the Internet or an intranet network where FrontPage will be used, you also must have installed the TCP/IP protocols (see Chapter 1 for a discussion of this) on a dialup network using a modem and/or on a local area network (LAN) with its adapter card. If you are using an Internet browser with Windows 95 or Windows NT, you probably have already installed and correctly configured TCP/IP. If you are just now coming up on the Internet or a network, you need to install TCP/IP. For the Internet, the best source (and it's free) is simply to install Microsoft Internet Express 3.0 with Internet Mail. It includes all the TCP/IP capability that you need. An alternative is Microsoft Plus for Windows 95, which provides all the necessary programs, installation wizards, and lots of instruction. For an intranet you need to work with your network administrator or other source of technical information to set up your network for TCP/IP. One of the best references is *LAN Times Encyclopedia of Networking* by Tom Sheldon (Osborne/McGraw-Hill, 1994).

What Components You'll Find in FrontPage

Within FrontPage itself there are a number of components, which are described in detail in Chapter 2. Among these are

- **FrontPage client software**, which allows you to create and edit webs (documents that you can deliver over the Internet or an intranet). It includes the FrontPage Explorer, the FrontPage Editor, the To Do List, and the FrontPage wizards. Most of this book discusses how to use this software.

- **FrontPage web server software**, which allows you to maintain and deliver webs to creators and users of them. It includes the FrontPage Personal Web Server, which is a full 32-bit web server for your PC that uses the HyperText Transfer Protocol (HTTP) and common gateway interface (CGI) standards, and the FrontPage Server Extensions, which provide additional programs and tools to use with the Personal Web Server. The FrontPage Personal Web Server is separate and distinct from the Microsoft Personal Web Server, which is included in the Bonus Pack. These two personal web servers are discussed further in the next section of this appendix and in Chapters 16 and 17.

- **FrontPage TCP/IP Test**, which will verify if your system is correctly configured with TCP/IP.

Installing Internet Explorer 3.0

If you don't have Internet Explorer 3.0 already installed, do so as your first step for two reasons: it will give you the TCP/IP capability if you need it, and the Microsoft Personal Web Server uses Internet Explorer for its administration. Even if you are a dyed-in-the-wool Netscape Navigator fan, it is good to have both browsers available to check your web sites against. Use these steps to install Internet Explorer 3.0:

1. Insert the FrontPage 97 with Bonus Pack CD. The dialog box that was shown in Figure A-1 should automatically be displayed. If you are installing FrontPage across a network, use the Windows Explorer to connect to the server and folder with the source files and double-click on Setup. The dialog box shown in Figure A-1 will appear.

2. From the FrontPage 97 With Bonus Pack dialog box click on the Internet Explorer 3.0 icon.

3. Click on Yes to accept the License Agreement (given that you do) and then on Yes again to select the optional Internet components to be installed. This shows you that Internet Mail and Internet News will be installed. Click on OK.

4. Click on OK again to accept the default installation location. Several message boxes and thermometer scales will inform you of the progress. You are then asked to restart your computer. Click on Yes.

5. When your computer restarts, double-click on the Internet Explorer icon on your desktop. The Internet Connection Wizard will open. Click on Next. Choose the type of Internet connection you want, as you can see in Figure A-2 (this is where TCP/IP and dialup networking are installed if you need them). Unless you have a good reason otherwise, like you already have an Internet connection installed, accept the default Automatic, and then click on Next.

   Depending on what you choose and how you are (or aren't) connected, the Internet Explorer will start and you may be connected to the Internet, to a local intranet, or just to a blank page. Where you connect (or don't) is not important. If you get an error message saying you can't connect, click on OK and ignore it for the moment.

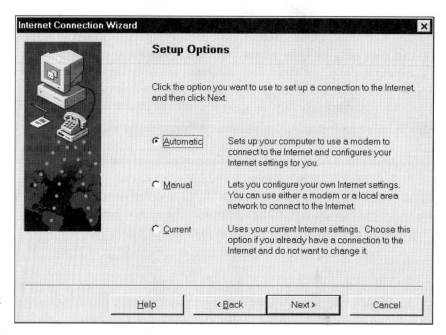

Internet
Connection
Wizard

FIGURE A-2

6. Open the View menu and choose Options. The Internet Explorer Options dialog box will be displayed, as shown in Figure A-3. Here you can specify settings to control how the Internet Explorer will operate.

7. Click on each of the tabs and look at the dialog boxes and options that are available. One in particular that you may want to consider changing is the Start Page Address in the Navigation tab. The default is http://home. microsoft.com/. You may want to change this to the address of your personal web server. You'll see this in the General tab of the Personal Web Server Properties dialog box after installing it in the next section.

By using the address of your personal web server as your Start Page, you will make it very easy to view the webs you create with FrontPage—all you need to do is type the web name at the end of the existing address.

8. When you have finished looking at the Internet Explorer Options dialog box and making any changes you wish to make, click on OK to close the dialog box. Then click on Close in the Internet Explorer itself.

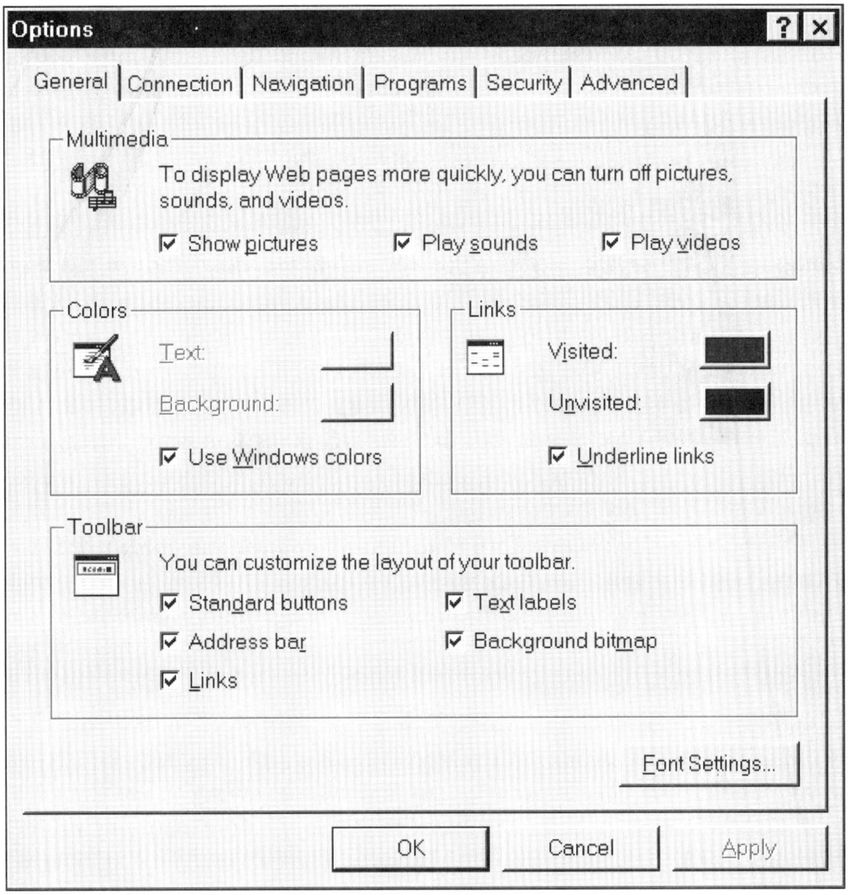

Internet Explorer Options dialog box

FIGURE A-3

Choosing and Installing a Server

FrontPage 97 with Bonus Pack comes with two personal web servers, the Microsoft Personal Web Server (MSPWS) and the FrontPage Personal Web Server (FPPWS). The MSPWS is a separate program that you must install. The FPPWS, although a separate program, is automatically installed with FrontPage unless it finds another web server already installed. This means that if you want to use the MSPWS, you must install it before installing FrontPage. Besides using the MSPWS or FPPWS, you can use any other web server that you have available, as long as the FrontPage

Server Extensions are installed on that server. For example, if you have the Microsoft Internet Information Server (IIS) with the FrontPage Server Extensions installed on your intranet, you can use that as your server with FrontPage. Unless you have very high-speed unlimited access to this server, you will be better served to install your own personal web server.

There are significant differences between the MSPWS and the FPPWS. The FPPWS is designed to function only with FrontPage, while the MSPWS is based on Microsoft's IIS and is more tightly integrated with Windows 95. IIS is included with Windows NT 4.0 Server and is all the web server you need to run a full World Wide Web site. Consequently, the MSPWS offers a broader range of features. For example, it allows you to also have an FTP (File Transfer Protocol) server available on your computer for the transfer of files between computers on your network in addition to a web server. MSPWS gives you a number of options that you can use to customize it to your needs, but the FPPWS gives you none. Most importantly, MSPWS allows you to create and support a large number of web sites, while FPPWS is limited to 18 or fewer webs.

There is no default server for FrontPage, so you can use either one for your web development. If you are upgrading from FrontPage 1.1, have modest intentions for what you are going to create with FrontPage, and are not connected to a network, you may want to use the FPPWS. It will only start when FrontPage is started and uses less computer resources.

If you are connected to a network, want to make your webs available to others on the network, and want to make extensive use of FrontPage, then MSPWS should be your choice. This book recommends and assumes that you are using MSPWS.

If MSPWS is your choice, you need to install it before installing FrontPage. Do that now with the following steps. If you want to use the FPPWS, skip the following steps. The FPPWS will automatically be installed when you install FrontPage.

1. If, after you reboot, the FrontPage 97 With Bonus Pack dialog box is not visible, either open and reclose your CD-ROM drive with the FrontPage 97 with Bonus Pack CD, or use the Windows 95 Explorer to locate the root directory of your CD and double-click on Setup. If you are installing FrontPage across a network, use the Windows Explorer to connect to the server and folder with the source files, and double-click on Setup.

2. Click on the Microsoft Personal Web Server for Windows 95 button. Click on I Agree, if you do, to the License Agreement, and the MSPWS will be installed (several message boxes will appear briefly, some with thermometer scales).

3. Click on Yes to restart Windows 95. When your system restarts, you'll see the MSPWS icon in the notification area on the right of your taskbar at the bottom of your screen, like this (on the left of the Volume control):

4. Double-click on the MSPWS icon in the notification area. The Personal Web Server Properties dialog box will open, as shown in Figure A-4. The General tab, which is the default, shows the HTTP address of your personal web server and the path on your disk to your default home page. You can see the home page and learn more about the MSPWS by clicking on the appropriate buttons on the General tab, but you must have a web browser such as the Microsoft Internet Explorer installed and identified as your default browser.

TIP: *The HTTP address of your personal web server is translated by the server to the physical disk address shown for your default home page. Use this address as the Start Page in the Internet Explorer to easily view your webs created in FrontPage, as suggested in the previous section.*

5. Click on the Startup tab. Here you will see that the MSPWS is currently running (you can stop it by clicking on Stop), that it is set to automatically run whenever you start your computer, and that its icon is to appear on the taskbar. Both of the latter states can be reversed by clicking on the appropriate check box.

6. Click on the Administration tab. Here you can open an Administration web on your default web browser, as you can see in Figure A-5. This lets you control how HTTP (the WWW option) and FTP will operate and who on your network can use your web server. Chapter 16 goes into these settings in more detail. (If you opened your web browser, close it to return to the Personal Web Server Properties dialog box.)

7. Click on the Services tab. This tab explains that the MSPWS provides both HTTP and FTP services, what those services are, and allows you to start and stop them, and control their properties.

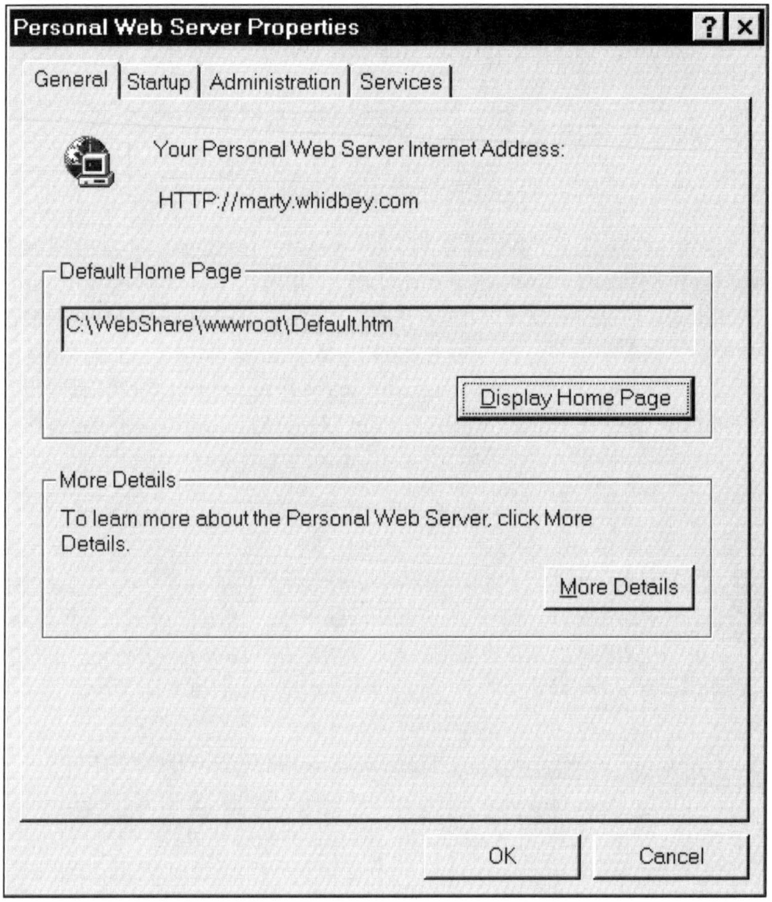

Personal Web Server Properties   ? ✕

General | Startup | Administration | Services |

Your Personal Web Server Internet Address:

HTTP://marty.whidbey.com

Default Home Page

C:\WebShare\wwwroot\Default.htm

Display Home Page

More Details

To learn more about the Personal Web Server, click More Details.

More Details

OK   Cancel

Personal
Web Server
Properties
dialog box

■ FIGURE A-4

8. Select the FTP service and click on Properties. The FTP Properties dialog box will open as you can see next. This and the HTTP Properties provide the same options. The FTP Properties dialog box allows you to choose between Manual and Automatic startup, with Automatic meaning the services are started whenever the computer is started and Manual requiring that you open the Personal Web Server Properties dialog box. You can also set the root directory used for FTP.

9. Close the FTP Properties dialog box and then the Personal Web Server Properties dialog box.

The MSPWS is a powerful web server and will support small- to moderate-size intranet sites very well.

Installing FrontPage 97

You may install FrontPage with either a Typical or a Custom installation procedure. If you choose Typical, recommended for most users, all FrontPage components will be installed. This is the choice assumed in this book and reflected in its examples and illustrations. If you choose Custom, you may choose which components to install.

Before you start, be prepared to specify one or two directory paths: one for installing FrontPage client software in any case, and another for the web server programs and the webs that you will create if you have chosen to use FPPWS. FrontPage will create default directories for you if you have no other preferences, and *that is the assumption and recommendation of this book.* Throughout the book you'll see the statement "if you

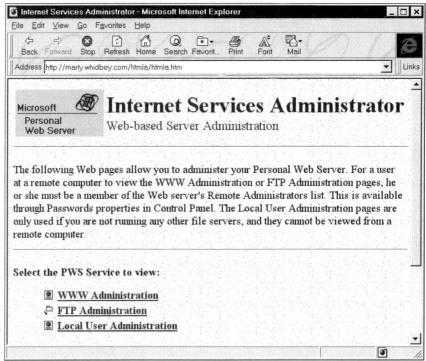

FIGURE A-5

followed the default installation procedure," which identifies the default directories
that the FrontPage Setup program will create for you.

 NOTE: *It is strongly recommended that you choose the Typical
installation and that you let the Setup program create the default directories
where FrontPage will be installed.*

Performing a Typical Installation

Follow these steps for a Typical installation:

1. Verify that the MSPWS is running by the presence of its icon in the
   taskbar *if* you do not want the FPPWS installed. Exit all other programs
   before installing FrontPage. Nothing should be running but Windows
   and MSPWS.

2. If you are installing FrontPage from the CD, insert (or reinsert) it into your drive, and the FrontPage 97 With Bonus Pack dialog box will appear as you saw in Figure A-1. If you are installing FrontPage across a network, locate the source files and double-click on Setup to get the same dialog box.

3. From the FrontPage 97 With Bonus Pack dialog box click on the FrontPage 97 Installation icon. If you have not installed MSPWS, you will be told that it is recommended and given a chance to do so now. If you wish to, click on Yes; if you want to install FPPWS, click on No.

4. After a minute you will see the "Welcome" message. After you have read it, click on Next to continue. Enter your name and company registration information, click on Next, confirm what you entered, and click on Yes. Enter your CD Key (located on the case of your CD) and click on OK.

5. If you are upgrading from FrontPage 1.1, Setup will tell you that it will examine your system to confirm the existence of the previous version. Click on Continue. If Setup can't find a qualifying product, a dialog box will appear telling you so. If you have FrontPage on another drive, or if you have already removed it, but have the original floppy disk, you need to tell Setup the drive to search. Click on Locate. A Locate Directory dialog box will appear. If you want a floppy searched, insert it in its drive. Select the correct drive and directory and click on OK.

6. In the Destination Path dialog box that opens next, you will see the Destination Directory where FrontPage client software will beplaced, as shown in Figure A-6. The default is C:\Program Files\Microsoft FrontPage.

7. If you want to install FrontPage into a different directory, choose Browse and select the Path to the destination directory you want. Do this by selecting the drive in the Drives field and choosing the directory in the Directories field. If you want to install FrontPage on another computer, click on Network and find the drive and directory on your network where FrontPage is to be installed. Choose OK (twice if you have selected a Network directory) when you have displayed the destination directory you want in the Path field. If the directory does not exist, Setup will create it for you.

8. Click on Next to accept the Destination Directory and continue.

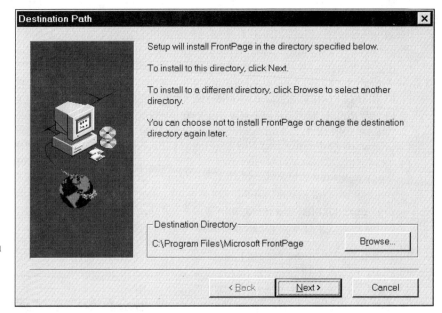

Asking for the directory in which to install FrontPage

FIGURE A-6

9. The Setup Type dialog box that appears allows you to select the type of installation, Typical or Custom, to perform. If it is not already selected, click on Typical to select it, and then click on Next to continue. (A Custom installation will be looked at later in this appendix.)

10. If you have one or more web servers already installed, a list of them will be displayed on which you can install the FrontPage Server Extensions. If you installed the MSPWS earlier, it will be listed. If only one server is listed, it will be selected. If you have several servers, select the one you want to use and click on Next.

11. If you want to use the FPPWS and have no other servers installed, the default directory for the FrontPage server software as well as the webs that you create will be displayed in the Choose Personal Web Server Directory dialog box. The default directory is C:\FrontPage Webs and is the recommendation assumed in this book.

12. If you want to choose another directory, click on Browse and select that directory as discussed in step 6. When the directory has been selected, click on Next to continue.

13. Your choices are confirmed in the Start Copying Files dialog box shown in Figure A-7. If all the information is correct, click on Next. If you need to change something, click on Back and correct it, click on Next to return to this dialog box, and finally click on Next to begin the copying.

14. You will see a summary of resources being used as the copying proceeds. The three bars represent the percentage of the current file being copied, the percentage of the current disk copied, and the percentage of your computer's disk space used.

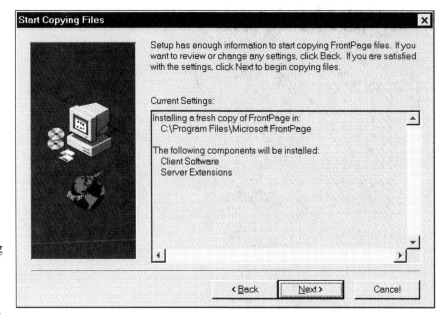

Confirming the installing steps

FIGURE A-7

15. If you are using the FPPWS, you are next asked to enter the account name and a password for the administrator and then to confirm the password. (You cannot use a blank password.) Do so and click on OK. Next the server extensions will be installed, and then, if you are using the MSPWS, you are asked if you want to restart the MSPWS to incorporate the server extensions. Click on Yes.

16. Finally you are told that Setup is complete and asked if you want to start the FrontPage Explorer. Verify that the check box is checked, and then click on Finish. The FrontPage Explorer will start and inform you that it is checking your host name and TCP/IP address. Click on OK. You will be informed of the host name and told you can now start using FrontPage. Click on OK. The Getting Started With Microsoft FrontPage dialog box will open, as shown in Figure A-8.

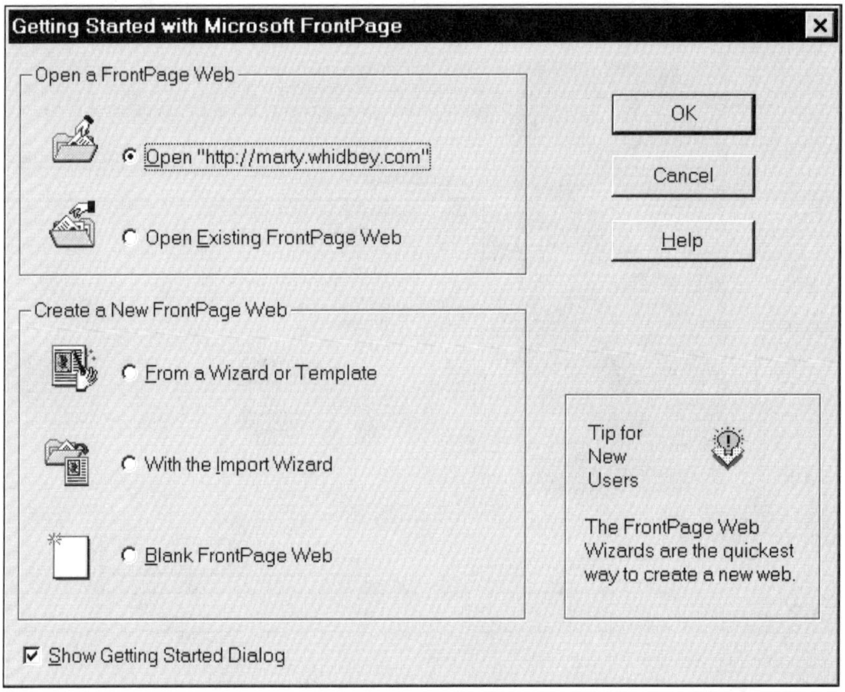

Getting Started With Microsoft FrontPage dialog box

FIGURE A-8

17. Click on Open Existing FrontPage Web and then on OK. The Open FrontPage Webs dialog box will open. Click on List Webs. The <RootWeb> should be selected; click on OK. If you are using the FPPWS, you'll be asked to enter your account name and password; do so, and click on OK. The default My Home Page will open in the FrontPage Explorer, as you can see in Figure A-9. (The default home page looks different depending on whether you are using FPPWS or MSPWS. Figure A-9 shows the MSPWS version. The FPPWS version does not have a counter available, names its home page differently, and has some different links.)

18. Double-click on the My Home Page (FrontPage Root Web with FPPWS) icon in the right pane of the FrontPage Explorer, and the FrontPage Editor will open, displaying the default Home page like that shown in Figure A-10. (Again, this page looks different if you are using FPPWS.)

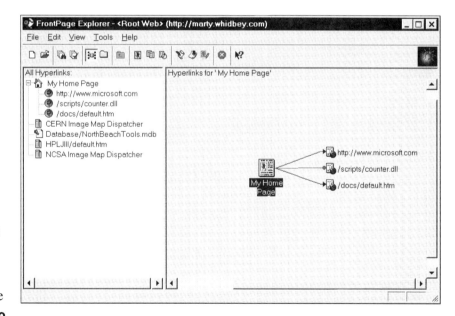

The FrontPage Explorer with the default home page

FIGURE A-9

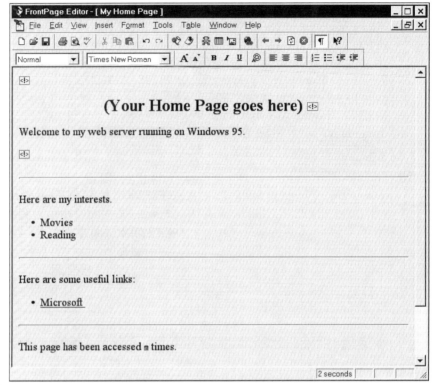

The FrontPage Editor with the default Home page

FIGURE A-10

19. Click on the Close buttons of FrontPage Editor and FrontPage Explorer. You have proven that the installation was completed successfully.

If for some reason your installation did not complete successfully, look carefully at the error messages you have received. Then correct any anomalies that are mentioned, like exiting from all programs except Windows and MSPWS that are running, or providing more disk space, and then rerun Setup.

If you installed FPPWS, it will automatically start when you start FrontPage Explorer, and it will remain running (although in an "idle" status) after you shut down FrontPage Explorer. You can tell that this is the case by the presence of the

Web Server task on the taskbar (the task is shown in the following illustration). You can shut down the FPPWS by clicking on it in the taskbar and then clicking on Close or selecting Exit from the File menu. You'll notice if you open the File menu that there are *no* options that you can control.

Performing a Custom Installation

Use the Custom installation when you want to install only some of the FrontPage component programs—for instance, if you are upgrading a previous copy of FrontPage. If you are installing FrontPage over a previous copy, you will want to use the same directory structure you used originally in order to preserve access to your webs. If you want to use a different directory, you will first have to uninstall the first copy and reinstall it to the desired directory.

To perform a Custom installation, follow these steps:

1. Follow the first eight steps in the Typical installation until the Setup Type dialog box appears. Click on Custom to select it, and then click on Next to continue.

2. The Select Components dialog box, displayed in Figure A-11, allows you to select the FrontPage components to be installed. If you do not want to install a component, click on its check box to clear it. (If you have already installed the MSPWS, the FPPWS will be dimmed, and if you are installing the FPPWS, the Server Extensions are dimmed, since they are automatically installed with the FrontPage Personal Web Server.)

3. If you find that your disk space is limited, you can search for additional space by clicking on Disk Space. As shown next, *Available* shows the disk space available on the selected disk drive. *Required* shows the disk space required for your selected components. Click on OK to close the Available Disk Space dialog box, and then click on Next.

4. If you have one or more web servers already installed, a list of them will be displayed on which you can install the FrontPage Server Extensions. If you installed the MSPWS earlier, it will be listed. If only one server is listed, it will be selected. If you have several servers, select the one(s) you want to use and click on Next.

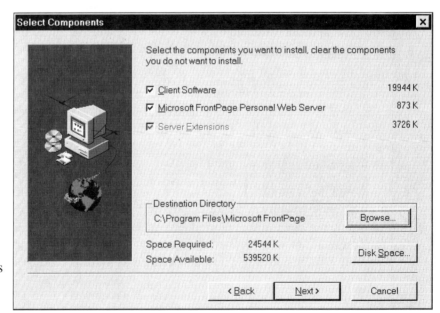

Specifying the components to be installed

FIGURE A-11

5. If you want to use the FPPWS and have no other servers installed, the default directory for the FrontPage server software as well as the webs that you create will be displayed in the Choose Microsoft FrontPage Personal Web Server Directory dialog box. The default directory is C:\FrontPage Webs and is the recommendation assumed in this book. Click on Next to select it, or first use Browse to choose a new directory.

6. The Start Copying Files dialog box will display your own selections for directories and components that will be installed. The defaults are shown in Figure A-12. If you agree with the selections, click on Next to copy the programs from the source to the destination directories. If you see something you want to change, click on Back as necessary to return to the original dialog box of the item that needs attention, change it, and then click on Next as necessary to return and begin the copying.

7. Complete the setup by following steps 14 through 19 of the Typical installation.

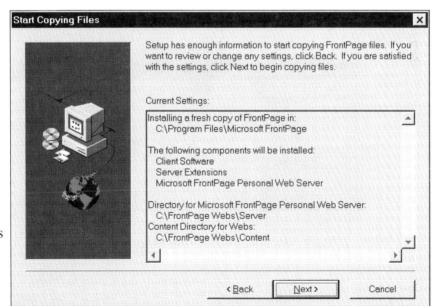

Components to be copied to the selected directories

FIGURE A-12

Checking Your Network Setup

The FrontPage package includes a program that tests whether you are properly set up on a network with the TCP/IP protocol, and what your host name and IP address are. Run that test as follows:

1. From the FrontPage Explorer open the Help menu, and click on About Microsoft FrontPage Explorer. In the About FrontPage Explorer dialog box click on Network Test. The FrontPage TCP/IP Test dialog box will open.

2. Click on Start Test. You may be asked if you want to connect to your Internet service provider (ISP). If you want to use a personal web server for the local creation of your webs, click on Cancel in the Connect To dialog box. (Use of a personal web server is assumed and recommended in this book.)

3. Your test results will appear. If all is well, they will look similar to those shown in the following illustration. If any of the boxes says "No," you have a problem. Listed next are several ideas to locate and solve these problems. Table A-1 explains each of the boxes in the FrontPage TCP/IP Test dialog box and what a negative answer might mean.

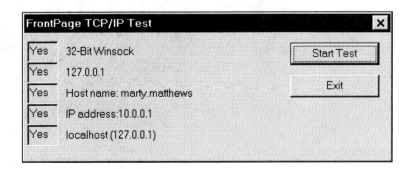

4. Click on Exit to close the FrontPage TCP/IP Test dialog box.

Element	Description
32-Bit Winsock	Verifies that the software connection between Windows 95/NT and TCP/IP networking is present. If this is not present, then either TCP/IP is not installed, or you have a Windows problem and probably need to reinstall it. See the following ideas and solutions for installing TCP/IP.
127.0.0.1	Verifies that you have a local web server available with this standard IP address. If this is false, and you want a local web server, you need to install a personal web server.
Hostname	Verifies the name of the web server that will be used by FrontPage. If this is not present and Localhost is confirmed, you can use "localhost." A negative response may mean that a web server is not installed or not functioning.
IP address	Verifies the IP address of the web server that will be used by FrontPage. If this is not present and Localhost is confirmed, you can use "localhost." A negative response may mean that a web server is not installed or not functioning.
Localhost (127.0.0.1)	Verifies that the name "localhost" and its IP address can alternately be used in place of the host name.

TCP/IP
Test Results

TABLE A-1

Here are some ideas of where to look for solutions:

■ Is a web server, personal or otherwise, running or available on your computer? If you haven't already, you need to install a web server (this is hard not to do because FrontPage Setup should have prompted you to install one), or you need to confirm your connection to your intranet or Internet web server.

- Do you have two web servers assigned to port 80? If you have two servers available, only one can be assigned to port 80; the other needs to be assigned to port 8080, which can also be addressed by FrontPage. A program, the FrontPage Server Administrator, and a help file are available to cure this and other server-related problems. These are located at C:\Program Files\Microsoft FrontPage\Bin\Fpsrvwin.exe and Fpsrvwin.hlp if you have a default installation.

- Is FrontPage installed properly? Uninstall and reinstall it using nothing but defaults, and make absolutely sure nothing but Windows and possibly MSPWS are running during installation.

- If you are on a network, make sure that the TCP/IP protocol has been set up. Do that by opening your Control Panel (Start menu, Settings, Control Panel) and double-clicking on Network. There you should see TCP/IP as a protocol, as you can see in Figure A-13 (you may only need it on either your LAN or your dialup network, and not necessarily on both, as shown in Figure A-13).

  If you don't have TCP/IP as one of your protocols, click on Add in the Network control panel, double-click on Protocol, click on Microsoft in the left list, and then click on TCP/IP on the right. Click on OK twice, and answer Yes to restarting your computer. There is also a special help file on this subject at C:\Program Files\Microsoft FrontPage\Bin\Fpnetwrk.hlp if you have a default installation.

- If you are using the Internet over phone lines, you need to have dialup networking installed and the TCP/IP protocol assigned to it. The easiest way to do that is to install Microsoft Plus for Windows 95 and to use it to install Internet capability. The help file mentioned in the last point also provides help in this situation.

Installing the Microsoft Image Composer

The FrontPage 97 with Bonus Pack includes a full, bitmap-image creation and editing program called Microsoft Image Composer, which is explained and demonstrated in detail in Chapter 6. Install that program next with these steps:

1. Insert or Reinsert the FrontPage 97 with Bonus Pack CD, or double-click on FrontPage Setup either locally or over a network to open the FrontPage 97 With Bonus Pack dialog box. Then click on the Microsoft Image Composer icon.

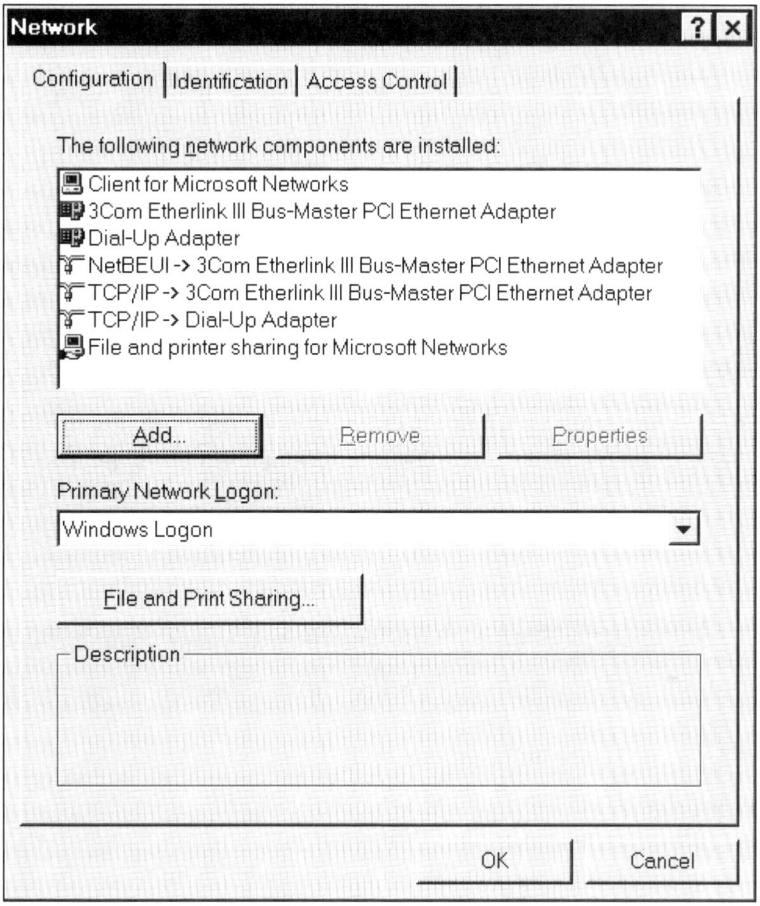

Network
control
panel
where
TCP/IP is
installed

FIGURE A-13

2. After several message boxes appear, the Microsoft Image Composer Setup Welcome message appears. Click on Continue. Enter and confirm your name and organization, clicking on OK after each step. Click on OK to acknowledge the Product ID number. Read the License Agreement and then, if you do, click on "I Agree."

3. Accept the default path for installing Microsoft Image Composer, and click on the Complete/Custom Install button. Select the options you want installed or accept the defaults and click on Continue. Accept the default

program group and click on Continue. The copying process will begin, and a thermometer bar will appear to inform you of the progress. Upon completion you will get a message of its success. Click on OK.

4. To make sure the program is available, open the Start menu, choose Programs, Microsoft Image Composer, and click on Image Composer 1.0. The Microsoft Image Composer window should appear, as you can see in Figure A-14.

5. Close the Microsoft Image Composer.

Installing the Web Publishing Wizard

The Web Publishing Wizard helps in transferring the web pages you create to the ultimate web server. If that server is not running the FrontPage Server Extensions,

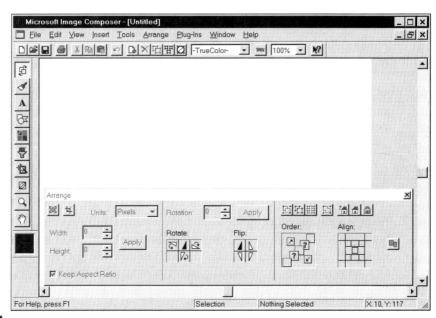

Microsoft Image Composer window

FIGURE A-14

the Web Publishing Wizard will help identify the parts of a web that need to be changed. Install the Web Publishing Wizard with the following instructions:

1. From the FrontPage 97 with Bonus Pack CD or over a network, open the FrontPage 97 With Bonus Pack dialog box, and then click on the Web Publishing Wizard icon.

2. Click on Yes to agree to the End-User License Agreement (if you do), and then you'll see several message boxes and thermometer bars informing you of the installation progress.

3. Upon completion you'll get a message on how to locate the Web Publishing Wizard. Click on OK. You'll then be told that you need to restart your computer. Click on Yes to do so.

4. Try out the Web Publishing Wizard by opening the Start menu; choosing Programs, Accessories, Internet Tools; and clicking on Web Publishing Wizard. The Web Publishing Wizard will appear, as shown in Figure A-15.

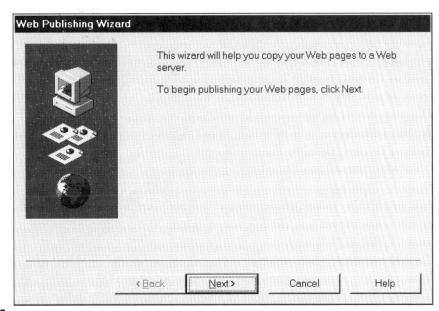

Web
Publishing
Wizard
dialog box

FIGURE A-15

5. Click on Cancel and then on Yes to confirm that you want to leave the Web Publishing Wizard. Chapter 17 describes how to use the Web Publishing Wizard.

All of your FrontPage products should now be installed and ready for you to use. Turn to Chapter 1 to begin doing so.

FrontPage 97 Software Developer's Kit

rontPage 97 includes a number of tools to make the web designer's job easier. These include templates for pages and webs, wizards, and WebBots. You can also create your own templates, wizards, and bots, as well as customize the FrontPage interface using the FrontPage 97 Software Developer's Kit (SDK). Some of the tools included with the FrontPage SDK require a knowledge of programming languages such as C++, Perl (Practical Extraction and Report Language), and Visual Basic, while others merely require a thorough knowledge of FrontPage. The SDK provides detailed information about the FrontPage file structure and Windows Registry entries, and a number of examples are included. This appendix is an overview of the FrontPage SDK tools and features that you can use to customize and expand the features of FrontPage.

Installing the FrontPage SDK

The FrontPage 97 SDK is available from Microsoft's FrontPage web site. These steps will take you through the process of downloading and installing the SDK:

1. In Windows Explorer create a new folder named **FPSDK**, for example, C:\FPSDK.

2. Open your web browser (your Internet connection should already be open), and then open Microsoft's FrontPage SDK download web page at http://www.microsoft.com/frontpage/softlib/fs_fp_sdk.htm. The FrontPage SDK license agreement is displayed.

NOTE: *Microsoft's FrontPage web site (http://www.microsoft.com/frontpage) contains a great deal of information and tools for working with FrontPage. You should familiarize yourself with what's available on the site and visit it often for the latest updates and news about FrontPage.*

3. If you agree with the terms of the license agreement, click on the "I have read and accept the terms of this agreement" hyperlink. The FrontPage SDK download page will be displayed.

4. Right-click on the "fp97sdk.exe" hyperlink, and select Save Target As from the context menu.

5. In the Save As dialog box that will be displayed, select the FPSDK folder you created and click on Save.

NOTE: *The fp97sdk.exe file download is about 900K and requires about 3.3MB of hard drive space when installed.*

B

6. When the download is complete, close your browser.

7. Click on the Start menu button on the taskbar, and then select Run from the Start menu.

8. In the Run dialog box click on Browse, and then open the folder where you have saved the download and select fp97sdk.exe. Click on OK.

9. In the Run dialog box type **-d** after the filename. Leave a space between the filename and the -d switch, as shown here:

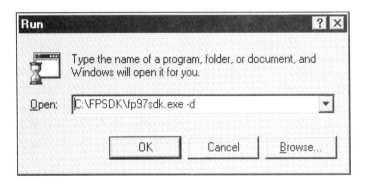

NOTE: *Extracting the file with the -d switch retains the directory structure of the FrontPage SDK. If you don't use the switch, or extract the files by double-clicking on it in the Windows Explorer, the directory structure will be lost, and all the files will be extracted to the same directory. You must extract the file with the -d switch.*

10. Click on OK. A DOS window will open and display the directories and files being extracted.

11. When the extraction is complete (the DOS window title bar will display "Finished – fp97sdk"), close the DOS window by clicking on the Close button in the upper-right corner.

12. In the Windows Explorer open the FPSDK folder. You may delete the fp97sdk.exe file if you want.

The fp97sdk.exe will have been extracted to six directories.

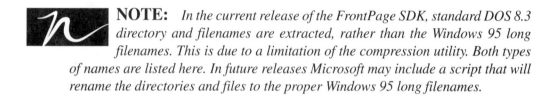 **NOTE:** *In the current release of the FrontPage SDK, standard DOS 8.3 directory and filenames are extracted, rather than the Windows 95 long filenames. This is due to a limitation of the compression utility. Both types of names are listed here. In future releases Microsoft may include a script that will rename the directories and files to the proper Windows 95 long filenames.*

- **CGI** Contains example CGI (common gateway interface) scripts using the standard CGI, programs to interface between the standard CGI and the Windows CGI (CGI-WIN), and an interface between the standard CGI and OLE (Object Linking and Embedding) server DLLs (dynamic link libraries). The CGI is used to exchange information between a web browser and executable files on the web server. These files resolve some problems in interfacing between the standard CGI and CGI-WIN, and in accessing the server OLE DLLs.

- **Designer HTML** (Design~1) is the term Microsoft uses to describe an extension of the WebBot HTML Markup component. This extension allows you to drag and drop HTML into a FrontPage web and create an alternate display in the FrontPage Editor for unknown HTML. (The standard display is a small icon with a question mark, shown in the margin.)

- **Template** Includes the Web Template Maker for creating FrontPage web templates.

- **Utility** Contains utility programs that you can use to work with the FrontPage API (application programming interface), to launch a FrontPage web and open a page for editing by clicking on a hyperlink, and to create web template directories based on a current FrontPage web.

- **WebBot** Contains information you need to create your own WebBot components, including a *hit-counter* (used to record and display the number of times a particular web page has been visited).

- **Wizards** Contains code samples and examples for creating your own FrontPage wizards.

In addition, the root directory contains the FrontPage SDK documentation (C:\FPSDK\ Fpdevkit.doc) in Microsoft Word format.

There are tools and examples that can benefit FrontPage users with almost any level of experience in the FrontPage SDK. In the following sections the contents of each directory are described in more detail, and some of the more useful examples and utilities are shown.

B

NOTE: *Examples that require a knowledge of programming languages such as C++ are not described in detail in this appendix. If you are a programmer, you will find many code samples and tools in the SDK to help you customize and expand the functions included with FrontPage.*

Using the Common Gateway Interface (CGI)

The CGI is a protocol used to pass data between a web page and an executable program on the web server. Information from forms is commonly processed by a CGI script or program, for example. CGI scripts are commonly written in Perl, though they can be written in any programming language supported by the server's operating system, such as Visual Basic or C++. The CGI scripts and programs are, by convention, usually placed in a directory named CGI-Bin on the server, though the directory name Scripts is also used (with Microsoft's Internet Information Server and the Microsoft Personal Web Server, for example). The name of the directory is not important as long as the hyperlinks in the web page contain the correct URL.

Executable files on a web server need to be placed in a separate directory for server security. Permission for anonymous users (users accessing the files over the Internet) to execute the files is granted, but permission to write files to the directory is not. This prevents anonymous users from uploading an executable program to a server and then running it, which could have disastrous consequences for the webmaster. (Read permission is normally all that is granted to anonymous users on a web server, though write permission is granted when the users will need to add or change the data stored on the server. An example would be the directory containing files for a discussion group.) The webmaster of your server can give you more information on how the CGI is implemented.

Problems with use of the CGI include the fact that the standard CGI, such as you would find on a UNIX server, is not exactly the same as the Windows CGI, which you would use on a Windows NT server. Also, the standard CGI does not allow easy access to API (application programming interface) DLLs (dynamic link libraries). A dynamic link library is a shared program that performs a specific task. DLLs are called by other applications during their execution. For Windows NT servers the FrontPage 97 server extensions are written as DLLs. (Previously, the FrontPage server extensions were standard programs.) DLLs are loaded into memory the first time they are called by an application and then stay memory resident. A standard program that performs the same task would be loaded and unloaded each time it was called. Using DLLs decreases the server response times and the size of programs that call them. Much of the Windows 95 and NT operating systems are DLLs.

These issues are primarily a concern of the server's webmaster. As a FrontPage author you simply need to know the correct URL to the CGI or Scripts directory and what scripts or applications are available for you to use—for example, a standard form handler. The utilities included in the FrontPage SDK CGI directory require a C compiler to create the executable files from the included source code.

Working with Designer HTML

This extension to the HTML Markup WebBot component is one that you may find extremely useful, and it doesn't require a knowledge of programming to use. With the normal HTML Markup bot you enter additional HTML in the FrontPage HTML Markup dialog box, either by typing the code directly into the dialog box or by pasting it in from the Windows Clipboard. With Designer HTML you can drag and drop the HTML into the FrontPage Editor, or use the File command from the Insert menu. In addition, you can also define a graphic or HTML code to be used to represent the inserted HTML. This makes it easy to see what type of HTML is inserted (for example, a JavaScript file). Designer HTML enables you to create a library of specialized HTML modules that can be easily inserted into any web page.

The examples included with the FrontPage SDK include a search page with predefined parameters, a JavaScript script that displays the current date and time, an image map with hotspots and hyperlinks predefined, and a replacement display for Excel Internet Assistant files.

Building your Own Templates

Working with and creating page and web templates is covered in Chapter 4, along with a discussion of the Web Template Maker included with the FrontPage SDK. The Template directory of the FrontPage SDK includes a template for a frameset with three equal rows, with the middle row divided into two columns; a page template with a one-row by three-column table; and two web templates: a corporate presence web and a web that can be used to test the custom WebBots included with the SDK. Use of this web will be covered in the section on WebBots.

Templates must be copied to the appropriate directories to be used with FrontPage. For the page template the default path is C:\Program Files\Microsoft FrontPage\Pages. For the web templates the path is C:\Program Files\Microsoft FrontPage\Webs. Chapter 4 further explains the placing of templates in the proper subdirectories.

Frameset templates differ from the other types. Page and web templates are basically identical to other pages and webs. *Frameset* templates consist of a text file (with the extension .FRM) that contains the specifications for the frameset. When the template file is loaded by the Frames Wizard, this text file is used to create the actual frameset. These templates are placed in the framewiz.wiz subdirectory of the Pages directory (C:\Program Files\Microsoft FrontPage\Pages\framewiz.wiz) by default.

Applying the SDK Utilities

In addition to the Web Template Maker mentioned in the previous section, the Utility directory contains two other utilities: APITest and FPlaunch. APITest is a resource for Visual Basic programmers, as it contains code for testing all the FrontPage OLE (Object Linking and Embedding) APIs. Figure B-1 shows the dialog box generated by the Apitests.exe application (C:\FPSDK\Utility\Apitests\Apitests.exe). Clicking on one of the buttons displays a dialog box with the information about the current FrontPage web. The dialog box displayed by clicking on the FrontPage Explorer Web Information button is shown in Figure B-2. The Built-in Key drop-down menu contains a list of the FrontPage built-in keys (name-value pairs that set FrontPage properties). The sections FrontPage Explorer Automation, FrontPage Editor Automation, and FrontPage To Do List Automation in the FrontPage SDK documentation contain detailed information about each of the calls supported by FrontPage.

```
 ■ FrontPage 1.1 API Tests                                    ☒

  INSTRUCTIONS: Open a familiar web in the FrontPage Explorer. Then click on the buttons
  below to exercise various parts of the FrontPage 1.1 API.

  ┌ FrontPage Explorer ──────────────────────────────────────────────┐
  │                                                                    │
  │  ┌ Web Information ┐  ┌ List Documents ┐  ┌ Open Web ┐  ┌ Put Documents ┐ │
  │                                                                    │
  │  ┌ Create/Remove ┐  ┌ Page Information ┐  ┌ Get Document ┐  ┌ Miscellaneous ┐ │
  │                                                                    │
  └────────────────────────────────────────────────────────────────────┘

  ┌ FrontPage Editor ────────────────────────────────────────────────┐
  │                                                                    │
  │  ┌ Open Web Page ┐  ┌ Query Web Page ┐  ┌ Bring to Top ┐  ┌ New Web Page ┐ │
  │                                                                    │
  └────────────────────────────────────────────────────────────────────┘

  ┌ FrontPage To Do List ────────────────────────────────────────────┐
  │                                                                    │
  │  ┌ Show/Hide ┐  ┌ Get Task Count ┐  ┌ Add Task ┐  ┌ Complete Task ┐ │
  │                                                                    │
  └────────────────────────────────────────────────────────────────────┘
```

FrontPage
API Tests
dialog box

■ FIGURE B-1

FPlaunch (C:\FPSDK\Utility\Fplaunch\Fplaunch.exe) is a utility that will open a FrontPage web in the FrontPage Explorer and then open the specified page in the FrontPage Editor to be edited. This utility is called by a hyperlink. The name of the web and file to open are stored in a text file with the extension .FPL. The .FPL file contains four lines:

- **Web Server Name** is the name of the server where the web is located.

- **Web Name** is the name of the FrontPage web.

- **Username** is the user name of the person editing the web and will be placed in the Login dialog box when FPlaunch is run (optional).

- **Page URL** is the URL of the page in the selected web that will be opened in the FrontPage Editor.

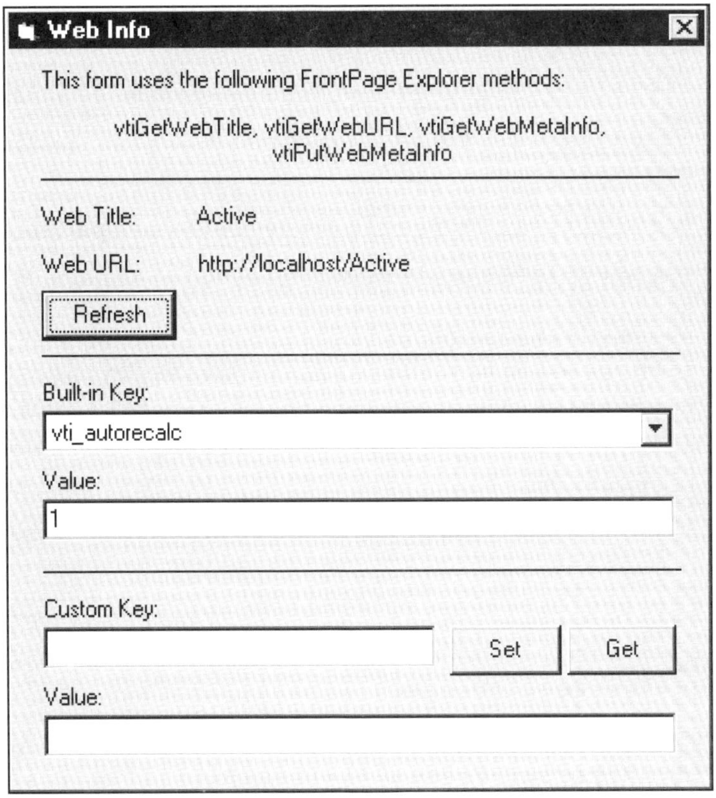

Web Info
dialog box

FIGURE B-2

For example:

```
http://mydomain.com
MyWeb
Administrator
Default.htm
```

To use the FPlaunch utility, you will need to create a new MIME type in your system configuration. You can configure your system and test the setup with these steps:

1. In Windows Explorer open the View menu and select Options.

2. Click on the File Types tab in the Options dialog box, and then click on the New Type button. The Add New File Type dialog box will open.

3. In the Description Of Type text box type **FPlaunch parameter file**.

4. Type **fpl** in the Associated Extension text box and press TAB.

5. Type **application/x-fplaunch** in the Content Type (MIME) text box, and then click on New. (If you get a message the "extension .fpl is already in use," click on OK and then Cancel, select the FPL type in the File Types tab of the Options dialog box, and click on Remove. Then start again with Step 2.)

6. In the New Action dialog box, type **open** in the Action text box, and then press TAB.

7. Click on the Browse button, and then locate the FPlaunch.exe file in the Open With dialog box (C:\FPSDK\Utility\FPlaunch\fplaunch.exe). Click on Open; then click on OK.

8. Clear the Confirm Open After Download check box. Your Add New File Type dialog box should look like Figure B-3.

9. Click on Close; then click on Close again.

Next you need to create an FPlaunch parameter file to test your configuration.

10. Open Notepad or another text editor.

11. Type **http://localhost** and press ENTER. Type **active** and press ENTER again.

12. If you used a user name and password with your FrontPage Active web, type the user name on this line, and then press ENTER. If not, press ENTER to leave a blank line. (The parameter file must be exactly four lines long, and the correct parameter must be on each line.)

13. Type **Default.htm**. Save the file in the FPlaunch directory (C:\FPSDK\ Utility\FPlaunch) with the name **Active.fpl**.

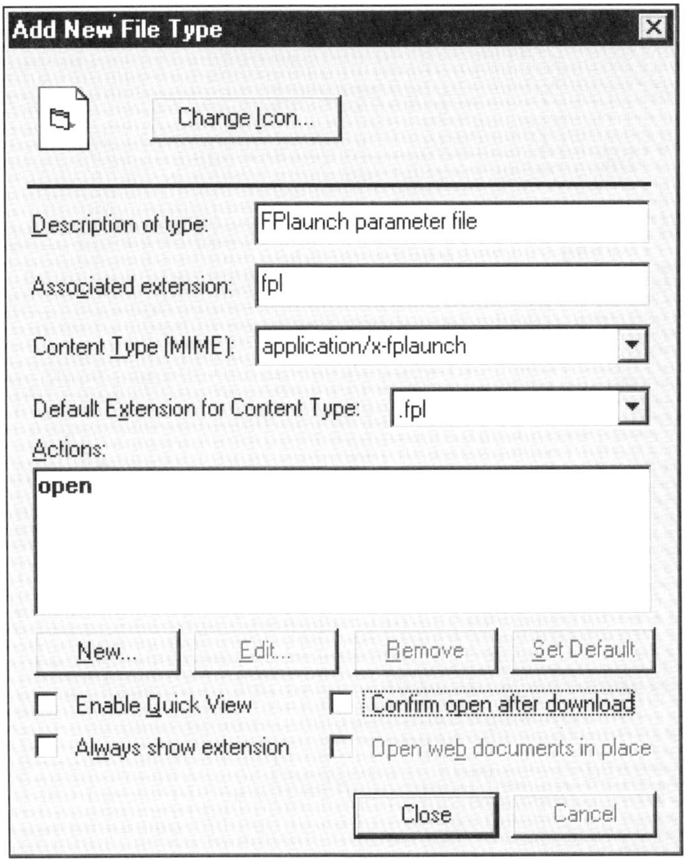

Add New File Type

Change Icon...

Description of type: FPlaunch parameter file

Associated extension: fpl

Content Type (MIME): application/x-fplaunch

Default Extension for Content Type: .fpl

Actions:

open

New... Edit... Remove Set Default

☐ Enable Quick View ☐ Confirm open after download
☐ Always show extension ☐ Open web documents in place

Close Cancel

B

Add New
File Type
dialog box

FIGURE B-3

14. Close Notepad or the text editor you used.

The final step is to create a hyperlink on a web page to call the FPlaunch utility.

15. Open the Active web in the FrontPage Explorer. Open the FrontPage Editor and create a new Normal page.

16. At the top of the page type **This link will open the home page for editing**.

17. Select the words "This link," and click on the Create Or Edit Hyperlink toolbar button.

18. In the Create Hyperlink dialog box, click on the World Wide Web tab, and then select Other from the Hyperlink Type drop-down menu.

19. In the URL text box type **C:\FPSDK\Utility\FPlaunch\Active.fpl** and then click on OK.

20. Save the web page with the title **FPlaunch Test Page** and the filename **FPlaunch.htm**.

21. Close FrontPage Editor and FrontPage Explorer.

22. Open your web browser and type **http:/serername/active/ FPlaunch.htm** in the Address or Location text box and press ENTER.

23. When the page is loaded, click on the "This link" hyperlink. The FrontPage Explorer will open, and then the FrontPage Editor with the Active Web Home Page loaded, ready for editing.

If you have a web where you regularly edit certain pages, you can use the FPlaunch utility to create a page of links to those pages. Then you can just load the page into your browser and select the hyperlink to the page you want to work on.

Creating Your Own WebBots

The are many examples of the standard WebBots included with FrontPage 97 in this book. With the tools and information included with the FrontPage SDK you can also create your own WebBots to automate tasks. WebBots must exist on the web server where your FrontPage webs are located in order to be used by a web. In other words, they are server-side components. Once the bots are on the server, they can be called by any FrontPage web page. The web page contains HTML that identifies the bot and calls it when the page is opened by the server. A complete explanation of this process is included in the FrontPage SDK documentation.

The WebBot directory of the FrontPage SDK contains source code in Visual C++, Perl, and TCL (Tool Command Language, pronounced "tickle"). Executables for Windows are also included (if you use a UNIX server, you will need to compile the source code for your platform). The Template directory of the SDK contains a template for creating a web to test the bots in the WebBot directory.

NOTE: *To use the WebBot components written in Perl or TCL, you must have these languages installed on your server, and the .INF files included in the SDK must include the URL of the language executables.*

Using the SDK's Wizards

In FrontPage you use wizards to create entire webs or pages. A wizard typically presents a series of dialog boxes that you make choices from, and then the wizard program uses the information entered to create the web or page. Wizards use FrontPage OLE calls to create the webs or pages, and so can be written in any programming language that supports OLE calls, such as Visual Basic or C++.

In the Wizards folder of the FrontPage SDK are two web wizards and two pages wizards. The web wizards included create a simple "Hello world" web and a web for real estate information. The page wizards create a "Hello world" page and a calendar page that uses HTML tables. To use the wizards, you first need to copy them to the appropriate directories. Web wizards are placed in the FrontPage Webs directory (C:\Program Files\Microsoft FrontPage\Webs) by default, and page wizards are placed in the Pages directory (C:\Program Files\Microsoft FrontPage\Pages). Each wizard is stored in a folder that has the .WIZ extension. To use these wizards, you also need to copy the Vb and Vc directories in the SDK to the FrontPage root directory (C:\Program Files\Microsoft FrontPage\ with the default installation).

If you plan to use FrontPage on a regular basis, you should download the FrontPage SDK and study the examples. There is a great deal of useful information included and, if you are a programmer, sample code that you can use in your own work.

B

NOTE:Page numbers in *italics* refer to illustrations or charts.

SYMBOLS

& (ampersand), HTML, 398
< (less-than character), HTML, 398
> (greater-than character), HTML, 398

A

Access. *See* Microsoft Access
access control, 503-519
 See also security
 firewalls, 517-519
 IIS (Internet Information
  Servers), 513-516
 IIS/Windows NT, *515*
 intranet, 517-519
 IP address control, 514
 lists (ACLs), 516, *517*
 NTFS (NT File System) control,
  516, *517*
 security, 503
 Server Extensions, 621
 setting up users and groups,
  509-512
 types of, 503
 user account control, 514
 virtual directory control, 514-516
 web server, 512-516, *517*
 web site, 504-509
Access Control Lists (ACLs), NTFS
 (NT File System), 516, *517*
ActiveX, 558-575
 Control Properties dialog box,
  561-564
 controls, 560, 561
 FrontPage and, 561-562
 installing ScriptActive plug-in,
  568-569
 Java comparison, 560, 575-576
 NCompass Labs plug-ins for
  Netscape Navigator, 567-569
 Netscape Navigator and, 562,
  566-568
 Netscape Navigator ONE (Open
  Network Environment),
  560-561
 OBJECT tag, 565-566, 567-568
 OBJECT tag attributes, *567*
 object-oriented programming, 560
 objects, 560
 OLE (Object Linking and
  Embedding) and, 559-560
 overview, 558-561
 resources, 560
Actual Size icon, Image Composer, *200*

Add A Product Confirmation page,
 North Beach Tools database, *496*
Add A Product page, North Beach
 Tools database, *492*, *494*
Add Choice dialog box, building
 forms, *319*
Add Editor Association dialog box,
 importing files from word
 processors, 367-368
Add New File Type dialog box,
 FPlaunch utility, 678, *679*
Add To Do Task dialog box, To Do
 Lists, *65*
Add Users dialog box, permissions,
 507, *508*
addresses
 See also hyperlinks; resources;
  URLs
 IP. *See* IP addresses
administration
 Internet Services Administrator,
  477
 ODBC Data Source
  Administrator dialog box, 469,
  471
 WWW Administrator Directory
  web page, 476-478, *479*
Administration tab, installing
 Microsoft Personal Web Server
 (MSPWS), 647-651
AFFI files, importing multimedia,
 381-383
Agenda.tem folder, .INF template
 information files, 129
Airbrush tool, Image Composer Paint
 tool and palette, 234, *235*
alignment
 form fields, 307
 Horizontal Alignment option (cell
  properties), *272*
 Vertical Alignment option (cell
  properties), *272*
Alignment option, table properties, *267*
Allprod.idc file, IDC files, 478-482,
 484
AltaVista
 home page, *5*
 search results, *6*
ampersand (&), HTML, 398
anchor tag attributes, HTML, *406*
animation
 See also multimedia files
 GIF graphics, 24
Animation Player, Microsoft
 PowerPoint, 380
annotation text, Personal Web
 template, 111
API Tests dialog box, SDK Utility
 directory, 675, *676*
Applet Properties dialog box, Java, *551*
APPLET tag attributes, Java, 553, *554*

applets. *See* Java
arguments, JavaScript, 584
ARPANET, history of Internet, 8
Arrange tool, Image Composer, 201,
 228
art. *See* clip art; graphics; Image
 Composer; word art
Art Effects tool and palette, Image
 Composer, 203
asymmetric cryptography. *See* public
 key encryption
attributes
 Extended Attributes dialog box,
  435-437
 HTML, 391
audio. *See* multimedia files; sound files
authentication
 SSL (Secure Sockets Layer),
  523-524
 user account control, 514
Author configuration variable,
 Substitution WebBot, *341*
authoring resources, HTML, 437-440
automatic confirmation forms, 325, *326*
automatic web template creation,
 149-151
 FrontPage Web Template Maker,
  150, *151*
automating web information. *See*
 WebBots
Available Disk Space dialog box,
 Custom FrontPage installations,
 658, *659*
AVI files, importing multimedia,
 381-383

B

backbone, Internet, 8
backgrounds, 46, 182-188
 Corporate Presence Wizard, 76
 Page Properties dialog box, *183*
 single image, 186-188
 solid color, 183-185
 textured, 185-186
bandwidth
 data throughput and, 18
 web publishing and, 619
Bar Net web site, 635-639
 home page, *636*
 Hosted Sites page, *637*
 questions and answers, 639
 Search page, *638*
A Beginner's Guide to HTML, HTML
 authoring resources, 438
Berners-Lee, Tim, World Wide Web
 creator, 9
bibliography
 See also resources
 security, 524-525

683

Bonus Pack CD-ROM
  See also installing FrontPage 97
    with Bonus Pack
  contents of, 642-643
  Web Publishing Wizard, 626-632
  Webtempl.exe (automatic web
    template creation), 150-151
The BookBay web site, 384-388
  home page, *385*
  questions and answers, 386-388
bookmarks, 242-243
  defined, 6-7, 242
  HTML, 405
  hyperlinks and, 244-246, *250*
  Personal Web template, 108-109
Border Size option, table properties,
  267
bots. *See* WebBots
breakpoints, Microsoft Script
  Debugger, 592-593
broken links, hyperlink management,
  262
browsers
  active features, 534-535
  defined, 4
  form validation, 310
  forms and, 324-328
  frames and, 59
  HTML and, 18-21
  imported files and, 378-381
  Preview In Browser feature, 31
  Table of Contents template, *124*
  tables and, 18, *19-20*
  testing hotspots with, 258
  testing hyperlinks with, 248-251
  Web design and, 18-21
Budget Home Page, building web
  templates, 139-143
Bugs page, Customer Support Web
  template, 117
bytecode, programming languages, 575

C

calibrating monitor color settings, 17
Caption, Cell, or Table Properties
  option, Table menu, *275*
CD-ROM in back of book. *See* Bonus
  Pack CD-ROM
Cell Padding option, table properties,
  267
cell properties, 271-274, *272*
Cell Properties dialog box, *271*
  HTX files, 483-484
Cell Spacing option, table properties,
  267
cells
  Cell Properties option (Table
    menu), *275*
  deleting, 277

Insert Cell option, *275*, 276
Merge Cells option (Table menu),
  275
Split Cells option (Table menu),
  275, 277-278
table, 264-265
certificates, public key, 524
CGI (common gateway interface)
  DLLs and, 674
  FrontPage SDK (Software
    Developer's Kit), 672, 673-674
  FrontPage Server Extensions and,
    620
  standard versus Windows, 674
cgi-bin directory
  manual web template creation,
    146-147
  web directory structure, *145*
character escape sequences, HTML,
  398, *400*
character styles
  FrontPage Editor, 42
  HTML, 395-398, *399-400*
Check Box Properties dialog box,
  forms, *319*
Clear Selection icon, Image Composer,
  200
client software, installing FrontPage 97
  with Bonus Pack, 644
client-side versus server-side
  validation of forms, 310
client/server relationships, HTTP and,
  11-12
clip art, Fantasy Travel web, 181-182
Clipboard, pasting text from, 353-354
color backgrounds, 183-185
Color Format icon, Image Composer,
  200
color names, HTML, 392
Color Picker dialog box
  Image Composer, *205*
  Image Composer text sprites, *225*
Color Ramp, Image Composer, 204
color settings, monitor, 15-17
Color Swatch and Color Picker, Image
  Composer, 204-206
color text, FrontPage Editor, 44, *45*
Color Tuning tool and palette, Image
  Composer, 203, *204*
columns
  Database Column Value dialog
    box (HTX files), 482-483
  Insert Rows Or Columns option,
    275, 276
  selecting table, 273, *275*, 277
Columns option, table properties, 267
combo boxes, defined, 5
commands, SQL statement, *451*
comment tags, JavaScript, 583
Comment WebBot, 331-332
compiling Java applets, 553-558

DOS windows, 556-558
  WordPad, 555-556
Composing Good HTML, HTML
  authoring resources, 438
configuration variables, Substitution
  WebBot, 341
configuring TCP/IP, 605-608
  TCP/IP Properties dialog box,
    606, 607, *609*
Confirm Save dialog box, HTML
  Conversion Utility, *571*
Confirmation Field WebBot, 332-335,
  336
  Component Properties dialog box,
    333
  described, *60*
  Literature Request form, *334*
  Settings For Saving Results Of
    Form dialog box, 334, *335*
Confirmation Form template, 119-120
confirmation forms, automatic, 325,
  326
contact information, Form Page
  Wizard, 302, *303*
content
  designing for World Wide Web, 22
  intranet, 600-601, 612-613
  planning for on webs, 155
controlling access. *See* access control
controls. *See* ActiveX
conversions, automatic graphic, 48
converting web sites to FrontPage with
  Import Web Wizard, 98-99
Corporate Presence Wizard, 74-94
  background and text color, 76
  Edit Hyperlink dialog box, 85-86
  Feedback page, 88-91
  Folder view, 78, *79*
  Home Page icon, 78
  home pages, 80-82
  HTML, 428-432, *433*
  Hyperlink view, 78
  Image Properties dialog box,
    84-85, *84*
  logo.htm, 83
  news.htm, 82
  presentation style options, 76, *78*
  Preview in Browser dialog box, 88
  Products & Services page, 83-87
  Properties dialog box, *80*
  Search page, 91-94
  Table of Contents page, 87-88, *89*
  To Do Lists, 77-78, *79*
  Under Construction icon, 77
  web server selection, 75
Create Hyperlink dialog box, *61*, *240*
  hotspots, *255*
Create New Data Source dialog box,
  defining System DSN (Data Source
  Name), 469, *470*
cryptography. *See* encryption

CU-SeeMe, multimedia files, 25-26
Custom Background option, cell properties, *272*
Custom Colors option, cell properties, *272*
Custom FrontPage installations, 659-661
    Available Disk Space dialog box, 659, *660*
    Select Components dialog box, 659, *660*
    Start Copying Files dialog box, 661
Custom Palette tab, Image Composer, 206
customer service, Feedback Form template, 120-121
Customer Support Web template, 116-118
    Bugs page, 117
    Drop-Down Menu Properties dialog box, *117*
    FTP transfers, 117, *118*
Customers table, North Beach Tools database, 456-457, 465-467

D

data authentication, 514, 523-524
Data Length option, Text Box Validation dialog box, *312*
data throughput
    bandwidth and, 18
    World Wide Web design and, 17-18
Data Type option, Text Box Validation dialog box, *312*
Data Value option, Text Box Validation dialog box, *312*
Database Column Value dialog box, HTX files, 482-483
Database Connector Wizard dialog box, IDC files, 479-480, *481*
database relationships, Microsoft Access, 462-464, *465*
databases, 441-498
    adding products to, 490-495
    defined, 442
    deleting records, 495-498
    error messages, *496*
    exporting data from with text files, 305
    fields, 442
    flat-file, 442
    FrontPage Web Settings dialog box, *472*
    HTTPODBC.DLL, 452
    HTX files, 446, 447-448, 482-485
    IDC files, 446, *447*, 475-482

IIS (Internet Information Servers), 442
    Microsoft Access, 445, 452-471
    Microsoft SQL Server, 445-446
    New Table dialog box, *455*
    North Beach Tools, 443, *444*, 452-462
    ODBC (Open Database Connectivity), 451
    one-to-many relationships, 443, *444*
    Open Connectivity. *See* ODBC
    overview, 442-445
    records, 442
    relational. *See* relational databases
    requests and web servers, 451-452
    SQL statements, 448-451
    Table Design view, *456*
    tables, 442
    web servers and requests, 451-452
dates, Timestamp WebBot, *60*, 346-347
decryption, security, 519
default directories, installing FrontPage, 651-652
default home pages, Typical FrontPage installations, 657, *658*
Default Hyperlink section, hotspot locations, 257
Default.htm
    Fantasy Travel web, 158
    frames, 287
    Properties dialog box (Substitution WebBot), *342*, *343*
Delete icon, Image Composer, *200*
deleting
    cells, 277
    form fields, 308
    records, 495-498
    webs, 625-626
Description configuration variable, Substitution WebBot, *341*
Designer HTML, SDK directories, 672, 674
designing for World Wide Web, 13-22
    browsers and, 18-21
    content, 22
    data throughput, 17-18
    monitor color settings, 15-17
    monitor resolution, 14-15, *16*
Destination Path dialog box, Typical FrontPage installations, 653, *654*
digital signatures, SSL (Secure Sockets Layer), 523
directories
    executable scripts and IDC files, 475-478
    file structure and, 143, *144*, *145*
    Pages subdirectory, 127, *128*
    root, 126-127, *128*, 143

SDK (Software Developer's Kit), 672-681
    server, 126-127
    template, 126-127, 143
    Webs subdirectory, 127
Disallow First Item option, Drop-Down Menu Validation box, 311
discussion groups, Project Web template, 114-116
Discussion Web Wizard, 94-98
    options, 95
    posting articles, 97-98
disk space, Available Disk Space dialog box, 659, *660*
disk-based webs, advantages of, 29
Display Name option, Text Box Validation dialog box, *312*
DLLs (dynamic link libraries)
    CGI and, 674
    FrontPage Server Extensions and, 620
DocActive, Netscape Navigator plug-in, 568
.DOC files, importing files from word processors, 357-358
domain names, ISPs and, 619
DOS windows, compiling TicTacToe Java page, 556-558
downloading
    data throughput and, 17-18
    Java Development Kit (JDK), 543-547
    Microsoft Script Debugger, 593
drag and drop, importing files via, 368-370
Drop-Down Menu Properties dialog box
    building forms, *320*
    Customer Support Web template, *117*
Drop-Down Menu Validation box, validating forms, *311*
Duplicate icon, Image Composer, *200*
duplicating sprites, Image Composer, 216-217

E

e-mail
    See also Discussion Web Wizard
    mailto hyperlinks, 161, 247, *248*, *251*
Edit Frameset Grid dialog box, Frames Wizard, 288, *289*
Edit Hyperlink dialog box
    Corporate Presence Wizard, 85-86
    managing hyperlinks, *260*
    Personal Web template, *110*
editing forms, 306-316

Editor. *See* FrontPage Editor
Elements of HTML Style, HTML
   authoring resources, 438
EMBED tag, HTML Conversion
   Utility, 572, 574
encryption, 519-522
   combined public and private key.
      See SSL (Secure Sockets
      Layer)
   private key, 519
   public key, 520
Eraser tool, Paint tool and palette
   (Image Composer), 236
error messages, North Beach Tools
   database, *496*
escape sequences, HTML characters,
   398, *400*
Excel. *See* Microsoft Excel
executable scripts (IDC files),
   directories for, 475-478
Explorer. *See* FrontPage Explorer;
   Microsoft Internet Explorer
exporting
   graphics, 179
   web form and database data with
      text files, 305
Extended Attributes dialog box,
   HTML, 435-437
extensions
   hypertext files. *See* HTX files
   server. *See* Server Extensions
eye dropper icon, Image Composer,
   205

F

Fantasy Travel web, 157-190
   backgrounds, 182-188
   clip art, 181-182
   creating and inserting graphics,
      177-180
   current specials list, 163-165, *166*
   Default.htm, 158
   entering Travel Options offerings,
      170-172
   footers, 161-162
   frames, 286-293
   graphics, 177-190
   home page titles, 163
   horizontal lines, 180-181
   HTML example, 426-428
   hyperlinks and hotspots, 237-262
   importing tables, 176
   importing Travel Options
      offerings, 172-176
   inserting graphics, 177-180
   list of current specials, 163-165,
      166
   Page Properties dialog box, 159
   permissions, 504-512

   posting to hosts with Server
      Extensions, 623-625
   Save As dialog box, 159-160
   scanned images, 188-190
   scanner text imports, 172-173
   starting, 157-160
   tables and frames, 263-293
   text, 160-176
   titles, 163, 167-170
   Travel Options section, 165-167,
      170-176
Feedback Form template, 120-121
Feedback page, Corporate Presence
   Wizard, 88-91
fields (form)
   aligning, 307
   creating, 49-51
   creation buttons, *49*
   databases and, 442
   deleting, 308
   Hidden fields property, 314
   labels and text, 307
   parsing, 585-586
   placement of, 309-310
   properties, 308-309
   sizing, 308-309
   types of, 316, *317*
   validating, 310-313
File DSNs, System DSN (Data Source
   Name), 469
file formats
   importing files from word
      processors, *352*
   importing native formats, 366-368
   multimedia, *383*
file structure, web directories, 143,
   144, 145
file-sharing
   installing TCP/IP on networks,
      608
   permissions and, 504
[FileList] section, .INF template
   information files, 130-131
fills. *See* Patterns And Fills tool and
   palette
filters
   packet. *See* packet filtering
   Warps and Filters tool and palette
      (Image Composer), 178, 202,
      203, 224-225
finding information. *See* search
   engines; Search pages; Search
   WebBot; searches
firewalls, 503, 517-519
   intranet, 615-616
flat-file databases, 442
flipping sprites, Image Composer,
   216-217, 218-219
floating frames
   HTML, 434-435, *436*
   Netscape Navigator, 414

focus function, JavaScript, 586
Folder view
   Corporate Presence Wizard, 78, *79*
   FrontPage Explorer, 34
font styles, FrontPage Editor, 40-42
FONT tag, FrontPage Editor and, 40
fonts, FrontPage CD-ROM, 219-221,
   222
footers
   Fantasy Travel web, 161-162
   paragraph styles, 161
For-Next loops, JavaScript, 585, 587
Form Handler property, 313
Form Page Wizard, 301-316
   contact information, 302, *303*
   editing forms, 306-316
   Formatted paragraph style, 306,
      307
   FrontPage Editor and, *54, 55*
   generating forms, 301-305
   handling form input, 324-328
   question lists, 304, *305*
   question types, 301, *302*
Form Properties dialog box, 313, *314*
Form tags, HTML, 407, *408-409*
form validation, JavaScript, 310,
   576-588
Form Validation page, JavaScript, *578*
Formatted paragraph style
   Form Page Wizard, 306, 307
   FrontPage Editor, 40
formatting forms, 306
formatting text
   Fantasy Travel web, 160-176
   FrontPage Editor, 39-46
forms, 48-51, 299-328
   Add Choice dialog box, *319*
   aligning fields, 307
   automatic confirmation, 325, *326*
   browsers and, 324-328
   building from scratch, 316-324
   Check Box Properties dialog box,
      319
   Confirmation Form template,
      119-120
   defined, 313
   deleting fields, 308
   Drop-Down Menu Properties
      dialog box, *320*
   editing, 306-316
   exporting data with text files, 305
   Feedback Form template, 120-121
   Feedback page, 88-91
   fields. *See* fields
   Form Handler property, 313
   Form Page Wizard, 301-316
   Form Properties dialog box, 313,
      314
   Formatted paragraph style, 306,
      307
   formatting, 306

handling input, 324-328
Hidden Fields property, 314
IDC files, 485-487
labeling fields, 307
Max Length text box, 308-309
Personal Web template, 111
properties, 313-316
Push Button Properties dialog
    box, *322*
Radio Button Properties dialog
    box, *321*
Save Results WebBot, 50
scrolling text boxes, 316, *322*
Settings For Saving Results Of
    Form dialog box, *51*, *315*, 323
sizing fields, 308-309
Text Box Properties dialog box,
    317, *318*
Text Box Validation dialog box,
    51, *52*, *309*
text fields, 307
toolbar buttons, *49*
validating, 310-313
WebBots and, 300
FPlaunch utility, 676-680
    Add New File Type dialog box,
        678, *679*
    FrontPage Editor and, 676-680
    MIME types, 678
    parameter files, 678-680
frame pages, HTML, 410
Frame tags, HTML, 413, *416-417*
frames, 286-293
    See also tables
    advantages of, 293
    browsers and, 59
    caveats, 292
    default.htm, 287
    floating, 414, 434-435, *436*
    framesets, 286
    FrontPage Editor and, 55, *58*
    HTML, 410-418
    Jay's Seafood Restaurant web
        site, *193*
    tables comparison, 286
Frames Wizard, 286-292
    Edit Frameset Grid dialog box,
        288, *289*
    Pick Template Layout, 287, *288*
    Table of Contents Frame, 290
    target frames, 290
    Top Navigation Bar Frame, 290,
        291
Frameset tag, HTML, 410-413
FROM command, SQL statements, 449
FrontPage
    ActiveX and, 561-562
    advantages of, 31-32
    automatic graphic conversions, 48
    components of, 28-29, 32-66, 644

creating database webs with,
    472-498
Editor. *See* FrontPage Editor
Explorer. *See* FrontPage Explorer
graphic formats, 46-47
HTML generation, 418-437
Image Composer, 197-236
importing files into, 350-383
installing, 651-661
Java and, 550-553
overview, 28-30
Script Wizard, 591-592, *593*
SDK (Software Developer's Kit),
    669-681
Server Extensions. *See* Server
    Extensions
SSL (Secure Sockets Layer) and,
    522
Web Servers. *See* FrontPage
    Personal Web Server
    (FPPWS); Microsoft Personal
    Web Server (MSPWS)
wizards, 71-102
FrontPage Editor, 38-64
    character styles, 42
    colored text, 44, *45*
    described, 28
    drag and drop, 370
    font styles, 40-42
    FONT tag and, 40
    Form Page Wizard, *54*, *55*
    Formatted paragraph style, 40
    formatting text, 39-46
    forms, 48-51
    FPlaunch utility, 676-680
    frames, 55, *58*, 59
    graphics, 46-48
    hotspots, 60-64
    HTML and, 38-39
    HTX files, *483*
    hyperlinks, 60-64
    Image Properties dialog box, *47*
    list styles, *43*, *44*
    logical font styles, 41
    New Page dialog box, 53
    Normal Web template, 105-106
    opening, 36, 38
    Page Properties dialog box, 44,
        45, 46
    page wizards and templates, 53-58
    paragraph styles, 39-40
    physical font styles, 41
    Table of Contents template, *124*
    tables, 51-53
    WebBots and, 59, *60*
    window, *38*
    wizards and templates, 53-58,
        56-57
FrontPage Explorer, 33-37
    described, 28
    drag and drop, 368-369

Folder view, 34
Hyperlink view, 33, *34*
New FrontPage Web dialog box,
    35
Normal Web template, 106-107
web page hierarchy, 34-35
wizards and templates, 35-36, *37*
FrontPage Personal Web Server
    (FPPWS)
    choosing and installing servers,
        647-651
    described, 28
    Microsoft Personal Web Server
        (MSPWS) comparison, 29
FrontPage Server Extensions. *See*
    Server Extensions
FrontPage Web Settings dialog box
    Advanced tab (JavaScript), *578*
    database webs, *472*
FrontPage Web Template Maker,
    automatic web template creation,
    150, *151*
FTP Properties dialog box, installing
    Microsoft Personal Web Server
    (MSPWS), 650, *651*
FTP servers, Web Publishing Wizard,
    627
FTP transfers, Customer Support Web
    template, 117, *118*
functions, JavaScript, 583-584

G

geometric shapes (Image Composer),
    225-230
    Arrange tool, 228
    creating, 226-228
    manipulating, 228-230
    Oval tool, 227
    Polygon tool, 227
    Rectangle tool, 227
    Save As command, 229-230
    Shapes tool, 226-228
Getting Started with Microsoft
    FrontPage dialog box
    Typical FrontPage installations,
        656
    web wizards, 72, *74*
GIF graphics, 23-24
Glossary of Terms template, 121-122
goals, web-planning, 154-155
graphic design. *See* designing for
    World Wide Web
graphics, 23-26, 177-190
    automatic conversions, 48
    background images, 46
    backgrounds, 182-188
    clip art, 181-182
    creating and editing. *See* Image
        Composer

creating and inserting, 177-180
exporting, 179
Fantasy Travel web, 177-190
formats acceptable to FrontPage, 46-47
formats acceptable to Image Composer, 198
GIF, 23-24
horizontal lines, 180-181
hotspots, 60-64, 254-257
hyperlinking, 251-258
image maps. *See* hotspots
Image Properties dialog box, *47*
inserting, 177-180
inserting with FrontPage Editor, 46-48
inserting into web templates, 139
JPEG, 24
linking, 251-258
linking to external webs, 252-254
multimedia files, 25-26
scanned images, 188-190
Scheduled Image WebBot, *60*, 337-338
separating from text with tables, *285*
single link, 252
sources of, 177
titles, 179, *180*
word art, 177
Great Web Site Contest
Bar Net, 635-639
Jay's Seafood Restaurant, 191-195
NeedhamOnline, 526-531
Surfrider Foundation Australia, 67-70
Winnov, Ltd. web site, 294-298
greater-than character (>), HTML, 398
groups, security setups, 509-512, *513*
guest books, NeedhamOnline web site, 526-527, *528*

H

hard disks, Available Disk Space dialog box, 659, *660*
Header Cell option, cell properties, *272*
headings
Include WebBot and, 337
single-page templates, 135-136
HEIGHT attribute, HTML, 404
Hidden Fields property, forms, 314
hierarchy of web pages, 34-35
Highlight Hotspots button, 257
hints, Image Composer, 214
hits, defined, 2
Home Page icon, Corporate Presence Wizard, 78
Home Page Properties dialog box, Normal Web template, *105*

Home Page Template, single-page templates, 137-138
home pages
AltaVista, *5*
Bar Net web site, *636*
The BookBay web site, *385*
Budget, 139-143
Corporate Presence Wizard, 80-82
creating. *See* Fantasy Travel web
default, 657, *658*
hyperlinks and hotspots, 237-262
Jay's Seafood Restaurant web site, *191*
multiple. *See* Project Web template
My Home Page icon, *657*
naming, 80
North Beach Tools database, 474
Personal Home Page Wizard, 99-102
renaming, 132-133
sample. *See* Fantasy Travel web
single-page templates, 134-138
titling, 163
Horizontal Alignment option, cell properties, *272*
horizontal lines, Fantasy Travel web, 180-181
host names, TCP/IP Test, 662-664
Hosted Sites page, Bar Net web site, *637*
hotspots, 254-257
See also hyperlinks; image maps
Create Hyperlink dialog box, *255*
Default Hyperlink section, 257
defined, 254
FrontPage Editor and, 60-64
Highlight Hotspots button, 257
HTML, 405
testing with browsers, 258
HTML (HyperText Markup Language), 12-13, 389-440
See also hyperlinks
adding to FrontPage webs, 433-434
ampersand (&), 398
anchor tag attributes, *406*
attributes, 391
authoring resources, 437-440
basic set of tags, *393-394*
bookmarks and, 405
browsers and, 18-21
character escape sequences, 398, *400*
character styles, 395-398, *399-400*
color names, 392
Corporate Presence Wizard, 428-432, *433*
Designer, 672, 674
example, 425-426
Extended Attributes dialog box, 435-437

Fantasy Travel sample, 426-428
floating frames, 414, 434-435, *436*
Form tags, 407, *408-409*
frame pages, 410
Frame tags, 413, *416-417*
frames, 410-418
Frameset tag, 410-413
FrontPage Editor and, 38-39
FrontPage-generated, 418-437
greater-than character (>), 398
HEIGHT attribute, 404
hotspots, 405
hyperlinks and bookmarks, 404-406
image maps, 402-403, 405
Image tag, 402-403, *404*
importing files from Microsoft Excel, 370-374, *381*
importing files from Microsoft PowerPoint, 374-377
importing files from word processors, 358, *359*, 366
intranets and, 597
less-than character (<), 398
multimedia and, 418
multimedia tags, *419-421*
overview, 390-391
paragraph styles, 392-395, *396-397*
scrolling marquees, 535-537
simple example, 425-426
standards and, 390
style sheets, 401-402
table modification with, 435-437
table tags, *411-413*
tables, 409-410
tags, 12-13, 390-392, *393-394*
viewing FrontPage, 421-425
WIDTH attribute, 404
HTML Conversion Utility, 569-575
Confirm Save dialog box, *571*
EMBED tag, 572, 574
IITML Markup dialog box, *573*
Import file To FrontPage Web dialog box, *571*
OBJECT tag, 572, 574
Page Properties dialog box, *571*
HTML Markup dialog box, HTML Conversion Utility, *573*
HTML Markup WebBot, Designer HTML extension, 674-675
The HTML Reference Library, HTML authoring resources, 439
HTTP (HyperText Transfer Protocol)
client/server relationships, 11-12
intranets and, 597
HTTPODBC.DLL, processing IDC and HTX files, 452
HTX files, 482-485
Cell Properties dialog box, 483-484

Database Column Value dialog
box, 482-483
finding specific files, 487-490
FrontPage Editor and, *483*
If-Then conditional statements,
487, *488*
keywords, *450*
North Beach Tools database,
482-485, 487-490, 493-494
Selectprod.htx page, *489*
web databases and, 446, 447-448
Hue Ramp, Image Composer, 204
Hyperlink view
Corporate Presence Wizard, 78
FrontPage Explorer, 33, *34*
hyperlinks, 238-262
See also hotspots; URLs
assigning to graphics, 251-258
assigning to text, 239-251
bookmarks, 6-7, 242-243,
244-246, *250*
broken links, *262*
Create Hyperlink dialog box, *61*,
240
defined, 238
Edit Hyperlink dialog box, 85-86,
110, *260*
FrontPage Editor, 60-64
HTML and, 404-406
mailto, 161, 247, *248*, *251*
managing, 258-262
mouse pointers and URLs, 249,
250
navbar activation, 241
Personal Web template, 110
Recalculate Links command, 261
reciprocal links, 633
setting to other than web sites,
246-247
testing with browsers, 248-251
types of, *247*
underlines and, 7
Verify Hyperlinks dialog box, 31,
259, *261*
on web pages, 6-7
hypermedia, defined, 4
Hypertext Extension files. *See* HTX
files

IDC files, 475-482
creating Allprod.idc file, 478-482,
484
creating directories for executable
scripts, 475-478
Database Connector Wizard
dialog box, 479-480, *481*
forms, 485-487

Internet Database Connector
Wizard dialog box, 479-480,
481
Internet Services Administrator,
477
Microsoft Personal Web Server
(MSPWS), 475
North Beach Tools database,
475-482, 485-487, 493
Personal Web Server Properties
dialog box, *476*
required and optional parameters,
447
SQL commands and, 485-487
web databases, 446
WWW Administrator Directory
web page, 476-478, *479*
If-Then conditional statements, HTX
files, 487, *488*
IIS (Internet Information Servers)
access control, 513-516
publishing database-enhanced
webs on Internet, 442
Image Composer, 197-236
Actual Size icon, *200*
Arrange tool and palette, 201
Art Effects tool and palette, 203
Clear Selection icon, *200*
Color Format icon, *200*
Color Picker dialog box, *205*
Color Ramp, 204
Color Swatch and Color Picker,
204-206
Color Tuning tool and palette,
203, *204*
Custom Palette tab, 206
Delete icon, *200*
Duplicate icon, *200*
eye dropper icon, 205
fills. *See* Patterns And Fills tool
and palette
geometric shapes, 225-230
graphic formats acceptable to, 198
hints, 214
Hue Ramp, 204
image objects. *See* sprites
Insert Image File icon, *200*
installing, 664-666
menus, 199-200
Paint tool and palette, 201,
233-236
palettes, 200-206
Pan tool, 204
Patterns And Fills tool and
palette, 202, 230-232
Select All icon, *200*
setting up, 207-208
Shape tool and palette, 202
sizing images, 208
sprites, 207, 209-225
Text tool and palette, 201

toolbar, 199-200
toolbar buttons, *200*
toolbox, 200-206
Warps and Filters tool and palette,
202, *203*
Whiteness Ramp, 204
window, 198-206, *199*
Zoom Percent icon, *200*
Zoom tool, 204
image maps
See also hotspots
HTML, 402-403, 405
image objects. *See* sprites
Image Properties dialog box
Corporate Presence Wizard,
84-85, *84*
graphics, 47
single image backgrounds, *187*
Image tag, HTML, 402-403, *404*
images. *See* graphics
images directory, web directory
structure, *145*
Images subdirectory, web templates,
131
Import File To FrontPage Web dialog
box
HTML Conversion Utility, 571
importing Java applets, 550-551
Import Web Wizard, 98-99
intranet content, 612-613
imported files, browsers and, 378-381
importing
tables, 176
text with scanners, 172-173
Travel Options offerings for
Fantasy Travel web, 172-176
importing files, 350-383
drag and drop, 368-370
legacy files on intranets, 377-378,
612-613
Microsoft Excel, 370-374
Microsoft PowerPoint, 374-377
multimedia, 381-383
word processors, 351-368
Include WebBot, 336-337
described, *60*
headings and, 337
Project Web template, 112-114
indexed color, GIF graphics, 23
Index.htm, renaming home pages,
132-133
indexing, Glossary of Terms template,
121-122
.INF template information files,
127-132
Agenda.tem folder, 129
[FileList] section, 130-131
[info] section, 129-130
[MetaInfo] section, 132
[TaskList] section, 132, *133*
Insert Caption option, Table menu, *275*

Insert Cell option, Table menu, *275*, 276
Insert Image File icon, Image Composer, *200*
Insert Rows Or Columns option, Table menu, *275*, 276
Insert Table dialog box, 265, *266*
Insert Table option, Table menu, *275*
inserting graphics, 177-180
    into web templates, 139
inserting sprites, Image Composer, 209-211
inserting tables into web templates, 141
installing
    FrontPage, 651-661
    FrontPage SDK, 670-673
    FrontPage Server Extensions, 620-622
    Java SDK, 542-547
    Microsoft Image Composer, 664-666
    Microsoft Internet Explorer, 645-646, *647*
    Microsoft Personal Web Server (MSPWS), 648-651
    ScriptActive ActiveX plug-in, 568-569
    servers, 647-651
    TCP/IP on networks, 602-605
    Web Publishing Wizard, 666-668
installing FrontPage 97 with Bonus Pack, 641-668
    choosing and installing servers, 647-651
    contents of FrontPage 97 and Bonus Pack CD-ROM, 642-643
    FrontPage components, 644
    FrontPage Server Extensions and, 648
    installing FrontPage, 651-661
    requirements, 643-644
    TCP/IP Test, 662-664
interlaced images, GIF graphics, 24
Internet, *502*
    See also intranets; World Wide Web
    backbone, 8
    graphics, 23-26
    history of, 8-9
    HTML, 12-13
    HTTP, 11-12
    IP (Internet Protocol), 10
    multimedia files, 25-26
    path confirmations, 630, *631*
    protocols, 8, 9-13
    security, 503
    Service Providers. *See* ISPs
    TCP (Transmission Control Protocol), 10-11
    TCP/IP, 9-11

World Wide Web and, 2-3
Internet Assistant Wizard, Microsoft Excel, *372*
Internet Connection Wizard, installing Internet Explorer, 645, *646*
Internet Database Connector files. *See* IDC files
Internet Development Toolbox, HTML authoring resources, 439
Internet Explorer. *See* Microsoft Internet Explorer
Internet Information Servers
    access control, 513-516
    publishing database-enhanced webs on Internet, 442
Internet Protocol (IP), 10
Internet Services Administrator, IDC files, *477*
InterNIC, IP address registration, 10
intranets, 595-616
    See also Internet; World Wide Web
    access control, 517-519
    benefits of, 599-600
    building FrontPage, 602-613
    configuring TCP/IP, 605-608
    content, 600-601, 612-613
    defined, 596
    firewalls, 615-616
    HTML and, 597
    HTTP and, 597
    Import Web Wizard, 612-613
    installing TCP/IP on networks, 602-605
    LANs and, 3-4, 602
    legacy files on, 377-378, 612-613
    Microsoft SourceSafe, 613-615
    NetBEUI protocol, 603
    Network dialog box, *603*, *605*
    overview, 596-598
    path confirmations, 630, *631*
    reasons for, 598-600
    security, 615-616
    Select Network Component Type dialog box, *604*
    Select Network Protocol dialog box, *604*
    Subnet Mask text box, 608
    TCP/IP and, 597-598
    Tcptest.exe, 611
    troubleshooting, 611
    using FrontPage, 608-612
    Volcano Coffee Company, 598, *599*
IP addresses, 10
    access control, 514
    configuring TCP/IP, 607-608
    TCP/IP Test, 662-664
IP (Internet Protocol), 10
ISPs (Internet Service Providers), 618-632
    bandwidth and, 619

cost and services, 618-619
deleting webs from servers, 625-626
domain names and, 619
FrontPage Server Extensions, 619-625
posting to without FrontPage Server Extensions, 626-252

J

Java, 537-558
    ActiveX comparison, 560, 575-576
    adding to web pages, 550-553
    Applet Properties dialog box, *551*
    APPLET tag attributes, 553, *554*
    applets, 7, 540-542
    compiling applets, 553-558
    defined, 7
    Development Kit (JDK), 543-547
    finding applets, 540-542
    high performance of, 540
    Import File To FrontPage Web dialog box, 550-951
    installing SDKs (Software Development Kits), 542-547
    interactivity of, 539
    object-oriented programming, 537-538
    platform independence, 539
    resources, 538, 542
    robustness of, 539
    safety of, 538
    System Configuration Editor, 546, *547*
    TicTacToe page, 548-549, *550*
    working with, 547-550
JavaScript, 576-588
    arguments, 584
    comment tags, 583
    For-Next loops, 585, 587
    form validation, 310, 576-588
    Form Validation page, *578*
    form validation script, 581-588
    FrontPage Web Settings dialog box Advanced tab, *578*
    functions, 583-584
    parsing fields, 585-586
    SCRIPT tag, 583
    Text Box Validation dialog box, 579, *580*
    variables, 584-585, 586
Jay's Seafood Restaurant web site, 191-195
    frames, *193*
    home page, *191*
    questions and answers, 194-195
    table of contents, *192*

JPEG graphics, GIF graphics comparison, 24-25

K

keywords, HTX files, *450*

L

LANs
    intranets and, 3-4
    resources, 602
layers of sprites, Image Composer, 207, 212
layout
    planning webs, 155-157
    table enhancements, 281-286
legacy files on intranets, 377-378, 612-613
less-than character (<), HTML, 398
lines, horizontal, 180-181
links. *See* hyperlinks
list of current specials, Fantasy Travel web, 163-165, *166*
list styles, FrontPage Editor, *43, 44*
Literature Request form, Confirmation Field WebBot, *334*
local area networks. *See* LANs
logical character styles, HTML, 395
logical font styles, FrontPage Editor, 41
logo.htm, Corporate Presence Wizard, 83
lossless compression, GIF graphics, 23
lossy compression, JPEG graphics, 24

M

mailto hyperlinks, 161, 247, *248, 251*
manually creating web templates, 144-148
    cgi-bin directory, 146-147
    New FrontPage Web dialog box, 147-148
    _private directory, 146-147
    _vti_shm directory, 146-147
manuals, legacy files on intranets, 377-378, 612-613
maps, image. *See* hotspots; image maps
marquees
    scrolling, 535-537
    Winnov, Ltd. web site, 295
Max Length text box, sizing form fields, 308-309
menus
    Drop-Down Menu Properties dialog box, *117*
    Drop-Down Menu Validation box, *311*
    Image Composer, 199-200

Table, 276-278
Merge Cells option, Table menu, *275*
message digests, SSL (Secure Sockets Layer), 523
[MetaInfo] section, .INF template information files, 132
Microsoft Access, 445, 452-471
    adding records to, 465-469
    building databases, 452-462
    creating database relationships, 462-464, *465*
    Customers table, 465-467
    defining System DSN (Data Source Name), 469-471
    Relationships dialog box, 463, *464, 465, 466*
    Show Table dialog box, *463*
Microsoft Excel
    importing files from, 370-374
    Internet Assistant Wizard, *372*
Microsoft FrontPage. *See* FrontPage
Microsoft Great Web Site Contest
    Bar Net, 635-639
    Jay's Seafood Restaurant, 191-195
    NeedhamOnline, 526-531
    Surfrider Foundation Australia, 67-70
    Winnov, Ltd. web site, 294-298
Microsoft Image Composer. *See* Image Composer
Microsoft Internet Explorer
    client-side form validation, 310
    downloading graphic, *21*
    HTML and, 18, *19*
    installing, 645-646, *647*
    Microsoft Script Debugger, 592-594
    Options dialog box, *647*
    scrolling marquees, 535-537
    tables in, 280, *281*
Microsoft Internet Information Servers. *See* IIS
Microsoft Office, importing files from, 350-370
Microsoft Personal Web Server (MSPWS)
    described, 28
    FrontPage Personal Web Server (FPPWS) comparison, 29
    IDC files, 475
    installing, 648-651
    security setups, 509-512
Microsoft PowerPoint
    Animation Player, 380
    importing files from, 374-377, *382*
Microsoft Script Debugger, 592-594
    breakpoints, 592-593
    downloading, 593
Microsoft SourceSafe, 613-615
    FrontPage Server Extensions and, 614

Microsoft SQL Server, 445-446
Microsoft Word, importing files from, 351-368
MIME types, FPlaunch utility, 678
Minimum Width option, cell properties, *272*
ModifiedBy configuration variable, Substitution WebBot, *341*
monitor color settings, 15-17
    calibrating, 17
monitor resolution, World Wide Web design, 14-15, *16*
Mosaic
    HTML and, 18, *20*
    tables, *283*
mouse pointers and URLs, hyperlink displays, 249, *250*
.MOV files, importing multimedia, 381-383
moving sprites, Image Composer, 211-212, *213*, 217-219
MPEG, multimedia files, 25
multimedia, defined, 4
multimedia files
    CU-SeeMe, 25-26
    formats, *383*
    HTML, 418
    importing, 381-383
    MPEG, 25
    RealAudio, 26
multimedia tags, HTML, *419-421*
My Home Page icon, Typical FrontPage installations, *657*

N

naming home pages, 80
native formats, importing files from word processors, 366-368
navbar activation, Home Page returns, 241
NCompass Labs plug-ins for Netscape Navigator, 567-569
    DocActive, 568
    ScriptActive, 568-569
NCSA, *A Beginner's Guide to HTML*, 438
NCSA Mosaic
    HTML and, 18, *20*
    tables, *283*
NeedhamOnline web site, 526-531
    guest book, 526-527, *528*
    questions and answers, 530-531
    Search page, 529
NetBEUI protocol, installing TCP/IP on networks, 603
Netscape Navigator
    ActiveX and, 562, 566-568
    client-side form validation, 310
    downloading graphic, *21*

floating frames, 414, 434-435, *436*
HTML and, 18, *19*
HTML authoring resources, 439
NCompass Labs plug-ins for ActiveX, 568-569
Open Network Environment (ONE), 560-561
tables, *282*
Network control panel, installing TCP/IP, *665*
Network dialog box, installing TCP/IP on networks, *603*, *605*
networks, local area. *See* LANs
New FrontPage Web dialog box
FrontPage Explorer, *35*
manually creating web templates, 147-148
web templates, 104
web wizards, 72, *73*
New Page dialog box, FrontPage Editor, 53
New Table dialog box, databases, *455*
news.htm, Corporate Presence Wizard, 82
No Wrap option, cell properties, 272
Normal Web template, 104-107
FrontPage Editor, 105-106
FrontPage Explorer, 106-107
Home Page Properties dialog box, *105*
North Beach Tools database, 452-462
Add A Product Confirmation page, *496*
Add A Product page, *492*, *494*
adding products to, 490-495
building, 454-462
Customers table, 456-457, 465-467
database webs, 472-498
deleting records, 495-498
error messages, *496*
finding specific products, 485-490
home page, *474*
HTX files, 482-485, 487-490, 493-494
IDC files, 475-482, 485-487, 493
Orders table, 460-461, *462*
Products table, 457-458, *459*, 468-469
relationships, *444*
SalesReps table, 458-459, *460*, 467-468
tables, 443
notes, Comment WebBot, 331-332
NSFNET, history of Internet, 8
NT. *See* Windows NT
NTFS (NT File System), Access Control Lists (ACLs), 516, *517*
Numeric Format option, Text Box Validation dialog box, *312*

O

OBJECT tag
ActiveX controls, 565-566, 567-568
attributes, *567*
HTML Conversion Utility, 572, 574
object-oriented programming
ActiveX, 560
Java, 537-538
objects
ActiveX, 560
defined, 560
image. *See* sprites
OCR (Optical Character Recognition), importing scanned text, 172-173
ODBC Data Source Administrator dialog box, defining System DSN (Data Source Name), 469, *471*
ODBC (Open Database Connectivity), 451
HTTPODBC.DLL, 452
web servers and requests, 451-452
Office. *See* Microsoft Office
OLE (Object Linking and Embedding), ActiveX and, 559-560
ONE (Open Network Environment), Netscape Navigator, 560-561
one-to-many relationships, databases, 443, *444*
Open Database Connectivity. *See* ODBC
Open File dialog box, importing files from word processors, 360-363
Open FrontPage Webs dialog box, Typical FrontPage installations, 657
Open Network Environment (ONE), Netscape Navigator, 560-561
opening
files onto New Pages, 360-363
FrontPage Editor, 36, 38
To Do Lists, 36, 64
Orders table, North Beach Tools database, 460-461, *462*
Oval tool, Image Composer, 227

P

packet filtering
intranet, 615-616
security and, 517
packets, IP (Internet Protocol), 10
Page Properties dialog box
Background tab, *183*
Fantasy Travel web, 159
FrontPage Editor, 44, *45*, 46
HTML Conversion Utility, 571
page templates, 118-125

Confirmation Form template, 119-120
Feedback Form template, 120-121
FrontPage Editor, 53-58
Glossary of Terms template, 121-122
Images subdirectory, 131
Search Page template, 122, *123*
Table of Contents template, 123-125
web template comparison, 126
page wizards
FrontPage Editor, 53-58
listed, *99*
Personal Home Page Wizard, 99-102
Page-URL configuration variable, Substitution WebBot, *341*
pages. *See* home pages; web pages
Pages subdirectory, 127, *128*
Paint tool and palette (Image Composer), 201, 233-236
Airbrush tool, 234, *235*
Eraser tool, 236
Paintbrush tool, 233, *234*
Pencil tool, 234, *235*
Smear tool, 235
palettes, Image Composer, 200-206
Pan tool, Image Composer, 204
paragraph styles
footers, 161
FrontPage Editor, 39-40
HTML, 392-395, *396-397*
parameter files, FPlaunch utility, 678-680
parsing fields, JavaScript, 585-586
passwords, user access control, 514
pasting text from Clipboard, importing files from word processors, 353-354
path confirmations, Web Publishing Wizard, 630, *631*
Patterns And Fills tool and palette, Image Composer, 202, 230-232
Pencil tool, Paint tool and palette, 234, *235*
permissions, 504-512
Add Users dialog box, 507, *508*
dialog box, *505*
file-sharing and printer-sharing, 504
levels of, 504
NTFS Access Controls Lists, 516, *517*
setting up users and groups, 509-512
Personal Home Page Wizard, 99-102
Personal Web Server Properties dialog box
IDC files, *476*
installing Microsoft Personal Web Server (MSPWS), 649, *650*

security setups, 509, *510*
Personal Web Servers. *See* FrontPage Personal Web Server (FPPWS); Microsoft Personal Web Server (MSPWS)
Personal Web template, 107-111
    annotation text, 111
    bookmarks, 108-109
    Edit Hyperlink dialog box, *110*
    forms, 111
    hyperlinks, 110
    plain text, 108
    timestamps, 111
    URLs, 111
physical character styles, HTML, 395
physical font styles, FrontPage Editor, 41
Pick Template Layout, Frames Wizard, 287, *288*
pictures. *See* clip art; graphics; Image Composer; word art
plain text, Personal Web template, 108
planning webs, 154-157
    content, 155
    goals, 154-155
    layout, 155-157
    organization, 155
platform independence, Java, 539
plug-ins, Netscape Navigator, 568-569
Polygon tool, Image Composer, 227
posting articles, Discussion Web Wizard, 97-98
posting to hosts
    with Server Extensions, 623-625
    without Server Extensions, 626-632
PowerPoint. *See* Microsoft PowerPoint
presentation style options, Corporate Presence Wizard, 76, *78*
press releases, promoting web sites, 633-634
Preview In Browser feature
    Corporate Presence Wizard, 88
    web creation and, 31
printer-sharing
    installing TCP/IP on networks, 608
    permissions and, 504
_private directory
    manually creating web templates, 146-147
    web directory structure, *145*
private key encryption, 519
    public key encryption and. *See* SSL (Secure Sockets Layer)
productivity files, importing, 350-381
Products & Services page, Corporate Presence Wizard, 83-87
Products table, North Beach Tools database, 457-458, *459*, 468-469

Project Team Questionnaire, handling form input, 324-328
Project Web template, 111-116
    Include WebBot, 112-114
    searches and discussion groups, 114-116
promoting web sites, 632-634
    press releases, 633-634
    reciprocal links, 633
    search engines and, 632-633
    Yahoo! submission area, 632, *633*
properties
    cell, 271-274
    form, 313-316
    form field, 308-309
    table, *267*, 268-271
Properties dialog box, Corporate Presence Wizard, *80*
protocols
    defined, 8
    HTTP, 11-12
    Internet, 8, 9-13
    TCP/IP, 9-11
    World Wide Web, 9
proxy servers, security, 517-519
public key encryption, 520
    certificates, 524
    private key encryption and. *See* SSL (Secure Sockets Layer)
publishing web pages, 618-632
    FrontPage Server Extensions, 618-625
    Web Publishing Wizard, 626-632
Push Button Properties dialog box, building forms, *322*

Q

question lists, Form Page Wizard, 304, *305*
question types, Form Page Wizard, 301, *302*
QuickTime .MOV files, importing multimedia, 381-383

R

Radio Button Properties dialog box, building forms, *321*
Radio Button Validation box, validating forms, *311*
RealAudio sound files, 26
Recalculate Links command, managing hyperlinks, 261
reciprocal links, promoting web sites, 633
records
    defined, 442
    deleting, 495-498

Microsoft Access, 465-469
Rectangle tool, Image Composer, 227
relational databases, 442, 443-445
    deleting records, 495-498
relationships, North Beach Tools database, *444*
Relationships dialog box, Microsoft Access, 463, *464*, *465*, *466*
Relief option, Warps And Filters tool and palette, 178
renaming home pages, 132-133
requests, web servers and, 451-452
resolution, monitor, 14-15, *16*
resources
    ActiveX, 560
    HTML authoring, 437-440
    Java, 538, 542
    LAN, 602
    security, 524-525
Rich Text Files. *See* .RTF files
root directories, 126-127, *128*, 143
rotating sprites, Image Composer, 217-218
rows
    Insert Rows Or Columns option, *275*, 276
    selecting table, 273
Rows option, table properties, *267*
RSA keys, SSL (Secure Sockets Layer), 520, 521, 523-524
.RTF files, importing files from word processors, 359-360

S

SalesReps table, North Beach Tools database, 458-459, *460*, 467-468
Save As command
    Fantasy Travel web, 159-160
    Image Composer, 229-230
Save As Template dialog box, single-page templates, *136*
Save Results WebBot, creating forms with, 50
scanned images, 188-190
scanners, importing text with, 172-173
Scheduled Image WebBot, 337-338
    Component Properties dialog box, *338*
    described, 60
Scheduled Include WebBot, 336-337
    described, 60
Script Debugger. *See* Microsoft Script Debugger
SCRIPT tag, JavaScript, 583
Script Wizard, 591-592, *593*
    List view, *592*
ScriptActive Netscape Navigator plug-in, 568-575

HTML Conversion Utility,
569-575
installing, 568-569
scripting languages, 575-594
bytecode, 575
JavaScript, 576-588
Microsoft Script Debugger,
592-594
overview, 575-576
programming languages
comparison, 575
Script Wizard, 591-592, *593*
VBScript, 588-591
scripts, CGI, 620, 672, 673-674
scrolling marquees, 535-537
scrolling text boxes in forms, 316, *322*
SDK (Software Developer's Kit),
669-681
CGI directory, 672, 673-674
Designer HTML directory, 672,
674
installing FrontPage, 670-673
Template directory, 672, 675
Utility directory, 672, 675-680
WebBot directory, 673, 680-681
Wizards directory, 673, 681
search engines, promoting web sites,
632-633
Search Page template, 122, *123*
Search pages
Bar Net web site, *638*
Corporate Presence Wizard, 91-94
NeedhamOnline web site, 529
WebBot Search Component
Properties dialog box, 93, *94*
Search WebBot, 339-341
described, *60*
excluding pages from, 341
Search pages, 91-94
WebBot Search Component
Properties dialog box, *340*
searches, Project Web template,
114-116
Secure Sockets Layer. *See* SSL
security, 499-531
access control, 503
access control to intranets,
517-519
access control to web servers,
512-516, *517*
areas where needed, 500-503
bibliography, 524-525
decryption, 519
encryption, 519-522
firewalls, 503, 517-519
Internet, 503
intranet, 615-616
Microsoft Personal Web Server
(MSPWS), 509-512
Microsoft SourceSafe, 613-615
packet filtering, 517

permissions, 504-509
Personal Web Server Properties
dialog box, 509, *510*
private key encryption, 519
proxy servers, 517-519
public key encryption, 520
setting up users and groups,
509-512
Select A File dialog box, importing
text files, *174*
Select All icon, Image Composer, *200*
Select Cell, Row, Column, or Table
option, Table menu, *275, 277*
SELECT command, SQL statements,
449
Select Components dialog box,
Custom FrontPage installations,
659, *660*
Select Network Component Type
dialog box, installing TCP/IP on
networks, *604*
Select Network Protocol dialog box,
installing TCP/IP on networks, *604*
selecting
rows and columns, 273
sprites, 211-214
Selectprod.htx page, HTX files, *489*
separating text and graphics with
tables, *285*
server directories, 126-127
Server Extensions, 619-625
access control, 512-516, *517*, 621
availability of, *622*
CGI and, 620
described, 29-30
DLLs and, 620
downloading address, 66
installing, 620-622, 648
ISPs and, 619-625
Microsoft SourceSafe and, 614
posting to hosts with, 623-625
posting to hosts without, 626-632
publishing web pages, 618-625
web server access control,
512-516, *517*
server selection, Corporate Presence
Wizard, 75
server software, installing FrontPage
97 with Bonus Pack, 644
server-side versus client-side
validation of forms, 310
servers
authenticating, 523-524
choosing and installing, 647-651
proxy, 517-519
requests and, 451-452
web. *See* web servers
Service Providers, Internet. *See* ISPs
Services tab, installing Microsoft
Personal Web Server (MSPWS), 649
setting up

access control for users and
groups, 509-512
Image Composer, 207-208
Settings For Saving Results Of Form
dialog box, *51, 315*
building forms, 323
Confirmation Field WebBot, 334,
335
Setup Type dialog box, Typical
FrontPage installations, 654
Shape tool and palette, Image
Composer, 202
shapes, geometric. *See* geometric
shapes (Image Composer)
Shapes tool, Image Composer, 226-228
sharing files and printers
installing TCP/IP on networks,
608
permissions and, 504
Show Table dialog box, Microsoft
Access, *463*
signatures, digital, 523
single-image backgrounds, 186-188
Image Properties dialog box, *187*
single-link graphics, 252
single-page templates, 134-138
headings, 135-136
Home Page Template, 137-138
Save As Template dialog box, *136*
sizing
form fields, 308-309
Image Composer images, 208
Image Composer sprites, 216-217
sizing handles, selecting sprites with,
211
Smear tool, Paint tool and palette
(Image Composer), 235
software
ActiveX, 558-575
Developer's Kit. *See* SDK
FrontPage 97 with Bonus Pack,
641-668
Java, 537-558
scripting languages, 575-594
version control with Microsoft
SourceSafe, 613-615
solid-color backgrounds, 183-185
sound files
See also multimedia files
RealAudio, 26
Source view, VBScript, 589
SourceSafe, 613-615
FrontPage Server Extensions and,
614
Split Cells option, Table menu, *275,*
277-278
spreadsheets, importing files from
Microsoft Excel, 370-374
sprites (Image Composer), 209-225
defined, 207
duplicating, 216-217

flipping, 216-217, 218-219
inserting, 209-211
layers of, 207, 212
moving, 211-212, *213*, 217-219
rotating, 217-218
selecting, 211-214
sizing, 216-217
text, 219-225
SQL Server, 445-446
SQL statements, 448-451
  commands, *451*
  FROM command, 449
  IDC files and, 485-487
  SELECT command, 449
SSL (Secure Sockets Layer), 520-524
  authentication, 523-524
  certificates, 524
  digital signatures, 523
  FrontPage and, 522
  implementing, 521
  message digests, 523
  overview, 520-521
  RSA keys, 520, 521, 523-524
Start Copying Files dialog box
  Custom FrontPage installations, 661
  Typical FrontPage installations, 655
Startup tab, installing Microsoft
  Personal Web Server (MSPWS), 649
Structured Query Language. *See* SQL
  Server; SQL statements
Style Guide for Online Hypertext,
  HTML authoring resources, 438
style sheets
  HTML, 401-402
  Winnov, Ltd. web site, 297
Subnet Mask text box, installing
  TCP/IP on networks, 608
Substitution WebBot, 341-344
  configuration variables, 341
  Default.htm Properties dialog
  box, *342, 343*
  described, *60*
Sun Microsystem. *See* Java; JavaScript
Surfrider Foundation Australia web
  site, 67-70
  home page, *68*
  membership form, *68*
  questions and answers, 70
symmetric cryptography. *See* private
  key encryption
System Configuration Editor,
  downloading JDK, 546, *547*
System DSN (Data Source Name),
  469-471
  Create New Data Source dialog
  box, 469, *470*
  File DSNs, 469

ODBC Data Source
  Administrator dialog box, 469,
  471
User DSNs, 469

T

TAB key, moving through layers of
  sprites with, 212
Table of Contents Frame, Frames
  Wizard, 290
Table of Contents page
  Corporate Presence Wizard,
  87-88, *89*
  Jay's Seafood Restaurant web
  site, *192*
Table of Contents template, 123-125
  browsers and, *124*
  FrontPage Editor and, *124*
Table of Contents WebBot, 344-345
  browsers and imported files,
  378-381
  Component Properties dialog box,
  345
  described, *60*
  web templates, 141, *142*
Table Design view, building databases,
  456
Table menu, 276-278
  options, *275*
table properties, *267*, 268-271
  dialog box, *270*
  width, 268, *269*
tables, 51-53, 264-286
  See also frames
  browsers and, 18, *19-20*
  building, 278-281
  cell properties, 271-274
  cells, 264-265
  defined, 442
  displaying data in, 265-281
  frames comparison, 286
  HTML and, 409-410, *411-413*,
  435-437
  importing, 176
  Insert Table dialog box, 265, *266*
  inserting into web templates, 141
  layout enhancements with,
  281-286
  Microsoft Internet Explorer, 280,
  281
  NCSA Mosaic, *283*
  Netscape Navigator, *282*
  North Beach Tools database, 443
  properties, *267*, 268-271
  selecting rows and columns, 273
  separating text and graphics with,
  285
  Table Properties option (Table
  menu), *275*

tabular data, importing files from
  Microsoft Excel, 370-374
tags, HTML, 12-13, 390-392, *393-394*
target frames, Frames Wizard, 290
[TaskList] section
  .INF template information files,
  132, *133*
  To Do List Task Details dialog
  box, *134*
tasks. *See* To Do Lists
TCP/IP, 9-11
  configuring, 605-608
  installing on networks, 602-605
  intranets and, 597-598
  IP addresses, 514, 607-608
  IP (Internet Protocol), 10
  Network control panel, *665*
  TCP (Transmission Control
  Protocol), 10-11
  Tcptest.exe, 611
  troubleshooting, 663-664
TCP/IP Properties dialog box,
  configuring TCP/IP, *606, 607, 609*
TCP/IP Test, 662-664
  results, *663*
  troubleshooting, 663-664
Template directory, SDK (Software
  Developer's Kit), 672, 675
templates, 103-151
  creating, 125-151
  defined, 126
  directories and, 126-127
  Frames Wizard—Pick Template
  Layout, 287, *288*
  FrontPage Editor, 53-58, *56-57*
  FrontPage Explorer, 35-36, *37*
  Home Page Template, 137-138
  .INF information files, 127-132
  page, 118-125, *126*
  Save As Template dialog box, *136*
  single-page, 134-138
  .TEM directory, 126-127
  types of, 126
  web, 104-118, *126*
.TEM directory
  [FileList] section, 130-131
  FrontPage directory structure,
  126-127
testing
  hotspots with browsers, 258
  hyperlinks with browsers, 248-251
text
  colored, 44, *45*
  Fantasy Travel web, 160-176
  formatting in FrontPage Editor,
  39-46
  hyperlinking, 239-251
  importing from word processors,
  351-368
  importing with scanners, 172-173
  pasting from Clipboard, 353-354

Personal Web template, 108, 111
  separating from graphics with
    tables, *285*
  word art, 177
Text Box Properties dialog box, forms,
  317, *318*
Text Box Validation dialog box
  forms, 51, *52, 309*
  JavaScript, 579, *580*
  options, *312*
text boxes, scrolling, 316
text color, Corporate Presence Wizard,
  76
text files
  exporting web form and database
    data with, 305
  importing from word processors,
    351-353
Text Format option, Text Box
  Validation dialog box, *312*
text sprites (Image Composer), 219-225
  Color Picker dialog box, *225*
  creating, 221-223
  enhancing, 224-225
  fonts on FrontPage CD-ROM,
    219-221, *222*
  Warps And Filters toolbox and
    palette, 224-225
Text tool and palette, Image Composer,
  201
textured backgrounds, 185-186
threaded replies, web wizards, 73
throughput, data, 17-18
TicTacToe Java page, 548-549, *550*
  compiling, 555-558
  WordPad, 555-556
Timestamp WebBot, 346-347
  Component Properties dialog box,
    346
  described, *60*
  Personal Web template, 111
titles
  graphics, 179, *180*
  home page, 163
  non-home page, 167-170
To Do List Task Details dialog box,
  [TaskList] section, *134*
To Do Lists, 64-65
  Add To Do Task dialog box, *65*
  Corporate Presence Wizard,
    77-78, *79*
  described, 28
  opening, 36, 64
toolbar, Image Composer, 199-200
toolbar buttons, Image Composer, *200*
toolbox, Image Composer, 200-206
Top Navigation Bar Frame, Frames
  Wizard, 290, *291*
Travel Options section, Fantasy Travel
  web, 165-167
troubleshooting

intranets, 611
TCP/IP Test, 663-664
Typical FrontPage installations,
  658
.TXT files, importing files from word
  processors, 355-356
typefaces. *See* font styles; fonts
Typical FrontPage installations,
  652-659
  default home pages, 657, *658*
  Destination Path dialog box, 653,
    654
  Getting Started with Microsoft
    FrontPage dialog box, 656
  My Home Page icon, *657*
  Open FrontPage Webs dialog box,
    657
  Setup Type dialog box, *654*
  Start Copying Files dialog box,
    655
  troubleshooting, 658
  upgrades, 653

U

Under Construction icon, Corporate
  Presence Wizard, 77
underlines, hyperlinks and, 7
UNIX, web pages and, 6
upgrades, Typical FrontPage
  installations, 653
uploading files, data throughput and,
  17-18
URLs (Uniform Resource Locators),
  5-6
  See also addresses; hyperlinks
  mouse pointers and hyperlink
    displays, 249, *250*
  Page-URL configuration variable
    (Substitution WebBot), *341*
  Personal Web template, 111
  promoting web sites, 632-634
  Web Publishing Wizard, 628, *629*
User DSNs, System DSN (Data
  Source Name), 469
users
  access control, 509-512, 514
  adding to groups, 511-512, *513*
  authenticating, 523-524
Utility directory (SDK), 675-680
  API Tests dialog box, 675, *676*
  described, 672
  FPlaunch, 676-680
  Web Info dialog box, 675, *677*

V

validating forms, 310-313
  client-side versus server-side, 310

Drop-Down Menu Validation
  box, *311*
Radio Button Validation box, *311*
Text Box Validation dialog box,
  51, *52, 309*
Text Box Validation dialog box
  options, *312*
validation, JavaScript form, 310,
  576-588
variables
  configuration (Substitution
    WebBot), 341
  JavaScript, 584-585, *586*
VBScript, 588-591
  Source view, 589
  Visual Basic and, 588
  Web Settings dialog box
    Advanced tab, 589
Verify Hyperlinks dialog box, 31, 259,
  261
version control, Microsoft SourceSafe,
  613-615
Vertical Alignment option, cell
  properties, *272*
vertical navbar, Winnov, Ltd. web site,
  295
video
  See also multimedia files
  GIF graphics, 24
viewing FrontPage HTML, 421-425
virtual directory control, access
  control, 514-516
Visual Basic, VBScript and, 588
Volcano Coffee Company intranet,
  598, *599*
_vti_bin directory, web directory
  structure, *145*
_vti_cnf directory, web directory
  structure, *145*
_vti_pvt directory, web directory
  structure, *145*
_vti_shm directory
  manually creating web templates,
    146-147
  web directory structure, *145*
_vti_txt directory, web directory
  structure, *145*

W

Warps And Filters tool and palette
  Image Composer, 202, *203*
  Relief option, 178
  text sprites, 224-225
.WAV files, importing multimedia,
  381-383
web browsers. *See* browsers
Web Etiquette, HTML authoring
  resources, 438

Web Info dialog box, SDK Utility directory, 675, *677*
web information, automating. *See* WebBots
web pages, 4-8
    adding graphics to, 46-48
    adding Java applets to, 550-553
    AltaVista, *6*
    converting to FrontPage with Import Web Wizard, 98-99
    creating, 30-32
    defined, 4
    deleting, 625-626
    excluding from Search WebBot, 341
    frames, 286-293
    hierarchy of, 34-35
    hyperlinks, 6-7
    hyperlinks and hotspots, 237-262
    intranet and World Wide Web, 4
    linking. *See* Table of Contents WebBot
    multiple. *See* Project Web template
    publishing. *See* Fantasy Travel web
    sample. *See* Fantasy Travel web
    single-page templates, 134-138
    Timestamp WebBot, *60*, 346-347
    UNIX and, *6*
    URLs, 5-6
    version control with Microsoft SourceSafe, 613-615
    WebBots and, 331-347
Web Publishing Wizard, 626-632
    dialog box, *667*
    folder and file selection, 628
    FTP servers and, 627
    installing, 666-668
    path confirmations, 630, *631*
    Publish FrontPage Web dialog box, 627
    URLs, 628, *629*
    web site names, 628
web scripting languages. *See* scripting languages
web security. *See* security
web servers
    See also FrontPage Personal Web Server (FPPWS); Microsoft Personal Web Server (MSPWS)
    access control, 512-516, *517*
    installing FrontPage Server Extensions, 620-622
    requests and, 451-452
    selecting with Corporate Presence Wizard, 75
Web Settings dialog box
    Advanced tab (VBScript), 589
    database webs, *472*
web sites
    access control, 504-509

adding Java applets to, 550-553
The BookBay, 384-388
converting to FrontPage with Import Web Wizard, 98-99
creating, 30-32
deleting, 625-626
disk-based, 29
hyperlinks and hotspots, 237-262
intranet. *See* intranets
Jay's Seafood Restaurant, 191-195
linking graphics to external, 252-254
linking pages. *See* Table of Contents WebBot
naming with Web Publishing Wizard, 628
permissions, 504-509
planning, 154-157
Preview In Browser feature, 31
promoting, 632-634
publishing, 618-632
sample. *See* Fantasy Travel web
security. *See* security
Surfrider Foundation Australia, 67-70
WebBots and, 331-347
Winnov, Ltd., 294-298
Web Template Maker, automatically creating web templates, 150, *151*
web templates, 104-118
    automatically creating, 149-151
    creating, 138-151
    Customer Support Web template, 116-118
    FrontPage Explorer, 35-36, *37*
    Images subdirectory, 131
    inserting graphics, 139
    inserting tables, 141
    manually creating, 144-148
    New FrontPage Web dialog box, 104
    Normal Web template, 104-107
    page template comparison, 126
    Personal Web template, 107-111
    Project Web template, 111-116
    Table of Contents WebBot, 141, *142*
web wizards, 72-99
    Corporate Presence Wizard, 74-94
    Discussion Web Wizard, 94-98
    FrontPage Explorer, 35-36, *37*
    Getting Started with Microsoft FrontPage dialog box, 72, *74*
    Import Web Wizard, 98-99
    New FrontPage Web dialog box, 72, *73*
    threaded replies, 73
WebBot Confirmation Field Component Properties dialog box, Confirmation Field WebBot, *333*

WebBot directory, SDK (Software Developer's Kit), 673, 680-681
WebBot Search Component Properties dialog box
    Search page, 93, *94*
    Search WebBot, *340*
WebBots, 59, *60*, 329-347
    Comment bot, 331-332
    Confirmation Field bot, 332-335, *336*
    creating, 680-681
    forms and, 300
    Include and Scheduled Include bots, 336-337
    Scheduled Image bot, 337-338
    Search bot, 339-341
    Substitution bot, 341-344
    Table of Contents bot, 344-345
    Timestamp bot, 346-347
webs. *See* web pages; web sites
Webs subdirectory, 127
Webtempl.exe, automatic web template creation, 149-151
Whiteness Ramp, Image Composer, 204
width
    cell properties, 273-274
    table properties, *267, 268, 269*
WIDTH attribute, HTML, 404
Windows NT, IIS (Internet Information Servers) and access control, 513-516
wine, building tabular data tables, 278-281
Winnov, Ltd. web site, 294-298
    individual product data sheet, *297*
    marquee, 295
    product array, *296*
    questions and answers, 298
    style sheet, 297
    vertical navbar, 295
wizards, 71-102
    FrontPage Editor and, 53-58, *56-57*
    FrontPage Explorer and, 35-36, *37*
    page, 99-102
    web, 72-99
Wizards directory, SDK (Software Developer's Kit), 673, 681
Word, importing files from, 351-368
word art, defined, 177
word processors, importing files from, 351-368
WordPad, compiling TicTacToe Java, 555-556
World Wide Web
    See also Internet; intranets
    designing for, 13-22
    Internet and, 2-3
    protocols, 9

The World Wide Web Complete Reference, HTML authoring resources, 440

World Wide Web Consortium, HTML authoring resources, 439

wrapping text, No Wrap option (cell properties), *272*

WWW Administrator Directory web page, IDC files, 476-478, *479*

Y

Yahoo! submission area, promoting web pages, 632, *633*

Z

Zoom Percent icon, Image Composer, *200*

Zoom tool, Image Composer, 204